AF696857

ASIAN AMERICANS AND THE LAW

Historical and Contemporary Perspectives

Series Editor

CHARLES McCLAIN

University of California, Berkeley

LAW LIBRARY

FEB 14 1995

GOLDEN GATE UNIVERSITY

A GARLAND SERIES

Series Contents

KF
4846
.J37
1994

VOLUME

2

JAPANESE IMMIGRANTS AND AMERICAN LAW

THE ALIEN LAND LAWS AND OTHER ISSUES

Edited with introductions by

CHARLES McCLAIN

GARLAND PUBLISHING, INC.
New York & London
1994

Introductions copyright © 1994 Charles McClain
All rights reserved

Library of Congress Cataloging-in-Publication Data

Japanese immigrants and American law : the alien land laws and other issues / edited with introductions by Charles McClain.
p. cm. — (Asian Americans and the law ; v. 2)
Includes bibliographical references.
ISBN 0-8153-1850-2 (acid-free paper)
1. Japanese—Legal status, laws, etc.—United States.
2. Japanese Americans—Legal status, laws, etc.—United States.
3. Land tenure—Law and legislation—United States. 4. Aliens—United States. I. McClain, Charles, 1943- . II. Series.
KF4846.J37 1994
346.7301'3—dc20
[347.30613] 94-29033
CIP

Printed on acid-free, 250-year-life paper
Manufactured in the United States of America

For Laurie

Contents

Series Introduction

According to the 1990 census there are now more than seven million persons of Asian ancestry living in the United States, representing close to three per cent of the total U.S. population. In California Asians represent almost ten per cent of the state's residents and that figure seems likely to increase in the years ahead. Asians (Chinese immigrants, in particular) have been present in significant numbers in the United States since the 1860s. What may not be known is that Asians have been deeply implicated in the legal history of this country since that time, as well. The law has had a profound, though often negative, impact on the experience of Asian communities in the United States. In turn the struggles of Asian Americans to vindicate their right to equal treatment under the law have contributed significantly to shaping the American legal order.

This Garland anthology gathers together some of the best writings on the large subject of Asian Americans and the law. As one might infer from the title, the orientation of this anthology is primarily historical. Most articles deal with past events, but they often make an effort to relate these events to contemporary developments. Furthermore, their authors come from a variety of disciplines besides history, including Asian American studies, law, and political science. Together they open up the possibility of a multidisciplinary understanding of the episodes and issues that are discussed. Finally, lest it be thought that the series focuses exclusively on the past, there are a number of articles in the collection that deal explicitly and in depth with contemporary themes, including themes that transcend individual Asian groups.

The series consists of four volumes and attempts to be comprehensive in its coverage. The first volume concerns Chinese immigrants and focuses on their struggles in the U.S. courts against discriminatory state and federal laws. Two volumes are dedicated to the Japanese, a group whose immigration dates from the 1890s, and who likewise encountered their share of discriminatory legislation. The first of these documents the rise of anti-Japanese agitation in the western states, the enactment of laws aimed at ousting the Japanese from their position in the agricultural economy, and the immigrant community's response. The second is devoted almost entirely to the forcible evacuation and mass internment of civilians of Japanese ancestry during World War II, a topic that has generated a torrent of literature and that constitutes a most extraordinary chapter in the legal history of Asians in this country. The last volume in the series is devoted to other Asian groups—Filipinos, Koreans, Asian Indians, Southeast Asians. These immigrant communities, whose size has increased dramatically in the last two decades, have had significant interactions with the American legal process. The volume also includes articles on the impact of the law on the indigenous population of Hawaii.

In the course of preparing this anthology I have incurred several debts of gratitude that I would like to acknowledge. I am very grateful to Roger Daniels and Neil Gotanda for their suggestions concerning articles to include in this collection. Naturally, the ultimate responsibility for the selection of articles is my own. I also want to express my thanks to Leo Balk, Carole Puccino, and the production staff of Garland Publishing for their patient assistance throughout this project.

Introduction

By the first decade of the twentieth century, the number of Chinese in America had fallen substantially as a result of federal exclusion legislation. Chinese immigrants were no longer occupying Caucasian consciousness on the West Coast as once they had, but for many Caucasians a new "yellow peril" had arisen to take their place. Modest numbers of Japanese immigrants had begun to arrive in the United States in the 1890s, but these figures increased dramatically during the first decade of the twentieth century and by the time of the 1910 census over 90,000 Japanese were present in the United States, overwhelmingly in the Pacific Coast states. The Japanese initially pursued a range of occupations, but they came to concentrate in agriculture, first as laborers, many later as landowners or tenant farmers. In this capacity they prospered, especially in such special fields as fruit and vegetable farming.

The western states reacted to this new influx of Asian immigrants in the same way they had to the nineteenth-century Chinese immigration. They sought through their laws to make life as unattractive as possible for the Japanese and thereby to discourage their residence. The articles in this volume concern the rise of anti-Japanese attitudes on the West Coast, the passage of anti-Japanese state laws and the immigrant community's response to these laws.

As several of the articles in Volume I of this series make clear, the Chinese cases of the nineteenth century firmly established the principle that resident aliens, regardless of race, were protected by the Fourteenth Amendment against many forms of invidious state discrimination. But constitutional law gave the states more maneuvering room to discriminate when it came to the Japanese. In a number of cases dating back to the immediate post-Civil War period, the Supreme Court affirmed that states, in the absence of overriding treaty provisions, could deny aliens the right to own real property within their borders. Farming, as noted above, was the preponderant occupation of the Japanese immigrants. The treaties between the United States and Japan, while guaranteeing certain rights to Japanese immigrants, said nothing about agricultural land. Here then was an opening for the western states to accomplish their objectives, and California led the way.

In 1913, California passed its first Alien Land Law. It limited the right of aliens ineligible for citizenship to own agricultural land, allowing only three-year leaseholds. (Though there was no authoritative court ruling on the question, Japanese were thought generally to be ineligible to become U.S. citizens.) Lands illegally acquired were to escheat to the state. Japanese farmers responded to the law in a variety of ingenious ways. They took title in the names of their citizen children and had themselves declared guardians of their children's estates. They formed corporations for the purpose of holding agricultural property. They took advantage of the leasing exemption in the law.

In 1920 the California electorate passed an initiative designed to close these "loopholes." Like the 1913 statute, the 1920 initiative was artfully couched in racially neutral terms. But the voter pamphlets explaining the measure were completely frank in acknowledging its overriding purpose to drive the Japanese immigrants out of their agricultural holdings. It prohibited ineligible aliens from acquiring shares in corporations that owned agricultural land. It made it illegal for them to become guardians of their minor citizen children's land and established a presumption that an ineligible alien who paid the consideration for land held in the name of an eligible landholder did so with intent to evade the law. It eliminated the three-year leasehold exemption contained in the 1913 measure. Finally, it added criminal penalties to the civil remedies that existed under the original act. Washington and Oregon followed suit with laws of their own modelled after California's. Eventually, some eleven states, mainly on the West Coast, would enact similar legislation. Arkansas, a state with negligible Japanese population, would pass its own alien land law during World War II.

Several articles in this volume discuss the severe strains that California's racially discriminatory legislation introduced into the federal government's foreign relations with Japan. Articles by Yuji Ichioka and Browning Carrott discuss the legal challenges to the laws mounted by the Japanese immigrant community. (Ichioka also chronicles efforts made contemporaneously by Japanese immigrants to vindicate in the courts a right to become naturalized citizens.) The first efforts met with success. In *Estate of Tetsubumi Yano,*[1] the California Supreme Court nullified the portion of California's law that prohibited ineligible aliens from serving as guardians of the agricultural estates of their minor citizen children. Challenges to other portions of the alien land laws of California in subsequent years met a different fate, however. In its October 1923 term, in a series of opinions authored by Justice Pierce Butler, the Supreme Court validated all the challenged provisions.[2] In a separate opinion it affirmed the constitutionality of the state of Washington's law.[3] The following year the legislative and executive branches of the national government dealt their own blow to the Japanese with the passage of the Immigration Act of 1924, which contained a provision barring all future Japanese immigration to the United States.

Robert Higgs, an economic historian, argues in his article that the 1924 act defused anti-Japanese sentiment in California and caused the state to lose interest in enforcing the Alien Land Law. At the same time, market forces were acting to undermine the law's effectiveness. In the end, Higgs contends, the law failed to accomplish its objective to drive the Japanese immigrants out of California agriculture. This point is disputed by other scholars. No one could deny however, and Higgs himself stresses this point, that these measures were oppressive, causing real hardship to the Japanese immigrants, and that the laws were incongruent with the principle of equality of treatment.

The Japanese mounted a new challenge to California's Alien Land Law after World War II. During the war California passed several amendments tightening the law and began a new series of escheat actions against Japanese farmers (in this volume, "The Japanese Problem in Oregon" describes parallel developments in the state of Oregon). One such action involved the family of Kajiro Oyama, a man who had purchased land in the name of his citizen son and become guardian of his estate. Like other Japanese, he was at the time in an internment camp, having been forcibly evacuated there by executive order at the war's outset. Upon his return he and his son brought suit to stop the proceedings, and the matter ultimately found its way to the Supreme Court of the United States. Among the lawyers representing the Oyamas in their appeal was the future Secretary of State, Dean Acheson.

While the case was pending before that tribunal, two articles in the *California Law Review*, both included in this volume, dissected the legislation before the court, pointing out its anomalies (one purported justification for discriminating against the Japanese stated that noncitizens took no long-term interest in the state's welfare, yet the state allowed eligible aliens who chose not to naturalize to own as much agricultural land as they wanted) and laying bare the deep racial bias behind it. Edwin Ferguson, a government attorney, described the law as "a symbol of racial intolerance and prejudice" and suggested that the court ought to find the law invalid under the equal protection clause of the Fourteenth Amendment.[4] (There was some irony here. Ferguson had served during the war on the legal staff of the War Relocation Authority, the agency that supervised the forced relocation of the Japanese to internment camps.)

The Supreme Court, however, chose not to do this. Instead of confronting the racism in the law and the injustice it was doing to California's Japanese alien residents, it focused exclusively—over the passionate objection of Justice Frank Murphy—on the law's effects on the rights of Oyama's citizen son. It held that by burdening the citizen son with the presumption that his father's purchase of land for him was done with the express intention of evading the law, while not making a similiar presumption for citizen children of eligible aliens, the California statute denied the son equal protection under the law.[5] The following year, a law note commenting on the decision criticized the court for dodging what it saw as the principal issue raised by the case. The Alien Land Law was, the author wrote, "a manifestation of racial prejudice which has no place in a nation avowedly dedicated to individual liberty and opportunity." The U.S. Supreme Court would never again confront the issue of the constitutionality of alien land laws. But in 1952 the California Supreme Court, following the lead of its sister tribunal in Oregon, held that *Oyama* had not foreclosed further consideration of that issue. It concluded that California's statute had been adopted for the purpose of effectuating racial discrimination and as such violated the Fourteenth Amendment.[6]

Wartime hysteria led not only to the amendment of the Alien Land Law and an upsurge in escheat actions against Japanese farmers, it also produced a new piece of anti-Japanese legislation. In 1943 California amended its Fish and Game Code to bar the issuance of fishing licenses to "aliens ineligible for citizenship" (as originally introduced the statute had read "alien Japanese," but the authors, on reflection, thought it might not be a good idea to make the law's racial animus so blatant and fell back on the time-honored circumlocution). In justification of the measure the state relied upon another somewhat esoteric doctrine of constitutional law, the so-called "common property" or "special public interest" doctrine. Under this doctrine, a state was seen as owning the natural resources within its borders and was free to discriminate against citizens of other states when it came to their management and use. If it could discriminate against citizens of other states, California argued, it could, *a fortiori*, discriminate against foreigners. But the U.S. Supreme Court rejected this argument, holding in the case of *Takahashi v. Fish and Game Commission*[7] that California was in effect attempting to bar lawfully admitted aliens from earning a living, something states were not permitted to do under established Fourteenth Amendment principles. Again, as in *Oyama,* the court seemed reluctant to address the question of the racial bias behind the law in any meaningful way. Included in this volume are two comments published shortly after *Takahashi* was handed down that provide able discussions of the decision.

The articles in this volume are by legal scholars, historians, political scientists, and others. They approach their subjects from a variety of different disciplinary perspectives and thus help to illuminate them better. Readers will notice that a fair number of the articles date from the 1920s and 1930s. I have chosen them for the continuing strength of their analyses and also, in part, by default. The law reviews and other scholarly journals have in recent years had their full share of articles on the subject of the forcible evacuation and internment of Japanese Americans during World War II and the major court cases to which they gave rise (see Volume III of this series). By contrast they contain much less in the way of law-related scholarship on the anti-Japanese discrimination of the pre-war period—a fact that seems surprising given how significant an episode it constitutes in the legal and political history of the United States and in view of the deep connections that exist between this episode and the latter one.

Notes

1. 188 Cal. 645 (1922).
2. *Porterfield v. Webb*, 263 U.S. 225 (1923); *Webb v. O'Brien,* 263 U.S. 313 (1923); *Frick v. Webb,* 263 U.S. 326 (1923).
3. *Terrace v. Thompson*, 263 U.S. 197 (1923).
4. A student note to the same effect was published contemporaneously in the *Yale Law Journal*. See "The Alien Land Laws: A Reappraisal," 56 *Yale L.J.* 1017.
5. In 1925 the U.S. Supreme Court had sustained that portion of the California law that raised a presumption of intent to evade the law if land was transferred to a citizen but paid for by an ineligible alien. *Cockrill v. California,* 268 U.S. 258 (1925).
6. *Sei Fujii v. State of California*, 38 Cal. 2d 718 (1952). In 1949 the Oregon Supreme Court had invalidated its state's alien land law. *Kenji Namba v. McCourt,* 185 Ore. 579 (1949).
7. 334 U.S. 411 (1948).

Further Reading

Frank F. Chuman, *The Bamboo People: The Law and Japanese Americans,* Publisher's Inc., 1976.

Roger Daniels, *The Politics of Prejudice: The Anti-Japanese Movement in California and the Struggle for Japanese Exclusion,* University of California Press, 1962.

Bill Hosokawa, *JACL: In Quest of Justice,* W. Morrow, 1982.

Yuji Ichioka, *The Issei: The World of the First Generation Japanese Immigrants, 1885-1924,* Free Press, 1988.

Milton Konvitz, *The Alien and the Asiatic in American Law*, Cornell University Press, 1946.

Japanese Immigrants and American Law

SOME LEGAL ASPECTS OF THE JAPANESE QUESTION

By Raymond Leslie Buell
Harvard University

It would be difficult to find a better illustration of the dependence of politics upon law [1] than in America's Japanese problem. Our attitude toward the Oriental has been crystallized in legislation. And much of the popular prejudice against the Japanese arises out of a conflict of legal principles over which they as individuals have no control. This article does not propose to discuss the policy which should be followed in regard to Japanese immigration or to the treatment of Japanese residents already here. But it merely attempts to set forth the legal aspects of the problem which must be considered before it can really be solved.

NATURALIZATION

Unlike an European, a Japanese alien cannot become a citizen of the United States. Different courts have ruled that he is "ineligible to citizenship."[2] Yet Congress has never passed a law barring Japanese from naturalization as it has the Chinese.[3] Despite the rulings of lower tribunals, many Japanese contend that the term "free white person"[4]—who may be naturalized—should be interpreted so as to include themselves. Their argument has been as follows:

In 1873–1874 the Revised Statutes of the United States were for the first time compiled, Title XXX of which dealt with naturalization (sections 2165–2174). Section 2165 of this Title declared, "*An alien* may be admitted to become a citizen of the United States in the following manner, *and not otherwise*." Section 2169 declared, "The provisions of this Title shall apply to aliens of African nativity and to persons of African descent."[5] Nowhere in this Title was any reference made to "free white persons." Under section 2165, aliens of all races were eligible. But how was section 2169 to be interpreted? If it was really a restrictive clause, limiting the scope of section 2165, it meant that no aliens except negroes were eligible to citizen-

[1] Cf. Bluntschli, *Lehre vom Modernen Stat*, Vol. I, p. 3.

[2] *In re Saito*, 62 Fed. 126; *In re Yamashita*, 30 Wash. 234, 70 Pac. 482; *In re Buntaro Kumagai*, 163 Fed. 922; *Bessho* v. *U. S.*, 178 Fed. 245.

[3] Chinese Restriction Act of 1882, 22 Stat. 61, ch. 126, sec. 14.

[4] This phrase was originally used in the first naturalization statute, approved March 26, 1790, 1 Stat. 103, ch. 3.

[5] The right of naturalization was first extended to negro aliens in the act of July 14, 1870. 16 Stat. 256, ch. 254, sec. 7.

ship—a ridiculous interpretation. But if it was a clause introduced merely to emphasize the revolutionary fact that negroes now could acquire citizenship, section 2165 would make all aliens, including negroes (and Japanese), eligible to be naturalized.

When Congress awoke to the omission of the words "free white persons," it amended section 2169 in 1875 so as to read, "The provisions of this Title shall apply to aliens [being free white persons, and to aliens] of African nativity and to persons of African descent."[6] But section 2165 was left unchanged[7]—"an alien" might still be naturalized "in the following manner, and not otherwise." As we have just seen, section 2165 must have been the controlling section between the years 1873–1875. It is the contention of the Japanese that the alterations made in section 2169 in 1875 did not convert it from an explanatory into a restrictive clause, but that the words "free white persons" were merely introduced for the sake of emphasis. If this argument is sound, section 2165, which is substantially incorporated in section 4 of the Naturalization Act of 1906, would still be the controlling section, and Japanese would be eligible to citizenship.

In the second place, the Japanese claim that they are not Mongolian, but Caucasian in origin, and that, therefore, they are "free white persons" from the standpoint of anthropology and of ethnology—a subject into wihch it is not necessary here to enter.[8]

Thirdly, they also assert that the term "free white person" is a catch-all phrase, including all races and nationalities not specifically mentioned by statute. For example, the state and federal censuses for a long time enumerated only whites, negroes and Indians.[9] All those who were not negroes or Indians were classified as "white." A race such as the Hindus might thus be listed as white, until they became numerous enough to be classified separately. When this was done the "whites" would be cut down, but they might still include members of other races not numerous enough to be mentioned separately. Now the Japanese have never been specifically mentioned in the naturalization laws, although negroes and Chinese have.[10] But if "free white person" is a catch-all term, the Japanese would be included under it, and eligible to citizenship.

[6] 18 Stat. 318, ch. 80, par. 14.

[7] Sections 2165–2169 of the Revised Statutes are still in force unless expressly repealed by later changes in the naturalization laws. *U. S.* v. *Meyer*, 170 Fed. 983; *In re Alverto*, 198 Fed. 688; *In re Geronimo Para*, 269 Fed. 643; *Bessho* v. *U. S.*, *supra; In re Rallos*, 241 Fed. 686; *In re Lampitoe*, 232 Fed. 382; *U. S.* v. *Balsara*, 180 Fed. 694; *Sato* v. *Hall*, 34 *Calif. Appellate Decisions*, 678.

[8] See the brief, "Japanese Naturalization Case, October Term, 1916, No. 222, *Takao Ozawa* v. *the United States*. On a certificate from the U. S. Circuit Court of Appeals for the Ninth Circuit." On racial origin, cf. W. E. Griffis, *The Mikado, Institution and Person*, (1915), p. 9; K. S. Latourette, *The Development of Japan* (1918), pp. 13–14.

[9] See Judge Lowell's learned opinion, *In re Halladjian*, 174 Fed. 834, 842.

[10] Nevertheless Chinese were declared ineligible to citizenship before they were barred by statute. *In re Ah Yup*, 5 Sawy. C. C. 155; cf. also *In re Gee Hop*, 71 Fed. 274.

Finally, the Japanese have claimed the right of naturalization by virtue of the act of May 9, 1918,[11] which declared that "any alien" serving in the army or navy of the United States might file a petition of naturalization without proof of the five years' residence otherwise required. Although section 2 of this act said, "Nothing in this act shall repeal or in any way enlarge section twenty-one hundred and sixty-nine of the Revised Statutes, except as specified in the seventh subdivision of this Act . . . ," the Japanese claimed that the phrase "any alien" included themselves. The Hawaiian courts were so impressed by this argument that they permitted the naturalization of a number of Japanese serving in the Hawaiian national guard.[12]

Federal courts have rejected all four of these arguments in favor of the eligibility of Japanese to American citizenship. In *In re Halladjian* the court ruled that section 2169 was really a restrictive clause, limiting the right of naturalization to free white persons and to negroes.[13] *In Ex parte Shahid* it was said that the term "free white persons" means "persons as then understood to be of European habitancy or descent"—which despatched with the ethnologic argument of the Japanese.[14] The repeated denial of citizenship to Japanese, as in the cases cited above, shows that the courts have refused to accept the "catch-all" interpretation of "free white person." Finally, it has been ruled that the Act of May 9, 1918 is controlled by the "color" provisions of the Revised Statutes.[15]

Nevertheless, the decisions of the naturalization courts have not been uniform. In the 1910 census there were more than four hundred naturalized Japanese in this country.[16] It was not until November, 1922, that the United States Supreme Court handed down a decision on this subject. As early as 1916 Takao Ozawa filed a brief in the Supreme Court. He had lived in American territory for twenty years and had been educated in American schools. His personal qualifications for citizenship were conceded, but the District Court of Hawaii, in which he applied for citizenship, denied it because of section 2169 of the Revised Statutes. He thereupon appealed to the Circuit Court of Appeals for the Ninth Circuit and that court certified the case to the Supreme Court, asking to be instructed on these questions (1) Is the Naturalization Act of June 29, 1906, limited by the provisions of Section 2169 of the Revised Statutes of the United States? (2) If so limited, is the appellant eligible to naturalization under

[11] 40 Stat. 542, ch. 69.

[12] *Survey of Education in Hawaii*, Dept. of the Interior, Bureau of Education, Bull. No. 16, 1920, p. 32.

[13] 174 Fed. 834, 836.

[14] 205 Fed. 812, 815; also *Ex parte Dow*, 211 Fed. 486.

[15] *In re Geronimo Para, supra; Petition of Easurk Emsen Charr*, 278 Fed. 207; cf. also *In re Bhagat Singh Thind*, 268 Fed. 683; and the letter of W. B. Wilson, Secretary of Labor to Senator Phelan, *Cong. Record*, Feb. 19, 1921, p. 3660; and *Sato* v. *Hall, supra.*

[16] 1910 Census, Vol. I, p. 1070; apparently these figures are not given in Volume I of the 1920 census.

that section? The Ozawa case was decided by the Supreme Court along with a similar case—*Yamashita* and *Kono* v. *Hinkle*. In the latter case a superior court in the State of Washington duly naturalized the plaintiffs who, on May 5, 1921, requested Hinkle, the Secretary of State of Washington, to accept a copy of articles of incorporation for a real estate company they had formed. Hinkle refused to file these articles on the ground that the plaintiffs, being Japanese, could not be admitted to citizenship and that, under the laws of Washington, they were not entitled to form such a corporation. The Washington Supreme Court decided the case in favor of Hinkle, upon which the Japanese appealed.

In view of the historic interpretation of the "color" provisions of the Revised Statutes, there was only one way which the Supreme Court could decide. Justice Sutherland rendered the opinion in which he said that "In all of the naturalization acts from 1790 to 1906, the privilege of naturalization was confined to white persons (with the addition in 1870 of those of African nativity and descent), although the exact wording of the various statutes was not always the same. If Congress in 1906 desired to alter a rule so well and so long established it may be assumed that its purpose would have been definitely disclosed and its legislation to that end put in unmistakable terms." In regard to the contention that the Japanese were "white," Justice Sutherland said that the intention of the framers of the naturalization law "was to confer the privilege of citizenship upon that class of persons whom the fathers knew as white, and to deny it to all who could not be so classified."[17]

But the court admitted that the interpretation of "white person" as "a person of Caucasian race" does not "establish a sharp line of demarcation between those who are entitled and those who are not entitled to naturalization but rather a zone of more or less debatable ground outside of which, upon the one hand, are those clearly eligible and outside of which, upon the other hand, are those clearly ineligible to citizenship. Individual cases falling within this zone must be determined as they arise from time to time by what this court has called, in another connection (*Davidson* v. *New Orleans*, 96 U. S., 97, 104) 'the gradual process of judicial inclusion and exclusion.' "

This rule the courts have followed in the past and with somewhat illogical results. They have naturalized a native of Mexico who could neither read nor write, and who admitted that he could not understand the constitution.[18] They have admitted a Syrian,[19] and an Armenian,[20] and a Hindu,[21] and a

[17] *Ozawa* v. *the U. S.*, No. 1—Oct. Term, 1922, "Supreme Court of the United States"; *Yamashita and Kono* v. *Hinkle*, No. 177—Oct. Term, 1922, "Supreme Court of the United States"; both decided Nov. 13, 1922. The decision in the Ozawa case is printed, *infra.*, p. 151.

[18] *In re Rodriguez*, 81 Fed. 337.

[19] *In re Najour*, 174 Fed. 735; *Dow* v. *U. S.*, 226 Fed. 145.

[20] *In re Halladjian, supra.*

[21] *In re Akhay Kumar Mozumdar*, 207 Fed. 115.

Parsee.[22] But other courts have denied citizenship to a Syrian,[23] a Burmese,[24] and a Filipino.[25]

Delving into racial metaphysics is not properly a judicial task; and it would be much better if Congress would pass a new naturalization law, either placing the admission of aliens to citizenship on a purely personal basis, or specifically banning races which it deems objectionable. It is entirely possible, moreover, to negotiate a treaty with Japan, making Japanese eligible to American citizenship.[26]

DUAL CITIZENSHIP

A second question closely connected with naturalization is dual citizenship. According to the fourteenth amendment to the Constitution of the United States, every Japanese born in the United States is an American citizen.[27] But according to Japanese law, he is also a subject of Japan.[28] This is the old conflict between *jus soli* and *jus sanguinis* familiar to all students of international law.[29] The rule of *jus sanguinis*, still adhered to by Japan, was followed by the United States up to 1907;[30] and it is now followed by most of the countries in Europe and several countries in South America.[31]

Every Japanese man is liable to conscription between the ages of 17 and

[22] *U. S.* v. *Balsara, supra.*

[23] *Ex parte Shahid, supra.*

[24] *In re Po*, N.Y. S. 383.

[25] *In re Alverto*, 198 Fed. 688, where a quarter-breed Spaniard and Filipino was excluded. Also *In re Lampitoe, supra.*

[26] Although Art. I, sec. 8, par. 4 of the Constitution authorizes Congress to "establish a uniform rule of naturalization," a treaty conferring the right of naturalization undoubtedly would be constitutional. Congress also has the power to regulate foreign commerce, but we have negotiated dozens of treaties of commerce and navigation. Naturalization has been conferred on Indians by treaty, *Elk* v. *Wilkins*, 112 U. S. 94, 100; *Wiggan* v. *Conolly*, 163 U. S. 56. The former cites a large number of treaties with Indian tribes in which naturalization is conferred. Citizenship was conferred on the inhabitants of the Louisiana territory by the treaty of 1803 between France and the United States, Moore, *Digest of International Law*, Vol. III, p. 313. Cf. the Treaty of Guadalupe Hidalgo of 1848, and the Alaskan treaty of 1867, Moore, *ibid.*, p. 319. See also Van Dyne, *Naturalization* (1907), "Naturalization by Treaty," p. 273 ff.

The naturalization of the Japanese has been discussed in S. L. Gulick, *American Democracy and Asiatic Citizenship* (1918), pp. 54–79; and in R. Malcolm, "American Citizenship and the Japanese," *Annals of the Academy of Political and Social Science*, Vol. XCIII, No. 182.

[27] Children born of parents ineligible to citizenship in this country are nevertheless citizens of the United States, *United States* v. *Wong Kim Ark*, 169 U. S. 649.

[28] "A child is a Japanese if his or her father is a Japanese at the time of his or her birth." Law of Nationality, No. 66, Article I, April 1, 1899; de Becker, *Civil Code of Japan*, Vol. 3, Appendix I.

[29] For the origin of these conflicting theories, see Sir Henry Maine, *Ancient Law*, Ch. IV.

[30] Cf. sec. 1993 of the Revised Statutes, and the Law of 1907, 34 Stat. 1228, which provides that a child born abroad of American parents loses the protection of the United States unless he declares his intention of becoming a resident, etc., of the United States.

[31] Borchard, *Diplomatic Protection of Citizens Abroad*, sec. 255.

40.[32] Under Japan's Nationality Law, it would appear, therefore, that every Japanese born in America, and an American citizen under our law, is liable to serve his time in the Japanese army, and to fight for Japan in time of war. In order to enforce this allegiance, the Japanese government keeps a record of all Japanese born abroad. Japanese subjects are required to register births with the local Japanese consulate. A birth certificate is also forwarded to the district in Japan where the parents originally lived. Thus when these Japanese reach the age of seventeen, they are placed on the military register.[33]

But the legal severity of these provisions is mitigated, first, by the failure of many Japanese parents to register the birth of children born in America. Out of a total of 2,345 Japanese births in the State of Washington for the years 1915–1917, only 1,770 were registered with the Japanese consulate. Secondly, the Japanese Government does not actually require Japanese living abroad to return home and perform military service. They may secure annual "exemption" slips which postpones their service, until the age of 37 when they are freed practically of this obligation.[34] Finally, the Japanese government has made possible the expatriation of Japanese born abroad by the Expatriation Law of March 15, 1916.[35] Expatriation is the act by which a person divests himself of citizenship in one nation and accepts, if he does not already hold, citizenship in another.[36] The Japanese Expatriation Law provides for expatriation in three ways: a Japanese minor born abroad can free himself of Japanese nationality first, if below the age of fifteen, at the request of a legal representative; second, if between the ages of fifteen and seventeen, only with the consent of his parent or guardian; third, if above the age of seventeen, only after serving in the Japanese army or navy, or being released from such an obligation. In all of these cases, the consent of the Minister for Home Affairs is necessary.

[32] There is considerable confusion in regard to the Japanese military service. Cf. Porter, *The Full Recognition of Japan* (1911), p. 220; McGovern, *Modern Japan*, (1920), p. 215; *Japan Year Book*, 1920–1921, p. 683–684; G. Ogawa, *Conscription System in Japan*, (1921), Part I.

[33] *Japanese Immigration*, Hearings of the House Committee on Immigration and Naturalization on the Pacific Coast, Government Printing Office, 1921, p. 1189.

[34] *Japan Year Book*, 1921–1922, p. 293.

[35] This law was first published in English in *California and the Oriental*, Report of the California State Board of Control (1920), pp. 186–187. I have followed the translation given in *Japanese Immigration*, Hearings, *cited*, p. 711.

[36] Expatriation may be effected either under law or under a treaty. In England, the Naturalization Act of 1870 provides that any person who, by reason of birth within the realm, is a natural-born subject, may renounce such citizenship if he wishes to do so. 33 Vict., ch. 14, sec. 4. The United States has negotiated some seventeen "naturalization" treaties with foreign nations, each of which provides that when a national of one state chooses to become naturalized in the other, the first nation agrees to relinquish its claim to allegiance. See Malloy, *Treaties and Conventions of the United States*, index, "Naturalization Conventions."

Because of the limitations of this law, it has often been regarded as a mere sham. The restrictions on the expatriation of Japanese of military age might be justified in cases which have occurred in France and Germany, where boys often emigrated to America solely to escape conscription.[37] But such is not the case with Japanese children born here. If through the negligence or ill-will of their parents, Japanese children do not become expatriated before the age of seventeen, they cannot become expatriated until they have served their time in the Japanese army—a provision equally unsatisfactory to the United States and to the individual Japanese. It is also unnecessary from the standpoint of the Japanese Government because immediately after military service is performed, Japan loses the allegiance of the Japanese wishing to acquire American citizenship.

Despite the restrictions of this law, a number of Japanese have taken advantage of it. Up to August, 1922, one hundred and forty Japanese filed expatriation papers in the territory of the Consulate General of Japan for California (with the exception of the nine southern counties), Utah, Nevada, and Colorado.[38]

Nevertheless, this problem is not entirely solved because of the limitations of the Expatriation Law of 1916. It may be settled by (1) a more liberal expatriation law on the part of the Japanese Government; (2) a treaty between Japan and the United States, automatically releasing from Japanese citizenship all Japanese born in this country who continue to reside here, and also all Japanese naturalized in the United States; (3) an amendment to the Constitution of the United States, now advocated by the Exclusion League and the American Legion, which would make ineligible to citizenship all children born in the United States of parents who are ineligible to citizenship. Regardless of its desirability, it is unlikely that such an amendment will ever be enacted. The South probably would not agree to it unless negroes were also barred from citizenship. But it is not likely that the North would ever accept this *quid pro quo*.

ANTI-JAPANESE LAND LEGISLATION AND THE TREATY OF 1911

Some twenty states in the Union deny to aliens the same right to acquire real property as are held by citizens.[39] But this legislation has had serious consequences only on the Pacific Coast where California, Washington, and Arizona have enacted land laws directed against the Japanese farmer.[40] In

[37] See Moore, *Digest*, Vol. III, pp. 518–551; for the subject of expatriation, see *ibid.*, Vol. III, pp. 552–735.

[38] Letter from the Consulate General of Japan, August 14, 1922. It is very interesting to note that with a growing knowledge of this expatriation law, an increasing number of Japanese are taking advantage of it. In 1917 there were only seven Japanese who became expatriated. In 1921, there were 58, and in the first six months of 1922, there were 56.

[39] For these laws, see *Alien Land Laws and Alien Rights*, House Doc. 89, 67th Cong., 1st sess., pp. 32–34.

[40] 1913 *California Statutes*, ch. 113, p. 206; Arizona, *Session Laws*, 1921, ch. 29, p. 25; Washington Constitution, Art. 2, par. 33, *Session Laws*, 1921, ch. 50, p. 156.

1913 the California legislature passed a land law which provided that aliens ineligible to citizenship can acquire and dispose of real property "in the manner and to the extent and for the purpose prescribed by any treaty now existing between the government of the United States" and the nation of which the alien in question is a subject, but not otherwise. The 1913 law permitted this class of aliens, the Japanese, to lease agricultural land for three years.[41] But in 1920 this provision was repealed by an initiative measure, which also attempted to prohibit alleged evasions of the 1913 law.[42]

This land legislation has been criticized on the ground that it abridges privileges granted Japanese residents in the United States by the treaty of 1911 between Japan and the United States. But by its very terms, the California land law is in accord with our treaty obligations—the Japanese are entitled to acquire property in the manner prescribed by treaty. The real question is whether the treaty of 1911 authorizes Japanese generally to acquire real property in the United States. In the enforcement of the laws of 1913 and 1920, the California executive officials have interpreted the treaty narrowly: they will bring action against any Japanese who purchases real property or leases it for agricultural purposes, on the ground that the treaty of 1911 does not grant such privileges. On the other hand, the Japanese have claimed these privileges because of three provisions of the treaty, as follows:

The provision granting the privilege "to enter, travel and reside" in the

[41] The Constitution of the State of California (Art. I, sec. 17), adopted in 1879, originally gave persons eligible to citizenship the same rights in regard to property as citizens. *Norris* v. *Hoyt*, 18 Cal. 217; *State* v. *Smith*, 70 Cal. 156. Section 671 of the California Civil Code later extended these privileges to all aliens, by declaring, "Any person, whether citizen or alien, may take, hold, and dispose of property, real or personal, within this State." The land laws of 1913 and 1920 returned in a sense to the rule laid down originally in the State constitution. The history of the anti-Japanese movement on the Pacific Coast is traced in R. L. Buell, "The Development of the Anti-Japanese Agitation in the United States," two parts, *Political Science Quarterly*, December, 1922, and March, 1923.

[42] 1921 *California Statutes*, pp. lxxxvii–xc. This act provides: (1) Aliens eligible to citizenship may acquire, hold, and transmit real property in the same manner as citizens of the United States; (2) all aliens "other than those mentioned in section one" may acquire property in the manner prescribed by any treaty now existing between the United States and the country of which the alien is a subject, and not otherwise; (3) any corporation of which a majority of members are aliens ineligible to citizenship, or in which a majority of issued capital stock is owned by such aliens, may acquire land only as prescribed by treaty; (4) a Japanese cannot act as guardian of a minor's estate which consists of property which the Japanese himself cannot hold; (5) every "colorable" transfer of real property is prohibited, if made to evade the law, and a presumption to that effect exists if (a) the land is paid for by a Japanese although some one else buys the property, (b) or if the property is acquired by a corporation, the controlling shares of which are paid for by Japanese but held by citizens of the United States. Any land acquired in violation of this act, shall escheat to the State of California. Section 10 of the Act punishes conspiracies to violate it with imprisonment up to two years and fine up to $5,000. This section was attacked on the ground that the act did not declare such conspiracy to be a crime. But it was sustained as it stood in *In re Akado* (May 16, 1922), 63 *Cal. Dec.* 577.

United States "to carry on trade, wholesale and retail, to own or lease and occupy houses, manufactories, warehouses and shops . . . , to lease land for residential and commercial purposes, and generally to do anything incident to or necessary for trade upon the same terms as native citizens or subjects. . . ."

The provision granting them "the most constant protection and security for their persons and property."

The provision granting them most-favored-nation treatment "in all that concerns commerce and navigation."[43]

It has been contended that the provision "to do anything incident to or necessary for trade" entitles the Japanese to lease land for agricultural purposes because, it is argued, agriculture is incidental to trade.[44] This argument was dispatched with by a federal court, in the recent case of *Terrace* v. *Thompson*, where it was said: "In the most liberal construction of this language that may be indulged in, it cannot be fairly said that truck-farming is incidental to trading . . . in the products of a farm, any more than conducting a sheep-ranch or growing mulberry trees is incidental to the dry-goods trade."[45]

Moreover, the provision guaranteeing the Japanese "most constant protection and security" merely protects property already acquired. It does not give them the privilege to acquire it generally for purposes not authorized by the treaty. The treaty between the United States and Italy of 1871 is very similar in the privileges it guarantees Italians in this country to the treaty of 1911 with Japan.[46] But the Supreme Court of the United States has ruled that the Italian treaty does not invalidate State legislation excluding aliens from employment on public works, and from killing wild birds, etc.[47] In the case of *Patsone* v. *Pennsylvania*, Mr. Justice Holmes declared that, "The prohibition of a particular kind of destruction and of acquiring property in instruments intended for that purpose establishes no inequality in either respect."

The land legislation under consideration is not confiscatory—it does not affect vested rights. If a Japanese owned a farm before 1913, he still owns it as far as the land laws are concerned.[48]

[43] Sections 1 and 3 of Article I, and Article XIV, Treaty of 1911, *Foreign Relations of the United States*, 1911, pp. 315–319.

[44] This was the official argument, printed in the pamphlet distributed to voters in regard to initiative measures, against the anti-Japanese measure of 1920.

[45] 274 Fed. 841, 846. The court merely followed out the Supreme Court's past distinction between commerce and agriculture or manufacture. See *U. S.* v. *E. C. Knight*, 156 U. S. 1; *Kidd* v. *Pearson*, 128 U. S. 1; *Capital City Dairy Co.* v. *Ohio*, 183 U. S. 238; *Delaware, Lackawanna & Western R. R. Co.* v. *Yurkonis*, 238 U. S. 439.

[46] For the treaty with Italy, see Malloy, *Treaties and Conventions of the United States*, p. 969.

[47] *Heim* v. *McCall*, 239 U. S. 175; *Patsone* v. *Pennsylvania*, 232 U. S. 138.

[48] Many Japanese wrongly assume that this legislation is confiscatory, see A. Kinnosuke, "What Japan Wants," *Nation*, February 2, 1921.

The California land law obviously discriminates between Japanese who cannot acquire real property and Europeans, etc., who can.[49] The Japanese Government has officially protested against this discrimination on the ground that it violates "most-favored-nation" treatment guaranteed in the treaty of 1911.[50] But the American State Department has pointed out, in its correspondence with the Japanese Government, that that treaty was merely a treaty of commerce and navigation, and that it did not apply to broad civil or political privileges. In support of its contention, it cited our protest in 1879 against the Mexican land law as a violation of the "most-favored-nation" clause in the treaty of 1831 between the United States and Mexico.[51] The Mexican Government made an unanswerable reply that this treaty was limited to commerce and navigation and did not extend to general property rights. In its correspondence with the Japanese Government, the State Department also asserted that whenever the United States has wished to grant most-favored-nation treatment in regard to real property, it has done so by special treaty.[52]

The treaty of 1911 does not expressly authorize Japanese to own land of any kind, or to lease land for agricultural purposes. That privilege cannot be implied as being incidental to trade, or from the most-favored-nation clause. The conclusion is unavoidable that the land laws of the western states do not violate the treaty of 1911.[53] This conclusion has been reached

[49] The California land law may possibly exclude all non-resident aliens from land ownership, except by treaty, for they are not eligible to citizenship if living abroad. Cf. McMurray, "Legal Aspects of the Japanese Question," *The Pacific Review*, December, 1920.

[50] "Protest of Japan against the Land Laws of the State of California," *Foreign Relations of the United States*, 1913, pp. 625–653; *ibid.*, 1914, pp. 426–434. In its final note, the Japanese Government said, "It is a matter of great regret . . . to find in the communications so far received from the United States Government, little that appears to answer in a fundamental manner to the main complaint of the Imperial Government, so as to shake their original convictions which dictated the present protest, namely, that the new California statute is invidiously discriminatory against the Japanese nation, that it is contrary to the letter as well as spirit of the existing treaty, and that it is incompatible with the sentiment of amity and friendship which has always characterized the intercourse between our two nations." *U. S. For. Rel.*, 1914, p. 433.

[51] Moore, *Digest of International Law*, Vol. VI, p. 702; *U. S. For. Rel.* 1913, p. 647.

[52] In a note of February 21, 1911, Baron Uchida admitted to Secretary Knox that the treaty of 1911 did not control land tenure, because he said, "In return for the rights of land ownership which are granted Japanese by the laws of the various States of the United States . . . the Imperial Government will by liberal interpretation of the laws be prepared to grant land ownership to American citizens from all the States, reserving for the future, however, the right of maintaining the condition of reciprocity with respect to the separate states." *U. S. For. Rel.* 1913, p. 643.

[53] Although the treaty of 1911 does not encroach upon the powers ordinarily reserved to the states in regard to land tenure, (cf. *U. S.* v. *Fox*, 94 U. S. 315), the Federal Government has the power to negotiate a treaty which would give Japanese the right to own agricultural land in California or any other State in the Union. Cf. *Society for the Propagation of the Gospel* v. *New Haven*, 8 Wheat. 464; *Ware* v. *Hylton*, 3 Dal. 199; *Chirac* v. *Chirac*, 2 Wheat. 259; *Geofroy* v. *Riggs*, 133 U. S. 258; *Hauenstein* v. *Lynham*, 100 U. S. 483; *Orr* v. *Hodgson*,

by the District Court for Washington in regard to the Washington land law, and by the Los Angeles District Court in regard to the California statute of 1920.[54]

ANTI-JAPANESE LAND LEGISLATION AND THE FOURTEENTH AMENDMENT

The fourteenth amendment to the Constitution of the United States (section 1) says that no State shall deprive any person of life, liberty, or property without due process of law; nor deny to any person within its jurisdiction the equal protection of the laws. The protection of this amendment extends to "persons" which includes aliens, whether eligible to citizenship or not.[55] It has been frequently asserted that in discriminating between aliens eligible and aliens ineligible to citizenship, this land legislation is a violation of these provisions of the fourteenth amendment.

But the land laws of the Pacific Coast States do not deprive aliens ineligible to citizenship of real property they had before the legislation went into force. These laws contain no provisions which actually deprive them of their property. They simply prohibit them from acquiring real property in the future.

The equal protection clause of the fourteenth amendment prohibits a State from arbitrarily discriminating between different classes of persons.[56]

4 Wheat. 453; *Carneal* v. *Banks*, 10 Wheat. 181; *Fairfax* v. *Hunter*, 7 Cranch, 627; *Hughes* v. *Edwards*, 9 Wheat. 489; *Wunderle* v. *Wunderle*, 144 Ill. 40; *People* v. *Gerke*, 5 Cal. 381; *Blythe* v. *Hinckley*, 127 Cal. 431, also 180 U. S. 333; *In re Turner's Estate*, 196 Pac. 807; *Missouri* v. *Holland*, 252 U. S. 416. See also E. S. Corwin, *National Supremacy* (1913), and Senator F. B. Kellogg's address, *Reports of the American Bar Assn.*, 1913, pp. 331–392.

For a protest against this view see Dean Tucker's *Limitation on the Treaty-Making Power*, (1915), Ch. X, and J. H. Boyd, "The Treaty-making Power of the U. S. and Alien Land Laws in States," 6 *California Law Review*, pp. 279–94.

For Californians' protest against such a treaty, see *Sacramento Bee*, August 27, 1920; and Montaville Flowers, *Japanese Conquest of American Opinion* (1917), p. 35. But State Attorney-General Webb, in an address before the states attorneys-general of the United States, in San Francisco, admitted that such a treaty could be negotiated. *Los Angeles Times*, August 9, 1922.

[54] *Terrace* v. *Thompson*, (July 25, 1921), 274 Fed. 841; *Porterfield* v. *Webb*, (December 19, 1921), 279 Fed. 114. For a comment on recent decisions affecting these laws, see M. E. Harrison, "Alien Land Legislation on the Pacific Coast," *American Bar Association Journal*, August, 1922; and "Comments on Cases," 10 *California Law Review*, *passim*, which discuss these decisions more from the standpoint of private law.

An interesting conflict between a law and a treaty has arisen lately in France. The Chamber of Deputies has passed a bill forbidding foreigners to hold real estate in France or to lease property for more than nine years without formal governmental approval. The American State Department has protested against this law on the ground that it violates the Franco-American Consular Convention of 1853, Article VII of which, the Department believes, gives reciprocal rights in regard to the ownership of real estate. New York *Times*, Nov. 24, 1922.

[55] *Yick Wo* v. *Hopkins*, 118 U. S. 356; *U. S.* v. *Wong Kim Ark*, *supra; Lau Ow Bew* v. *U. S.*, 144 U. S. 47; *Lem Moon Sing* v. *U. S.*, 158 U. S. 538; *Ex parte Virginia*, 100 U. S. 339; *Missouri* v. *Lewis*, 101 U. S. 22; *Pace* v. *Alabama*, 106 U. S. 583.

[56] *Yick Wo* v. *Hopkins*, *supra.*

But a State does have the power to make classifications, provided they are reasonable.[57]

If aliens were allowed freely to acquire real property, it would become legally possible for them to gain control of a great deal of the real property of the State, which might very well be considered a danger, especially in time of war. The reason why aliens were denied these privileges in ancient England were set forth, with unconscious humor, by the judges in Calvin's case: "It followeth next in course to set down the reasons, wherefore an alien born is not capable of inheritance within England, and that he is not for three reasons: 1. The secrets of the realm might thereby be discovered. 2. The revenues of the realm (the sinews of war, and ornament of peace,) should be taken and enjoyed by strangers born. 3. It should tend to the destruction of the realm. . . . First, it tends to destruction *tempore belli;* for then strangers might fortify themselves in the heart of the realm, and be ready to set fire on the commonwealth, as was excellently shadowed by the Trojan horse in Virgil's second Book of the *Æneid,* where a very few men in the heart of the city did more mischief in few hours, than ten thousand men without the walls in ten years. Secondly, *tempore pacis,* for so might many aliens born get a great part of the inheritance and freehold of the realm, whereof there shall follow a failure of justice (the supporter of the commonwealth) for that aliens born cannot be returned of juries for the trial of issues between the king and the subject, or between subject and subject." [58]

For these reasons, under the English law an alien could not lease land for agricultural purposes,[59] and he could not hold real property[60] against the king who might take it away from him at any time by a procedure known as "office found."[61] By a law passed in the reign of Queen Victoria, aliens residing in Great Britain were permitted to hold personal property of all kinds, *except chattels real.* Likewise they might hold land or houses for *residence or business* for a period not exceeding twenty-one years.[62] It was

[57] *Mo. Pacific R. R. Co.* v. *Mackey,* 127 U. S. 205; *Walston* v. *Nevin,* 128 U. S. 578; *Barbier* v. *Connolly,* 113 U. S. 27; *Bell's Gap R. R. Co.* v. *Pa.,* 134 U. S. 232; *Clark* v. *Kansas City,* 176 U. S. 114; *St. John* v. *New York,* 201 U. S. 633; *Gulf, etc. R. Co.* v. *Ellis,* 165 U. S. 150; *Home Insurance Co.* v. *N. Y. State,* 134 U. S. 594.

[58] Calvin's case, *Coke's Reports* (J. H. Thomas ed., 1826), Part VII, p. 32.

[59] *Coke on Littleton,* (Day's edition, 1812), ch. 1, sec. 1, 2b.

[60] For the common law rights of aliens, see Coke, *cited;* and the cases cited in T. A. Walker. *History of the Law of Nations,* (1899) p. 121; *Fairfax* v. *Hunter,* 7 Cranch 620; *Geofroy* v. *Riggs,* 133 U. S. 265; Blackstone, *Commentaries* (Lewis' edition) Book I, pp. 331 ff.; Kent, *Commentaries,* Vol. II, p. 71.

[61] *Osterman* v. *Baldwin,* 6 Wall. 121; *Fairfax* v. *Hunter, supra*; *Craig* v. *Leslie,* 3 Wheat. 589; *Craig* v. *Radford,* 3 Wheat. 599; *Cross* v. *De Valle,* 1 Wall. 13; *Hauenstein* v. *Lynham,* 100 U. S. 484. Cf. *Suwa* v. *Johnson,* 203 Pac. 414; and *Mork* v. *Mellett,* 205 Pac. 664.

[62] 7–8 Vict., ch. 66, secs. 4 and 5.

not until the Naturalization Act of 1870 that aliens were placed on the same footing as subjects in regard to real property.[63]

The reason for drawing a line between aliens and citizens for certain purposes has been so obvious that the Supreme Court has dismissed the contention that such discriminations violated the fourteenth amendment, in almost a summary manner. In *Crane* v. *N. Y.* a law, which prohibited aliens from being employed on public works, was attacked on the ground that the classification was unreasonable, under the fourteenth amendment. In delivering the opinion, Mr. Justice McKenna said, "There is added the view that a distinction between aliens and citizens violates the principle of classification. We think this view is also without foundation."[64] In *Toop* v. *Ulysses Land Co.*, a Nebraska law, incapacitating aliens from inheriting or holding real estate, was also attacked on constitutional grounds. But this "contention that the state statute forbidding the ownership of real property by aliens was repugnant to the Fourteenth Amendment," Chief Justice White said, "is too frivolous to afford a basis of jurisdiction."[65]

In 1909 the State of Pennsylvania passed a law which made it unlawful for any unnaturalized foreign born resident to kill any wild bird or animal except in defense of person or property, and "to that end" made it unlawful for such foreign born person to carry or own a shotgun or rifle. This statute was attacked on constitutional grounds in the case of *Patsone* v. *Pennsylvania.* But it was sustained by the court, Mr. Justice Holmes saying:

> . . . A State may classify with reference to the evil to be prevented, and . . . if the class discriminated against is or reasonably might be considered to define those from whom the evil is mainly to be feared, it properly may be picked out. A lack of abstract symmetry does not matter. The question is a practical one, dependent upon experience. The demand for symmetry ignores the specific difference that experience is supposed to have shown to mark the class. It is not enough to invalidate the law that others may do the same thing and go unpunished, if, as a matter of fact, it is found that the danger is characteristic of the class named . . . The State "may direct its law against what it deems the evil as it actually exists without covering the whole field of possible abuses. . . ." The question therefore narrows itself to whether this court can say that the legislature of Pennsylvania was not warranted in assuming as its premise for the law that resident unnaturalized aliens were the peculiar source of the evil that it desired to prevent. . . .
>
> Obviously the question, so stated, is one of local experience on which this court ought to be very slow to declare that the state legislature

[63] 33 Vict., ch. 14, sec. 2. Cf. 32 Hen. 8 ch. 16, sec. 13, and Woodfall, *Landlord and Tenant*, p. 91; and Earl of Halsbury, *The Laws of England*, Vol. I, "Rights and Duties of Aliens"; Pollock and Maitland, *History of English Law* (1895), Vol. I, pp. 442 ff.

[64] 239 U. S. 195, 198.

[65] 237 U. S. 580, 583; cf. *Blythe* v. *Hinckley*, 180 U. S. 333, 340; and *Sullivan* v. *Kidd*, 254 U. S. 433.

> was wrong in its facts. . . . If we might trust popular speech in some States it was right; but it is enough that this court has no such knowledge of local conditions as to be able to say that it was manifestly wrong.[66]

This is a very sweeping doctrine. It would seem to follow from it that if a state has the power to incapacitate aliens generally from holding real property,—which has been repeatedly upheld—it has the power to incapacitate certain classes of aliens who may be "the peculiar source of the evil that it desired to prevent." A State law specifically barring the Japanese from owning land might therefore be constitutional.

If the classification between aliens and citizens in regard to holding real property is a reasonable one, it is only a step further to say that the classification between aliens eligible and aliens ineligible to citizenship is reasonable. As the court declared in *Terrace* v. *Thompson*:

> It is obvious that one who is not a citizen and cannot become one lacks an interest in, and the power to effectually work for the welfare of the state and so lacking, the state may rightfully deny him the right to own and lease real estate within its boundaries. If one incapable of citizenship may own or lease real estate it is within the realm of possibility that every foot of land within the state might pass to the ownership or possession of noncitizens. Such a result would leave the foundation of the state but a pale shadow, and the structure erected thereon but a Tower of Babel, from which the tenant in possession might, when the shock of war came, bow themselves out, because they were not bound as citizens to defend the house in which they lodged.[67]

In the light of these different decisions and the reasoning underlying them, it is very probable that the Supreme Court will hold that this classification between aliens eligible and aliens ineligible to citizenship is reasonable, so far as the ownership of real property is concerned. Under the English law, an alien could lease land for commercial purposes, but not for agriculture, a distinction followed in the treaty of 1911 between Japan and the United States.[68] It is very probable also that the power of the State will be upheld to forbid aliens even to lease land for agricultural purposes. The land laws of the Pacific Coast States bar them from acquiring any "interest" in real property. And the court in *Terrace* v. *Thompson*, (*supra*) ruled that the State legislature has the power to define a lease as real, rather than personal property.[69]

But there is a difference between holding an "interest" in real property through ownership or lease, and merely *using* land for commercial or agricultural purposes, a question which will be discussed presently.

[66] 232 U. S. 138. Cf. *Central Lumber Co.* v. *South Dakota*, 226 U. S. 157; *Tragesser* v. *Grey*, 73 Maryland 250, 9 A. L. R. 780; *Wunderle* v. *Wunderle*, *supra*.

[67] 274 Fed. 849–850.

[68] For the English law on this point, see authorities cited in footnote 60.

[69] 274 Fed. 851; cf. *State ex. rel. Winston* v. *Morrison*, 18 Wash. 664; *State ex. rel. Winston* v. *The Hudson Land Co.*, 19 Wash. 85; but cf. also *Jeffres* v. *Easton*, 113 Cal. 345.

While California's actions in regard to the Japanese have been, strictly speaking, legal, they have severely disturbed the foreign relations of the nation as a whole; they have really controlled foreign policy. No state should have this power; for as long as the state is as free as it now is in regard to aliens, the interests of the Union may be jeopardized by one State.[70]

Very little actual violence has been used against the Japanese in California. However, in the summer of 1921 some fifty Japanese workmen were driven out of the melon fields in Turlock. The ringleaders of this outrage were tried in the Superior Court of Stanislaus County, between April 25 and May 5, 1922; but all of them were acquitted. This is a minor example of the failure of State courts to punish offenses against aliens. Nominally, an alien thus outraged has the right to sue in a federal court for tort in violation of the law of nations or of a treaty of the United States. *Rev. Stat.*, Title XIII, ch. 3, sec. 563, par. 16. But the federal government cannot now punish criminal offenders. Many presidents, such as President Harrison (see Message of December 9, 1891, *Messages and Papers of the Presidents*, National Literature Edition, p. 5618) have advocated a law giving federal courts jurisdiction of all offenses, civil and criminal, against aliens, involving the breach of treaty rights.[71] On June 2, 1921 Senator Kellogg of Minnesota introduced a bill (S. 1943, 67th Congress, 1st session), which would authorize the President to file a bill of equity against any person threatening to violate the rights of a subject of a foreign country; and this provision was to apply to acts threatened by State officers under the alleged justification of a law of the legislature of the State concerned. It also would authorize the United States Attorney General to remove any action against any alien to enforce an act passed by the State legislature, to the proper district court of the United States. It would declare any act committed in a State in violation of the treaty rights of aliens, a crime against the United States, punishable in the Federal courts. In his special message to Congress on the industrial situation, of August 18, 1922, President Harding asked that Congress pass this legislation, in order that such offenses as those just committed at Herrin, Illinois, could be adequately punished.

Although the land legislation is constitutional, it seems that the State cannot legally prohibit its evasion through the means of guardianships and of "croppage contracts." After the passage of the land law of 1913, Japanese aliens, it is alleged, became guardians of their children born in America

[70] For a suggested remedy of this defect in our federal system, see R. L. Buell, "The New States-Rightism," *Nation*, August 17, 1921.

[71] A committee of the American Bar Association once questioned the constitutionality of such a law. See *Reports American Bar Association*, 1892, pp. 406–407. But President Taft rebutted its seven objections, in *The United States and Peace*, p. 59 ff. The Supreme Court in *Baldwin* v. *Franks*, 120 U. S. 678, 683, ruled in favor of the constitutionality of such legislation.

(and therefore, American citizens), solely for the purpose of acquiring agricultural land in their children's name.[72] In order to prevent this evasion of the land law, the 1920 measure prohibited a Japanese alien from acting as guardian of a minor's estate when it consisted of property which the Japanese himself could not hold. But in the important case of *In re Yano,* the California Supreme Court has declared this provision unconstitutional. The court said, "It needs no argument to demonstrate the proposition that a law which gives to one person the right or privilege of becoming the guardian of his child and withholds it from another, both being alike competent in all respects, is not equal as between the two persons. The person from whom it is withheld is not in such a case accorded the protection of equal laws. In this respect the initiative act of 1920 is clearly a violation by this state of the guarantee contained in the fourteenth amendment, that no state shall deny to any person the equal protection of the laws." [73] The court admitted that the classification between aliens eligible and aliens ineligible to citizenship was reasonable so far as acquiring real property was concerned, but "the right or privilege of a father to be the guardian of his own minor child does not in any respect depend upon or arise out of his nationality or his eligibility to citizenship in this country." Thus a classification may be reasonable for some purposes, but unreasonable for others.

This statement was challenged by Justice Lawlor, in a strong dissent. He said that the classification was reasonable in both cases, because if the Japanese could establish guardianships and acquire land in the name of their children, the alien land law, the constitutionality of which the court admitted, could be circumvented. In his words, "To hold that under the federal guarantee of equal protection of the laws, the state is powerless to prevent the circumvention of a law it had the authority to enact, is in effect to declare that it cannot, by an exercise of its sovereign will, effectuate the purpose of the original legislation." [74]

But in reply, the majority asserted that: "A guardian neither acquires, possesses, or enjoys the property belonging to the ward, in any accurate or legal meaning of those terms. . . . He controls it as trustee only, and is held to strict accountability to the child for all the benefits accruing from the use of it." The question therefore reduces itself to the privileges of the Japanese minor born in this country. He is an American citizen and there-

[72] Japanese guardianships established in good faith were upheld by the Superior Court of Riverside in *People of the State of California* v. *Yukiehi Harada et al.*, Superior Court of the State of California in and for the county of Riverside, No. 7751. Filed, County Clerk of Riverside, decided October 22, 1918. But other courts severely scrutinized the manner in which Japanese aliens fulfilled their trusts. If the land thus held was not used strictly for the benefit of the minor, the guardianship was dissolved. See the cases reported in *Hearings, cited*, 873 ff.

[73] *In re Estate and Guardianship of Yano*, California Decisions, May 5, 1922, No. 3348, p. 520.

[74] He cited the case of *Patsone* v. *Pennsylvania*, 232 U. S. 138.

fore can acquire real property freely upon reaching the age of twenty-one. According to *In re Yano*, he may also acquire it through his father, acting as guardian, from the day of birth. Although from the legal standpoint, this is not an evasion of the land law, from the economic and social standpoint, the law becomes practically worthless, because it does not necessarily weaken the hold of the Japanese on the land.

A second means of evasion, the "croppage contract" has also been sustained. In this form of contract the owner of the land ordinarily agrees to furnish the "cropper" or tenant, in this case, a Japanese, with housing accommodations, tools, farming implements, and horses for the cultivation of the crop; while usually he promises to haul the crop to delivery points. The contract specifically states that the cropper has no interest or estate in the land; but the owner agrees to give him as his wage, one-half or some such proportion of all crops grown. The cropper, on the other hand, agrees to maintain and keep up the personal property and to return it to the owner at the expiration of the contract. He also promises to keep the land in shape, maintain the irrigation ditches, harvest and pack the crops. Finally, the owner promises not to sell or mortgage the property without the written consent of the cropper.

Even when three-year leases were permitted, many Japanese farmers and white landlords used the "croppage contract." Its advantage then was that it might run for a longer time than the three-year lease; that the owner furnished more of the equipment than he ordinarily did under the lease; and that the landowner's share of the crop could not be attached for the employee's obligations, whereas under the ordinary cash-lease, his portion might be attached while it was being carried from the ranch to the packing house or railroad.[75]

The California land law of 1920 said nothing about "croppage contracts." But it did forbid aliens ineligible to citizenship from holding "any interest" in real property, and it punished severely all evasions of this provision.[76] The question was whether or not the croppage contract established an "interest" in real property or whether it was merely a personal employment contract. The State Attorney-General, in informal rulings, expressed the opinion that the Japanese had no right to "the possession and enjoyment of lands" even through a croppage contract, which he believed to be a mere subterfuge. But the district court for northern California, in *O'Brien* v. *Webb*, has ruled that "in a cropping contract, the cropper has no estate in the land. He may be physically upon the land, and have possession of the crops. Yet such possession is that of a servant, who receives his pay in a certain proportion of the crop." The owner only can maintain action for trespass. The court cited a large number of State decisions upholding the general principle that "croppage contracts" were personal contracts,

[75] Although such portion cannot be attached before delivery begins or after it is made.
[76] Cf. secs. 5, 9, and 10.

and did not give any "legal interest" in the land, within the meaning of the statute. The cropper has no "estate" in the land or ownership in the crops, as one would have in a lease or in ownership. The court declared that "a forced construction should not be put on the contract, in order to bring it within the prohibition of the law." [77]

From the legal standpoint, this decision is probably sound. But its practical result would seem to be that the Japanese will continue to remain upon California's land. There has been some agitation for further legislation which will prohibit Japanese even from making croppage contracts. But it is likely that any such legislation would be unconstitutional because of the equal protection clause of the fourteenth amendment. It was in order to give effect to this amendment that Congress passed Section 1977 of the Revised Statutes which declared, "All persons within the jurisdiction of the United States shall have the same right in every State and Territory to make and enforce contracts, to sue, be parties, give evidence, and to the full and equal benefit of all laws and proceedings for the security of persons and property as is enjoyed by white citizens, and shall be subject to like punishment, pains, penalties, taxes, licenses and exactions of every kind, and to no other."

An alien, therefore, is authorized by the statutes of the United States, "to make and enforce contracts." Consequently, he can make and enforce croppage, labor, or personal employment contracts by which he may obtain the *use* of agricultural land. That such contracts are included within the meaning of this statute and of the Fourteenth Amendment is shown by the decision in *In re Tiburcio Parrott*, in which Justice Sawyer said: "And contracts to labor, such as all others make, are contracts which they [aliens such as Chinese] have a right 'to make and enforce', and the laws under which others' rights are protected are the laws to which they are entitled to the 'equal benefit', 'as is enjoyed by white citizens.'" [78] It is also shown by the decision of the United States Supreme Court in *Truax* v. *Raich*, involving an Arizona constitutional amendment prohibiting the employment by any firm, of less than 80 per cent "qualified electors or native-born citizens." Thus only two out of each ten employees could be aliens. This provision was declared unconstitutional, Justice Hughes saying, "Being lawfully an inhabitant of Arizona, the complainant [an alien] is entitled under the Fourteenth Amendment to the equal protection of the laws. . . . The discrimination here involved is imposed upon the conduct of ordinary private enterprise." The state police power did not extend to such discriminations. It cannot "deny to lawful inhabitants, because of their race or nationality,

[77] 279 Fed. 117, 119, 123, decided December 20, 1921. See also "The Status of a Cropper." (Notes) 36 *Harvard Law Review*, 209, December, 1922. This case has been appealed to the U. S. Supreme Court, along with *Porterfield* v. *Webb*. In the case of *In re Yano*, a petition for rehearing was denied.

[78] 1 Fed. 481, 509. Cf. *Coppage* v. *Kansas*, 236 U. S. 1, 14.

the ordinary means of earning a livelihood. . . . It is no answer to say, as it is argued, that the act proceeds upon the assumption that 'the employment of aliens unless restrained was a peril to the public welfare.' The discrimination against aliens in the wide range of employments to which the act relates is made an end in itself and thus the authority to deny to aliens, upon the mere fact of their alienage, the right to obtain support in the ordinary fields of labor is necessarily involved. . . . The authority to control immigration—to admit or exclude aliens—is vested solely in the Federal Government. . . . The assertion of an authority to deny to aliens the opportunity of earning a livelihood when lawfully admitted to the State would be tantamount to the assertion of the right to deny them entrance and abode, for in ordinary cases they cannot live where they cannot work."

Neither could the State of Arizona declare that it had not *totally* denied aliens the opportunity to work. For "if the State is at liberty to treat the employment of aliens as in itself a peril requiring restraint, regardless of kind or class of work," it can prohibit absolutely such employment. "The restriction now sought to be sustained is such as to suggest no limit to the State's power of excluding aliens from employment. . . . The discrimination is against aliens as such in competition with citizens in the described range of enterprises and in our opinion it clearly falls under the condemnation of the fundamental law." [79]

From these different decisions, the following summary may be made: A State may legally prohibit aliens ineligible to citizenship from owning real property or leasing it for agricultural purposes, since such a power in their hands might conceivably endanger the State; but a State cannot, because of the fourteenth amendment, prohibit aliens from making croppage contracts, which do not give them any control over the land, but under which they may continue to till agricultural land; nor can a State prohibit Japanese guardianships whereby land may be acquired by Japanese minors born in the United States.[80]

OTHER ANTI-JAPANESE LEGISLATION

At least three other kinds of laws have been aimed at the Japanese on the Pacific Coast. The first has been the alien poll tax which was adopted by the people of California in the election of 1920. Although the tax applied to all aliens, it was aimed at the Japanese. The California Supreme Court, however, made short shift of it, declaring it unconstitutional on the ground

[79] 239 U. S., 33, 39, 41, 43.

[80] Before the passage of the 1920 land law in California, State political leaders admitted that the State had no power to prevent the *use* of land by Japanese. See Governor Stephen's letter to Secretary Colby, *California and the Oriental*, Report of the State Board of Control, p. 13; also Chester H. Rowell, "California and the Japanese Problem," *New Republic*, September 15, 1921.

that it violated Article I of the treaty of Japan of 1911, providing for equal taxation, and also that it violated the fourteenth amendment of the Constitution of the United States.[81] Secondly, the State legislature has passed a law regulating foreign-language schools. These are schools maintained by Japanese in which Japanese children are taught the Japanese language, before or after regular school hours. They have been accused of fostering anti-Americanism and Emperor worship.[82] Although a demand was made for their abolition, the 1921 State legislature followed Hawaii's example,[83] and enacted a regulatory law. It provided (1) that no person shall conduct such a school without a permit from the superintendent of public instruction; (2) that no such permit shall be granted unless the applicant "is possessed of the ideals of democracy, knowledge of American history and institutions, and knows how to read, write and speak the English language"; (3) that each applicant must file an affadavit promising to make his pupils "good and loyal American citizens"; (4) that no private language school shall be conducted in the morning before school hours or during hours while the public schools are in session; and that no pupil shall attend a private language school for more than an hour a day; (5) that the superintendent of public instruction shall have full power to prescribe the course of study and text books in these schools and also the power of inspection.[84]

This legislation is undoubtedly constitutional because it is based on the police power and the State's control of its educational system.[85]

Finally, some states have passed laws prohibiting aliens from fishing. Oregon and Washington prohibit aliens from engaging in nearly every kind of fishing.[86] Certain kinds of fishing are also prohibited to aliens in Alaska. An attempt was unsuccessfully made in the 1921 California legislature to bar Japanese fishermen from coastwise waters. It is a question whether they now have a right to fish or at least to operate vessels in American waters, under the laws of the United States. According to Revised Statutes 4377 the master of a vessel engaged in coastwise trade or fishing, which requires a license, must swear that he is a citizen of the United States and that the vessel is wholly the property of citizens of the United States. Because of an oversight, the statute contains no penalty for violations of the law. But even if this is corrected, the law can still be easily evaded by the present practice of canneries of themselves owning fishing boats and permitting Japanese to use them. The constitutionality of State laws barring aliens from the privilege of fishing probably will be upheld by the Supreme Court,

[81] *Ex parte Terui*, 200 Pac. 954; *Ex parte Kotta*, 200 Pac. 957.

[82] See V. S. McClatchy "Japanese in the Melting Pot," *Annals, cited*, pp. 31–32. *Hearings, cited*, pp. 926 ff., 976.

[83] *Japan Review*, December, 1920; *Survey of Education in Hawaii*, p. 112.

[84] 1921 *California Statutes*, ch. 683.

[85] *Marshall* v. *Donovan*, 10 Bush (Ky.), 681; *Ward* v. *Flood*, 48 Cal. 36; *Berea College* v. *Kentucky*, 211 U. S. 45; Freund, *Police Power*, secs., 266, 698.

[86] *California and the Oriental*, pp. 94–96.

on the ground that fish is public property the use of which is reserved only to citizens.[87]

There is also a California statute which prohibits aliens from holding any public employment, except as teachers, etc.;[88] but this affects but few Japanese.[89]

[87] *McCready* v. *Virginia*, 94 U. S. 391; *Patsone* v. *Pennsylvania*, *supra*; *Geer* v. *Connecticut*, 161 U. S. 519; *Manchester* v. *Massachusetts*, 139 U. S. 240; *Ex parte Powell*, 70 Fla. 363; *People* v. *Setunsky*, 161 Mich. 624. Cf. also *Consanti* v. *Darwin*, 102 Wash. 402. However, in *In re Ah Chong*, 5 *Pacific Coast Law Journal* 451, also 2 Fed. 733, 737, the federal court overthrew a California law of 1880, which prohibited aliens "incapable of becoming electors" from fishing in the waters of the State, on the ground that it violated the equal protection of the laws, guaranteed by the fourteenth amendment.

[88] 1915 *Cal. Stat.*, ch. 417. The constitutionality of such statutes has been upheld in *Atkins* v. *Kansas*, 197 U. S. 207, and in *Heim* v. *McCall*, 239 U. S. 175. There are a few occupations from which aliens may be excluded, involving an oath of allegiance, etc. See "The Legal Status of Aliens," *Immigrants in America Review*, March, 1915.

[89] It should be reiterated that a discussion of the wisdom of the policy pursued by the United States toward Japanese residents is beyond the scope of this article. But the writer does not wish any part of it to be construed as favoring such a policy. On the contrary, he believes that it intensifies the Japanese problem on the Pacific Coast, and that it injures the relations of the United States and Japan. See R. L. Buell, *The Washington Conference*, (1922), p. 302 ff.

THE DEVELOPMENT OF THE ANTI-JAPANESE AGITATION IN THE UNITED STATES

1. *The Beginnings*

When President Fillmore called the attention of the Congress of the United States to the rude treatment accorded shipwrecked mariners unhappily cast upon Japanese shores, he unknowingly opened up a problem which has already perplexed the western world for three-quarters of a century.[1] Before this time there had been no Oriental problem. It had been forestalled by the stern intolerance of Toyotomi Hideyoshi who, in the seventeenth century, banished all foreigners, whether priests or traders, from Japan, and commanded all Japanese, under penalty of death, to remain at home.

But the pressure of trade and of ideas perforce brought this isolation to an end. In 1853 the Black Ships of Commodore Perry steamed into Yedo Bay. Five years later Townsend Harris signed the first treaty between Japan and the United States. With these acts, Japan was placed in contact with the western world. Intercourse between nations in the past has usually been marred by discord. And in the case of Japan, the opportunity for misunderstanding has been increased by the factor of race.

Immigration was the first cause of friction between Japan and the United States. As early as 1851[2] a few shipwrecked Japanese were tossed upon the Pacific Coast. But the first actual immigrants were brought into this country by a Hollander

[1] Third annual message, December 6, 1852, *Messages and Papers of the President* (Bureau of National Literature edition), p. 2703. For the very early activities of Japanese abroad, see Chapman, *A History of California* (1921), chapter iv, "The Japanese Opportunity in the Pacific".

[2] Treat, *Japan and the United States* (1921), p. 253. For the opening of Japan to the western world, see the same writer, *The Early Diplomatic Relations between the United States and Japan 1853-1865* (1917); also Satow, *A Diplomat in Japan* (1921).

who, driven from the employ of the Japanese Court, sought refuge in America.[1] In 1880 there were only about one hundred and fifty Japanese in the entire country. But their number rapidly increased after the legalization of emigration by the Japanese government in 1885.[2] As early as 1889 some Japanese were employed as section hands at Portland. About the same time others gradually sifted into Vancouver and spread out along the Pacific Coast, entering the mines, the fisheries and the farms. Beginning with 1891, over a thousand Japanese entered America yearly, subject only to the restriction of the general immigration laws. In 1898, the number of immigrants was 2,000; two years later, it jumped to 12,000.

There were three reasons for Japanese emigration to America. The first was economic. Wages averaged about fourteen cents a day in Japan,[3] where the pressure of population had already made the food problem acute. Little wonder that stories of two-dollar-a-day wages in America led the Japanese to forsake the home of their ancestors! In fact, the greatest number of emigrants came from those provinces where agricultural conditions were the worst and where poverty was most widespread.

Secondly, Japanese emigration was caused by the labor shortage in California, which had arisen partly because of the fact that Chinese labor had been excluded by the Acts of 1882 and 1892. Negroes, Mexicans, Filipinos, Hindus, Porto-Ricans and Japanese were now eagerly sought after by California farmers.[4] According to one eye-witness, "568,943 acres of farm land were put out of cultivation. From Bakersfield to Redding, banks had mortgages on farm lands that could not be made productive because Chinese labor had been driven out".[5]

[1] Carey, *A History of Japanese Immigration,* unpublished manuscript taken from Japanese sources, furnished me by Dr. G. W. Hinman.

[2] Ichihashi, *Japanese Immigration, Its Status in California* (1916), p. 7.

[3] Yoshida, "Sources and Causes of Japanese Emigration," *Annals of the American Academy of Political and Social Science,* vol. 34, no. 2, p. 162.

[4] Coolidge, *Chinese Immigration* (1909), pp. 384-385.

[5] Testimony of J. P. Irish, Hearings before Committee on Immigration and Naturalization, H. of R., *Japanese Immigration* (Government Printing Office, 1921), pp. 43-44. Hereafter cited as *Hearings.*

It was not until the year 1885 that the Japanese government authorized the emigration of Japanese. In that year it was permitted, but with express stipulation that the emigrants should never lose their allegiance to the Mikado. Each Japanese subject was required to register in his native prefecture, which he could leave only with the permission of the authorities. If he wished to go out of the country it was necessary to procure a passport which provided that he must return within three years.[1]

Based as it was upon a paternal feudalism, the Japanese government attempted to make certain that its emigrants abroad should creditably represent their fatherland, and that in case of destitution they should return home. With this purpose in view, the "Emigrants' Protection" Law was enacted by the Japanese parliament in 1896. It provided that every laborer leaving the country should have some responsible surety at home who could be compelled to provide for his care during sickness and, if necessary, for his return.[2]

Despite the excellent intentions of this law, it actually stimulated the emigration of Japanese to the United States. The requirements were so stringent that few laborers could individually meet them. Consequently, a number of emigration companies sprang up which provided every laborer with a surety, furnished him with transportation, and gave him a job at his destination. Working in connection with labor contractors in the United States, these companies built up a business of great profit. In order to regulate their activities, the government required a guarantee. It was necessary also that their foreign agents be approved. These emigration societies soon began to wield a tremendous power in Japan. The aggregate capital of twelve of them was 558,999 yen, and stock was held by the leading business men and politicians of the country.[3]

[1] Rice, *Immigration of Japanese*, House Doc. No. 686, 56th Congress, 1st sess., May 14, 1900, p. 4.

[2] *Third Report of the Commissioner of Labor on Hawaii*, Bulletin of Bureau of Labor, no. 66, September, 1906, p. 505.

[3] Rice, *op. cit.*, p. 5.

Six of these companies maintained agents in the United States and Canada.

As a result, emigration to the United States and Hawaii increased tremendously. In the five years between 1899 and 1903 the number of emigrants going to foreign countries, excluding Korea and China, was 84,576. Eighty per cent went to the United States.[1] In the year 1900, four times as many Japanese entered America as in the previous year. Naturally this irritated the sensibilities of California—easily aroused after a riotous twenty-year struggle with Chinese immigrants.

California's attention was first attracted to Oriental labor in 1888 when a San Francisco shipowners' association manned several of its vessels with Japanese. In 1891 a Mr. Doyle, a former resident of Japan, came to San Francisco and proposed to bring in 5000 Japanese from the Hawaiian islands—a suggestion which was immediately protested by the city Trades' Council.[2] The first real protests against the Japanese were not made, however, until 1900. In March of that year symptoms of bubonic plague appeared in San Francisco. Immediately Mayor Phelan and the Board of Supervisors quarantined the Chinese and the Japanese quarters, but no other part of the city.[3] This discrimination led the Japanese to form the "Japanese Association of America" for the purpose of protecting their interests. Feeling was further heightened by a belief that stories of the plague were based on unfounded evidence, and that they were being circulated purely for political purposes.[4] Partly because of the excitement stirred up over the plague and partly because of the increased number of Japanese immigrants, a mass meeting was held in Metropolitan Hall, on May 7, under the auspices of the San Francisco Labor Council. After listening to addresses by Professor Ross, then of Stanford University, and Mayor Phelan (who later became

[1] Yoshida, *op. cit.*, pp. 160, 161.

[2] *San Francisco Chronicle,* March 20, 1905; special article by Walter Macarthur.

[3] *Ibid.*, March 7, 1900.

[4] *Ibid.*, May 30, 1900; editorial, "Phelan in the Rôle of a Fakir".

United States Senator), the meeting passed a resolution urging the extension of the Chinese Exclusion laws to include the Japanese.[1] In the same year, the State Labor Commissioner also referred to the sudden increase in Japanese laborers;[2] while Governor Henry T. Gage called the attention of the legislature to the "Japanese problem" in his message of January 8, 1901.[3]

As a result of this agitation, the Japanese government showed the conciliatory disposition which it has usually held toward American opinion, by amending the Emigration Act of 1896. In July, 1900, the Foreign Department announced that henceforth no passports whatever would be issued to Japanese coolies wishing to go to the United States.[4] As a result, the number of Japanese arrivals declined one-half in 1901.[5] This voluntary limitation was the first "Gentlemen's Agreement." However, it did not satisfy many elements in the State. In November, 1901, a Chinese Exclusion Convention was called in San Francisco by the Board of Supervisors. Its official purpose was to urge upon Congress the necessity of re-enacting the Chinese exclusion laws which were soon to expire. But it also adopted a resolution which recognized "in the character and rapidly increasing numbers of Japanese and other Asiatic immigrants a menace to the industrial interests of our people." Likewise, the American Federation of Labor, in its convention in San Francisco, November, 1904, demanded that the exclusion laws be applied to Japanese immigrants. However, there was no vigorous movement against the Japanese on the Pacific Coast until 1905. In order to understand this agitation, which for intensity recalled the days of Dennis Kearney and his stormy Sand-lotters, and very nearly involved the country in war, it is necessary to take some account of the political situation in California at this time. Partly because of the Chinese

[1] *Ibid.,* May 8, 1900.

[2] *Ninth Biennial Report of the Bureau of Labor Statistics,* 1899-1900, p. 15.

[3] *San Francisco Chronicle,* January 9, 1901.

[4] Statement of K. Uyeno, Japanese Consul-General, *San Francisco Chronicle,* April 5, 1905.

[5] From 12,626 in 1900 to 4,909 in 1901.

agitation, extending between 1855 and 1882, the Workingmen's Party had won control of the State, and in 1879 was strong enough to frame a constitution which is still in force. But the position of Union Labor was soon to be contested. In 1888 San Francisco capitalists organized themselves into a number of different associations, resolved to drive the workingman from power.[1] A period of financial depression so strengthened them that they were able to lower wages and to establish the "open shop" in politics and in industry as well. The Workingmen's Party by this time had disappeared.

However, between 1898 and 1901, San Francisco underwent a period of unrivaled prosperity. The annexation of Hawaii, the opening of the Alaskan gold mines, and the outbreak of the Spanish-American War increased the business of San Francisco and revived the drooping industries of the whole state. An unfilled demand for workingmen now strengthened the labor forces. Determined on revenge, the labor leaders organized the State Federation of Labor in January, 1901. Its fight against the Employers' Association culminated in the San Francisco teamsters' strike of July—a strike caused by the refusal of the organized teamsters to deliver goods to a non-union express company.[2] The issue was clearly Unionism *versus* non-Unionism. The Employers' Association refused to negotiate with the men, and the men refused to have anything to do with the employers.

There was nothing peaceful about the strike which ensued. One shipping company employed prize fighters to act as strike-breakers. Union men attacked non-union teamsters carrying goods away from railroad yards.[3] In order to protect these men, the chief of police placed two policemen on each truck. Labor leaders demanded that the policemen be removed. The mayor replied that it was his duty to secure public order. At a meeting held September 23, 1901, he was said to have de-

[1] Eaves, *A History of California Labor Legislation* (1910), p. 50 *et seq.*

[2] Hichborn, *"The System", as Uncovered by the S. F. Graft Prosecution* (1915), p. 11 n.

[3] *San Francisco Chronicle,* September 22, 1901.

clared that if the workmen did not want to be clubbed, they should go back to their jobs. This story, which was later proved to be false, turned the labor forces against the Phelan administration and resulted in the organization of the Union Labor Party.

This new party was successful enough to win the election of November, 1901, and place Eugene E. Schmitz in the mayor's chair. Schmitz was a man of little education, with no experience in politics. He had been hired as a musician in a San Francisco theater, and was a member of the Musicians' Union. Under the leadership of this man, San Francisco was governed for five years which were to be truly momentous in California's history. During this period, San Francisco was to be visited by a devastating earthquake and fire, interpreted by many to be a divine judgment on a wicked city. Corporations were beginning their exploitation of the boundless resources of a magnificent state. Telephone companies struggled for franchises; the water supply was vested in a private monopoly; the United Railroads strangled San Francisco's transportation facilities; the Southern Pacific Company actually retained legislators and subsidized newspapers to make certain the political control of the State.[1]

Naturally the victory of the Union Labor Party, headed by an ignorant and self-seeking man, was eagerly seized by these interests, and an attempt was made to transform California into a *latifundium* which would have done credit to the patricians of Rome. Schmitz, in fact, owed his position, not to the long-suffering workingmen of San Francisco, but to the genius of the most able and most crooked political boss San Francisco has ever seen. This was Abraham Ruef—a Jew, a lawyer, a college graduate, a Republican. Schmitz made an admirable tool with which Ruef could work. The latter contributed $16,000 to Schmitz's first campaign fund.

Under the leadership of Schmitz and Ruef, San Francisco went through a period of political corruption which would make the blackest deeds of Boss Tweed look as harmless as

[1] Fremont Older, *My Own Story* (1919), p. 23 *et seq.*

politics in a woman's club. Franchises were bought and sold; the United Railroads bribed the supervisors with the fat sum of $200,000; the city tax-collector ran off with an adventuress and several hundred thousand dollars of the tax-payers' money; houses of ill-fame maintained a fixed schedule of prices by which police officials, from captains to patrolmen, were systematically bribed; gamblers shared their ill-gotten gains with the mayor; "French Restaurants"—infamous houses of assignation—paid Abe Ruef large sums to secure liquor licenses, and half of this tribute was turned over to Schmitz. Boodling was rampant everywhere.

So firmly did the Machine have control of the processes of justice in California, and so cleverly did it conceal the magnitude of its crimes, that the greatest skill of detective William J. Burns and attorney Francis J. Heney was necessary finally to dig out the poisonous roots of San Francisco's life.

When Ruef and Schmitz were finally brought to trial in 1906, the working of the "system" became more vigorous and more desperate than ever. Ruef attempted to flee. When this failed, an effort was made to secure the passage of a change of venue bill by the state legislature which would free the culprits on a technicality. Jurors were bribed; Fremont Older, the dauntless editor of the *San Francisco Call*, who led the campaign against the boodlers, was kidnapped; a gunman was hired to murder him, and only the ruffian's loss of nerve saved Older's life. Francis J. Heney was shot while in court by an ex-convict who was a juryman on a former Ruef trial, and whom Heney had exposed.[1]

This disgraceful situation in San Francisco was intimately related to the Japanese agitation. First, the Labor party was in power, and Japanese immigration affected workingmen vitally. Secondly, the Schmitz administration would naturally seize upon every means and occasion to divert public attention from its own crimes.

[1] Ruef was finally convicted for bribery, and was recently pardoned. Schmitz was freed on a technicality and ran again for mayor in 1919.

But in addition to the political situation, there were four other causes which led to the outbreak against the Japanese in 1905 and 1906. In the first place, the Gentlemen's Agreement of 1900 had not been enforced. Japanese laborers kept dribbling in from Japan, despite the limitation which the Japanese government had imposed. The chief reason was that the administration of the Japanese passport law was placed in the hands of local officials, from whom it was not difficult for the powerfully financed emigration companies to purchase passports.

Furthermore, the restriction had not applied to the laborers wishing to go to Hawaii. Passports were still issued to this destination. Originally the Japanese had been invited by the Hawaiian Government to work on the sugar plantations.[1] In 1886 Hawaii and Japan entered into an agreement providing for the importation of Japanese laborers. When Hawaii was annexed to the United States in 1898, this official encouragement came to an end. But the planters of the island still wished cheap labor.[2] Moreover, the emigration companies continued to bring Japanese in, not only to supply the labor market in Hawaii but also to transport them later to the Pacific Coast. The Japanese, on the other hand, were willing to leave Hawaii for the mainland because of the higher wages paid in California—and because of the irksome restraints imposed upon them by the sugar plantations.

This is a typical advertisement, printed in a Hawaiian Japanese paper:

Special Notice

In the next three months we shall recruit 1,000 laborers of Niigata Province, Japan, for the mainland. Apply at the hotel below. Don't

[1] *Third Report, Commissioner of Labor on Hawaii,* cited, p. 503.

[2] The charge has been made that the Planters' Association of Honolulu later contributed to the funds of the Asiatic Exclusion League, in order to keep Japanese laborers in Hawaii, and thereby keep wages down. King, *Report of the Royal Commission appointed to inquire into the methods by which oriental laborers have been induced to come to Canada.* Quoted in "Immigration Situation in Other Countries", *Senate Documents,* vol. 22, 61st Cong., 3rd sess., 1910-11.

miss a good chance! The Industrial Corporation of Japanese of Niigata Province have sent a representative to Hawaii to encourage their countrymen to go to America. This representative, Mr. Seisku Kuroishi, assists applicants in every way. Yamaichi Hotel, February 1, 1905.[1]

It was apparently impossible to arrest the activities of these emigration companies under the authority of the Contract Labor Laws of the United States. There was nothing but an oral understanding between the companies and the Japanese. But for all purposes the latter were contract laborers: when a boatload of Japanese landed in San Francisco, they were lined up in companies, marched to Japanese boarding houses, and then assigned to contractors along the entire coast.

As a result of the activities of these companies, emigration from Hawaii to the mainland increased alarmingly. The figures follow:

January 1–September 30, 1902	1,054
October 1–September 30, 1903	2,119
October 1, 1903–June 30, 1904	3,665
July 1, 1904–December 31, 1905	13,803[2]

The next factor was the Russo-Japanese War, which began in February, 1904. American opinion was at first sympathetic toward Japan in a war which the latter was apparently fighting to check an imperial Pan-Slavism. The pluck of this new nation, with scanty resources and limited manpower, aroused the admiration of the English-speaking world. But with the progress of the war and the repeated victories of the armies of Nippon, the enthusiasm for the yellow man, at least along the Pacific Coast, began to wane. The Kaiser's extravagant warning of the "Yellow Peril" found instant response among the workingmen of California. Congressmen lent themselves unconsciously to this propaganda. Mr. Hull, chairman of the House Committee of Military Affairs, declared that if Japan won the war with Russia, she would fight a "bloody war with

[1] *Immigration Commission Reports* (42 vols., 1911), vol. 23, p. 15.

[2] *Third Report of Commissioner of Labor on Hawaii*, p. 378.

the United States over the Philippines."[1] The *Ogden Standard* declared that the Japanese "feel quite confident of their ability to defeat the American navy and humiliate our army."[2] And Senator Selvage likewise declared: "Those who have followed the course of events in Asia for the past few months have not failed to discover therein a great, a serious menace, not only to California, but to the Nation." The excessive demands of Japan at the Portsmouth conference and her gradual absorption of Korea did nothing to allay California's fear.

Of more practical importance was the possibility that at the close of the war the desire of the Japanese to come to the United States would be greater than ever. Tired of the struggle into which they had been drafted, and fearful of the economic hardships which the war imposed on those who remained in Japan, they would seize every opportunity to migrate to El Dorado across the seas. It was the fear of this "invasion" which fortified California's outcry for ironclad exclusion.

Finally, the workingmen of California had already felt the pinch of Japanese competition. They could therefore easily imagine the effect of an increased Asiatic population upon their well-being. The Japanese were accused of maintaining sweatshops; of driving white female domestics out of employment; of forcing two hundred shoe-repairing men out of San Francisco; of invading the fruit districts of Vacaville, Fresno and Visalia; of controlling all unskilled labor on the railroads and in the beet-fields; of cutting into the white laundry business; and of underbidding white building contractors from twenty to sixty per cent.

To these economic grievances were added political and racial denunciations. The Japanese were accused of perpetual allegiance to the Mikado. Rumors that Japanese at American army posts were gaining detailed knowledge of American fortifications, were persistently circulated. Finally, it was charged that the Japanese were actually crowding American children out of schools. The *Chronicle* declared against "the daily

[1] *San Francisco Chronicle,* March 16, 1905.

[2] Quoted, *ibid.,* March 23, 1906.

contact of young girls with adult men of Asiatic birth and training."

It is impossible to tell the amount of truth there was in these charges. Suffice it to say that they, in company with the charges made later, were grossly exaggerated. Nevertheless, the ineffectiveness of the limitation imposed in 1900 and the activities of Japanese imperialism abroad, easily led to violent protests. It was just before the siege of Mukden that the *San Francisco Chronicle* chose an opportune time to launch the anti-Japanese campaign in California. On February 23, 1905, it printed a nine-column article, covering nearly two pages, on the dangers of Japanese immigration. "It contains as much of a menace as the Chinese immigration ever did", declared the *Chronicle*. The number of Japanese then in the United States was placed at 100,000—a greatly exaggerated figure. The first result of the article was to arouse the state legislature. On the first of March the senate unanimously adopted a resolution declaring against the unrestricted immigration of the Japanese, and asking the federal government for immediate protection.[1] The *Chronicle* graphically reported the adoption of this resolution in these words: "The resolution was not the product of the moment; it was not the result of an indignant mass meeting, but was deliberated upon and discussed, in a great measure, calmly and dispassionately by men of affairs—men who have 'made good'—many of whom, if they so desired, need take no interest in the welfare of the laborer, having amassed a competence sufficient to maintain themselves and their families in comfort. But many of the Senators were born here, and they are proud of the name their forbears made for the State of California, synonymous everywhere with things big, broad, and great, from the biggest things in nature to men and money. Their fathers wrested the State from a foreign power, riveted it to the Union with their bayonets, and today their sons acted on a proposition that a California should hold what a California has"![2]

[1] For the ten charges then made against the Japanese, see Senate Joint Resolution, No. 10, *California Statutes*, 1905, p. 1060. This resolution passed the lower house the next day.

[2] March 2, 1905.

At the instigation of this newspaper, the leadership of the anti-Japanese movement now passed into the hands of union labor, which was at this time so firmly intrenched in San Francisco politics. On March 10, 1905, the Labor Council of San Francisco, then the largest labor body in the country west of Chicago, held a meeting in which the campaign against the Japanese was definitely launched under the leadership of Olaf Tveitmoe, a Swedish laborer who served a term in a Minnesota state prison for forgery and who later was to be convicted for complicity in the MacNamara dynamite plots.[1] Boycotts on the Japanese were now urged—even on white merchants or manufacturers employing Japanese. The campaign was on in earnest.

On Sunday, May 7, 1905, a mass meeting was held at Metropolitan Hall to launch the Japanese and Korean Exclusion League. The *Chronicle* was lurid in its description of this gathering. Publishing a picture of a group of swarthy, foreign-featured laborers, who composed the "convention," it said: "Some present owned their own little homes; while a majority know what it is to sit with the good wife of an evening, figure on approaching rent day and make up the cash on hand to see if there is enough to carry the family over to the next day." Men of "swelling muscles" attended this meeting—and grimly cheered fulminations against the yellow men who were keeping them from having "lace curtains on the windows"!

As a result of this agitation, the Japanese government for the second time showed its good-will, by first limiting the number of Japanese who might emigrate to Hawaii to 500 per ship, and finally by suspending temporarily all emigration to Hawaii (April, 1905). But even this did not satisfy the Exclusion League. On the contrary, it redoubled its activities by recruiting members, by pledging political candidates to an exclusion law, and by attempting to organize all of the western states in a concerted movement to force Congress to grant its desires. A platform was constructed of five planks which declared:

[1] *Los Angeles Times*, March 23, 1913. He was freed from the federal penitentiary on a technicality.

(1) that the Chinese exclusion laws be extended so as to exclude all classes of Japanese and Koreans, except those exempted by the terms of the Chinese Act, from the United States and its insular territories; (2) that the members of the League should pledge themselves not to employ or patronize Japanese nor to patronize any person or firm employing Japanese or dealing in products coming from such firms; (3) that the action of the School Board in adopting a policy segregating Japanese from white children be approved; (4) that a propaganda campaign calling the attention of the President and Congress to this "menace", be undertaken; (5) that all labor and civic organizations in California be asked to contribute a fixed assessment to the cause.

It is a mistake to believe, however, that California was united in its opposition to the Japanese. On March 20, 1905, the Methodist ministers of San Francisco declared that "not one of these charges [against the Japanese] could be substantiated." David Starr Jordan of Stanford University said that an exclusion measure would mean "war between the United States and Japan." President Eliot of Harvard also spoke of the "insolence of excluding Japanese from this country because of their inferiority." Finally, the fruit-growers of San Joaquin and Santa Clara valleys formally protested against legislation excluding Japanese labor, on the ground that such legislation would make it impossible to harvest their crops.

Meanwhile, a lull came in the anti-Japanese storm. The peace negotiations between Japan and Russia, the effort made in the East to modify the stringent administration of the Chinese exclusion laws, the attempt on the part of the *Chronicle* and other forces to defeat Schmitz for reelection in 1905—all consumed the attention of the anti-Japanese forces. But the defeat of John S. Partridge, the *Chronicle's* candidate for mayor, caused this journal once more to turn its broadsides against the Japanese. The Exclusion League was also doggedly pursuing its campaign. California congressmen had agreed to introduce exclusion bills in the next Congress, which was to meet in the fall of 1905. However, an unexpected obstacle to their carefully laid plans was found in the person of President

Roosevelt. In his annual message of December 5, 1905 [1], he urged a non-discriminatory immigration policy which would not single out a man on account of his color or his creed. But he dealt his most vigorous blow at the suggested exclusion of the Japanese in an informal manner. A committee of California congressmen and others had obtained an interview with the President in regard to the proposed exclusion bills. When hearing of the contemplated legislation Roosevelt is reported to have become furious. "What on earth did you Californians mean by introducing such a bill?" he roared. "Didn't you know such a thing is preposterous? With our great trade openings in the Orient, and our peculiar relations with those countries, and with our solemn treaty with Japan, which is the supreme law of the land? Do you suppose I would approve a bill that would be a violation of a treaty and an affront to Japan? Why, I would veto it if it were passed unanimously". The President then asked who these people were who were backing the bill. On being informed that they were headed by one Livernash, the President gritted his teeth, pounded his desk, and exploded, "Send them to me! Send them to me! I'll veto the bill and deport Livernash!" Speaker Joe Cannon expressed similar and nearly as violent sentiments when he declared to one of the bill's sponsors, "Loud, what in hell do you fellows in California mean by introducing a bill to exclude the Japanese from the United States? . . . You'd better leave well enough alone."

In this overbearing manner, the President poked holes in the exclusion dikes of which the League had so blissfully dreamed. The President was wrong in his premises: the exclusion of Japanese labor did not violate our treaty with Japan of 1894. The last paragraph of Article II of this treaty expressly declared that the provisions of the treaty should not "in any way affect the laws, ordinances and regulations with regard to trade, *the immigration of laborers*, police and public security which are in force or *which may hereafter be enacted* in either of the

[1] *Messages and Papers of the President*, p. 7388.

[2] *San Francisco Chronicle*, December 7, 1905.

two countries"[1]. The President was also wrong in intimating that the treaty was the "supreme law of the land" in the face of contradictory laws enacted later by Congress. Even if the treaty of 1894 had guaranteed the admission of Japanese labor to America, Congress had the *legal* right to abrogate that treaty at any time by the mere passage of an exclusion law. This point President Hayes had admitted in regard to the Chinese Exclusion Laws; and the Supreme Court has upheld this position repeatedly.[2] Despite these mistakes, Mr. Roosevelt thoroughly frightened the California congressmen; exclusion was temporarily dead.

2. *The San Francisco School Incident*

Japanese laborers continued to enter the United States. Worse still, the federal government had refused to recognize the necessity of keeping them out. It was well aware that any restrictions placed on Japanese immigration would be deeply resented by Japan. President Roosevelt had refused almost insolently to consider California's case. It was not strange, therefore, that the politicians of San Francisco resolved to take matters into their own hands; to substitute local for national action; to become town-heroes by defying the national will. Consequently the Exclusion League continued its activities. It demanded that the anti-Japanese boycott be intensified. It even asked that every union man in the state contribute one cent a month toward the campaign. Plans were made for a "monster" mass meeting to be held on May 6, 1906. But this meeting was thwarted by a disaster which has seldom been equaled in the annals of an unreasoning Nature. On April 18, San Francisco was visited with an earthquake and fire which cut off the city completely from the outside world. It was bereft for days of all transportation facilities, of gas, of water, of light, of all means of communication, even of food. It is remarkable that only five hundred lives were lost in a disaster

[1] Malloy, *Treaties, Conventions, etc. of the United States*, p. 1030.

[2] See his veto message, *Messages and Papers of the President*, pp. 4470-4471. Also *The Head Money Cases*, 112 U. S. 580; *Cherokee Tobacco Case*, 11 Wall. 616; *Fong Yue Ting, v. U. S.*, 149 U. S. 698.

which damaged property to the extent of $350,000,000 and which sent skyscrapers reeling to the ground. This great tragedy, of course, postponed anti-Japanese propaganda. The Japanese showed their good-will toward San Francisco by contributing, through the Red Cross, almost $250,000 to the sufferers.

But the reconstruction of the city again resurrected anti-Japanese sentiment. Ten thousand Japanese had been affected by the fire. In an effort to find new homes and business locations, many invaded the western districts of San Francisco which hitherto had been "white man's land."

Meanwhile other sources of irritation manifested themselves. Immigration by no means had ceased. For the first six months of 1906 the excess of Japanese arrivals over departures in San Francisco alone was 5772, a figure which led the *Chronicle* to declare, "If the next Congress does not act in this matter it will assume very grave responsibilities." At this time also occurred the Japanese sealing incident. Sailors on a Japanese ship landed on St. Paul's Island, and, contrary to law, killed a great number of female seals. This caused the *Chronicle* again to protest that "The lower classes of Japanese . . . are born thieves." Increasing evidence of Japanese imperialism in Manchuria and Korea did nothing to sooth the troubled waters. Furthermore, a crime wave was sweeping over San Francisco. It was caused partly by the opportunity which the fire had given, and partly by the Schmitz administration which by its own example encouraged crime. Within two months there were nine murders and twenty-two robberies. The Japanese restaurants were among the first to be caught in this wave. Before the fire there were in San Francisco only eight Japanese restaurants which served meals to Americans. Following the earthquake, however, about thirty of these restaurants opened in the devastated districts, and for a time did a flourishing business with workingmen engaged in rebuilding the city. As early as June 25, 1906, the Exclusion League protested that many union men were patronizing these restaurants. With the plea, "White men and women, patronize your own race", the League unsuccessfully attempted to keep them from being frequented.

When this failed, violence in many instances was resorted to; many restaurants were invaded and their property destroyed.[1]

Furthermore, Japanese stores were burglarized and one bank president murdered. The distinguished Japanese scientist, Dr. F. Omori of the Imperial University of Tokyo, while examining the ruined districts, was besieged with tomato cans and stones by a gang of hoodlums, one of whom was a post-office messenger. These assaults attracted but little attention in San Francisco. But they were immediately and widely reported in Japan, where they had a profoundly irritating effect.[2]

In the fall of 1906 another political campaign took place in which congressmen were to be elected. Of course the Japanese question became a popular issue. Both the Democratic and Republican State Conventions declared for the exclusion of the Japanese in no uncertain terms. On September 16, the Exclusion League held a "mass meeting," addressed by congressional candidates, at which it was announced that the membership of the League had reached a total of 78,500 and that its program had been endorsed by independent organizations composed of nearly four and a half million members.

On October 11, 1906, the School Board of San Francisco passed a special resolution which brought the anti-Japanese crisis to a white heat. As part of a well-organized plan, the School Board had first decided to establish separate schools for Japanese and Chinese on the day before the first convention of the Exclusion League was held (May 6, 1905). The legal right to segregate white from Mongolian school children in this manner was based on a school law which authorized school boards to establish separate schools for Indian, Chinese and Mongolian children, at their own discretion.[3] The law, however, did not mention the Japanese by name. Presumably, they were "Mongolians". The reasons which prompted the first action of the San Francisco Board were set forth in this resolution:

[1] *Immigration Commission Reports,* vol. 23, p. 200 *et seq.*

[2] For other instances of violence, see *Senate Document No. 147,* 59th Congress, 2nd session.

[3] Article X, Section 1662, *Political Code of the State of California,* p. 379.

Resolved that the Board of Education is determined in its efforts to effect the establishment of separate schools for Chinese and Japanese pupils, not only for the purpose of relieving the congestion at present prevailing in our schools, but also for the higher end that our children should not be placed in any position where their youthful impressions may be affected by associations with pupils of the Mongolian race.

As this resolution was not carried out, it did not create the furor which similar action later aroused. The reason for the failure to carry out at once this policy of segregation was lack of funds. The Board of Supervisors, which had been petitioned for a new building in which to house the Orientals, asserted that it did not have the money necessary to erect it. The old system therefore was maintained. But on October 22, 1905, the Exclusion League voted unanimously to petition the Board to carry out this policy. During the discussion, it was established beyond question that the School Board, the members of which were appointed by the mayor, was under the absolute control of Schmitz and Ruef.[1] No further action could be expected until these bosses had given the word, and they would wait until their own interests would be served by a renewal of the anti-Japanese agitation.

On July 23, 1906, the schools, which had been closed by the fire, were opened with an attendance of 25,000. After a tour of inspection, the president of the Board of Education announced that there was very little over-crowding. He said nothing about the dangers of the Japanese. But nearly three months later, on October 11, the Board suddenly ordered all Japanese children, after October 15, to attend the Oriental school in Chinatown. The resolution was scarcely noticed in the San Francisco papers. At that time the city was occupied with the famous investigations which Heney and Burns were making of the music-master's administration. On November 15, Ruef and Schmitz were indicted for bribery and embezzlement. In addition a gubernatorial campaign was in progress—Gillett, the Republican candidate, was running against Bell, a Democrat.

[1] *San Francisco Chronicle*, October 23, 1905.

Aroused by this school order, the secretary of the Japanese Association of America immediately protested to the School Board. Upon its refusal to modify the order, the secretary sent word to the newspapers in Japan. And it was the frenzied outbursts of Japanese opinion against a measure which it considered to be a treaty violation and a national insult, that first attracted the attention of the city of San Francisco to the act of its own authorities. The views of the Japanese government were brought to the attention of Washington by a telegram from Ambassador Wright in Tokyo to Secretary Root. On October 23, 1906, Mr. Root telegraphed Ambassador Wright that "The United States will not for a moment entertain the idea of any treatment of the Japanese people other than that accorded to the people of the most friendly European nations." How different the course of events might have been if this promise had been kept! Two days later Ambassador Aoki formally protested against the school measure to Secretary Root, on the ground that it denied rights expressly conferred by the treaty of 1894. The Japanese colony of San Francisco was also indignant. A mass meeting was held at which funds were raised to fight the measure in court. Meanwhile President Roosevelt dispatched Secretary of Commerce and Labor V. H. Metcalf to investigate the situation in San Francisco. In an effort to appease the ruffled feelings of Japan, President Roosevelt, in his annual message to Congress of December 3, 1906, denounced San Francisco's action in no uncertain terms: "To shut them [the Japanese] out from the public schools," he said, "is a wicked absurdity." [1] He then made two radical recommendations: (1) That an act be passed specifically providing for the naturalization of the Japanese; (2) that the statutes of the United States be amended so as to enable the President to enforce the treaty rights of aliens. Meanwhile Secretary Metcalf had proceeded to San Francisco, and, after investigating the situation, sent two reports to the President, the second of which was delivered to the Senate on December 18. In this latter report Mr. Metcalf

[1] *Messages and Papers of the President*, pp. 7434-7436.

discussed the actual number of Japanese in the schools, the anti-Japanese boycotts, and the anti-Japanese agitation generally.[1]

What, indeed, was the necessity for the School Board's action? Out of 25,000 school children in the city there were only 93 Japanese. Of these 68 were born in Japan and 25 in the United States. On the face of it, the charge that the Japanese were crowding out and holding back American children, was ridiculous: there were too few of them. However, if it were true that these Japanese were adults, their contact with American children might prove to be morally and intellectually harmful. This situation could have been remedied merely by fixing an age-limit applicable to all students in the schools. But the Board repeatedly refused to restrict the scope of the resolution in this manner, even after Roosevelt himself had suggested it. As a matter of fact, however, only two of the Japanese students were over twenty years of age, one being in the eighth grade and the other in the sixth. Only three were above nineteen, and four above eighteen. Colonel John P. Irish is authority for the statement that "no oral or written protest was ever made against the Japanese pupils by the parents of white pupils in those schools"; and "that no Japanese pupil in those schools was ever under the slightest suspicion of immoral or disorderly conduct"[2].

That the act of the Board was unwarranted was also proved by the attitude of the leading educators of the State. School principals in San Francisco, the superintendent of the Los Angeles city schools, the state convention of school superintendents, President Jordan of Stanford and President Wheeler of the University of California—all, in one way or another, intimated their disapproval of this drastic action. A number of chambers of commerce interested in developing trade with the Orient resented any measure discriminating against Japanese already here, although few of them favored unrestricted immigration.

[1] *Senate Document 147,* 59th Congress, 2nd session.

[2] *Oakland Tribune,* January 20, 1907; quoted in Johnson, *Discrimination Against the Japanese,* p. 23, a compendium of opinion in regard to this period.

There was little moral justification for the School Board's order. But it did serve as an occasion for an outburst of feeling against the Japanese and as a warning to the East that Japanese immigration must be stopped. More important still, it enabled Schmitz and Ruef to make "martyrs" of themselves at a time when their other activities should have received the universal condemnation of the city.

Moreover, the action of the School Board in excluding the Japanese from the schools was attacked on the ground that it was unconstitutional. As we have seen, the Board derived the authority for its action from a state law which authorized school boards to establish separate schools for children of "Mongolian" descent. It was contended, in the first place, that the Japanese were not Mongolian. Secondly, it was asserted that the ordinance was an unreasonable discrimination against the Japanese in violation of the Fourteenth Amendment of the Constitution of the United States, which guaranteed to all persons the equal protection of the laws. It is improbable, however, that the mere establishment of separate schools for different races would have been declared unconstitutional provided *equal* facilities for study were afforded for both races. On this ground the Supreme Court has upheld the constitutionality of Jim Crow cars, etc.[1] Even if separate schools were sustained on the general principle that the accommodation afforded the Japanese was *equal* to that given Americans, the San Francisco ordinance would not have been necessarily valid because of the location of the Oriental school. This school was set up in the midst of the Chinese settlement; but the Japanese population was scattered all over the city. In the words of Secretary Metcalf, "If the action of the Board stands, and if no schools are provided in addition to the one mentioned, it seems that a number of Japanese children will be prevented from attending the public schools, and will have to resort to private instruction." In other words, the ordinance would actually result in depriving them of public school facilities.

[1] *Plessy v. Ferguson*, 163 U. S. 537; *McCabe v. A. T. & S. F. Ry.*, 235 U. S. 151; *Berea College v. Kentucky*, 211 U. S. 45; Freund, *Police Power* (1904), sec. 698.

On that ground, it would have probably been pronounced invalid, although this legal defect could have been remedied by increasing the number of separate schools for the Japanese.

In the third place, it was asserted that this ordinance and the law upon which it was based violated the treaty of 1894 between the United States and Japan. This treaty granted most-favored-nation treatment to Japanese in the United States in all "rights of residence";[1] and it was contended that the right to attend public schools was a "right of residence". If a state law stood in the way of a treaty which was the supreme law of the land, the state law must be set aside.

Finally, it was said that the federal government had a right to control action of the schools when they involved the foreign relations of the United States, especially because it had contributed to the support of these schools by the grant of public lands on the understanding that they be conducted in accordance with the Constitution and treaties of the United States.

In order to settle these legal questions, President Roosevelt instructed the attorney-general, acting through United States Attorney Devlin, to bring an action against the School Board in the courts. Consequently, two suits were entered, on January 17, 1907: one was brought in the supreme court of California in the name of a Japanese child for the purpose of obtaining a writ of mandamus to compel his admission into the public schools; and the second was brought in the federal circuit court, where the federal government asked an injunction against the School Board restraining it from excluding Japanese pupils.

After the message of the President to Congress in which he denounced the action of San Francisco as a "wicked absurdity", the city became thoroughly incensed, although at first it had passed over the incident in silence. The *San Francisco Chronicle* scored Roosevelt's message by saying, "The President has degraded his position by assertions which are untrue, assumptions which have no basis in fact, recommendations which can only excite ridicule, implied threats which he has

[1] Malloy, *Treaties, Conventions, etc. of the United States,* p. 1030.

no power to execute. . . ."[1] California congressmen also showed their belligerency by again introducing bills favoring exclusion.[2]

As a result of the great furor stirred upon in the West, Roosevelt retreated from his original position. In a special message transmitting Metcalf's report to the Senate, he admitted that "there would be no objection whatever to excluding from the schools any Japanese on the score of age."[3] Furthermore, it was persistently rumored that negotiations were in progress between the President and the Japanese government which would settle all points of dispute between the two nations, including the most pressing problem of immigration.

But the Exclusion League would have nothing to do with a diplomatic form of settlement; it demanded an ironclad exclusion law. Moreover, its feelings were deeply hurt by the intrusions of the federal government into what it considered a purely municipal affair. Just before Christmas, a protest meeting was held which was presided over by none other than the mayor himself. This meeting, supposedly held under the auspices of the Labor Party and the Exclusion League, was an evidence of the connection between Schmitz and the anti-Japanese agitation. The mayor did not confine himself to calling the federal government names. He attempted to use the whole meeting—in fact, the whole agitation—to defend himself against the criminal charges recently made against him. The *Chronicle* was vehement in its denunciation:

In a speech the other evening to a meeting which he should never have been permitted to address, Mayor Schmitz lugged in an attempted defense of himself which was utterly out of place, and in the course of his remarks he said: "I find myself against a bottled-up judge." A condition of affairs under which an indicted criminal presumes to thus attack the judge before whom he is to be tried, is outrageous.[4]

[1] Editorial, December 5, 1906.

[2] H. R. 160 and H. R. 8975, 59th Congress, 2nd session.

[3] *Senate Document No. 147*, 59th Congress, 2nd session.

[4] Editorial, December 8, 1906.

In view of the hubbub raised on the Pacific Coast and in Japan over the San Francisco controversy, it was not in the least remarkable that the European press predicted that war between the United States and Japan was imminent. The President was well aware of the seriousness of the situation. By this time he realized that Japanese immigration must be stopped. In a letter written November 27, 1907, to Secretary Metcalf, the President declared that in a conversation with the Japanese Ambassador he had expressed the wish that the Japanese government "would stop their coolies, all their working men, from coming either to the United States or to Hawaii." [1] But the President added that "the great difficulty in getting the Japanese to take this view is the irritation caused by the San Francisco action." Roosevelt set out to eradicate this cause of discord.

Consequently, in the latter part of January, 1907, Mr. Roosevelt requested the San Francisco Board of Education to come to Washington and confer with him in regard to a settlement which would be agreeable to all. In the meantime, he suggested that all anti-Japanese agitation be suspended, in order not to prejudice a diplomatic settlement of the immigration question.

It took Schmitz a week to decide whether to permit the School Board to go to Washington, and then he decided to go with them. Word was circulated that he, an official charged with disreputable crimes, was to go to Washington to defend the children of San Francisco against the Japanese! In the first week of February, Schmitz and his docile Board left for Washington to be away until March 6. According to press reports, members of his following "were frankly delighted with the prospects of the indicted Mayor returning from the national capital covered with glory, and acclaimed the savior of the country from a war with Japan." [2]

[1] This letter was made public for the first time when it was placed on exhibition in the New York Public Library by the Roosevelt Memorial Association, in January, 1922. It was published in *The New York Times*, January 11, 1922.

[2] Hichborn, *op. cit.*, pp. 127-128.

But the Exclusion League refused to silence its guns, as the President had requested. On February 3, a meeting was held at which President Tveitmoe scored Schmitz for obeying the "command of President Roosevelt." In referring to the suggestion that the Japanese be excluded by treaty, he declared, "Exclusion by treaty never excludes. Roosevelt and Root may hedge and scheme and try to throw dust in the eyes of the people of the Pacific Coast, but we know what the Oriental invasion means." Nothing short of an exclusion law would satisfy these Chauvins of the West. While the Washington conference was in session, Tveitmoe telegraphed Schmitz not to desert the laboring man. "If President wants to humiliate the American flag," he wired, "let him tell California's Governor and Legislature to repeal the law, but he cannot coerce free Californians to bow in submission to the will of the Mikado. Roosevelt's power will not make one white man out of all the Japs in the Nipponese Empire. California is the white man's country, and not the Caucasian graveyard[1]"!

Not to be outdone by the Exclusion League, the California legislature likewise showed complete disregard for the President's request that the agitation against the Japanese temporarily cease. The 1907 session was heaped full of anti-Japanese bills. There was the Sanford resolution protesting against Roosevelt's suggestion that Japanese be naturalized; the Black resolution in favor of an exclusion treaty; the Caminetti bill providing that Japanese be expressly included among those for whom separate schools might be established; the Keane bill providing for a referendum on the question of exclusion; and the Drew bill prohibiting land ownership by aliens. On March 11, Governor Gillett telegraphed to President Roosevelt to find out what his attitude was toward this legislation. The President replied:

I earnestly deprecate the passage of any legislation affecting the Japanese. The National Government now has the matter in hand, and can in all human probability secure the results that California desires, while at the same time preserving unbroken and friendly rela-

[1] *San Francisco Call,* February 11, 1907, as in Johnson, *op. cit.*, p. 13.

tions between the United States and Japan . . . Any such action as that you mention would merely hamper the National Government in the effort to secure for California what only the National Government can secure.

In the meantime the President had been endeavoring to win the San Francisco School Board, then in Washington, over to his point of view. He declared that the national government would "meet every reasonable wish and every real need of the people of California or any other State in dealing with the people of a foreign power."[1] At the same time, he insisted that the federal government was charged exclusively with the conduct of foreign relations, and that it could tolerate no action on the part of a state or municipality which impaired this national function. As a result of this conference, Schmitz and the School Board capitulated, despite the intransigence of the labor leaders in San Francisco. The solution agreed upon was: (1) that the School Board would rescind its resolution ordering Japanese children to attend the Oriental School; (2) that the President would prevent Japanese in Hawaii, Canada and Mexico from entering the United States on passports issued by Japan only to those destinations; (3) that the President would undertake to restrict Japanese emigration coming directly to the United States from Japan, by diplomatic means; (4) that the federal government would withdraw the suits instituted to test the constitutionality of the California school law.

After agreeing to this settlement, the School Board returned to San Francisco, and on March 13, 1907, rescinded its school resolution in so far as it applied to the Japanese. This was followed by the dismissal of the suits against the law by District Attorney Devlin. Finally, the President undertook to stop emigration from Hawaii, Canada and Mexico. It will be remembered that the chief complaint against Japanese immigration concerned that from Hawaii. Once there, Japanese immigrants hitherto could not be restrained from coming to the United States because the island was American territory. If this immigration could be stopped, therefore, the greatest

[1] *Theodore Roosevelt—An Autobiography* (1913), p. 379.

grievance against the Japanese would be removed. As a final part of the compromise Congress inserted a provision in the Act of February 20, 1907,[1] which authorized the President to refuse entrance to immigrants who, to obtain entrance to the mainland, were using passports originally issued to "any country other than the United States." Under the authority of this act, the President issued the proclamation of March 14, 1907, which ordered that "Japanese or Korean laborers, skilled and unskilled, who have received passports to go to Mexico, Canada or Hawaii, and come therefrom, be refused permission to enter the continental territory of the United States."[2]

This executive order solved only half the difficulty. It had nothing to do with the immigration of Japanese coming *directly* from Japan to the United States. As we have seen, the President was attempting to stop this immigration by an agreement with the Japanese Government. But Ambassador Aoki met his advances with the argument that the Japanese should be treated exactly on the same footing as the immigrants of any other nationality. But the President did not let this logic trouble him. In reply he said that "what we had to do was to face facts . . . and that it was not possible to admit Japanese laborers into the United States."[3]

Negotiations continued fruitlessly throughout the summer and into the fall. But the Japanese government refused to agree to an exclusion treaty. In November, however, Foreign Minister Hayashi announced that the Japanese government would itself restrict emigration to the United States—a promise which had been made in 1900. This announcement apparently was not put into effect because of the opposition of the emigration companies. At any rate 30,226 Japanese entered this country, including Hawaii, in 1907—twice as many as in 1906. They also came in from Canada on bogus passports, which Japanese already here would mail to them for prices ranging

[1] 34 *Stat.* 898, c. 1134, par. 1.

[2] See Rule 21, Immigration Regulations, Department of Commerce and Labor, Doc. No. 78, *Immigration Laws and Regulations of July 1, 1907* (1907).

[3] Quoted from a letter to Secretary Root, July 13, 1907.—Bishop, *Theodore Roosevelt and His Time, Shown in His Letters* (1920), vol. II, p. 65.

from five to twenty-five dollars. It was also charged that despite the order of March, 1907, 10,000 Japanese had come in from Mexico within the last few months. These facts and these rumors increased the uneasiness of the Pacific Coast until finally open agitation against the Japanese broke out anew. As early as July, 1907, the San Francisco authorities had refused to grant licenses to Japanese employment agencies—a measure which was doubtless unconstitutional. Exclusion bills also became thick in Congress. At first they were laid aside at the President's request. But there was a limit to the patience of Congress. In February, 1908, hearings on the subject of Japanese immigration were opened. War-talk was also revived. Rumors were broadcast that Japanese warships were hovering near Hawaii. The mayor of Portland publicly announced that Japanese spies had secured detailed maps of the roads and pipelines leading into the city. A Japanese "spy" was arrested at Fort Rosecrans. Captain Richmond Pearson Hobson wrote a series of articles estimating the number of men Japan could land on the Pacific Coast. It was reported that Japan was manufacturing more munitions than at any time since the Russian war.

President Roosevelt's decision to send the fleet around the world intensified the crisis. There were doubtless many other reasons for this unprecedented action, taken without consulting Congress. But the President admitted that the Japanese problem was the crux of the whole matter. In a letter to Secretary Root, he said, "I am more concerned over the Japanese situation than almost any other. Thank Heaven we have the navy in good shape. It is high time, however, that it should go on a cruise around the world."[1] The fleet left for the Pacific in December, 1907, in the midst of the negotiations between the State Department and Japan.

For some reason which has never been satisfactorily explained, the Japanese Ambassador at Washington, Viscount Aoki, was now recalled. On his way home he gave out a very important statement in San Francisco in which he said that

[1] Bishop, *op. cit.*, p. 64.

diplomatic negotiations over the immigration question were at an end, and that the Japanese government itself had undertaken to regulate immigration.[1]

This vague intimation of the "Gentlemen's Agreement" was not confirmed by the State Department. In fact, little credence was placed in the statement of a recalled ambassador who later was dismissed from the service. And the appointment of Baron Takahira as the next ambassador led to the supposition that negotiations would be reopened. The press reported an interchange of notes at the end of December and the first of January, 1908, after which, on January 25, Washington pronounced the position of Japan toward immigration "satisfactory." In all probability, these notes confirmed the "Gentlemen's Agreement," by which Japan undertook voluntarily, and upon her own responsibility, to restrict emigration to the United States. But if an agreement was reached at that time, the public was kept in the densest ignorance—a fact proved by the continued agitation in Congress for the passage of exclusion laws.

Another indication that some understanding had been reached came in the latter part of January, 1908, when the Japanese government announced that after February 1 it would permit emigration to Hawaii only of those laborers returning to resume a former residence, or of immediate relatives of those already there.

It is apparent, therefore, that great secrecy surrounded the negotiation of this mysterious agreement. At the same time a similar understanding was being reached between Canada and Japan, concerning which a public statement was made. Japanese immigration had sorely vexed some of the provinces of Canada—particularly British Columbia.[2] About 1900 Canada and Japan entered into an agreement by which the Emperor promised to limit emigration to Canada. But this agreement had been repeatedly violated at the instigation of such firms as

[1] *San Francisco Chronicle,* January 5, 1908.

[2] On the Japanese in Canada, see W. G. Smith, *A Study in Canadian Immigration* (1920), p. 156 *et seq.*

the Canadian Pacific Railroad, which wished Japanese labor for construction purposes. In January, 1907, there were about 7500 Japanese in British Columbia, but in the following ten months, 4,429 entered.[1] This great increase led to race riots in Vancouver, and finally to the dispatch of the Canadian minister of labor, Rodolphe Lemieux, to Japan in the latter part of October, 1907, to bring about a diplomatic settlement of the question. On December 23 of the same year, Foreign Minister Hayashi sent a note to Lemieux which defined the basis on which the Japanese government agreed to restrict immigration to Canada. Hayashi insisted that the treaty between the two countries guaranteed to Japanese subjects "full liberty to enter, travel and reside" in any part of Canada; but that the Japanese Government would not insist upon the right when its exercise "would involve disregard of special conditions" which may prevail there "from time to time." For that reason the Japanese government would undertake to meet "the desires of the government of the Dominion as far as is compatible with the spirit of the treaty and the dignity of the state."[2] This was interpreted to mean that only 480 Japanese emigrants might go to Canada annually. This statement illustrates the precarious and the indefinite nature of an agreement presumably similar to that entered into with the United States at approximately the same time.

Although the agreement with the United States was apparently negotiated in January, 1908, the first official announcement of it did not appear until the annual report, July, 1908, of the United States Commissioner-General of Immigration. In this report it was stated that "an understanding was reached with Japan that the existing policy of discouraging the emigration of its subjects of the laboring classes to continental United States should be continued and should, by cooperation of the governments, be made as effective as possible. This understanding contemplates that the Japanese Government shall issue

[1] Report of 1909, W. L. MacKenzie King, deputy minister of labor, III-VII, Oriental Immigration, 9-10 Edward VII, Sessional paper No. 36, p. 77.

[2] *Ibid.*, pp. 99-100.

passports to continental United States only to such of its subjects as are non-laborers or are laborers who, in coming to the continent, seek to resume a formerly-acquired domicile, to join a parent, wife or child residing there, or to assume active control of an already possessed interest in farming enterprise in this country. . . . With respect to Hawaii, the Japanese Government of its own volition stated that, experimentally at least, the issuance of passports," to laborers coming there would be limited to former residents or relatives of residents.[1]

It had required seven years to bring about the prohibition of Japanese immigration. The first step had been taken in 1900 when Japan voluntarily prohibited the emigration of laborers to the United States. Upon the failure of this voluntary restriction, President Roosevelt took the second step, in March, 1907, when he prohibited the emigration of Japanese from Hawaii, Mexico and Canada without proper passports. The third step came in December, 1907, when Japan entered into a Gentlemen's Agreement with Canada, which affected materially the United States, because it made smuggling over the Canadian border less probable. The fourth step came when an informal agreement to prohibit emigration to the United States was reached—an agreement which carried out and strengthened the restraints imposed in 1901, and which also prohibited, at least temporarily, emigration from Japan to Hawaii. Thus by 1908 the emigration of Japanese laborers to the United States, to Canada and Hawaii had been severely restricted. As a result the San Francisco school controversy came to an end, and the agitation which had accompanied it temporarily died down.

There doubtless had been an economic basis for the early beginnings of the anti-Japanese movement in California and on the Pacific Coast. Japanese had come into California and Washington by thousands. They competed with the white man as white men compete with each other. But they differed from other immigrants in that they worked harder than most

[1] *Reports of Department of Commerce and Labor,* 1908, "Report of Commissioner-General of Immigration, pp. 221-222.

laboring men, possibly had a lower standard of living[1], and were of a different skin. Their ignorance of American customs and their disposition to organize into "gangs" made possible their exploitation by contractors, often resulting in the undercutting of white men. San Francisco was in the hands of the unions, the policy of which was to diminish the supply even of white labor. Hence their hostility to any immigration was natural. There is little evidence, however, that the Japanese were actually driving white men from employments. The menace from the Japanese lay not in the present, but in the future. From this standpoint, the attempt to prohibit immigration, the end which the San Francisco agitation had in view, was legitimate.

But even this did not justify the tactics employed by the Exclusion League and Schmitz's henchmen. Such politicians were perhaps not expected to be adequate judges of the *means* to be used. They may have been ignorant of the grievous effects of their appeals to race prejudice, their boycotts, and their violence, on the relations between America and Japan. But it was not so much ignorance on the part of these politicians as it was deliberate intent, which led them to choose the means they did. Schmitz used the School Board and the Exclusion League to shield himself, though unsuccessfully, from the Grand Jury. The order of the School Board came out only a few weeks before his indictment. But the agitation arising from it and his junket to Washington to "keep the country out of war" did not occur until afterward. Even leaders in the demand for exclusion denounced Schmitz's manipulation of the issue. On March 12 the *Chronicle* declared:

Schmitz had no business to go near Washington at all. He was not invited, but butted himself in with the obvious intent to divert public attention from his impending trial for alleged boodling. Schmitz had nothing to do with the action of the Board of Education except on the

[1] The Japanese standard of living is lower than that of the north-European immigrant, but probably no lower than the south and central European; see *Reports of the Immigration Commission,* vol. 23, pp. 137-138.

assumption that its members are mere puppets arranged to jump when Schmitz pulls the wires. Even if that is the case, there was no need of making an indecent exposure of it.[1]

Although Schmitz failed personally to profit by the anti-Japanese agitation, he established a precedent which less desperate politicians since have followed.

Inasmuch as the Japanese were for the most part located in the cities, the agitation of 1905–1907 originated largely with the labor unions. Those Japanese who had gone to the country were hard and willing workers, during a period of labor scarcity; as yet they were willing to remain wage-earners. Consequently, the farmer had little complaint to make against them. In succeeding years, however, the Japanese, because of increasing immigration, city boycotts, and accumulating capital, have moved *en masse* to the country and have begun to compete with the white farmer. As a result, the protest against the Japanese on the Pacific Coast during the last ten years has come more and more from the rural districts and interests and it has taken the form of legislation attempting to drive the Japanese off the land back into the cities. This phase of the agitation will be discussed in the concluding section of this article.

[1] The *Los Angeles Times* (quoted in Johnson, *op. cit.*, p. 18) in referring to the indicted mayor's declaration that if necessary he would lay down his life in battle against the Japanese, caustically remarked: "It is a notable fact that his Honor has never laid down anything of value. His promise, however, would almost reconcile anyone to a war with Japan." The *Los Angeles Express* also declared that "nothing less than the hanging of the Japanese by the toes would satisfy some of the anti-Japanese agitators in San Francisco."

RAYMOND LESLIE BUELL

HARVARD UNIVERSITY

THE DEVELOPMENT OF ANTI-JAPANESE AGITATION IN THE UNITED STATES II

The California Land Laws

I

DISSATISFIED with half-measures, the Exclusion League showed no disposition to give the Gentlemen's Agreement a trial.[1] It had no faith in the "honor" of the Japanese government, and it placed little hope in an agreement which was modeled after the signally unsuccessful "understanding" of 1900. In the first annual convention of the League, held in Seattle, February, 1908, a memorial addressed to Congress was adopted which declared against "any agreement which will permit the ruler of any foreign country to make stipulations as to what class of persons and in what numbers shall leave said foreign country for the purpose of immigration to the United States."[2]

Neither was the State legislature pleased. It shared the Exclusion League's distrust of the Agreement as a means of prohibiting future immigration. Furthermore, it considered the Japanese already on the Pacific Coast a "menace" to American life. The Gentlemen's Agreement had nothing to do with the latter problem. And the legislature was insistent that this aspect should also be solved. It had no right directly to expel the Japanese or any one else from the State.[3] But it attempted to accomplish the same end by making conditions so disagreeable for the Japanese that they would "voluntarily" leave. By the agitation which inevitably accompanies the passage of irritating legislation, it also hoped to arouse an apa-

[1] See "The Development of Anti-Japanese Agitation in the United States I", POLITICAL SCIENCE QUARTERLY, vol. XXXVII, pp. 605-638.

[2] *Immigration Commission Reports,* vol. 23, p. 170.

[3] *In re Ah Fong,* 3 Sawy. 144. Measures indirectly excluding the Chinese, by head-taxes, etc., have been also declared unconstitutional. See Coolidge, *Chinese Immigration* (1909), chap. v.

thetic country to the necessity of "solving" California's racial problem.

In the 1909 session of the legislature about seventeen anti-Japanese measures were introduced. These were narrowed down to three bills: (1) The Drew Alien Land Law, which compelled every alien landholder[1] to become a citizen within five years or dispose of his holdings—a measure which would effectually exclude the Japanese from ownership as they could never become citizens;[2] (2) the Anti-Japanese School Bill, which provided for the segregation of Japanese children in the public schools—a revival of the old agitation; and (3) the Municipal Segregation Bill which authorized municipalities, in order to "protect the health, morals and peace of their inhabitants", to restrict "undesirable, improper and unhealthy persons" within certain prescribed districts.[3]

At the intervention of Governor Gillett and of President Roosevelt,[4] these bills were finally dropped, although not without a good deal of grumbling. One assemblyman declared, "Since yesterday I have changed my views. I thought there were three departments in this Government, but I find that I was mistaken. I recognize the error of my youthful belief. I know that the Legislature and the Executive are one, or rather that the Executive is the Legislative." The only anti-Japanese action taken by the legislature was a resolution advocating the extension of the Chinese exclusion laws to the Japanese,[5] and

[1] The early hostility of political parties toward alien land ownership may be seen in Davis, *Political Conventions in California*, pp. 458, 529, 548.

[2] Federal courts have ruled that Japanese are not "free white persons" and therefore not eligible to citizenship under our naturalization laws. In November, 1922 the U. S. Supreme Court confirmed these decisions. *Ozawa v. the U. S.*, 43 Sup. Ct. Rep. 65. For a detailed discussion of this and other legal questions, such as dual citizenship, the treaty of 1911, and anti-alien land legislation, see R. L. Buell, "Some Legal Aspects of the Japanese Question", *Americal Journal of International Law*, January, 1923.

[3] Hichborn, *Story of the California Legislature of 1909*, pp. 202 *et seq.*

[4] See Roosevelt's letter to Mr. P. A. Stanton, speaker of the Assembly. *Theodore Roosevelt—An Autobiography*, pp. 382-384. On Roosevelt's views regarding exclusion at this time, see his letter of Jan. 29, 1909, to Congressman William Kent, reprinted in "Japanese Immigration and Colonization", *Senate Doc. No. 55*, 67th Cong., 1st session, p. 62.

[5] Joint Resolution, *California Statutes*, 1909, p. 1346.

a law appropriating funds in order that the State Labor Commission might collect statistics concerning them.[1]

Another source of agitation was found in the launderers. In March, 1908, an "Anti-Japanese Laundry League" was organized to protect white laundries from yellow competition. Laundry proprietors and employees paid regular dues to this organization. The League attempted to prevent the issuance of licenses to the Japanese, to reduce their patronage, and to prevent them from securing laundry equipment.[2] Billboard advertising was skillfully utilized. One poster read:

> Foolish woman!
> Spending your man's
> Earnings on Japs.
> Be fair, patronize
> Your Own.
> We support You.

From the very start, it is evident that neither the laboring men nor the politicians were satisfied with the Gentlemen's Agreement.

California's apprehension in regard to the Japanese was further aroused by the negotiation of a new treaty with Japan in 1911. It will be remembered that the treaty of 1894 contained a provision at the end of Article II which virtually said that each country might exclude the laborers of the other. The Japanese government had strenuously objected to this provision, and finally agreed to it only because the removal of extraterritoriality in Japan depended on the ratification of this treaty. Shortly afterward, Count Hayashi wrote in his *Secret Memoirs*, "In a few years, the time will come for the denunciation of that treaty, and a new treaty will be made, which will have no restriction on the freedom of the Japanese to immigrate to America."[3] This prophecy proved to be correct. The Treaty of 1911 (Article 1) read, "The citizens or subjects

[1] *Ibid.*, p. 227.

[2] *Immigration Commission Reports*, vol. 23, pp. 195-196.

[3] *Secret Memoirs of Count Tadasu Hayashi* (1915) edited by A. M. Pooley, p. 249.

of each of the high contracting parties shall have liberty to enter, travel and reside in the territories of the other. . . ." No qualification in regard to the admission of laborers was made. The only safeguard against immigration was the Declaration accompanying the treaty, signed by Count Uchida, the Japanese Ambassador to America, which stated that Japan would continue to enforce the Gentlemen's Agreement.[1] The elimination of the exclusion provision of 1894 from the treaty of 1911 alarmed the California legislators, who believed that, despite the Declaration, we had now surrendered the control of our borders to the Japanese government.[2] The legislature was in session when the Japanese treaty was pending. Naturally, vigorous opinions were expressed in regard to its terms. The senate went so far as to pass a land bill denying to aliens ineligible to citizenship the right to hold land, by a vote of 29 to 3. But at the intercession of President Taft, the legislature finally dropped the measure.

II

A presidential year came in 1912. The Republican party had been in power at Washington since 1896. It was also in control of the California legislature. Consequently, President Roosevelt had been able to restrain the latter body whenever its anti-Japanese measures threatened to embarrass the federal government. This, despite the bad grace with which the legislature had usually marred its acquiescence. Not that the Democrats were inspired by any loftier motives than the Republicans—on the contrary, they seized upon the timorous restraint of their opponents as a high horse upon which they themselves might ride to power. In the 1912 campaign the state Democratic party declared that Roosevelt believed that "the Japanese should be allowed to overrun the lands in California", and "that grown Japanese men should be allowed to mingle in the public schools with white boys and girls of tender years"!

[1] See Charles, *Treaties and Conventions, etc. of the United States*, p. 82.

[2] Roosevelt also thought the treaty to be a mistake.—*Autobiography*, p. 389.

Such sabotage had no effect on the smoothly greased wheels of Hiram Johnson's political machine. In the elections of 1912 the Progressives carried the state for Roosevelt, and the state legislature became Progressive and Republican. But at Washington, a Democrat, Woodrow Wilson, had driven the Grand Old Party from power. Never before during the Japanese controversy had a Republican (or Progressive) legislature existed in Sacramento simultaneously with a Democratic President in Washington. Furthermore, California's Governor, Hiram Johnson, apparently had an eye on the Presidential chair. Consequently, the legislature which had hitherto bowed to the will of President Roosevelt now was to treat the remonstrances of Washington, with respect, but with total disregard.

When the Sacramento legislature was convened in the winter of 1913, about forty anti-Japanese measures were introduced. Many of them dealt with the right of aliens to own land. After conducting hearings on these bills, the Judiciary Committee of the assembly reported out a measure, on April 2, 1913, which declared that: (1) an alien might acquire real property and hold it for one year, (2) he might lease land for five years, (3) corporations, a majority of the stock of which was owned by aliens *ineligible to become citizens*, were declared to be aliens.[1] With the exception of the last provision, this bill treated all aliens alike. For this very reason, the measure was vigorously opposed by assemblymen from districts in which foreign capital was invested. But despite their objections, the assembly passed the bill in its original form.

Likewise, the senate Judiciary Committee framed a law which was even less discriminatory than the Assembly bill. It fixed the leasing period at three years and also excluded from the rights of ownership all corporations the majority of stock of which was owned by aliens of whatever race. On the 18th of December, Secretary Bryan telegraphed that the senate bill was greatly to be preferred over that of the assembly. He advised especially against the use of the words, "ineligible to citizenship."

[1] Hichborn, *Story of the California Legislature for 1913*, p. 236.

If this bill had been enacted, it would have been unobjectionable from the diplomatic standpoint. It could not have become by any possible interpretation a source of international dispute; and it would have protected the resources of California more thoroughly than a measure limited merely to "aliens ineligible to citizenship"—or the Japanese. But the California senate would not have it so. Many of its politicians wished to make out of the Japanese question an international issue—otherwise they would attract little notoriety. Furthermore, European capitalists did not relish the loss of possible investments in California, especially in minerals and oil. Consequently, they organized a powerful lobby which was successful in causing the state senate to defeat the non-discriminatory bill.[1] Just what European interests participated in this lobby, it is difficult to determine. But in 1913, Andrew Weir, a large ship-owner in England, representing a prominent group of Englishmen, undertook to gain control of the Union Oil Company of California. This group actually purchased twenty-five per cent of the company's stock and secured an option on the remainder.[2] The passage of a land law which applied to all aliens would have prevented the acquisition of the Union Oil Company by this English syndicate. It would have prevented the operation of another alien corporation, the Royal Dutch Shell Company, which became incorporated on July 30, 1915. It would have prevented the operation of new mines, in Shasta County, by the Mountain Copper Company, a British syndicate which owns one of the largest smelters in the state.

Whatever these interests were, they brought tremendous pressure to bear on the senate. As a result, that body amended previous measures so as to exempt practically all European and Canadians from their operation.[3] The bill as it now stood permitted aliens "eligible to citizenship"—and no others—to own

[1] Hichborn, *op. cit.*, p. 243.

[2] This option expired on the outbreak of the war.

[3] It made three amendments: (1) corporations, the majority of the stock of which was held by citizens eligible to citizenship, might hold land; (2) aliens eligible to citizenship might also own mining and oil-well property; (3) the leasing period was limited to four years.

mining and oil-well property. This discrimination against aliens who could not become citizens, obviously the Japanese, was immediately protested by President Wilson. In a telegram he declared, "Invidious discrimination will inevitably draw in question the treaty obligations of the Government of the United States. I register my very earnest and respectful protest against discrimination in this case." On the 23rd of April, the President again wired that he could not understand the situation and asked permission to send Secretary of State Bryan to Sacramento.

For some strange reason, the legislature did not take umbrage at his request; and both houses dispatched an invitation to Mr. Bryan to confer with them. The Secretary arrived in Sacramento on April 28th, and stayed for about a week. But all of his efforts to obtain the passage of a land law which would not discriminate against the Japanese failed. He left Sacramento a defeated man. His visit probably was a mistake. Very likely, if Mr. Wilson had kept his hands off a Republican legislature, it would not have dared to pass legislation bound to cause international trouble. But the state legislature had been balked by a Republican President for at least six years. Each time that it had withdrawn anti-Japanese legislation it had felt humiliated; yet because of the mutual party interests in state and federal government it had obeyed. Now, however, there was no reason why it should suffer yet another rebuke from a President who had come to power because of a division in Republican ranks. Furthermore, Japan demanded that its rights be redressed. If there is anything which disgusts a California politician—and indeed many of its people—it is talk about the "rights of Japan." In the face of the protests of a Democratic President and of an "impudent" Japan, a Republican legislature believed that it could never face "the people at home" if it acquiesced in the demands of both. Consequently, the senate stood firm.

But in order to make the proposed legislation conform to the treaty obligations of the United States, the Webb-Heney bill was finally agreed upon. This bill left to aliens ineligible to citizenship all rights to real property granted by treaty, *but no others*—except the right to lease land for three years. As the treaty of 1911 did not grant Japanese the right to acquire land, they now had no rights in regard to the acquisition of real property whatever.[1] But all aliens eligible to citizenship were given the same rights to real property as citizens. In this form the Webb-Heney bill passed the senate on May 2, 1913. The European investors had been spared; but the Japanese, less able to defend themselves, were singled out for attack; and they were denied rights granted to aliens from other countries. The assembly also accepted the bill. Despite the opposition of the Panama-Pacific Exposition, of the Asiatic Exclusion League (the members of which believed that the law would hurt the fight for exclusion), and of President Wilson, the bill now became law.[2]

Because of its discriminatory nature, this legislation immediately brought forth protests from Japan. The Japanese Foreign Office emphasized the importance of "the discriminatory phase of the legislation in those affairs of international commercial concern, in which nations usually accord to peaceful and friendly aliens equal treatment, either as a matter of comity or by application of the principle of the most favored nation."[3] These protests, official and popular, led to the revival of war talk. After the remonstrances of the Japanese ambassador, the *Los Angeles Examiner* frantically declared, "Not since the guns of Fort Sumter boomed out over Charleston Harbor in

[1] See my article, "Some Legal Aspects of the Japanese Question".

[2] The land law which went into effect on August 10, 1913, contained the following provisions: (1) aliens eligible to citizenship may acquire, hold and transmit real property in the same manner as citizens of the United States; (2) all aliens "other than those mentioned in section one" may acquire property in the manner prescribed by any treaty now existing between the United States and the country of which the alien is a subject; and in addition, may lease land for agricultural purposes for a term not to exceed three years; (3) any corporation of which a majority of members are aliens ineligible to citizenship, or in which a majority of issued capital stock is owned by such aliens, may acquire land only as prescribed by treaty; (4) any property acquired in violation of this law shall escheat to the State of California.—*1913 California Statutes*, p. 206.

[3] *Foreign Relations of the United States*, 1913, p. 630. See also *ibid.*, 1914, pp. 426-434.

1861 has the nation fronted so serious a threat as it does to-day."[1] The militarists of America were matched by the militarists of Japan, who silently chuckled at the resentment of their people against California's action. White-Perilism meant larger budgets for the navy!

This land law did nothing more than prevent the acquisition of real property by the Japanese *in the future.* It did not deprive them of land which they already owned. It did not even prevent them from leasing any amount of land they might wish in the future. Although the leasing term was limited to three years, they might legally renew the lease and remain on the land indefinitely. The law, therefore, was absolutely ineffective in removing the Japanese from the land. Efforts were now to be made to make the legislation more stringent.

III

But despite attempts made to abolish the leasing privilege in the 1915 and 1917 legislatures, nothing more was done in regard to the Japanese until 1919. Now that the war had come to an end, and the American Legion had been organized,[2] and a national election was approaching, the Japanese again became a target of attack. Attention was called to the "enormous" increase in acreage made by the Japanese during the war. The acreage owned by the Japanese, which in 1913 was 26,707, had increased in 1918 to 29,105 acres; while the amount held by lease, etc., increased to 336,721. It was alleged that these increases were brought about by subterfuge and the evasion of the law. The means taken by the Japanese to evade the law and acquire title to real property were: (1) by dummy cor-

[1] April 23, 1913.

[2] The head of the Stockton American Legion has testified as follows: "We were the first—I know that we were the first in Stockton—to agitate the question and circulate the anti-Japanese-Asiatic petitions . . . and we feel that we are more or less responsible for the movement in California." — *Hearings,* pp. 475-76. Another witness testified: "Yesterday . . . we were accosted by a young man who wanted us to sign the initiative measure and we started to examine it, when he said, 'It is not necessary to examine it.' We said that we did not want to sign it without reading it, and he said that there was not one in 500 that read it. He said, 'The American Legion is behind this, and the American Legion is behind Senator Phelan.'"—*Ibid.,* p. 570.

porations in which the majority of the stock was held by American citizens (who might be Japanese children born here) but paid for and controlled by Japanese, themselves ineligible to own land;[1] (2) by trusteeships, where Japanese paid American citizens to purchase land and hold it for them or for their children; (3) by guardianships, in which the Japanese parents, as guardians of their American-born children, purchased land in their name, but used it for themselves. The amount of land thus acquired by the Japanese was not very large. In the nine counties of Southern California only 518 acres of farm land and 47 city lots were acquired in the names of Japanese children in the seven years following 1913. Nevertheless, the Anti-Japanese League exhorted against the shocking immorality of the Japanese who stooped to such practices. But they failed to recognize that the evasions had been brought about by American lawyers, and that Americans themselves utilize every possible means of side-stepping laws affecting their own interests.

Furthermore, the state already had the power of dissolving fictitious guardianships. In the case of *People v. Harada*, decided in 1918, the court held that when a Japanese father acquired property in good faith for his children and administered it for their interests, the law could not intervene. This decision was interpreted to mean that the state had no power to dissolve guardianships obtained by Japanese purely to circumvent the land law of 1913.[2] This interpretation, however, was illogical inasmuch as the court, in the case cited, insisted that the guardianship must rest on good faith. But all Japanese guardianships obviously have not rested on that basis. In fact, in the so-called Visalia cases, the court terminated letters of guardianship on the ground that the Japanese concerned had rendered no account of his guardianship; that he had used the property as his own; and that his purpose in applying for letters of guardianship was merely to gain title and

[1] For a list of these corporations, see *Hearings*, pp. 420 *et seq.*

[2] For the case, see *People of the State of California v. Yukiehi Harada et al.*, in the Superior Court of the State of California in and for the County of Riverside, No. 7751. Filed, County Clerk of Riverside, decided October 22, 1918.

control of land which otherwise he could not have.[1] The court declared that it was an absurd construction of the law to hold that the state did not have power to terminate such fictitious relationships.

Despite these decisions which show that the state already possessed the power to deal with this means of evasion, the politicians seized upon it as a pretext to amend the 1913 land law. It was during the Peace Conference at Paris that such action was commenced. On April 1, 1919, two senators asked that the legislature permit the introduction of anti-Japanese bills, one concerning "picture brides" and the other abrogating the leasing provisions of the 1913 land law.[2] The passage of these laws would incense Japanese opinion, as it had formerly done, and at a time when the American peace program might be seriously affected. Consequently the senate committee to which these requests were referred, recommended that they be denied.[3] It was finally decided to continue the consideration of the requests until a cablegram could be sent to the Secretary of State at Paris asking whether or not the introduction of such measures would embarrass the United States at the Conference. Such a dispatch was sent on April 3, 1919, A week later M. Lansing replied that it would be particularly unfortunate to have these bills introduced or pressed at the present time. . . ."[4] As a result of this cable, the senators withdrew their requests and the anti-Japanese legislation was dropped.

[1] *In the matter of the Estate and Guardianship of Fumiko Kawahara,* November 24, 1919; also *In the matter of the Estate and Guardianship of Kimiko Okasaki, et al.,* January 5, 1920. For other cases, see *Hearings,* pp. 873 *et seq.*

[2] The California legislature, which meets biennially, has the unique practice of dividing each session into two parts; in the first part, bills are introduced, after which a recess of a month is taken in which the legislators may learn the opinions of their constituents. According to the Constitution (Article IV, section 2) no bill can be introduced after the reassembling of the Legislature, without the consent of three-fourths of the members of the house. This is why the senators were obliged to ask the consent of the senate to introduce these bills.

[3] *Senate Journal,* 1919, p. 999.

[4] *Senate Journal,* 1919, p. 1277. On April 10th, the senate replied to Lansing urging federal action in regard to Japanese immigration (p. 1377).

But the "people" felt no such responsibility to the nation. After the Peace Conference was terminated by the signature of the Treaty of Versailles on June 28, 1919, the diplomatic restraints which had been clapped on anti-Japanese talk were thrown to the winds. The Hearst papers and the anti-Japanese politicians again raised the spectres of Japanism—land monopolies—increasing Japanese immigration—picture brides—Emperor worship and dual citizenship. The Immigration Hearings in Washington, held to frame a new policy for the United States, gave Senator Phelan and others an opportunity to harp *ad nauseam* on the Japanese menace to the country. But it was Japanese imperialism which really fed the fires of anti-Japanese agitation. The universal indignation at the award of Shantung to Japan and cumulative evidence of the broken pledges of Japan in international affairs increased the suspicion of many honest people in California that Japan would show no scruples in violating the Gentlemen's Agreement, the only bar to an inundating wave of Orientalism. It made little difference to the popular mind that the berry hucksters who plowed California's fields had nothing to do with Japanese imperialism. For all that they knew, the Japanese government might be using them to accomplish by covert means what it was more openly doing in Korea, Manchuria and Siberia! The responsibility, therefore, for a large share of anti-Japanese agitation in California is due to the militarists of Tokyo.

In September, 1919, a committee was appointed to revive the old Exclusion League, which had been dormant since 1909.[1] Once organized it secured the affiliated membership of such organizations as the American Legion, the State Federation of Labor, and the Native Sons and Daughters. It adopted this "five-point" program:

1. Cancellation of the "Gentlemen's Agreement."
2. Exclusion of "Picture Brides." [2]

[1] *Los Angeles Examiner*, September 18, 1919.

[2] When a Japanese resident in the U. S. has been too poor to return to Japan and find a wife, he has arranged for his relatives, etc., to pick out a bride and to have a proxy marriage ceremony performed in Japan, whereupon the "wife" proceeds to the United States to join her husband. Her picture is sent on

3. Rigorous exclusion of all Japanese as immigrants.

4. Confirmation and legalization of the policy that Asiatics shall be forever barred from American citizenship.

5. Amendment of the Federal Constitution providing that no child born in the United States shall be given the rights of an American citizen unless both parents are of a race eligible to citizenship.

This organization, as well as many of the members of the state legislature, now demanded that Governor Stephens call a special session of the state legislature. The governor refused, his position being that no action should be taken until the State Board of Control should conclude an investigation of the Japanese situation which it had just undertaken. His refusal to call a special session took a tremendous amount of courage, for it brought down upon his head abuse from organs such as the *Grizzly Bear*, which demanded the recall of the governor and of all the other "pro-Japs in California", in order that the state might remain what "it has always been and God Himself intended it shall always be—the White Man's Paradise." [1]

But even such diatribes did not shake the governor in his determination not to call a special session that would, to use the words of the *San Francisco Chronicle*, only "complicate international relations" and be a "waste of the public money." [2]

Having failed to secure a special session of the legislature, the anti-Japanists now turned "to the people." Despite the journeys of different "peace" commissions to Tokyo, one going from the San Francisco Chamber of Commerce,[3] the

ahead, hence the name "picture bride". The Japanese Government refused to issue passports to "picture brides" after February 29, 1920, as a concession to American sentiment against the practice. But apparently this prohibition did not apply to passports to "picture brides" to Hawaii, since in its report to the Secretary of Labor, released January 25, 1923, the Hawaiian Labor Commission emphatically recommended that the importation of "picture brides" be stopped, because "these practices have defeated the purpose of the so-called 'Gentlemen's Agreement'".

[1] *Grizzly Bear,* March, 1920.

[2] October 30, 1919.

[3] See the interview with Mr. Wallace Alexander, *San Francisco Call,* April 26, 1920.

propaganda against the Japanese showed no signs of abatement. The agitation was aided by the report of the State Board of Control, entitled *California aud the Oriental*, which appeared in June, 1920; and by the hearings conducted by the House Committee on Immigration and Naturalization on the Pacific Coast in July and August, 1920. While the facts brought out in both inquiries were, for the most part, correct, they were immediately misinterpreted by "anti-Jap" agitators; and the House hearings allowed some people to write their views on the pages of a government document, when otherwise they would have obtained little publicity.

As a result of this movement, two initiative measures were placed upon the ballot for the general election of November, 1920. The first was an amendment to the land law of 1913. It deprived aliens not eligible to citizenship of the right to lease agricultural land; it prevented a Japanese alien from acting as guardian for a minor, even if born in this country and an American citizen, when his estate consisted of property which the Japanese himself could not hold under the law. It punished every "colorable" transfer of property, made to evade the law; a transfer was presumed to be "colorable" if an American acquired real property when a Japanese furnished the money with which to buy it; or when a corporation acquired real property when a majority of its stock, although held by Americans, was actually paid for with Japanese money.[1]

The second measure provided for a poll tax of ten dollars on male aliens resident in California, and for their registration.[2] This measure was aimed primarily at the Japanese, since, with the possible exception of the Mexicans, they are the largest group of aliens in the state. The Exclusion League was apparently ignorant of the provision of the treaty of 1911, which guarantees that Japanese in this country "shall not be compelled, under any pretext whatever, to pay any charges or taxes other or higher than those that are or may be paid by native citizens or subjects." [3]

[1] 1921 *Calif. Statutes*, pp. lxxxvii–xc.

[2] *Ibid.*, ch. 424, enacted to carry out the constitutional amendment adopted at the polls.

[3] Article I, par. 2, Treaty of 1911, Charles, *op. cit.*

There was little of general interest in the campaign waged to secure the adoption of these two measures at the polls. The Hearst papers, the Exclusion League, and the American Legion led the movement against the Japanese. The latter organization not only entered vigorously into a political campaign, but it used methods which cannot be too strongly condemned. It sponsored one of the most vicious examples of propaganda ever witnessed in the state—a moving picture, entitled *Shadows of the West*. Graphically illustrating every charge made against the Japanese, this picture depicted a ridiculously mysterious room fitted up with a wireless apparatus by which a head-Japanese ticked out prices which controlled a state-wide vegetable market! It showed Japanese dumping fish and vegetables into harbors in order to keep prices high. Worse still, it invented a Japanese spy system, and it "exposed" the headquarters of a secret government. It did not hesitate to appeal to the deepest instincts of racial prejudice by picturing the abduction of two white girls by Japanese; an attempted assault; and a melodramatic rescue by the "legion boys" after a bloody race war! Furthermore, local posts of the Legion, notably in the Imperial valley, deliberately interfered with meetings conducted by those opposed to the anti-alien land law.[1]

Politicians also profited by the anti-Japanese issue. Candidates for Congress and the Senate could not denounce the Orientals too strongly, because the latter had no votes! The presidential candidates were more restrained—they realized the international issue at stake. Both Mr. Harding and Mr. Cox said the question must be settled by measures "consistent with our national honor."[2]

It was a foregone conclusion that the land law would pass. Leaders of the Exclusion League prophesied that it would carry 9 to 1. Many citizens believed that it would remove the Japanese from the state. Others realized that the land law would not solve California's Japanese problem, because it

[1] *El Centro Progress*, October 23, 1920; *Calexico Chronicle*, October 23, 1920.

[2] "The Japanese Question in the Campaign", *Literary Digest*, Oct. 9, 1920.

would not necessarily remove any Japanese from the state or even, because of constitutional reasons, drive them off the land. But people nevertheless voted for this law because they felt that if it was defeated, the remainder of the country would believe that California had no grievances against the Japanese. The alien land law measure was in reality, therefore, an exclusion measure. It is safe to say that ninety per cent of the arguments made in the campaign had nothing to do with the Japanese on the land, but with the racial differences between Orient and Occident—which the law in no way remedied. In view of these different circumstances, it is surprising that the land law did not carry by a greater majority than it received. When the votes were counted, it was found that the law had received 668,483 votes, while 222,086 were cast against it.

Thus the last popular demonstration against the Japanese on the Pacific Coast came to an end. But its effects were left upon the state legislature, the members of which had made extravagant anti-Japanese election pledges. This body considered a bill appropriating $50,000 for the purpose of spreading "anti-Japanese" propaganda throughout the country. To the credit of the legislature, it failed to become law. The only definite action taken was the passage of a bill regulating foreign-language schools[1] and several resolutions asking the federal government to bring about the absolute exclusion of Japanese immigration.[2]

The actual attitude of the politicians toward the Japanese was revealed when a bill was introduced barring Japanese from fishing in the coastwise waters of the state. This bill passed the senate by a vote of 30 to 4. But when it came before the assembly a tremendous protest was made, not by Japanese, but by American cannery men who realized that this law would kill the cannery business of the state, which was dependent on Japanese fishermen.[3] As a result of this opposition, the assembly tabled the bill. The legislature previously had passed land

[1] Section 1534, Calif. Pol. Code.

[2] 1921, *Calif. Statutes*, p. 1774.

[3] See *California and the Oriental*, Report of the State Board of Control, p. 96; also *Los Angeles Examiner*, April 17, 1921.

and other legislation which did no material damage to anyone except the Japanese. But now a measure had come before it which would actually injure American capital. The racial, political and economic "menace" of the Japanese in the fisheries was just as great to the state as was the "menace" of the Japanese in agriculture. Yet the legislature refused to pass any anti-Japanese laws which might hurt the pocketbooks of Americans. Racial antagonism is all right until it becomes expensive—then people choose to be "liberal."

IV

The last chapter in the anti-Japanese movement on the Pacific Coast has been written since the campaign of November, 1920. In the summer of 1921, Japanese contractors under-bid the American Fruit Workers' Union, an organization of "fruit tramps," in the melon fields of Turlock, California. White farmers insisted that the union asked a price they could not afford to pay, and they continued to employ Japanese. On the night of July 18, a band of several hundred white men, by means of motor trucks and with the apparent connivance of the police, aroused 58 Japanese laborers from their beds, placed them on board a freight train, and warned them not to return. Although the mob was armed, no violence was employed, obviously because the Japanese offered no resistance.[1] The Turlock incident was a direct result of the campaigns of incitement against the Japanese which have featured in many California elections. These working men merely carried into action the sentiments which the politicians had limited to talk. The incident shows, moreover, that the means employed by the Pacific Coast to "solve" its Japanese problem merely increase the ill-feeling between the Oriental and the whites, and still further alienate the Japanese from American life.[2]

Within recent months, the futility of these anti-Japanese

[1] *Farmers' Daily Journal*, July 19, 20, 21, 22, 1921; *San Francisco Call*, July 22, 1921.

[2] As to the effect on the relations of Japan and the United States, see R. L. Buell, *The Washington Conference* (1922), p. 362.

campaigns has been demonstrated from another angle. The state supreme court has declared the alien poll-tax unconstitutional because of the treaty of 1911 with Japan, and the Fourteenth Amendment to the Constitution of the United States.[1] Although federal courts have upheld the constitutionality of the chief provisions of anti-alien land legislation,[2] they have upheld the legality of "croppage contracts" through which Japanese farmers may continue to use California's farm land as long as they and the white owner may wish.[3] The state cannot prohibit such contracts because of the Fourteenth Amendment, which protects aliens and citizens in certain rights.[4] Moreover, the state supreme court has declared unconstitutional the provision of the land law that a Japanese alien cannot serve as a guardian for a minor born in the United States.[5] The land legislation may therefore be evaded through "croppage contracts" and through guardianships. For constitutional reasons, it has been rendered ineffective.

A Solution

As brought out in the last few pages, the fundamental cause for the agitation against the Japanese on the Pacific coast has been the demand for the exclusion of Japanese immigration. The necessity for exclusion is now universally recognized. But the *means* now utilized to enforce exclusion—the Gentlemen's Agreement—is, from the popular standpoint, inherently unsatisfactory. The enforcement of this Agreement, whose very terms, incidentally, are not known to the public, is in the hands of Japan alone. She promises to keep her laborers at home, although non-laboring classes may enter this country. But we are apparently forced to accept Japan's interpretation of what

[1] *Ex parte Terui*, 200 Pac. 954; *Ex parte Kotta*, 200 Pac. 957.

[2] *Terrace v. Thompson*, 274 Fed. 841; *Porterfield v. Webb*, 279 Fed. 114; *Frick v. Webb*, 281 Fed. 407.

[3] *O'Brien v. Webb*, 279 Fed. 117.

[4] *Cf.* Sec. 1977 of the Revised Statutes; *In re Tiburcio Parrott*, 1 Fed. 481, 509; *Truax v. Raich*, 239 U. S. 33; *Coppage v. Kansas*, 236 U. S. 1; *Lem Moon Sing v. the U. S.*. 158 U. S. 538; *Yick Wo. v. Hopkins*, 118 U. S. 356.

[5] *In re Estate and Guardianship of Yano*, Calif. Dec., May 5, 1922, No. 3348, p. 520.

constitutes a "laborer"; and we are forced to accept every passport issued to Japanese coming to America.[1] We have no means of telling whether Japan is keeping her word; we have no part in enforcing the Agreement. The popular distrust of such a one-sided arrangement, into we have entered with no other nation, is increased with the militaristic nature of Japan's government and its violation of past promises in the Orient.

A good deal of paper has been wasted to prove that emigration of Japanese to the United States has actually declined under the Gentlemen's Agreement. A great deal of paper has been wasted in figuring out the increases of the Japanese population in the United States, and in making absurd deduc-

[1] In a letter to Senator Phelan, May 22, 1916, Secretary of Labor Wilson defended the agreement as follows: "If it is found in any case (and I am glad to say that this department's experience has been that such cases are extremely rare) that a passport to the United States has been issued by Japanese authorities inadvisedly or erroneously, the matter is promptly brought to the attention of the Japanese government through diplomatic channels, with request that proper steps be taken to prevent any recurrence of the mistake. Requests of this sort have always received prompt and careful attention."—*Cong. Record*, vol. 54, pt. I, p. 254. Yet even this statement is an admission that the final authority in the matter is the Japanese government alone.

But apparently Secretary Wilson's Commissioner General of Immigration did not agree with him. In the Report of the Commissioner General of Immigration for 1920, Mr. Caminetti has this to say about the Gentlemen's Agreement: "The too general terms of the agreement itself and the *ex parte* determination by officials of Japan, both in that country and in the United States, of matters arising under its terms, have not been conducive at all times to the production of the results anticipated by both countries when the agreement was conceived. Not only is clarification of the agreement needed if its main purpose in keeping laborers from coming to the United States is to be effected but systematic enforcement thereof by joint administrative effort, not only with relation to the mainland but to our island possessions as well, should be brought about by both nations. Frauds against both would thereby be materially checked if not entirely prevented and the rights of all concerned protected."—*Department of Labor, Annual Reports for 1920*, p. 299.

Before 1917 either the Japanese government or the President of the United States could terminate the Gentlemen's Agreement, with the result that Japanese immigrants could then enter this country as freely as any other immigrants, being subject only to our general immigration laws. But in order to prevent this, Congress inserted a clause in section 3 of the Act of February 5, 1917, which read: "And no alien now in any way excluded from, or prevented from entering the United States shall be admitted to the United States." Thus in the event of the termination of the Agreement by executive action, our immigration officials would have power to exclude the Japanese.

as to the consequence of such increases.[1] But these mathematical acrobatics don't get anywhere. At present the Japanese constitute only three per cent of the population of California, and they control only two per cent of the farm land in the State. While it is true that their birth rate is three times that of the whites and that when working for themselves, they will accept lower prices than Americans, there is absolutely no racial characteristic which is responsible for either of these traits. If their standard of living is raised by the processes of Americanization, those traits which are due to economic causes will disappear.[2] But at present, the Pacific Coast will have nothing to do with an Americanization program for the Oriental because of the fear that, under the Gentlemen's Agreement, the Japanese population is increasing. And it realizes well enough that it will be impossible to Americanize, even to the slightest extent, a steady stream of Oriental immigrants.

There are four possible ways of "solving" the problem. The first is by amending the terms of the present Gentlemen's Agreement, so as to limit more strictly the classes of Japanese who may enter this country. But mere tinkering with the Gentlemen's Agreement will not alter its fundamental defect—Japan's sole responsibility for administering its terms.

The second is by the passage of a Japanese exclusion law, similar to that which now excludes the Chinese.[3] But an exclusion law would violate the policy which originated with President Roosevelt's stand against such legislation in 1905. Ever since 1911 general immigration bills have contained a clause barring immigrants "ineligible to citizenship", unless already excluded by treaty or agreement.[4] But at Japan's

[1] For a complete statement of the anti-Japanese case, see "Japanese Immigration and Colonization", *Senate Document 55*, 67th Congress, 1st sess.

[2] In Hawaii, the Japanese have a birth rate lower than that of some other races. See the table, *Survey of Education in Hawaii*, Department of the Interior, Bureau of Education, Bulletin No. 16, 1920, p. 15. See also *Immigration Commission Reports*, vol. 28, "The Fecundity of Immigrant Women", pp. 146, 805; Commons, *Races and Immigrants in America* (1904), p. 203.

[3] *Cf.* Chinese Restriction Act of 1882, 22 Stat. 61, and Act of 1904, 33 Stat. 394.

[4] See statement by W. W. Hubbard, Commissioner General of Immigration, in Jenks and Lauck, *The Immigration Problem* (1922), p. 434.

protest against the mere use of these delicate words, although they did not change the status of Japanese immigration, they have always been dropped. In the immigration bill introduced into Congress on March 30, 1916 (H. R. 10384) there was a provision which would exclude Hindus and persons who cannot become eligible to citizenship "unless otherwise provided for by existing agreements as to passports or by existing treaties, conventions or agreements, or by treaties, conventions, or agreements that may hereafter be entered into."[1] But the Japanese government again protested against the use of the words "ineligible to citizenship."[2] And as a result, the final act of February 5, 1917, omitted this clause and substituted for it the "Barred Zone" provision, which excludes aliens from within certain degrees of latitude and longitude.[3] Amendments proposed by Senators Phelan and Poindexter barring "picture brides" and aliens ineligible for citizenship were rejected for the same reason.

Apparently indifferent or oblivious to this policy, the House Committee on Immigration has virtually written an exclusion law into the new immigration bill.[4] On February 5, 1923 this committee adopted a plan which would exclude all immigrants "not eligible to citizenship", with the exception of a few specified classes such as government employees and tourists. This measure goes much farther than the original immigration bill of March, 1916. It not only uses the phrase "not eligible to citizenship" but it actually excludes Japanese, when hitherto they have been excepted because of an "existing agreement" covering their immigration. In other words, it is a Japanese exclusion law. If enacted, it would be a violation of the treaty with Japan of 1911. Article I of this treaty says that the citizens and subjects of each of the high contracting parties shall

[1] See *H. R. Reports*, vol. I, no. 95, 64th Cong., 1st sess., January 13, 1916. Also letter of Secretary of Labor Wilson, May 22, 1916, *Cong. Record*, vol. 54, p. 254.

[2] New York *Times*, Feb. 8, 1916; April 22, 1916; April 25, 1916.

[3] *Senate Reports*, vol. II, no. 352, April 17, 1916; 39 Stat. Ch. 29, sec. 3, p. 876.

[4] *Cf.* H. R. 12237, 67th Cong., 2nd sess.; New York *Times*, February 6, 1923.

have liberty to enter, travel and reside in the territories of the other. Laborers are not excepted from this rule, as they were in the treaty of 1894. The treaty of 1911 is merely accompanied by a Declaration in which Japan promises to continue the Gentlemen's Agreement in force.[1] An exclusion law would certainly violate the terms of this treaty, granting Japanese liberty to enter and reside in this country, as long as the treaty is in existence.

An exclusion law would be an affront to the Japanese people, who are racially self-conscious to a much greater extent than Anglo-Saxons; it would be a weapon in the hands of the Japanese military party and might be used to convince the Japanese people that American "liberalism" is meant, not for the colored races, but for the Nordics alone. At the Paris Peace Conference, the American Delegation was partly responsible for the defeat of a "racial equality" clause which the Japanese representatives proposed for incorporation in the Covenant of the League of Nations. This clause would guarantee "to all alien nationals of States Members of the League, equal and just treatment in every respect, making no distinctions, either in law or fact, on account of their race or nationality."[2] Despite the fact that this clause could easily be interpreted to have nothing to do with immigration, it was defeated principally by the United States. But because of this position, the American delegation could not very well hold out against Japan's claims to Shantung. Having defeated Japan's claim to racial equality, the American delegation was forced to make concessions elsewhere. In a similar manner, the Japanese government may use an exclusion law to secure concessions from us in its foreign policy. In 1913 and 1914 Japan protested vigorously against a state discrimination—the California Land Law. But if an exclusion law is enacted, similar to the one which the House Committee has just proposed, the discrimination becomes national, and Japan's basis for a protest will become greater than ever. If there is any possible means of avoiding

[1] Charles, *Treaties and Conventions of the U. S.*, p. 82.

[2] R. S. Baker, *Woodrow Wilson and World Settlement* (1922), vol. II, p. 234.

it, the United States cannot afford to jeopardize the good feeling established at the Washington Conference between Japan and America, by the passage of this legislation.

A third means of "remedying" the evils of Japanese immigration would be by applying the principles of our "percentage" legislation to the Japanese. According to the Immigration Restriction Act of May 19, the number of immigrants of any nationality who may be admitted to the United States in any fiscal year is limited to three per cent of the number of foreign-born persons of such nationality resident in the United States, as determined by the census of 1910. But the provisions of this Act do not apply to "aliens from countries immigration from which is regulated in accordance with treaties or agreements relating solely to immigration"—in other words, immigration from Japan.[1]

This exception was apparently made because of the belief that the Gentleman's Agreement more effectively excludes the Japanese than would the three per cent restriction. But this has not proved to be true. In 1910, there were 67,744 foreign-born Japanese in continental United States and 59,786 in Hawaii—a total of 127,530,[2] three per cent of which would be 3826, the number of Japanese eligible to admission if the Percentage Act applied to them.[3] But under the Gentlemen's Agreement, 9279 Japanese were admitted in 1920 and 7531 in 1921,[4] or twice the number that would be admitted under a general Restriction Act.

In the bill adopted by the House Committee in February, 1923, it was proposed to adopt the census of 1890 as a basis, and to admit only two per cent of the numbers here, as based

[1] *U. S. Statutes*, 67th Congress, 1st sess., ch. 8, sec. 2 (5).

[2] *U. S. Census, 1910*, vol. I, p. 781; vol. III, p. 1160.

[3] The Act of May 19, 1921 defines the United States so as to include any waters, territories, or other places subject to its jurisdiction, except the Canal Zone and the Philippines. But if the Act had been intended to apply to the Japanese, Hawaii would have doubtless been also excluded, because of the excessive number of Japanese there. If the population only of the foreign-born Japanese in continental United States were considered, the number who could be admitted annually would be 2032 instead of 3826.

[4] *Statistical Abstract of the U. S., 1921*, p. 107.

on that census. If this plan should be extended to the Japanese, they would be excluded nearly as effectually as under an exclusion law. In 1890 there were only 2292 persons in this country who had been born in Japan, two per cent of which number would be forty-six [1]—surely not much of a Yellow Peril! The advantage of applying the percentage plan to the Japanese is that it would be non-discriminatory; the Japanese would be on exactly the same basis as the European immigrant.[2] But this type of immigration restriction is not likely to be permanent; manufacturers and capitalists are already demanding freer immigration of European laborers. If Congress is induced to let down the bars in this respect, the question of Japanese exclusion would again arise.

The best means, therefore, of handling this question is through a treaty. An exclusion treaty would accomplish the same end as an exclusion law, but without offense to Japan. A treaty is a bilateral agreement; it is brought about by the joint and friendly discussion of two governments. If made reciprocal, an exclusion treaty would be non-discriminatory. It should apply to American labor wishing to go to Japan and Japanese labor wishing to come to America. This treaty should guarantee to Japanese residents already in this country most-favored-nation treatment in all *civil* rights, and make them eligible to American citizenship on the same basis as any other aliens.[3] Japanese born in this country are already citizens under the fourteenth amendment. If Japanese immigration is effectively prohibited in the future no conceivable danger would arise from giving the vote to a few thousand additional Japanese.[4] The concession of such a privilege would be added

[1] *U. S. Census, 1890,* vol. I, p. 609.

[2] A similar plan was originally suggested by Dr. S. L. Gulick, *The American Japanese Problem* (1914), ch. xvii.

[3] The British Empire has solved the question of Hindu immigration on somewhat the same basis as this. Each dominion may exclude Hindus; but once they are admitted, they should be granted citizenship. See *Work of the Prime Ministers, Official Report; Transactions of the Imperial Conference, 1921;* "Position of British Indians in the Empire", *Round Table,* no. 44, p. 756.

[4] The Japanese population in continental United States in 1920 (*U. S. Census, 1920,* vol. III, p. 11) was 111,010. But this included American-born Japanese,

incentive for them to adapt themselves to American life.[1] But the greatest advantage of such a concession is that it would prove to the Japanese people that we insist on exclusion, not because of racial inferiority, but because of racial difference.

The treaty of 1911 was negotiated only for a period of twelve years. It will therefore expire on July 17, 1923; and negotiations of some sort must shortly take place.[2] If the American State Department should attempt to negotiate such a treaty, it is practically certain that it would now meet with the approval of Japan. Such a treaty would meet Japan's objection against discrimination. And the Japanese government would doubtless realize that if it refused to agree to such a treaty, Congress would probably pass an exclusion law, which is the last thing the Japanese desire.

minors and others who could not meet the general naturalization tests, or who would not choose to become naturalized. In California there were 47,566 Japanese over twenty-one in 1920 (*ibid.*, p. 128); but it is doubtful if half of them would become citizens if eligible.

[1] On the question of assimilation, see L. Aubert, *Américains et Japonais,* (1908), ch. iv.

[2] Article XVII, Treaty of 1911.

RAYMOND LESLIE BUELL.

HARVARD UNIVERSITY

THE CALIFORNIA-JAPANESE QUESTION.

The intense prejudice of California against the Japanese is partly racial, partly economic. There is the feeling of white superiority, and there is the dislike of the workmen to be pitted against a competitor who is willing to work harder and live cheaper than himself.

It began with the hostility to the Chinese, invaluable as these people were in California's development. The treaty of 1868, Art. 5, with China had "recognized the inherent and inalienable right of man to change his home and allegiance, and also the mutual advantage of the free migration and emigration of their citizens and subjects respectively." But in 1880, this "inalienable right" was denied by Art. 1 of the treaty of that year, in these words: "Whenever in the opinion of the United States, the coming of Chinese laborers to the United States or their residence therein, affects or threatens to affect the interests of that country" it may regulate, limit or suspend such coming or residence, but may not absolutely prohibit it. This restriction was to apply to laborers only and must be "reasonable."

Still the Pacific Coast was not satisfied, and at its insistence the Geary Act was passed by Congress excluding Chinese laborers altogether, followed (though it should have been preceded) by the convention of 1894, which by Art. 1 sanctioned such exclusion for ten years, to be followed by another term of ten years unless terminated at six months notice. It is curious to note the preamble of this treaty: "And whereas the Government of China, in view of the antagonism and much deprecated and serious disorders to which the presence of Chinese laborers has given rise in certain parts of the United States, desires to prohibit the emigration of such laborers into the United States."

There was for a long time no such emigration of Japanese subjects to the United States as of Chinese, and no similar regulation and exclusion were demanded. Moreover, the development of the two countries diverged. China remained weak, loosely organized, clinging to her ancient ways. But Japan adopted modern ideas, introduced universal education, and grew in national self-consciousness and pride. The treaty with her in 1894, accordingly, was a compact between equals. Article 1 reads:

> In whatever relates to rights of residence and travel; to the possession of goods and effects of any kind; to the succession to personal estate by will or otherwise; and the disposal of property of any sort and in any manner whatsoever which they may lawfully acquire, the citizens or subjects of each contracting party shall enjoy in the territories of the other the same privileges, liberties and rights, and shall be subject to no higher imposts or charges in these respects than native citizens, or subjects of the most favored nation.

Article 2 adds, however, this proviso:

> It is, however, understood that the stipulations contained in this and the preceding article do not in any way affect the laws, ordinances and regulations with regard to trade, the immigration of laborers, police and public security which are in force or which may hereafter be enacted in either of the two countries.

This was a treaty of commerce and navigation. It was almost the first to surrender those exterritorial privileges which our nationals had, like other foreigners, enjoyed in Japan. The new status further developed Japanese pride and power.

Then came the war with China over Corea, an easy victory for Japan but ending in her humiliation in being shorn of the full fruits of victory by the intervention of Russia, Germany and France. To avoid such intervention in future, there was framed an alliance with Great Britain, defensive in character, to preserve the status quo in the East.

This series of events testifies to the position of equality in the Society of Nations which Japan had attained. This position was, of course, greatly enhanced by her victory over Russia. This made her one of the great Powers. As the writer interprets the Treaty of Portsmouth, one of its important features was the increase of the Japanese food supply, cereals in Corea and Manchuria, fish in Saghalien and along the Siberian coast. This would argue the desire of the Japanese Government to retain, feed and employ its surplus population within contiguous territory. It was the same problem which faced the Germans, but solved in a legitimate way.

If this surmise is correct, Japanese policy and Pacific Coast prejudice are quite compatible, both desiring to confine the Japanese population within the jurisdiction of the Empire, both discouraging a constant overflow of the surplus of that race into Christian countries. This was coupled in Japan, however, with the penetration of China and a strangle-hold upon Corea.

Consider now the present friction with Japan growing out of the public laws of California since the Russian War. These laws affect the Chinese also, in fact result from the permitted attitude of the State toward the Chinese.

They relate to three questions, that of the schools, that of restricted immigration, that of land holding.

The elementary schools of California are open to children between the ages of six and twenty-one; also to adults "if the governing body of the district deems such admission advisable." Alien adults in pursuit of the English language may well have been on a par scholastically with much younger students. There developed a dislike that white children should mix at school with colored children. There was also objection to propinquity between young white girls and Japanese adults. This found expression in the statute which gave school boards power to exclude "children of filthy or vicious habits; or children suffering from contagious or infectious diseases, and also to establish separate schools for Indian children and for children of Chinese or Mongolian descent." In the last-mentioned case, such children are not to be admitted to the regular schools. These statutes were amended and repealed from time to time. I quote from the law of 1909.

The coupling together in the same sentence of vicious, diseased and Oriental children, was a slap in the face. The separate treatment of those of Mongolian descent was discrimination, setting them apart from other aliens. It would have been possible, one would think, to settle all genuine grievances arising from the mixture of races and ages at school, by giving equality of treatment to all aliens. Then no one race could have complained. But when a proud, highly educated people found itself classed with Indians, Coreans and Chinese, discriminated against and despised, it naturally remonstrated and insisted that its treaty right of the most-favored-nation treatment should be observed. This topic was discussed by Mr. Root with great force and clarity in the first volume of this JOURNAL.

Then there was the immigration question. This related to laborers only. The prejudice and the arguments were much the same as in the case of the Chinese twenty years before. But Japan is not a Power to be treated as China was then treated, without remonstrance. Moreover, as has been argued, the Japanese Government itself was not desirous that its laborers should emigrate. A solution for this difficulty therefore was found in appeals to Governor and Legislature in California to stop action which, by direct violation of treaty, tended to embroil the two Powers, and in the substitution for an exclusion statute of a private understanding, a so-called gentlemen's agreement, to the same purport. This is now operative.

And now comes the land question to disturb our relations. In accordance with the Treaty of 1894, nationals of each contracting party had the "full liberty to enter, travel, or reside in any part of the territories" of the other; access to its courts to defend their rights; and property rights as already recited. Safeguarded by this treaty, came a small but continuous stream of immigration. A considerable percentage sought and worked the land. These Japanese immigrants were naturally gregarious. They were regarded by the white Californians with growing suspicion and dislike. The hostility to the Chinese had been largely urban; hostility to the Japanese is largely agricultural and rural. Agitation of the familiar kind was set on foot and sought expression in State legislation. After the gentlemen's agreement was reached, this legislation was aimed at land-holding rights under the treaty. By Act 129, approved 1913, Sec. 1, it took this form: "All aliens eligible to citizenship may acquire, possess, enjoy, transmit and inherit real property or any interest therein" like native citizens of the United States.

Since Japanese are incapable of naturalization under our laws and judicial decisions, this amounted to a prohibition of Japanese land owning, slightly camouflaged. But what was to become of their treaty rights? Under our Constitution, no State can make, no State may violate, a national treaty. Therefore, Sec. 2 added that aliens ineligible to citizenship might acquire real property "in the manner and to the extent and for the purposes described by any treaty now existing," etc., "and may in addition thereto lease lands in this State for agricultural purposes for a term not exceeding three years.

If this provision under Sec. 2 is fairly interpreted and carried out, perhaps no injustice is done and no treaty right violated. Nevertheless, as in the school matter, there is a discrimination against those of Mongolian descent as compared with other aliens, a denial of that equal treatment which the most-favored-nation clause demands.

Unfortunately this is not the end. The writer has not been able to obtain the text of the additional legislation as to alien land holding, passed by the people of California by initiative at the November election. But its purport seems only too clear. It prohibits absolutely land ownership by Japanese. It forbids them to lease farm land. It prevents their working land as guardians of their children, who being capable of citizenship might in collusion with their parents evade the prohibition. Nor may Japanese become shareholders in any farm land company. Whether this legislation is aimed at Japanese by name or at persons of Mongolian descent or at persons incapable of citizenship, I am not informed. In any case its intent to debar certain aliens and not others, is evident. It has the same taint of illegal discrimination that has been already remarked. But it is also to all appearance a plain violation of the Treaty of 1894. To excuse it by alleging that Americans cannot own land in Japan, even if this be true, is not to the point, unless it can be shown that our nationals are unequally treated, that they are debarred while other aliens are permitted the privilege.

This then is the parting of the ways. A single State of these United States arrogates to itself the right to change a national treaty. We have seen a long course of aggressive anti-Oriental legislation in California, gradually encroaching upon treaties which are the law of the land, and now culminating in open violation of treaty. Whether Californian prejudice and the action resulting are justified or not, has nothing to do with our question. What we ask is, whether one State is greater than the whole, whether one State may alter at will a treaty made by the United States?

There are three conclusions, growing out of this historical recital, which California should take to heart.

1. If it has a grievance against a foreign Power or its subjects, redress lies not with itself but with the National Government and Congress.

2. If one of the States violates a treaty of the United States, the latter is responsible for the act of the former.

3. Being thus responsible, it must have a power commensurate. If no efficient control exists over State legislative action affecting a foreign Power and its treaty rights, then such control must be provided, not a theoretical control merely, but one prompt and drastic.

It has been reported from time to time that negotiations are under way with Japan to frame a new treaty, that an agreement has been reached, but that the "advice and consent" of the Senate are to be taken before the terms of the treaty are made known. It is well that the Senate's part in treaty-making is again recognized. It is well that our relations with Japan, so needlessly disturbed by the unfriendly acts of California, are to be settled by joint harmonious action. It is all the more necessary that Californian anti-Japanese legislation must be inoperative until a new basis of intercourse is reached.

THEODORE S. WOOLSEY.

THE JAPANESE EXCLUSION BILL OF 1924

(An Historical Sketch)

EARL H. PRITCHARD

In the spring of 1924 the anti-Japanese forces of the Pacific Coast, by a union with the anti-immigrant forces of the East and Middle West, succeeded in inserting a clause into the general immigration bill which in effect excluded Japanese immigrants from the United States. The exclusion of the Nipponese marked the culmination of a long series of attacks upon Japanese immigration, the causes of which need not be mentioned here.[1] The purpose of this paper is simply to trace the development of the particular exclusion bill which became law in 1924, and to note the various forces which influenced it from its first introduction to its final passage.

The elemental ideas and phrases which constituted the exclusion sections had already been in existence for some time before 1924. For example, the idea of excepting from the general operation of the bill "officials, teachers, students, merchants, or travelers for pleasure or curiosity" dates back at least to the Chinese exclusion law of 1888.[2] The convenient phrase, "alien ineligible to citizenship," was formulated in idea, if not in words, in the California Alien Law of 1913,[3] and was definitely used as a basis of discrimination in the Louisiana Alien Land Law of 1921.[4] Finally, the idea of establishing certain classes not subject to the main immigration laws was more definitely formulated in the immigration bill of 1921 by the inclusion of the phrase, "aliens from countries immigration from which is regulated in accordance with treaties or agreements relating solely to immigration."[5]

A study of the immigration bills and committee reports upon them introduced into Congress during the year 1921 will show that the idea of Japanese exclusion did not very seriously occupy the minds of most

[1] For a discussion of the Japanese immigration problem consult the facts and figures relating to Japanese immigration given in the **Annual Reports** of the Commissioner General of Immigration. See also, Raymond Leslie Buell, **Japanese Immigration** (Boston, 1924); Roy L. Garis, **Immigration Restriction** (New York, 1927), Chap.X; K. K. Kawakami, **The Real Japanese Question** (Chicago, 1917); H. A. Millis, **Japanese Problem in the United States** (New York, 1915).

[2] K. S. Inui, **The Unsolved Problem of the Pacific**, p. 353. See text of law.

[3] Ibid., p. 425 for text of the law.

[4] Ibid., p. 455 for text of the law.

[5] **U. S. Statutes at Large**, V. 42, Part 1, Chap. 8, p. 5.

congressmen;[6] furthermore, the immigration bill of that year passed Congress without dissent upon the clause especially excepting from the quotas, "aliens from countries immigration from which is regulated in accordance with treaties or agreements relating solely to immigration."[7] Apparently Congress was not yet vitally interested in Japanese exclusion.

The force, however, which was to change the attitude of leaders in the House Committee on Immigration from a passive policy toward the Japanese to a militantly exclusive one was already at work. This was the Japanese Exclusion League which had the support of other adherents of the exclusion policy. The work of this group and its allies, linked with various investigations held by the Congressional Committees on Immigration, served, in the course of a few years, to mobilize public opinion both in and out of Congress in favor of exclusion.

Historically, the exclusion clause of 1924 must date from April 4, 1921, when the Japanese Exclusion League of California, representing officially such organizations as the American Legion, War Veterans, Native Sons and Native Daughters of the Golden West, State Federation of Women's Clubs, State Federation of Labor, and with the approval of the Los Angeles County Anti-Asiatic Association, and the Japanese Exclusion League of Washington, was able to introduce into the California Senate a joint resolution calling for the

> Absolute exclusion for the future of all Japanese immigration not only male but female, and not only laborers, skilled and unskilled, but 'farmers' and the men of small trades and professions, as recommended by Theodore Roosevelt.
>
> Permission for temporary residence only for tourists, students, artists, commercial men, teachers, etc.[8]

This resolution was eventually endorsed by the Senate and Assembly and copies of it were sent to the President, to the Secretary of State, and to each member of the California delegation at Washington.[9] It

[6] **Congressional Record,** V. 61, April 18, 1921; **House Report** No. 4, 67 Cong., 1st sess.; **Senate Report,** No. 117, 67 Cong., 1st. sess. For two exceptions to this see **Congressional Record,** V. 61, pp 182 and 520.

[7] **U. S. Statutes at Large,** V. 42, Part 1, Chap. 8, p. 5; see also **Congressional Record,** V. 61, pp. 495, 967, 1426-28, and 1592. This clause exempted Japanese from the action of the quotas.

[8] California, **Senate Journal,** 44th sess., April 4, 1921, p. 1040. For text, see **Congressional Record,** V. 61, pp. 182 and 520.

[9] California **Senate Journal,** 44th sess., 1921, pp. 1255, 1345, 1899.

reached Congress at a time when the quota bill for that year was in Conference and had no appreciable effect upon it, but it marked the beginning of a movement which culminated in Japanese exclusion.[10]

The Exclusion League followed the California resolution with a brief prepared by V. S. McClatchy, editor of the *Sacramento Bee* and secretary of the League. It was a highly sensational document purporting to show the dangers from Japanese immigrants and pointing out why they should be excluded. It was presented to the Secretary of State with the endorsement of the entire California delegation in Congress.[11] On July 27, 1921, Senator Johnson of California introduced it into the records of the Senate with these words, "The brief is pertinent to a pending matter of very great consequence to the West and to the Nation too."[12]

During the summer and fall of 1921 the campaign against the Japanese continued to grow; and when Congress met, the question of immigration in general came up again, but this time a demand for Japanese exclusion also made its appearance in the Capitol. Definite action upon Japanese exclusion was postponed until after the passage and approval, on May 11, 1922, of the joint resolution extending the quota bill of 1921 to June 30, 1924.[13] On June 26, Mr. Johnson, chairman of the House Committee on Immigration, introduced H. R. 12169,[14] and on June 27 Mr. Raker introduced H. R. 12193.[15]

Relative to his bill Judge Raker said in a speech on June 29,

> One of the vital and important provisions of this bill (H. R. 12193) is that which relates to ineligible aliens, which reads as follows:
>
> > 'That no alien ineligible to citizenship under the laws of the United States shall be admitted to the United States.'
>
> The bill also provides for the elimination and abrogation of what is known as the "Gentlemen's Agreement."[16]
>
> This bill was the first ever introduced in Congress carrying the provision that 'no alien ineligible to citizenship should be admitted to the United States."[17]

Mr. Raker, not Mr. Johnson, was the author of the first bill to exclude "aliens ineligible to citizenship," and during these early stages he seems to have been the leader in the House for Japanese exclusion.

[10] **Congressional Record,** V. 61, May 7, 1921, p. 1145.
[11] **Senate Document,** No. 55, 67 Cong. 1st sess.
[12] **Congressional Record,** V. 61, July 27, 1921, p. 4332.
[13] **Ibid.,** V. 62, June 29, 1922, p. 9689.
[14] **Ibid.,** V. 62, June 26, 1922, p. 9489.
[15] **Ibid.,** V. 62, June 27, 1922, p. 9540.
[16] **Ibid.,** V. 62, June 29, 1922, p. 9689.
[17] **Ibid.,** V. 65, May 15, 1924, p. 8639.

These bills apparently were introduced not with the idea of passage during that session of Congress but rather to act as advance agents for bills to be introduced in 1923.[18] On June 30, 1922, Mr. Johnson introduced a new immigration bill, which apparently satisfied Mr. Raker, and which was to serve as the basis for the summer's investigation and the model for future thinking on immigration.[19]

The Congress which met in the fall of 1922 was slow to take up definite consideration of the immigration question. It would appear that both Houses were holding back, neither willing, until better informed, to take a definite step.[20] It was also evident that opinion in the House had swung far more toward exclusion than had opinion in the Senate.[21] On February 5, 1923, the Senate, showing its desire to avoid the issue, passed a bill to enable certain political refugees from the Near East to enter the United States.[22] The House was goaded into action by this move. Mr. Johnson, on February 9, introduced a bill to restrict immigration, and on February 10, Mr. Miller (of Washington) introduced a bill to exclude "aliens ineligible to citizenship."[23] These two bills the House Committee on Immigration and Naturalization combined into one which it submitted to the House on February 15, in the form of an amendment to the Senate bill.[24]

The immigration bill, found in *House Report* No. 1621 for 1922-23, was very comprehensive, and served as a model for those bills introduced into the first session of the 68th Congress in 1923-24.[25]

In section 3, the above mentioned measure defined *an immigrant* as any alien departing from a place outside of the United States destined for the United States, except: (1) government officials, their families and servants; (2) aliens visiting the United States temporarily as tourists or for business or pleasure; (3) aliens in continuous transit through the United States; (4) aliens lawfully admitted who in transit from one part of the United States to another go through

[18] **Ibid.**, V. 62, June 29, 1922, p. 9689.

[19] **Ibid.**, V. 62, June 30, 1922, p. 9879.

[20] According to the **Congressional Record**, V. 64, there were prior to Feb. 9, 1923, ten bills introduced into Congress relating to immigration, but only one of them was ever reported back by the committees. See pp. 24, 207, 502, 732, 843, 1212, 1273, 1447, 2043, and 2291.

[21] **Ibid.**, V. 64, March 3, 1923, pp. 5435-38.

[22] **Ibid.**, Feb. 5, 1923, pp. 3034-36.

[23] **Ibid.**, Feb. 9 and 10, 1923, pp. 3380 and 3444.

[24] **Ibid.**, Feb. 15, 1923, p. 3735. (See **House Report**, 1621.)

[25] **Ibid.**, March 2, 1923, pp. 5181-82—Johnson's report on the work of the Committee on Immigration and Naturalization.

foreign contiguous territory; (5) and bona fide seamen. It also, in section 4, defined *non quota immigrants* as (c) immigrants who have previously been lawfully admitted to the United States and who are returning from a temporary trip abroad; (e) ministers or professors; and (h) students over sixteen years of age.

It then proceeded to say

> An *immigrant not eligible to citizenship* shall not be admitted to the United States unless such immigrant is admissible as a non-quota immigrant under the provisions of subdivision (c) (e) or (h) of sec. 4, or (2) is the wife or unmarried minor child of an immigrant admissible under subdivision (e) and is accompanying or following to join him.[26]

In connection with this it must be explained that the United States nationalization laws denied citizenship to all persons except free whites and persons of African nativity or of African descent.[27] The provision thus worked effectively to exclude all Asiatics, Japanese included. It will be noted that no provision was made for guarding the treaty rights of Asiatic peoples.

This bill never came to a vote, although some interest in Asiatic exclusion was manifested by a memorial from the Oregon Legislature which arrived on February 19.[28] Mr. Johnson, however, in a speech supporting the bill, gave notice that during the next session a second measure embodying these principles would be introduced.[29]

During the recess between the last session of the 67th Congress and the first meeting of the 68th, which had been elected in the fall of 1922 partly, at least, upon the issue of immigration restriction or freedom, the propaganda to convince the country and the new Congress of the necessity of Japanese exclusion continued. The California Legislature early in May adopted two memorials to be sent to the Congress of the United States. One demanded the exclusion of aliens ineligible to citizenship, and the other asked that the Constitution of the United States be so amended as to make all persons born in the United States of parents ineligible to citizenship also ineligible to citizenship.[30]

---

26 House Report, No. 1621, 67 Cong., 4th sess., pp. 2 and 5.

27 Inui. op. cit., pp. 418-19; see also decision of the Supreme Court in the case of Takao Osawa vs. United States, 1922, in Buell, op. cit., pp. 345-46.

28 Oregon Senate and House Journal, 1923, pp. 60-61; Congressional Record, V. 64, Feb. 19, 1923, pp. 3931-32.

29 As explained by Mr. Johnson, fear that filibustering would prevent passage of the bill and so preclude the relief measures for the Near Eastern refugees kept it from coming to a vote. See Congressional Record, V. 64, March 2, 1923, pp. 5181-82.

30 California, Senate Journal, 45th sess., 1923, pp. 755-56, 1827, 2089.

When Congress opened in December, 1923, the matter of immigration was given immediate consideration. Several bills were introduced into the House to regulate immigration and out of these Mr. Johnson drafted H. R. 6540 which was introduced on February 1, 1924.[31] On February 9, 1924, the Committee on Immigration reported the bill back to the House (H. Report 176).[32] The majority report was favorable. Its main features corresponded exactly with the bill introduced during the previous session. Its only change in purport was to raise the age of students exempted from exclusion from sixteen to eighteen years, and to lower the age for the exemption of unmarried children of professors and preachers from twenty-one (minors) to eighteen.[33] It also failed to protect treaty rights.

On February 8, Secretary Hughes addressed a reply to Mr. Johnson's earlier letter of inquiry relative to bill 6540. He objected to the bill for two reasons: First, it violated existing treaties of commerce and navigation, especially that with Japan. To remedy this he suggested that an additional class of people be added to those defined as non-immigrants, to include "an alien entitled to enter the United States under the provision of a treaty." Second, he objected to the clause excluding aliens ineligible to citizenship, because of its unjust discrimination against the Japanese. The clause, he thought, was not only unnecessary, but would not accomplish its ostensible purpose as well as would further executive agreement with Japan. He asked that the clause be struck out, and the Japanese placed upon a quota basis.[34] This protest arrived too late to influence House Report 176.

As a result of the protest and certain technical considerations, Mr. Johnson, on March 17, introduced H. R. 7995 which was ultimately enacted into statute.[35] This bill was reported back from the Committee (H. R. 350) on March 24.[36] The Committee after due consideration had decided not to eliminate the exclusion clause. It had, however, added the following subdivision to section 3 defining non-immigrants, who would escape the exclusion proviso, as "aliens entitled to enter the United States solely to carry on trade under and in pursuance of

[31] **House Journal**, 68 Cong., 1st. sess., 1923-24, pp. 19, 21, 31, 74, 85, 94, 113, 114, 121, 132, 133, 159, 173, 194, and 218.

[32] **Ibid.**, p. 239.

[33] **House Report**, No. 176, 68 Cong., 1st sess., 1923-24.

[34] **International Conciliation**, No. 211, "Diplomatic Relations between the United States and Japan 1908-1924," pp. 176-81.

[35] **House Journal**, 68 Cong., 1st sess., 1923-1924, p. 343.

[36] **House Report**, No. 350, 68 Cong., 1st sess., p. 2, and **House Journal**, 68 Cong., 1st sess., p. 365.

the provisions of a present existing treaty of commerce and navigation."[37] This provision guarded the treaty rights of aliens, but carefully limited these rights to the strict letter of the Japanese treaty of 1911.[38] In this form the bill adhered to the letter of existing treaties, but without any respect for the sensibilities of the Japanese, baldly excluded them as a group.

In the meantime the Senate, with less zeal but with equal effectiveness, had taken up the problem of immigration. Several bills were introduced to limit it, and on February 20, 1924, Mr. Reed, of Pennsylvania, introduced Senate Bill 2576 which was to serve as the contribution of the upper house to the immigration legislation of the year.[39] This bill had the advantage of Secretary Hughes' suggestion that it should not contain an exclusion proviso. It also proposed to include in the non-immigrant classes, "an alien entitled to enter the United States under the provision of a treaty."[40] In this form the measure eliminated both points to which Mr. Hughes had objected in House Bill 6540.

The bill now went to the Committee on Immigration, of which Senator Colt, an opponent of exclusion, was chairman. On March 11, Secretary Hughes addressed a letter to the Senator reiterating his suggestions of February 8 to Mr. Johnson, and urging him to "avoid the affront of the enactment of any exclusion provision."[41] Upon the basis of this recommendation and other considerations of expediency, the Senate Committee, on March 27, reported the bill back with a further concession.[42] This was done despite special demands for exclusion which were introduced into the Senate on March 13 from ex-Senator Phelan, of California;[43] and on March 25 from the Japanese Exclusion League and its supporters, the American Federation of Labor, the American Legion, the National Grange; and from the Long Beach (California) Committee Regarding Japanese Immigration.[44]

The concession which the Committee proposed was an amendment to be added to the treaty exception provision, above mentioned, to make it read, "an alien entitled to enter the United States under the provision of a treaty, or *an agreement relating solely to immigration.*"[45]

[37] House Report, No. 350, 68 Cong., 1st sess., pp. 1-9.
[38] William M. Malloy, Treaties and Conventions of the U. S., V. 3, pp. 2712-13.
[39] Senate Journal, 68 Cong., 1st sess., pp. 6, 78, 71, 104, 136, and 161.
[40] Congressional Record, V. 65, April 2, pp. 5409-10 and 5415.
[41] Letter of Hughes to Senator Colt, March 11, 1924, in Buell, op. cit., p. 357.
[42] Congressional Record, V. 65, April 2, 1924, p. 5415, and March 27, 1924, pp. 5055-56.
[43] Ibid., March 13, 1924, p. 4073.
[44] Ibid., March 25, 1924, pp. 4923-25.
[45] Ibid., April 2, 1924, p. 5415.

This would have recognized the "Gentlemen's Agreement" and would have avoided all possible discrimination against the Japanese. On March 27, 1924, the two Houses, therefore, stood in direct opposition in regard to the Japanese exclusion question.

On April 7, Mr. Hughes addressed letters to Mr. Johnson and Mr. Frothingham, both of the House of Representatives, advising against the passage of the exclusion provision.[46] The next day Mr. Free, addressing the House, spoke of the menace of the "Yellow Peril," and bewailed the fact that the Japanese were acquiring control of all the land and industries in California and that their birth rate was dangerously high. He also charged the "Gentlemen's Agreement" with allowing thousands to come in, and demanded that it be abolished and the Japanese excluded.[47]

On April 12, the bill came up for a vote in the House, and the exclusion clauses as reported by the Committee were passed by an overwhelming majority.[48] Mr. Burton alone voiced a protest because he felt it unwise to offend a friendly nation in order to exclude the forty-six immigrants[49] which would enter under the quotas. He further believed that upon the basis of Japan's attitude the question might be successfully settled by diplomacy.

If the Senate Committee on Immigration was not disposed to exclude the Japanese, these sentiments were not shared by all the Senators. On April 2, when Senate Bill 2576 came up for first discussion[50] Senator Shortridge, of California, was ready with two amendments. One proposal was to add a new paragraph excluding aliens ineligible for citizenship with certain excéptions, while the second was to limit the treaty exemption clause by amending it to read, "an alien entitled to enter the United States solely to carry on trade under and in pursuance of the provisions of a present existing treaty of commerce and navigation."[51] These amendments would have brought the bill into almost exact conformity with that of the House.

By April 14 when the bill came up for consideration a great change in attitude had come over the Senate.[52] This was due to a sentence in Ambassador Hanihara's letter of April 10 to Secretary Hughes in

[46] Ibid., pp. 5840 and 5882.
[47] Ibid., April 8, 1924, pp. 5924-26.
[48] Ibid., April 12, 1924, p. 6258.
[49] Ibid., pp. 6249-51. The number 46 was given by Mr. Burton but seems to be inaccurate.
[50] Ibid., April 2, 1924, p. 5393.
[51] Ibid., pp. 5410-11.
[52] Ibid., April 14, 1924, p. 6302.

which he discussed the "Gentlemen's Agreement." In protesting against the exclusion clause found in the House bill, he referred to "the *grave consequences* which the enactment of the measure retaining that particular provision would inevitably bring upon the otherwise happy and mutually advantageous relations between our two countries."[53] This letter was introduced into the Senate on April 11.[54] This phrase, which taken in its true setting was perfectly harmless, was viewed as a "veiled threat" by certain members of the Senate. It, together with an earlier appeal to the American people against discriminatory legislation, issued by Japan's Foreign Minister through the Associated Press on February 7,[55] was considered an impertinent attempt on the part of Japan to influence domestic legislation, and caused many Senators to vote for exclusion as a protest against such interference.[56]

Senator Reed who had formerly been opposed to Japanese exclusion by statute now declared himself forced "on account of that veiled threat, to vote in favor of the exclusion, and against the committee amendment."[57] Senator King suggested the possibility of executive abrogation of the agreement as a means to avoid "brutal and rude" action.[58] Senator Sterling alone pleaded against such narrow-minded legislation and asked that, "If we are going to exclude Japanese immigrants, let us exclude them because it is . . . . wholesome."[95]

The opinion of the Senate had, however, turned against Japan, and the Committee amendment to the treaty-exemption clause, "or an agreement relating solely to immigration," was defeated by a large majority.[60] Senator Reed immediately proposed to make the clause read, "an alien entitled to enter the United States solely to carry on trade under and in pursuance of the provisions of a present existing treaty of commerce and navigation." The amendment was passed.[61] Two days later the Senate in Committee of the Whole, passed an exclusion provision similar to that of the House. On April 18 the Senate further amended the bill so that it would take effect at once,[62]

[53] Hanihara to Hughes, April 10, 1924, in Buell, op. cit., pp. 358-62. Italic is the writer's insertion.
[54] Congressional Record, V. 65, April 11, 1924, pp. 6073-74.
[55] Ibid., Feb. 25, 1924, p. 3034.
[56] Ibid., April 14, 1924, p. 6305 for statement of Senator Lodge.
[57] Ibid., p. 6305 .
[58] Ibid., p. 6306.
[59] Ibid., p. 6308.
[60] Ibid., pp. 6314-15.
[61] Ibid., pp. 6315-16.
[62] Ibid., April 16 and 18, 1924, pp. 6460 and 6644.

and changed the age at which students would be admitted from eighteen to fifteen.[63] The bill as amended was agreed upon and sent to the House with a request for a Conference.[64]

The House and Senate bills which were now to be united in the Conference were practically identical in so far as the exclusion clauses were concerned. During the Conference, and prior to May 1, the President attempted to secure a modification of the bill. He suggested that the exclusion clause should not take effect until March 1, 1926, with the proviso,

> That the provisions of this paragraph shall not apply to the nationals of those countries with which the United States, after the enactment of this act, shall have entered into treaties by and with the advice and consent of the Senate for the restriction of immigration.[65]

The Conference refused to do this, and proceeded, on May 6, to hold its final meeting, in which the only recorded change was the adoption of the age of fifteen as the lower limit for admittance of students.[66] So nearly complete was the work of the Conference that it issued a statement to the press and determined to meet the 7th to consummate the agreement. The next morning President Coolidge, upon the request of Mr. Johnson, invited the Republican members to the White House and suggested that the following be added to the exclusion clause:

> That this subdivision shall not take effect as to exclusion until March 1, 1925, before which time the President is requested to negotiate with the Japanese Government in relation to the abrogation of the present arrangement on this subject.

The Republican majority of the Conference accepted this suggestion, and it was added to the Conference Report.[67]

This report was submitted to the House on May 9. Furious debate arose, and telegrams poured in from Washington and California demanding that the amendment be rejected.[68] The House and Senate were afraid that the amendment would in some way leave room for a treaty regulating immigration, or lead to other complications by setting a precedent, so the bill was recommitted to the Conference with instructions that the amendment be struck out.[69] On May 15 the Con-

[63] Senate Journal, 68 Cong., 1st sess., 1923-24, p. 281.
[64] Ibid., pp. 270 and 281.
[65] Congressional Record, V. 65, May 9, 1924, p. 8235.
[66] Ibid., pp. 8231-35; House Journal, 68 Cong., 1st sess., p. 505.
[67] Congressional Record, V. 65, May 9, 1924, pp. 8231-2, 8235-36.
[68] Ibid., pp. 8233-34 and 8237-38.
[69] Ibid., p. 8249. For details of debates in House see pp. 8218-49. Discussion in Senate see May 8, 1924, pp. 8085-87.

ference Report was returned with the objectionable feature removed, and it passed the House by a vote of 308 for, 62 against, and 63 not voting.[70]

As has been indicated the immigration bill of 1924 was the result of a union of anti-Japanese and anti-immigration ideas, the latter being of interest to a far larger group of people than the former. An analysis of the petitions and memorials presented to Congress shows that the East was interested primarily in limiting European immigration.[71] The West was willing to cooperate with the East, but its main interest was in the exclusion of the Japanese.[72] The Pacific Coast thus took advantage of the interest of the East in general immigration restriction to secure, during the excitement, a bill excluding Asiatics. Had the question of exclusion been determined entirely upon its own merits, it seems unlikely that the anti-Japanese party could have mustered so much support.

The most noticeable thing about the entire course of the argument upon the exclusion bill was that it constantly avoided the real issue. Most people were willing to concede that the exclusion of Japanese immigration, or at least a very severe restriction of it, was necessary and desirable. The real question at issue, then, was *how* it should be done. The leaders of the anti-Japanese group, however, almost completely ignored this fact, and centered their energy upon pointing out the economic, social, political, and cultural dangers resulting from immigration. People became so aroused over these arguments that they could not see that friendly cooperation with Japan in restriction, plus the quotas, which put a maximum of 146,[73] would be a far more effective limitation than the exclusion bill which aroused dislike in Japan and terminated Japanese cooperation.

The State Department and the President alone remained calm and looked at the problem in its true light. They, however, accomplished nothing for their trouble, while the diplomatic protests of Japan served

[70] Ibid., May 15, 1924, p. 8652.

[71] Based upon a study of the petitions delivered to the Senate in 1923-24, found in Senate Journal, 68 Cong., 1st sess.

[72] There is in the Senate Journal for the 68 Cong., 1st sess. but one petition from an exclusively Eastern organization demanding exclusion. This was from the United American Mechanics, of Newton, N. H., and was introduced on April 24 (See p. 297). On the other hand, there are four petitions representing Eastern churches; the Association to Abolish War, of Boston; and the Women's Christian Temperance Union, of Lisbon, Ohio, protesting against exclusion (pp. 313 and 368). The greater part of the active support outside of Congress to Japanese exclusion apparently came from the West.

[73] See Buell, op. cit., p. 361.

as a goad to the resolute Senate. The main objections to Japanese immigration which were advanced, such as non-assimilation, economic competition, vice, high birth rate, and the like, although good arguments if the country had been threatened with a deluge of Orientals, really missed the point at issue. The best argument which the friends of exclusion had was that the Japanese could not become citizens and, therefore, little good would come through increasing the number in the United States. The contention that the matter must be settled now, for all time, also had some foundation. On the other side the argument was simply that it was bad diplomacy to exclude by statute, and so discriminate against the nationals of a friendly power, when the same end might be better accomplished by friendly agreement.

On May 15, 1924, the final Conference Report was passed upon in the House and was sent to the Senate.[74] The following day the Senate agreed to the report,[75] and on May 19 it was sent to the President.[76] On the 26th President Coolidge signed the document and it became the law of the land.[77] The President gave his consent to the exclusion features with regret, as was shown by his statement upon signing the bill.[78]

As finally passed and approved, the measure excluded from the United States all persons ineligible to citizenship except:

> (1) a government official, his family, attendants, servants, and employees, (2) an alien visiting the United States temporarily as a tourist or temporarily for business or pleasure, (3) an alien in continuous transit through the United States, (4) an alien lawfully admitted to the United States who later goes in transit from one part of the United States to another through foreign contiguous territory, (5) a bona fide seaman serving as such on a vessel arriving at a port of the United States and seeking to enter temporarily the United States solely in the pursuit of his calling as a seamen, (6) an alien entitled to enter the United States solely to carry on trade under and in pursuance of the provisions of a present existing treaty of commerce and navigation, (7) an immigrant previously lawfully admitted to the United States, who is returning from a temporary visit abroad, (8) professors and preachers, (9) the wives or unmarried children under eighteen years of age of the above professors and preachers, and (10) bona fide students at least fifteen years old.[79]

[74] **House Journal,** 68 Cong., 1st sess., p. 534.
[75] **Ibid.,** p. 540.
[76] **Ibid.,** p. 558.
[77] **Ibid.,** p. 616.
[78] See Buell, **op. cit.,** p. 371.
[79] **U. S. Statutes at Large** (1923-25), V. 43, Part I, Chap. 190, pp. 154-162.

Into the Japanese protest and the exchange of diplomatic notes which followed the passage of this bill we need not go. Suffice it to say that clear-headed thinking on the part of the diplomats of both countries helped to smooth over difficulties which might easily have led to severe complications. As time has passed, agitation has died down and friendly relations have been established between the two great peoples, but the Japanese are still waiting for the time when America will do an about-face and right what they consider an unjustifiable wrong.

California, Japan, and the Alien Land Legislation of 1913

Thomas A. Bailey

The division of powers between the federal and state authority in the United States, although for the most part satisfactory, has now and then resulted in a situation highly embarrassing to the national government and altogether incomprehensible to foreign nations.[1] Twice within a period of seven years, in 1906 and again in 1913, California took advantage of the absence of federal jurisdiction over aliens within her borders and involved the government at Washington in international complications of a most serious nature. For at least half a century prior to this time the people of the state had shown themselves to be more than ordinarily sensitive when the question of color was involved, and in the two incidents just mentioned the problem was basically one of prejudice against the Japanese as a race. In the San Francisco school imbroglio of 1906, when this feeling for the first time came to a head, Roosevelt bludgeoned the state into submission and promised relief through the Gentlemen's Agreement. Dissatisfied with Roosevelt's high-handed methods and the solution proposed, successive legislatures considered bills designed to annoy and restrict orientals. Every session during the six years prior to 1913 witnessed the introduction of anti-alien land bills and other intentionally discriminatory measures.[2] In fact, the situation became so delicate that Roosevelt and Taft had to intervene to force a Republican majority to withhold action.[3]

[1] Presidents Tyler, Harrison, McKinley, Roosevelt, Taft, and Harding recommended, without result, that Congress give the federal government jurisdiction over aliens in such cases. See *Congressional Record,* 67 cong., 2 sess., 11590.

[2] See Chester Rowell, "The Japanese in California" in *World's Work,* June, 1913, 200.

[3] Franklin Hichborn, *Story of the Session of the California Legislature of 1909* (San

In the state campaign of 1912 the Democrats, alone of the three major parties, included an anti-alien land plank in their platform. Despite this declaration, a strong Progressive Republican majority was returned, many of the members of which were privately understood to favor drastic action against the Japanese.[4] During the early days of the 1913 session the usual batch of anti-Japanese measures, this time more than thirty in number, was introduced, and caused the usual stir both in Washington and in Japan.[5] Interest, however, was centered on the proposed anti-alien land legislation.

The initial demand for a land law appears to have come from labor organizations and to a certain extent from those agricultural areas in which the Japanese were most heavily concentrated.[6] On the other hand, the anti-union elements, a number of large land owners, and certain business and commercial interests were anxious to defeat anti-alien legislation. Although the Japanese government had already agreed to be generously represented at the San Francisco exposition in 1915, rumors of the pending discrimination led to the demand in certain quarters in Japan that the exhibit be cancelled.[7] Believing that Japanese cooperation was essential for the success of their enterprise, the exposition officials brought pressure to bear on the legislature of 1911 to block the passage of anti-Japanese measures, and in 1913, even before the opening of the session, they used their influence to prevent the introduction of objectionable bills.[8] When the legislature convened and

Francisco, 1909), 205-214; Franklin Hichborn, *Story of the Session of the California Legislature of 1911* (San Francisco, 1911), 343-344; R. L. Buell, "The Development of Anti-Japanese Agitation in the United States" in *Political Science Quarterly,* XXXVIII, 58-60.

[4] Franklin Hichborn, *Story of the Session of the California Legislature of 1913* (San Francisco, 1913), 214. Hereafter cited as Hichborn, *Legislature of 1913.*

[5] See Chester Rowell, "Alien Land Laws and the Japanese Situation" in *California Outlook,* April 26, 1913, 5; Edwin Maxey, "Japanese-American Relations" in *Forum,* July, 1913, 70-71.

[6] Hichborn, *Legislature of 1913,* 225; New York *Times,* April 6, 22, 1913; *Literary Digest,* April 19, 1913, 878.

[7] Sacramento *Union,* April 2, 1913; New York *Times,* April 9, 1913; *Literary Digest,* May 3, 1913, 1002.

[8] Sacramento *Union,* April 3, 4, 1913; Hichborn, *Legislature of 1913,* 216-219.

committee hearings were begun, the arguments of the farmers, who believed that the sacrificing of the exposition was preferable to permitting Japanese penetration to continue unchecked, proved more effective than those of the exposition attorneys.[9] Furthermore, it was obvious that Japan would not hasten to deprive herself of the commercial advantages of the exposition, even though offended by California.

The alleged Japanese menace in California requires a brief explanation. In 1913, out of a total population approaching 2,500,000, the Japanese, by a liberal estimate, numbered about 50,000.[10] Of approximately 27,000,000 acres of improved or unimproved land in the state, the Japanese owned 12,726 acres in 1912, much of which they had reclaimed themselves.[11] These few figures are eloquent, and they explain why Easterners were unable to understand the necessity for immediate and drastic action. Some of the more intelligent and disinterested Californians admitted that no menace existed, but, with the example of Hawaii before them, they argued that legislation was necessary to avert an unendurable future condition.[12]

The first alien land bill to receive serious consideration by the assembly in 1913 placed severe restrictions on the ownership of land by all aliens. The only discriminatory feature of this measure was directed at corporations controlled by aliens who were ineligible to become citizens of the United States. On April 15, 1913, the bill passed the assembly, 60-15.[13]

In the meanwhile, the senate had begun consideration of a drastic measure which avoided the discriminatory features of that of the assembly by applying to all aliens alike.[14] Imme-

[9] In deadly earnest, the farmers spoke of the inevitability of armed outbreaks. *Ibid.*, 225.

[10] Estimates based on the census returns of 1910 and 1920.

[11] *Fifteenth Biennial Report of the Bureau of Labor Statistics of the State of California*, 1911-1912, 634.

[12] Chester Rowell, "Alien Land Laws and the Japanese Situation" in *California Outlook*, April 26, 1913, 5.

[13] *Journal of the Assembly during the Fortieth Session of the Legislature of the State of California*, 1574. Hereafter cited as *Assembly Journal*. See also Hichborn, *Legislature of 1913*, 236-241.

[14] *Journal of the Senate during the Fortieth Session of the Legislature of the State of*

diately the senate was flooded with protests from the representatives of foreign investors, and the Washington legations of several of the nations concerned showed uneasiness.[15] After it had been made evident that California would suffer commercially as a result of pursuing the course proposed, a poll of the senate was taken on April 18, 1913, and it was demonstrated that a bill including all aliens could not pass. The Californians had no desire to cripple themselves in their efforts to get at the Japanese; consequently, there would have to be a discriminatory anti-Japanese measure or none at all.[16]

The Wilson administration was watching the situation in California with considerable apprehension. The Democratic party, the historic defender of state rights, had included in its platform of 1912 an unusually strong plank denouncing the usurpations of the federal government under the Republican regime.[17] The direct methods of Roosevelt and Taft were consequently out of the question if charges of inconsistency were to be avoided. Furthermore, both of these Presidents had dealt with Republican legislatures; and the patronage club had helped to hold them in line.[18] The new legislature, predominately Progressive Republican, was not only out of sympathy with the Democrats in Washington, but it had political advantages to gain and no patronage to lose by embarrassing the Wilson administration. The stage was obviously set for trouble.

As early as March, 1913, when the bills were before the committees, Wilson began to study the situation carefully. From time to time he let it be known that the federal government could not and would not interfere, and that the regularly constituted agencies, including the courts, were competent to smooth out any subsequent difficulties.[19] Nevertheless, no effort

California, 1309-1312. Hereafter cited as *Senate Journal*. See also Hichborn, *Legislature of 1913*, 242-247.

[15] Sacramento *Union*, April 10, 17, 1913; New York *Times*, April 19, 1913.

[16] *Ibid.*, April 22, 1913; Sacramento *Union*, April 19, 1913.

[17] Kirk H. Porter, *National Party Platforms* (New York, 1924), 322-323.

[18] See Buell, *loc. cit.*, 60.

[19] D. F. Houston, *Eight Years with Wilson's Cabinet* (Garden City, 1926), I, 51; New York *Times*, April 6, 10, 12, 13, 17, 1913; Sacramento *Union*, April 8, 10, 12, 1913.

was made at Washington to conceal the fact that the administration, through pressure on prominent Californians, was privately attempting to get the bill into as unobjectionable form as possible.[20]

It seems likely that Wilson would have continued indefinitely his policy of non-intervention had not the press of the United States, on the morning of April 18, 1913, carried reports of an enormous mass meeting of protest in the city of Tokyo. These accounts, doubtless exaggerated but nevertheless disquieting, stated that on this occasion speakers denounced the submissive attitude of the government and that twenty thousand people hysterically cheered the demand for war.[21] Although the responsible newspapers of Tokyo deplored the meeting as the work of demagogues and declared that there was no foundation to the war talk, circumstantial evidence and contemporary opinion indicate that this outburst so disturbed Wilson as to persuade him to authorize the first federal intervention in California.[22] On April 18, 1913, the day after the reported Tokyo meeting, Secretary of State Bryan telegraphed to Governor Johnson of California and, while recognizing the right of the state to legislate on the subject, courteously asked that the legislature consider the international character of the problem.[23]

Despite this request from the national administration, the senate amended the pending bill, on April 21, 1913, to meet the demands of European investors by permitting their corporations to own land while denying that privilege to orientals. The senate bill, as well as that of the assembly, was now discriminatory.[24] On the next day, Wilson, not his secretary of state, sent a telegram to Johnson and to the legislature earnestly and respectfully urging that the latter refrain from discrimination.[25]

20 *Ibid.*, April 16, 17, 1913; New York *Times*, April 15, 17, 19, 1913.

21 *Ibid.*, April 18, 1913.

22 Sacramento *Union*, April 19, 1913; London *Times*, April 21, 1913; New York *Times*, April 22, 1913.

23 *Senate Journal*, 1582.

24 See *ibid.*, 1666-1670.

25 *Ibid.*, 1717.

On the same day the governor telegraphed a somewhat evasive reply.[26]

Apparently dissatisfied with the results of his overtures, Wilson sent three telegrams to California on the next day, April 23, 1913. One was addressed to the governor, another to the president of the senate, and another to the speaker of the assembly. The President expressed his inability to understand adequately the situation at that distance, and ventured to inquire whether it would be agreeable to have Bryan come to Sacramento to aid the legislature in framing a satisfactory law.[27]

On April 23, 1913, the day of Wilson's inquiry, Johnson wired his willingness to consult with Bryan, and both houses of the legislature resolved that "while this Senate [Assembly] respectfully maintains the right of the Legislature . . . to legislate on the subject of land ownership . . . it will be entirely agreeable to this Senate [Assembly] to have the Secretary of State . . . visit Sacramento for the purpose indicated in the President's telegram. . ."[28]

A stormy debate developed over the state rights clause in this resolution. One Democratic leader denounced the Progressives for playing politics at a critical time and another accused them of directly insulting the President. Statements such as these from the Democrats, who for the past six years had been insisting that the state had full power to enact any kind of land law that it desired, indicate that consistency was being sacrificed in an attempt to make Wilson's position less difficult. The Progressives, on the other hand, pointed to the President's assurance of their right to act and denied political motives.[29] The attempt of the Democrats in the senate to secure a satisfactory amending of the resolution was defeated, 28-7, and it was then approved 35-3, eight Democrats voting affirmatively.[30] In the assembly, the proposal to strike out the state rights clause was rejected without roll call, and the resolu-

[26] Sacramento *Union*, April 23, 1913; New York *Times*, April 23, 1913.

[27] *Senate Journal*, 1785-1786.

[28] *Ibid.*, 1786.

[29] Sacramento *Union*, April 24, 1913; New York *Times*, April 24, 1913.

[30] *Senate Journal*, 1786-1787.

tion was adopted 59-11.[31] The legislature, therefore, without actually extending an invitation to Bryan, expressed acquiescence in the plan for his coming to Sacramento.

This unprecedented situation requires a further word of comment. Anomalously enough, a state rights President was asking for an invitation to send a state rights secretary of state across the continent to plead with California. More than one observer noted that Roosevelt had not degraded the federal executive by deferring to a state as to an equal, but in 1906 had summoned the San Francisco officials to come to him. But more surprising is the fact that there was no real protest voiced by the legislature against Wilson's proposal. One would have expected the Progressive majority to administer a stinging rebuke to a Democratic President by flatly refusing his request; but perhaps the unpopularity of the state at that time in the East made for moderation. In any event, the rebuff was eventually administered in a more exasperating manner.

Bryan was in an unenviable position. When Wilson proposed the California trip to him, Bryan said that he was far from eager to go but that he would do what the President thought best.[32] After the reply of the legislature had been received, on April 23, 1913, it was announced that the secretary of state would leave for California for the purpose of persuading the legislature to avoid giving offense to Japan.[33] As a matter of fact, this objective was a hopeless one. Up to the very eve of Bryan's arrival, there was every indication of a determination on the part of the legislature to pass some kind of anti-Japanese measure.[34] The gleeful demonstration in the senate when Wilson's first telegram was read, would indicate that federal intervention, to some extent at least, strengthened that determination.[35] To expect Bryan, a Democrat of the Democrats, to make

31 *Assembly Journal,* 1988.

32 Houston, *op. cit.,* I, 60; see *Senate Journal,* 2900.

33 New York *Times,* April 24, 1913.

34 See A. W. Lane and L. H. Wall (eds.), *The Letters of Franklin K. Lane* (Boston, 1922), 136; Hichborn, *Legislature of 1913,* 254; New York *Times,* April 6, 24, 25, 26, 28, 1913; Sacramento *Union,* April 6, 28, 29, 1913.

35 *Ibid.,* April 23, 1913.

satisfactory headway with a Progressive legislature already prepared to act was to expect what was well-nigh impossible.

Bryan arrived in Sacramento on April 28, 1913, and that same day he attended two joint conferences of both houses of the legislature. He specifically stated at these meetings that he was merely the spokesman of the President, and that he would keep in constant telegraphic communication with Washington. On behalf of Wilson, Bryan suggested two general courses: first, delay, in order that a new treaty might be drawn up; and second, legislation that would apply equally to all aliens.[36]

A dramatic touch was given to the proceedings of the second conference. Johnson had been watching the situation warily, and he was apparently displeased by developments, particularly by evidence that Bryan was winning some of the Progressive leaders over to a policy of delay. He therefore arose, and in a statement of considerable warmth asserted that California had a right to pass a law similar to that which eight other states had already enacted without protest, and he served notice that the Progressive majority would push through an alien land bill. This vigorous intervention by the governor, who appears to have had the Progressives well under his control, helped to counteract any headway that Bryan may have been making.[37]

In the meantime considerable progress had been made in the framing of a bill that was within the letter, if not the spirit, of the treaty of 1911 with Japan. That agreement had provided that Japanese should be permitted to own property in the United States for residential and commercial purposes, but they were not guaranteed the privilege of owning agricultural land.[38] The Webb bill, which in modified form eventually became law, provided that aliens eligible to citizenship could own property without limitation, but that all others could own land only as specified in existing treaties. Such a law would

[36] *Ibid.*, April 29, 1913; New York *Times*, April 29, 1913.

[37] Sacramento *Union*, April 29, 1913; New York *Times*, April 29, 1913; San Francisco *Chronicle*, April 29, 1913; Hichborn, *Legislature of 1913*, 257.

[38] For treaty see *Papers Relating to the Foreign Relations of the United States*, 1911, 315-319. Hereafter cited as *Foreign Relations*.

therefore bar Japanese from owning agricultural land in California as a result of a distinction made by the federal government, and it would put the Wilson administration in the embarrassing position of asking a state to grant a privilege which the national government had been unwilling to accord to the Japanese. Because the statement has been made that Bryan's influence secured this deference to treaty obligations, it would be well to point out that the Webb bill had been drawn up in rough form and distributed several days before the secretary of state reached Sacramento.[39]

On the day after Bryan's arrival, the senate voted, with almost indecent haste, to bring the Webb bill up for consideration.[40] It is difficult to determine whether this action was designed as a rebuke to Bryan, or whether it was an effort to compensate for the brief delay occasioned by his trip. The efforts of the Democrats to secure postponement were defeated, and on May 1, 1913, Wilson telegraphed to Johnson warning him of the possibility of long and delicate litigation as a result of the proposed law. The governor wired a noncommittal reply on the same day.[41]

As originally introduced, the Webb bill prohibited aliens from either owning or leasing agricultural land. The owners of large tracts in California who were interested in leasing their property to Japanese immediately voiced their protest.[42] After their views had been presented and after it had become evident that a non-leasing bill probably could not pass the assembly, the senate voted, on May 2, 1913, to insert a clause giving the orientals leasing privileges for a period of three years.[43] Those who had been insisting on drastic legislation at once condemned the bill for not weakening the Japanese hold on California, while at the same time affronting a powerful nation.[44] The Progressives argued, however, that the amend-

---

39 Hichborn, *Legislature of 1913*, 261.

40 See Sacramento *Union*, April 30, 1913.

41 New York *Times*, May 2, 1913.

42 See Sacramento *Union*, May 2, 3, 1913.

43 *Senate Journal*, 2311. The vote was 25-13.

44 See Sacramento *Union*, May 5, 1913; San Francisco *Argonaut*, April 12, 1913, 227.

ment was a step forward, and that in a few years it would be a simple matter to strike out the leasing provision. In the meantime, it would be possible for both the whites and the Japanese in California to make adjustments with a minimum loss to both.[45]

Bryan was still in Sacramento when this amendment was added, and he was not unnaturally given credit in the East for the change.[46] The evidence is strong, however, that he had nothing whatever to do with the leasing clause. Both Johnson and the senate leaders were emphatic in declaring that the subject of leases was never mentioned by Wilson and Bryan.[47] This statement is further supported by the fact that the Wilson administration was striving desperately to prevent the passage of any discriminatory alien land law, with or without a leasing clause. Furthermore, as Johnson pointed out, every other alien land bill previously introduced had contained a leasing provision, and the amendment was merely a correction necessary before the measure could be passed.[48]

In the end, the obstructionist tactics of the Democrats proved unavailing, and on May 2, 1913, the senate passed the Webb bill, 35-2, one of the two dissentients being a Democrat.[49] On the following day, May 3, 1913, the assembly passed the measure, 72-3, two Republicans and one Democrat voting negatively.[50] It will be observed, therefore, that during the six days between the arrival and the departure of Bryan the bill was introduced and passed. Even a cursory glance at the legislative records indicates that it was pushed through with unusual haste.

Several significant observations may be made on the voting. Although there were thirty-five Democrats in the legislature, only two respected the wishes of Wilson and voted against the bill. The explanation appears to be that while the Democrats

[45] New York *Times*, May 5, 1913; Sacramento *Union*, May 4, 5, 1913.

[46] See New York *Times*, May 3, 1913; Sacramento *Union*, May 4, 1913.

[47] New York *Times*, May 5, 1913; Sacramento *Union*, May 4, 5, 1913.

[48] New York *Times*, May 5, 1913; Hichborn, *Legislature of 1913*, 267.

[49] *Senate Journal*, 2324.

[50] *Assembly Journal*, 2495. For Webb law see *The Statutes of California*, 1913, 206-208.

sought to amend or to postpone the measure, they did not dare to violate their platform promises and vote against it. They apparently preferred to redeem their pledges to their constituents rather than offend them and please the national administration. It should also be noted that the five dissentients represented large agricultural counties in the southern part of the state where a number of land owners were eager to sell to the Japanese.[51]

During the six days of his stay, Bryan maintained his headquarters across from the senate chamber, in effect a transplanted portion of the federal government, while the senate, representing the state, speedily went its way. The secretary of state kept the wires to Washington busy, consulted with various leaders, and visited Florin, where the social and economic effects of Japanese occupation could be seen in their most acute form.[52] In various conferences Bryan continued to present Wilson's instructions, the most significant of which was a definite promise to remove California's grievances by diplomatic means if delay could be secured.[53] After the Webb act had passed both houses, Bryan delivered a farewell address to a conference of the legislature, on May 3, 1913, in which he stated unchanged his previous views, criticized the discriminatory features of the bill, and hinted that the people might resort to the referendum.[54] He then took his leave.

A number of prominent California Democrats favored a referendum on the ground that the Webb act was too weak to be effective and that it embarrassed the administration at Washington.[55] Johnson, however, advised the use of the initiative if the voters wanted direct action, for a referendum would deprive the state of a land law until the general election some nineteen months later.[56] Although it was reasonable to suppose

[51] Fresno, San Diego, Los Angeles, and Kings county were represented by the five.

[52] Bryan was shown a school in which there were 20 white children and 22 Japanese. He was noncommittal. Sacramento *Union,* May 2, 1913.

[53] *Ibid.,* April 30, May 3, 1913.

[54] *Senate Journal,* 2900-2902.

[55] See Sacramento *Union,* May 20, 1913.

[56] *Ibid.,* May 21, 1913.

that a delay of almost two years would facilitate a diplomatic adjustment, a bitter anti-Japanese campaign would have stirred up extreme feeling in the state. Besides, there was little evidence that such a referendum would be supported by the voters.[57] The Wilson administration therefore discouraged the proposal, and nothing came of it.[58]

Johnson was pleased with the passage of the bill, but he promised to wait "a reasonable time" before affixing his signature. This delay would permit Bryan to reach Washington, confer with the President, and lodge any protest that the administration cared to make.[59] On May 11, 1912, Johnson received a telegram from Bryan suggesting a veto and promising, in such an event, to secure a remedy for the existing problems.[60] Johnson's lengthy reply, which he telegraphed on May 14, 1913, was an able presentation of California's case and a further expression of the governor's determination to sign. The fact was stressed that the federal government had already established the precedent for discrimination against orientals and that other states had similar laws; consequently, if there was any discrimination it was against California.[61]

In the meantime, the center of interest had shifted to Washington. As early as April 5, 1913, the press reported that Ambassador Chinda of Japan had lodged an informal protest against the proposed action of California.[62] During the ensuing weeks he conferred frequently with Wilson and the Department of State, making known the wishes of his government, and on May 9, 1913, after the Webb act had passed both houses but before it was signed, he filed a formal protest which declared that the bill was unfair, inequitable, discriminatory, prejudicial to the rights of Japanese in California, inconsistent with the

[57] Chester Rowell predicted that the vote would have been as overwhelming as that of the legislature. *California Outlook,* May 24, 1913, 3.

[58] See Houston, *op. cit.,* I, 62.

[59] Sacramento *Union,* May 4, 5, 1913.

[60] New York *Times,* May 12, 1913.

[61] *Ibid.,* May 15, 1913. According to Johnson, eight other states and the District of Columbia had similar laws. See Sacramento *Union,* April 22, 1913.

[62] *Ibid.,* April 5, 1913; New York *Times,* April 5, 1913.

treaty of 1911, and opposed to the spirit of amity existing between the two nations.[63] After Bryan's return, this note was discussed in cabinet meeting, where Houston reported that "the offensive character of the protest was something of a shock, especially in view of what the government has done and was doing and of Japan's own laws against aliens." On this occasion some of the members expressed the fear that Japan was eager to start trouble before the opening of the Panama Canal; others thought that the protest was purely for home consumption. In view of the fact that the Webb act specifically safeguarded treaty rights, Wilson was of the opinion that the protest was unfair. It was agreed, however, that the note should not be published, lest an outburst of public opinion should result, and Bryan was authorized to tell Chinda informally that his language in certain places was objectionable. Wilson further requested the secretary of state to determine from the tone of the conversations if the Japanese were as greatly disturbed as the protest would indicate, and he added that if the note were to be taken at its face value "it is impossible to exaggerate the seriousness of the situation."[64]

On May 13, 1913, the revised Japanese protest was considered by the cabinet. The portions offensive to California had been omitted, as well as the demand that the federal government declare the law invalid. Wilson, however, still thought that Japan had a weak case.[65] On May 19, 1913, immediately after Johnson's signing of the Webb act, Bryan presented the reply of the United States to the protest of May 9, 1913. This note squarely denied an attitude of unfriendliness on the part of the United States, referred to the efforts of the federal government to secure less drastic legislation, pointed to the specific treaty guarantees in the Webb law, asserted that the difficulty was rooted in economic conditions in California, and suggested that Japan resort to the courts if still dissatisfied.[66]

---

[63] *Foreign Relations,* 1913, 629-631.

[64] Houston, *op. cit.,* I, 61-62; see also New York *Times,* June 26, 1914.

[65] Houston, *op. cit.,* I, 65.

[66] *Foreign Relations,* 1913, 631-632.

On June 4, 1913, more than two weeks after Bryan's reply, Chinda presented another protest, accompanied by an *aide-mémoire* and a telegram from the Japanese minister of foreign affairs. The ambassador maintained his previous objections, denied that the legislation was based solely on economic grounds, and asserted that diplomacy, rather than court action, would provide the most acceptable means for a solution.[67] This statement did not excite undue apprehension, and Bryan waited almost a month and a half before replying to it.[68] On July 16, 1913, he submitted to Chinda a note accompanied by an *aide-mémoire,* and the burden of his argument was that the situation in California was primarily an economic one, although the racial problem was to some extent incidental. He added, however, that the United States was ready to compensate California Japanese for losses incurred as a result of the Webb law.[69]

Not content to let the matter drop, the Japanese government instructed Chinda to lodge a third protest, which was presented to the Department of State on August 26, 1913. The arguments of treaty infraction and racial discrimination were repeated, and it was further stated that California's action was mortifying to Japan and disregardful of the susceptibilities of her people.[70] Apparently realizing that he had nothing new to say and that no good would come of further correspondence, Bryan contented himself with conversations rather than a formal reply.[71]

After this diplomatic interchange, the two governments entertained proposals to adjust their difficulties by a special convention. On June 10, 1913, shortly after a change in the Japanese ministry, Chinda delivered instructions in which the minister of foreign affairs stated that a convention would be more likely to create new difficulties than to compose past misunderstandings. He therefore declined to proceed further with the negotiations, requested a continuance of correspondence looking

[67] *Ibid.,* 632-641.

[68] See Houston, *op. cit.,* I, 72.

[69] *Foreign Relations,* 1913, 641-650.

[70] *Ibid.,* 651-653.

[71] See New York *Times,* January 22, 1914.

toward a diplomatic settlement, and, in the hope of facilitating such a solution, suggested making public the notes that had been exchanged on the subject.[72] By mutual consent, the correspondence was published on June 25, 1914, more than a year after the first interchange. At the same time it was announced that Bryan had replied, on June 23, 1914, to the last Japanese protest.[73] When this answer was finally published it further revealed Bryan's unwillingness to admit that racial, not economic, factors were the basis of the difficulty.[74] A final note from Chinda, dated November 25, 1914, reviewed the situation and stated that compensation for damages to individual Japanese would not be an adequate substitute for diplomatic action.[75]

Various proposals for the solution of the difficulty were subsequently discussed, such as the issuance of a federal injunction suspending the operation of the law until adjudicated by the courts, arbitration by the Hague tribunal, and court action at the instance of the federal government or of the Japanese government. The latter, however, did not care to appear as a suppliant in the courts of the United States, and the former foresaw difficulties in presenting what was considered a domestic problem to an international tribunal. It was widely believed that Japan would seek the right of naturalization for her subjects, thus invalidating the law, but apparently the time was not deemed propitious for such a move. In the end, it was left for individual Japanese to bring suit in the federal courts. It was not, however, until 1923 that the Supreme Court of the United States passed upon the Webb law, then made more drastic by amendment, and the decision was that the California anti-alien land legislation was not in violation of the treaty of 1911.[76]

Several important questions remain unanswered. First of all, how far was the Webb law the result of purely partisan

72 *Foreign Relations*, 1914, 426-427.

73 New York *Times*, June 26, 1914.

74 *Foreign Relations*, 1914, 427-428.

75 *Ibid.*, 428-434.

76 The two important cases decided by the Supreme Court in 1923 were Webb vs. O'Brien and Frick vs. Webb, 263, *U.S. Rep.*, 313, 326.

politics? In this connection it should be observed that Johnson, about April 1, 1913, suddenly changed from an attitude of opposition to land legislation to one of support and played a leading part in pushing the legislation through. Whether this summersault was due to presidential aspirations, or to a desire to get on the bandwagon, or to an eagerness to increase the difficulties of the Wilson administration is something that can not be definitely settled.[77] As for the legislature, there can be little doubt, especially in view of the facts presented, that a desire to embarrass the Democratic administration played some, although probably not a decisive, part in the passing of the measure.[78] There is also little doubt that a Progressive Republican President could have elicited a greater measure of cooperation from the legislature, but politics or no politics, so definitely crystallized was public opinion in California on this subject that probably not even a Roosevelt could have prevented action.

The element of spite was widely discussed at the time. It was charged that the legislature passed the Webb bill largely because of resentment at the outbursts of the populace in Tokyo. It will be recalled, however, that the first assembly bill was passed on April 15, 1913, and that significant demonstrations in Japan were not reported in the United States until two or three days later. It was also charged that the legislature took action because the Japanese government was so ill-advised as to lodge a protest. The informal protest of Chinda, early in April, made no appreciable stir in California, and the first formal protest was not made until six days after the Webb act had passed both houses. It was further alleged that the bill was hurried through because of Wilson's effrontery in interfering and dispatching Bryan. But the first Washington telegram, that of April 18, 1913, from Bryan, was not forthcoming until after the assembly bill had passed and until it had become

[77] Sacramento *Union*, April 3, 5, 19, 23, 29, May 10, 1913; *Lane Letters*, 136; *California Outlook*, May 10, 1913, 5; San Francisco *Argonaut* during 1913, April 12, 227, May 3, 281-282, 10, 297, June 21, 394.

[78] See London *Times*, April 24, 1913; Sacramento *Union*, April 24, 1913.

evident that the enacting of a discriminatory measure was practically inevitable.

It was frequently asserted that the majority of the people of California did not favor an anti-alien law, but that the members of the legislature were misled by the clamor of the labor unions and the tactics of the demagogues. If this statement were confined to the thinking people of California, as it sometimes was, much could be said in its support.[79] But public opinion appears to have favored an anti-Japanese measure. The overwhelming majorities in the legislature, despite great pressure from within and without the state, would indicate as much. Dozens of legislators testified that the people demanded an alien land law, and several stated that if it were not forthcoming the people would resort to the initiative.[80] Of the forty-nine expressions of opinion that poured in upon the legislature from within the state, most of them from organizations representing considerable numbers, only seven were opposed to the legislation. The press of the state, in general, strongly favored the land bill.[81] The San Francisco *Argonaut,* although bitterly opposed to Johnson and to land legislation, admitted that if a referendum were held the law would be sustained by a majority of five or ten to one.[82]

79 See New York *Times,* April 15, 28, 1913; Sacramento *Union,* April 19, 1913.

80 Sacramento *Union,* April 29, May 1, 3, 1913; *Assembly Journal,* 2495; *California Outlook,* May 10, 1913, 5. State Senator Sanford wired to Congressman Raker that sentiment in California seemed to actively favor legislation, 5 to 1. Sacramento *Union,* April 9, 1913.

81 The California newspapers examined were the Sacramento *Union,* the San Jose *Mercury-Herald,* the Los Angeles *Tribune,* the Los Angeles *Times,* the San Francisco *Call,* the San Francisco *Chronicle,* and the Palo Alto *Times.* The two important California weeklies, the San Francisco *Argonaut* and the *California Outlook,* were also consulted. Only three of these publications opposed the passing of the legislation at that time: the San Francisco *Argonaut,* the San Francisco *Chronicle,* and the Los Angeles *Times.* The last named was particularly outspoken, and its editorials attracted wide attention in the East. It should be noted, however, that it was strongly anti-union, and that, in common with the other two journals, it was bitterly hostile to the governor and the Progressive legislature. Nevertheless, both the San Francisco *Argonaut* and the San Francisco *Chronicle* were willing to admit that the people of California overwhelmingly opposed ownership of land by the Japanese. See San Francisco *Chronicle,* April 30, 1913; San Francisco *Argonaut,* May 10, 1913, 297; *Current Opinion,* June, 1913, 447; *California Outlook,* May 24, 1913, 2; Sacramento *Union,* May 1, 1913.

82 San Francisco *Argonaut,* May 10, 1913, 297. It may also be noted that in 1920 Cali-

There was little sympathy for the course of California outside the Pacific Coast area. As a rule the Eastern newspapers regarded the state as perversely attempting to provoke a war which the other states would have to support.[83] The Japan Society of New York conducted a poll of 800 leading newspapers, and it discovered that of the 232 taking a definite position, 207 condemned and only 25 supported California.[84] Southern newspapers and Southern Congressmen, quick to sympathize when the questions of color and state rights were involved, accorded a considerable measure of support to the state.[85] Altogether there was misunderstanding on both sides: the Californians failed to appreciate the seriousness of the difficulties that they were causing the federal government, and the Easterners failed to realize that serious social and economic problems frequently arise when large bodies of orientals dwell among whites.[86]

The Japanese were naturally offended by the discrimination of California. Numerous mass meetings were called to discuss the issues involved, but the government and the better classes expressed disapproval of all jingoistic efforts.[87] An attempt was made to initiate a boycott of American goods, but this plan was discouraged.[88] In fact, much of the agitation was interpreted in certain quarters as an attempt on the part of a small political group to embarrass the government.[89] The mass of the population was restrained, and the attitude of the Japanese

fornia, by initiative action, dropped the leasing clause from the Webb law by a vote of 668,483 to 222,086. Buell, *loc. cit.*, 72.

83 New York *Times*, April 26, 29, 1913; San Francisco *Chronicle*, April 29, 1913; *Outlook*, May 3, 1913, 22-24; San Francisco *Argonaut*, May 10, 1913, 298; June 21, 1913, 393; *Independent*, November 6, 1913, 236.

84 New York *Times*, May 10, 1913.

85 *Ibid.*, May 1, 1913; Sacramento *Union*, May 1, 1913; Maxey, *loc. cit.*, 76. As Johnson pointed out, Missouri, Kentucky, Oklahoma, and Texas had anti-alien land laws. Sacramento *Union*, April 22, 1913.

86 It was suggested that Bryan's visit, by focusing attention on conditions in California, did a good deal to clarify the problem for and explain it to Easterners. See *ibid.*, May 2, 1913.

87 New York *Times*, April 16, 19, 22, May 2, 15, 16, 1913; Sacramento *Union*, May 6, 1913.

88 *Ibid.*, May 2, 1913; New York *Times*, June 5, 1913.

89 *Ibid.*, April 22, 1913.

government in endeavoring to keep the situation in hand was unobjectionable.[90]

The possibility of war between the United States and Japan was seriously discussed, but the situation appears to have been considerably less acute than it was in 1906.[91] Nevertheless, affairs were in such a posture that a wrong move by either nation might easily have led to grave consequences. It was evident that Wilson was greatly worried over developments and that he was making every effort to quiet war talk. One of the obvious dangers was that the popular clamor in Japan might become so great as to force the government into a belligerent attitude. As it was, the Japanese notes were friendly, though firm, and merely represented the use of a legitimate instrument by a government seeking to protect its subjects' interests. Unfortunately, even responsible persons in the United States aggravated the situation by jingoistic utterances, particularly Representative T. U. Sisson of Mississippi, who attracted widespread attention by a fiery war speech in Congress, but who appears to have cooled down after a conference with Wilson.[92]

In a cabinet meeting shortly after the first protest, the possibility of war was discussed, and some comfort was derived from the fact that Japan appeared to be financially unprepared for hostilities.[93] This same idea seems to have been foremost in the minds of many California editors, who, quite in contrast with those of the East, displayed an amazing indifference to the possible consequences of the course that the legislature was pursuing.[94] In another cabinet meeting, on May 13, 1913, Wilson expressed the belief that there would be no war but

[90] On June 18, 1913, some unknown Japanese desecrated the walls of the American embassy in Tokyo. The Japanese government sent both a formal message of regret and an apology. *Ibid.*, June 21, 1913.

[91] See *ibid.*, April 22, 1913.

[92] See *Congressional Record*, 63 cong., 1 sess., 632-637, 1712 ff.; New York *Times*, April 29, May 22, 1913.

[93] Houston, *op. cit.*, I, 61-62.

[94] Several of the newspapers were immersed in local politics, others gave little space to the subject in their news columns, and others had practically no editorials on it. See San Francisco *Argonaut*, May 10, 1913, 297.

that the situation would have to be watched. Secretary Daniels submitted a report from his naval staff, which concluded that in the event of hostilities the Philippines, Hawaii, and Alaska would be lost to Japan. It may have been, as was rumored in Washington, that Great Britain, a nation which had no great difficulty in seeing the point of view of California as a result of having encountered somewhat the same problem in her dominions, brought pressure to bear on her ally in the interests of moderation.[95] Again, on May 16, 1913, the matter was discussed in the cabinet, and Wilson stated that not until the day before, when he noted the extreme perturbation of Chinda, had he entertained the thought of such a criminal possibility as war.[96] When it was suggested that ships in Chinese waters should be dispatched for the defense of Manila, Wilson asserted that he would make no warlike preparations for fear of precipitating hostilities, even though he should be criticized for inaction in the event of war.[97] This precaution is further evidence that the President was doing all that he could to avert a crisis, and by May 19, 1913, war talk had quieted down to a gratifying degree.[98]

The mission of Bryan has frequently been sneered at as fruitless. Although he was received with every outward evidence of courtesy, and although he conducted himself with dignity and restraint, his visit had no demonstrable effect on the provisions of the Webb bill, and it probably accelerated the passage of that measure.[99] But it should be remembered that in diplomacy the object sought is not always the object avowed. It now seems clear that Wilson, who avoided intervention until the passage of a discriminatory measure appeared practically certain, had little hope of preventing legislation. He felt, how-

[95] Houston, *op. cit.*, I, 65.

[96] It may have been, however, that Chinda was disturbed over the fate of the home government. *Ibid.*, 66.

[97] Even routine troop movements to Hawaii were sensationally headlined, and on May 16, 1913, it was reported that Wilson had issued orders against any military movement that might cloud the situation. New York *Times*, May 16, 1913.

[98] See *ibid.*, May 19, 1913.

[99] See Sacramento *Union*, May 4, 1913.

ever, that the tension between Japan and the United States would be greatly relieved by such an open gesture of friendliness as the sending of Bryan to California.[100] This appears to have been Wilson's main objective, and although it was not announced as such at the time, a number of discerning observers could clearly see what the President was trying to do.[101] Federal intervention undoubtedly did mollify Japanese public opinion to a gratifying extent. A marked disappearance of the bitter tone in the Japanese press was immediately noted, and Japanese organizations and leaders in Japan, and Japanese groups and individuals both in California and in the Eastern states, expressed their deep appreciation of Wilson's efforts in their behalf.[102] Probably this gesture of friendliness, though barren of tangible results, did more than any other one thing to avert a serious crisis.

In the early stages of this difficulty it appeared to the federal government that California could not possibly achieve her purpose of discriminating against the Japanese without violating the treaty of 1911. Nevertheless, a clever wording of the bill enabled the state to remove this objection, at least to the satisfaction of the Wilson administration and, later, of the Supreme Court, although Japan persistently denied the inapplicability of the treaty and made out a good case for her point of view. It may be concluded, then, that the question was not basically one of a state violating a treaty, but, in the last analysis, merely a matter of comity—whether a state would accede to a reasonable request from the national authority, which consistently admitted that California had a perfect right to pass any

100 Houston, *op., cit.*, I, 60; see also *Lane Letters*, 136.

101 See San Francisco *Argonaut*, May 10, 1913, 297; *Literary Digest*, May 17, 1913, 1108; *Harper's Weekly*, May 3, 1913, 3; *Independent*, May 1, 1913, 946.

102 See Sacramento *Union*, April 21, 1913; New York *Times*, April 21, 26, 29, May 5, 16, 19, 1913; London *Times*, April 29, 1913. Telegrams of appreciation came to Wilson from the Japanese Association of America, the Japanese American Association of Japan, the Japan Society of New York, the Executive Committee of the Japan Society, and a mass meeting of five hundred Japanese residents in New York. Ambassador Chinda and Baron Makino were both reported to have expressed their satisfaction with Wilson's move. See Sacramento *Union*, May 3, 1913; New York *Times*, April 24, 26, 28, May 1, 1913; London *Times*, May 6, 1913.

kind of legislation, constitutional or unconstitutional. Yet one of the distressing features about the whole affair was that even if the action of California had been in flagrant violation of treaty rights, the federal government, as on previous occasions, would have been equally powerless to act. The authority for effective intervention, despite former difficulties, simply did not exist. Taft had summarized this difficulty admirably in 1909:

> It puts our Government in a pusillanimous position to make definite engagements to protect aliens and then to excuse the failure to perform those engagements by an explanation that the duty to keep them is in States or cities, not within our control. If we would promise we must put ourselves in a position to perform our promise. We can not permit the possible failure of justice, due to a local prejudice in any State or municipal government, to expose us to the risk of a war which might be avoided if federal jurisdiction was asserted by suitable legislation. . .[103]

Once again attention was focused on the anomaly that the Constitution is so regardful of the rights of states that it allows one of them to provoke war while forbidding it to make war, and on May 23, 1913, Representative Richard Bartholdt introduced a joint resolution in the House to the effect that Congress should have exclusive power to legislate on all questions affecting the rights of aliens in the United States, but nothing came of this effort.[104] Despite his unhappy experience, Wilson was still enough of a Democrat to be unwilling to shear the states of any of their existing rights, and in his annual messages of 1913 and 1914 he completely ignored the subject.[105]

To summarize and conclude: there can be little doubt that the Webb law was the result of prejudice, reasonable or unreasonable, against the Japanese in California and that it was designed to be discriminatory.[106] Although partisan politics

[103] *Congressional Record,* 61 cong., special session of Senate, 4.

[104] *Ibid.,* 63 cong., 1 sess., 1730.

[105] Wilson was reported as saying that federal legislation on this subject was not feasible, and that each alleged discrimination could be dealt with on its merits. New York *Times,* December 16, 1914.

[106] By refusing to ratify the Fifteenth Amendment, by inserting a clause in the constitution of 1879 against aliens ineligible to citizenship, and by outbursts against the

probably accelerated its passage, the desire for legislation of this kind had been thwarted for so long that its passage in 1913 appears to have been inevitable. Furthermore, the evidence indicates that the measure was supported by a strong majority of the Californians. The belief that the law was passed because of resentment against Japanese protests has little basis in fact. With the exception of the Southern states, the course of California was extremely unpopular east of the Rockies, and Republicans and Democrats alike united to condemn the state and to praise Wilson. For a President subscribing to state rights views, Wilson appears to have done all that could have been expected to avert a crisis. The attitude of the Japanese government, though firm, was correct. Although war could easily have broken out had the wrong move been made, the situation was probably not so serious as in 1906. Bryan's unprecedented personal lobby had no demonstrable effect in shaping the Webb bill, and it probably hastened the passage of that measure. Nevertheless, by showing the Japanese government the friendly intentions of the national administration, this trip probably did more than any other one thing to prevent a crisis.

The dispassionate observer finds little to justify the conduct of California at this time. Although there were undeniably localized problems connected with Japanese immigrants, there was no menace of any kind that demanded immediate action. With much more courtesy than had been shown by Roosevelt, the Wilson administration made the request that the state delay action for a short time, and promised to secure redress through diplomatic means. A delay of two years would not have aggravated the alleged menace appreciably, and a satisfactory diplomatic adjustment would have provided greater security than

Chinese, the Californians had early shown themselves not incapable of race prejudice. Houston, however, drew certain pertinent conclusions as a result of conversations with a number of Californians. The people of that state did not object particularly to Chinese and negroes, who were racially different but who stayed in their place. But they did object to the Japanese because they were efficient, thrifty, ambitious, and, above all, unwilling to remain "mudsillers." See Houston, *op. cit.*, I, 51-52. State Senator Sanford frankly admitted that the people of California were "after the Japanese." Sacramento *Union*, April 29, 1913.

a statute of doubtful constitutionality. If the federal government had been unable to redeem its promise within the two year period, the state could then, with more show of reason, have gone ahead with legislation. Why California should have been so disregardful of its obligations to the other forty-seven states as to ignore this altogether fair request is difficult for an outsider to understand. Perhaps Dennis Kearney and the spirit of '77 suggest the answer.

THOMAS A. BAILEY

Stanford University

PREJUDICE GOES TO COURT

The Japanese & the Supreme Court in the 1920s

M. Browning Carrott

In May 1905, the San Francisco Board of Education drafted a plan to establish separate schools for Asian students because it believed association with children of the Mongolian race was detrimental to Caucasian children. Japanese children, the board claimed, were particularly vicious and immoral. Although one Japanese third grader, Kazuye Togasaki, later became a physician and a San Francisco's Woman of the Year—symbolizing the waning of overt anti-Japanese discrimination in the decades which followed—during the first half of the twentieth century, Japanese in the United States were barred from citizenship, land ownership, and even from attending Japanese language schools. Far from protecting their rights against incursions by demogogic newspaper editors, politicians, and a frightened racist public, the U.S. Supreme Court issued a series of decisions in the 1920s which further institutionalized anti-Japanese prejudice.

Although Japanese immigration to the continental United States began in the last decades of the nineteenth century, fewer than 25,000 had arrived by 1900. Thereafter, the pace of immigration quickly accelerated, however, and by 1910 over 72,000 Japanese resided in the continental United States. In 1908, under pressure from the United States, the American and Japanese governments entered into a "Gentlemen's Agreement" in which Japan agreed to withhold passports from those who applied to enter the

The author is a constitutional historian at Southern Illinois University, Carbondale.

From 1925 to 1929 this largely conservative United States Su Court thwarted cases involving attempts by Japanese immig obtain citizenship and own land. The roster: (seated, from l James C. McReynolds, Oliver Wendell Holmes, Jr., Chief Jus William Howard Taft, Willis VanDevanter, Louis D. Brande (standing) Edward T. Sanford, George Sutherland, Pierce Bu Harlan Fiske Stone.

The right to naturalized citizenship became a primary issue California Japanese families like that of restaurant owner N Kumataru. CHS, San Francisco

After 1900 Japanese immigrants concentrated in largely agricultural counties. In this view c. 1910, the mostly male patrons of Mr. Tamaki's general store and hotel in Sacramento posed for a visiting photographer.

United States as laborers, thus reducing for a few years the flow of Japanese to the West Coast.[2]

Because many early Japanese immigrants came from agricultural areas of Japan, they initially found work as farm laborers. Others took jobs on railroads, in canneries and forests, and in mining, meatpacking, and salt production industries. Hard-working, uncomplaining, and willing to work for low wages, the Japanese quickly incurred the enmity of unions and other employee organizations. In urban centers, the Japanese had more difficulty finding employment, particularly in better-paying industries such as cigar, shoe, and clothing manufacturing. As a result many turned to agriculture, where they sought to acquire land of their own—and where they became economic competitors with white American farmers. This was particularly true in California, which by 1910 contained over half of the Japanese in the United States. In California, the Japanese became concentrated in the Alameda, Fresno, Los Angeles, Sacramento, San Francisco, and San Joaquin counties, with Los Angeles County leading in numbers.[3]

Ozawa possessed all qualifications to be a good citizen [but] the U.S. District Court in Hawaii dismissed his petition for naturalization in 1916.

As the Japanese immigration to California accelerated after 1900, popular attitudes towards them became increasingly hostile. In the February 23, 1905, issue of the *San Francisco Chronicle*, a typical story appeared under the front-page banner: "The Japanese Invasion, The Problem of the Hour." On December 20, 1906, the Hearst press began its own thirty-five year campaign against Japan with this statement in the *San Francisco Examiner* warning of Japanese spies: "Japan Sounds Our Coast—Brown Men Have Maps and Could Land Easily." A few days later the *Examiner* claimed that Japanese troops had arrived in Hawaii in the guise of coolies in order to prepare secretly for hostilities, and that these troops practiced infantry drill with rifles two or three nights a week after dark. In 1916, the International Film Service, another part of the Hearst empire, continued the campaign against the Yellow Peril with a motion picture, *Patria*, which showed Japanese troops invading California with the aid of Mexico and committing atrocities against the local population. A few years later, a prominent state politician, U.S. Senator James D. Phelan, warned a special session of the California legislature in 1919 that a "Jap is a Jap" and that "the native Japanese are as undesirable as the imported."[4]

This rising hostility and antagonism toward the Japanese of course meant that they had a difficult time securing equal treatment under the law, and in the 1920s, the Supreme Court effectively validated discrimination against Japanese immigrants. Under the leadership of Chief Justice William Howard Taft, whom President Warren Harding appointed in 1921, the Court adhered to a conservative position in its willingness to strike down any measure regulating property and its unsympathetic attitude towards personal rights. On many occasions, Justice Oliver Wendell Holmes, appointed in 1902, and Louis Brandeis, appointed in 1916, objected to Taft's view of the Constitution, but they were unsuccessful in undermining the basic conservatism which dominated the 1920s Court. Accordingly, those who asserted the rights of minority groups before the nation's highest court during this decade faced a steeply uphill fight.[5]

Cases concerning the Japanese which came before the Court during the 1920s arose in three main areas: the right to acquire U.S. citizenship, the right to

possess land for agricultural use, and the freedom to use the Japanese language in private schools.

Because Congress had never made it possible for Asians to become naturalized citizens, the right to citizenship became a primary issue. In the United States, Congress alone determines eligibility for naturalization, and racism has consistently influenced policymaking on this matter. The first Naturalization Act of 1790 allowed only free white aliens to become American citizens; in 1870, after the abolition of slavery, Congress extended this privilege to aliens of African nativity and descent. At that time, the Senate debated the naturalization of Asians, but senators from the West Coast successfully opposed Massachusetts Senator Charles Sumner's efforts to remove racial restrictions from the law. Since there were 63,000 Chinese in the United States in 1870 and only 55 Japanese, senators limited their discussion to the former group; most probably never considered the status of Japanese. With the 1882 Chinese Exclusion Act, Congress not only barred Chinese from entering the country but also made them ineligible for naturalization. Although Congress drafted a comprehensive Naturalization Act in 1906, it merely dealt with procedural issues and did not consider the question of eligibility for citizenship. Prior to the 1920s, however, the lower federal courts had permitted the naturalization of many Asians.[6]

The Supreme Court decided the issue of citizenship for Asians in November 1922 in the landmark case of Ozawa vs. United States. Takao Ozawa, a Japanese alien, had applied for naturalized U.S. citizenship. Ozawa had resided in California and Hawaii for twenty years, had attended the University of California, Berkeley, for three years, and had educated his children in American schools. His family attended American churches, and family members spoke English at home. As the opinion of the Supreme Court indicated, Ozawa possessed all qualifications to be a good citizen. However, the U.S.

District Court in Hawaii dismissed his petition for naturalization in 1916, and the Ninth Circuit Court of Appeals certified or officially requested answers to three questions by the Supreme Court in 1917. The first question asked whether the Naturalization Act of 1906, which omitted any mention of race and therefore did not specifically exclude anyone from citizenship, had superseded earlier laws limiting naturalization to white persons and those of African descent. The second question asked if a person of the Japanese race, born in Japan, could acquire citizenship through naturalization. The third question inquired whether, assuming that the 1906 Naturalization Act had *not* by implication repealed earlier laws barring citizenship to non-whites and non-African Americans, an alien of the Japanese race could ever obtain citizenship.[7]

Political and diplomatic considerations kept the Supreme Court from answering these questions for five years. In June 1918, Secretary of State Robert Lansing asked Solicitor General John W. Davis to delay further consideration of the case until the end of World War I, mentioning Japan's assistance in the war against Germany and the Japanese sensitivity on the citizenship issue. Davis fully acceeded to Lansing's request. Lansing also requested that the Japanese Embassy persuade Ozawa to drop the case. Ambassador Ishii told Lansing that although he agreed with Lansing's position, he could not dissuade the plaintiff from pressing his suit.[8]

The delay continued into the postwar period because both the federal government and Ozawa's attorney, the prominent George W. Wickersham, felt that political considerations required a further postponement.[9] Relations between the two countries had become more sensitive because of American concern over rising Japanese power in the Far East, especially in China. The leading naval powers had called the upcoming Washington Naval Conference, scheduled for November 1921, to negotiate limits on naval armaments. As a country with a growing navy, this subject was of particular interest to the Japanese.

Small businesses such as Mr. Fujita's Mikado Fish Market in Sacramento served the needs of growing Japanese communities.

Because of these delaying tactics, the Supreme Court did not hear the Ozawa case until the fall of 1922. The brief filed with the Court on Ozawa's behalf argued that since the Naturalization Act of 1906 had not specifically excluded the Japanese, they were definitely eligible to become American citizens. It said that this statute had so overhauled naturalization laws and procedures that it had superseded earlier provisions restricting this right to white persons and those of African descent and nativity. Building a case for citizenship, the brief used an argument designed to show Japanese superiority to other Asians: "The Japanese are 'free.' They are, or at least the dominant strains, are 'white persons,' speaking an Aryan tongue and having Caucasian root stocks; a superior class fit for citizenship. . . . The Japanese are commonly called 'The Yankees of the Orient.' " It was not uncommon for the Japanese themselves to use similar racist arguments based on supposed Japanese superiority to the Chinese or Japanese identification with Caucasians.[10]

The brief for the Justice Department submitted by Solicitor General Beck insisted that the Japanese were not white and that the Naturalization Act of 1906 did not extend the privileges of citizenship to those not previously eligible. An *amicus curiae* brief, filed by Attorney General U.S. Webb of California, strongly praised the national policy of denying naturalization to Asians, using the familiar argument that they could never assimilate with white Americans. Furthermore, he maintained, the Asian posed a particular threat to American farm life:

> The American family reared along the lines of American traditions with the father managing the farm, the mother presiding in the home, and the children during their younger years attending school, cannot compete with the Oriental farm life wherein children and mother join with the father in the actual farm labor, and in addition do not enjoy conditions of life which are demanded by the American standard of living.[11]

Speaking through Justice George Sutherland, the Supreme Court, without dissent, rejected Ozawa's claim to citizenship.[12] Sutherland viewed the Naturalization Act of 1906 as a procedural measure which did not alter the previous substantive policy of limiting naturalization to whites and African-Americans. If Congress had desired to make this important change, according to the opinion, it would have so indicated in a more affirmative manner. In rejecting the argument of the petitioner that at least some of the Japanese belonged to the white race, the justice said that skin color did not provide an adequate test for determining citizenship since color varied greatly among members of the same race.

Hard-working, uncomplaining, and willing to work for low wages, the Japanese quickly incurred the enmity of unions and other employee organizations.

In May 1925, the Supreme Court rejected another Japanese claim for citizenship in the case of Hidenitsu Toyota vs. United States. Because of Toyota's service in the U.S. Coast Guard during World War I, the U.S. District Court in Massachusetts accepted his 1921 petition for naturalization based on a law passed in 1918, stating that any alien who had served in the armed forces during wartime could file for citizenship without meeting the normal five-year residency requirement. At the behest of the government, however, the District Court had cancelled the certificate of naturalization in 1923, ruling that the law did not apply to Asian aliens. The First Circuit Court of Appeals then certified or raised the question to the Supreme Court. Speaking through Justice Pierce Butler, the Court accepted the government's

Mr. Motoyama operated a San Joaquin Valley farm boasting 162 acres of orchards and asparagus. California's Alien Land Act of 1913 denied him the right to own the land.

contention that Toyota had no valid claim to American citizenship. (Chief Justice Taft dissented without opinion.)[13]

The Toyota decision remained in effect for only eleven years; in 1936 Congress enacted a law which permitted the naturalization of all aliens who had served in the armed forces during World War I and who had maintained a permanent residence in the United States.[14] Since there is no record of the congressional debate, it is difficult to determine why the subject came up at that time. Perhaps Congress decided that Asian veterans of World War I deserved better treatment.

Skin color did not provide an adequate test for determining citizenship since color varied greatly among members of the same race.

In the 1920s, the Supreme Court also decided the extent to which the states could restrict the right of the Japanese to own and lease land. The Japanese had become a target in this matter because of their intensive farming of fruits and vegetables, their profitable adoption of experimental techniques for farming desert and swampy land which others regarded as unfit for cultivation, and their abilities as businessmen. Therefore, as the Japanese increased in number and enjoyed greater economic success, particularly in truck farming, a number of states passed laws limiting landholding by aliens who were not specifically mentioned as eligible for citizenship. Since the Japanese were concentrated in California, the first restrictions appeared there.[15] Historian Spencer Olin analyzes some of the reasons:

> The Japanese began to acquire land and to employ as workers members of their own race exclusively, thereby reducing the farm labor pool. As the Japanese land owners began to monopolize such cheap farm labor, they incurred the animus of both large and small growers. The Japanese were no longer a convenient source of manpower, but had gradually become active competitors for farm labor, farm land, and agricultural markets.[16]

In their quest to obtain land, the Japanese easily antagonized both large and small farmers. Smaller operators resented the competition of those who excelled at the intensive truck farming methods, while larger operators dislike their inroads into their labor supply. Furthermore, rising racial prejudice made the Japanese an even more appealing target. Passage of a restrictive law giving vent to this hostility—the 1913 Alien Land Act—was almost inevitable.[17]

The Alien Land Act was preceded by similar attempts to prevent Japanese land ownership, but in each case presidential objections to the passage of measures offending Japan prevented these bills from becoming law. In 1907 a bill was introduced into the California legislature prohibiting all aliens from owning land for more than five years and limiting leasing of land to one year. Objections from President Theodore Roosevelt and Governor James Gillett, however, proved decisive in defeating this measure. Pressure from President Roosevelt convinced Governor Gillett and the legislature that a similar bill, proposed in 1909, would have an unfortunate impact on relations between the United States and Japan. In 1911 the California Senate again passed a law forbidding aliens ineligible for citizenship to own land, but opposition from President Taft helped bring about the demise of this bill in the Assembly.[18]

Increasing ownership and leasing of land by the Japanese led to further attempts to impose restrictions. According to one study, based on Japanese figures which may have been somewhat inflated, Japanese ownership of land in California between

1910 and 1913 rose from 17,000 to 27,000 acres, while land tenancy went from 177,000 acres to 255,000 acres.

In response to this dramatic increase, and despite objections from President Wilson and Secretary of State William Jennings Bryan that Japan would bitterly resent this measure, the California Senate and Assembly overwhelmingly passed the Alien Land Act in 1913. Governor Hiram Johnson said that because the measure had been approved by such a large majority, he felt compelled to sign it. (Governor Johnson approved the law not only to enhance his own popularity, but also to challenge President Wilson, his political rival, who as a Democrat would have had little chance of convincing the strongly Republican state to rescind the embarrassing measure.[19])

Section one of the Act permitted all aliens eligible for citizenship to acquire, possess, enjoy, transmit, and inherit real property. Section two said that the right of all other aliens to own property depended solely on any existing treaty between the United States and the nation of which the alien was a citizen. Section three imposed similar restraints on the holding of land by corporations where aliens ineligible for citizenship owned a majority of the capital stock. Sections five and six established procedures by which land acquired in violation of the statute would revert (or escheat) to the state.[20]

The California law of 1913 referred to the Treaty of 1911 between the United States and Japan which allowed the citizens of each country the rights to enter, travel, and reside in the territories of the other, to carry on trade, to own or lease and occupy houses, manufactories, warehouses, and shops, and to lease land for residential and commercial purposes upon the same basis as citizens. While the treaty did not mention the ownership of land or its leasing for agricultural uses, the California law allowed aliens ineligible for citizenship to lease farm land for three years.[21]

California's Alien Land Act of 1913 was the first

measure depriving the Japanese of any substantial rights in the United States, and its passage testified to the growing hostility toward the Japanese. Many California Japanese, however, could evade the Alien Land Act by placing land in the name of their children, who held American citizenship because of birth in the United States, or in the name of a Caucasian friend. Furthermore, the law did not completely prohibit the purchase of stock in a farming corporation. Ironically, during World War I Japanese agriculture in California entered its most prosperous years, with the Japanese estimated at war's end to have owned or leased 1 percent of the land under cultivation, which produced 10 percent of the dollar value of the state's crops.[22]

After World War I, racist antipathy towards the Japanese grew as their hard work brought noticeably greater economic success. Other states then followed California's lead in enacting alien land laws: Arizona passed a similar measure in 1917, Louisiana in 1921, New Mexico in 1922, Idaho, Montana, and Oregon in 1923, and Kansas in 1925. But the greatest animosity toward the Japanese developed in California and Washington, the states with the most Japanese residents. Out of a total Japanese population in the United States of 111,000 in 1920, California claimed 71,900 and Washington 17,3000. Census figures for 1920 suggest why Japanese agriculture became such a target in these two states.[23]

In California in 1920, only 4.4 percent of all farm operators were Japanese, and they worked only 1.2 percent of all the farmed land. But while Japanese holdings were small when compared with the total figures, they were concentrated in certain counties. In California, where the Japanese constituted a large proportion of non-white farmers, five counties had a substantial number of Japanese farmers:[24]
Not many Japanese owned farms, but they made up a sizable percentage of the tenant farmers in these five counties.

Similarly, in Washington Japanese farmers operated

Even prosperous Westernized Japanese such as automobile parts dealer Tahashi Mitani could not become naturalized citizens because of their race.

only 1 percent of all farms and farmed only .2 percent of all acres farmed. But almost 11,000 of the 17,300 Japanese living in Washington resided in King County, which included the City of Seattle. This concentration attracted attention and hostility.[25]

After World War I, both California and Washington reacted against their Japanese residents' economic gains. According to one account "Returning soldiers and dismissed war workers saw in the Japanese barriers to their re-establishment as farmers and to their obtaining jobs."[26] The xenophobic nationalism stirred up by World War I and the succeeding Red Scare, the nativist pressure exerted by such groups as the American Legion, the Native Sons and Daughters of the Golden West, the California State Federation of Labor, and the California State Grange, and the difficult postwar economic adjustments further sharpened already existing hostility towards the Japanese.

In November 1920, the voters of every county in California approved through the initiative process a new alien land act designed to plug the loopholes of the earlier law. This measure did not allow Asians to lease land for agricultural purposes or to acquire any stock in a corporation authorized to hold farm land, and it established a prima facie presumption of illegality if a person eligible to hold real estate took title to it after an ineligible person provided the funds. The state could punish violations of the law by bringing an action to claim the land in question (called escheatment).[27]

In 1921, a year after California enacted its new alien land act, the Washington state legislature passed a measure which prohibited the ownership, possession, or use of land by an alien who had not in good faith declared his intention of becoming a U.S. citizen. The act neatly prevented aliens ineligible for citizenship such as the Japanese from owning land, for they could never declare their intention of becoming American citizens. This provision also applied to corporations where aliens owned a majority of the capital stock.[28]

Two years later, in November 1923, the U.S. Supreme Court handed down four decisions on California and Washington's alien land laws, all detrimental to the Japanese. In Terrace vs. Thompson, Terrace, a white American, desired to lease his agricultural property for five years to Nakatsuka, a Japanese alien. Attorney General L.L. Thompson threatened to sue if the parties carried out the leasing agreement. Terrace and Nakatsuka then brought suit against Thompson to restrain him from enforcing the state law, claiming that the Act violated the 1911 treaty with Japan and violated the Fourteenth Amendment by depriving the plaintiffs of their liberty and property without due process and denying them equal protection under the laws.[29]

The U.S. District Court for the Western District of Washington had held in 1921 that the Treaty of 1911 did not give the Japanese the right to lease land for farming. Further, it had added that Congress had passed the Fourteenth Amendment primarily to as-

	COUNTIES				
	Alameda	*Fresno*	*Los Angeles*	*Sacramento*	*San Joaquin*
Farms operated by owners	1,886	7,291	8,578	1,840	3,290
Non-white owners	25	154	69	76	12
Farms operated by tenants	821	1,338	3,174	1,049	1,083
Non-white tenants	154	437	1,481	504	282

Young Japanese children worked side-by-side with their parents harvesting hops in Wheatland in 1935. Dorothea Lange Collection, © City of Oakland, Oakland Museum

sist freed slaves, not to aid other groups. The wording of the opinion displayed the unselfconscious racism that permeated jurisprudence at the time:

> The yellow or brown race color is the hallmark of Oriental despotism, or was at the time the original naturalization act was enacted. It was deemed that the subjects of these despotisms, with their fixed and ingrained pride in the type of their civilization, which works for its welfare by subordinating the individual to the personal authority of the sovereign, as the embodiment of the state, were not fitted and suited to make for the success of a republican form of government. Hence, they were denied citizenship.

In November 1920, the voters of every county in California approved a new alien land act designed to plug the loopholes of the earlier law.

The District Court concluded that an alien not eligible for citizenship lacked the interest to work effectively for the welfare of the state.[30]

The appellants' petition to the Supreme Court in 1923 stressed that the Washington law of 1921 violated the due process clause since it prohibited aliens from engaging in a common occupation of the community and since it stopped the landowner from lawfully leasing his property; it deprived Nakatsuka of the equal protection of the laws because the state did not have a valid reason for discriminating against aliens who had not declared their intent to become citizens. In addition, the appeal read, the 1921 law contravened the part of the Treaty of 1911 which allowed Japanese to carry on trade and to lease land for commercial purposes. To counter these points, the brief for the attorney general stated that the Fourteenth Amendment did not give aliens the right to own or lease property, the Treaty with Japan did not apply to the leasing of land for farming, and the state must have the power to protect itself against Asians controlling a large amount of land. The underlying argument was that Americans could not compete with Orientals in agriculture: "This is so because their standards of living are incomparably different. The Oriental works his wife and his family in the fields practically during all the hours of daylight, and his standard of living could not be adopted by an American."[31]

In its 1923 decision the Supreme Court concluded that the state had the authority to forbid aliens from holding land, and it would lose this power only if its actions were repugnant to the Fourteenth Amendment or to a treaty. Since the state had followed the federal policy of discriminating only against certain aliens, the justices held that Washington's law was reasonable. Nor could the plaintiffs receive any protection from the Treaty of 1911, according to the opinion, because it did not give the Japanese the right to own or lease farming property. The Court concluded on a note of patriotic fervor: "The quality and allegiance of those who own, occupy, and use the farm lands within its borders are matters of highest importance and affect the safety and power of the state itself."[32]

The Supreme Court's three other alien land cases involved California suits. In Porterfield vs. Webb, as in Terrace vs. Thompson, the plaintiffs, a Japa-nese alien and a white citizen who had made a contract for the rental of farm land, in Los Angeles County, sued California Attorney General Webb to restrain him from pressing a suit for the land. The plaintiffs lost in the lower court, and after they appealed to the Supreme Court, the attorney general of California submitted a brief reiterating the theme that because of differing family work habits the Japanese would achieve a dominant position in agriculture if not stopped by special restrictions. Jus-

tice Pierce Butler relied largely on the Terrace case in upholding the Alien Land Act of California.[33]

In Webb vs. O'Brien, a white landowner and a Japanese alien had entered into a cropping agreement in Santa Clara County which would have allowed the alien to raise crops on the land in return for the owner taking one-half of the output. The U.S. District Court for Northern California granted an injunction in 1921 prohibiting the state from attempting to escheat or take over the land on the basis that the cropper could not have any legal rights to it. In the brief filed with the Supreme Court, State Attorney General Webb reemphasized the need to contain the activities of the Japanese. Agreeing with this position, Justice Butler held that if the Court sanctioned this cropping arrangement, aliens ineligible for citizenship would threaten the security of the state by controlling much of its farm land. He therefore reversed the decision of the lower court.[34]

In the third case, Frick vs. Webb, a white American had agreed to sell stock in a company owning 220 acres of farm land in Merced County to a Japanese alien. When the attorney general threatened to institute an action to forfeit the share to the state, both the U.S. District Court for Northern California and the Supreme Court refused to issue a restraining order on the grounds that ownership of stock in a farm corporation was the same as holding an interest in the land.[35]

In none of these four land cases did the Supreme Court reach a unanimous verdict. Justice George Sutherland did not participate in any of those decisions, and Justices Brandeis and James McReynolds dissented on the technicality that where the parties had not actually executed the contracts, the court had no grounds for hearing the cases.[36]

In 1925, in Cockrill vs. California, the Supreme Court made its last attempt to crack down on people attempting to evade the 1920 Alien Land Act by registering land in their children's name. The Superior Court of Sonoma County convicted the defendants of conspiracy to transfer real estate in violation of

state law, the Court of Appeal upheld the verdict, and in 1923 the California Supreme Court declined to hear the case, after which it was taken to the U.S. Supreme Court.[37]

Cockrill, an American citizen, had made a contract with Ikada, a Japanese alien, to purchase a piece of farm land with Cockrill taking title and Ikada furnishing the money and assuming possession of the property. While the state contended that the parties had conspired to evade the Alien Land Act, the defense maintained that Ikada had acquired the land for his children who were native-born, even though Ikada never actually placed the land in his children's name. Speaking for a unanimous Supreme Court, Justice Butler said that the state had established a reasonable and constitutional method of controlling attempts to evade the Alien Land Act and therefore the Superior Court's original ruling against Cockrill was valid. Property could not be purchased by aliens for their native-born children.

A 1922 decision by the California Supreme Court in In Re Tetsubumi Yano's Estate ensured that the legal impact of the Cockrill decision for Japanese who put land in their children's name would be limited. After Yano had purchased fourteen acres of land in Sutter County and conveyed it to his four-year old daughter expressly to evade the Alien Land Act, he applied for guardianship over her person and property, knowing that the Act specifically prohibited a guardian's appointment over the estate of minor children if it consisted of property which the guardian could not legally hold. In this case the state Supreme Court held that this provision violated the equal protection clause of the Fourteenth Amendment by discriminating arbitrarily against guardians who could not become American citizens; the right of a father to be guardian, it reasoned, had no reasonable relationship to citizenship. As a result, through the guardianship procedure Japanese aliens with American-born children were able to circum-

The Supreme Court upheld the right of families like that of Morimoto Masayoshi (or Seikichi) to attend private schools conducted in the Japanese language, although state courts maintained that these schools taught disloyalty to the United States government.

vent the Alien Land Act.[38]

Despite the ensuing widespread use of this loophole, 1930 census figures show that the number of Japanese farmers declined in California from 5,152 in 1920 to 3,956 in 1930, while acreage farmed dropped from 361,000 acres to 191,000 acres. Scholars have debated the degree to which this decline resulted from passage of the Alien Land Act. According to Roger Daniels, "The measure was an attempt to lock the door after the horse had been stolen. Had it been enacted in 1913, when native-born Japanese were less numerous, it would have seriously inhibited Japanese acquisition of agricultural land. By 1920 its enactment was an empty gesture, an ineffective irritant." Historian John Modell, however, states that the decline in Japanese agriculture, at least in Los Angeles County, came about largely from increasing urban encroachment, not from lackadaisical enforcement of the Act.[39]

On the other hand, some scholars have concluded that the Alien Land Act of 1920 had a severely damaging effect on Japanese agriculture. Masakazu Iwata holds that in 1921 the Japanese produced 12.3 percent of the total farm products in California, but by 1925 this figure had dropped to 9.3 percent. He ascribes this decline to the agricultural depression of the 1920s, the Alien Land Act, and the Exclusion Act of 1924 which barred further Japanese immigration. Similarly, Harry Kitano believes that although the Japanese could evade the specific legal implications of the Act, it still presented a symbolic threat:

> An alien, denied the right to citizenship, denied the right to own or lease land, and finding himself under continuous harassment, would think twice before investing hard-earned money in land which might be taken away from him at any time. And in a capitalistic system where property rights are highly valued, the inability to own land is a tremendous handicap.[40]

T. Scott Miyakawa supports this conclusion, observing that "the anti-alien land laws made land ownership speculative and unpredictable, subject to the pressure of the anti-Japanese leaders and the inclination of the district attorneys, rather than rational predictable capital."[41]

The movement to curb the rights of the Japanese in the 1920s extended to the Hawaiian Islands, where their number had increased to over 100,000. As with the alien land laws on the mainland which were aimed primarily at the Japanese, schools conducted in the Japanese language became a principal target, perhaps because 147 of the islands' 163 foreign language schools were Japanese. Despite a number of court cases challenging the existence of foreign language schools, however, racist legislation against the Japanese in the area of education found less secure footing. In February 1927, in fact, the Supreme Court handed down a decision which was a major victory for Japanese language schools, and the impact of Farrington vs. Tokushige was felt by all Japanese in America, nowhere more strongly than in California.[42]

The attorney general of California reiterated the theme that because of differing family work habits the Japanese would achieve a dominant position in agriculture.

The first measure regulating language in schools enacted by the Hawaiian territorial legislature provided for the licensing of all schools conducted in any language except English and Hawaiian. The purpose of the law was purportedly the Americanization of aliens, and the Department of Public Instruction was given the right to prescribe a school's course of study and to insist on use of the English language. Teachers were also required to sign a pledge that they would observe the terms of the act and make the students loyal Americans. In 1925 the Department of Public Instruction significantly tightened these restrictions by ruling that until pupils had reached the age of fourteen or had completed the eighth grade, they could spend only one hour a day at foreign language schools.[43]

Alleging that such burdensome requirements would force the closure of their schools, the operators of the private Japanese schools secured an injunction in 1925 from the U.S. District Court in Hawaii against the enforcement of these regulations. The following year the Ninth Circuit Court of Appeals affirmed that the plaintiffs had the freedom to operate foreign-language schools, that teachers had the right to teach in them, and that students could receive instruction therein. The decision relied heavily on two earlier cases: Meyer vs. Nebraska (1923) and Pierce vs. Society of Sisters (1925), both of which used the Fourteenth Amendment to uphold the rights of private schools and their teachers. In the Farrington case, the Court of Appeals held that the presence of a large Japanese population in the Hawaiian Islands and the fear that it would soon constitute a majority of the electorate did not justify the drastic measure against the Japanese language schools.[44]

Through the guardianship procedure, Japanese aliens with American-born children were able to circumvent the Alien Land Act. Despite this, the number of Japanese farmers declined.

In the brief submitted to the U.S. Supreme Court defending the licensing regulations, the attorney general of Hawaii said that Hawaii should not have to "watch its foreign-born guests conduct a vast system of schools of American pupils . . . teaching them loyalty to a foreign country and disloyalty to their own country, and hampering them during their tender years in the learning of the home language in the public schools. . . ." On the other hand, the brief for the plaintiffs stressed that the Japanese schools taught complete loyalty to the United States and that Hawaii could not rightfully interfere with the parents' fundamental freedom to direct the education of their children.[45]

Speaking through Justice McReynolds, the U.S. Supreme Court affirmed the verdict of the Court of Appeals. Insisting that Japanese parents had the same liberty as others to control their children's education, McReynolds ruled that the Hawaiian provisions went far beyond mere regulation of privately supported schools. Lest there be doubt about the Court's sentiment, however, the opinion concluded that "we, of course, appreciate the grave problems incident to the large alien population of the Hawaiian Islands."[46]

The Farrington decision proved to be a boon for Japanese language schools in California, since the Court ruled that no state could now unduly regulate them. These schools reached their peak of popularity between 1930 and 1942, when wartime evacuation and internment of the Japanese disrupted them irreparably. In 1939 around 10,000 Japanese children in Los Angeles alone attended such schools, but by the mid-1960s only 2,000 remained in attendance.[47]

Although conceived by the Founding Fathers to be the guardian of individual rights and liberties, the Supreme Court of the 1920s succumbed to popular racist arguments that the Japanese in the United States should receive as few rights as possible. Never did the Court seriously resist the nativist fears of white Americans, especially on the West Coast, that the Japanese posed a major threat to their way of life. The justices accepted the alien land laws, denied claims by Japanese aliens and other Asians to citizenship, and upheld the Japanese only in the relatively less important area of language in private schools.[48] The Japanese, for their part, strongly desired to acquire citizenship in order to gain more protection against discriminatory legislation like the alien land acts, which interfered with one of their most important means of livelihood. Their chief victory came in a case where the Court had little choice; because of the precedents established by the Meyer and Pierce decisions, the justices were forced to uphold the rights of Japanese private schools.

Since Congress had never specifically authorized naturalization for Asians, it is more difficult to criticize the Court's failure to grant citizenship to Japanese aliens, but its decisions clearly revealed a willingness to adopt the prejudice that immigrants from northern Europe would make the best U.S. citizens.[49]

Most open to question is the Court's handling of the alien land issue. In these cases the justices interpreted the Fourteenth Amendment to uphold burdensome and arbitrary economic restrictions, while in other decisions they used this amendment to strike down state regulation of private property. While Justices Brandeis and Holmes in particular filed dissenting opinions on the latter decisions, Holmes remained silent in the alien land cases, and Brandeis noted only procedural dissents.[50] In most of its opinions the Court reflected the same anti-Japanese prejudice common in this era to the nation's most vitriolic yellow journalists and opportunistic politicians.

Notes

1. Frank Chuman relates this incident in *The Bamboo People: The Law and Japanese-Americans* (Del Mar, 1976), p. 20. See also Roger Daniels, *The Politics of Prejudice: The Anti-Japanese Movement in California and The Struggle for Japanese Exclusion* (Berkeley and Los Angeles, 1962); Harry H.L. Kitano, *Japanese Americans: The Evolution of a Subculture* (Englewood Cliffs, 1969); and William Petersen, *Japanese Americans: Oppression and Success* (New York, 1971).
2. *Twelfth Census of the United States* (Washington, 1922), Part I, CXXIII, *Thirteenth Census of the United States* (Washington, 1913), I, 125; Chuman, *Bamboo People*, 33-7.
3. Kitano, *Japanese Americans*, 15-16 162; Daniels, *Politics of Prejudice*, 13.
4. Chuman, *The Bamboo People*, 32, 77; Daniels, *The Politics of Prejudice*, 70, 76.
5. For an overview of the Court in the 1920s, see Alpheus Mason, *William Howard Taft: Chief Justice* (New York, 1965). For information on the dissenters, see Alpheus Mason, *Brandeis: A Free Man's Life* (New York, 1946), and Francis Biddle, *Justice Holmes, Natural Law and the Supreme Court* (Washington, 1945).
6. 1 Stat. 103; 16 Stat. 256; *Congressional Globe*, 41st Cong., 2d. Session, 5, 148-77; John H. Wigmore "American Naturalization and the Japanese," *American Law Review*, XXVIII (November-December, 1894), 819-20; Milton Konvitz, *The Alien and the Asiatic* (Ithaca, 1946), pp. 83, 85-6; 22 Stat. 58; 34 Stat. 596-607; Konvitz, *The Alien and the Asiatic*, 81, 85.
7. 260 U.S. 178; On Certificate from the Circuit Court of Appeals, Ninth Circuit, 2-3, Ozawa v. United States, *Records and Briefs of the United States Supreme Court*, 260 U.S. 178.
8. Lansing to Davis, June 3, June 8, June 11, 1918, Ozawa v. United States, Record Group 60, General Records of the Department of Justice, National Archives, Washington, D.C.
9. Alex King, Solicitor General, to Senator James Phelan, June 16, 1919; King to James D. Faher, Clerk of the Supreme Court, October 2, 1919; Wickersham to Solicitor General William Frierson, September 16, 1920; Wickersham to Solicitor General James Beck, July 15, 1921; Beck to S.C. Haber, U.S. Attorney in Hawaii, August 13, 1921; and Wickersham to Beck, September 15, 1921, ibid.
10. Brief for Petitioner, 5-10, 16-22, 54, 58, *Records and Briefs*.
11. Brief for Government, Ozawa v. United States, 260 U.S. 186-9; Brief of Attorney General of California, 120, 123 *Records and Briefs*.
12. Sutherland, appointed to the Supreme Court in 1922, was regarded as a conservative justice. See Joel Paschal, *Mr. Justice Sutherland: A Man Against the State* (Princeton, 1951).
13. 268 U.S. 402; 290 F. 971. Like Sutherland, Butler was a conservative appointed to the Supreme Court in 1922. See Francis J. Brown, *The Social and Economic Philosophy of Pierce Butler* (Washington, 1945).
14. 49 Stat. 397-8.
15. Kitano, *Japanese Americans*, 16-7, and T. Scott Miyakawa, review of Daniels' *The Politics of Prejudice* in *Southern California Quarterly* (March, 1964), 107. See also John Modell, *The*

The photograph of the Supreme Court is from Melvin I. Urofsky and David W. Levy, eds., **Letters of Louis D. Brandeis**, *vol. 5 (Albany, 1978). All the other photographs except the one by Dorothea Lange are from* **Japanese in California—A Pictorial History**, *Kaibara, ed. (Nichi Bei Times, 1911[?]).*

Economics and Politics of Racial Accomodation: The Japanese of Los Angeles (Urbana, 1977), p. 46 and Roger Daniels and Harry H.L. Kitano, *American Racism: Exploration of the Nature of Prejudice* (Englewood Cliffs, 1970), p. 51.

16. Spencer C. Olin, Jr., "European Immigrant and Oriental Alien: Acceptance and Rejection by the California Legislature of 1913," *Pacific Historical Review*, XXXV (August 1966), 309.
17. Carey McWilliams, *Factories in the Fields* (Boston, 1939), pp. 111-3; Jacobus ten Broek, Edward N. Barnhart, and Floyd Matson, *Prejudice, War and the Constitution* (Berkeley and Los Angeles, 1954), pp. 50-1; Modell, *Economics and Politics of Racial Accomodation*, 31-2; Fred H. Matthews, "White Community and 'Yellow Peril'," *Mississippi Valley Historical Review*, L (March 1964), 612-33; Daniels, *Politics of Prejudice*, ch. 5; Daniels and Kitano, *American Racism*, 52; Thomas Bailey, "California, Japan and the Alien Land Legislation of 1913," *Pacific Historical Review*, I (March 1932), 58; and Charles H. Sullivan, "Alien Land Law: A Reevaluation," *Temple Law Quarterly*, XXXVI (Fall 1962), 33.
18. Ichihashi, *Japanese in the United States*, 261, 263-4.
19. Ibid., 194; Ibid., 269-70; Daniels and Kitano, *American Racism*, 51.
20. Cal. Stats., 1913, ch. 113, 206-8.
21. 37 Stat. 1504; Cal. Stats., 1913, 207.
22. Kitano, *Japanese Americans*, 17; Modell, *The Economics and Politics of Racial Accomodation*, 38; Daniels and Kitano, *American Racism*, 50.
23. Dudley O. McGovney, "The Anti-Japanese Land Laws of California and Ten Other States," California Law Review, XXXV (March, 1947), 7-8; *Fourteenth Census of the United States* (Washington, 1922), III, 19, 106, 1,082.
24. Ibid., VI, Part 3, 337, 344-8.
25. Ibid., 258; III, 1,085.
26. Edwin E. Ferguson, "The California Alien Land Law and the Fourteenth Amendment," *California Law Review*, XXXV (March, 1947), 69.
27. Cal. Stats., 1921, Initiative Act of 1920, LXXXVII, LXXVII, LXXVIII, LXXXIX; Daniels, *The Politics of Prejudice*, 90.
28. Washington, Remington's Revised Statutes (1922), III, 2,929-30. See also Jack D. Freeman, "The Rights of Japanese and Chinese Aliens in Land in Washington," *Washington Law Review*, VI (June, 1931), 127-31 and Joseph Lanza, "Some Effects of the Alien Land Act in Washington," *Washington Law Review*, VIII (January, 1934), 131-36.
29. 263 U.S. 197. The alien land cases are discussed in Thomas Reed Powell, "Alien Land Cases in United States Supreme Court," *California Law Review*, XII (May, 1924), 259-82.
30. 274 F. 841; 274 F. 849.
31. Brief of Appellants, 50-62, 119, Terrace v. Thompson, *Records and Briefs*, 263 U.S. 197; Brief of Appellee, 16-66, ibid.
32. 263 U.S. 221.
33. 263 U.S. 225; 279 F. 117; Brief for Appellees, 25, *Records and Briefs*.
34. 263 U.S. 313; 279 F. 117; Brief for Appellants, 46-7; Webb v. O'Brien, *Records and Briefs*, 263 U.S., 313.
35. 281 F. 407; 263 U.S. 326.
36. McReynolds, appointed to the Court in 1914, was probably its most conservative member in the 1920s. See Stephen T. Early, "James Clark McReynolds and the Judicial Process" (Unpublished Ph.D. dissertation, Department of History, University of Virginia, 1954).
37. 268 U.S. 258; 62 Cal. App. 22.
38. 188 Cal. 645.
39. *Fifteenth Census of the United States* (Washington, 1932), IV, 302; Daniels, *Politics of Prejudice*, 88; Modell, *Economics and Politics of Racial Accomodation*, 104.
40. Masakazu Iwata, "The Japanese Immigrants in California Agriculture," *Agricultural History*, XXXVI (January, 1962), 31-2; Kitano, *Japanese Americans*, 18.
41. Miyakawa, review of *Politics of Prejudice*, 108; a similar position is expressed in Olin, "European Immigrant and Oriental Alien," 315.
42. *Fourteenth Census of the United States*, III, 1,172; 273 U.S. 284.
43. This background information comes from the opinion of the Court, 273 U.S. 290-7, and Gavin Daws, *Shoal of Time: A History of the Hawaiian Islands* (New York, 1968), 308-10.
44. 11 F. 2nd. 710; 262 U.S. 390; 268 U.S. 510.
45. Brief of Attorney General of Hawaii, 19, Farrington v. Tokushige, *Records and Briefs*, 273 U.S. 284; Brief for Respondents, 3-12.
46. 273 U.S. 299.
47. Kitano, *Japanese Americans*, 24-5.
48. The Japanese also won less significant victories in Asakura v. Seattle, 265 U.S. 332 (1924), and Jordan v. Tashiro, 278 U.S. 123 (1928).
49. This principle was written into the National Origins Act of 1924, which sharply restricted immigration into the United States and which heavily favored immigrants from Northern Europe. Immigration policies in the 1920s are discussed in John Higham, *Strangers in the Land: Patterns of American Nativism, 186051925* (New Brunswick, 1955), ch. 11.
50. See, for example, Truax v. Corrigan, 257 U.S. 312 (1921); Pennsylvania Coal Company v. Mahon, 260 U.S. 393 (1922); Wolff Packing Company v. Court of Industrial Relations, 262 U.S. 522 (1923); Jay Burns Baking Company v. Bryan, 264 U.S. 504 (1924); and Frost and Frost Trucking Company v. Railroad Commission of California, 271 U.S. 583 (1926). Holmes and Brandeis dissented in Truax v. Corrigan, Jay Burns Baking Company v. Bryan, Frost and Frost Trucking Company v. Railroad Commission of California.

"The Most Thankless Task": Bryan and the California Alien Land Legislation

PAOLO E. COLETTA

The author is professor of history in the U.S. Naval Academy. He has published the first volume of a projected longer life of Bryan.

SECRETARY OF STATE William Jennings Bryan's first contact with a problem involving the Far East arose on March 5, 1913, when the Japanese ambassador, Viscount Sutemi Chinda, spoke with him about renewed Japanophobia on the west coast and forwarded copies of anti-Japanese bills being considered by the legislatures of California and Washington.[1] Noting that there was no anti-Japanese disturbance anywhere in the United States except on the west coast, where Japanese had congregated in numbers large enough to create what he believed was economically motivated unhappiness, Bryan wrote to President Woodrow Wilson that he could solve the problem by getting Japan to agree to "the dispersion of the Japanese in this country so as to relieve the economic pressure which has aroused the protest." Wilson thought the plan would spread rather than eliminate the problem and wisely vetoed it.[2] On March 11 Bryan took home for study a draft on the subject prepared by Robert Lansing, aide to Counselor John Bassett Moore.[3] On March 23, at Wilson's request, he wrote to Governor Ernest Lister of Washington

[1] Baron Shidehara to Bryan, with enclosures, March 7, 1913, State Department File, NA, 811.52/32; and Shidehara to Ransford S. Miller, March 15, 1913, *ibid.*,/33. Hereafter, this file will be cited as SD with number.

[2] Bryan to Wilson, March 8, 1913, Wilson to Bryan, March 8, 1913, Bryan-Wilson Correspondence, NA. Bryan would reduce the number of Japanese in California by half by encouraging them to move to other states, with the understanding that not more than a thousand would go into any other state and no more than a hundred into any one county.

[3] Bryan to Wilson, March 11, 1913, William Jennings Bryan Papers, Division of Manuscripts, Library of Congress.

that "the President hopes that the Pacific States will go as far as they can in helping him to promote amicable relations with the Asiatic nations." Rather than seeking to bar state action that would prohibit resident Japanese aliens from owning agricultural land, Wilson desired only that the states "avoid *discrimination*,"—that the bill "be so drawn as to make ownership depend upon something other than race." [4]

When a similar bill was considered by the California legislature which met in March, 1913, Bryan asked state senator Anthony Caminetti, who had helped thrust the Japanese question into local politics, to oppose it and suggested that Wilson speak with Democratic members of the congressional delegations from the Pacific coast, adding that he did not think that Governor Hiram Johnson of California, a "Roosevelt Republican," would prove amenable to reason.[5] He himself had long opposed Oriental immigration; it was all right to take Christianity to the Far East, but it was not desirable that its peoples leave home to seek it in the United States. Wilson had supported the exclusion of Oriental immigrants and in 1912 had declared "We cannot make a homogeneous population out of a people who do not blend with the caucasian race." [6] Yet he suggested to such Californians as James D. Phelan, Senator John D. Works, and Representative William Kent that, in the light of the most-favored-nation clause in the Japanese-American treaties of 1894 and 1911[7] and of

[4] Bryan to Lister, March 23, 1913, Woodrow Wilson Papers, Division of Manuscripts, Library of Congress; and Bryan to Wilson, March 23, 1913, *ibid.*

[5] In 1910 the 50,000 Japanese in California owned only 233 out of its 66,632 farms (William C. Redfield to Bryan, April 30, 1913, SD 811.52/75). In 1912, of a total of about 27,000,000 acres in the state, they owned 12,726, or one-tenth of one per cent, and leased another 17,600, a decline of 2,700 acres since 1909 (Thomas A. Bailey, "California, Japan, and the Alien Land Legislation of 1913," *Pacific Historical Review,* I [1932], 38; and editorial, "Secretary Bryan in California," *Harper's Weekly,* May 3, 1913, p. 3). For California's Japanophobia, see Dorothy S. Thomas and Richard S. Nishimoto, *The Spoilage* (Berkeley, 1946); Jacobus ten Broek *et al., Prejudice, War and the Constitution* (Berkeley, 1954); Yamata Ichihashi, *Japanese in the United States* (Stanford, 1932); R. L. Buell, "Development of Anti-Japanese Agitation in the United States," *Political Science Quarterly,* XXXVII (1922), 605–638, and XXXVIII (1923), 57–81; and Fred H. Matthews, "White Community and the 'Yellow Peril,'" *Mississippi Valley Historical Review,* L (1964), 612–633.

[6] Cited in Matthews, "White Community and the 'Yellow Peril'," 620.

[7] Article I of the Treaty of Commerce and Navigation between the United States and Japan of 1911 stated: "The citizens or subjects of each of the High Contracting Parties shall have liberty to enter, travel and reside in the territories of the other to carry on trade, wholesale and retail, warehouses and shops, to employ agents of their choice, to lease land for residential and commercial purposes, and generally to do anything incident to or necessary for trade upon the same terms as native citizens and subjects...." Article XIV contained a most-favored-nation clause, but the treaty did not

the great irritation of Japan, the law avoid singling out the Japanese by forbidding "aliens ineligible to citizenship" to own land. He suggested the District of Columbia Act of 1887 as a model. Representative Kent, who avidly supported an alien land law, passed Wilson's suggestions on to Governor Johnson, who intimated that Wilson would do better to contact him directly.[8]

The California Democratic platform of 1912 included an anti-alien land plank. Bryan knew that such California Democrats as Caminetti and Phelan had vied with Progressive Republicans in 1912 in demanding that Japanese be prohibited from owning land and in using the race issue to embarrass corporation politicians.[9] He also knew that the twilight zone between federal and state powers enabled states to pass laws in contravention of treaties. He, therefore, prevailed upon Caminetti to act in his behalf in trying to convince California's legislators and labor leaders to oppose anti-alien legislation—for which Caminetti was later made United States Commissioner of Immigration.

However, Secretary of the Interior Franklin K. Lane, a Californian, told Wilson that his state would pass such legislation;[10] Phelan telegraphed both Bryan and Lane that public sentiment was "overwhelmingly" in favor of an alien land law, adding, "Don't fail to tell the President the wisdom of hands off";[11] and Champ Clark, speaker of the house of representatives, observed that "It is a question if the national government has a right to negotiate a treaty which interferes with the undeniable right of the state to regulate ownership of land." [12] Bryan knew that Japanese official as well as public opinion was inflamed and that Japan might not extend the treaty of arbitration of 1908, which would expire in June, 1913. Chinda had person-

give Americans the right to own real estate in Japan. Joseph K. Goodrich to Bryan, April 5, 1913, SD 811.52/35.

[8] Wilson to John D. Works, April 9, 1913, William Kent to Bryan, April 7, 1913, Kent to Wilson, April 9, 1913, Wilson to Kent, April 19, 1913, Works to Wilson, April 8, 1913, Wilson to James D. Phelan, April 9, 1913, Kent to Hiram Johnson, April 7, 1913, Hiram Johnson to Kent, April 8, 1913, Wilson Papers. Part of Wilson's letter to Phelan is printed in Ray S. Baker, *Woodrow Wilson: Life and Letters* (Garden City, 1927–1939), IV, 78.

[9] Anthony Caminetti to Bryan, April 6, 1913, SD 811.52/67; April 17, 1913, SD 811.52/69; George E. Mowry, *The California Progressives* (Berkeley, 1951), 88–89, and *Theodore Roosevelt and the Progressive Movement* (Madison, 1946), 92–94; James D. Phelan, "Japanese Question from a California Standpoint," *The Independent*, June 19, 1913, pp. 1439–1442.

[10] Franklin K. Lane to Wilson, April 7, 1913, Wilson Papers.

[11] Phelan to F. K. Lane, telegram, April 7, 1913, *ibid.*

[12] New York *Tribune*, April 30, 1913.

ally objected on March 5 against the action impending in both Washington and California. He heard of threats to cancel Japan's arrangements for exhibits at the forthcoming San Francisco exposition.[13] In mass meetings in Tokyo, demands were made that ships be sent to California and that Japan seize the Philippines and Hawaii.

A. Bailly-Blanchard, the American chargé in Tokyo, in receipt of a flood of protests, warned Bryan that the Japanese foreign minister, Baron Nobuaki Makino, with "deepest emotion," had asserted that he had no recourse "but to make a solemn appeal to the American Government to take suitable steps after *further* consideration to prevent such a development of affairs as might lead to very serious misunderstanding between the two peoples" and appealed to the president and secretary of state "to use their good offices to prevent unfair and discriminate treatment of the Japanese." [14] On April 11, after discussing the problem with the cabinet, Makino cabled Viscount Chinda to

> impress upon the President and Secretary of State that the [California] measures are clearly contrary to the spirit of good relations and good intercourse which Japan has endeavored to foster and encourage, and you will strongly urge them to take such steps as may be necessary to prevent the proposed bills from becoming law. You will say that the Japanese Government cannot but regard this question as the most serious and important.

As Makino told Blanchard in person, Japanese public opinion was deeply aroused, and the enactment of the bills would be prejudicial to the friendship of the two countries and very injurious to their important commercial relations.[15]

These warnings and threats impelled Bryan to grasp Governor Johnson's suggestion for direct contact and to appeal to him to avoid offending the Japanese. The president, he told Johnson, intended to

[13] Chinda to Bryan, April 6, 1913, SD 811.52.207; New York *Times*, April 9, 1913.

[14] A. Bailly-Blanchard to Bryan, April 11, 1913, SD 811.52/40, and April 12, 1913, SD 811.52/47. The state of Japanese public opinion is described in these and other letters from Bailly-Blanchard to Bryan; in letters from individual Japanese and Christian-Japanese groups, as in K. Okura to Bryan, April 14, 1913, Baron Shibusa to Bryan, April 30, 1913, Viscount Kanelo to Bryan, received April 24, 1913, State Department Papers; Christian Endeavorers of Kyoto to Bryan, April 27, 1913, SD 811.52/37; and in such newspapers as the New York *Times*. Minority groups in the United States, like the Negroes, Italians, and Spaniards, defended the Japanese.

[15] Minister for foreign affairs to the Japanese ambassador, received April 11, 1913, SD 811.52/50; Bailly-Blanchard to Bryan, two telegrams, April 14, 1913, SD 811.52/73 and /74.

respect to the utmost the unquestioned prerogatives of his government; he himself wished he would

> allow this Department as long a time as possible under the constitutional provisions of the State for the consideration of the measure in view of the treaty obligations of the Government, so that, if necessary, the questions and the possible embarrassments involved may be laid before you before the measure becomes law by your signature.[16]

Johnson and certain state leaders wished to be conciliatory, but they were nonetheless determined to have their way on the land ownership matter. "The fundamental basis of all legislation upon this subject . . . has been, and is, race undesirability," declared the state attorney general, U. S. Webb,[17] and on April 15 the California Assembly, by a vote of 60 to 15, passed a bill barring all persons "ineligible to citizenship" from owning land and discriminating only against corporations controlled by aliens ineligible for citizenship.[18]

Unlike Theodore Roosevelt, who had brandished his Big Stick at California when San Francisco had proposed to segregate Oriental school children in 1906,[19] both Wilson and Bryan believed in state rights. In 1906 Bryan had upheld the right of California to control "matters purely local," and the Democratic national platform of 1912 contained a strong plank denouncing the usurpations by the federal government. Rather than use federal power to coerce a state, they would use friendship to conciliate both California and Japan. On April 14 Bryan furnished to Chinda and Wilson copies of the measure passed by California's assembly and favorably reported by a senate committee,[20] and for several days he carried on a telegraphic campaign to persuade Governor Johnson to obtain wording in the final bill that would not offend the Japanese.[21]

Unknown to Bryan, Henry White had had a long talk with Chinda in Washington early in April and then appealed to Roosevelt to use his influence to restrain California. Roosevelt telegraphed Johnson

[16] Bryan to Hiram Johnson, April 10, 1913, Wilson Papers.

[17] Ichihashi, *Japanese in the United States*, 275.

[18] Hiram Johnson to Bryan, telegram, April 15, 1913, SD 811.52/53, and letter of April 16, 1913, Wilson Papers.

[19] Thomas A. Bailey, *Theodore Roosevelt and the Japanese-American Crisis* (Stanford, 1934), 90.

[20] Bryan to Chinda, April 14, 1913, SD 811.52/46.

[21] Hiram Johnson to Bryan, telegrams, April 14, 15, 1913, SD 811.52/48; Bryan to Hiram Johnson, April 15, 1913, *ibid*. Bryan also sent to Wilson a copy of the District of Columbia law of 1887. Bryan to Wilson, *ca*. April 15, 1913, Wilson Papers.

on April 20 that state laws of an international character raised questions with which the federal government must necessarily deal and that in this instance, as in 1906, California's congressional delegation should "bring the matter promptly before the Administration and insist on whatever measure of relief the needs of California's people demand." He added that this was the course he had followed in 1906, "and I then as President kept friendly relations with Japan and yet secured the exclusion of the Japanese laborers as the people of California requested and met completely the then needs of California." [22] He might have put it better by saying that he had delayed rather than settled the problem.[23]

Meanwhile Bryan told Wilson that the District of Columbia law of 1887 was a "find" whose wording was inoffensive and also sent him an Illinois law that Wilson believed would provide a "valid and sensible solution" if adopted by California. On April 18 Bryan wrote to Governor Johnson that "the President recognizes the right of a state to legislate on the subject of land tenure" but that recognition should be given to the "international character" of such legislation. The friendly relations existing between Japan and the United States should be preserved, and the president

> very respectfully, but most earnestly, advises against the use of the words "ineligible to citizenship." He asks that you bring this view to the attention of the legislators. He believes the Senate bill as telegraphed to the Department of State is greatly to be preferred. That bill limited ownership to citizens and to those who had declared their intention of becoming citizens.[24]

And on April 20 he asked Yachichiro Yamashita, the Japanese boy he had helped through the University of Nebraska, to "urge Japanese to await final action before judging." [25]

Aware that Wilson would not interfere and eager to make political capital, the California senators dumped the bill favored by Bryan and Wilson in favor of the Webb bill, which used the very words they had been asked to avoid but extended the prohibition of land owner-

---

[22] Theodore Roosevelt to Hiram Johnson, April 20, 1913; Allan Nevins, *Henry White: Thirty Years of American Diplomacy* (New York, 1930), 316–317.

[23] Henry F. Pringle, *Theodore Roosevelt: A Biography* (New York, 1931), 412.

[24] Bryan to Hiram Johnson, April 18, 1913, Wilson Papers; New York *Times*, April 22, 1913.

[25] Bryan to Yamashita, April 20, 1913, SD 811.52/61A. For Yamashita, see my *William Jennings Bryan. I. Political Evangelist, 1860–1908* (Lincoln, 1964), 362.

ship from individuals to corporations in which the majority of stockholders were "aliens ineligible to citizenship." In another long and strong appeal from Wilson, including a request that Bryan be received,[26] the president said:

> ... If [the people, the Governor, and the legislature of California] deem it necessary to exclude all aliens who have not declared their intention to become citizens from the privileges of land ownership, they can do so along lines already followed in the laws of many of the other states and of many foreign countries, including Japan herself. Invidious discrimination will inevitably draw in question the treaty obligations of the Government of the United States. I register my very earnest and respectful protest against discrimination in this case.[27]

Governor Johnson replied that his state was acting within its rights, that the law would not violate any treaty obligations, and that a visit by Bryan would be welcome.[28]

Stating publicly that perhaps Governor Johnson was playing politics,[29] as Josephus Daniels and others had asserted in cabinet meeting, a disturbed Wilson consulted his cabinet again on April 22. Was a state bound by treaty? he asked.[30] Bryan talked about the issue at some length, then asked if it would be possible to have the Japanese matter submitted to a referendum in California. With the state's attitude so well known, the cabinet disapproved. Wilson then asked Bryan if he would go to California. Bryan replied that he was not soliciting the long trip but that "he had but one spirit in coming into the Cabinet and that was to help and be ready to do anything that the members of the Cabinet and the President thought he ought to undertake. His idea was that nobody should go unless invited by the California people." [31] Daniels demurred at Bryan's going, saying that

[26] "Anomalously enough, a state rights President was asking for an invitation to send a state rights secretary of state across the continent to plead with California" (Bailey, "California, Japan, and the Alien Land Legislation of 1913," 42).

[27] Quoted in Japanese ambassador to the secretary of state, Nov. 25, 1914, SD 811.52/271; Wilson telegrams to the governor, the president of the senate, and the speaker of the house of the state of California, April 22, 1913, Wilson Papers; also printed in New York *Times*, April 24, 1913, and New York *Tribune*, April 24, 1913.

[28] Hiram Johnson to Wilson, telegram April 22, 1913, Wilson Papers.

[29] New York *World*, April 24, 1913.

[30] See Edward S. Corwin, *National Supremacy. Treaty Power vs. State Power* (Gloucester, Mass., 1965 [reprint of 1913]), and *The Constitution and World Organization* (Princeton, 1946), chap. III; Harley Notter, *The Origins of the Foreign Policy of Woodrow Wilson* (Baltimore, 1937), 237.

[31] Josephus Daniels Diary, Josephus Daniels Papers, Division of Manuscripts, Library of Congress (entry of April 22, 1913); David F. Houston, *Eight Years in Wilson's Cabinet* (Garden City, 1926), I, 60.

he would "waste his time." Secretary of War Lindley M. Garrison also objected, stating that Wilson would establish a precedent of "invasion of 'state rights.' " Lane, however, said that Bryan was popular in California and that "if any man had to go, Bryan was the one." Wilson asserted that it was his "duty" to put all the information available before Johnson and that, if the governor preferred political stunts to statesmanship, he must take the responsibility.[32] Actually, Bryan went on what he knew was an impossible task, for he told Daniels, "Wish me well, my friend, in what promises to be the most thankless task I ever undertook." [33]

Japanese had long looked upon California with special concern; anything that tended to damage their status therein caused "a lively emotion or motion," an American with a Japanese wife wrote to Wilson.[34] On the other hand, thirty-four anti-Japanese bills had been introduced in the California legislature between March and May, 1913, and California's organized farmer and labor groups solidly approved of the alien land bill under consideration. The three leading parties—Democratic, Republican, and Progressive Republican—heartily approved of it. A large majority of both houses were pledged to it, the progressive administration had nothing to lose by embarrassing Wilson, Wilson had no power of patronage with which to hold California in line, and California Democrats had the choice of repudiating their platform pledges or Wilson.[35]

Moreover, the mayor of San Francisco had gone to see President Roosevelt in Washington to learn of the national government's attitude toward the Japanese agitation of 1906, and in some quarters Bryan's going to California to seek the views of a state was deemed "not altogether consonant with National dignity." [36] "We do not believe that the president of the United States will allow the citizens of this sover[e]ign state of California . . . to be humiliated by the ag-

---

[32] Daniels Diary, May 13, 1913.

[33] Josephus Daniels, *The Wilson Era. Years of Peace, 1910–1917* (Chapel Hill, 1946), 162. Roosevelt had wisely used a Californian, Secretary Metcalf, to investigate the San Francisco situation.

[34] James S. de Benneville to Wilson, May 5, 1913, SD 811.52/37.

[35] Editorial, "Secretary Bryan in California," *Harper's Weekly*, May 3, 1913, p. 3; William Inglis, "Playing with Dynamite," *ibid.*, pp. 7, 26; editorial, "California and the Japanese," *American Review of Reviews*, XLVII (1913), 648.

[36] Lawrence Abbot to the secretary of the interior, April 25, 1913, Wilson Papers; editorial, "Mr. Bryan's Mission to California," *The Outlook*, May 3, 1913, p. 7.

gression of any foreign power," one Californian wrote to Wilson.[37] "Build up a big navy and have it ready for instant use," advised another.[38] And, although Speaker Champ Clark refused to criticize Bryan's mission to California, he noted that "to my mind California is within her rights in fixing whatever reasonable restrictions she deems necessary upon the ownership of land by aliens." [39] Finally, by directing Bryan not to advise the Californians but proferring advice himself, Wilson made Bryan's success improbable.[40] Indeed, his going may have strengthened the determination of the Progressive Republican legislature to resist federal intervention at the hands of state-rights Democrats like Bryan and Wilson.[41]

Soon after arriving in Sacramento on April 28, where he was a house guest of Governor and Mrs. Johnson, Bryan addressed an executive joint session of the legislature. He did not approve of secrecy in government, he said, but on this occasion it was warranted because he could speak "with frankness not otherwise allowable, and also take matters up in a confidential way." Wilson desired a solution to the problem, he went on, that would please California yet work "the least hardship on anyone." He was aware that the assimilation of the races, not land ownership, was the crux of the question, but he held the question of immigration to be an independent one with which he would not deal. He pleaded for delay in legislation or for a bill that would not offend the Japanese. If California could wait two years, it should "set up an investigating committee and avoid . . . unfriendliness." Meantime, California could study the less offensively worded statutes of Illinois and of the District of Columbia and follow one of them if it must. At all costs it should avoid using the words "ineligible to citizenship." He asked:

Who is able to look into the future and tell us what it may mean to do that which may be regarded as a declaration to the world of inferiority, that which cannot but wound the pride of a nation that has made wonder-

[37] Thomas Jefferson Hammer to Wilson, Jan. 29, 1913, SD 811.52/37.

[38] Ernest T. Carter to Wilson, Oct. 23, 1913, *ibid.* Wilson's papers contain angry denunciations of California's proposed action from such minority groups as Negroes; religious groups such as the Christian Endeavorers; and, from Tokyo, the America and Japan Fellowship Association. Letters and telegrams, *ibid.*, April 27–30, 1913.

[39] William J. Bryan, *The Commoner,* May 9, 1913.

[40] Ray S. Baker, "Memorandum of an interview with John Basset Moore, November 9, 1928," Ray S. Baker Papers, Division of Manuscripts, Library of Congress. Incidents of similar nature were among the reasons Moore resigned in 1914.

[41] Bailey, "California, Japan, and the Alien Land Law of 1913," 42–43.

ful progress, a nation which is our friend and ought to remain our friend?"[42]

The session lasted two and a half hours, after which Bryan spent two more hours answering questions. He reported his progress to Wilson and asked him for his opinion on how next to proceed. For his pains he was rewarded by the admonition not "to sanction particular statutes or forms of legislation" but to restrict himself to advice "along general lines" and to remember that "we are acting in a merely advisory character and not undertaking to settle beforehand questions of law or policy that may subsequently arise."[43] Even as he telegraphed, Roosevelt wired Johnson a criticism of the Wilson administration for trying "to restrain California without itself providing a remedy."[44]

On the next day the California Senate responded to Bryan's pleading with a modified bill that provided that all aliens "eligible to citizenship" could own land and that other aliens could own land as prescribed by treaty.[45] Wilson wired Johnson via Bryan that such a bill "would involve an appeal to the courts on question of treaty rights and bring on what might be long and delicate litigation."[46] Bryan confronted the legislature again, this time with a message from Wilson stating that the phrase "eligible to citizenship" was as offensive to the Japanese as the words "ineligible to citizenship" and pleaded that he be given an opportunity to settle the question by diplomacy.[47] Sensing that Bryan was winning some Progressive leaders to his view, Johnson delivered an impassioned defense of the right of the state to pass a law similar to that enacted without protest in eight other states.[48] Bryan was unwilling to discuss aspects of the

[42] Bryan to Wilson, April 28, 1913, SD 811.52/217; Bryan to Wilson, April 29, 1913 enclosing speech of April 28, 1913, Wilson Papers; "Minutes of the Executive Joint Conference of the Senate and Assembly of the State of California, April 28, 1913," copy in Bryan Papers; William Jennings Bryan and Mary Baird Bryan, *The Memoirs of William Jennings Bryan* (Philadelphia, 1925), 366–367.

[43] Bryan to Wilson, April 29, 1913, Wilson to Bryan, telegram, April 29, 1913, Wilson Papers.

[44] Roosevelt to Johnson, telegram, April 28, 1913, cited in Nevins, *White*, 317.

[45] Bryan to Wilson, April 30, 1913, Wilson Papers; New York *Times*, April 30, 1913; New York *World*, April 30, 1913; Franklin Hichborn, *Story of the Session of the California Legislature of 1913* (San Francisco, 1913), 255–256.

[46] Wilson to Bryan, April 30, 1913, Wilson Papers.

[47] Bryan to Wilson, May 1, 2, 1913, SD Papers; Bryan to Wilson May 1, 3, 1913, Wilson Papers; San Francisco *Examiner*, April 30, 1913; New York *Tribune*, April 30, 1913; New York *Times*, May 4, 5, 1913.

[48] New York *Times*, April 29, 1913; Hichborn, *California Legislature of 1913*, 257.

legislation involving the race problem and asked Wilson how long he should remain in California.[49]

Meanwhile, the Curtin resolution, which would amend the Webb bill to give the administration time to settle the Japanese problem by diplomacy, was defeated in the senate by an almost strict party vote, and Bryan's third and final plea fell on deaf ears.[50] On May 3 the legislature approved the Webb bill as amended to enable aliens eligible to citizenship to own any property and provided that aliens ineligible to citizenship could lease agricultural land for a period of no longer than three years, with only one Democrat in each house voting against the measure. This was within the letter, if not in the spirit, of the Treaty of 1911, which provided that the Japanese could own residential and commercial properties but did not guarantee the privilege of owning agricultural land and put the onus for the limitation upon the federal rather than the state government.[51] The vote was 35 to 2 in the senate and 72 to 3 in the assembly. That Bryan's influence had nothing to do with the amendment providing for lease is clear from his wiring Wilson that "The nearly unanimous vote shows Governor back of bill." The Democrats had tried to delay action, he added, and then to amend the bill when they found they could not change it. He himself must now leave, for to remain after the bill had passed "would in my judgement do no good and might irritate," yet he hoped that Governor Johnson would delay signing the bill until he reached Washington, and Wilson asked the governor not to act until he had spoken with Bryan and had had time to consider the bill before taking "final action." [52] Johnson told Bryan that he would allow a "reasonable" time to elapse before signing the bill so that Wilson could study it, comment on it, and submit it to the Japanese ambassador.[53] He had thirty days to sign if the legislature remained in session, ten days if it adjourned.

At 9 p.m. on May 3 Bryan boarded the train for his return to Washington. As he traveled, ex-President William Howard Taft wrote to Elihu Root:

... When I saw that Wilson was sending Bryan to California to stop the

[49] Bryan to Wilson, May 1, 1913, Wilson Papers.

[50] Bryan to Wilson, telegram, May 2, 1913, *ibid.*

[51] Bailey, "California, Japan, and the Alien Land Legislation of 1913," 43–45.

[52] Bryan to Wilson, telegrams, May 3, 4, 1913, Wilson to Hiram Johnson, May 6, 1913, Wilson Papers.

[53] Bryan to Wilson, May 1, 1913, *ibid.*

demagogue and the fool performances of the California legislature under that arch-Demagogue and fraud Johnson, I laughed to myself that Bryan should finally find himself in a position of responsibility where he was being criticized instead of being the critic, and I have enjoyed the thought ever since.... However I think that Wilson has gotten off on the right foot.[54]

Bryan would have disagreed with Taft, for en route he wrote to his brother, Charles, that he had been on a

very delicate mission and I think we were fortunate in escaping without more friction than was manifested.... I think that my going has served a very useful purpose, although no concessions were made by the state government. Japan appreciates the efforts that were made, and for that reason it will be easier for us to deal with the Japanese government.[55]

On April 29 Chinda had called on Counselor Moore to repeat Japan's protests against the impending California law and ask for a private interview with Wilson.[56] Moore temporized as to a secret conference. On May 1 Chinda called on Moore to warn that his government could not accept the California law, to intimate that the Wilson administration "had perhaps not gone so far as President Roosevelt did at the time [of] the school question to prevent undesirable action in California," and to ask that Wilson have the law declared invalid with "prompt and decisive action." [57] A week later, using language as strong as peacetime diplomacy allowed, Chinda made an "urgent and explicit" protest that

[54] Taft to Root, May 5, 1913, Elihu Root Papers, Division of Manuscripts, Library of Congress.

[55] Bryan to Charles W. Bryan, May 5, 1913, Silas Bryan Papers. (These papers were made available to the author through the courtesy of Silas Bryan, son of Charles.)

[56] J. B. Moore, "Memorandum of an interview held with the Japanese Ambassador on the afternoon of April 29, 1913," Wilson Papers.

[57] J. B. Moore to Wilson, May 1, 1913, *ibid.* On May 2, Roosevelt sent Henry White copies of his earlier telegrams to Hiram Johnson but said he would not publish them because "the attitude of President Wilson and Mr. Bryan has been hopelessly weak, so as to render it quite impossible to stand up for them. Wilson's duty, according to my view, was perfectly clear. He should in the first place have asserted the power of the Federal Government to act as regards all treaties, and in the next place acknowledge its duty to safeguard California's interests. The Japanese must not, as a class, own agricultural land." He admitted that the task of Wilson and Bryan was more difficult than his in 1906 because "With their usual fatuity, Taft and Knox, surrendered the proper position by the treaty [of 1911]...for they abandoned our right to keep out Japanese laborers.... Wilson has told California that it was all right, but tried to coax it not to exercise its rights, and offered no adequate remedy." He concluded that "Well! grape juice diplomacy under Wilson does not bid fair to be much better than dollar diplomacy under Taft." Roosevelt to White, May 2, 1913, Nevins, *White,* 317–318.

the act in question is essentially unfair and discriminatory, and it is impossible to ignore the fact that it was primarily directed against my countrymen. [The measure was] unjust and inequitable ... prejudicial to the existing rights of Japanese subjects ... inconsistent with the provisions of the treaty actually in force ... and opposed to the spirit and fundamental principles of amity and good understanding.[58]

On May 8 Chinda had sent Bryan an outline of the formal complaints he would make. The character of Bryan's intended reply may be gauged from the pencilled memorandum he made on the communication:

The federal government will consider any claim for damages that may arise in the actual enforcement of the law and, as far as the administration can (remembering that the co-operation of Congress is necessary), save the subjects from pecuniary loss. The federal government will facilitate, insofar as it can, recourse to the courts and hasten final adjudication.[59]

Wilson asked Bryan to have Chinda use less forceful language. Bryan tried. While Moore prepared a reply to the note, Wilson on May 13 read it to the cabinet. Its language was "very strong," he said, and some of its statements "unfair." Although neither he nor Bryan noted any hostile intentions on the part of Japan, he refused to have it published.[60]

Meanwhile, America's leading military men, who knew how weak the United States was in the Pacific and sensed the possibility of war, directed all army and navy commanders in the United States, Hawaii, and the Philippines to stand by for orders[61] while the Joint Board of the Army and Navy met to decide what to do. Admiral Bradley A. Fiske, aide for operations, wrote to Secretary of the Navy Daniels that "war is not only possible, but even probable," [62] and the joint board advised that three American gunboats in the Yangtze River be sent to aid the puny Asiatic Fleet in the defense of Fort Corregidor in Manila.[63] Secretary of War Garrison asked Daniels to endorse the joint board's advice. When Daniels refused, saying that these ship movements would excite the Japanese without appreciably enhanc-

[58] The Japanese ambassador to the secretary of state, May 9, 1913, SD 811.52/164.

[59] Chinda to Bryan, May 8, 1913, SD 811.52/164, with Bryan's memorandum attached.

[60] Daniels Diary, May 13, 1913; Houston, *Eight Years,* I, 65.

[61] New York *World,* May 16, 1913.

[62] B. A. Fiske to Daniels, May 14, 1913, Daniels Papers.

[63] Daniels Diary, May 15, 1913.

ing the protection of the Philippines, both men proceeded to the White House. Wilson, infuriated by American newspaper accounts of war preparations, vetoed the ship movements but said that the cabinet would discuss the proposal next day, which they did for two hours.[64] When Garrison upheld the joint board and indicated that its decision were of more value than those of the cabinet, Bryan, just returned from California,

> got red in the face and ... thundered out that army and navy officers could not be trusted to say what we should or should not do, till we actually got into war; that we were discussing not how to wage war, but how not to get into war, and that if ships were moved about in the East, it would incite war.[65]

William C. Redfield, William G. McAdoo, and Joseph McReynolds supported Garrison; David F. Houston, Lane, William B. Wilson, and Daniels upheld Bryan. Quipping that he would go on other missions if the president sent him but that he would not have time to attend to the duties of his office, Bryan left at that point to quell a revolt in the Pennsylvania Assembly at Harrisburg.[66]

On May 15 Bryan wrote to Wilson after a visit by Chinda that Chinda had been "personally more disturbed than he has appeared to be at any previous time" and that he himself was pleased to learn that Wilson supported his ideas on how to deal with Japan.[67] Wilson later told Daniels that the joint board looked at problems from the military viewpoint, whereas he and Bryan sought a diplomatic solution. He assumed personal responsibility for keeping the ships in the Yangtze and told the press that rumors of war preparations were false and that he sought a policy that would mollify Japan.[68] To help down the rumors of war preparations in the United States, Bryan told Chinda that the recommendations by the joint board had not been

[64] *Ibid.*, May 13, 15, 1913; William C. Redfield, *With Cabinet and Congress* (Garden City, 1924), 71.

[65] Houston, *Eight Years,* I, 66.

[66] Daniels Diary, May 13, 16, 1913.

[67] Bryan to Wilson, May 15, 1913, Wilson Papers.

[68] New York *Times,* May 17, 1913; Redfield, *With Cabinet and Congress,* 72. When the joint board protested the president's decision and Fiske urged Daniels to present a memorandum to Wilson recommending that all destroyers and torpedo boats on the California coast be sent to Hawaii, Daniels did so. Wilson told Daniels that he had made his decision on ship movements, that the joint board had no right to discuss the matter further or to seek to change a decision already made, and asked Daniels to tell the board that "if this should occur again, there will be no General or Joint Boards. They will be abolished." Daniels Diary, May 13, 17, 1913.

approved and directed the newly arrived American ambassador to Japan, George W. Guthrie, to categorically deny any such action, thereby assuring Japan that no warlike actions would be taken while negotiations for peace were pending.[69]

On May 18, by arrangement, Chinda called personally on Bryan. Chinda was suave and diplomatic in his language, but his hands and voice shook with tenseness as he presented first his government's compliments and then its complaints. Bryan sought to set him at ease by telling of his pleasant visit to Japan and admiration for the Japanese people, but Chinda would not be mollified. The name of Japan had been aspersed and what Bryan said did not restore its dignity. Bryan replied that dignity was not involved; it was merely an economic matter which could be resolved if the California Japanese would resort to the courts. He refused to guarantee action on the part of the federal government against California or to give any hope that the United States would permit the naturalization of Japanese but would consider submitting the problem for investigation by a special international commission if Japan would accept a cooling-off treaty. The discussion proceeded for some time, with neither man retreating from his stand. Chinda asked if the California law would hold. Bryan said it would. Chinda then arose and said, "I suppose, Mr. Secretary, this decision is final." Bryan arose, extended his hand, and said in some of the most inspired phraseology he thought he had ever devised, "There is nothing final between friends, my dear Ambassador." Chinda sat down again, and at the end of the hour-and-a-half session a proposal was adopted to reach an agreement in which the dignity of Japan would be restored without interfering with California's economics.[70]

After the California legislature adjourned, Governor Johnson had ten days to act on the Webb bill. Despite repeated urgings from Wilson that he be permitted to respond to Chinda's protests and handle the problem by diplomacy, Johnson spoke of the "menace" of the Japanese. "We believe we are within our legal and our moral right, and that we are doing only what is imperatively demanded for the protection and preservation of our State," he wrote to Wilson. Moreover, the bill was in accord with the Treaty of 1911.[71] Finally, say-

[69] *The Commoner,* June 6, 1913; Daniels, *The Wilson Era,* 167–168.

[70] Bryan to Wilson, May 18, 1913, Wilson Papers; Daniels Diary, May 20, 1913; Bryan, *Memoirs,* 367.

[71] Hiram Johnson to Wilson, May 4, 1913, Wilson Papers.

ing that "We have prevented the Japanese from driving the root of their civilization deep into California soil," he signed the bill, on May 19.[72] The Japanese ministry appreciated Bryan's efforts and sought to "control public opinion and keep public calm," Chargé Blanchard cabled to Bryan. Japan complained less about the violation of the letter than of the spirit of the Treaty of 1911, spoke of their case as "equitable" rather than "technical," and indicated that they would continue to press for relief by a special treaty or by the grant of the right to Japanese to acquire American citizenship.[73] But, to mollify Japan while contending that the California law was not in contravention of the treaty, called for the full use of Bryan's great conciliatory powers, particularly when the Hearst press was running scare headlines about a possible war with Japan and some magazine writers patronizingly patted him on the back for a good try but said his mission to California had been hopeless. Wilson adopted Bryan's proposal to recommend to Congress that money be appropriated to compensate any Japanese citizen if the California law caused him financial loss, and Bryan directed the American embassy in Tokyo to emphasize:

> the extraordinary efforts made by the Washington Government to prevent passage of law. Explain freedom of action allowed states under our constitution; advise restraint and calmness. Suggest that nothing is final between friends and express confidence that a satisfactory solution can be found for all questions if the parties approach the subject with patience and in the right spirit.[74]

Moreover, Japan should be assured that the United States did not intend to strengthen its defenses in the Pacific. Later Bryan told Secretary Houston that there would be no war with Japan, for "I've seen the Japanese Ambassador and I'm letting the old man down easy." [75]

The formal American reply to the Japanese note of May 9, prepared by Wilson, Bryan, and Moore, contained the expressions Bryan had already conveyed to Chinda and cabled to Japan but also stressed that the California law was "not political in its spirit and object but

[72] San Francisco *Examiner,* May 4, 1913; New York *Times,* May 4, 1913; *The Commoner,* May 9, 16, 1913.

[73] Bailly-Blanchard to Bryan, May 17, 1913, SD 811.52/117.

[74] Bryan to Bailly-Blanchard, May 18, 26, 1913, SD 811.52/117.

[75] Houston, *Eight Years,* I, 67.

wholly economic" and added that Japanese subjects adversely affected by it might appeal for redress to the federal courts.[76] Both the Japanese reply to this note, on June 4, and an *aide-mémoire* of explanation contained expressions of unhappiness. The Japanese saw the California law as "intentionally racially discriminatory," without economic basis, and in violation of privileges granted by treaty. With reference to Bryan's proposal that the Japanese in California could have recourse to the federal courts, the Japanese asserted that "the wrong complained of is directed against my countrymen as a nation" and that Japan had diplomatic relations not with the state of California but with the United States.[77]

On June 19 Bryan summarized for Wilson his ideas on how to reply to Japan's note of June 4. He would not take up the issue of naturalization, he would "recommend compensation in case actual pecuniary loss is caused by the law when put into operation," but he was not willing to declare the law either unconstitutional or in violation of the Treaty of 1911.[78] After talking with Counselor Moore, he sent a revised draft[79] and on July 3 Wilson replied:

> I am sending you with this the note which Mr. Moore prepared in reply to the last Japanese note, I think it is admirable. I do not see how it can be answered.
>
> At the same time, I am perfectly willing that the amendments you suggested to Mr. Moore should be embodied, particularly the one regarding the purchase by the Government of the lands now owned by Japanese which they are willing, or desire, to sell.
>
> I have some doubt as to the omission of the passage concerning naturalization. I would not like to seem to avoid or dodge *any* of the points made in the last Japanese note, and Mr. Moore's reply to the portion concerning naturalization seems to me quite as excellent and quite as conclusive as the rest of the paper.[80]

[76] The secretary of state to the Japanese ambassador, May 19, 1913, SD 811.52/164. The first and final drafts of the note are in the Wilson Papers. The date of the note was the same as that of the signing of the alien land law by Governor Johnson. See "California Alien Land Tenure Law," *American Journal of International Law,* VIII (1914), Supplement, 177–179; *The Commoner,* May 23, 1913.

[77] Japanese ambassador to the secretary of state, June 4, 1913, SD 811.52/165; "Aide Memoire in Explanation and Support of Viscount Chinda's Notes of May 9 and June 4, 1913," July 3, 1913, SD 811.52/181; editorial comment, "The American-Japanese Discussions Relating to the Land Tenure Law of California," *American Journal of International Law,* VIII (1914), 571–578.

[78] Bryan to Wilson, June 19, 1913, SD 811.52/295a.

[79] Bryan to Wilson, July 1, 1913, SD 811.52/295b.

[80] Wilson to Bryan, July 3, 1913, SD 811.52/296, enclosing Moore's "Reply to the Aide Memoire presented by . . . Chinda on July 3, 1913."

Bryan and Moore studied some supplemental matter Japan forwarded late in June and considered it while working on the final draft of the American reply.[81] Meantime the Japanese began to reveal a definitely conciliatory attitude. On June 28 the Japanese ambassador revealed a friendly spirit by signing the Bryan protocols extending the Japanese-American arbitration treaty, and the emperor granted a very cordial reception to the new American ambassador, Guthrie. Late in June or early in July both Bryan and Moore were invited to meet a special Japanese commission at dinner at the Japanese embassy. Although he did not disclose what transpired, Moore later asserted that "it was one of the most significant incidents of the entire transaction." [82]

On July 16, with additional help from Moore and Wilson, Bryan presented to Japan a detailed reply, again denying that the California law was an expression of "any national discriminatory policy" or that it violated the Treaty of 1911 and again offering to compensate any Japanese subject for loss sustained by its operation.[83] However, the unhappy Japanese foreign minister, Makino, continued to protest against the "unjust and obnoxious" California statute which was "discriminatory" and "mortifying" to Japan and "disregardful of the national susceptibilities of the Japanese people." The California law was "clearly indicative of racial antagonisms"; no justification for such enactment could be found in Bryan's assertion that it was "the emanation of economic conditions." His government, he concluded, could not consider the question settled "so long as the existing state of things is permitted to continue." [84] Henceforth,

[81] Telegram received by the Japanese embassy on June 30, 1913 from the minister of foreign affairs, SD 811.52/181; Bryan to Wilson, June 30, 1913, SD 811.52/165; Bryan to Wilson, June 19, 1913, SD 811.52/295a; Bryan to Wilson, July 3, 1913, SD 811.52/296; Bryan to Wilson, June 21, July 1, 1913, Wilson Papers.

[82] Moore to R. S. Baker, June 24, 1929, R. S. Baker Papers. Moore volunteered this information after reading at Baker's request what he had written on the California question for his *Woodrow Wilson: Life and Letters.*

[83] Bryan to Wilson, June 19, July 1, 1913, Wilson to Bryan, July 3, 1913, Wilson Papers; the secretary of state to the Japanese ambassador, July 16, 1913, SD 811.52/165; *aide-mémoire* to the Japanese embassy, July 16, 1916, SD 811.52/181.

[84] The Japanese minister for foreign affairs to the Japanese ambassador, Aug. 22, 1913, SD 811.52/190 (received at the state department Aug. 26, 1913); "A New Japanese Note," *American Review of Reviews,* XLVIII (1913), 294. The note of July 16 pointed out that the Treaty of 1911 was silent on the question of ownership of agricultural land and that until this time Japan's attitude toward reciprocal landownership had been that: "In return for the rights of landownership which are granted Japanese by laws of the various States of the United States the Imperial Government will by liberal interpretation of the law be prepared to grant landownership to American citizens from all the States, reserving for the future, however, the right of maintaining the condition of

Bryan talked with Chinda but did not exchange additional informal notes with him.

On August 19, Japan proposed the writing of a new treaty in which, in part, the United States would have confirmed those land titles acquired by Japanese subjects in California before passage of the alien land law.[85] Bryan's sense of justice and fair play moved him, and he was willing to accept such a treaty. "If the alien land laws are desired they should be made to apply to all aliens alike. It is not fair for a state to endanger international peace by acting independently of the rest of the states on a matter that concerns other nations," he wrote to Wilson.[86] But Wilson thought otherwise, and Bryan had the unpleasant task of telling Chinda that Wilson would not recommend to the senate a treaty that limited the rights of the states to legislate on racial and national distinctions and also that such a treaty at the time was a political impossibility.[87]

However, the Japanese had also suggested a convention which would in the future confer the mutual right to persons and corporations of land ownership on the most-favored-nation principle but not affect existing laws in either country.[88] Busy with tariff reform, Wilson could not study the convention in detail but approved of it in theory.[89] Bryan approved too and went over it carefully with E. T. Williams and other aides in the far eastern division of the department of state and with Chinda. But he questioned how the senate would react to it and was particularly unwilling to enter into any agreement without discussing it with the senate foreign relations committee, which had given him a great deal of trouble over his treaties with Colombia and Nicaragua. When Wilson refused to risk a Democratic division on the proposal but stated that he would submit it without recommendation when it could be done "safely" and "ascertain what is possible," Bryan explained the situation to Chinda, who understood, and Guthrie explained to the Japanese minister for foreign affairs, who acknowledged that the senate's failure to confirm

reciprocity with respect to the separate States." The Japanese ambassador to the secretary of state, Feb. 21, 1911, *Papers Relating to the Foreign Relations of the United States, 1913*, 626–627.

[85] Guthrie to Bryan, Aug. 19, 1913, SD Papers; telegram from the minister of foreign affairs, Tokyo, received Aug. 19, 1913, given by Bryan to Chinda, copy in Wilson Papers.

[86] Bryan to Wilson, Sept. 17, 30, 1913, Wilson Papers.

[87] Bryan to Wilson, Sept. 17, 1913, *ibid.*

[88] Copy of convention, *ca.* Sept. 15, 1913, SD 811.52/194.

[89] Bryan to Wilson, Sept. 9, 1913, SD 811.52/207a; Wilson to Bryan, Sept. 11, 1913, Wilson Papers.

the convention would be accepted by Japan as "unavoidable."[90] However, Makino's failure to win satisfaction from the United States was an important ingredient in toppling the ministry in the elections held in September, 1913, and public opinion in Japan continued bitter against the United States. Hypersensitive to any hint of inferiority, the Japanese were using the California law to oppose not only the United States, but Christianity. As Guthrie told Bryan, irate Japanese said that when Americans spoke of "the fatherhood of God" and the "brotherhood of man" they meant only "white men." Guthrie also noted that the California act caused Japan to lose face in the Orient and expressed his belief that the act was unconstitutional because in contravention of the non-discrimination clause of the Fourteenth Amendment.[91] In turn, a San Franciscan wrote to Commissioner Caminetti,

> We cannot compete with [the Japanese], as they live on about half what the white man does and breed like rabbits or rats, and it is only a question of a generation or two when they will dominate California as they now do Hawaii.[92]

When Congress in January, 1914, discussed a bill pushed by the California delegation restricting immigration and adopted an amendment excluding all Asiatics, Wilson and Bryan came out strongly against the amendment, and by great majorities the house rescinded it.[93] With tariff reform and currency reform out of the way, on January 14, 1914, Wilson talked with Bryan and on January 15 asked him to tell the senate committee on foreign relations that

> it would be right, as it is desirable, to enter into a treaty with Japan which would assure her that her citizens would receive the same treatment as the citizens of other foreign countries, so far as their personal rights and privileges in the United States might be concerned.[94]

Bryan immediately told Chinda of Wilson's desire, and Chinda was so eager to save face that he was willing to desist in his demand for a treaty confirming the land titles acquired by Japanese subjects in

[90] Bryan to Guthrie, Sept. 23, 1913, SD 811.52/198; Guthrie to Bryan, Sept. 23, 1913, SD 811.52/198 and Sept. 25, 1913, /199.

[91] Guthrie to Bryan, Oct. 13, 1913, SD 811.52/214.

[92] R. Rothemel to Caminetti, March 7, 1914, SD 811.52/37.

[93] J. O. Davis to Joseph Tumulty, Jan. 4, 1914, SD 811.52/234; "Japan," *American Review of Reviews*, XLIX (1914), 267.

[94] Wilson to Bryan, Jan. 15, 1914, Wilson Papers.

California before the passage of the alien land law. Bryan added that the concession would go far in winning over the senate and that he would consult Moore on how to phrase the treaty. Baron Makino cabled his delight at the progress being made, for he had found the United States position thus far to be "not at all satisfactory." [95] In February the senate foreign relations committee asked Wilson for all the correspondence on the California question. Bryan wrote to Wilson:

> Our experience with that committee makes me fearful that if the matter is laid before it it might leak out, and the kind of leaking we have had is worse than publicity. . . . We had better decline this information for the present, even if it results in the delay of our Japanese arbitration treaty.[96]

Wilson respected Bryan's wish. However, the new ministry which assumed power in Japan on April 16 was led by Count Shigenobu Okuma, an aggressive nationalist embittered by the American discussion of Japanese exclusion and known to favor pressing the United States on the California Japanese question. He disdained the treaty and convention proposed in August and September, 1913, and the new foreign minister, Baron Takaaki Kato, requested from Bryan an answer to the last Japanese protest, that of August 26, 1913, and suggested that the correspondence on the California question be published.[97] Bryan agreed to the proposals and to the publication of the strictly official part of the correspondence and added his sincere regret that the Japanese laid so much emphasis on the element of racial discrimination and repeated his assurance that "the legislation of which your Government complains rests upon an economic basis, as does legislation of other countries, including your own, affecting immigration and the ownership of land by aliens." [98] However, when California Representative John Edward Raker proposed new immigration legislation to exclude all Asiatic *laborers,* Chinda complained

---

[95] Bryan, "Memorandum of a conversation with the Japanese Ambassador, January 23, 1914," SD Papers; Guthrie to Bryan, Jan. 22, 29, 1914, both SD 811.52/209.

[96] Bryan to Wilson, Feb. 11, 1914, Wilson Papers.

[97] The Japanese minister for foreign affairs to the Japanese ambassador, June 9, 1914, SD 811.52/292; Bryan to the Japanese ambassador, June 23, 1914, SD 811.52/292; Guthrie to Bryan, June 15, 1914, SD Papers; Guthrie to Bryan, June 20, 1914, SD 811.52/242; Guthrie to Bryan, July 3, 1914, SD 811.52/244; "Fall of the Japanese Cabinet," *American Review of Reviews,* XLIX (1914), 545.

[98] Bryan to Chinda, June 24, 1913, SD 811.52/292. See also L. H. Woolsey, "Memorandum of discussion between Chinda and Lansing, June 25, 1914," SD 811.52/274.

to Bryan that United States policy was one of "steadily increasing forcefulness." [99]

Seventeen months had passed since the California question had arisen. Bryan had persistently refused to regard the California law as infringing upon treaty rights. Japan had as obdurately seen in the California law "a local policy of discrimination against Japanese subjects *qua* Japanese subjects, and that it was a manifestation of racial antagonism."

On November 25, 1914, Chinda bluntly reminded Bryan that Wilson objected not to California's discriminating against the Japanese but only to "invidous discrimination." Talk about war against the United States continued in Japan, fanned partly by what Japan believed to be too friendly an American attitude toward China during the early months of the Great War and partly by renewed fear that the state government elected in California in November would pass additional anti-Japanese legislation.[100] On this latter point, Bryan cabled to Guthrie on December 15: "Have communicated with influential people in California. Cannot of course guarantee that nothing will be done but the prospects are against any such legislation being attempted and we shall do our best in that direction." [101]

Fortunately, the newly re-elected Governor Johnson opposed more stringent laws and declared that he would veto any introduced.[102] Moreover, a federal court at San Francisco declared unconstitutional an Arizona anti-alien employment act, and Japan hoped that the decision might have some bearing on the California alien land law if its constitutionality were ever tested. Although Wilson vetoed the John L. Burnett immigration bill on the ground of its literacy test provision, many Japanese believed that his defense of the primarily Roman Catholic and Jewish immigration against which the bill aimed might lead to a just and friendly settlement of the California question consonant with Japan's self-respect.[103]

[99] "Japan," *American Review of Reviews,* L (1914), 154.

[100] Sidney L. Gulick to Wilson, Oct. 13, 1914, SD 811.52/37; Guthrie to Bryan, Nov. 7, 1914, Bryan Papers.

[101] Bryan to Guthrie, Dec. 15, 1914, SD 811.52/262a.

[102] Undated newspaper clipping in Curtis H. Lindley to Secretary F. L. Lane, Jan. 24, 1915, forwarded by Lane to Wilson, Jan. 25, 1915, SD Papers. When the Californians seemed to be at the point of passing objectionable legislation, Chinda had again protested to Henry White as the friend of Roosevelt. Upon taking the matter up with Roosevelt, White found that he had written to Governor Johnson three weeks earlier urging him to prevent the passage of the bill which was worrying Chinda. Johnson had replied that he expected no more trouble with the anti-Japanese agitators—and there was none. Roosevelt to White, Dec. 8, 1914, Nevins, *White,* 319.

[103] New York *Sun,* Jan. 9, 1915; Lansing to Guthrie, Jan. 13, 1915, SD 811.52/276a;

Such was not to be the case. If a threat of war had ever existed, however, it now vanished. Official correspondence on the question ceased with Japan's summary of its case to Bryan on November 25, 1914, but it remained unsettled, for the supreme court ruled on November 12, 1922, that Japanese were ineligible to citizenship by naturalization (*Ozawa* v. *United States*), even though it held on November 19, 1923, (*Obrien* v. *Webb*) that the California law was not in violation of the Treaty of 1911. Between 1921 and 1925 Arizona, Arkansas, Delaware, Idaho, Kansas, Missouri, Montana, Nebraska, Nevada, New Mexico, Oregon, Texas, and Washington passed alien land laws similar to California's, and the Japanese temper was mightily exascerbated when Congress, on May 26, 1924, adopted a rigid quota system for immigrants and totally excluded those ineligible to citizenship, including Japanese. Not until 1952 (*Sei Fujii* v. *California*) did the California Supreme Court overrule Bryan's contention by deciding that the alien land law violated the Fourteenth Amendment.

Bryan and Wilson were of fairly like mind in their attitude toward Oriental immigration and belief that friendly overtures would win over the Californians and the Japanese. Being state-rights Democrats, they hesitated to challenge the police power of a state with the superior federal authority available under the treaty-making power, but Bryan was convinced that California's land laws did not violate the Treaty of 1911, and the best legal opinion available to him sustained him.[104] Bryan had visited Japan, provided a home for a Japanese boy for five years, liked the Japanese, and opposed laws that discriminated against them, whereas Wilson had no such sympathy for them as he had for the Chinese. Busy with reform legislation and other foreign matters, Wilson could not devote full energy to the California question.

Bryan revealed a Jovian patience in his dealings with Chinda, and his statement that "Nothing is final between friends" was a tactful diplomatic touch. While he admitted that his trip to California had accomplished nothing, he believed the time and effort expended worthwhile; he had comported himself with dignity and restraint,

---

Guthrie to Lansing, Feb. 15, 1915, SD 811.52/277. On Dec. 14, 1914, Wilson had bid godspeed to Dr. Shailer Matthews, of the University of Chicago, who had embarked on a mission to bring about a better understanding with Japan (letter, Wilson Papers).

[104] L. H. Woolsey, "Japanese Land Question in the United States," June 16, 1914, SD 811.52/238 1/2; Ambassador Morris in *Papers Relating to the Foreign Relations of the United States, 1921,* II, 338–339. See also Raymond L. Buell, "Some Legal Aspects of the Japanese Question," *American Journal of International Law,*" XVII (1923), 29–49.

and he had won some time in which to secure a remedy by diplomacy. Redfield spoke of Bryan's having "rendered a great service to his country" by preventing Japanese-American relations to become acute and threaten war, and Houston concurred.[105] Said Daniels:

His spirit was one of conference and exchange of views. He disarmed criticism by displaying no Big Stick. He sought a method of doing what Californians were set on doing, without singling out Japan, which was overwrought and whose people were talking militantly. In the end, while it did not satisfy the Japanese government, the law that Governor Johnson signed served to keep the dispute in diplomatic channels. The gesture of the Washington government in trying to adjust matters assuaged the war party in Japan and gave cooling time.[106]

John Bassett Moore later wrote:

I do not hesitate to affirm . . . that Bryan's inquiry regarding the part he should play in certain circumstances in California was prudent and sensible. It was just such an inquiry as it was the duty of a person in his situation to make, and is cogent proof of the fact that he understood his business.[107]

The nation's eastern press, which generally questioned his capabilities, in this case endorsed his efforts. Said the New York *Times* in a unique exception to its perennially caustic treatment of him:

It must be noted that Mr. Bryan's policy of treating every apparently acute disagreement with a prescription of endless conversations has worked well. If the matter is still unsettled and a settlement is not in sight, at least the attitude of both countries has changed. It is difficult to realize . . . how high passion rose . . . especially in Japan, and how close appeared a real breach. It is Secretary Bryan's belief, and he acts on it with a courage proof against ridicule, that even when everything seems definitely at an end, it is good diplomacy to go on talking about it.[108]

In strange contrast to his demand for the repeal of the Panama Canal tolls exemptions because a treaty right was being broken, Wilson would not admit that the California law violated any treaty right. He utterly ignored the whole issue in his annual messages of 1913 and 1914, but he correctly feared defeat if he sought a treaty which

[105] Redfield, *With Cabinet and Congress;* 71; Houston, *Eight Years,* I, 65–66.
[106] Daniels, *The Wilson Era,* 162.
[107] Moore to R. S. Baker, June 24, 1929, Baker Papers.
[108] New York *Times,* June 24, 1914.

would satisfy the wishes of the Japanese but not of Californians, and he was no more willing than Bryan to use Rooseveltian methods in coercing a state. His objective was never to prevent the passage by California of a law that it had the perfect right to pass, whether constitutional or not; rather it was to relieve the tension between Japan and the United States by sending Bryan to California as a gesture of friendship. Bryan's trip gained this short-run objective and averted a serious crisis.[109] Nevertheless, resultant ill feeling made the solution of subsequent problems with Japan, as of the "Twenty-One Demands" on China, ever more difficult for Bryan, and the Japanese "racial equality" question blew up into a storm of serious proportions which Wilson had to weather at Versailles.

[109] Bailey, "California, Japan, and the Alien Land Law of 1913," 55–56.

CONSTITUTIONAL LAW: EQUAL PROTECTION OF THE LAWS: PRESUMPTION OF INTENT TO EVADE ESCHEAT IN CALIFORNIA ALIEN LAND LAW.

A recent United States Supreme Court decision[1] declares unconstitutional one important provision of the California alien land law and raises

[1] Oyama v. California (1948) 332 U. S. 633.

doubt as to the basic validity of the act. The California alien land law, first passed by the legislature in 1913,[2] strengthened and re-enacted by the Initiative Act of 1920,[3] in effect denies to alien Japanese the right to own any legal or beneficial interest in agricultural land.[4] It provides that land acquired in violation of the statute shall escheat to the state as of the date of acquisition,[5] and that any conveyance made with intent to thwart escheat shall likewise result in escheat.[6] Further, a prima facie presumption of such intent arises when an ineligible alien pays the consideration for land conveyed to a citizen or eligible alien.[7]

In 1923, the United States Supreme Court approved the Washington and California alien land laws.[8] The Court found that there was no denial of equal protection of the laws; the distinction between aliens eligible for citizenship and those ineligible for citizenship was a reasonable classification because it was borrowed from a rule established by Congress. In the view of the Court it was evident that ineligible aliens lacked an interest in, and the power to work effectively for, the welfare of the state, and consequently that, as landowners, they might endanger its security. The right to own agricultural land was distinguished from the protected right of aliens to work for a living in a common occupation.[9]

---

[2] Cal. Stats. 1913, p. 206.

[3] Cal. Stats. 1921, lxxxiii, as amended by Cal. Stats. 1923, p. 1020; *id.* 1927, p. 880; *id.* 1943, pp. 2917, 2999; *id.* 1945, pp. 2164, 2177; see also *id.* 1945, pp. 2552, 2739. For the present law in full, see CAL. GEN. LAWS, Acts 260, 261 (Supp. 1947).

[4] CAL. GEN. LAWS, Act 261, §§ 2, 3, (1944). The act provides for ownership of real property by ineligible aliens "to the extent and for the purposes prescribed by any treaty now existing between the government of the United States and the nation or country of which such alien is a citizen or subject, *and not otherwise* . . . ." (Italics added.) Because the treaty with Japan, (1911) 37 STAT. 1504, specifically protected the right of Japanese nationals to own interests in land for residential and commercial purposes, the act affects only agricultural land. But the abrogation of the treaty, effective January 26, 1940, 1 DEP'T. STATE BULL. 81 (1939), has made it doubtful whether Japanese aliens in California still may own or rent a home or business. Palermo v. Stockton Theatres (1946) 172 P. (2d) 103 held that the abrogation of the treaty did not deprive Japanese aliens of the right to rent a building for business purposes. The reasoning was that the reference in the act to the treaty must be regarded as specific in order to avoid the attack that it unconstitutionally delegates to the federal government the state's power to legislate; and if regarded as specific, the provisions of the treaty, as of the date of the alien land law, are incorporated in the act. Hearing granted, Palermo v. Stockton Theatres, Inc. (October 31, 1946) 29 A. C. No. 6, minutes p. 2.

[5] CAL. GEN. LAWS, Act 261, §§ 7, 8 (Supp. 1947).

[6] *Id.* § 9.

[7] *Ibid.* " . . . A prima facie presumption that the conveyance is made with such intent shall arise upon proof of any of the following group of facts: (a) The taking of the property in the name of a person other than [an ineligible alien] if the consideration is paid or agreed or understood to be paid by an alien [ineligible to citizenship] . . . . In each of the foregoing instances, the burden of proof shall be upon the defendant to show that the conveyance was not made with intent to prevent, evade, or avoid escheat . . ."

[8] Terrace v. Thompson (1923) 263 U.S. 197; Porterfield v. Webb (1923) 263 U.S. 225 (lease); Webb v. O'Brien (1923) 263 U.S. 313 (cropping contract); Frick v. Webb (1923) 263 U. S. 326 (sale of stock of corporation owning agricultural land). At common law, the sovereign has the power to forfeit land belonging to an alien. 5 TIFFANY, REAL PROPERTY § 1377 (3d ed. 1939) McGovney, *The Anti-Japanese Land Laws of California and Ten Other States,* (1947) 35 CALIF. L. REV. 7, at 18-24.

[9] Truax v. Raich (1915) 239 U.S. 33.

Before the war, Kajiro Oyama, an ineligible alien Japanese, paid for two parcels of agricultural land and caused the deeds to be executed to his minor American-born son, Fred. In 1942, the Oyama family was evacuated from the West Coast with all other persons of Japanese ancestry, and in 1944, while they were still unable to return, the State of California commenced proceedings to declare the two parcels escheated[10] on the ground that the conveyances to the son had been effected with intent to evade the alien land law. The trial court held for the State and the Supreme Court of California affirmed the judgment,[11] both courts relying strongly upon the statutory presumption that a conveyance is made with intent to avoid escheat if an ineligible alien pays the consideration and the property is taken in the name of one eligible to hold land.[12] On certiorari, the United States Supreme Court reversed,[13] primarily on the ground that the application of the presumption deprived the citizen son of equal protection of the laws as guaranteed by the Fourteenth Amendment.[14]

The rationale of the leading opinion was that, whereas generally in California when a parent pays for a conveyance of land to his child the law presumes a gift to the donee rather than a resulting trust to the donor,[15] the effect of the presumption in the alien land law is to change that rule as to children of ineligible aliens and instead presume a resulting trust.[16] Such a

---

[10] Of the 73 escheat actions instituted by California since the act was enacted, 59 were begun after Pearl Harbor when it was felt that war hysteria would support vigorous enforcement. Ferguson, *The California Alien Land Law and the Fourteenth Amendment* (1947) 35 CALIF. L. REV. 61 at 72. Prior to the war, the alien land law was not seriously enforced. One observer argued that the reason was that anti-Japanese forces gained more politically from the process of opposing Japanese farmers than from eliminating them. MCWILLIAMS, PREJUDICE 65 (1944).

[11] People v. Oyama (1946) 29 Cal. (2d) 164, 173 P. (2d) 794.

[12] Other grounds for the decision were an inference of intent to avoid escheat from the fact that the conveyance ran to a minor child, and an inference of lack of good faith at the time of the original transaction from the fact that the father failed to file annual guardianship reports.

[13] Oyama v. California, *supra* note 1. Vinson, C. J., wrote the opinion of the Court, Frankfurter, J., joining. Black, J., was joined by Douglas, J., in one concurring opinion, while Rutledge, J., joined Murphy, J., in another. Reed and Burton, J.J., agreed in one dissent and Jackson, J. dissented alone. Neither the separate concurring opinions nor the separate dissents will be distinguished in this note because of similarity in substance.

[14] The opinion of the Court did not discuss two of the three attacks advanced against the alien land law—that the father was denied "equal protection" by the act, and that the act violated "due process" by authorizing a taking of property after expiration of the applicable limitations period—because it thought the escheat judgment reversible under the initial challenge.

[15] Gomez v. Cecena (1940) 15 Cal. (2d) 363, 101 P. (2d) 477; RESTATEMENT, TRUSTS §§ 440, 442 (1935).

[16] The Court pointed to statements in Estate of Yano (1922) 188 Cal. 645, 650, 206 Pac. 995, 998 and in People v. Fujita (1932) 215 Cal. 166, 170, 8 P. (2d) 1011, 1012, that, where aliens are prohibited from holding land, an implied trust by operation of law will not arise in their favor, as indicating an inconsistency by the California Supreme Court in applying the statutory presumption in the instant case. Oyama v. California, *supra* note 1 at 642. But in those statements, the California court was considering the effect of Civ. Code § 853 which related generally to the presumed resulting trust arising out of a transfer of real property to one person and payment by another, and not the effect of the statutory presumption of the alien land law. Significantly, the paragraph

shift of the burden of proof is a discrimination based solely on the father's country of origin. Even if it be assumed that the basic provisions of the alien land law are valid, the majority concludes, a presumption regarded as necessary to carry out its purpose cannot be sustained if it conflicts with "the right of American citizens to own land anywhere in the United States."[17]

The two dissenting opinions insisted that if the basic aim of the alien land law be accepted as constitutional,[18] and if the protection against evasion by condemning conveyances made with intent to avoid escheat is not challenged, the statutory presumption relied upon at the trial is reasonable and necessary to effect the purposes of the act. The legislature may establish a presumption of one fact from the existence of others if there is a rational connection between the ones proved and the one presumed to follow.[19] The dissenters found such a rational connection. Since the presumption is rebuttable, the citizen can overcome it by proving a bona fide gift.[20] The application of the presumption did not deny the citizen child equal protection of the laws because it is the capacity of the donor to own land and not the ancestry of the donee which causes the presumption to arise. If the gift had been made by the elder Oyama to a person, other than his son, who was eligible to hold land under California law, there would still have been a prima facie evasion of the act, which the donee would have had the "onerous burden" of rebutting. Conversely, if the younger Oyama had received this land from a citizen or eligible alien, the presumption would not have been applicable. Admittedly there is a discrimination in this situation, but it flows from the fundamental provision of the act prohibiting agricultural land ownership by ineligible aliens.

The dissents' criticism of the logic of the leading opinion seems entirely justified. It pointed up, however, that the real issue was whether the twenty-five year old approval of the alien land laws should continue. The four concurring justices, after tersely indicating their agreement with the leading opinion, called for a clear overruling of *Terrace v. Thompson* and companion cases.[21] They showed that the historical roots of the California alien land law were deeply embedded in race prejudice, and that its purpose was to discriminate against members of a racial group in order to drive them from the state.[22] Such state action is enjoined by the Fourteenth Amendment's Equal Protection Clause, which applies to citizens and aliens alike.[23] Further, it conflicts with the exclusive power of Congress over immigration, since, by limiting the opportunity for Japanese aliens to make a living, it seeks to discourage those lawfully in the United States from coming into or remaining

---

in People v. Fujita, immediately following the statement referred to by the Court, interpreted the presumption just as it was used in the California courts in the instant case.

[17] Oyama v. California, *supra* note 1 at 647.

[18] At no point did the dissenting justices indicate their opinion of the constitutionality of the alien land law. It is obvious, however, that they were not prepared to declare it unconstitutional at this time.

[19] *See* Tot v. United States (1943) 319 U. S. 463, 467.

[20] People v. Fujita, *supra* note 16.

[21] Cases cited, *supra* note 8.

[22] McGovney, *supra* note 8 at 51. Ferguson, *supra* note 10 at 63.

[23] Truax v. Raich, *supra* note 9 at 39.

within one of its states. The holding of *Terrace v. Thompson,* that the Congressional classification of aliens into those eligible and those ineligible for naturalization is, in and of itself, a reasonable basis for the discrimination of the alien land laws, was sharply criticized. Distinctive treatment of a single class of persons is allowed under "equal protection" only if there is a rational ground for the discrimination in the particular situation. That a classification is reasonable for one purpose, naturalization,[24] does not necessarily justify its use for another purpose, land ownership. Other rationalizations for the act were also refuted. The argument that ineligible aliens tend to be disloyal and uninterested in the welfare of the state is unsound since those attributes are individual and not group traits.[25] The possibility that unrestricted land ownership by ineligible aliens could result in acquisition by them of all the agricultural land in the state is not only statistically inconceivable, especially in view of their diminishing number,[26] but also historically unconvincing, since a large part of Japanese landholding before the alien land law was in areas which had not been previously cultivated and which they reclaimed by their intensive farming methods.[27]

It is regrettable that one more Justice did not join the concurring group and allow a clear-cut decision to be rendered, because the case leaves the present status of the law very uncertain. The Attorney General of California has interpreted it as ending the practical utility of the alien land law, and has indicated his intention to dismiss all the escheat cases pending before the California courts.[28] As only the presumption was invalidated, a new trial could be held and a judgment that the conveyance was made with intent to avoid escheat could be reached on the evidence, without the use of the presumption. Should the Attorney General change his mind and press the case along this modified line, Fred Oyama would again be in danger of having his land declared escheated. However, Fred Oyama and others in his position could take advantage of the present official reaction to the Supreme Court decision by bringing suit to quiet their titles against the state, and, if they are successful, thereby preclude any future escheat declaration.[29]

---

[24] Murphy, J., concurring in Oyama v. California, *supra* note 1 at 664. Although thus far there has been no case limiting that power, Justice Murphy is probably referring to a possible "due process" objection to the racial criterion for naturalization.

[25] See Ferguson, *supra* note 10 at 83 for evidence of the loyalty of persons of Japanese ancestry in the last war.

[26] McGovney, *supra* note 8 at 17.

[27] Ferguson, *supra* note 10 at 81.

[28] San Francisco Chronicle, Jan. 28, 1948, p. 2, col. 6. California Attorney General Fred Howser said he thought that if the validity of the law came before the United States Supreme Court, the Justices "no doubt would invalidate the law as unconstitutional."

[29] CAL. CODE CIV. PROC. § 738.5. "An action may be brought against the State of California to determine whether or not an escheat has occurred . . . [under the alien land law] . . . . The State of California shall be the sole defendent in such action and no other matter may be adjudicated except the issue of the occurrence of an escheat . . ." As this code section, enacted in 1945, directs the public attorney to "perform duties similar to those required to be performed in escheat proceedings," the plaintiff risks a declaration of escheat. But in view of the Attorney General's intent not to prosecute escheat cases and his announced opinion as to the constitutionality of the alien land law, the risk of pressing suit now is probably less than the risk of a future change in administrative and judicial attitudes.

The California alien land law is a manifestation of racial prejudice which has no place in a nation avowedly dedicated to individual liberty and opportunity regardless of color, religion, or national origin. The result of the principal case, although encouraging as a major limitation of the act, is unsatisfactory both from a legal and a moral point of view. Not only do American citizens in the position of Fred Oyama suffer continued uncertainties because of a law based upon racial distinctions, but also another substantial denial of equal protection of the laws, the prohibition of land ownership by aliens ineligible to naturalization, is left intact. Thus, further judicial or legislative action is required to bring our law into conformity with our avowed ideals.

The California Alien Land Law and the Fourteenth Amendment

*Edwin E. Ferguson**

THE PAST few years have seen a surge of activity by California law-enforcement officers, aided by new state legislation and augmented appropriations, in the investigation of possible violations of the alien land law and the institution of escheat proceedings. By the summer of 1945 approximately thirty escheat actions had been begun, judgments in favor of the state had been entered in four of them, and out-of-court settlements of $100,000 and $25,000, respectively, had been effected in two others.[1] By the spring of 1946 some fifty actions were pending. All of these suits involved agricultural lands and were directed against persons of Japanese ancestry.[2] Additional suits have since been filed.[3]

The alien land law, first enacted in 1913, denies to aliens ineligible for citizenship the right to own, lease, or otherwise enjoy land, except to the extent provided by treaty.[4] Despite the manifest discrimination against one class of aliens and the deprivation of property rights involved, the United States Supreme Court in 1923 upheld the law, concluding that it did not violate the equal protection and due process guaranties of the Fourteenth Amendment.[5] The new wave of escheat actions has resulted in a new test of the law. Late in 1946, in an appeal from a judgment of escheat which again raised the equal protection and due process issues, the California supreme court reaffirmed the constitutionality of the law in *People v. Oyama*,[6] relying upon the rationale provided by the 1923 decisions.

This article, it is believed, will demonstrate that the alien land law was enacted and has been enforced solely as a discriminatory

*B.S. in Ed. 1931, LL.B. 1934, Drake University; J.S.D. 1937, Yale University. Assistant General Counsel, Federal Public Housing Authority; formerly Solicitor, War Relocation Authority; member of the Iowa Bar. The opinions expressed in this article are those of the author and do not necessarily reflect the official view of any organization with which he has been or is now associated.

[1] Business Week, Aug. 4, 1945, at 50.

[2] Pacific Citizen, Feb. 2, 1946, at 1.

[3] Pacific Citizen, Nov. 9, 1946, at 2.

[4] Cal. Stats. 1913, p. 206; *ibid.* 1921, p. lxxxiii.

[5] Porterfield v. Webb (1923) 263 U.S. 225.

[6] (1946) 29 A.C. 157, 173 P. (2d) 794.

law directed against the Japanese; that the rationale supplied by the United States Supreme Court in support of its constitutionality, and followed in the *Oyama* case, is premised upon untenable assumptions; and that the law serves no substantial public purpose. If this be true, the California court should have given the law the "rigid scrutiny" which the United States Supreme Court recently said should be given all legislation based on racial differences,[7] and declared it unconstitutional.[8]

GENESIS AND HISTORY OF THE LAW

Historians say that the purpose of the California alien land law was to discourage further immigration of Japanese aliens to California and to call to the attention of Congress and the rest of the country the desire of California that the "Japanese menace" be crushed.[9] That conclusion is amply supported by studies of the growth and strategy of anti-Oriental agitation in California.

The Japanese immigrants to the mainland of the United States were the legatees of a strong prejudice against Orientals which was originally directed toward the Chinese, who preceded the Japanese by almost fifty years. This prejudice began to build up with the large-scale immigration of the Chinese initiated by the gold-rush.[10] Those who led the campaign were labor unions, who feared the economic competition of the Chinese, and politicians, who sought the support of labor. In September, 1877, the San Francisco Trade and Labor Union broke with existing political parties to enter politics as the Working Men's Party of California. Of the 152 members of the convention to draw up a new state constitution in 1879, fifty-one were members of the working men's party.[11] Article XIX of this constitution was devoted exclusively to the expression of a policy intended to discourage residence in the state by Chinese.[12] Numerous laws and

---

[7] Korematsu v. United States (1944) 323 U.S. 214.

[8] *Cf.* Barnette v. West Virginia State Board of Education (S.D.W.Va. 1942) 47 Fed. Supp. 251, declaring a flag-salute regulation unconstitutional despite a prior Supreme Court decision holding a similar regulation valid.

[9] STRONG, THE SECOND-GENERATION JAPANESE PROBLEM (1934) 46; H.R. REP. No. 2124, 77th Cong. 2d Sess. (1942) at 85; see also, Rep. Cal. State Bd. Control, California and the Oriental (1920) at 11.

[10] Between 1850 and 1852 the number of Chinese in California increased from 1,000 to 20,000. HUNT and SÁNCHEZ, A SHORT HISTORY OF CALIFORNIA (1929) 529. In 1882 there were 132,300 Chinese in the state, the largest number ever recorded. See COOLIDGE, CHINESE IMMIGRATION (1909) 498.

[11] HUNT and SÁNCHEZ, *op. cit. supra* note 10, at 548.

[12] Section 4 of article XIX of the 1879 constitution opens with this language: "The presence of foreigners ineligible to become citizens of the United States is de-

municipal ordinances aimed at the Chinese were enacted shortly before and after the adoption of the constitution of 1879. They were obviously unconstitutional but they dramatized for the whole country the dissatisfaction of the Californian with his Chinese neighbor.[13] Popular feeling was fanned to such a pitch that many acts of violence against individual Chinese occurred.[14] Primarily as a result of this agitation, the first Chinese exclusion act became law in 1882.[15] Under a later amendment, Chinese laborers departing from the United States for China for visits were denied reentry.[16] The Chinese population in the state began immediately to decline. From 132,300 Chinese in 1882, it dropped to 107,488 in 1890; 89,963 in 1900; 71,531 in 1910; and 61,639 in 1920. With this decline in number, the agitation against the Chinese subsided.[17]

The pattern for dealing with the Chinese—local opposition by apparently competing economic groups, physical violence highly publicized, capitalization on racial and color prejudices by politicians, enactment of laws constitutional or otherwise to direct national attention to the "problem", followed by national legislation to deny admittance to the "undesirable" aliens—was destined to be followed in dealing with the Japanese.

The year 1900 saw the real beginning of anti-Japanese agitation.[18] In 1900, 12,628 Japanese entered the country.[19] Through the annexa-

---

clared to be dangerous to the well-being of the State, and the Legislature shall discourage their immigration by all the means within its power."

[13] *E.g.*, Chy Lung v. Freeman (1875) 92 U. S. 275; Yick Wo v. Hopkins (1885) 118 U. S. 356; *In re* Ah Fong (C.C.D. Cal. 1874) 1 Fed. Cas. 213; Ho Ah Kow v. Nunan (C.C.D. Cal. 1879) 12 Fed. Cas. 252; *In re* Ah Chong (C.C.D. Cal. 1880) 2 Fed. 733; *In re* Parrott (C.C.D. Cal. 1880) 1 Fed. 481; *In re* Quong Woo (C.C.D. Cal. 1882) 13 Fed. 229; *In re* Tie Loy (C.C.D. Cal. 1886) 26 Fed. 611; Ling Sing v. Washburn (1862) 20 Cal. 534.

[14] Rep. Cal. State Bd. Control, *op. cit. supra* note 9, at 7.

[15] 22 STAT. (1882) 58. This statute was enacted as a temporary measure but it later became permanent legislation. 23 STAT. (1884) 115; 27 STAT. (1892) 25; 32 STAT. (1902) 176; 33 STAT. (1904) 428; 8 U. S. C. (1940) 263. The Chinese exclusion laws were repealed during World War II, however, and Chinese are now admitted on a quota basis. 57 STAT. (1943) 600.

[16] 23 STAT. (1884) 115.

[17] ICHIHASHI, JAPANESE IN THE UNITED STATES (1932) 161.

[18] The failure of attempts to arouse any measurable antipathy prior to 1900 was due to the comparatively small number of Japanese immigrants. In 1890 there were only 2,039 Japanese in California. ICHIHASHI, *op. cit. supra* note 17, at 53. Annual Japanese immigration first exceeded 1,000 in 1891, and had risen to only 2,844 in 1899. REP. COMM'R IMMIG. 1900, at 35. During this period, however, there were isolated labor outbreaks against Japanese. ICHIHASHI, *op. cit. supra* note 17, at 229.

[19] REP. COMM'R IMMIG. 1900, at 10.

tion of Hawaii in 1898, all indentured labor contracts in the Islands had been automatically abrogated, thus liberating thousands of Asiatic peons.[20] Many of them came to the mainland. The influx directly from Japan was accelerated by steamship lines and emigration companies.[21] This increased migration gave rise to the first wave of resentment by the white workers of the state, an attitude which was adroitly exploited by the political agitators anxious to secure the labor vote.

On May 7, 1900, a mass meeting in San Francisco, held to discuss the Bubonic Plague, adopted a resolution that the Chinese exclusion act be extended to apply to the Japanese.[22] In response to a recommendation by the governor in January, 1901, the California legislature adopted its first resolution urging Congress to protect American labor by restricting Japanese immigration.[23] In November, 1904, the American Federation of Labor at an annual convention in San Francisco adopted a resolution to exclude Japanese and Koreans as well as Chinese laborers. The San Francisco Chronicle followed with a series of inflammatory articles against the Japanese in California which was highly effective in whipping up popular feeling against them.[24] In March, 1905, the California legislature passed a second resolution demanding action to limit the immigration of Japanese laborers.[25]

In May, 1905, the Asiatic Exclusion League, originally the Japanese and Korean Exclusion League, was organized in San Francisco. The avowed purpose of the league was to prevent or minimize the immigration of Asiatics. This organization favored the segregation of Japanese in separate schools and a boycott against Japanese workers and businessmen. It claimed a membership in California alone of 110,000 by February, 1908. Of the 238 affiliated bodies composing the league, 202 were labor unions; the rest were fraternal, civic, benevolent, political, and military societies.[26]

---

[20] PAJUS, THE REAL JAPANESE CALIFORNIA (1937) 5.

[21] ICHIHASHI, *op. cit. supra* note 17, at 88. The number of Japanese in this country swelled from 24,326 in 1900 to 72,157 in 1910. See 15th Census of the United States: 1930, Population, Vol. II, p. 32. Most of these Japanese settled in California.

[22] Buell, *The Development of the Anti-Japanese Agitation in the United States* (1922) 37 POL. SCI. Q. 605, 608.

[23] ICHIHASHI, *op. cit. supra* note 17, at 231.

[24] MCWILLIAMS, PREJUDICE (1944) 17.

[25] ICHIHASHI, *op. cit. supra* note 17, at 250.

[26] 25 REP. IMMIG. COMM. (1911) 169; Buell, *op. cit. supra* note 22, at 617. The Asiatic Exclusion League was believed to have received contributions from the Hawaiian planters' associations to assist in agitation which would discourage Japanese in Hawaii

In October, 1906, the San Francisco Board of Education by resolution ordered the segregation of Japanese pupils in the public schools. Protests were immediately made to the Japanese government and its intercession caused President Theodore Roosevelt to send Secretary Metcalf to investigate. In his message to Congress of December 4, 1906, the President denounced the segregation measure as "wicked absurdity". A survey showed that there were only 93 Japanese pupils in a total school population of 29,000. In January, 1907, President Roosevelt summoned the San Francisco School Board to Washington and in return for his agreement to end Japanese immigration, the Board agreed to rescind the resolution.[27] Ensuing negotiations with the Japanese government resulted in the so-called gentlemen's agreement, announced in July, 1908, under which the Japanese government agreed to limit passports for the United States to nonlaborers or to such laborers as had already established a domicile in this country, and to persons who were seeking to join a parent, wife or child resident in the United States, or who intended to assume control of an already acquired farming enterprise.[28]

These developments, however, did not appease the agitators. At the California legislative session of 1909, no less than seventeen anti-Japanese bills were introduced. The intervention of the President defeated a school segregation bill. The first alien land bill directed at the Japanese failed when at the President's suggestion it was amended to apply to all aliens.[29] The only anti-Japanese measures which became law were a resolution favoring exclusion, which was sent to both houses of Congress without results, and an appropriation for gathering and publishing statistics regarding Japanese in the state.[30]

In the California election campaign of 1910 the Republican, Democratic and Socialist parties urged exclusion.[31] An exhaustive report completed by the state commissioner of labor in 1910, which

from seeking better economic opportunities on the mainland. Report, Royal Commission Appointed to Enquire into the Methods by which Oriental Laborers have been Induced to Come to Canada (1907) 41. See also, ICHIHASHI, *op. cit. supra* note 17, at 249.

27 STRONG, *op. cit. supra* note 9, at 41; ICHIHASHI, *op. cit. supra* note 17, at 244. "Although various explanations of this resolution were given at the time, the real reason was to start the process of discrimination which would eventually lead to the enactment of an exclusion law." TREAT, JAPAN AND THE UNITED STATES (1921) 254. President Roosevelt's weak stand was undoubtedly due to alignment of the solid south with California on the racial issue involved. MCWILLIAMS, PREJUDICE (1944) 29-34.

28 REP. COMM'R IMMIG. 1908, at 221; Buell, *op. cit. supra* note 22, at 634.

29 ICHIHASHI, *op. cit. supra* note 17, at 250.

30 25 REP. IMMIG. COMM. (1911) 171; ICHIHASHI, *op. cit. supra* note 17, at 251.

31 25 REP. IMMIG. COMM. (1911) 117; ICHIHASHI, *op. cit. supra* note 17, at 252.

concluded that the continued importation of Japanese labor was necessary for the development of California agriculture, was disapproved and suppressed by the California Senate.[32] The following year that body memorialized the President and Senate of the United States to disapprove the 1911 treaty with Japan, protesting the lack of an exclusion clause.[33]

In the 1911 California legislative session a bill prohibiting land ownership by aliens not eligible for citizenship passed the Senate by a vote of twenty-nine to three but died in committee in the Assembly. Presidential intervention once more was instrumental in killing the bill.[34] Opposition also came from the Panama Pacific Exposition Company and its supporters, who feared the effect of the measure upon Japan's participation, and possibly that of other countries as well, in the forthcoming exposition at San Francisco.[35]

By 1913 the political situation was ripe for the passage of an anti-Japanese land law. The state administration in California remained Progressive Republican while the national administration became Democratic and exercised less influence over the state legislature. The Exposition had progressed to the point where the appeal for its success was no longer sufficiently effective. Opposition to the bill came only from a few relatively ineffective groups.[36]

The choice presented to the legislature was the enactment of a law applicable only to aliens ineligible for citizenship, or of a law applicable to all aliens. The latter would have affected large European holdings and strong pressure against it was brought by the San Francisco real estate board, chambers of commerce, boards of trade, merchants associations, and foreign oil and copper syndicates.[37] At this juncture Secretary of State Bryan visited California "for the purpose of counseling with the members of the Legislature and co-operating with them in framing a law which would meet the views of the People of the State and yet leave untouched the international obligations of the United States" (*i.e.*, conform to the 1911 treaty with Japan).[38]

---

[32] ICHIHASHI, *op. cit. supra* note 17, at 253; CAL. SENATE J. (1910) 39.

[33] ICHIHASHI, *op. cit. supra* note 17, at 255.

[34] *Ibid.* at 264.

[35] HICHBORN, STORY OF THE CALIFORNIA LEGISLATURE OF 1911 (1911) 342; MILLIS, THE JAPANESE PROBLEM IN THE UNITED STATES (1915) 200.

[36] *Ibid.* at 204; ICHIHASHI, *op. cit. supra* note 17, at 265.

[37] MILLIS, *op. cit. supra* note 35, at 202; Buell, *The Development of Anti-Japanese Agitation in the United States II* (1923) 38 POL. SCI. Q. 57, 62.

[38] HICHBORN, STORY OF THE CALIFORNIA LEGISLATURE OF 1913 (1913) 248; MILLIS, *op. cit. supra* note 35, at 206.

Shortly after his departure, a bill was passed by overwhelming majorities in both houses and became law in May, 1913. The law prohibited aliens ineligible for citizenship (hence, Japanese aliens)[39] from acquiring, possessing, enjoying, or transferring real property or any interest therein except to the extent prescribed by existing treaties. A similar prohibition applied to corporations a majority of whose members were ineligible aliens or a majority of whose issued capital stock was owned by such aliens. An exception was made permitting the lease of land for agricultural purposes for a term not exceeding three years; land already owned by ineligible aliens, or acquired in satisfaction of existing liens, might be retained. Property acquired or held in violation of the law was subject to escheat by the state, acting through the attorney general, title passing upon entry of final judgment.[40]

Since the treaty with Japan in 1911 specifically protected the right of Japanese nationals to lease land for residential and commercial purposes and to own residential and business property in the United States,[41] the new law was effective only to proscribe the ownership or long-term lease of agricultural land. However, a large number of the Japanese were engaged in agriculture.[42] By 1909 they were a dominant element in the farm labor supply.[43] Like other immigrant groups, they had begun seeking the stability and increased income opportunities of land tenure. Japanese-controlled farms in California had increased from 29 units (4,698 acres) in 1900[44] to 1,816 units (99,254 acres) in 1910.[45] These facts largely explain the concerted and finally successful efforts of the anti-Japanese groups, balked in their attempts to obtain federal action completely barring further Japanese immigration, to secure passage of the alien land law, even though it would prohibit only acquisition of agricultural lands in the case of

---

39 The right to naturalization was at that time restricted to white persons and persons of African nativity or descent, although it has since been extended to descendants of races indigenous to the western hemisphere, persons of Chinese nativity or descent, Filipinos, and persons of races indigenous to India. See 8 U. S. C. A. § 703; Pub. L. No. 483, 79th Cong. 2d Sess. (July 2, 1946.) Japanese aliens are not "white persons" within this statute. Ozawa v. United States (1922) 260 U. S. 178; *In re* Saito (C. C. D. Mass. 1894) 62 Fed. 126; *In re* Yamashita (1902) 30 Wash. 234, 70 Pac. 482.

40 Cal. Stats. 1913, p. 206.

41 37 STAT. (1911) 1504.

42 An estimated 30,000 Japanese were employed in California agriculture in 1909, of whom about 24,000 were farm laborers. 23 REP. IMMIG. COMM. (1911) 33, 61.

43 MILLIS, *op. cit. supra* note 35, at 105.

44 *Ibid.* at 137.

45 U. S. Census Bureau Bull. No. 127 (1914).

the Japanese. It was reasoned that such legislation would largely discourage their further inflow and encourage those already here to return to their homeland.[46]

The period immediately following the enactment of the alien land law was relatively an era of good will toward Japanese aliens. On January 22, 1915, a bill was introduced in the Assembly proposing to delete the clauses in the alien land law which allowed aliens to lease farm lands for a period of three years, but it met opposition from the press and political leaders of the state.[47] With the war came a demand in rural districts for labor to meet the void caused by the departure of white farm laborers to industrial centers. Japanese farmers, as laborers and tenants, were again in good repute and they took advantage of their opportunities.[48] Two factors, however, bode for further trouble. Despite the alien land law, Japanese immigration continued almost unabated and Japanese farming activities in California continued to expand. From 1913 to 1920, the year in which the initiative alien land law was adopted, 77,936 Japanese aliens came to this country; 59,098 departed, leaving a net gain of 18,838.[49] The gentlemen's agreement apparently was not observed too closely during these years, although many of those admitted, such as wives and children, were not subject to its provisions.[50] The increase in the number of women was coincident with and reflected the advance in status of the Japanese from farm laborers to farm operators. In 1919, the state board of control reported that the Japanese in California owned or had contracted to buy 74,769 acres of agricultural land and leased or held by contract 383,287 acres.[51]

---

[46] U. S. Webb, co-author of the 1913 law, frankly stated in a speech before the San Francisco Commonwealth Club on August 13, 1913: "The fundamental basis of all legislation upon this subject, State and Federal, has been, and is, race undesirability . . . . It [the 1913 law] seeks to limit their presence by curtailing their privileges which they may enjoy here; for they will not come in large numbers and long abide with us if they may not acquire land." ICHIHASHI, *op. cit. supra* note 17, at 275. See also, PAJUS, *op. cit. supra* note 20, at 71.

[47] *Ibid.* at 73-78.

[48] *Ibid.* at 32, 78; Dearborn Independent, Sept. 11, 1920, at 8 (Wallace, Waving the Yellow Flag in California).

[49] See ICHIHASHI, *op. cit. supra* note 17, at 62.

[50] The earlier immigrants were almost exclusively males. During this period many aliens brought in their wives and children. See CALIFORNIA FARMERS CO-OPERATIVE ASSOCIATION, JAPANESE IMMIGRATION AND THE JAPANESE IN CALIFORNIA (1920) 9. The number of males per 100 females among the Japanese declined from 694.1 in 1910 to 189.8 in 1920. 14th Census of the United States: 1920, Population, Vol. III, p. 15.

[51] Rep. Cal. State Bd. Control, *op. cit. supra* note 9, at 47. These figures indicate that the alien land law was not enforced at all rigorously during this period. It is also

Hostilities of World War I had been ended only a short time when agitation against the Japanese in California was renewed. The increase in immigration during the war and the increase in land ownership and control furnished effective ammunition. Returning soldiers and dismissed war workers saw in the Japanese barriers to their reestablishment as farmers and to their obtaining jobs. Politicians manipulated this potential hostility to their own advantage.[52]

At the governor's request the state board of control issued a report in 1919 on the leasing of land in California to aliens ineligible for citizenship. The report dealt only with Japanese, Chinese and Hindus. It dwelt only briefly upon the Hindus, who were negligible in number, and the Chinese, who (the report concluded) were generally engaged in small commercial enterprises and could not be considered a menace because of the Chinese exclusion acts. Nearly the entire report was given over to the Japanese problem—population, birth rate, land ownership and control, financing, labor, the fishing industry, immigration, etc. Aliens and citizens were lumped together in figures on population and land ownership, and much emphasis was placed on the allegedly high birth rate of the Japanese. The governor transmitted the report to the secretary of state under a letter urging control of Japanese immigration.[53] But any anti-Japanese legislation at that time was blocked by a request that such legislation be delayed because of the unfortunate effect it would have upon negotiations for a peace treaty.[54] However, in the off-year of the legislature, and during the election year, 1920, an initiative measure went on the ballot. The chief pressure group supporting the measure was the Joint Immigration Committee, composed of members of the old Exclusion League, the American Legion of California, the State Federation of Labor, the Native Sons of the Golden West, the California State

---

true, however, that the Japanese were by various devices able to circumvent the law, as by purchase in the name of their minor citizen children, trust arrangements, and by use of dummy corporations nominally controlled by citizens. *Ibid.* at 12, 69; Pajus, *op. cit. supra* note 20, at 72; Buell, *op. cit. supra* note 37, at 66.

52 The governor of California in a speech on January 21, 1920, said: "In my opinion the present agitation in California was inspired by candidacy for office. It is true that many worthy citizens have now allied themselves with it for laudable purposes. The fact remains, however, that the dominant factors in the movement are actuated by their desires for political preferment." Kawakami, The Real Japanese Question (1921) 84; see Treat, *op. cit. supra* note 27, at 261.

53 Rep. Cal. State Bd. Control, *loc. cit. supra* note 9.

54 *Ibid.* at 12.

Grange, and other individuals who had long been active in "saving" California from the "yellow peril".[55]

The initiative measure continued in effect the prohibitions of the 1913 law, and deleted the provision authorizing leases of agricultural land for not over three years. In order to plug loopholes in the 1913 law,[56] the measure forbade membership or acquisition of any stock by ineligible aliens in corporations authorized to acquire agricultural land, prohibited such aliens from serving as guardians of estates which they could not properly own or enjoy themselves,[57] required yearly reports from persons acting as guardians, trustees, or agents of ineligible aliens or their minor children, and established a presumption of intent to avoid escheat where a conveyance was made to an eligible person and the consideration was paid by an ineligible alien. Conspiracy to violate the law was made a criminal offense.[58]

The campaign for the law was a bitter one. All of the old prejudices were raked over by the press and the organizations supporting the law. Exaggerated statements were made of the number of Japanese in the state and no factual data was available to refute them since the 1920 census figures were not yet available.[59] It was charged that the birth rate of the Japanese was so high that they would eventually replace the white people.[60] The "low standard of living" of the Japanese, and its alleged eventual effect on the whole society, was effectively used as a scare.[61] Overshadowing economic objections and the claim of nonassimilability of the aliens and their citizen children —"once a Jap always a Jap"—were stressed continuously.[62] This propaganda was sufficiently effective to insure the adoption of the initiative act by a vote of 668,438 to 222,086.[63]

---

[55] MEARS, RESIDENT ORIENTALS ON THE AMERICAN PACIFIC COAST (1928); Buell, *op. cit. supra* note 37, at 70.

[56] *Supra* note 51.

[57] This provision was held unconstitutional in Estate of Tetsubumi Yano (1922) 188 Cal. 645, 206 Pac. 995 as denying equal protection of the laws to the alien and equal privileges and immunities to the ward.

[58] Cal. Stats. 1921, p. lxxxiii.

[59] TREAT, *op. cit. supra* note 27, at 267.

[60] Rep. Cal. State Bd. Control, *op. cit. supra* note 9, at 37. See HEARINGS ON JAPANESE IMMIGRATION BEFORE HOUSE COMMITTEE ON IMMIGRATION AND NATURALIZATION, HOUSE OF REPRESENTATIVES, 66th Cong. 2d Sess. (1920) pt. 1, at 220, 346.

[61] Rep. Cal. State Bd. Control, *op. cit. supra* note 9, at 103, 110; Buell, *op. cit. supra* note 37, at 72; see Phelan, *Why California Objects to the Japanese Invasion* (1921) 93 ANNALS 16.

[62] HEARINGS, *supra* note 60, at 240-244.

[63] TREAT, *op. cit. supra* note 27, at 281.

The campaign against the Japanese did not stop here, however. The Joint Immigration Committee and its allied organizations continued their relentless campaign for exclusion. The proposal of a 1923 amendment expressly forbidding cropping agreements by Japanese and making escheat retroactive to the date of wrongful acquisition[64] gave the pressure groups an opportunity to renew the numerous charges against the Japanese. They also took their case to Congress. Resolutions favoring exclusion were adopted by the legislature in both 1921 and 1923[65] and a provision generally prohibiting admission into this country of aliens ineligible for citizenship was inserted in the immigration act of 1924.[66] President Coolidge expressed his regret that the bill contained the provision but nevertheless approved the measure.[67] A representative of the Joint Immigration Committee stated in 1942 that the committee considered itself instrumental in securing the adoption of the exclusion provision.[68]

Japanese agricultural interests declined in the period following the adoption of the exclusion law. California farm land controlled by Japanese dropped from 321,276 acres in 1920 to 191,427 acres in 1930.[69] The groups in California traditionally opposed to Japanese continued active, however, as guardians of the exclusion clause and as sponsors of additional restrictive legislation. An amendment to the alien land law in 1927 prescribed additional statutory presumptions to facilitate prosecution of escheat proceedings and criminal actions.[70]

---

64 The proposed amendments became law. Cal. Stats. 1923, p. 1020. The retroactive escheat provision apparently divested the aliens of their common-law power to convey good title at any time prior to escheat proceedings. *Cf.* Mott v. Cline (1927) 200 Cal. 434, 253 Pac. 718. Its practical effect was to make uncertain all titles to agricultural land since the land might conceivably have been held after 1923 by a person acting *sub rosa* for an ineligible alien. Presumably to rectify this situation the California legislature recently authorized quiet title actions against the state. Cal. Stats. 1945, p. 2552.

65 *Ibid.* 1921, p. 2165; *ibid.* 1923, p. 1657.

66 43 Stat. (1924) 162, 8 U. S. C. (1940) § 213(c).

67 Ichihashi, *op. cit. supra* note 17, at 309.

68 Hearings Before Select Committee Investigating National Defense Migration, House of Representatives, on H. R. 113, 77th Cong. 2d Sess. (1942) 11069.

69 14th Census of the United States: 1920, Agriculture, Vol. II, p. 313; 15th Census of the United States: 1930, Agriculture, Vol. IV, p. 302.

70 Cal. Stats. 1927, p. 880. One presumption created by this amendment (that the defendant was an ineligible alien if the state proved that he has been in use or occupation of real property and was a member of a race ineligible for citizenship) was upheld in Morrison v. California (1932) 125 Cal. App. 282, 13 P. (2d) 800, appeal dismissed (1933) 288 U. S. 591. The other presumption (that the defendant in a criminal action was an ineligible alien where the state alleged such ineligibility and proved the acquisition of real property) was held to deny due process in Morrison v. California (1934) 291 U. S. 82.

A campaign in the early thirties to repeal the exclusion provision of the immigration act of 1924 was countered by agitation in California involving propaganda in the press contending that oriental competition was sapping the American economy, suits against Japanese merchants for alleged patent infringement, a movement to boycott Japanese-produced commodities, and introduction of legislation to squeeze the Japanese from agriculture entirely.[71] At the same time, however, the alien land law was apparently not seriously enforced; one observer reported in 1934 that the law was virtually a dead letter in many if not all parts of the state.[72] This condition continued until shortly after the outbreak of war with Japan in December, 1941.[73]

The historically anti-Japanese forces took advantage of Pearl Harbor to urge the evacuation of all resident Japanese from the west coast, a policy adopted by the military in February, 1942. Mass removal and ultimate deportation were, of course, a logical result of the earlier campaign for exclusion. It became apparent by the end of 1942, however, that the program of the War Relocation Authority for the further resettlement of the evacuees throughout the country would seriously jeopardize the success of any attempt to deport the evacuees or keep them from eventually returning to the west coast. There followed an amazing and vicious campaign, emanating largely from California, to reactivate west coast prejudice and stir up national feeling against the evacuees.[74] One by-product of this campaign was a 1943 amendment to the alien land law enacting stricter reporting requirements from ineligible alien guardians, providing criminal penalties for violation of the law (as distinguished from conspiracies to violate it), raising the maximum penalty, and authorizing injunction and declaratory judgment suits as additional enforcement procedures.[75] Another offshoot was a renewed alien land law enforcement program.[76]

After initial successes the campaign failed, chiefly because of

---

71 McWilliams, *Once Again the "Yellow Peril"*, The Nation, June 26, 1935, at 735; PAJUS, *op. cit. supra* note 20, at 165.

72 STRONG, *op. cit. supra* note 9, at 211.

73 See MCWILLIAMS, PREJUDICE (1944) 65. The lack of any serious, concerted attempt to enforce the law lends credence to the conclusion that the benefits derived by the anti-Japanese factions from pushing for adoption of alien land laws "were not dependent upon the actual presence or absence of the Japanese farmers, but rather upon the process of opposing them." *Ibid.*

74 *Ibid.* 231-273.

75 Cal. Stats. 1943, pp. 2917, 2999.

76 See REP. W. R. A. Jan.-June 1944, at 44.

WRA's country-wide educational program, the excellent record of relocating evacuees, the excesses of the race-baiters themselves, and the brilliant exploits of the Japanese-American combat team in Italy and France. The west coast was reopened to evacuees in January, 1945.[77] A wave of terrorism in California against returning evacuees arose in the spring but subsided after (if not because) it became apparent that the nation was wholly out of sympathy with such activities and that the inflow of evacuees was continuing.[78] A rear-guard action in the 1945 session of the legislature, however, resulted in a $200,000 appropriation to enforce the alien land law,[79] and additional amendments designed to remove escheat actions from the operation of any statute of limitations,[80] to centralize responsibility for supervising enforcement in the attorney general, and to provide an incentive for local enforcement by splitting the proceeds of successful escheat actions with the counties in which the land is situated.[81]

As mentioned previously, there were some fifty actions pending in California to escheat agricultural lands by the early spring of 1946. All of them were against persons of Japanese ancestry. The majority of the suits were centered in the lower San Joaquin Valley, in Fresno and Tulare counties. It had been announced that fifteen additional suits were ready for filing in Fresno county, and that 150 farms in Tulare county were under investigation.[82] It may be significant that most of the reported instances of terrorism in the spring of 1945 occurred in these two counties.[83]

THE SUPREME COURT DECISIONS

The validity of the 1920 alien land law came before the Supreme Court in 1923 in *Porterfield v. Webb*,[84] which involved a proposed

77 Pub. Proc. 21, War Dept., Dec. 17, 1944, 10 FED. REG. (1945) 53; Pub. Proc. WD-2, War Dept., Jan. 20, 1945, 10 FED. REG. (1945) 889.

78 REP. SEC. INT. 1945, at 275.

79 Cal. Stats. 1945, p. 2739.

80 *Ibid.* p. 2177.

81 *Ibid.* p. 2164. The proponents of the alien land law suffered a definite setback, however, in the 1946 election. So-called Proposition 15, to validate all legislative amendments subsequent to the 1920 initiative act, was decisively defeated. Pacific Citizen, Nov. 9, 1946, at 1.

82 *Ibid.* at 2.

83 Pacific Citizen, Feb. 2, 1946, at 1. Every reported case arising under the California alien land law that the writer has been able to discover involved Japanese, with the exception of several that were not escheat or criminal actions brought by the state. See Mott v. Cline (1927) 200 Cal. 434, 253 Pac. 718; Alfafara v. Fross (1945) 26 Cal. (2d) 358, 159 P. (2d) 14.

84 (1923) 263 U.S. 225.

lease of agricultural land to a Japanese alien. The Court also had before it *Terrace v. Thompson,*[85] testing the constitutionality of the Washington alien land law which prohibited aliens who had not in good faith declared their intention to become citizens from owning and leasing certain lands, and which likewise involved a lease of agricultural land to a Japanese alien. A decision was handed down first in the *Terrace* case. Justice Butler, speaking for the Court, concluded that legislation which denied aliens the right to own real property did not violate the due process guaranty for the reason that the Fourteenth Amendment did not divest the states of those police powers reserved at the time of adoption of the Constitution; and that one of those powers, in the absence of a treaty provision to the contrary, was the authority to deny aliens the right to own land within the state. With respect to the equal protection issue, Justice Butler found "real differences" between a declarant and a nondeclarant alien in the renunciation of allegiance to his former country by a declarant alien. He denied that a person who was ineligible for naturalization was discriminated against since "The rule established by Congress on this subject, in and of itself, furnishes a reasonable basis for classification in a state law withholding from aliens the privilege of land ownership",[86] and "If one incapable of citizenship may lease or own real estate, it is within the realm of possibility that every foot of land within the State might pass to the ownership or possession of noncitizens."[87] He also distinguished the denial of the right to own or lease land from the right to earn a living in the common occupations on the ground that the "quality and allegiance of those who own, occupy, and use the farm lands within its borders are matters of highest importance and affect the safety and power of the state itself."[88]

In the *Porterfield* case the Court relied almost entirely upon its analysis in the *Terrace* decision, stating that the cases were similar and that the Court could not "say that the failure of the California Legislature to extend the prohibited class, so as to include eligible aliens who have failed to declare their intention to become citizens of the United States, was arbitrary or unreasonable."[89]

[85] (1923) 263 U. S. 197.

[86] *Ibid.* at 220.

[87] *Ibid.*

[88] *Ibid.* at 221.

[89] 263 U. S. at 233. At the same term the Court disposed of two other cases arising under the California law. The prohibition of stock ownership in corporations authorized to own agricultural land was sustained in Frick v. Webb (1923) 263 U. S. 326. In Webb v. O'Brien (1923) 263 U. S. 313, the Court held that a cropping contract gave a Japanese

Equal Protection.

The equal protection clause of the Fourteenth Amendment does not, of course, forbid classification for legislative purposes; it only requires that all classifications be based upon substantial differences having a reasonable relation to the objects or persons dealt with and to the public purpose sought to be achieved.[90] By its very nature this standard is not susceptible of precise definition. Great weight is given to the legislature's appraisal of local conditions, and the usual presumption of constitutionality arises. Nor is it essential that the complete source of the evil sought to be cured be treated by the legislation.[91] But a classification arbitrary on its face or shown to be arbitrary by evidence or judicially cognizable facts will not be sustained.[92]

It is well established that aliens are entitled to the protection of the Fourteenth Amendment and for this reason the courts have stricken down laws which had the effect of denying aliens the right to engage in the "common occupations".[93] At the same time the courts have been loathe to invalidate restrictions upon aliens in certain professions or occupations where some special public interest may conceivably be served.[94] And even prior to the 1923 alien land law decisions the courts consistently assumed that the power of the states to restrict alien land ownership, carried over from the common law, was unaffected by the Fourteenth Amendment.[95]

---

alien use, control, or benefit of agricultural land that was prohibited, reversing the lower court's decision [(N. D. Cal. 1921) 279 Fed. 117] and in effect refusing to follow the state court's interpretation of the law prior to the 1923 amendment which specifically proscribed cropping contracts [*In re* Okahara (1923) 191 Cal. 353, 216 Pac. 614].

In the recent Oyama decision, *supra* note 6, the California supreme court added nothing to the rationale of the Porterfield decision, except to hold that the "clear and present danger" test applicable to restrictions upon civil liberties was not relevant, and that it was enough if there was (as the court found) a "rational basis" for the classification.

[90] Southern R. Co. v. Greene (1910) 216 U. S. 400; Frost v. Corporation Comm. (1929) 278 U. S. 515; Old Dearborn Co. v. Seagram Corp. (1936) 299 U. S. 183.

[91] Clarke v. Deckebach (1927) 274 U. S. 392.

[92] Weaver v. Palmer Bros. (1926) 270 U. S. 402.

[93] Yick Wo v. Hopkins (1886) 118 U. S. 356 (laundry business); Truax v. Raich (1915) 239 U. S. 33 (restaurant cook); Templar v. State (1902) 131 Mich. 254, 90 N. W. 1058 (barbering); *In re* Opinion of Justices (1911) 207 Mass. 601, 94 N. E. 558 (hotel and restaurant business); State v. Sinchuk (1921) 96 Conn. 605, 115 Atl. 33 (news dealing).

[94] Clarke v. Deckebach, *supra* note 91 (operation of poolrooms); Trageser v. Gray (1890) 73 Md. 250, 20 Atl. 905 (sale of liquor); *In re* Yamashita (1902) 30 Wash. 234, 70 Pac. 482 (practice of law).

[95] *Cf.* Hauenstein v. Lynham (1879) 100 U. S. 483; Phillips v. Moore (1879) 100 U. S. 208; Blythe v. Hinckley (1901) 180 U. S. 333.

It is exceedingly doubtful whether there is any real social purpose served by restrictive state legislation against aliens as a class, at least in the field of land ownership. The arguments pointing to this conclusion are inextricably intermingled with considerations of due process and are therefore reserved for discussion under that section. Even if it be assumed, however, that the denial of the privilege of land ownership to *all* aliens does not violate the equal protection guaranty and is a proper exercise of state police power, the California law is subject to inquiry for its discrimination against one class of aliens—those ineligible for citizenship—and its application in practice against one group of aliens within that class, the Japanese.

The first of Justice Butler's justifications for the discrimination against ineligible aliens was no more than the fact that Congress had not seen fit to make them eligible for naturalization:

> "Two classes of aliens inevitably result from the naturalization laws, —those who may and those who may not become citizens. The rule established by Congress on this subject, in and of itself, furnishes a reasonable basis for classification in a state law withholding from aliens the privilege of land ownership as defined in the act."[96]

This statement assumes that the criteria for state classification are the same as for the particular federal classification. Congressional power to restrict or extend naturalization to designated classes of aliens is plenary. Justice Butler set up the judgment of Congress on a purely political issue—a judgment at that with which many thoughtful persons disagree[97]—as a ground for deciding a constitutional question involving fundamental rights of persons under state law. He ignored the well-established principle that each statutory classification must be tested in the light of the purpose for which the statute was enacted. Surely some more substantial rationale must be provided than this.

Another justification for the discrimination was that if ineligible aliens could lease or own real estate it was within the "realm of possibility" that noncitizens might acquire "every foot of land" within the state. It would be difficult to find a better example of judicial ostrich-ism. Even at the time of the 1923 decisions, the immigration laws absolutely prohibited the immigration of natives of countries within the so-called "barred zone", including the large East Indies

[96] Terrace v. Thompson, *supra* note 85, at 220.

[97] *E.g.*, Gordon, *The Racial Barrier to American Citizenship* (1945) 93 U. of Pa. L. Rev. 237; *In re* Po (1894) 28 N. Y. S. 383, 7 Misc. 471.

islands, French Indo-China, Siam, India, Persia, Afghanistan, and most of China.[98] Chinese were separately excluded by the Chinese exclusion acts.[99] Japanese immigration was severely restricted by the gentlemen's agreement.[100] The only ineligible aliens whose immigration was not prohibited or severely restricted at that time were Koreans and nonwhites of the Central and South American countries; there is nothing to indicate that they constituted any problem whatever.[101]

Only two of the restricted nationalities—the Chinese and the Japanese—had ever migrated to California in appreciable numbers. The Chinese in California had diminished in number from 132,300 in 1882 to 61,639 in 1920, and even California admitted that they were no menace to the future of the state.[102] The California Japanese population in 1910 was 41,356—1.74 per cent of the state's population—and 4,502 of this total were American-born. The corresponding figure for 1920 was 71,952—2.1 per cent of the state's population—but by this time over one-third of the total was American-born;[103] the ratio of aliens to total population did not increase at all during this period. With respect to agricultural lands, the percentage of California farms controlled by Japanese, *aliens and citizens alike,* increased only from 2.1 to 4.4, and the acreage involved in 1920 was merely 1.2 per cent of the state's agricultural land.[104]

The year following the Supreme Court decisions saw the enactment of the immigration act of 1924 generally prohibiting further immigration of aliens ineligible for citizenship.[105] From 1920 to 1940 the total Japanese population in the state increased only from 71,952 (one-third American citizens) to 93,717 (two-thirds American citizens).[106] During the same period the percentage of Japanese-controlled farms decreased from 4.4 to 3.9, and the acreage involved from 1.2 to 0.7.[107] Since these figures include bona fide holdings by citizens, the proportionate decrease in alien holdings has, of course, been even more marked. It is readily apparent that there is no factual

---

98 Immigration Act of 1917, § 3, 39 STAT. (1917) 875, 876, 8 U. S. C. (1940) § 136(n).

99 *Supra* note 15.

100 *Supra* p. 65.

101 *Supra* p. 69.

102 *Ibid.*

103 ICHIHASHI, *op. cit. supra* note 17, at 320.

104 H. R. REP. No. 2124, 77th Cong. 2d Sess. (1942) 127.

105 43 STAT. (1924) 162, 8 U. S. C. (1940) § 213(c).

106 H. R. REP. No. 2124, 77th Cong. 2d Sess. (1942) 96.

107 *Ibid.* at 122.

basis whatever to support a conclusion that it is even within "the realm of possibility" for the land holdings of Japanese aliens in California to increase, much less dominate California agriculture.

No one will disagree with Justice Butler's general assertion that the quality and allegiance of persons who own and occupy lands within a state "are matters of highest importance and affect the safety and power of the State itself." The only additional justification given for separate treatment of ineligible aliens in this connection, however, is the quotation, without amplification, from the lower court's decision in the *Terrace* case:

> "It is obvious that one who is not a citizen and cannot become one lacks an interest in, and the power to effectually work for the welfare of, the state, and, so lacking, the state may rightfully deny him the right to own and lease real estate within its boundaries."[108]

The charge that those who cannot become citizens lack an interest in state welfare is merely a generalization unsupported by facts. The vast majority of ineligible aliens in this country are domiciled here. Their economic security lies in the businesses and occupations in which they have established themselves. They have largely reared their children here, children who by virtue of their birth in this country are United States citizens, and who have attended our schools and whose futures are clearly identified with this country. Clearly these aliens have as much at stake in the economic, social, and political ills or good fortunes of the state as anyone else, regardless of citizenship.[109] It is simply unrealistic to conjecture that ineligible aliens as a class have less interest in the welfare of their communities and their states than have other aliens simply because they are denied the privilege of becoming United States citizens.

Nor did Justice Butler choose to elucidate his assertion that aliens who cannot become citizens lack the power effectually to work for the state. Presumably he meant that they lacked the power to vote and to hold public office. The franchise is a privilege withheld from aliens by the state; lack of power to vote is not a disability in-

---

[108] 263 U. S. at 220.

[109] Compare the following statement by Mr. Justice Black in *Ex parte* Kawato (1942) 317 U. S. 69, 71, upholding the right of a Japanese enemy alien to sue in the federal courts: "Nothing in this record indicates, and we cannot assume, that he [the petitioner] came to America for any purpose different from that which prompted millions of others to seek our shores—a chance to make his home and work in a free country, governed by just laws, which promise equal protection to all who abide by them."

herent in their status.[110] Except with respect to the highest federal offices, the same is true of occupancy of public offices.[111] Here again, it is a dangerous doctrine to permit political discrimination to justify additional discrimination. Even today residents of the District of Columbia are disfranchised but their disfranchisement could hardly justify denying them the right to own land on the theory that they cannot work for the welfare of the state. With ineligible aliens as well as any other disfranchised group, the potential to work constructively for the state exists despite any state-imposed disability to participate in the affairs of government. Actually the ineligible aliens who migrated to this country have played an important historical role in the development of our resources, and they continue to function as an integral segment of our society. As a class their roots are here. No one would deny that during World War II they contributed to the war effort, directly and indirectly, in as many ways as did their adopted countrymen. Again, it is unrealistic to conclude that categorically they cannot or will not work in the interest of the state simply because of their political disability.

The complete artificiality of Justice Butler's political justification is demonstrated by the discrimination in favor of aliens who have the opportunity but prefer not to become citizens. The California law permits such aliens to own land under precisely the same conditions as citizens. It is not even necessary that aliens be living in the United States in order to enjoy the right to own California land if they are not of a race ineligible for naturalization. Obviously the reasoning of Justice Butler with respect to lack of interest in and incapability of working for the welfare of the state would, if valid at all, apply even more strongly to aliens who fail or refuse to take advantage of the privilege of naturalization extended to them and aliens who do not even live in this country.

Hardly more need be said to demonstrate the lack of substantive basis for Justice Butler's rationalization to support the California law's discrimination against ineligible aliens as a class. But we should not stop here. The unsavory truth is that the law was aimed solely at the Japanese, and during its spotty history of enforcement was used only to throttle them. It should be further tested for its actual dis-

---

110 United States v. Wong Kim Ark (1898) 169 U.S. 649; Dorsey v. Brigham (1898) 177 Ill. 250, 52 N.E. 303; see Aylsworth, *The Passing of Alien Suffrage* (1931) 25 AM. POL. SCI. REV. 114.

111 Connell v. State (1924) 196 Ind. 421, 144 N.E. 882; but *cf.* State *ex rel.* Off v. Smith (1861) 14 Wis. 539; Opinion of the Justices (1877) 122 Mass. 594.

crimination against a racial group within the more general category.[112] All legal restrictions which curtail the civil rights of a single ethnic or racial group are immediately suspect. "Pressing public necessity may sometimes justify the existence of such restrictions; racial antagonism never can."[113]

Most of the writings of the times on the "Japanese menace" are totally unreliable. One observer, commenting on the charges made against the Japanese during this period, has said:

> "Determined to stop the Japanese immigration, the agitators proceeded to convince a majority of the voters of the Pacific Coast of this necessity and to annoy the Japanese already here so much that they would voluntarily depart for Japan. . . . And so the agitators struck at the Japanese in every possible way. Many of the political leaders among these agitators were experienced in such matters. . . . Every significant thing about the Japanese, whether favorable or unfavorable, was seized upon and twisted about until it made a suitable weapon for injuring the newcomers. Hence, if they asked less than the going wage, they were threatening the American standard of living; if they demanded better wages, they were avaricious; if they were successful in farming and saved enough to buy their own ranch, they were driving the whites out; if they were unsuccessful they were 'wearing out the land.'
>
> "As an actual fact, the specific charges made against the Japanese have very little significance in themselves. They were merely the smoke pouring up from a bonfire; they gave evidence of a fire and that was about all. This the Japanese and their friends discovered when they attempted to answer the charges with facts. It was as useless to answer the charges as to pour water on smoke."[114]

The most common cry against the Japanese during the campaign for adoption of the 1920 law was that they would soon acquire all of the agricultural land of the state. Justice Butler accepted this possibility as a justification for the discrimination. The cold fact, conclusively demonstrated earlier in this article, is that Japanese aliens never have controlled more than an infinitesimal acreage of California land. With continued prohibition of or severe restrictions upon Japanse immigration certain, and with the resident aliens, the great

---

[112] Yick Wo v. Hopkins, *supra* note 93 (enforcement only against Chinese of restrictive laundry ordinance purporting to be of general applicability held to be denial of equal protection); see also Quong Wing v. Kirkendall (1912) 223 U. S. 59.

[113] Korematsu v. United States, *supra* note 7, at 216.

[114] STRONG, *op. cit. supra* note 9, at 125. See also WAR RELOCATION AUTHORITY, MYTHS AND FACTS ABOUT THE JAPANESE AMERICANS (1945).

majority of whom came here before 1924, rapidly dying off, the next few decades will see the percentage of alien holdings approach zero.

Another charge, more relevant to the public interest, if true, than the mere quantity of land controlled by the Japanese, was that the Japanese were destroying the productivity of the soil more than were other races of aliens. No reliable factual support for the assertion has been found. To the contrary, there is evidence that they were excellent farmers and preserved the soil.

> "The complaint that the Japanese 'skin' the land and ruin the orchards is frequently heard. Most of the Japanese are tenants, and tenant farming is likely to have such results. No case can be made against the Japanese as against other tenants, however. On the contrary, while one finds rather numerous instances in which the landowners have been dissatisfied with the Japanese tenants they have had, the general opinion is that the Japanese are good farmers and give rather more than less interest than is usual among tenants to the care and conservation of the properties leased by them. At Sacramento recently the president of one large fruit-shipping firm and the treasurer of another said that the Japanese were among the most careful and painstaking orchardists. At Fresno, a prominent Armenian told me that he would rather lease his vineyards to Japanese than to farmers of his own race because they took better care of them. The charge that the Japanese ruin the farms is a charge, which, like many others, one hears less of the closer he gets to the place where the damage is presumed to have taken place. On the whole the Japanese are regarded as good farmers and good tenants."[115]

It was charged that the Japanese drove "white" farmers from the soil by their long hours of work and low standards of living, that the "white" farmer could not maintain his usual standard of living and compete with the Japanese. Even assuming the truth of this charge, it is anomalous that efficiency and productive ability should ever be a valid ground for discrimination against any group. The charge was nevertheless largely false.

Writing in 1924, Robert Welles Ritchie said:

> "The three areas of greatest Japanese concentration then, in 1920, as now, were in the cantaloupe and winter-lettuce fields of the Imperial Valley, in the extreme southeastern part of the state; in the mountain fruit center of Placer County; and in the strawberry fields and the potato, celery, onion and asparagus districts roughly embraced in the term, the Delta, which lies in the exact center of the state. Let us be very blunt in this context and say that in the Imperial Valley and the

[115] MILLIS, *op. cit. supra* note 35, at 148.

> Delta country the Japanese never displaced white men, for white men would not work there; and in the mountain fruit district the Chinese, and after them the Japanese, came in—after nearly every white man had quit—and made a go of a crippled industry."[116]

Other sources bear out this conclusion.[117] The Japanese turned primarily to intensive farming, which required painstaking care and long, hard hours of toil, and in which the ordinary American farmer was slow to engage.[118] By and large they created their own niche in California agriculture without replacing white farmers to any great extent. In so doing they contributed greatly to the development of the agricultural wealth of the state.

Admittedly the standard of living of the Japanese was at first low. The living standard of any people is determined mainly by opportunities to make a decent living. There is ample evidence that the Japanese were constantly striving to overcome the handicaps that forced them, when they first arrived as immigrants, to accept low wages or starve.[119] They were no different from any other first-generation group in that they of necessity worked hard and long hours to get their foothold. As their economic status improved, their living standards rose. The natural effect of the alien land law was to restrict their opportunities to better themselves.

The remaining charges made against the Japanese relate to alleged cultural and political allegiance to Japan and inability to be assimilated in this country, telescoped in the charge "Once a Jap always a Jap". General De Witt grasped at them in his post-mortem justification for the west coast evacuation of the Japanese in 1942; Mr. Justice Murphy summarizes them in his dissent in the *Korematsu* decision as follows:

> "Individuals of Japanese ancestry are condemned because they are said to be 'a large, unassimilated, tightly knit racial group, bound to an enemy nation by strong ties of race, culture, custom and religion.' They are claimed to be given to 'emperor worshipping ceremonies' and to 'dual citizenship.' Japanese language schools and allegedly pro-Japanese organizations are cited as evidence of possible group disloyalty, together with facts as to certain persons being educated and residing at length in Japan. It is intimated that many of these

116 The Country Gentleman, March 1, 1924, p. 1.

117 See MILLIS, *op. cit. supra* note 35, at 145; 23 REP. IMMIG. COMM. (1911) 86.

118 MILLIS, *op. cit. supra* note 35, at 89.

119 *Ibid.* at 164; H. R. REP. No. 2124, 77th Cong. 2d Sess. (1942) 64; PALMER, ORIENTALS IN AMERICAN LIFE (1934) 55.

> individuals deliberately resided 'adjacent to strategic points,' thus enabling them 'to carry into execution a tremendous program of sabotage on a mass scale should any considerable number of them have been inclined to do so.' "[120]

It would follow from these charges, particularly if there were any factual basis for the assertion that the Japanese were rapidly gaining control of all the agricultural lands in the state, that in time of international crisis the Japanese might constitute a special hazard to the security of the state. The argument might then be made that the state, while prohibited by treaty from dealing with all sources of the evil, could nevertheless minimize the danger by striking at the ownership of agricultural land.

Accepting for the moment the premise that the Japanese aliens might have constituted a special risk, and the implicit assumption as to the inadequacy of the federal war power, the argument is unsound. Prohibition of ownership of agricultural land by aliens inevitably increases the likelihood of their gravitation to other better income opportunities, which could be found only in urban areas. Under conditions of modern warfare the greater danger to internal security from espionage and sabotage is found in the city. Urban centers provide the factories necessary for war production, the warehouses, the heart of the transportation and communication systems, the concentration of vital information needed by the enemy. And surveillance of enemy agents' activities is infinitely more difficult among tightly-packed masses of humanity than it is in sparsely settled rural areas. If there was any real danger from the resident Japanese in California, the alien land law tended to increase it by driving them from the farms.

But like the other accusations leveled against the Japanese, these charges were also a mass of misrepresentations, distortions, and exaggerations. Mr. Justice Murphy was clearly correct in his conclusion that every charge "relative to race, religion, culture, geographical location, and legal and economic status has been substantially discredited by independent studies made by experts in these matters."[121] We have just finished a bitter struggle with Japan that put the observations of these experts to the test. It is reported that no case of espionage or sabotage by any person of Japanese ancestry domiciled in Hawaii or on the mainland was uncovered during the entire course

[120] Korematsu v. United States, *supra* note 7, at 237.

[121] *Ibid.* at 240. See also, WAR RELOCATION AUTHORITY, *loc. cit. supra* note 114.

of the war. Thousands of the aliens in the relocation centers streamed out to plant and harvest sugar beets and other vital war crops. Many others found maintenance jobs on railroads, employment at ordnance depots, positions in military language schools and war agencies, and other war-connected service. Probably no better proof of the assimilation of the Japanese exists than the record of the 23,000 Japanese-American lads, the sons of the aliens so vilified by the race-baiters, who fought brilliantly in both the European and Pacific war theaters. The simple truth is that the vast majority of the Japanese in this country are bound to us by the most powerful economic, family, and personal considerations. Discrimination against them in the ownership of land on the basis of inability to be assimilated or because of closer ties to the motherland than other groups of immigrants is unwarranted.

Due Process.

In the *Terrace* decision it was concluded that legislation denying aliens the right to acquire real property did not violate the due process guaranty for the reasons that: (1) the Fourteenth Amendment did not take away from the states those police powers that were reserved at the time of the adoption of the Constitution; and (2) one of those powers, in the absence of any treaty provision to the contrary, was to deny aliens the right to own land. Admittedly the Fourteenth Amendment did not deprive the states of the power to safeguard the public health, safety, and welfare. And at common law an alien's rights in real property were, generally speaking, subject to forfeiture to the sovereign.[122] Nevertheless, a control sanctioned by the common law does not forever remain inviolate. What may once have been thought to be a reasonable restriction in the common interest may by changing circumstances or upon reexamination be shorn of its social justification.[123] And the due process clause of the Fourteenth Amendment is operative to protect the individual, whether he be alien or citizen, against state interference with private rights that cannot be more

[122] An alien could acquire real property by act of the parties, although not by operation of law. In the case of leases of houses by merchants who were alien friends, their rights were apparently indefeasible. In all other instances they held subject to the possibility of forfeiture to the sovereign. Co. LITT. *2.b; 1 BL. COMM. *371; Fairfax v. Hunter's Lessee (1813) 11 U. S. 602; Dutton v. Donahue (1932) 44 Wyo. 52, 8 P. (2d) 90.

[123] Compare cases relating to the effect of changed circumstances on constitutionality of statutes, *e.g.*, Nashville C. & St. L. Ry. Co. v. Walters (1935) 294 U. S. 405; Chastleton Corp. v. Sinclair (1924) 264 U. S. 543.

than offset by public benefit. This balance of convenience is the heart of the due process issue. Justice Butler disposed of it by ignoring it.

What public benefit is served by state restrictions on alien land ownership? The justification at common law rested primarily upon the security of the realm.[124] But under our federal system the responsibility for security against attack or infiltration by foreign nations rests primarily in the federal government. Congress has plenary power over immigration.[125] All aliens may be and are required to register themselves as such.[126] Persons acting on behalf of other countries must similarly register, and copies of any political propaganda such persons disseminate must be filed with the government.[127] On outbreak of war enemy aliens are subject to summary apprehension and internment;[128] persons can be evacuated from critical defense areas regardless of citizenship where the federal government deems it a military necessity and there is a rational basis for that judgment;[129] curfew may be imposed as a precautionary measure under similar conditions.[130] Or where the need is imperative, martial law can be established.[131] In addition to these restraints, summary federal seizure or other control of alien assets, real property as well as tangible and intangible personalty, that might conceivably be utilized against the best interests of the country is fully authorized in time of emergency.[132]

The potential security hazard created by our alien residents can, for that matter, easily be overexaggerated. Aliens constitute but a small fraction of our population, and their number is decreasing.[133] Severe quantitative and qualitative restrictions upon immigration preclude any substantial threat from new immigrants.[134] More im-

124 See Calvin's Case (1609) 77 Eng. Rep. 377.

125 Fok Yung Yo v. United States (1902) 185 U. S. 296.

126 8 U. S. C. (1940) § 452; Hines v. Davidowitz (1941) 312 U. S. 52.

127 22 U. S. C. (1940) § 611.

128 50 U. S. C. (1940) § 21.

129 Korematsu v. United States, *supra* note 7.

130 Hirabayashi v. United States (1943) 320 U. S. 81.

131 See Fairman, *The Law of Martial Rule and the National Emergency* (1942) 55 HARV. L. REV. 1253.

132 50 U. S. C. APP. SUPP. V. (1946) §§ 1-31, 616. For discussion, see *Enemy Property* (1945) 11 LAW & CONTEMP. PROB. 1 *et seq.*

133 The 1940 alien registration disclosed 4,889,770 aliens in this country, 3.7 per cent of our then total population of 131,669,275. (Information received from Bureau of the Census.) In 1920 the alien population was 7,430,809, and in 1930 it was 6,284,613. See Fellman, *The Alien's Right to Work* (1938) 22 MINN. L. REV. 137.

134 The total annual immigration quota, computed under the immigration act of 1924, as amended [8 U. S. C. (1940) § 211], is now 153,879, or slightly over 0.1 per cent

portant, this country has always been an in-migrant nation, and the great bulk of the immigrants have taken root here. By and large their interests have merged with the interests of the American people.[135]

The lack of need for state controls on alien land ownership as a security measure is strongly indicated by the action taken by New Jersey and New York during World War II. In 1943 New Jersey, which had previously limited to alien friends the right to hold real property, placed resident enemy aliens in the same category as alien friends if they were not interned, their property had not been confiscated, and they were permitted to do business by the federal government.[136] In 1944 New York, upon recommendation of the law revision commission, conferred upon all aliens the same rights to hold land as native-born citizens, a privilege theretofore reserved to nonenemy aliens. It was pointed out in a footnote to this amendment that control over enemy alien property was left solely to the federal government, "which has already acted for the protection of the nation through the Trading with the Enemy Act and various proclamations and executive orders."[137]

What other legitimate justifications there could be for restrictions upon alien land ownership are difficult to conceive. Aliens have no inherent special privileges if permitted to own land. Like citizens they must pay taxes[138] and obey all applicable laws.[139] There is nothing inherently injurious to morals or dangerous to the public health or safety in the mere fact of land ownership or control; the cases upholding discrimination against aliens in the right to engage in certain

---

of our 1940 population. The quota has never been filled in recent years, and the net inflow has been considerably reduced by emigration. Thus, from 1931 to 1936 there was a net emigration of 103,142. Fellman, *loc. cit. supra* note 133. During the following three years the total net immigration was 149,958, less than one year's quota. Note (1940) 17 N. Y. U. L. Q. 242, 253. In the pre-war years of 1940 and 1941 net immigration figures were 48,295 and 34,661, respectively. (Statistics furnished by Immigration and Naturalization Service.)

Qualitative requirements are strict. The law excludes, among others, persons mentally or physically defective, paupers or others likely to become a public charge, felons, immoral persons, contract laborers, and persons believing in or affiliated with organizations that believe in forcible overthrow of the government. 8 U. S. C. (1940) § 136.

135 For judicial recognition of this fact, see the quotation from *Ex parte* Kawato, *supra* note 109.

136 N. J. Laws 1943, p. 395.

137 N. Y. Laws 1944, p. 627.

138 They are entitled to equal taxation, however. *Ex parte* Kotta (1921) 187 Cal. 27, 200 Pac. 957.

139 Carlisle v. United States (1872) 83 U. S. 147.

occupations that may be specially affected with a public interest[140] have no application here. On the contrary, by bringing aliens into closer contact with our institutions and giving them a stronger economic interest in the public well-being, alien land ownership appears to be socially desirable.

If anything, restrictive land laws would seem to affect the public interest adversely. By narrowing economic opportunities they limit full utilization of the natural capacities of the aliens to contribute to the development of economic wealth. By the very fact of overt discrimination they tend to breed distrust and disillusionment and to retard assimilation. At the same time they tend to prostitute the naturalization process by making the economic motive a primary incentive for seeking American citizenship.

In eighteen states aliens are expressly authorized by statute or constitutional provision to acquire and dispose of real property as if they were citizens.[141] Aliens who establish residence in the state have the same rights in six additional jurisdictions.[142] It is hardly credible that any real public purpose is served by restrictions on alien land ownership when half the states have seen fit to confer upon all aliens

---

140 Cases cited *supra* note 94.

141 ALA. CONST. art. I, § 34; ALA. CODE (1940) tit. 47, § 1; COLO. CONST. art. II, § 27; COLO. STAT. (1935) c. 7, § 6; CONN. GEN. STAT. (1930) §§ 5055-5056; DEL. REV. CODE (1935) §§ 3655-3657; FLA. CONST., Declaration of Rights, § 18; FLA. STAT. (1941) § 731.28; ME. REV. STAT. (1944) c. 154, § 2; MASS. LAWS (1932) c. 184, § 1; MICH. CONST. art. XVI, § 9; MICH. COMP. LAWS (1929) § 13493; NEV. COMP. LAWS (1929) § 6365; New York Laws 1944, p. 627; N. C. GEN. STAT. (1943) § 64-1; N. D. REV. CODE §§ 47-0111, 56-0116; OHIO CODE (Throckmorton, 1940) § 10503-13; R. I. GEN. LAWS (1938) c. 432; S. D. CONST. art. VI, § 14; S. D. CODE (1939) §§ 51.0205, 56.0120; TENN. CODE (Williams, 1934) §§ 7187-7190; W. VA. CONST. art. II, § 5; W. VA. CODE (1943) § 3541; WIS. CONST. art. I, § 15; WIS. STAT. (1943) §§ 234.22, 234.23.

Alaska and Hawaii permit unrestricted land ownership by aliens resident in the United States [8 U. S. C. (1940) §§ 71-77] and Georgia, Maryland, and New Jersey by alien friends [GA. CODE (1933) §§ 79-303, 79-304; MD. CODE (Flack 1939) art. 3, § 1; N. J. REV. STAT. (1937) §§ 3:3-13, 46:3-18]. There are only acreage limitations in Indiana, Minnesota, Pennsylvania, and South Carolina [IND. STAT. ANN. (Baldwin, 1934) §§ 14707, 14708; MINN. STAT. (1941) § 500.22; PA. STAT. (Purdon, 1936) tit. 68, §§ 22-32; S. C. CONST. art. III, § 35; S. C. CODE (1942) §§ 8687, 8907, 8908, 7790].

142 Arkansas, Iowa, Mississippi, New Hampshire, Oklahoma, and Wyoming. ARK. CONST. art. I, § 20; IOWA CONST. art. I, § 22; IOWA CODE (1939) §§ 10214, 10215; MISS. CODE (1942) § 842; N. H. REV. LAWS (1942) c. 259, § 19, c. 340, § 9; OKLA. CONST. art. XXII, § 1; OKLA. STAT. (1941) tit. 60, §§ 121-127; WYO. CONST. art. I, § 29; WYO. REV. STAT. (1931) § 88-4004. Recently enacted Arkansas and Wyoming statutes prohibiting land ownership by persons of Japanese descent and by ineligible aliens, respectively (Ark. Laws 1943, p. 74; Wyo. Laws 1943, p. 33) clearly run afoul state constitutional provisions guaranteeing alien residents equal rights with citizens in land ownership. See Applegate v. Luke (1927) 173 Ark. 93, 291 S. W. 978.

or upon resident aliens the same rights as citizens, states ranging from hinterland agricultural states with negligible alien populations, such as Arkansas and Iowa, to heavily industrialized and urbanized states like Massachusetts and New York with large alien concentrations.[143]

Balanced against the dubious need for state alien land restrictions of any kind is the interference with private rights that flows from the California law. An agricultural landowner is denied the right to sell land to or avail himself of the services of a Japanese alien except as employer, with consequent master-servant liability; he must pay cash for the alien's services and cannot share the risk through share-cropping arrangements. The alien is prohibited from advancing beyond the status of an ordinary laborer in one of this country's major occupations. He cannot utilize his skill or his savings to better himself economically in what is often the one field of endeavor he knows. If either the landowner or the alien violates the law, he is subject to criminal prosecution, and the alien's interests are subject to escheat as of the date of acquisition, thus rendering the alien accountable for any interim profits. This is in sharp contrast with the comparatively liberal common-law provisions which attached no criminal penalty to alien ownership and permitted the alien to acquire and enjoy land until forfeiture proceedings were instituted. These are substantial invasions of private rights; no court should uphold them in the absence of positive evidence of a corresponding public benefit. The writer believes the conclusion to be inescapable that no such benefit can be shown.

Furthermore, because the 1911 treaty with Japan was terminated in January, 1940,[144] the California law might now deny Japanese aliens the right to own or lease residential and commercial property as well as agricultural land. This depends upon whether the provision authorizing acquisition of land by ineligible aliens only to the extent provided by "any treaty now existing" is construed to incorporate the 1911 treaty in the law, irrespective of subsequent changes in or abrogation of the treaty. The state attorney general has taken the position that the treaty was incorporated in the law, citing usual rules of statu-

---

[143] In 1940 the percentage of aliens (including persons whose citizenship was not ascertained by census enumerators) in these four states, in the order named was 0.15, 1.2, 8.2 and 8.2. (Computed from statistics in 16th Census of the United States: 1940, Population, Vol. II.)

[144] H. R. Doc. No. 339, 78th Cong. 1st Sess. (1943) vol. II, p. 189.

tory construction;[145] a superior court which had taken the contrary view, and held that the law is now applicable to commercial leases, was reversed on appeal,[146] but the California supreme court has not yet ruled on the issue. It is clear that the Washington statute upheld in the *Terrace* decision now cuts practically a clean sweep with respect to Japanese aliens.[147] The absurdity of the doctrine casually enunciated in the 1923 land law decisions—that state power to prohibit alien land ownership is limited only by treaty provisions—could hardly be better illustrated. If the Japanese alien evacuees returning to their domiciles are by law prohibited from purchasing or leasing any real property whatever, those not fortunate enough to have acquired business properties before abrogation of the treaty—and to have retained them through all the vicissitudes of evacuation—are relegated to the position of wage earners. In effect the law would deny them the right to engage in any common occupation which in ordinary business practice requires the ownership or lease of real property.[148] Similarly—and this is even more fundamental—those without homes to return to would be unable to buy or lease houses in which to live.[149] It is inconceivable that any court should hold that such a harsh and repressive law did not deprive aliens of due process of law.

* * * * *

The California Alien Land Law is a symbol of racial intolerance and prejudice. Its genesis and history are part and parcel of the whole sordid spectacle of anti-Japanese agitation in California. In such a context it should not be enough to indulge in speculative justifications of the law as the Supreme Court did in 1923 or to plead ignorance of local conditions and the "possibility" of a "rational basis" for the legislative judgment.[150] Restrictive legislation stemming from race

---

145 3 OP. ATT'Y GEN. (1944) 112. And *cf. In re* Heath (1892) 144 U. S. 92; *In re* McNabb (D. Ore. 1909) 175 Fed. 511; Fischer v. Simon (1902) 95 Tex. 234, 66 S. W. 447, 882.

146 Palermo v. Stockton Theatres, Inc. (1946) 76 A. C. A. 26, 36, 172 P. (2d) 103, 109, hearing granted (Oct. 31, 1946).

147 The Washington law excepts only mineral lands and lands necessary for their development or manufacture of products therefrom. See WASH. REV. STAT. (Remington, 1933) §§ 10581, 10582.

148 *Cf.* cases cited *supra* note 93.

149 While a license to use a house might not be forbidden since it constitutes no interest in land, the likelihood of finding landlords willing to grant revocable licenses is exceedingly remote. For all practical purposes the alien's right to live in the state would be meaningless.

150 *Cf.* Clarke v. Deckebach, *supra* note 91; People v. Oyama, *supra* note 6.

prejudice, particularly against a minority that is unable to participate in the political process, calls for a more searching judicial inquiry.[151] Such an inquiry would reveal, it is submitted, that the alien land law is unjust and unjustifiable legislation, and that it clearly violates rights protected by the Fourteenth Amendment.

---

151 See United States v. Carolene Products Co. (1938) 304 U.S. 144, 152, n. 4; *cf.* Nixon v. Herndon (1927) 273 U.S. 536; Smith v. Texas (1940) 311 U.S. 128; Korematsu v. United States, *supra* note 7.

Landless by Law: Japanese Immigrants in California Agriculture to 1941

Besides racial prejudice against them, the Japanese are not allowed the privilege of becoming full citizens of the United States, thus being prevented from developing along many lines. Among these, the most noteworthy is the California Alien Land Law and the consequent laws which prohibit Japanese from possessing land unless they are citizens. Under these circumstances, can it justly and fairly be claimed that the Japanese are non-assimilable?

Kiichi Kanzaki, *California and the Japanese*, 1921

THE Japanese occupy a unique place in the history of America's immigrants. They were denied the privilege of naturalization (until 1952), forbidden to purchase or lease farm land (in California, 1913-1956), driven from their homes by the wartime evacuation and confined in concentration camps (1942-1945). Yet the Japanese are now one of the most successful of all ethnic groups in America. The narrative of this remarkable experience has been written often and well, and detailed studies of its political, legal, and social aspects have been made. Economic historians, however, have done relatively little to analyze and learn from the Japanese-American experience.

My paper, which attempts to fill this gap, offers a brief sketch of the involvement of the Japanese in California agriculture during the half century before the Second World War. I then consider two related issues in the economic history of discrimination against the Japanese in America: first, the discrimination against them in the agricultural labor and land rental markets; second, the legal discrimination against them required by the alien land laws of California. A concluding section takes a broad view of and offers some generalizations about this historical experience.

IMMIGRATION AND EMPLOYMENT

Substantial numbers of Japanese immigrants arrived for the first time in the mainland United States during the 1890s. The volume of

Journal of Economic History, Vol. XXXVIII, No. 1 (March 1978). Copyright © The Economic History Association. All rights reserved.

I have received valuable advice and bibliographical assistance from Tetsuden Kashima and Frank Miyamoto at the University of Washington; through correspondence, Masakazu Iwata (Biola College) and Harry H. L. Kitano (UCLA) were helpful. To all of them, my sincere gratitude.

arrivals increased sharply at the turn of the century, and the period 1900-1908 witnessed the greatest influx. The United States census of 1910 counted more than 72,000 Japanese in the continental United States, but this enumeration was especially defective and the actual number was perhaps as much as 20,000 larger.[1] After the Gentlemen's Agreement went into effect in 1908, Japanese immigration declined and included a much larger proportion of women. Although the United States census of 1920 showed a total increase of almost 39,000 Japanese during the preceding decade, the increase was less than 14,000 for foreign-born males, and much of that apparent increase was probably spurious, reflecting only the greater completeness of the 1920 count. With the new immigration law in effect after 1924, Japanese immigration became negligible. Although natural increase pushed the resident population up, a considerable net emigration pulled it down, and by 1940 the Japanese population, including both the native- and the foreign-born, numbered only 127,000.[2]

The first Japanese immigrants found a wide variety of jobs, scattered throughout the western states. Railroads, logging and lumbering camps, mines, canneries, and domestic service provided a large part of their employment during the 1890s. After 1900, however, the immigrant workers, predominantly young unmarried males, tended to migrate away from such jobs to find employment in agriculture; increasingly they concentrated in California, especially in the areas where the acreage of labor-intensive crops was being expanded in the Central Valley and near Los Angeles. The Immigration Commission estimated that California agriculture provided employment for 30,000 Japanese during the summer months of 1909.[3] According to the records of the Japanese associations in California, two-thirds of those gainfully occupied in 1910 worked in agriculture.[4] From this peak, the relative importance of agricultural employment declined somewhat, and the absolute number of Japanese involved also fell. Still, as

[1] U.S. Bureau of the Census, *Chinese and Japanese in the United States, 1910*, Bulletin no. 127 (Washington, 1914), p. 7; H. A. Millis, "Some of the Economic Aspects of Japanese Immigration," *American Economic Review*, 5 (Dec. 1915), 789.

[2] U.S., Congress, House, Tolan Committee, *National Defense Migration*, 77th Cong., 2d sess., 1942, no. 2124, p. 94; Dorothy Swaine Thomas, "Some Social Aspects of Japanese-American Demography," *Proceedings of the American Philosophical Society*, 94 (Oct. 19, 1950), 459-62; William Petersen, "A Note on Statistics," in his *Japanese Americans: Oppression and Success* (New York, 1971), pp. 14-19.

[3] U.S., Immigration Commission, *Reports*, XXIII (Washington, 1911), p. 61.

[4] *Japanese American Yearbook* of 1911, cited in Edward K. Strong, *The Second-Generation Japanese Problem* (Stanford, 1934), p. 216. H. A. Millis, *The Japanese Problem in the United States* (New York, 1915), p. 103, cites similar estimates by the California Commissioner of Labor.

late as 1940, more than 17,000 found employment in California agriculture, and just over half of the Japanese males employed in the state remained in farming. In the production of vegetables, berries, fruit, and grapes, they exerted themselves prodigiously. In 1941 they accounted for an estimated 30-35 percent of the value of all commercial truck crops grown in California.[5]

During the period 1900-1920 many Japanese in California agriculture left work as wage laborers and became farm tenants and, less frequently, owner operators. The federal census of agriculture in 1920 enumerated more than 5,000 Japanese farm operators, nine-tenths of them tenants, in the state.[6] Skilled farmers, working intensely for long hours in a hot climate, often in a backbreaking stooped position, they proved formidable competitors in the land rental markets. As such they gained both the respect of the large white landlords and the enmity of the small white tenant farmers. Partly because of their success as independent farmers, they became the target of hostile land laws, enacted first in 1913 and strengthened by amendments in 1920, 1923, and 1927. On paper these laws left the Japanese immigrants no legal position in agriculture except that of wage laborer, but in practice, as we shall see, the laws became dead letters.[7]

MARKET DISCRIMINATION

During the earliest period of their employment in California agriculture, the Japanese generally worked for wages, and they received lower wages than whites for similar work. Although this racial difference tended to narrow after the turn of the century, two extensive surveys reveal that it remained substantial as late as 1909.

In that year the California Commissioner of Labor undertook, at the special request of the state legislature, a study of California's Japanese population. The agricultural portion of the inquiry involved visits to 4,102 farms scattered over 36 counties; of the farms investigated, 1,733 were operated by Japanese owners or tenants, 2,369 by white operators equally divided between those employing only white laborers and those employing racially mixed labor forces.[8] Some findings of the study with respect to wages appear in Table 1.

[5] *House Reports* [Tolan Committee], pp. 105, 117-18.

[6] U.S. Census, *Agriculture, 1920,* V (Washington, 1922), p. 312.

[7] For a much longer and more detailed survey of the subjects discussed in this section, see Masakazu Iwata, "The Japanese Immigrants in California Agriculture," *Agricultural History*, 36 (Jan. 1962), 25-37.

[8] [J. D. Mackenzie], "A Summary by Labor Commissioner J. D. Mackenzie of the Report of the 'Special State Investigation of 1909' of the Japanese in California. Given to the Press May 30,

TABLE 1
DAILY WAGE RATES (WITHOUT BOARD) PAID BY WHITE EMPLOYERS TO WHITE AND JAPANESE LABORERS, SELECTED FARM OCCUPATIONS, CALIFORNIA, 1909

	Whites		*Japanese*	
Occupation	*Number reporting*	*Average wage*	*Number reporting*	*Average wage*
Berry pickers	9	$1.86	59	$1.63
Celery cutters	20	1.50	101	1.50
Cultivators	141	1.69	127	1.34
Farm hands	1,187	1.70	2,026	1.47
Fruit pickers	1,424	1.73	3,186	1.58
Grape pickers	147	2.00	929	1.75
Hoers	273	1.88	274	1.69
Laborers	186	1.84	1,067	1.45
Packers	165	1.78	440	1.55
Pruners	225	1.36	1,408	1.39
Teamsters	454	2.05	59	1.74
Total	5,189	1.80	10,676	1.54

Source: California Commissioner of Labor, *Fourteenth Biennial Report*, insert, p. 270, as reproduced in H. A. Millis, *The Japanese Problem in the United States* (New York, 1915), p. 120.

The table shows that the average wage rate of Japanese workers hired by white employers fell 26 cents per day, or 14 percent, below that of white workers, although wage rates were about the same in two occupations, pruning and celery cutting. The Commissioner's report cautioned, however, that $1.54 per day "cannot be taken as the average earnings of the Japanese, for 49.2 per cent of the entire number employed were working by contract or piecework, under which condition the earnings of the Japanese are much larger than those of the whites." The report also noted that Japanese farm operators hired 17,784 workers, of whom 96 percent were Japanese, and paid an average wage of $1.65 per day without board, "showing that the Japanese were better paid by their own countrymen than by the white farmer."[9]

Also in 1909, agents of the U.S. Immigration Commission collected information from 5,793 wage laborers in California agriculture, and their findings closely paralleled those of the Labor Commissioner. The Immigration Commission's report observed that wages varied considerably among districts, but in most places "there is a discrimination of

1910," printed in Sidney L. Gulick, *The American Japanese Problem* (New York, 1914), pp. 316-23.

[9] Ibid., pp. 317-18.

about 25 cents per day in favor of white men as against Japanese and other Asiatics engaged in the same work." In a few places, daily wages for seasonal work were reported to be the same for both races. Most seasonal workers, however, received piece-rate wages, and on this basis the Japanese made "from 10 to 100 per cent larger average earnings per day than at day rates," the earnings of some individual workers reaching $6 or more per day. The Japanese earned more than whites on the piece-rate system because they worked "longer hours and with closer application to their work, for piece rates are now usually the same for all races."[10] The report also confirmed that Japanese workers received higher wages when hired by Japanese employers, and it noted, insightfully, that "the higher wages paid by the Japanese farmers have . . . tended to compel white farmers to pay more to their Japanese employees."[11]

This competitive pressure increased rapidly after 1909, and within a few years racial discrimination against the Japanese in the farm labor market had virtually disappeared. Millis reported in 1915 that "lower payment of Japanese than of white men engaged in the same occupations is almost entirely a matter of the past." In addition, piece rates remained uniform for white and Japanese laborers.[12] After the Gentlemen's Agreement went into effect in 1908, the influx of Japanese laborers fell dramatically. Resident alien workers increasingly moved into positions as tenants or, less frequently, as owner operators. This shift reduced the ranks of potential victims of discrimination and swelled the number of nondiscriminating employers in the wage labor market. More and more the Japanese wage laborers found jobs with Japanese employers. In 1920 the State Board of Control averred that "there are probably more white laborers working for Oriental farmers than there are Oriental laborers working for American farmers," and some observers adduced evidence that in 1919-1920 the Japanese actually received higher wages than whites, the premium being compensation for superior work and the performance of particularly onerous tasks.[13]

While the transition from wage labor to tenancy played a central role in eliminating racial wage discrimination, the newly-established tenants immediately encountered another form of discrimination in

[10] U.S., Immigration Commission, *Reports*, XXIII, pp. 66-67; see also pp. 61-67.
[11] Ibid., XXIV, p. 40; see also pp. 33-43.
[12] Millis, *The Japanese Problem*, p. 124; idem, "Economic Aspects," p. 796.
[13] State Board of Control of California, *California and the Oriental: Japanese, Chinese, and Hindus*, rev. ed. (Sacramento, 1922), pp. 58, 60, 115, 229, 239-40.

the land rental market. All sources agree that the Japanese paid higher rental rates than white tenants. The Immigration Commission concluded in 1909 that "the offer of comparatively high rents, though not universal, is fairly general." Six years later Millis observed that the racial difference in rental rates had probably diminished but had not yet disappeared. Then, noting that the higher rents paid by the Japanese had never been a matter of dispute, he abruptly dropped the subject, remarking that "further detail need not be added."[14]

Further detail would have been illuminating, however, for neither the reports of the Immigration Commission nor the later observations by Millis established the magnitude of the discrimination faced by Japanese tenants in the land rental market. Table 2 sheds some light on this matter. The data shown there were originally collected in the federal agricultural census of 1920 but were neither compiled nor published by the Census Bureau. Early in the 1920s Clyde Chambers, a USDA economist, obtained permission to draw a sample of the data, and the evidence in Table 2 is taken from his study.[15] The 1,901 Japanese tenant farms that were sampled were located in eight different counties, and they provide a reliable basis for judgment; the 1,745 white tenant farms that were sampled furnish a substantial comparative standard.

The table supports several conclusions. First, the Japanese tenants invariably occupied more valuable land than their white neighbors; in some places, such as Alameda, Orange, Sacramento, and Solano Counties, much more valuable land. Second, the Japanese invariably paid higher rent per acre than their white counterparts. (Neither of these related racial differences, of course, implies anything about racial discrimination.) Third, and most importantly, the Japanese generally paid higher rents relative to land values than did their white counterparts, the only exceptions being the longer-term tenants in Alameda and Orange Counties. In some cases the racial differences in the ratio of rent to value were small and would probably fall short of standard significance levels in a statistical test (which cannot be performed in the absence of the individual observations from which the averages were computed). In many cases, however, the racial differences were large and almost certainly significant: in four cases the Japanese ratio exceeded the white by three percentage points or

[14] U.S., Immigration Commission, *Reports*, XXIII, p. 82; Millis, *The Japanese Problem*, pp. 142-43.

[15] Clyde R. Chambers, *Relation of Land Income to Land Value*, USDA Bulletin no. 1224 (Washington, June 11, 1924).

Table 2

AVERAGE RENT, AVERAGE VALUE, AND RATIO OF RENT TO VALUE FOR FARMS CLASSIFIED BY RACE OF TENANT AND PERIOD OF OCCUPANCY, SELECTED COUNTIES, CALIFORNIA, 1920[a]

County and period of occupancy of farm	*Whites*				*Japanese*			
	Number of farms	*Ave. cash rent/acre*	*Ave. value/acre*	*Ratio*	*Number of farms*	*Ave. cash rent/acre*	*Ave. value/acre*	*Ratio*
Alameda								
Total	194	$5.19	$152	3.4	88	$27.00	$913	3.0
1 year	50	11.66	338	3.5	25	31.76	562	5.7
2 or More	144	4.50	132	3.4	63	25.97	989	2.6
Imperial								
Total	509	19.96	176	11.3	272	27.08	209	13.0
1 Year	343	20.96	176	11.9	178	29.58	216	13.7
2 or More	166	18.24	178	10.3	94	23.68	200	11.9
Los Angeles								
Total	442	12.88	506	2.5	996	23.06	743	3.1
1 Year	223	15.34	505	3.0	358	23.55	738	3.2
2 or More	219	11.50	507	2.3	638	22.81	745	3.1
Orange								
Total	30	8.15	292	2.8	41	23.11	699	3.3
1 Year	12	7.69	411	1.9	12	24.23	494	4.9
2 or More	18	8.44	218	3.9	29	22.79	757	3.0
Sacramento								
Total	141	5.96	128	4.6	259	24.45	380	6.4
1 Year	61	7.89	125	6.3	60	25.82	353	7.3
2 or More	80	5.24	129	4.0	199	24.03	388	6.2
San Joaquin								
Total	210	$12.53	$250	5.0	119	$23.67	$314	7.5
1 Year	101	13.46	233	5.8	58	24.57	324	7.6
2 or More	109	11.79	264	4.5	61	22.53	301	7.5

TABLE 2 (CONTINUED)

AVERAGE RENT, AVERAGE VALUE, AND RATIO OF RENT TO VALUE FOR FARMS CLASSIFIED BY RACE OF TENANT AND PERIOD OF OCCUPANCY, SELECTED COUNTIES, CALIFORNIA, 1920[a]

County and period of occupancy of farm	*Japanese*				*Whites*			
	Number of farms	*Ave. cash rent/acre*	*Ave. value/ acre.*	*Ratio*	*Number of farms*	*Ave. cash rent/acre*	*Ave. value/ acre*	*Ratio*
Santa Clara								
Total	106	8.95	290	3.1	83	23.29	537	4.3
1 Year	35	12.32	310	4.0	22	22.06	442	5.0
2 or More	71	7.99	285	2.8	61	23.68	568	4.2
Solano								
Total	113	6.57	113	5.8	43	29.65	301	9.9
1 Year	45	5.51	96	5.7	9	71.12	683	10.4
2 or More	68	7.00	119	5.9	34	26.46	272	9.7

[a] Data apply only to tenants unrelated by kinship to landlords and to farms of 10 acres or more.

Source: Clyde R. Chambers, *Relation of Land Income to Land Value*, USDA Bulletin no. 1224 (Washington, June 11, 1924), pp. 74-76.

more (first-year tenants in Orange and Solano, longer-term tenants in San Joaquin and Solano Counties). Given that the cash rents were accurately reported and that the average land values were unbiased estimates, the conclusion is inescapable that landlords, as late as 1920, effectively discriminated against the Japanese in the land rental market. The average Japanese tenant probably paid a rental premium equal to one or two percent of the land's estimated value.

I shall not stop to judge whether this premium was "large" or "small." A more intriguing question is why it existed at all. Contemporaries adduced plausible reasons why the Japanese were willing or able to pay higher rents than whites: more ambition; greater willingness to bear risk; the ability to work harder, longer, and more efficiently; more unpaid family labor; lower standards of living; fewer alternative opportunities—all were advanced to account for the willingness of the Japanese to outbid white tenants.[16] There the matter was allowed to rest, the question of why the Japanese tenants found it *necessary* to pay a rental premium never having been raised. To my knowledge, only one contemporary recognized the inadequacy of explanations referring exclusively to the tenants' side of the market. Anticipating Gary Becker's model of the economics of discrimination by more than 30 years, Chambers wrote: "Japanese tenants can and will pay considerably more for the use of the land than the white tenants. *Since the landowners prefer to rent to white tenants without this rent premium*, the Japanese have to pay this premium in order to get the use of the land." Chambers, however, was too good an economist to stop there, and he added, insightfully:

> The fact alone, that the Japanese have to pay higher rents than the white tenants in order to get the use of the land does not explain why the Japanese rents are higher relative to the value of the land. If the Japanese were found grouped in large communities which the buyers and sellers of land regarded as stable, and if the Japanese could not become owners of this land, as is the case, then the buyers and sellers of land in these communities would base their values on the income the farms would earn when leased to Japanese tenants. Then the ratios of rent to value in these communities would be the same as the ratios in communities of white tenants, although the rents would probably be higher. The fact that the Japanese were paying relatively higher rents than the white tenants would not alter the situation, for the values would be directly based upon those rents, regardless of the factors determining them. The percentage of Japanese tenants, however, is small and the permanent value of the land is based upon what white operators can make it earn.[17]

[16] Ibid., p. 58; U.S., Immigration Commission, *Reports*, XXIII, p. 82; Millis, *The Japanese Problem*, pp. 141-44; idem, "Economic Aspects," p. 800.

[17] Chambers, "Relation of Land Income," pp. 58-59 (italics added).

This is excellent economic analysis, and Chambers' model offers a coherent explanation of the prevailing discrimination against the Japanese in the land rental market, *provided one accepts his assertion* that the landowners (all of them?) preferred white tenants unless the Japanese paid a rental premium.

My uneasiness with this explanation arises from my skepticism about the realism of its pivotal assumption. If a substantial number of landlords preferred wealth to the pleasures of discriminating against the Japanese, then competition among landlords would have tended to reduce the prevailing racial difference in rental rates. In fact, the Japanese in California were not without friends, chief among whom were the large landlords raising labor-intensive crops and operating their ranches with tenant labor.[18] Such landlords could have had a profound impact on the market, especially after 1920, when the rapid rise in the number of Japanese tenants halted and then reversed itself. My conjecture is that the existence of a racial rental premium in 1920 represented a disequilibrium situation: competitive forces had yet to overcome the discrimination exerted during the years 1900-1920 when the Japanese were rushing headlong into the rental markets of a few districts. This conjecture suggests that the discriminatory rental premium should have disappeared during the period 1920-1940. Unfortunately, I have been unable to find any systematically compiled data on the rents paid by tenants of the two races during these years. I greatly regret the lack of such evidence, for without it one cannot conduct a clearcut test of whether competition or racial discrimination ultimately triumphed in this important market.

LEGAL DISCRIMINATION

The Japanese, in the eyes of the California whites, were indistinguishable from the Chinese, and hence the whites' longstanding anti-Chinese hostilities inevitably descended on the newcomers from the Orient. Although they seldom suffered from the mob violence that had often plagued the Chinese of California in the nineteenth century, the Japanese became a similar target for legal discrimination and exclusion. Pure racism supplied the main impetus for the whites' desire to discriminate, but the success of the Japanese in agriculture

[18] Millis, *The Japanese Problem*, pp. 204, 223-24; T. Iyenaga and Kenoske Sato, *Japan and the California Problem* (New York, 1921), pp. 123-24; C. McWilliams, "Once again the 'Yellow Peril,' " *Nation*, 140 (June 26, 1935), 736; Roger Daniels, *The Politics of Prejudice* (Berkeley, 1962), p. 48.

certainly heightened preexisting hostilities. By concentrating in a few districts, the Japanese farmers made their accomplishments more conspicuous, and their gains in land tenure and crop production were easily exaggerated by those who despised them on racial grounds or feared them as economic competitors. Seldom have so few innocuous people inspired so much irrational hatred and apprehension.

In these circumstances some form of legal discrimination against the Japanese was highly probable, and after several years of agitation by politicians and organizations representing a variety of labor, agricultural, and civic interests the state legislature passed the Alien Land Law of 1913.[19] Its authors openly designed the law to make life unpleasant for the state's Oriental aliens. In the words of the law's co-author, State Attorney General U. S. Webb, the objective was "to limit their presence by curtailing their privileges which they may enjoy here; for they will not come in large numbers and long abide with us if they may not acquire land."[20]

Still, in a feeble attempt to disguise the affront to Japan, the law was written without any mention of the Japanese. On its face it appeared only to define certain property rights of "all aliens eligible to citizenship under the laws of the United States." It provided, however, that "all aliens other than those" could enjoy only such property rights as "prescribed by any treaty now existing between the government of the United States and the nation or country of which such alien is a citizen or subject"; the single exception was that aliens ineligible for citizenship could "lease lands in this state for agricultural purposes for a term not exceeding three years." As the Japanese were legally ineligible for naturalization, and as the treaty of 1911 between Japan and the United States gave the Japanese no explicit rights to own or lease agricultural land in the United States, and as the Chinese had long been denied the privilege of immigration, the act in effect applied only to the Japanese. To plug a potential loophole, the restrictions of the act were also placed upon corporations of which a majority of the members were aliens ineligible to citizenship or which had issued a majority of their stock to such aliens. The state attorney general was empowered to institute escheat proceedings against property acquired in violation of the act.

[19] Cal. Stats., Ch. 113, 1913 (May 19, 1913) took effect Aug. 10, 1913. On the political machinations that surrounded the passage of this law, see Daniels, *Politics of Prejudice*, pp. 46-64.

[20] Speech before the Commonwealth Club of San Francisco, Aug. 9, 1913, cited in Frank F. Chuman, *The Bamboo People: The Law and Japanese-Americans* (Del Mar, Calif., 1976), p. 48.

Under the Alien Land Law of 1913, the only interest in agricultural land that a Japanese alien could legally acquire was a leasehold for a term not exceeding three years. But the law was immediately, openly, and widely evaded, and the Japanese continued to acquire ownership rights and unrestricted leaseholds. Three evasive devices played important roles during the years 1913-1920.

Probably the most significant was the purchase of land in the names of native-born (citizen) sons and daughters. As almost all the offspring were then minors, such purchases required the appointment of a legal guardian or properly qualified trustee. Usually the alien parent of the citizen child applied for and was granted guardianship, and few objections to this practice arose until after the First World War. In 1919 and 1920, with the renewal of widespread agitation against the Japanese, some courts adopted a hostile stance, refusing to grant such guardianships or rescinding those already granted. The character of the presiding judges became decisive. "If the man was liberal-minded," observed Jean Pajus, "the harried litigants who appeared before him were treated leniently; if he happened to be rabidly contra-alien, his victims did not have the ghost of a chance." In a guardianship case brought before him in 1920, a judge in Santa Clara County remarked: "I will deal with it . . . just as I do with white children; there is no distinction . . . . We can't sit here and punish people according to our notions." Only a year earlier, however, a judge in Tulare County had ruled quite differently. Not content to deny the application for guardianship of a Japanese mother who had earlier purchased an orchard in her daughter's name, the judge used the occasion to rail against "this contract . . . made purely as an evasion of the law to prevent Japanese from buying property in this state"; he reproachfully advised that "the attorneys of this state should refrain, as far as possible, from handling any such proposition as this."[21]

Japanese purchasers of land could avoid the potential difficulties of guardianships by "borrowing the name" of an American citizen of legal age. Sometimes Hawaiian-born Japanese, who were generally older than those born on the mainland, supplied their names for this purpose. Hawaiian-born Kazuo Miyamoto tells in his autobiography how distant relatives approached him during his senior year at Stan-

[21] Jean Pajus, *The Real Japanese California* (Berkeley, 1937), pp. 131-34; see also pp. 135-36; and U.S., Congress, House, Committee on Immigration and Naturalization, *Japanese Immigration: Hearings*, 66th Cong., 2d sess., 1921, pp. 404, 873-76.

ford University to present this proposition: "The whole crux of the arrangement is in the getting of a trustworthy citizen who will not betray the Japanese farmers. Since you are twenty-one years old, you can lease these farms for us. What do you think? In return Mr. Tanaka will guarantee the expense to put you through medical school." For financially straitened Miyamoto, "nobody could have planned anything more convenient at such an opportune time."[22] Sympathetic white citizens also provided names, often as trustees. L. M. Landsborough, of the Florin district, near Sacramento, testified before a House Committee in 1920 that he had purchased six different parcels, containing over 100 acres, for Japanese farmers, taking the deeds in his name. Paid only for the clerical work involved, he acquired no substantive interest in the properties and later transferred the deeds to native-born Japanese children when payment for the land had been completed. By steadfastly refusing to admit any wrongdoing to his inquisitors, Landsborough provoked Congressman John Raker to say that "on the face of the record, here is the Japanese who has no title to or who is not entitled to own the land; he is running it, farming it, controlling it, just the same as though he owned it, but using you and your name, and, through you, is violating the law; isn't that right?" Momentarily intimidated, Landsborough confessed, "Well, I think it is."[23]

The third major device employed to evade the Alien Land Law of 1913 was the formation of "dummy" corporations. Provided that American citizens constituted a majority of the stockholders and held a majority of the issued stock, a corporation did not violate the law. Such a corporation could be easily formed by a Japanese couple with two native-born children, assisted by a cooperative American attorney. Each person could be a stockowner, three citizens and two aliens making citizens a majority of the members; and enough of the stock owned by the children could be issued to the attorney, acting as their trustee, to give the citizens a majority ownership of the issued stock. A handful of lawyers specialized in this exotic branch of corporate law: of 30 Japanese farming corporations in Merced County in 1920, 23 issued large blocks of stock to trustees Albert H. Elliot and Guy C. Calden, who served as attorneys for the Japanese Association of America.[24] An official of the State Board of Control in 1920 compiled a

[22] Kazuo Miyamoto, *Hawaii: End of the Rainbow* (Rutland, Vt., 1964), pp. 237-39.

[23] House Committee, *Japanese Immigration*, p. 263. For Landsborough's full testimony, see pp. 244-74. See also Dorothy Swaine Thomas, *The Salvage* (Berkeley, 1952), p. 181.

[24] House Committee, *Japanese Immigration*, pp. 428-34; see also pp. 215-20, 325-26, 503-8,

list of 302 Japanese farming corporations owning almost 48,000 acres.[25] In his unpublished research, Masakazu Iwata has identified 416 companies formed before 1921 ("370 were organized to operate farms and the remainder formed for the specific purpose of land purchase and floricultural operations") which held almost 66,000 acres.[26] Concerned about this practice, the State Board of Control complained: "It is a source of deep regret that there are attorneys in the state who despite their oath to support the constitution and the laws of this state, nevertheless sell their legal talent in aiding this breach of the spirit and purpose of the Alien Land Law."[27]

The Alien Land Law of 1913 simply did not accomplish what its proponents had intended. Through its wide loopholes, multitudes of Japanese farmers adroitly passed. With the end of the war and the onset of renewed agitation against the Japanese, the dogs of racism howled for an amended law. Political feuds prevented passage of new legislation in 1919. The next year the legislature did not convene, but the anti-Japanese forces managed to place an initiative proposal before the electorate at the general election. In this way they secured, by a margin of three-to-one, passage of the Alien Land Law of 1920.[28]

This law sought to close all the loopholes of the 1913 act. In effect, it denied Japanese aliens all rights of ownership *and* leasehold over agricultural land, forbade them to become members of or acquire shares in any corporation entitled to hold agricultural land, and prohibited them from acting as guardians for minors owning or leasing land. The law provided for escheat proceedings to be brought by the attorney general or any district attorney against illegally held interests in land. It defined several *prima facie* presumptions of intent to evade the law, including the taking of an interest in real estate in the name of a citizen when consideration was paid by an ineligible alien. Criminal penalties were established (up to two years imprisonment and five thousand dollars fine) for those who conspired to violate the law. The final section of the act, a clear confession of legal insecurity, declared: "If any section, subsection, sentence, clause or phrase of this act is for any reason held to be unconstitutional, such decision shall not affect the validity of the remaining portions of this act."

841-42, 900 for additional evidence on the services of attorneys for Japanese farming corporations.

[25] Ibid., pp. 420-24.

[26] Personal correspondence, Masakazu Iwata to the author, June 22, 1977 and Aug. 5, 1977.

[27] State Board of Control, *California and the Oriental*, p. 69.

[28] Cal. Stats., 1921, Initiative Act of 1920, p. lxxxiii (approved Nov. 2, 1920; became effective Dec. 9, 1920). On the political machinations that surrounded the passage of this law, see Daniels, *Politics of Prejudice*, pp. 79-91.

In general, the courts upheld the constitutionality of the Initiative Act and its subsequent amendments.[29] In several cases decided in 1923 the U. S. Supreme Court held that the act was not arbitrary and unreasonable in its discrimination against aliens ineligible to citizenship and that it did not deny them due process of law.[30] Said Justice Butler: "The allegiance of the farmers to the state directly affects its strength and safety. We think it within the power of the state to deny to ineligible aliens the privilege to use agricultural lands within its borders."[31] Exactly how the operation of a few thousand small vegetable and fruit farms by the Japanese threatened the strength and safety of California was not explained by the learned Justice.

While these cases were still moving through the federal courts, however, the Supreme Court of California decided a separate case of far-reaching importance. In *Estate of Tetsubumi Yano*,[32] the court concluded that "the provisions of the Initiative Act of 1920 forbidding the appointment of an alien resident, ineligible to citizenship, as guardian of the farming land of his native-born child, and authorizing the removal of such parent, if previously appointed as such guardian, are invalid," being denials of equal protection of the law. This decision opened a crack in the law through which many Japanese farmers would subsequently squeeze by making "gifts" of land to their minor children, for whom they acted as legal guardians and farm managers.[33]

The Japanese also employed other devices to circumvent the alien land laws after 1920. Probably the most common were collusive, unwritten arrangements whereby the alien leased a farm *de facto* while acting only as a salaried manager *de jure*. By 1928 Eliot Mears perceived that "over the state there is a general lack of enforcement" of the alien land laws. Edward K. Strong, after directing a survey (10 percent sample) of the California Japanese in 1930, observed that "on many occasions men reported that they were managers or foremen,

[29] The most important amendments were: 45 Cal. Stats. 1020 (June 20, 1923), declaring sharecropping agreements to constitute an interest in real property; and Cal. Stats., 1927, Ch. 528, Sec. 9a and 9b, placing the burden of proof on the alleged ineligible alien in cases of contested citizenship.

[30] *Porterfield v. Webb*, 263 U.S. 225 (Nov. 12, 1923); *Webb v. O'Brien*, 263 U.S. 313 (Nov. 19, 1923); *Frick v. Webb*, 263 U.S. 326 (Nov. 19, 1923).

[31] The best treatments of the legal and constitutional aspects of the alien land laws are Chuman, *Bamboo People*, passim, and Dudley O. McGovney, "The Anti-Japanese Land Laws of California and Ten Other States," *California Law Review*, 35 (Mar. 1947), 7-60.

[32] 188 Cal. 645 (May 1, 1922).

[33] Pajus, *The Real Japanese California*, pp. 136-41; Chuman, *Bamboo People*, p. 119; McGovney, "Anti-Japanese Land Laws," pp. 28-30. The *Yano* doctrine was later sustained in *People v. Fujita*, 215 Cal. 166 (1932) and in *Kiyoko Nishi v. Downing*, 21 C.A. 2d 1 (May 11, 1937).

only to admit later that they were renting or had purchased the land. As far as could be discovered by our interviewers, the land law is non-operative in many sections of the state if not in all parts." One large landowner told Strong that he had never heard of the alien land laws and that many white landowners in his district rented to Japanese tenants.[34] A decision by the U. S. Supreme Court in 1934 made it virtually impossible for the state to invoke the criminal sanctions of the alien land laws by proving that a conspiracy had transpired.[35] In 1935 Carey McWilliams declared the law a dead letter: "It is no longer enforced," he said, "nor is there any sentiment for its enforcement."[36]

White landlords and Japanese farmers evaded the law because both parties gained wealth by doing so. Many contemporary observers noted that strict enforcement of the law would have severely damaged the interests of large landowning whites, and "when it is to the advantage of the whites to lease their land to Japanese, they find a way to do it."[37] Local district attorneys, acting with self-serving circumspection, rarely brought escheat proceedings against violators of the law.[38] In some districts landlords and tenants simply ignored the law without resorting to any evasive devices whatever.[39] Finally, as more and more native-born Japanese came of age in the 1930s, evasion became unnecessary, land titles and leaseholds being taken in the names of adult citizen members of Japanese families.

Under the alien land laws, as amended in 1923, aliens ineligible to citizenship could not legally "acquire, possess, enjoy, use, cultivate,

[34] Eliot Grinnell Mears, *Resident Orientals on the Pacific Coast: Their Legal and Economic Status* (Chicago, 1928), p. 253; Strong, *Second-Generation Japanese Problem*, pp. 211-12; Thomas, *The Salvage*, p. 182.

[35] *Morrison v. California*, 291 U.S. 82 (Jan. 8, 1934).

[36] McWilliams, "Once again the 'Yellow Peril,' " p. 736. See also Grace Cable Keroher, "California's Anti-Orientalism," in Clarence A. Peters, comp., *The Immigration Problem* (New York, 1948), p. 183.

[37] Strong, *Second-Generation Japanese Problem*, pp. 45, 212. See also McWilliams, "Once again the 'Yellow Peril,' " p. 736; Edwin E. Ferguson, "The California Alien Land Law and the 14th Amendment," *California Law Review*, 35 (Mar. 1947), 72; Thomas, *The Salvage*, p. 24.

[38] Mears, *Resident Orientals*, p. 254. Chuman (*Bamboo People*, pp. 117-18) finds 16 reported escheat cases between 1920 and 1940. Undoubtedly others took place in the superior courts but were not appealed and hence not reported.

[39] "My own father who was a farmer seemed to have little difficulty in southern California in renting land without resorting to devious means to get around the law. The law was possibly not enforced with rigidity here" (personal correspondence, Masakazu Iwata to the author, June 22, 1977). "[I]n the 1920's it may have been necessary for father to rely on one of his Caucasian friends, a banker in San Fernando by the name of Walker, to sign lease papers. But as far as my own recollection goes, in the latter 1920's and the 1930's he acquired land simply on an oral promise. There seemed not to be any hassle regarding this as far as he was concerned" (idem, Aug. 5, 1977).

occupy, and transfer real property." As Justice Butler correctly observed, "the Act as a whole evidences legislative intention that ineligible aliens shall not be permitted to have or enjoy any privileges in respect to the use or the benefit of land for agricultural purposes."[40] But these sweeping intentions were never realized, nor were they even approximated. We have seen how the Japanese, in cooperation with white landowners and a handful of resourceful lawyers, devised means of circumventing the obstacles erected by the state legislature. It remains to examine the quantitative record of Japanese involvement in California agriculture as a final test of the laws' effects.

Clearly, the alien land laws did not drive the Japanese out of agriculture. A majority of the employed males still found employment in farming as late as 1940. Nor were they reduced to wage laborers. Table 3 shows that the number of self-declared owners rose continuously. The number of tenants probably reached a peak in 1920, as the table indicates, but the apparently precipitous drop from 1920 to 1930 was largely spurious. Much of this decline was offset by the greatly increased number describing themselves as "managers," a common ruse to evade the alien land laws. By 1940 the number declaring themselves managers had shrunk drastically, which is consistent with the evidence already marshalled on the changing modes of evasion and nonenforcement of the laws. The total number of Japanese farm operators in 1940 was virtually the same as it had been 20 years earlier. In this light, the alien land laws appear to have failed utterly.

Table 4 brings together scattered data on the acreage owned and leased by Japanese farmers. For all years except 1942, the data originated in surveys made by the Japanese Association of America. Although not completely accurate, these are the most reliable data available on acreage operated. (The federal census data, by comparison, are substantially smaller, for obvious reasons.) Total acreage reached a peak in 1920, fell abruptly during the next two years, then declined slowly for the duration of the period. Anticipating the new restrictions imminent in 1920, the Japanese simply bit off more than they could chew. Overextended, they almost certainly had to reduce their acreage sometime afterwards; the collapse of farm prices in 1921 must have hastened the day. Perhaps the Initiative Act of 1920 also contributed in those first dark days when many farmers were confused and uncertain about whether the new legal restrictions could be circumvented. Between 1932 and 1942 the owned acreage increased

[40] 45 Cal. Stats. 1020 (June 20, 1923); *Webb v. O'Brien*, 263 U.S. 313 (Nov. 19, 1923).

TABLE 3
U.S. CENSUS AND WRA ENUMERATIONS OF JAPANESE FARMS, BY TENURE STATUS OF OPERATORS, CALIFORNIA, 1910-1942

Date	*Owners*	*Tenants*	*Managers*	*Total*
1910	233	1,547	36	1,816
1920	506	4,533	113	5,152
1930	560	1,580	1,616	3,756
1940	1,290	3,596	249	5,135
1942	1,703	3,195	10	4,908

Sources: For 1910 and 1920, U.S. Census, *Agriculture, 1920,* V (1922), p. 312; for 1930 and 1940, U.S. Census, *Agriculture, 1940,* III (1943), p. 224; for 1942, War Relocation Authority evacuee property records, cited in Adon Poli and Warren M. Engstrand, "Japanese Agriculture on the Pacific Coast," *Journal of Land and Public Utility Economics,* 21 (Nov. 1945), 355.

considerably, while the rented acreage continued to decline. This difference suggests that something other than the land laws was at work. Evidently, a plethora of obstacles notwithstanding, Japanese farmers continued to climb upward on the "tenure ladder."

A final important element, neglected in most assessments of the effects of the land laws, was demographic change. The virtual cessation of immigration and substantial emigration after 1924, along with normal mortality, caused the population of alien adult males to decline steadily from about 32,000 in 1920 to only about 21,000 in 1940,

TABLE 4
FARM ACREAGE OPERATED BY JAPANESE OWNERS AND TENANTS, CALIFORNIA, 1905-1942

Date	*Acres owned (in 1,000's)*	*Acres rented or worked under annual labor contract (in 1,000's)*	*Total*
1905	2	60	62
1913	27	255	282
1920	75	383	458
1922	51	280	330[a]
1925	42	266	308
1932	38	250	288
1942	69	163	232

[a] Discrepancy due to rounding.

Sources: Except for 1942, the original authority for all years is the Japanese Association of America, as cited by Kiichi Kanzaki, *California and the Japanese* (San Francisco, 1921), p. 55; Yamato Ichihashi, *Japanese in the United States* (Stanford, 1932), p. 193; Edward K. Strong, Jr., *Japanese in California* (Stanford, 1933), p. 138. For 1942, the original authority is the War Relocation Authority evacuee property records, cited in Adon Poli and Warren M. Engstrand, "Japanese Agriculture on the Pacific Coast," *Journal of Land and Public Utility Economics,* 21 (Nov. 1945), 355.

a decline of approximately one-third.[41] In 1920 the census counted a total of 5,039 Japanese farm owners and tenants, virtually all of whom can be assumed to have been alien adult males. In 1940 there were 3,911 alien Japanese males who admitted that they were farmers or farm managers.[42] Inasmuch as the true manager component was negligible, the implication is that during the period of the most stringent land laws, 1920-1940, the number of *alien* Japanese farmers declined by about 22 percent, or *much less than the corresponding population*. In 1920 one of every 6.4 male adult aliens was a farm operator; in 1940 one of every 5.4. As the number of *rural* adult aliens had probably declined even more rapidly than the total,[43] the conclusion applies *a fortiori:* the Japanese immigrants substantially improved their tenure status in California agriculture during the two decades after the passage of the harsh Initiative Act of 1920.

MELTING POT BE DAMNED

One can write much of the economic history of the Japanese immigrants by employing the theme of discriminatory challenge and market response. Confronted by wage discrimination and limited opportunities for advancement in the farm labor market, the Japanese responded by going into business for themselves, mainly as tenants. Encountering discrimination in the land rental market, a growing number responded by acquiring ownership of farm land. In the face of highly restrictive land laws, they devised the means to continue operating their farms and, after a transitory reversal in the early 1920s, steadily advanced up the tenure ladder. On every occasion when attempts to discriminate against them took place, market counterpressures—the lure of wealth awaiting the nondiscriminators—worked to free them from discriminatory restraints. On the eve of the Second World War, the immigrant generation had attained an economic position of solid middle class dimensions. With a high rate of self-employment, considerable ownership of land and other property, and a comfortable standard of living, the Japanese of rural California could look back with well justified pride. They had, it appeared, triumphed over racial discrimination in both the market and the law.

Of course, there was another, less cheerful side to the story. To an

[41] U.S. Census, *Population, 1920*, III (1922), p. 128; U.S. Census, *Population, 1940: Characteristics of the Nonwhite Population by Race* (1943), p. 98.

[42] Table 3 above; and *House Reports* [Tolan Committee], p. 105.

[43] The alien rural Japanese population of all ages fell from 18,479 in 1920 to 8,915 in 1940, a decline of over half. See U.S. Census, *Population, 1940*, II (1943), p. 518.

important extent, the alien land laws had fallen into desuetude because they had been, in the minds of many of their initial supporters, no more than means to an end. That end was Oriental exclusion, and after its attainment in the immigration act of 1924, only a few felt threatened by the dwindling numbers of resident alien Japanese and their well-behaved children.[44] The Japanese and the large white landowners became, as Carey McWilliams expressed it in the mid-thirties, "partners in an unholy and highly profitable conspiracy." But, suspecting that the racists might only be sleeping, McWilliams sensed the imminence of new dangers and wondered: "Will their economic alliances protect them?"[45] We know now, of course, that their alliances did not protect them when the storm came, and in the hysteria of 1942-1945 the immigrant generation lost practically everything it had so arduously accumulated. Emerging from the concentration camps in 1945, the aging immigrants were too old to start anew. Their children, much younger and more vigorous, with excellent educations, would make extraordinary economic progress in the postwar era. But their great gains should blind no one to the vast losses of their parents, losses for which only token restitution was ever made.[46]

There was a time, especially in the early 1920s, when the question of Japanese immigrant assimilation provoked vigorous debate. The exclusionists adamantly maintained that the Japanese were unassimilable, hence undesirable, and ought not to be admitted to the country at all. More honest white spokesmen put the matter bluntly: "It is not a question of whether the Jap is assimilable or not," said an official of the Los Angeles Chamber of Commerce; "we do not want to assimilate him."[47] Kiichi Kanzaki, General Secretary of the Japanese Association of America, knew that assimilation was a phony issue and that the real issue was white racism. "If," he said,

> after establishing all sorts of barriers on the way of assimilation, it [is] always contended that the Japanese are nonassimilable, this is nothing but another way of stating that the whites are nonassimilable. . . . In other words, they want to assimilate others but they do not want to be assimilated by others. Their assumption is their racial superiority, and unless this is adjusted no question of assimilation can be permanently settled.[48]

[44] Mears, *Resident Orientals*, p. 178; *House Reports* [Tolan Committee], pp. 85-86; McGovney, "The Anti-Japanese Land Laws," pp. 51-52; Ferguson, "The California Alien Land Law," p. 72; Strong, *Second-Generation Japanese Problem*, p. 46.

[45] McWilliams, "Once again the 'Yellow Peril,' " p. 736.

[46] Petersen, *Japanese Americans*, pp. 104-8.

[47] Statement of Dr. George P. Clements, manager of the agricultural department, Los Angeles Chamber of Commerce, printed in House Committee, *Japanese Immigration*, p. 1008.

[48] Testimony of K. Kanzaki, ibid., p. 655.

The Japanese were quite willing to go more than half way in accommodating themselves to white culture, but white racism reared its head at every turn. "I know America is the melting pot," said Yo Suzuki of Stockton, ". . . and we are ready to melt, but some American people hate us; hate us by appearance, color of skin, and so on; and they say the Japanese can not be assimilated. I think that is wrong."[49] Most whites now would probably agree with Suzuki. But the white Americans' change of heart—if it really is that—came too late to save the immigrant victims of California's longstanding anti-Oriental racism.

ROBERT HIGGS, *University of Washington*

[49] Testimony of Yo Suzuki, president of Stockton Growers' Exchange, ibid., p. 516.

YUJI ICHIOKA

JAPANESE IMMIGRANT RESPONSE TO THE 1920 CALIFORNIA ALIEN LAND LAW

Japanese immigrants perceived the 1920 California Alien Land Law as a "bread-and-butter" issue (literally "life-and-death"). Seeing its enactment as a serious threat to their livelihood, they fought the law in many ways. Many scholars discount the effectiveness of the law, suggesting that Japanese farmers did not suffer from either its enactment or enforcement. They believe that the farmers successfully circumvented the law by one means or another.[1] Other scholars argue that the 1920 law and a post–World War I recession caused a sharp drop in Japanese agriculture during the twenties.[2] No scholar, however, has studied Japanese immigrant sources fully enough to substantiate either interpretation. Nor has any scholar presented a historical account and analysis of how the Japanese immigrants themselves responded to the 1920 law. Using previously unexamined Japanese immigrant sources, this essay will reexamine the question of the 1920 California Alien Land Law and its effect on Japanese farmers during the twenties from a Japanese immigrant perspective.

Statistics of Japanese farmholdings reflect the growth of Japanese

YUJI ICHIOKA is Research Associate, Asian American Studies Center, University of California, Los Angeles.

[1]Edward K. Strong, Jr., *Japanese in California* (Stanford, Calif.: Stanford University Press, 1933), 102-4; Emil T. H. Bunje, *The Story of Japanese Farming in California* (Berkeley: W.P.A. Project, 1937), 125-35; Carey McWilliams, *Prejudice: Japanese-Americans: Symbol of Racial Intolerance* (Boston: Little, Brown, 1944), 65; Roger Daniels, *The Politics of Prejudice* (New York: Atheneum, 1974), 88; John Modell, *The Economics and Politics of Racial Accommodation* (Urbana: University of Illinois Press, 1977), 100-103; and Robert Higgs, "Landless by Law: Japanese Immigrants in California Agriculture to 1941," *Journal of Economic History* 38 (March 1978): 221.

[2]Eliot G. Mears, *Resident Orientals on the American Pacific Coast* (Chicago: University of Chicago Press, 1928), 254-55; Yamato Ichihashi, *Japanese in the United States* (Stanford, Calif.: Stanford University Press, 1932), 279-80; and Jean Pajus, *The Real Japanese California* (Berkeley: James J. Gillick, 1937), 145-48. See also Masakazu Iwata, "The Japanese Immigrants in California Agriculture," *Agricultural History* 36 (January 1962): 31-32.

agriculture in California. According to U.S. Census data, there were only 37 Japanese farms in 1900 with a combined acreage of 4,674 acres.[3] The earliest Japanese figures indicate that 350 Japanese in 1902 farmed 17,260 acres in Northern California.[4] By 1910, and again based on U.S. Census data, the total acreage increased sharply to 99,524 acres on 1,816 farms.[5] The *Nichibei Shimbun*, the leading Japanese immigrant daily, compiled much higher statistics. The newspaper's acreage figures, broken down into four categories, from 1905 to 1913 are as follows:

TABLE 1. JAPANESE AGRICULTURAL LANDHOLDINGS IN CAIFORNIA, 1905-1913 (ACRES)

Year	Owned	Cash-Lease	Share-Lease	Contract	Total
1905	2,442	35,258	19,573	4,775	61,858
1906	8,671	41,885	24,826	22,100	97,452
1907	13,815	56,889	48,228	13,359	131,292
1908	15,114	55,971	57,578	26,138	155,581
1909	16,449	80,232	57,001	42,276	195,958
1910	16,980	89,464	50,399	37,898	194,742
1911	17,765	110,442	62,070	49,443	239,720
1912	26,571	124,656	56,053	38,473	245,753
1913	26,707	155,488	50,495	49,997	281,687

SOURCE: *Nichibei Nenkan* [Japanese American Yearbook], no. 3 (1907): 104-5; no. 4 (1908): 102-3; no. 5 (1909): app. 1, pp. 1-2; no. 6 (1910): 87-88; no. 7 (1911): 130-31; no. 8 (1912): 100-101; no. 9 (1913): 107-8; no. 10 (1914): 120-21.

NOTE: These figures do not always add up correctly, but the margin of error is small.

As can be seen, the 1910 aggregate figure of 194,742 acres is considerably higher than that of the corresponding U.S. Census total of 99,524 acres. The discrepancy is explainable by the newspaper's inclusion of acreage under contract, but only partially. The newspaper compiled its statistics from local Japanese Association reports which included the names of individual owners, lessees, and contract farmers and the acreage each farmed. The U.S. Immigration Commission conducted an extensive survey of Japanese immigrants in 1909 and checked these figures up to that time in a few areas. Its agents found them to be accurate on the whole.[6] Thus the *Nichibei Shimbun* statistics undoubtedly are more accu-

[3]U.S., Census Office, *Twelfth Census of the United States, 1900* (Washington, 1902), vol. 5: *Agriculture*, pt. 1, p. cxviii.

[4]Ueno Kisaburō to Komura Jutarō, 30 April 1902, enclosure no 2, in Gaimushō [Foreign Ministry], *Nihon Gaikō Bunsho* [Papers Relating to the Foreign Relations of Japan] (Tokyo: Gaimushō, 1957), 44: 697-99.

[5]U.S., Bureau of the Census, *Chinese and Japanese in the United States, 1910* (Washington: GPO, 1914), Bulletin 127, p. 44.

[6]U.S., Immigration Commission, *Reports of the Immigration Commission: Immigrants in Industries* (Washington: GPO, 1911), 24: 299.

rate than those of the U.S. Census, giving a truer picture of the dramatic rise and growth of Japanese agriculture after the turn of the century. By 1913 the 281,687 acreage was farmed by 6,177 farmers.

As Japanese immigrants were settling on the land, California enacted the 1913 Alien Land Law. The law itself avoided direct reference to the Japanese. Instead it employed the phrase "aliens ineligible to citizenship," but it was legislated with the Japanese in mind. The law prohibited individual Japanese and companies, the majority of whose members or stockholders were Japanese, from purchasing agricultural land and restricted the leasing of such land to three years. It also banned Japanese from bequeathing or selling agricultural land they already owned to any fellow immigrant. The *Nichibei Shimbun* expressed the anger felt by the Japanese. In an editorial it complained that the law manifested the "height of discriminatory treatment" to which Japanese immigrants were subjected. Ostensibly a people of a first-rate power, Japanese were being "accorded worse treatment than people of third-rate southern and eastern European nations living in the United States."[7]

Japanese farmers quickly took steps to protect existing landholdings. The immediate problem was the ban on the transfer or sale of agricultural land from one Japanese to another. A Japanese farmer could not bequeath his farm to his kin as long as they were aliens ineligible to citizenship. (Four actual cases arose. One was that of Yokoi Hideyoshi, a resident of Florin. He died on 6 September 1913, leaving a 36-acre farm and a will which stipulated that his land should be divided equally between his wife and parent.)[8] Neither could a Japanese farmer sell his land to another alien Japanese, even if he wished to divest himself of his holding. Yet the law did not prohibit the transfer and sale of stocks in landholding companies. Governor Hiram Johnson signed the law on 19 May and it became effective on 10 August. As early as June, the *Nichibei Shimbun* strongly urged Japanese farmers to form land companies to solve this problem.[9] According to a comprehensive report of the Japanese consul in San Francisco, Japanese owned a total of 29,735 acres in California as of the end of 1913.[10] There were 141 land companies at the end of

[7]*Nichibei Shimbun* [Japanese American News], 26 April 1913.

[8]See the documents relating to Yokoi Hideyoshi and others in Japanese American Research Project, Japanese Foreign Ministry Archival Documents (hereafter JARP JFMAD).

[9]*Nichibei Shimbun*, 12 June 1913.

[10]Numano Yasutarō to Katō Takaaki, 14 October 1914. (Unless otherwise noted, all Japanese consular reports cited in this essay are in JARP JFMAD.) This particular report includes a comprehensive listing of all landholdings as of the end of 1913. A detailed list of individual owners and their acreage is appended to it. The total owned acreage of 29,735 acres is higher than the *Nichibei Nenkan* [Japanese American Yearbook] figure of 26,707 for 1913. The 1914 *Nichibei Nenkan* total was 31,828, but the newspaper noted that the increase was in part attributable to omissions in the 1913 total. The 1913 consular total is doubtless more accurate. The data on the number of landholding companies below are drawn from this report too.

1913, of which 100 held agricultural land totaling 10,249 acres. Out of the 100 companies, at least 65 were organized in 1913, the overwhelming number in July and early August just before the effective date of the law.

Japanese farmers also had the problem of meeting payments on land purchased before the 1913 law. The case of the Yamato Colony offers an excellent example. In 1906 the American Land and Produce Company purchased 3,200 acres of undeveloped land in Livingston, Merced County. This company was headed by Abiko Kyūtarō, publisher of the *Nichibei Shimbun* and immigrant leader who encouraged Japanese laborers to take up farming. The land company subdivided this large tract of land into 40-acre parcels and sold them to those who wanted to settle down on land. A handful of pioneer settlers moved onto the land in 1907 to form what was to be called the Yamato Colony.[11] In February 1914 Abiko applied for a $56,000 loan to the San Francisco branch of the Yokohama Specie Bank.[12] As one reason for his loan request, Abiko stressed the paramount importance of retaining existing landholdings in view of the prohibition against the purchase of additional land. Of the original 3,200 acres bought by the American Land and Produce Company, 1,500 acres had been paid off, while 1,000 acres had been lost in 1910 with the liquidation of the Japanese American Bank, a Japanese immigrant bank which had held the mortgage. The loan application was for the balance of 720 acres and the $56,000 was for making outstanding payments and developing this acreage.

Japanese immigrants had always lacked adequate banking facilities. Before 1911 there had been nine immigrant banks varying in size.[13] By 1910 all but two had gone out of existence; the two biggest ones, the Golden Gate Bank and the Japanese American Bank, were liquidated in 1910.[14] The two surviving banks were the Nippon Bank of Sacramento and the Industrial Bank of Fresno. Most Japanese farmers managed without the aid of immigrant banks. The outstanding exception was the farmers of the Yamato Colony whose land had been purchased with the backing of the Japanese American Bank. As editor of the *Hokubei Nōhō*, a monthly journal devoted to the promotion of Japanese agriculture,

[11]Shakuma, "Rekishi Inmetsu no Tan [The Destruction of History Lamented], pts. 93-96, JARP, Oka Papers. This source is a series of ninety-seven articles published in the *Nichibei Shimbun* in 1922 on the early history of Japanese immigrants. Shakuma is the pen name of Washizu Bunzō, a pioneer immigrant. For a history of the Yamato Colony, see Kesa Noda, *Yamato Colony: 1906-1960* (Livingston-Merced: Livingston-Merced JACL Chapter, 1981).

[12]Abiko Kyūtarō, "Shakkan Moshikomisho" [Loan Application], 10 February 1914, JARP JFMAD.

[13]Zaibei Nihonjinkai [Japanese Association of America], *Zaibei Nihonjin Shi* [History of Japanese in America] (San Francisco: Zaibei Nihonjinkai, 1940), 278.

[14]California State Superintendent of Banks, *First Annual Report* (Sacramento, 1910), 535-38.

Chiba Toyoji lamented the lack of financial assistance available to Japanese farmers.[15] The Japanese immigrant-style rotating credit union could not generate large capital. The *Nichibei Shimbun* likewise bemoaned the lack of an adequate rural bank and the insufficiency of rotating credit unions.[16] Because of the desire to preserve existing landholdings in the light of the 1913 law, this problem took on added urgency in 1914. In Abiko's opinion, the two surviving immigrant banks of Sacramento and Fresno were too small and did not have the resources to lend large sums of money. Uncertainties had been generated regarding the position of Japanese farmers, and however well disposed a few American banks may have been, the risks foreclosed possibilities of loans from them.[17]

The only institution to which Japanese farmers could turn was the Yokohama Specie Bank, with branches in San Francisco and Los Angeles. With the disappearance of immigrant banks, the branches of this bank had a virtual monopoly over immigrant savings from 1911. Operating as an exchange bank, the Yokohama Specie Bank did not lend money to Japanese immigrants. So a situation arose where the bank absorbed immigrant savings, but offered very little in return. The branches did provide the service of remitting money to Japan, but that was a far cry from granting loans to help the immigrants develop economically. As of the end of September 1913, the Yokohama Specie Bank held $11 million in immigrant savings deposited in the two branches and in Japan.[18] In 1913 Japanese grape growers of Bowles had requested a loan of $30,000 from the bank. The branch heads of San Francisco and Los Angeles were not authorized to grant loans. They only extended short-term loans to Mitsui Bussan and other trading firms with the approval of the home office. Hence the San Francisco branch rejected the Bowles grape growers' request. Despite the endorsement of the local consul, Abiko's loan application met the same fate. The Yokohama Specie Bank took the position that it was not a commercial bank in the business of lending money.[19] This early experience with the lack of adequate financial institutions was to recur in an acute form in later years, but it did not hinder the expansion of Japanese agriculture at this juncture.

Indeed, notwithstanding the 1913 Alien Land Law and lack of bank loans, Japanese agriculture expanded between 1914 and 1920. Japanese statistics indicate the following growth in acreage (see table 2). Until the

[15]Chiba Toyoji, "Zairyū Dōhō Nōgyō Kinyū Mondai" [Financial Problems of Japanese in America], *Hokubei Nōhō* [North American Agricultural Review] 2 (May 1911): 1-3.

[16]*Nichibei Shimbun*, 10 December 1913, 11 August 1915.

[17]This was the judgment of the San Francisco consul, Numano Yasutarō. See Numano to Makino Shinken, 1 November 1913.

[18]Ibid.

[19]Numano to Katō, 27 April 1914.

TABLE 2. JAPANESE AGRICULTURAL LANDHOLDINGS IN CALIFORNIA, 1914, 1918, 1920 (ACRES)

Year	Owned	Cash-Lease	Share-Lease	Contract	Total
1914	31,828	155,206	72,040	41,300	300,474
1918	30,306	336,721[a]		23,608	390,635
1920	74,769	192,150	121,000	70,137	458,056

SOURCES: Figures for 1914 and 1918 are drawn from *Nichibei Nenkan,* no. 11 (1915): 123-24; and no. 12 (1918): 5-6. The 1920 data are from Eliot G. Mears, *Resident Orientals on the American Pacific Coast* (Chicago: University of Chicago Press, 1928), 255.

[a]The figure between columns is combined cash-and-share.

economic boom ushered in by World War I, the growth was characterized exclusively by increases in the acreage of leased land. From a combined cash and share acreage of 227,246 in 1914, this acreage rose to 336,721 by 1918, while the owned acreage decreased slightly in the corresponding span of time.[20] But in 1919 and 1920 the acreage of owned land rose sharply. World War I caused a great expansion in American agriculture. With a sudden demand for agricultural commodities accompanied by rising prices, American farmers enjoyed unprecedented prosperity during the wartime years. Sharing in the general prosperity, Japanese farmers increased their landholdings in these two years. Purchasing land in the names of American-born Nisei children or land companies, they more than doubled the 1918 total of 30,306 acres to 74,769 by 1920.[21] The 1918 total acreage of 390,635 peaked to 458,056 acres by 1920, the highest total acreage Japanese farmers were ever to cultivate.

It would be wrong, however, to claim that the law had no negative effects. In 1917 Chiba Toyoji, managing director of the Japanese Agricultural Association, presented a perceptive critique.[22] According to his analysis, in the few cases in which landowners died with deeds still in their names, their land sold for 30 to 40 percent less than the going market value at public auctions. The three-year leasing limitation discouraged many farmers from cultivating fruit, grapes, and other crops which required a longer investment of money, time, and labor. On the other hand, it encouraged "speculative" agriculture in one-year crops. More-

[20]Mears used the statistics of the Japanese Association of America in his study. The 1920 Census records a total acreage of only 361,276 acres. See U.S., Bureau of the Census, *Fourteenth Census of the United States, 1920* (Washington, 1922), vol. 5, *Agriculture: General Report and Analytical Tables,* 313. Since the census figures are so much lower than Japanese statistics, I have relied upon the latter.

[21]There is no statistical breakdown on the acreage purchased in the name of Nisei children and in the name of land companies.

[22]Chiba Toyoji, "Kashū Tochihō no Dageki Eikyō Ippan" [General Impact of the California Land Law], *Kashū Chūō Nōkai Geppō* [Japanese Agricultural Association Monthly] 2 (December 1917): 1-3.

over, given the uncertain future of Japanese farmers, it also reinforced their desire to return to Japan as soon as possible, causing many to neglect their housing and physical environment. Finally, and most important, the 1913 Alien Land Law forced all Japanese to live with the stigma of being aliens ineligible to citizenship and subject to discriminatory treatment.

Designed to plug up the loopholes in the 1913 law, the 1920 California Alien Land Law had the undisguised purpose of driving Japanese farmers out of California agriculture. This law prohibited aliens ineligible to citizenship not only from purchasing but also from leasing agricultural land. It also denied them the right of buying and selling stock in land companies which owned or leased agricultural land and disqualified them from being appointed guardians of minors who had interest in such land. Like the 1913 law, it banned the transfer or sale of agricultural landholdings from one alien ineligible to citizenship to another. To punish violators of the law, strict penalties and escheat provisions were included. This stringent 1920 law originated as an initiative measure which appeared on the November ballot. The California electorate passed it overwhelmingly, and it became effective on 9 December.

This new law threatened the economic foundation of Japanese immigrant society. Starting as laborers at the bottom of California agriculture, the Japanese had worked their way up to become farmers of one kind or another only to be confronted now with the prospect of being reduced again to laborers. Farmers whose leases were due to expire had very few choices open to them. One option seemed to offer some hope. Relying on the distinction between an employment agreement and a lease, tenant farmers thought they would be able to continue farming through so-called cropping contracts. Under such contracts, they would become employees of landowners rather than tenants. In exchange for cultivating and harvesting crops, they would be paid by landowners either by a set share or in cash with the amount determined by the total value of the crop. Since lease agreements were banned, cropping contracts, if drawn up carefully, seemed the best way of approximating share-lease agreements without violating the 1920 law.[23] The choices were limited in any event, and the overall future was bleak in the light of the 1921 economic outlook for agriculture. Agricultural prices plummeted beginning in 1921 as the postwar years witnessed a contraction in demand for agricultural commodities.[24] Matsumoto Ryōsaku, who replaced Chiba Toyoji as the man-

[23]Matsumoto Ryōsaku and Satō Nobutada, "Kashū Nihonjin Nōgyōsha no Jitsujō" [Actual Condition of Japanese Farmers in California], November 1921, JARP JFMAD. This report was submitted by the Japanese Agricultural Association to the Japanese Embassy.

[24]From 1917 to 1920 the average wholesale price index for farm commodities was 146.3 during the boom years. From 1921 to 1924 the average dropped to 95.2. See Pajus, *The Real Japanese California*, 148.

aging director of the Japanese Agricultural Association, estimated that of the approximately 300,000 acres leased as of November 1921, the leases of 90,000 acres were due to expire.[25] In short, in 1921 Japanese farmers faced not only the stringent 1920 law, but also looked at a declining state of agriculture.

Feeling endangered by the 1920 law, Japanese immigrants quickly took their fight into court. At the outset the Japanese of Northern and Southern California went to court under the separate leadership of the Japanese Association of America and the Central Japanese Association of Southern California. As events unfolded, however, the two associations cooperated with each other, making the legal battle a coordinated struggle of all Japanese in California. Four basic types of cases found their way into court.[26] The first dealt with the legality of cropping contracts; three others challenged the prohibition against the leasing of land, the appointment of guardians, and the holding of stock in landholding companies. Of the four types, the litigation on cropping contracts and leasing began first.

The legal status of cropping contracts was unclear at the beginning of 1921. Were they prohibited by the 1920 Alien Land Law? The answer hinged on whether or not an employment agreement gave Japanese the possession and enjoyment of agricultural land in a legal sense. State Attorney U.S. Webb did not take a position on this question until the summer. Because he did not, Japanese farmers thought they had the hope of continuing farming under such contracts. In July 1921 Webb suddenly announced that cropping contracts were illegal. They were like lease agreements, he said, since they gave employees the same rights as those granted to tenant farmers.[27] In late September Webb declared that cropping contracts "seek to accomplish what the statute prohibits without incurring its penalties."[28]

[25]Matsumoto and Satō.

[26]It is not my intent here to write a legal history of these cases. For the legal details, see San Francisco Consulate General, *Documentary History of Law Cases Affecting Japanese in the United States, 1916-1924* (San Francisco: Consulate General of Japan, 1925), vol. 2; Pajus, *The Real Japanese California*, 91-144; Dudley O. McGovney, "The Anti-Japanese Land Laws of California and Ten Other States," *California Law Review* 35 (March 1947): 7-59; Edwin E. Ferguson, "The California Alien Land Law and the Fourteenth Amendment," ibid., 60-90; Milton R. Konvitz, *The Alien and the Asiatic in American Law* (Ithaca, N.Y.: Cornell University Press, 1946), 148-70; Frank F. Chuman, *The Bamboo People: The Law and Japanese-Americans* (Del Mar: Publisher's Inc., 1976), 72-89; and Moritoshi Fukuda, *Legal Problems of Japanese-Americans* (Tokyo: Keio Tsūshin, 1980), 123-213.

[27]*Sacramento Bee*, 8 July 1921. Webb's announcement coincided with county grand juries being authorized to investigate alleged violations of the alien land law.

[28]*Sacramento Bee*, 22 September 1921. In August the Stockton Chamber of Commerce had asked Webb about cropping contracts on behalf of local landowners. This was his answer.

This interpretation eliminated the one option Japanese farmers had and impelled them to action. Under the auspices of the Japanese Agricultural Association, the farmers of Northern California convened two emergency meetings on 2 September and 10 October to discuss the ominous turn of events.[29] On the day following the second meeting, the Japanese Association of America and its affiliated locals convened an extraordinary session of their delegate assembly.[30] The Japanese Agricultural Association had solicited the assistance of the Japanese Association of America. The delegates acted by establishing a land litigation committee. To finance the cost of litigation, they passed a budget of $25,000, half to be collected from farmers and the balance from other Japanese residents. This committee then had a bill of complaint filed in Santa Clara County on 13 October. Seeking a temporary injunction against the 1920 law, the complaint was filed on behalf of J. J. O'Brien and J. Inouye who wished to enter into a cropping contract. Believing that the question of cropping contracts was the most pressing one, Japanese farmers and immigrant leaders of Northern California acted in this decisive manner.

Independent of the Japanese Association of America, the Central Japanese Association of Southern California took a leasing test case to court. Thinking the ban on leasing more crucial, the leadership of this association sought to contest this prohibition. A land litigation committee had been formed earlier in August with a projected budget of $20,000.[31] This committee brought the Porterfield and Mizuno case before the Federal District Court on 18 October. The owner of eighty acres of land in Los Angeles County, Porterfield desired to lease his land to Mizuno for the purpose of raising vegetables. This case was also in the form of a bill of complaint which asked for a preliminary injunction.

Subsequently, the two associations cooperated and pursued common goals. Representatives of the two land litigation committees met on 5 November and agreed to form a joint committee whose decisions would be binding on both associations.[32] They also agreed to share all litigation expenses. In anticipation of going to the Supreme Court, the Japanese Association of America assumed the responsibility of finding an appropriate lawyer to handle all appeals. In January 1922 the joint committee engaged Louis Marshall on the recommendation of the Japanese Association of America.[33] The need to hire a lawyer for the appeal process

[29]Matsumoto and Satō, and *Shin Sekai* [New World], 3 September, 11 October 1921.

[30]*Shin Sekai* 12, 13 October 1921.

[31]Fujioka Shirō, *Beikoku Chūō Nihonjinkai Shi* [History of the Central Japanese Association of America] (Los Angeles: Beikoku Chūō Nihonjinkai, 1940), 99.

[32]Fujioka, 102-3, and Ōyama Ujirō to Uchida Yūya, 5 November 1921.

[33]Ōyama to Uchida, 24 January 1922. A partner in the New York law firm of Guggenheimer, Untermeyer and Marshall, Marshall was an expert on constitutional law with experience arguing cases before the U.S. Supreme Court.

had become necessary because of the outcome of the first two cases. The O'Brien and Inouye case ended in a momentary victory for Japanese farmers. The court ruled on 20 December that cropping contracts did not violate the 1920 law, reviving the hopes of Japanese farmers and giving them a short breathing spell to continue farming under such contracts. On the other hand, the Japanese lost the Porterfield and Mizuno case. On 19 December the court upheld the ban on leasing. Both decisions were appealed, the first by the State of California and the second by the Japanese.

In January 1922 the joint committee made decisions regarding two other cases. Having lost the leasing case, it decided to challenge the prohibition against the buying and selling of stock in land companies. On 7 February the Frick and Satow case was brought before the San Francisco Federal District Court, and again the Japanese side asked for a preliminary injunction. The bill of complaint stated that Raymond L. Frick wished to sell to Satō Nobutada twenty-eight shares of capital stock in the Merced Farm Company, an agricultural landholding company. On 23 May 1922 the court ruled that such a transaction was prohibited by the 1920 law. Whereupon the Japanese side appealed the decision.

The second case was the Yano guardianship case which began in October 1920. Prior to this test case, a number of guardianship cases had appeared in court, but none had been appealed.[34] Yano Hayao purchased fifteen acres of land in Butte County before the 1920 law and placed the deed in the name of his minor daughter. On 23 October 1920 he filed a petition to be appointed guardian to administer her estate. The presiding judge denied his petition on the ground that he had placed the deed in her name in order to evade the 1913 Alien Land Law. Since the state then instituted escheat proceedings, Yano's attorney appealed the decision to the California Supreme Court. In January 1922 the joint committee considered the case as a possible guardianship test case. But at the time Yano's appeal had not been accepted by the State Supreme Court. When the court accepted his appeal, the committee fully supported his case. The State Supreme Court rendered its decision on 1 May. Ruling that the State could deny a petition of guardianship only on the basis of proven incompetency, it overturned the lower court decision and ordered the appointment of Yano as the guardian of his daughter's estate. This meant that the court had invalidated that section of the 1920 law pertaining to the prohibition against the appointment of aliens ineligible to citizenship as guardians of minors who had title to agricultural land.

This first round of court action engendered optimism among Japanese immigrants. The *Nichibei Shimbun* editorialized in January 1922 that it "expected final victory" in the cropping contract and leasing test cases

[34]For these cases, see Pajus, *The Real Japanese California*, 130-36, and San Francisco Consulate General, *Documental History of Law Cases Affecting Japanese in the United States, 1916-1924*, 2: 913-1013.

at the U.S. Supreme Court level.[35] It also applauded the Yano decision as "just" and expressed great satisfaction that Japanese immigrants had been able to defend their constitutional rights through the case.[36] The Yano decision caused the *Shin Sekai*, another Japanese immigrant newspaper, to reaffirm its faith in this country by declaring that "justice still exists in America.[37] By the spring of 1923 the three key test cases on cropping contracts, leasing, and stockholding were ready to be argued before the high court. The *Nichibei Shimbun* in March 1923 confidently stated that "all preparations have been made." "Although it is hard to predict whether we will win or lose," it asserted, "we are generally optimistic."[38]

Six months prior to the high court decisions, the California legislature strengthened the 1920 law. The 1920 law did not prohibit cropping contracts explicitly. To correct the oversight and to counter the decision in the O'Brien and Inouye case, the legislature amended the 1920 law, broadening its restrictive provisions to include the usage, cultivation, and occupancy of agricultural land for beneficial purposes. This amendment made it difficult, if not impossible, to draw up employment agreements which granted Japanese farmers rights akin to those in share-leases. The decision in the Yano case moved the legislature to act too. It added a new section to the California Code of Civil Procedure. This section prohibited the appointment of aliens ineligible to citizenship, or companies the majority of whose members or stockholders were such aliens, to act as guardians of any estate that included real property. These new enactments made it all the more imperative, from the Japanese farmers' point of view, for the high tribunal to hand down favorable decisions.

But such decisions never came to pass. The Supreme Court ruled against Japanese farmers in November 1923. On 12 November the court affirmed the lower court decisions in two leasing test cases. In addition to the Porterfield and Mizuno case, there was another one which originated in Washington state. The Northwest American Japanese Association of Seattle had challenged the ban on leasing contained in the 1921 Washington Alien Land Law in the Terrace and Nakatsuka case. Having lost at the lower court level, the Association had appealed this case.[39] The

[35]*Nichibei Shimbun,* 16 January 1922.

[36]Ibid., 3 May 1922.

[37]*Shin Sekai,* 9 May 1922.

[38]*Nichibei Shimbun,* 23 March 1923.

[39]Seihokubu Renraku Nikkai [Northwest American Japanese Association], *Kaimu Hōkoku* [Transactions], Seattle, 1 March-31 August, 1921. The Northwest American Japanese Association acted more quickly than its counterpart in California. Influenced by the enactment of the 1920 California law, the Washington legislature passed its own version of an alien land law in March 1921. In contrast to the California law, the Washington legislature made the distinction between an alien who "in good faith declared his intention to become a citizen" and an alien who did not. Inasmuch as Japanese immigrants were unable to declare an intent to naturalize, they were subject automatically to the new law.

U.S. Supreme Court upheld the lower court decision in the Terrace and Nakatsuka case and applied its decision to the Porterfield and Mizuno case. A week later, on 19 November the court overturned the lower court decision in the O'Brien and Inouye case and affirmed the same in the Frick and Satow case. Finding the California and Washington Alien Land Laws in violation of neither the constitution nor the 1911 U.S.-Japan Treaty of Commerce, the high tribunal upheld the prohibition against the leasing of agricultural land, the purchasing of stock in land companies, and even cropping contracts. The two-year legal battle ended in defeat for Japanese farmers.

All Japanese immigrants were stunned by the defeat. They had been confident that they would not lose every case. If they lost the leasing test cases, they expected to fare better in the others. And if by chance they lost the Frick and Satow case, they believed the Supreme Court would not deny them the right to enter into cropping contracts. In reporting on the effects of the decisions, the San Francisco consul observed:

> The land law decisions have dealt a severe blow to Japanese immigrants, spiritually as well as materially.... They had previously won a favorable decision...on cropping contracts. As lease agreements expired, the majority switched to these contracts. Nearly everyone anticipated victory in this case. Just at the point when they firmly believed that they could solve all land law difficulties through cropping contracts, the case ended in failure. The sense of despair it aroused is hard to imagine.[40]

All Japanese immigrant newspapers expressed disbelief. On 21 November the *Nichibei Shimbun* said:

> The defeat...in the cropping contract and corporation stock test cases was wholly unexpected, taking not only our newspaper staff but also Japanese in general by surprise. No, not just Japanese, it also took not a few Americans by surprise. As far as we know, even the American legal profession was taken aback since the defeat of the State in these two cases was anticipated.[41]

When the *Shin Sekai* learned of the 12 November decisions, it still retained "a slim hope" that the high court would rule favorably on cropping contracts.[42] Hearing of the 19 November decisions, it stated flatly, "There is nothing more to say." Convoluted legal arguments now were useless. Japanese immigrants "have fallen to a lot worse than Mexicans, Armenians, Poles, and Negroes."[43]

[40] Ōyama Ujirō, "Gasshūkoku Daishinin no Kashū Tochihō Hanketsu no Eikyō Gaikyō" [General Effects of the United States Supreme Court Decisions Relating to the California Land Law], 26 February 1924, JARP JFMAD.

[41] *Nichibei Shimbun*, 21 November 1923.

[42] *Shin Sekai*, 13 November 1923.

[43] Ibid., 20 November 1923.

The *Rafu Shimpō* of Los Angeles described the situation in Southern California:

> The extreme dejected spirit of the Japanese . . . cannot be concealed. Some people are thinking of returning to Japan. Some are seeking safe havens outside the State or country. Some are planning to change occupations despite the lack of experience. Each person is planning according to his personal situation. And this is not limited to farmers who bear the brunt of the failure in litigation. The number does not stop with them. Businessmen who handle agricultural produce and many merchants who have farmers as their main customers have also been affected greatly.[44]

In the Pacific Northwest, the *Taihoku Nippō* said that the decisions caused "a great panic" among Japanese immigrants and decried the fact that the United States treated the immigrants as Japan treated her "eta" or pariah caste.[45] This immigrant reaction was understandable in view of the implication of the Supreme Court decisions. All Japanese farmers who did not own land and who desired to continue in agriculture would be reduced to working as laborers. By upholding the alien land laws, the decision undermined the economic foundation of Japanese immigrant society.

The Japanese Association of America and the Central Japanese Association of Southern California both convened emergency meetings with their affiliated locals after the Supreme Court decisions. Association leaders realized that they had no choice but to abide by the decisions. To make sure Japanese farmers understood them, they explained the sole option open to land leasing and cropping contract farmers.[46] That choice was to farm as wage-earners through employment agreements that provided neither a share of the crop nor a cash remuneration relative to its value. In January 1924 State Attorney General Webb conferred with county district attorneys to seek their cooperation in the enforcement of the alien land law. He announced that he would enforce it fully, except for existing cropping contracts which would be allowed until the end of the harvest season.[47] In other words, Japanese farmers who had such contracts would be permitted to fulfill them. But after the 1924 harvest season, they would be subject to the full enforcement of the law.

Japanese statistics from 1920 to 1925 indicate the drastic effects of the 1920 law. (See table 3.) The total acreage dropped from the 1920 peak of 458,056 acres to 330,653 in 1922 and to the lowest level, 307,966, by

[44]*Rafu Shimpō* [Los Angeles Japanese Daily], 27 November 1923.

[45]*Taihoku Nippō* [Great Northern Daily], 28 November, 4 December 1923.

[46]*Shin Sekai,* 1, 2 December 1923, and Fujioka, *Beikoku Chūō Nihonjinkai Shi,* 128-33. A number of farmers had renewed leases for three years just before the 1920 law became effective on 9 December. These leases all expired in December 1923.

[47]*Los Angeles Times,* 13-15 January 1924.

TABLE 3. Japanese Agricultural Landholdings in California, 1920, 1922, 1925 (acres)

Year	Owned	Cash-Lease	Share-Lease	Contract	Total
1920	74,769	192,150	121,000	70,137	458,056
1922	50,542	104,228	175,883[a]		330,653
1925	41,898	76,397[a]		189,671	307,966

source: Eliot G. Mears, *Resident Orientals on the American Pacific Coast* (Chicago: University of Chicago Press, 1928), 255.

note: The Japanese Foreign Ministry published slightly different figures for 1922, recording 51,000 owned acres, 152,000 leased acres, and 145,000 contract acres for a total of 348,000 acres. Gaishmushō Tsūshōkyoku Iminka [Foreign Ministry, Bureau of Commerce, Emigration Section], *Kashū Oyobi Kashū Tochihō Sosho Keika Gaiyō* [Summary of Litigation Relating to the California and Washington State Land Laws] (Tokyo: Gaimusho, 1923), 27. These figures do not change the substance of the argument, however.

[a]The figures between columns are combined cash-and share, and combined share and contract.

1925. The leased acreage plummeted from the 1920 total of 313,150 acres to 76,397 acres by 1925, the latter figure reflecting the full enforcement of the law after 1924. The acreage of owned land also fell sharply, from 74,769 acres in 1920 to 41,898 acres by 1925. The 1925 contract acreage of 189,671 acres includes the acreage of former tenant farmers who continued farming as managers or foremen.

The loss of owned acreage was caused by the inability to make payments. As exemplified by Abiko Kyūtarō and the Yamato Colony in 1914, this was an old problem that resurfaced in an acute form. During the wartime boom years, Japanese farmers purchased additional land; with the sudden postwar slump, these farmers could not meet their payments. The Yokohama Specie Bank adhered to its policy of not lending money to Japanese farmers. The Sumitomo Bank, which established a San Francisco branch in 1917, had the same policy. The postwar financial dilemma was compounded by the general uncertainties created by the 1920 law. Given the precarious position of Japanese farmers, American banks refused to provide loans, even when the farmers were willing to put their land up as collateral.[48]

The Japanese Association of America surveyed the landholdings of Japanese farmers in Northern California. Of the land purchased prior to 1920, there were still 14,753 acres with an unpaid balance of $2,080,195 as of May 1924.[49] The bulk of this acreage was concentrated in Fresno

[48]Ōyama to Shidehara Kijurō, 26 September 1924. Consul Ōyama sympathized with the plight of the farmers, feeling that it was absurd for the Yokohama Specie Bank to adhere to its nonlending policy.

[49]Zaibei Nihonjinkai, "Chūka Chihō Tochi Shoyūsha Hogo ni Kansuru Seigan Riyūsho" [Rationale for the Petition to Protect Landowners in Central California], September 1924, JARP JFMAD.

and its vicinity and consisted of 7,601 acres with $1,705,450 outstanding. Of this unpaid balance, $646,705 was due in 1924 and 1925. To save this land from foreclosure, the Japanese Association of America petitioned the Foreign Ministry requesting assistance in September 1924. The Supreme Court had already rendered its decisions. Reasoning that it was urgent to preserve existing landholdings, the Association asked the Foreign Ministry to intercede and persuade the Yokohama Specie Bank to change its policy. The Yokohama Specie Bank and the Sumitomo Bank, according to the petition, held over 80 percent of all immigrant savings.[50]

Simultaneously, the Japanese Association of America submitted a loan application to the San Francisco branch of the Yokohama Specie Bank.[51] It asked for a long-term loan of $646,000 and requested that a loan division be opened within the San Francisco branch. As collateral for the loan, the application stated that Central California farmers were willing to put up their land, estimated as having a market value of $3,875,199. To assure that its petition to the Foreign Ministry would be given due consideration, in October 1924 the Association dispatched general secretary Takimoto Tamezō to Japan to negotiate directly with the Foreign Ministry and the Yokohama Specie Bank. While in Japan, Takimoto also sought the intercession of Shibusawa Eiichi, a prominent person in financial and business circles who was knowledgeable about Japanese immigrants in America.[52]

All of these efforts produced a small concession from the Yokohama Specie Bank: it agreed to provide limited loans. The head office instructed the San Francisco branch on 20 December 1924 that it could consider loans on an individual basis on three strict conditions.[53] No collateral could violate the California Bank Act, which prohibited commercial banks from lending money on second mortgages. This first condition meant that Japanese farmers had to put up collateral other than their lands which had first mortgages on them. This in itself severely restricted loan possibilities. The second and third conditions were straightforward. In considering loans, the San Francisco branch had to take into account the total balance of debts on farming equipment extending beyond 1925 and be assured of repayment within a reasonable time period.

Japanese farmers had never had access to adequate bank loans. The two small banks, the Nippon Bank of Sacramento and the Industrial Bank of Fresno, the sole surviving immigrant banks, both disappeared in the

[50]Ibid.

[51]Ōyama to Shidehara, 26 September 1924.

[52]Shibusawa Eiichi Denki Shiryō Kankōkai [Committee to Publish the Sources in the Life of Shibusawa Eiichi], *Shibusawa Eiichi Denki Shiryō* [Sources in the Life of Shibusawa Eiichi] (Tokyo: Shibusawa Eiichi Denki Shiryō Kankōkai, 1960), 33: 405-16.

[53]Ichinomiya Reitarō to Kojima Hisata, 20 December 1924.

twenties. The Industrial Bank was purchased in 1923 by the Valley Bank of Fresno, an American bank, and the Nippon Bank was sold to the Sumitomo Bank in 1925.[54] The concession of the Yokohama Specie Bank did not rescue Japanese farmers who owed payments. By 1926 the San Francisco branch had lent only $101,800 to farmers in the Fresno area, affecting 622 acres, a relatively small sum compared to the initially requested $646,000.[55] The loss of acreage in owned land, therefore, was caused by the inability of farmers to meet payments. But this inability was related to the negative climate generated by the 1920 law and the lack of sufficient loans available to them.

There were other negative effects of the 1920 law as well. After the autumn of 1924 Japanese farmers who were not landowners faced a dim future. As a last exercise in futility, the Central Japanese Association of Southern California supported two so-called bonus test cases in the summer of 1924.[56] This litigation was based on the subtle distinction between cropping contracts and employment agreements with bonuses. Cropping contracts had been a way of approximating share-leases; bonus contracts were a way of approximating cropping contracts. In cropping contracts, the payment of shares or cash percentages of crops to employees was the sole remuneration. In bonus contracts, this payment was in the form of bonuses on top of wages. In December 1924 the State Supreme Court ruled that bonus contracts were cropping contracts in disguise, and therefore illegal, too. The Japanese Association of America never endorsed this litigation in anticipation of this decision. The Central Japanese Association of Southern California supported the bonus test cases as a last legal straw to prevent tenant farmers from being relegated to the status of laborers. Thus from 1925 other ways of getting around the law had to be formulated.

Various methods were devised to mitigate the effects of the law.[57] One

[54]California State Superintendent of Banks, *Fourteenth Annual Report* (Sacramento, 1923), and *Sixteenth Annual Report* (Sacramento, 1925).

[55]Zai-Sōkō Nihon Teikoku Sō-Ryōjikan [San Francisco Consulate General of Imperial Japan], "Hompōjin Nōkōsha no Jōkyō ni Kansuru Chōsa Hōkokusho" [Investigative Report on the Situation of Japanese Farmers], pt. 1, September 1926, JARP JFMAD.

[56]These were the Noji and Makimoto bonus cases. For the legal details, see San Francisco Consulate General, *Documental History of Law Cases Affecting Japanese in the United States, 1916-1924,* 2: 795-816. For the activities of the Central Japanese Associaiton of Southern California, see Nanka Chūō Nihonjinkai, *Taishō Jūsannendo Nenpō* [Annual Report, 1924], Los Angeles, 31 January 1925.

[57]The primary source for this section of the essay is an extensive report on Japanese farmers in Northern California compiled by the San Francisco Japanese Consulate. Divided into two parts, it is titled "Hompōjin Nōkōsha no Jōkyō ni Kansuru Chōsa Hōkokusho" [Investigative Report on the Situation of Japanese Farmers], pt. 1, September 1926, and pt. 2, October 1926. All statistics cited below are drawn from this report. The report offers the best insights into how Japanese farmers mitigated the

method was the so-called middleman arrangement. Gaining the help of a citizen, a Japanese farmer had the person lease land for him. The lessee was the nominal farmer, who never cultivated the land. The Japanese did the actual farming and assumed the financial burden of operating the farm. To avoid prosecution for violating the alien land law, the middleman hired the Japanese as his manager or foreman in an employment agreement. All business transactions in the operation of the farm were carried out in the name of the lessee. Two separate but parallel accounts were kept, one covering the transaction between the middleman and the farmer and another between the middleman and the lessor. In return for the service rendered by the middleman, the farmer paid a "middleman fee." The fee varied from place to place and depended on the agreement between the two parties. It was a flat sum of money, a set percentage of the farmer's net profit, or so many dollars per acre leased. In 1926 the flat fee was $50-$70 in Florin, the percentage of net profit was 5 percent in Hollister, and the fee per acre leased was $3.00 in Stockton.

This middleman arrangement had its drawbacks. It was premised on mutual trust. The two parties had to have a clear understanding which they both honored. If the middleman tried to exact more money than the agreed-upon fee, the farmer found himself in a vulnerable position. Beholden to the middleman for his livelihood, he could not dismiss him lightly. When the middleman was an adult Nisei who was related by blood or an offspring of a friend or associate, no problems occurred. In the late twenties, however, there were only a few adult Nisei who had been born on the continental United States, and many farmers had to rely on Hawaii-born Nisei who had no real personal ties with local Japanese communities. Some of these Nisei blackmailed farmers to force them to pay higher middleman fees. This underhanded "squeeze" was by no means unique to Nisei middlemen, but was practiced by non-Japanese middlemen as well. Japanese farmers called these unscrupulous middlemen "parasites." Moreover, whether a middleman was a Nisei or not, if the person died suddenly the farmer had another serious problem. If the deceased middleman left no one to fulfill his obligations, the farmer stood to lose his entire investment in the operation of the farm. Because of these drawbacks, Japanese farmers did not consider the middleman arrangement the safest way of farming.

Not all Japanese communities engaged in it. In 1926 Japanese farmers in Courtland continued to farm 11,882 acres under various arrangements. Over half of this total (6,005 acres) consisted of land farmed in the name

effects of the alien land law. Thus far the principal source of information on this subject has been the short comments elicited from a few Japanese farmers by fieldworkers for Edward K. Strong's study. See Strong, *Japanese in California*, 103-4.

of Nisei. Of this figure, 850 acres were leased for cash, 2,880 acres for share, and 700 acres were farmed under contract, adding up to an aggregate of 4,430 acres; the balance of 1,575 acres consisted of leased land on which Japanese were hired as actual foremen. On the other hand, in Walnut Grove, just down the delta from Courtland, the figures were remarkably different. Out of the 10,753 acres cultivated by 61 Japanese farmers in 1926, only 350 acres were farmed by 3 farmers using the names of Nisei. Thirty-eight farmers were actual foremen on 8,470 acres of the total acreage. The remaining 20 farmers cultivated 1,933 acres under so-called oral agreements with landowners.

An oral agreement was another alternative. Rather than use a middleman, a Japanese farmer entered into two separate, direct agreements with a landowner, one public and another private. The landowner hired the Japanese as a foreman on his farm. The terms of employment were written into a public agreement which the landowner could show to local law enforcement officers. Based on an unwritten, mutual understanding, and in contrast to the public agreement, the Japanese cultivated the landowner's land as a cash or share tenant. To maintain the public facade that the Japanese was an employee, the two parties kept two different accounts parallel to the two agreements and similar to the system of accounting in the middleman arrangement. In general, landowners who had profited from leasing land to Japanese farmers opposed the 1920 Alien Land Law. To continue their profitable relationship with them, some landowners were amenable to oral agreements.

The prevalence of oral agreements was related to two key factors. First, there had to be mutual trust between a Japanese farmer and a landowner. If a landowner broke his oral agreement, the farmer had no legal recourse. Given the inherent risks, no Japanese was likely to enter into an oral agreement unless he was reasonably sure that the landowner could be trusted. Second, even where mutual trust existed, landowners themselves were unlikely to enter into oral agreements if local district attorneys were zealous enforcers of the alien land law. The influence of landowners in local county politics was crucial. If landowners were assured that local law enforcement officers would overlook oral agreements, they had no fear of prosecution. Otherwise they were reluctant to enter into such agreements. For Japanese farmers, oral agreements were not always satisfactory nor possible everywhere.

There was a third possibility for Japanese farmers: to have land companies lease land for them. In 1926 there were an estimated 414 or 415 Japanese-related land companies, of which 400 had been formed prior to the 1920 law. Almost all of the companies were located in Northern and Central California. Japanese farmers in this part of the state had the legal advice of Albert H. Eliot and Guy C. Calden, legal counsels of the Japanese Association of America, and 142 of the companies had some ties with their law firm. There were two types of land companies. One was formed for personal profit; the other was organized for the welfare of a group of farmers. Stock was issued, in both cases, to American friends or Nisei who generally had nothing to do with the operation of the companies.

The Lodi Corporation was an example of the second type. In 1926 this company leased 1,026 acres in the Lodi area. Managed by the local Japanese Association, it operated for the benefit of local farmers. When a farmer knew of a landowner who wished to lease land, the farmer asked the company to become the lessee. Once the company checked the economic feasibility of farming the land, it leased the land for the farmer. The company then hired the Japanese as a foreman. Ostensibly the foreman, the Japanese farmed the land as if he had signed the lease himself. The company and the farmer had their own private agreement. The farmer put up his own capital to operate the farm. As in the middleman agreement, instead of doing business in his own name, he had the company transact it in its name. To compensate the company for its service, the farmer paid 5 percent of his annual rental for cash leases and 5 percent of his net earnings for share leases. This income permitted the company to pay taxes and cover its administrative overhead. The secretary of the local Japanese Association managed the day-to-day affairs of the company. He negotiated with landowners on behalf of local farmers and handled all business transactions. Because this method of farming also demanded two separate accounting books, he recorded all transactions with farmers in one set and with landowners in another. In 1926 twenty-nine Japanese farmed under the auspices of the Lodi Corporation.

This third method was the safest way of farming. Assuming companies were managed efficiently, Japanese farmers had a sense of security. With stock in the hands of American friends or Nisei, the companies were organized and operated for their benefit. They eliminated the problem of middlemen making exorbitant additional demands and the fear of landowners breaking oral agreements. As long as books were kept up and taxes paid, neither land companies nor farmers could be prosecuted for conspiring to evade the alien land law. Landowners were safe from prosecution too. They dealt openly and legally with land companies. What occurred between the companies and Japanese farmers did not legally implicate them in any way. As far as the law was concerned, they signed legal lease agreements.

There are no precise figures for every farming community on the acreage farmed through the middleman arrangement, oral agreement, and land companies. The impression is one of extreme variation from community to community. The use of Nisei middlemen predominated in Courtland. This practice later increased in every community as many Nisei born on the continental United States reached adulthood during the thirties. No land companies operated in Courtland, Walnut Grove, or Isleton, while the Lodi Corporation played an important role in the Lodi area. Oral agreements were widespread in the Hanford and Salinas areas. One method did not preclude others, so that all three methods of farming may have coexisted in other areas. Some scholars have assumed *a priori* that these methods automatically nullified the effectiveness of the 1920 law. Without exact statistics, however, it would appear that the best interpretation is that they helped to mitigate, but not eliminate, the negative impact of the law.

The 1920 enactment had a final effect. It caused Japanese immigrants to entertain the idea of leaving the state, and even the country. In 1920 Japanese consuls considered dispersing the immigrants throughout the United States, attributing the hostility of Californians to the high Japanese concentration in the state. Short of the complete withdrawal of Japanese immigrants from America, the consuls believed that dispersal would solve the exclusion question. The New York consul first suggested that the Foreign Ministry should adopt this policy of dispersal, and the San Francisco and Los Angeles consuls concurred with his recommendation.[58] Nevertheless, the Foreign Ministry never acted on the idea.

The immigrants themselves toyed with the idea, but they did not give it serious consideration until the 1923 Supreme Court decisions. At the 1924 conference of the Pacific Coast Japanese Association Deliberative Council, held in April, the idea appeared on the agenda as a resolution to investigate conditions in other states.[59] The delegates passed this resolution with the possible future migration of Japanese farmers in mind. In the fall the Japanese Association of America sent Matsumoto Manroku, an agricultural expert, to survey the southern states on behalf of the Council. According to general secretary Takimoto Tamezō, fifty persons from Northern California had left on their own during the summer to places outside the state.[60] In his opinion, Japanese farmers should migrate only after careful planning, and in groups. Studies of the agricultural prospects, the attitudes toward Japanese, and the likeli-

[58]Kumazaki Kyō to Uchida, 22 July 1920, Ota Tamekichi to Uchida, 24 July 1920, and Ōyama to Uchida, 30 July 1920. New York consul Kumazaki made his recommendation just as exclusionists in California were securing the required number of signatures to get the 1920 alien land initiative on the November ballot.

[59]Taiheiyō Engan Nihonjinkai Kyōgikai [Pacific Coast Japanese Association Deliberative Council], "Gijiroku" [Proceedings], 9-11 April 1924.

[60]Takimoto Tamezō, "Gojin no Jūyō Mondai, Fuzoku Shorui Dai-Nigō: Beikoku Taiheiyō Engan Igai no Nōkōchi Chōsa ni Kansuru Ken" [Our Pressing Problem, Attached Document No. 2: Investigation of Farming Areas Outside of the Pacific Coast], 15 August 1924, JARP JFMAD.

hood of anti-Japanese agitation arising in other states had to be conducted. In November 1924 the Japanese Association of America published Matsumoto's report in which he concluded that Georgia, particularly its delta region, and Florida were ideal.[61]

Some immigrants considered leaving the country. A few people in Southern California looked at Mexico as a prospective new immigrant land; others looked further south toward Brazil. In the summer of 1924 the Rikkōkai, a Japan-based organization, proposed to resettle Japanese immigrants in the United States to Brazil where it was establishing an agricultural colony.[62] In earlier years the Rikkōkai had assisted many indigent students to emigrate to the United States. Two farmers actually left California and took up farming in Manchuria under the influence of Chiba Toyoji, who had been long associated with Japanese immigrant agriculture. Since 1910 he had edited the *Hokubei Nōhō;* and in 1916 he had assumed the post of managing director of the Japanese Agricultural Association and editor of its monthly bulletin. Because of the anti-Japanese agitation, Chiba withdrew from California in 1921. He desired, in his words, "to go to a place where Japanese national power had influence" and resettled in Dairen, Manchuria.[63]

Nonetheless, Japanese farmers did not migrate to other states or countries in any significant numbers. They already had too much invested in California to pull up stakes, not merely in terms of money and families but in less tangible items like time and familiarity. Yet, that immigrant leaders entertained the idea of leaving the state and country demonstrates the effectiveness of the 1920 law. That the law was not effective enough to cause an actual mass exodus from California in no way detracts from its oppressiveness.

In summary, viewed from a Japanese immigrant perspective, the 1920 California Alien Land Law was indeed a "bread-and-butter" issue. Japanese immigrant sources reveal that its enactment and enforcement, coupled with the post–World War I slump in agriculture, caused a sharp drop in Japanese agriculture during the twenties, supporting the contention of the scholars who have taken this position. The law was not "an ineffective irritant" which "in no wise significantly affected land tenure."[64] Nor was it "blithely ignored."[65] The contraction in the twenties was real,

[61]Zaibei Nihonjinkai, *Shūgai Shisatsu Hōkoku* [Survey of Other States] (San Francisco: Zaibei Nihonjinkai, 1924).

[62]Nagata Shigeshi, "Zaibei Nihonjin ni Atauru Sho" [A Proposal to the Japanese in America], *Rikkō Sekai* [Rikko World] (June 1924): 1-25.

[63]Chiba Toyoji, "Chiba Toyoji Ikō" [Posthumous Writings of Chiba Toyoji] (Dairen, 1944), 2: 616.

[64]Daniels, *The Politics of Prejudice*, 88.

[65]McWilliams, *Prejudice*, 65.

not "largely spurious." If all "managers" were actual tenants, then "much of this decline" can be said to have been "offset."[66] But since many (the exact number is unverifiable) were actual managers, this interpretation must be modified. In 1933 Edward K. Strong, Jr., concluded that the "land law is non-operative in many sections of the state, if not in all parts."[67] This assertion may be true, partially or wholly, for the thirties, but not for the twenties. During the thirties, the problem of finding trustworthy middlemen to sign leases was alleviated by the increasing number of Nisei born on the continental United States who reached adulthood. Through these Nisei, many onetime farmers who had been reduced to working as actual foremen and managers were able to resume farming as cash or share tenants.

To grasp the full meaning of the 1920 Alien Land Law, it is necessary to look at the broader historical context. From the Japanese immigrant perspective, it was a part of a series of events which culminated in their rejection by American society. In 1922 the immigrants had lost a naturalization test case. The Supreme Court upheld their ineligibility to citizenship in the noted Takao Ozawa case.[68] If the court had ruled otherwise, the land litigation would have become meaningless. But the Ozawa case actually made the land cases absolutely crucial, which is why the immigrants reacted so strongly when they lost every test case at the Supreme Court level. Soon after the shocking 1923 decisions, Congress enacted the 1924 Immigration Act barring the further admission of any alien ineligible to citizenship, which brought all Japanese immigration to an abrupt end. All of these events combined to produce a profound sense of rejection among Japanese immigrants, a feeling that they were deemed racially inferior and hence undesirable by white America. This left a legacy of bitter resentment which rankled in their hearts well into the decade of the thirties.

[66]Higgs, "Landless by Law," 221.

[67]Strong, *Japanese in California*, 103.

[68]Yuji Ichioka, "The Early Japanese Immigrant Quest for Citizenship: The Background of the 1922 Ozawa Case," *Amerasia Journal* 4 (1977):1-22.

THE JAPANESE PROBLEM IN OREGON*

THE year 1945 has witnessed the revival and development in this state of organized activity against the Japanese. While the condition is not yet alarming, it is nevertheless sufficiently grave to be a matter of concern to the thinking people of Oregon, for the problem involves not only the constitutional rights of American citizens, but also those fundamentals of justice and respect for human dignity upon which depends that racial harmony which is essential to the kind of world for which we are making sacrifices.

Your committee appointed to consider group and racial animosities engendered by the World War, has been requested by the president of the association to submit for the information of the bar a general report upon the Japanese problem existing in this state. Four main aspects of the situation seem to justify special consideration: (1) personal rights of resident alien Japanese; (2) dual citizenship; (3) alien land laws of Oregon; and (4) recent anti-Japanese activities.

I. Personal Rights of Resident Alien Japanese

Since approximately one-third of the Japanese residents of Oregon are aliens and ineligible for citizenship, it may be of interest to consider briefly what personal rights and privileges are extended to them under our laws.

Subject only to the provisions of any treaty and to the provisions of the Constitution of the United States, the rights of resident alien Japanese are to be determined by the Constitution and laws of the state of Oregon.

Since the Treaty of 1911 conferring upon alien Japanese the right to engage in business enterprises in this country and authorizing them to own or lease real property for residential and commercial purposes was by formal notice effective January 26, 1940, abrogated by the United States, their rights presently are only those granted by the Federal and state constitutions and the laws of Oregon.

Briefly stated, however, a resident alien enjoys in the main, along with citizens of the United States, the right to so employ himself as to gain a livelihood. Primarily, he has the same right and privilege as citizens under similar circumstances to engage in useful, gainful employment and occupations, unless they pertain to the regulation or distribution of the public domain, or to the common property or re-

* Report of a committee appointed by the president of the Multnomah Bar Association to report on the Japanese problem in Oregon. Members of the committee were Verne Dusenbery, chairman, Rupert R. Bullivant, Mark M. Matthiessen, Clarence D. Phillips, and Samuel B. Weinstein.

sources of the people of the state, or to the devolution of real property, or to public works, or to benefits to be received from public moneys.

The Japanese come squarely within the language of the Fourteenth Amendment to the Federal Constitution prohibiting the states from denying to any person within their jurisdictions the equal protection of their laws, or from depriving any person of life, liberty, or property without due process. As aliens, moreover, they are entitled to the protection of the provision against suspension of the privilege of habeas corpus, except in time of public danger, the provision against the passage of bills of attainder or ex post facto laws, the provision that no person shall be held to answer for a capital or other infamous crime unless on a presentment or indictment of a grand jury, or be twice put in jeopardy, or be compelled in any criminal case to be a witness against himself, the provision securing the right to defendants to have compulsory process for obtaining witnesses, and the guaranty against excessive bail and fines and cruel and unusual punishments.

Obviously, on the other hand, they are not entitled to the benefits of the constitutional prohibition upon the states against making or enforcing any law which abridges the privileges and immunities of citizens of the United States, because they are indeed ineligible to citizenship.

II. Dual Citizenship

Another question which is the subject of frequent discussion in connection with Japanese racial problems is that of "dual citizenship." In fact, the term is so frequently used in connection with the Japanese, and so little used in connection with other nationalities, that there is a widespread belief that the concept of dual citizenship was originated by Japan and is made use of only by that nation. A brief consideration of the facts may be of interest.

With respect to citizenship, some countries follow one theory of international law, called *ius sanguinis,* meaning that citizenship is a matter of blood and inheritance. Other countries hold to the theory of *ius soli,* meaning that citizenship is a matter of place of birth. Obviously where one country follows either of these theories and another country follows the other, the problem of dual citizenship arises between them. A large number of countries, including France, Germany, Italy, Spain, Norway, and Sweden, determine citizenship on the basis of blood and inheritance. Many other countries, including Great Britain and the self-governing dominions and most of the South American republics, determine citizenship according to the place of birth. Japan adheres to the doctrine that citizenship is determined by blood and not by place of birth, and so claims as citizens all persons of Japanese ancestry born in the United States (see exception below). On the other hand, the United States, with certain minor exceptions, determines citizenship according to the place of birth, and so claims as citizens all persons of Japanese ancestry born in the United States.

Prior to the adoption of the Fourteenth Amendment to the Federal Constitution, there was no established definition of citizenship in the United States. The only reference thereto in the original Constitution was in Article 4, Section 2, proclaiming that citizens of each state shall be entitled to all privileges and immunities of citizens in the several states.

Historically, it will be remembered that, under the *Dred Scott Case,* a man of African descent, whether a slave or not, was not and could not be a citizen of the United States. Consequently, the Fourteenth Amendment to the United States Constitution was adopted providing, among other things, that all persons born or naturalized in the United States and subject to the jurisdiction thereof, are citizens of the United States and of the state wherein they reside. The words, "subject to the jurisdiction," were intended to protect the citizenship of the representatives in this country of foreign governments, and recognized the extraterritoriality of ministers, ambassadors, and consuls of foreign countries.

Under the Fourteenth Amendment, all children of Japanese ancestry who are born in the United States are citizens of this country; but, as we are advised, under the laws of Japan these same children, if born before December 1, 1924 or if born since that date and properly registered with Japanese diplomatic representatives, would be considered Japanese citizens.

However, it is permissible under our statutes for one to renounce his citizenship in a foreign country, and such renunciation may be made whether he was born in this country or naturalized.

Under our present naturalization laws (Title 8, Sec. 703, U. S. C. A.), the right to become a naturalized citizen extends only to white persons, persons of African nativity or descent, descendants of races indigenous to the Western Hemisphere, and, by recent amendment, Chinese.

No problem of dual citizenship arises as to the Issei, born in Japan, since they are Japanese citizens by Japanese law as well as our own laws. Only the Nisei, persons of Japanese ancestry born in the United States, may be dual citizens. However, a Nisei can divest himself of American citizenship by expatriation. If he was born since December 1, 1924, he is not considered by the Japanese government as a citizen of Japan unless he was registered with a Japanese diplomatic representative within fourteen days of his birth. The effect of the Japanese statute, operative since December 1, 1924, has been to diminish the extent of dual citizenship, and was an attempt on the part of the Japanese government to conform to conditions in the United States. It made children born in the United States to Japanese parents, American citizens rather than dual citizens, if the parents failed to properly register them.

III. Alien Land Laws of Oregon

Alien land laws of the Pacific Coast states have made political and judicial history for more than three-quarters of a century. Originating in California, they later spread to Oregon and Washington. They were first directed against the Chinese, following extensive Chinese immigration after the settlement of California. They were then predicated upon a genuine fear that the sparsely settled coastal region would be inundated by waves of migrating Orientals. The Chinese Exclusion Act, and other Federal statutes prohibiting Oriental immigration and rendering most Orientals ineligible for citizenship, minimized the danger but did not entirely eliminate the fear.

In Article XV, Section 8, of the Oregon Constitution which was adopted in 1857, our forefathers with frontier directness prescribed that "no Chinaman" (except residents when the Constitution was adopted) should ever hold any real estate or mining claim in Oregon, and authorized the Legislature to carry the provision into effect.

There are now two statutes governing the rights of aliens to own and enjoy real property in this state. The most important of the two, Secs. 61-101 to 61-112 O. C. L. A. 1940, enacted in 1923, establishes the substantive rights and prohibitions on this subject, and is still in effect. This statute is supplemented by Senate Bill 274, enacted at the 1945 session of the Oregon Legislature, which adds certain criminal penalties and sets up certain disputable presumptions applicable to civil or criminal proceedings brought under either statute. Many of the provisions of each statute are similar to or identical with California legislation on the subject.

Alien Land Law of 1923. Under this statute, aliens eligible to citizenship under the laws of the United States may acquire, possess, enjoy, transmit, and inherit real property or any interest therein in the same manner and to the same extent as citizens of the United States except as otherwise provided by Oregon law. All other aliens (aliens not eligible to citizenship under the laws of the United States) may acquire, possess, enjoy, and transfer real property or any interest therein in the manner and to the extent and for the purpose "prescribed by any treaty *now existing* between the government of the United States and the nation or country of which such alien is a citizen or subject."

When the 1923 statute was enacted, there was in effect between the United States and Japan the Treaty of 1911 under which Japanese nationals were authorized "to own or lease and occupy houses, manufactories, warehouses and shops" and "to lease land for residential and commercial purposes." This treaty was not terminated until January 26, 1940. Construing the statute and the treaty together, it is obvious that the agricultural use and ownership of land by Japanese nationals was not permitted. On the other hand, the Oregon statute, when construed with the treaty, does permit ownership or leasing and occupancy of houses, manufactories, warehouses, and shops, and does permit leasing of land for the other uses specified in the treaty.

The committee feels that there is serious doubt whether the abrogation of the treaty either by governmental act or by war had the effect of terminating whatever pre-existing rights Japanese nationals may have had under our statutes to own and enjoy land. Since the privileges afforded by the treaty were incorporated in the Oregon law by reference, by the use of the language "any treaty now existing," the committee deems it likely that these privileges or rights still exist.

The statute (Sec. 61-103) prohibits the ownership and other related rights in land by corporations, a majority of whose members are ineligible aliens, beyond the extent permitted in any treaty then existing affecting such aliens. It also (Sec. 61-104) prohibits an ineligible alien and corporation of the type covered by the preceding section from being appointed as guardian of that portion of the estate of a minor which consists of property which such ineligible alien or corporation is prohibited from acquiring, owning, or enjoying.

The latter section is of doubtful constitutionality. In *Tetsubumi Yano's Estate,*[1] the California Supreme Court struck down the prohition on the ground that it denied aliens and their minor children rights guaranteed by the Fourteenth Amendment to the Federal Constitution. In 1924, the Washington Supreme Court, in *In re Fujimoto,*[2] sustained the validity of the same type of provision in the Washington law. There are no Oregon decisions on this question.

By Secs. 61-108 and 61-109 transfers and leases to ineligible aliens or corporations are declared unlawful and provision is made that property involved in such transfers or leases shall escheat to the state of Oregon in proceedings brought by the district attorney of the county in which the property involved is located. Sec. 61-110 provides that transfers in violation of the act are void and that the interests sought to be transferred shall escheat. It also establishes certain disputable

[1] 188 Cal. 645, 206 Pac. 995 (1922).
[2] 130 Wash. 188, 226 Pac. 505 (1924).

presumptions for use in legal proceedings involving such transfers. The Oregon statute does not provide for an automatic escheat of property but contemplates that escheat is not effective until proceedings are instituted and properly terminated. In the opinion of the committee, this means that titles to land which have passed through ineligible aliens are not voided simply because they have once been held by an ineligible alien or corporation.

The committee has found only one Oregon case construing the land-ownership and land-use provisions of the 1923 act, *Yoshida* v. *Security Insurance Company*,[8] in which the court held that Japanese tenants engaged in the hog-feeding business were conducting a "commercial" rather than an agricultural operation within the meaning of the 1911 Treaty between the United States and Japan. In this case a month-to-month tenancy for such purpose was declared valid under the statute, since the 1911 Treaty with Japan permitted Japanese subjects to lease land for residential and commercial purposes.

The 1945 Act. As stated earlier, this act (Senate Bill 274) did not supersede or repeal the 1923 statute but supplemented it in several particulars.

Sec. 1 provides that it shall be a criminal offense for any person to sign a lease, cropping agreement, or other agreement to acquire, use, transfer, possess, enjoy, cultivate, or occupy agricultural land or to transfer the beneficial use of real property used for agricultural purposes if such agreement is made in the name of the wife or child of an ineligible alien or in the name of any other person if an ineligible alien is permitted thereafter to farm such land or enjoy directly or indirectly the beneficial use thereof. The penalties are imprisonment for not to exceed two years and a fine of not to exceed $5,000. It is emphasized that this section applies only to agricultural land. The same section of the act also authorizes injunction suits to prevent violations of the section.

Sec. 2 provides for the establishment of a prima-facie presumption in any proceeding, criminal or civil, instituted by the state, that the defendant is ineligible for citizenship when it is proven that the defendant has been in the use or occupation of real property and that he is a member of a race ineligible for citizenship. When such presumption is established, the burden of proving citizenship or eligibility to citizenship as a defense then rests upon the defendant. The constitutionality of a similar provision of the California law was sustained by

[8] 145 Or. 325, 26 P. (2d) 1082 (1933).

the California court in *Morrison* v. *California*,[4] and sustained by the United States Supreme Court when an appeal was dismissed.[5]

Under sec. 3, if it is proven that a defendant in any civil or criminal action relating to the rights, powers, and disabilities of aliens is not a registered voter in the county in which the land involved is located, a prima-facie presumption is established that the defendant is an alien ineligible for citizenship. While the presumption is a rebuttable one, the committee directs attention to the fact that, under Oregon law, a presumption is evidence and does not disappear when rebutting evidence is produced. Because of the doctrine that statutory presumptions must be based on some rational connection in human experience or logic between the fact proved and the fact presumed, in order to be immune from constitutional attack, the committee believes that there is grave doubt as to the constitutionality of this section of the act.[6] The mere fact that an individual does not register as a voter has a very remote connection in human experience with the question as to whether or not such individual may be an alien ineligible to citizenship. There is a further question as to whether or not sec. 3 violates the equal-protection-of-the-laws provision of the Fourteenth Amendment to the Federal Constitution in that a burden is cast upon nonresidents of the state, who are not eligible to register for voting, which is not cast upon residents of the state who are eligible to register for this purpose.

Sec. 4 provides a prima-facie presumption that an ineligible alien who shall till, farm, or work land in the state or occupy the same in any capacity shall be presumed to be the owner of a leasehold or some interest in said land. This disputable presumption is subject to the same grave doubts as were expressed by the committee in connection with sec. 3 with respect to the problem as to whether there is any rational connection between the presumption and the fact required to be established in order to give rise to the presumption. Merely because an individual works on land, it does not seem to logically follow that he owns a legal interest in the land.

There is a further serious question as to the validity of sec. 4 arising from its indirect effect upon the right of an alien ineligible to citizenship to perform ordinary farm labor. Because the presumption is evidence, even though rebutting evidence is produced, any alien ineligible to citizenship is exposed to conviction of a crime simply because he works on agricultural land. If the statute is construed as a direct im-

---

[4] 125 Cal. App. 282, 13 P. (2d) 800 (1932).

[5] 288 U. S. 591 (1933).

[6] See in this connection: 20 AM. JUR. 40; 12 AM. JUR. 316; Wyckoff v. Mutual Life, 147 P. (2d) 227 (Or. 1944); Morrison v. California, 13 P. (2d) 800 (Cal. 1932), *appeal dismissed*, 288 U. S. 591 (1933); Tot v. U. S., 319 U. S. 463 (1943); Morrison v. California, 291 U. S. 82 (1934); Mobile Railroad v. Turnipseed, 219 U. S. 35 (1910).

pairment of the right to labor, a right possessed by ineligible aliens, it may also be subject to attack upon this ground.[7]

IV. Recent Anti-Japanese Activities

Within the last six months two distinct centers of anti-Japanese activity have developed in Oregon. The movements seem to have been of separate origin, one in Hood River County and the other in the Gresham district of Multnomah County. As the committee is now informed, there is no indication that similar movements are likely to originate in other counties, although the Gresham group is attempting to expand its activities throughout the state.

Both of the anti-Japanese groups have formed organizations and are incorporated as nonprofit corporations under the Oregon law. The Hood River group makes use of the innocuous and noncommittal name of "Hood River Citizens Committee, Inc." The professed objectives of the corporation are mild and beneficent:

> "The object, business or pursuit of this corporation is one of general public community welfare, peace, tranquility and the promotion of such projects and undertakings as shall tend to the betterment, understanding, and well being of the citizens of Hood River County, Oregon, to the end that their spirit of Americanism may be preserved, encouraged and perpetuated as an inheritance for future generations."

Even though the Oregon statute for the organization of nonprofit corporations is broad and elastic, the Gresham group experienced some difficulty in completing its corporate organization. The articles of incorporation first tendered, using the name "Oregon Anti-Japanese Inc.," were submitted by the corporation commissioner to the attorney general for his opinion as to the eligibility of the proposed corporation. In two well-considered opinions, dated January 23, 1945 and April 17, 1945, the attorney general advised that, while the declared objectives of the corporation were vague and difficult to construe, they did not definitely disclose any unlawful purpose. He pointed out, however, that the term "Anti-Japanese" in the corporate name implied discrimination against American citizens of Japanese ancestry, and suggested a change of name. Thereafter the name was changed to "Japanese Ex-

---

[7] See the following: Truax v. Raich, 239 U. S. 33 (1915); Ex Parte Case, 20 Ida. 128, 116 Pac. 1037 (1911); In re Tiburcio Parrott, 1 Fed. 481 (1880); Fellman, *The Alien's Right to Work* (1937) 22 MINN. L. REV. 137; O'Connor, *Constitutional Protection of the Alien's Right to Work* (1941) 18 N. Y. U. L. Q. REV. 483; Takiguchi v. State, 55 P. (2d) 802 (Ariz. 1936); Bailey v. Alabama, 219 U. S. 219 (1911); Taylor v. Georgia, 315 U. S. 25 (1942); Pollock v. Williams, 322 U. S. 1 (1944).

clusion League," and the articles were filed and a certificate of incorporation was issued on April 30, 1945.

The three objectives of the Japanese Exclusion League are declared to be:

(1) To conduct during the national emergency and by all lawful means, an educational program relating to the return to the Pacific Coast states of all people of the Japanese race.

(2) To make available to the United States government information obtained by members or officers of the corporation relating to the conduct of Japanese residing in the United States or any of its possessions.

(3) Upon the termination of the present national emergency, to assist by all lawful means the enactment of legislation, both state and Federal, "designed to exclude from United States citizenship all persons now ineligible for citizenship, as well as their descendants."

Since the proposed objectives of the corporation are vague and ambiguous, the legality of the corporation may ultimately depend upon the practical construction which the corporation itself places upon them by the activities in which it elects to engage. Thus the first objective of the corporation may become unlawful if the proposed "educational program" should be conducted to deprive citizens of Japanese ancestry of the right to return to and live in the state of Oregon. The second objective might also become unlawful if the corporation should, by a campaign of spying and snooping, attempt to deprive Japanese residents of fundamental personal rights, including the right of privacy. Likewise, the third objective might be unlawful if under it an attempt were made to deprive American-born Japanese of their citizenship.

Although both groups have been permitted to incorporate, the question is still open whether either of them is or shall continue to be a lawful enterprise. As stated by the attorney general in one of his opinions, the filing of the articles "in no way dignifies the corporate entity thus created, nor gives to the objects or powers set forth therein the stamp of legality." Regardless of its professed objectives, either corporation may render itself subject to dissolution by engaging in activities which are unlawful or against the public policy of the state.

As the committee is informed, there is one difference between the Hood River organization and the Gresham organization that is worthy of note. The Hood River group so far has confined its operations to the local community, and has not as yet shown any tendency to engage in a state-wide race crusade. On the other hand, the Gresham organization seems to have entered upon a more ambitious program. Its bylaws provide for an elaborate organization of local community groups to be formed wherever twenty-five or more members may be obtained. It charges an initiation fee of $10.00 and dues of $1.00 per month. It has obtained the services of professional organizers. According to the best information of the committee, the Japanese Exclusion League is now operating in Washington as well as in Oregon, and has plans for extending its activities to other states.

Opinions may differ as to the cause of the recent anti-Japanese movements in Oregon. Although these outbursts have arisen in wartime, the war seems to have furnished the occasion rather than the cause. The two decisions of the military authorities, first on the ground of military necessity to evacuate all Japanese from the Pacific Coast area and second to permit them to return when the military emergency had passed, were in all probability contributing factors. In the opinion of your committee, they cannot be explained on the basis of a spontaneous outburst of patriotic fervor engendered by the war. The movement cannot be traced to the men of the armed services who are fighting this war. Paradoxical as it may seem, the men in the service form one of the strongest bulwarks supporting the constitutional rights of Americans of Japanese ancestry.

Nor can the resurgence of anti-Japanese activity be explained on the ground of economic necessity—the historic argument upon which the entire anti-Oriental movement has been based. The census discloses that the Japanese have never been sufficiently numerous in Oregon to constitute an economic menace in any part of the state. Only about half of the Japanese population is engaged in agriculture. As disclosed by the table below, the Japanese percentage of the population was highest in 1900 when it was 0.6 per cent, and lowest in 1940 when it

THE JAPANESE POPULATION OF OREGON FROM 1900 TO 1940
AS SHOWN BY UNITED STATES CENSUS

Census year	*Total population of Oregon*	*Japanese in Oregon*		*% of foreign-born Japanese**
		Total numbers	*% of total population*	
1900	413,336	2,501	0.6	99.6
1910	672,765	3,418	0.51	96.0
1920	783,389	4,151	0.53	76.1
1930	953,786	4,958	0.52	52.4
1940	1,089,684	4,071	0.37	39.7

* This column shows the percentage of the total Japanese population in Oregon which was foreign-born. Since only Japanese born in the United States are citizens, the column shows the percentage of aliens in the Japanese group.

was 0.37 per cent. While the total Japanese population in Oregon rose slowly until 1930, when it amounted to 4,958, it declined 18 per cent between 1930 and 1940 to 4,071, the number revealed by the last census.

A special plea of economic necessity has been made by some of the backers of the Hood River movement, who assert that that county is especially menaced since the Japanese account for 10 per cent of the population. The percentage appears to be exaggerated. While it is true that Hood River County has a higher percentage of Japanese residents than any other region in the state, the 1940 census reveals 462 Japanese out of a population of 11,580, or approximately 4 per cent.

In the opinion of the committee, these uprisings cannot be accounted for as an expression of any spontaneous emotion; rather, they seem to have been initiated, guided, and directed by persons and groups who are chiefly motivated by hope of economic aggrandizement. The general objective of these active groups appears to be the prevention of the return of the Japanese to Oregon, or at any rate to the localities where the groups operate. Economic advantage may inure to them in two ways: (1) by making the lands owned by Japanese citizens available to white residents on favorable terms and (2) by relieving members of the groups from what is considered "tough" competition with Japanese farmers.

The Japanese are discouraged if not prevented from returning to Oregon by various means. In the first place, the existence of the organized movement is in itself a strong deterrent to their return. Clothed as they are with the corporate franchise of the state, these organizations confront the returning Japanese with a rather formidable reception. It is true that there has not been in Oregon in recent times any known case of violence against a Japanese. But there has been violence in California, and the dislocated Japanese contemplating a return to his land has no assurance that violence will not break out here.

There is also evidence of economic coercion. It is applied quietly but apparently with considerable effect. Most of the Japanese farmers in Oregon were engaged in growing green vegetables and similar produce. For the most part they are dependent upon making prompt sales of their produce direct to large consumers or disposing of it from day to day on the wholesale markets. The anti-Japanese operators quietly approach the large chain-store buyer or the independent grocer and threaten retaliation if purchases are made from Japanese. The committee has not been able to ascertain the extent to which this method of coercion has been carried on, or to trace the various known acts of coercion directly to either the Hood River or the Gresham group. It is known, however, that truck loads of produce otherwise in good demand have been brought to the wholesale market in Portland by Japanese and taken away because no one would purchase the produce; that dealers, who before the evacuation were accustomed to furnishing bread and similar items to Japanese operating roadside stands, are now refusing to supply such goods; that large purchasers of produce have refused to buy from Japanese; and that processors of fruit and vegetables have on occasion refused to make their facilities available for products grown by Japanese.

As the committee is advised, in most of the cases investigated by the War Relocation Authority the refusal to purchase Japanese produce has not been based upon the antipathy of the dealer toward the Japanese, but upon fear of reprisal by white growers, not a few of whom, strange as it may seem, are themselves recent emigrants from European countries. But in fairness to Oregon farmers it should be noted that economic coercion against the Japanese is also being practiced to some extent in the city of Portland. A commonly expressed excuse for refusal to deal with Japanese is, "I think right on this question, but my hands are tied."

Since the committee was requested to present a "factual" report on the Japanese problem, we have endeavored to confine the subject matter of our report to ascertained facts and legitimate inferences of fact to be drawn from them. We have therefore intentionally refrained from making any moral evaluation of the facts disclosed, or from submitting any recommendations for consideration by the association.

Prelude to Prejudice: Hiram Johnson, Woodrow Wilson, and the California Alien Land Law Controversy of 1913

BY HERBERT P. LE PORE

The year 1910 in California saw the emergence of a political personality who was to have great influence on the future of the Japanese in California. This was Hiram W. Johnson (1866-1945), a native California attorney whose father, Grove Johnson, had been one of the early advocates for Japanese exclusion during the late 1800s and early 1900s. In 1910, because of his reputation for honesty and reform, Hiram Johnson obtained the leadership of the Progressive movement in California and was elected governor. Although nominally a Republican, he bolted the Republican Party in 1912 and became Theodore Roosevelt's vice-presidential running mate in the Progressive or "Bull Moose" party. In 1914 he was reelected governor and in 1916 he became a successful candidate for the United States Senate.[1]

Hiram Johnson became the governor of California in 1911 at a time when legislative expression in the state was influenced by the Republican president, William Howard Taft. In fact, because of the Panama Exposition, which was to be held in San Francisco in 1915, Taft put pressure on the new governor-elect to guarantee that he would not push for a state exclusion act against the Japanese. Since the Japanese government was to be one of the major participants in the Exposition, Taft realized that such an untoward act would anger and humiliate that nation.[2]

President Taft went even further. To insure the maintenance of cordial relations between the United States and Japan, he had Secretary of State Philander Knox maintain correspondence with Johnson during the early months of Johnson's first term, reminding him that it was essential to refrain from allowing any legislation—be it anti-land or exclusion legislation—to be enacted against the Japanese, especially since Japan and the United States were in the process, not only of discussing Japan's participation at the Panama Exposition, but also were negotiating a treaty of commerce and navigation. Johnson repeatedly wrote Knox that he was doing his best to keep any anti-Japanese legislation in check, although doing so was increasingly difficult because of the growing antagonistic reaction of white Californians against Japanese increased land holdings.[3]

At this time, it should be noted that the Progressive era, in which Hiram Johnson served his first term as governor, was an era of white middle-class political leadership. The party was partially dedicated to the restoration of economic competition, yet determined to put limits on this compeition so as to avoid a revival of unencumbered business trusts and domination. In California, however, the limits on competition were extended against certain racial and color groups. Progressives in California believed that economic self-preservation was closely united with racial preservation. It was believed that, if the Japanese were allowed to make economic inroads, it would be only a matter of time before they would make racial inroads. Inter-marriage and propagation of their race would impair the Anglo-Saxon racial purity so important to the Progressives' concept of economic leadership.[4] Ironically, Johnson in his first campaign for the governorship made few references to the race issue; instead he let his Democratic opponent, Theodore Bell, monopolize the question.[5]

One of the most important issues during the 1910 gubernatorial campaign in California was the Japanese refusal to allow aliens to hold land in Japan. The fact that Japan in 1910 did decree that aliens could hold land in Japan if Japanese nationals were reciprocally allowed to hold land in other countries did not silence the vociferous antagonism of white Californians to Japanese land ownership in California.[6] And that year Japan protested vigorously the end of Article II in the Treaty of 1894, which said that either country—Japan or the United States—might exclude the laborers of the other country.[7]

With the ratification of the Treaty of Commerce and Navigation of 1911 between the United States and Japan, white Californians became more dissatisfied, possibly because the treaty was just and equal. Article I, possibly the most important article, read as follows:

> The citizens or subjects of each of the High Contracting parties shall have liberty to enter, hovel and reside in the territories of the other, to carry on trade, wholesale and retail, to own or lease and occupy houses, manufactories, warehouses, and ships to employ agents of their choice, to lease land for residential and commercial purposes, and generally to do anything incident to or necessary for trade upon the same terms as native citizens or subjects, submitting themselves to the laws and regulations there estabished.[8]

The citizens or subjects of both nations were to receive constant protection and security for their persons and properties in each other's territories and to have the same privileges as native citizens. These citizens and subjects would also be exempt from compulsory military service in each other's armed forces.

Whereas the treaty of 1894 had provided the right of exclusion or restriction, in itself a partial safeguard, this treaty had no provision for exclusion of immigration restriction of laborers. Despite Japan's assurance that it would continue to honor the existing provisions of the Gentlemen's Agreement about immigration, many Californians viewed the new treaty as a bad omen.

White Californians became especially upset over the provision of reciprocal residency rights, trading rights, and manufacturing rights, but what was most unacceptable to white Californians was the right of the Japanese to lease and own land in California—or anywhere in the United States. White Californians believed the Japanese were buying or leasing the best agricultural lands in California as a means of obtaining economic power. The ability to check or limit the leasing of land to the Japanese was a prerogative that white Californians thought should not be taken away by federal fiat or treaty.[9]

Ironically, while the treaty of 1911 was in the final drafting stages in late 1910, the California legislature was pressing for the enactment of alien land laws—with the Japanese especially in mind.[10] Approximately twenty-seven anti-Japanese measures were introduced in the first legislative assembly during Johnson's term as governor.[11] Although Johnson in his letters had promised Secretary Knox that he would do all he could to prevent passage of any alien land bills, it was not until pressure was put on the governor by President Taft that he initiated steps to have this anti-Japanese legislation tabled. For the remainder of 1911, there was little effort by the California legislature or newspapers to keep the question of Japanese immigration a major issue .

Immigration, however, was a big issue to Californians in the presidential campaign of 1912. Both the Republicans and the Democrats had anti-immigration planks in the presidential platforms. Woodrow Wilson, the Democratic candidate running against Republican candidate William Howard Taft and Progressive candidate Theodore Roosevelt, was not then a great champion of liberty and individual rights. He telegraphed to James Phelan from Princeton, New Jersey, on May 2, 1912: "Oriental coolieism will give us another race problem to solve, and surely we have already had our lesson regarding race." The following day he wired Phelan again:

> In the matter of Chinese and Japanese coolie immigration I stand for the national policy of exclusion (or restricted immigration). The whole question is one of assimilation of diverse races. We cannot make a homogenious population out of people who do not blend with the Caucasian race. Their lower standard of living as laborers will crowd out the white agriculturalist and is, in other fields, a most serious industrial menace.[12]

White Californians no doubt liked the substance of the telegrams, for Wilson lost California to Hiram Johnson and the Progressives by only 174 votes out of 700,000 votes canvassed. This was the best showing in California by the Democrats since Grover Cleveland had won the state in 1882.

The year 1913 saw the beginning of the two-term Wilson administration and marked the beginning of the California-federal government conflict over an alien land law.

The dominant rationale for an alien land law in California was that the Japanese were allegedly buying all the choice farm and orchard land. However, in 1913, according to the California State Board of Agriculture, the Japanese landholdings were 12,726 acres out of 27 million improved acres, divided into 331 farms with an assessed value of $478,990.[13] The Japanese in actuality owned only one acre out of every eight thousand acres in the state of California. By 1913 there were approximately thirty thousand Japanese—out of an estimated fifty thousand Japanese in California—engaged in farming on all levels.[14] This figure included all farm workers from field laborers to farm foremen and owners.

The initial demand for a land law appears to have come from labor organizations and from white farm groups in agriculutural areas where the Japanese were most heavily concentrated.[15] However, at the same time, there were groups that were anxious to defeat any anti-alien legislation. These were white farmers who owned large land tracts and employed the Japanese for their agricultural abilities, merchants who needed efficient labor, and large American firms who dealt with the Japanese at home and abroad.[16] The rest of the country tended to remain relatively aloof from the controversy.

When the California legislature was convened in the winter of 1913, about forty anti-Japanese measures were introduced, many of them concerning the rights of aliens to own land.[17] The first alien land bill to receive serious consideration by the California assembly in 1913 placed severe restrictions on the ownership of land by all aliens.[18] The only discriminatory feature of this measure was directed against corporations controlled by aliens who were ineligible to become citizens of the United States. On April 15, 1913, this bill passed the assembly, 60 to 15.

Hiram Johnson had some idea that the newly installed Wilson administration would ask him to put into abeyance any anti-Japanese legislation, as had the Taft administration.[19] Johnson could not fail to realize that the Wilson administration was watching with alarm what took place in the Sacramento legislative chambers in 1913.[20] But unlike his predecessors, Roosevelt and Taft, Wilson was a Democrat president and had little influence in the California legislature. As early as March 1913, he took a laissez-faire attitude toward the impending alien land legislation.[21] He gave the impression that there was little the federal government could do and that the courts were the only instruments which could, and should, attempt to change the California alien land legislation.

In early April 1913, the California senate discussed the passage of a measure which would have applied the alien land law to all aliens, not only to those ineligible for citizenship. However, protests from the representatives of foreign investors and nations were so bitter that the California senate, after taking a poll of its members, rescinded its efforts.[22] Part of the reason for this change was the realization that California would suffer commercially if the legislature made an alien land law all-inclusive.

The Japanese government during late 1912 and early 1913 watched what was taking place in California with great concern. President Wilson told Japanese Ambassador Chinda that there was nothing he or the federal government could do regarding California's adoption of an alien land law.[23]

The initial alien land law presented in the California assembly called for restriction on the ownership of land by all aliens—including foreign corporations.[24] However, this measure was aimed at corporations owned by aliens ineligible for citizenship. The only aliens not eligible for citizenship were Asians, including Japanese.

Secretary of State William Jennings Bryan, on behalf of President Wilson, sent a telegram to Governor Johnson on April 10, 1913, inquiring about the efforts of the California legislature to enact an alien land law.[25] Johnson replied that he expected passage of what was then the Birdsall Anti-Alien Land Bill in the next few days and that, if any part of the bill semed obnoxious to the State Department, the California legislature would be advised at once.[26] Immediately foreign corporations let their displeasure toward the bill be known, and Johnson had no choice but to press for rescinding the bill.

Governor Johnson, however, was buying time. While keeping Bryan posted by telegram on what was going on at the legislative sessions, Johnson himself was busy behind the scenes helping to formulate the Webb-Heney Act, which stated that land ownership should be restricted to those eligible for citizenship. The basic tenant of this act was that the Japanese—by allusion—could not own land for a period of three years but could only lease the land for a period of three consecutive years; they could own land they had purchased before the passage of the Webb-Heney Act only until their death. The land then had to be sold back to the state, to someone eligible for citizenship, or to a citizen.[27] The first attempt to deprive the Japanese in California of a substantial right, this law was circumvented until 1920 by Japanese parents giving land to their American-born children who were citizens by birth and retaining trusteeship or guardianship.

On April 18, 1913, a crowd of approximately 20,000 Japanese in Tokyo cheered wildly as a member of the Diet demanded the Japanese fleet to be sent to California to protect Japanese nationals and Japan's honor.[28] The reaction in America was two-fold: first, Wilson and Bryan were now determined to settle the alien land law affair as quickly as possible to placate the ire of the Japanese government; second, Governor Johnson and the California legislature became just as determined to pass the Webb-Heney bill into law as quickly as possible, partly out of anger and partly out of fear thtt national reaction might force shelving of the bill.[29]

On April 18, 1913—the same day as the Japanese demonstration in Tokoyo against the alien land law—Bryan acknowledged the California legislature's alien land bill by sending Johnson a telegram to the effect that President Wilson recognized the right of the people to legislate alien land laws, but he thought that the term "ineligible to citizenship" was harsh. The wording of the Webb-Heney bill was preferable: "limiting land ownership to citizens, and those who had declared their intentions to become citizens."[30] Johnson, to mollify Bryan, had the wording that Wilson wanted inserted in the bill.

President Wilson attempted to persuade Johnson and the legislature to reconsider their action because passage of this alien land law would run counter to the treaty obligation of the United States with Japan, stating that exclusion should be based on reciprocity, not on unilateral action.[31] Johnson blithely assured him that the California legislature would do nothing to embarrass the federal government and that any alien land act would be in concert with existing laws and statutes. It is difficult to determine what existing laws and statutes Johnson thought applicable to the passage of the alien land law bill.[32] The only law which might have been remotely related was the treaty of 1894, which did allow for immigration restriction or exclusion. However, that act had been superseded by the treaty of 1911, which had no provision for exclusion or restriction of immigration.

Wilson was not satisfied with Johnson's reply, especially when he received a letter from David Starr Jordan, president of Stanford University, which strongly intimated that the California legislature, under the leadership of Johnson, intended to make political capital of Wilson's indecisiveness in challenging Johnson about alien land legislation. Jordan told Wilson that the Japanese were living up to the Gentlemen's Agreement of 1907, that Japanese land ownership in California was no menace to white Californians, and that the Japanese were as "assimilable" as any southern European immigrants.[33] Thereupon Wilson requested from Johnson and speedily received an invitation for Bryan to come to Sacramento for consultation.[34] But by the time Bryan detrained in Sacramento, the California legislature probably had made up its mind to push through its anti-alien law legislation. In fact, Californa Democrats favored an alien land law, an attitude which certainly impeded Bryan's efforts to reduce the probability of the law's passage.

In a letter Herbert C. Jones, an advocate of anti-Japanese legislation, wrote to David Starr Jordan: "The white man and the Negro have come in conflict, and the Negro has submitted. The Japanese neither submit or die."[35] One notes a feeling of anger in Jones regarding the fact that the Japanese would not succumb to the white Californians' predudice. The white Californians were determined to make sure that, if the Japanese did not die, they would at least submit. However, the Japanese neither died nor submitted.

At this time, it might be noted that in a private letter to Johnson in March 1913, President Wilson asked that citizenship not be one of the prerequisites for land ownership.[36]

Few people at that time knew that while Bryan was en route to California, Johnson—along with Ulysses S. Webb, the state attorney general, and Francis J. Heney, a state legislator—drafted what was in essence a substitute bill. This bill, although it protected all rights under the 1911 treaty between Japan and the United States and replaced the phrase "aliens ineligible to citizenship" with the equally offensive phrases "all aliens eligible for citizenship" and "all aliens other than," did little to provide any just solution to Japanese land ownership.[37]

Bryan, although noted for his oratorical abilities, did little to dissuade the California legislators from their planned course of action.[38] His two days of secret hearings produced few significant results. He dined with several of the advocates of the bill, including Johnson, Phelan, and V.S. McClatchy, on an amiable basis; however, it is uncertain whether or not anything was accomplished—other than gastronomical satisfaction.[39]

Wilson did little to thwart the efforts of the California legislature. His indecisiveness regarding an open confrontation with Johnson, as well as the possible use of the federal courts and public opinion to force retraction of the alien land legislation, did little to force the issue to a head.

On May 3, 1913, while Secretary Bryan was still in Sacramento, both the California Senate and the Assembly passed the Webb-Heney Act—the Senate by a vote of 35 to 2, the Assembly by a vote of 72 to 3.[40]

Before leaving Sacramento for Washington that same day, Bryan expressed his dissatisfaction with the new legislation and attempted to have Johnson put the issue of the alien land law before the people.[41] Johnson demurred. Most likely the white California voters would have voted for the legislation in 1913 as they were to do in 1920. Johnson withheld signing it, giving the Wilson administration an opportunity to discuss the law and make comments about it to him.

With the realization that the alien land law bill would soon be law, Ambassador Chinda once again made strong protests to Wilson. Wilson, after consultation with his cabinet, had Bryan draft several notes to the Japanese government to the effect that the passage of the bill by the California legislature was based solely on economics and that the United States government was not engendering a policy of malice, either toward the Japanese government or toward the Japanese in California.[42]

In light of the fact that the federal government had heretofore passed legislation excluding Asian immigration in the Exclusion Act of 1882, one could not help questioning the veracity of the Bryan notes to the Japanese government. It was obvious—even in 1913—that an important issue behind the alien land law was race. The percentage of Japanese owning land at that time was not significant enough to warrant the passage of the act because of economic factors.

Hiram Johnson signed the bill on May 17, despite Bryan's request for a veto.[43] On August 10 the first alien land act in California became law.[44] The previous day Attorney-General Webb, in a speech before the Commonwealth Club of San Francisco, had said, "the fundamental basis of all legislation upon this subject (land ownership) has been, and is racial undesirability."[45] It certainly did not take this speech to make the Japanese government realize that race had been and would continue to be the basis of anti-Japanese legislation.

Wilson's role in the alien land law was ambiguous. Although he attempted to dissuade Hiram Johnson from allowing the passage of the alien land bill, he made little effort to force the hand of the California legislature. He certainly did not attempt to use the federal courts, especially the Supreme Court, to challenge the California law; nor did he take the issue to the people or Congress and thus force federal domination upon California.

Perhaps his Southern background had imparted a feeling of racial superiority and prejudice. Perhaps political ambitions influenced him. Perhaps he believed he could use the authority, as had his predecessors, to dissuade Hiram Johnson from pushing through any laws contrary to existing treaties. This did not happen.

It is not difficult to assess the role of Hiram Johnson regarding the alien land law of 1913. He was the stimulus that eventually influenced the California legislature to pass this legislation. An opportunist who did not move until he had carefully evaluated the dynamics of any situation, Johnson initially had remained silent regarding legislation against the Japanese, letting his Democratic gubernatorial opponent use such proposed legislation as part of the political platform. However, after the 1912 presidential election, in which the Progressive party of Roosevelt and Johnson defeated Wilson and the Democrats in California by a scant 177 votes, Johnson became more assertive, especially when he began to have presidential aspirations in 1913. Johnson also realized that in order to assure himself, not only of California Progressives, but also of independents, he had to present himself as one who could handle authority and power. The best way to do so, he thought, was to stand up to the Democratic president, Woodrow Wilson, who had supposedly won the election of 1912 only because of Republican factionalism.

Johnson was also shrewd enough to realize that, barring unforeseen circumstances, Wilson would stand for reelection in 1916 and would no doubt make a concentrated bid to win in California after having lost by such a narrow margin in 1912. The only way Wilson could foreseeably achieve this goal was by not doing anything that might turn Californians against him in the 1916 election. Both Johnson and Wilson would not forcefully oppose a Califoria law on alien land ownership.

Johnson was also fortunate in having a Progressive majority in both houses of the California legislature so that he was able to exert the influence he wanted, especially regarding the controversial alien land law. Although Johnson never did see the fruition of his desire to become president, he did achieve the lofty position of United States senator and served a long and relatively distinguished career in the Senate. Probably the greatest political and psychological victory that Johnson achieved was securing the passage of the alien land law—a law curtailing the rights of people whose welfare he had sworn to uphold.

NOTES

[1] Hiram W. Johnson Papers, Introductory page, Biographical Sketch, p. 1, Bancroft Library, University of California, Berkeley.

[2] Yamoto Ichihashi, *Japanese in the United States: A Critical Study of the Problems of the Japanese Immigrants and Their Children* (Stanford: Stanford University Press, 1932), p. 255.

[3] Letters, January 6-March 23, 1911, between Johnson and Knox, Johnson Papers.

[4] Dumas Malone and Basil Rauch, *The New Nation 1865-1917* (New York: Appleton-Century-Crofts, 1960), pp. 248-249.

[5] Roger Daniels, *The Politics of Prejudice* (Berkeley: University of California Press, 1962), p. 47.

[6] File on Japanese in California, James D. Phelan Papers, Bancroft Library, University of California, Berkeley.

[7] Raymond Leslie Buell, "The Development of Anti-Japanese Agitation in the United States," *Political Science Quarterly*, XXXVIII (1923), 59.

[8] File on Japanese in California, Phelan Papers.

[9] Daniels, *Politics of Prejudice*, p .51.

[10] James A.B. Scherer, *The Japanese Crises* (New York: Frederick Stokes Company, 1916), p. 99.

[11] Daniels, *Politics of Prejudice*, p. 50.

[12] Telegram from Woodrow Wilson, Princeton, N.J., May 2, 1912, to James D. Phelan, San Francisco, California, Phelan Papers.

[13] Koyoshi Kawakami, *Japan in World Politics* (New York: Macmillan Company, 1917), p. 75.

[14] Harry H.L. Kitano, *Japanese Americans: The Evolution of a Sub-Culture* (Englewood: Prentice-Hall Inc., 1969), p. 15.

[15] Thomas A. Bailey, "California, Japan and the Alien Land Legislation of 1913," *Pacific Historical Review,* II (1932), 37.

[16] Kitano, *Japanese Americans,* p. 26.

[17] Buell, "Anti-Japanese Agitation," p. 61.

[18] Bailey, "California, Japan and the Alien Land Legislation," 38.

[19] Letter from Hiram Johnson to Chester Rowell, Editor, Fresno *Republican,* March 17, 1913, Johnson Papers.

[20] Scherer, *The Japanese Crisis,* p. 103.

[21] Bailey, "California, Japan, and the Alien Land Legislation," p. 39.

[22] Buell, "Anti-Japanese Agitation," p. 62.

[23] Daniels, *Politics of Prejudice,* p. 58.

[24] Bailey, "California, Japan, and the Alien Land Legislation," p. 38.

[25] Telegram, W.J. Bryan to Hiram Johnson, April 10, 1913, Johnson Papers.

[26] Telegram, Johnson to Byran, April 11, 1913, Johnson Papers.

[27] Ichihashi, *Japanese in the United States,* p. 275.

[28] Daniels, *Politics of Prejudice,* p. 61.

[29] Buell, "Anti-Japanese Agitation," p. 63.

[30] Telegram, W.J. Bryan to Hiram Johnson, April 18, 1913, Johnson Papers.

[31] Telegram, Woodrow Wilson to Hiram Johnson, April 22, 1913, Johnson Papers.

[32] Telegram, Johnson to Wilson, April 22, 1913, Johnson Papers.

[33] Letter, David Starr Jordan to Woodrow Wilson, April 14, 1913, David Starr Jordan Papers, Hoover Library, Stanford University.

[34] Telegram Wilson to Johnson, April 23, 1913, Johnson Papers.

[35] Letter, Herbert C. Jones to David Starr Jordan, April 23, 1913, Jordan Papers.

[36] Henry W. Taft, *Japan and America: A Journey and A Political Survey* (New York: The Macmillan Company, 1932), p. 134.

[37] Daniels, *Politics of Prejudice,* p. 61.

[38] Albert M. Robbins, *Exclusionism as a Factor in the Relations of Japan and the United States* (Unpublished M.A. Thesis, University of Southern California, 1954), p. 27.

[39] Letter, David Starr Jordan to his wife, April 30, 1913, Jordan Papers .

[40] Robbins, *Exclusionism as a Factor in the Relations of Japan and the United States,* p. 28.

[41] Daniels, *Politics of Prejudice,* p. 63.

[42] Taft, *Japan and America,* p. 136.

[43] Telegram, Bryan to Johnson, May 11, 1913, Johnson Papers.

[44] Speech, August 9, 1913, Phelan Papers.

[45] Speech, August 9, 1913, Phelan Papers.

The Anti-Japanese Land Laws of California and Ten Other States*

Dudley O. McGovney†

THE LAW in nine states of the United States puts every alien in the world either completely or substantially on an equality with a citizen with respect to acquiring and holding real property within their borders, except aliens who are *racially* ineligible to naturalization under the laws of the United States. In these states both resident and nonresident aliens racially ineligible to naturalization, but no others, are denied the privilege of aquiring any legal interest in land for agricultural purposes. In some of these states, probably in all, they are also denied the privilege of owning, as distinguished from holding under lease, any land for any purpose whatsoever, even for residential purposes.

California began this discrimination between "ineligible aliens"[1] and all others in 1913.[2] The statute of that year was stiffened in 1920[3] and subsequent additions have made it even more drastic.[4] Eight states have followed her lead with variations on relatively minor points: Arizona in 1917;[5] Louisiana, 1921;[6] New Mexico,

*All rights to reprint any or all of this article are reserved by the author.

†A.B., 1901, Indiana University; M.A., 1904, Harvard University; LL.B., 1907, Columbia University. Professor of Law, University of California.

[1] In the remainder of this essay the expression "ineligible aliens" will be used to mean aliens who are ineligible to naturalization solely because of their race. While any alien is ineligible to naturalization, whatever his race, if he lacks any one of several other qualifications required for naturalization, the laws herein discussed have been interpreted as applying solely to those "ineligible aliens" whose ineligibility is due to their race.

[2] Cal. Stats. 1913, p. 206.

[3] Initiative Act of 1920, Cal. Stats. 1921, lxxxiii.

[4] Cal. Stats. 1923, p. 1020; *ibid.* 1927, p. 880; *ibid.* 1943, pp. 2917, 2999; *ibid.* 1945, p. 2164 (enjoining the Attorney General and district attorneys to enforce the law, and sharpening "escheat" proceedings); *ibid.* p. 2177 (declaring the statute of limitations inapplicable to "escheat" proceedings); *ibid.* p. 2552 (similar to the preceding); *ibid.* p. 2739 (appropriating $200,000 for investigation and prosecution of violation of the law). For the present law in full, see CAL. GEN. LAWS, Acts 260, 261.

[5] Ariz. Laws, 1917, p. 56; *ibid.* p. 25; ARIZ. CODE (1939) §§ 71.201-71.206.

[6] LA. CONST. (1921) art. XIX, § 21.

1922;[7] Idaho, 1923;[8] Montana, 1923;[9] Oregon, 1923;[10] Kansas, 1925[11] and Utah, 1943.[12]

Wyoming recently became the tenth state to enact laws aimed at racially ineligible aliens. By Act of February 10, 1943,[13] such aliens, except Chinese nationals,[14] were barred from acquiring any interest in real property "or having in whole or in part the beneficial use thereof." It seems, however, that insofar as this statute affects aliens residing in Wyoming, it is in violation of the state constitution, article I, section 29, which reads: "No distinction shall ever be made by law between resident aliens and citizens as to possession, taxation, enjoyment and descent of property." Thus the statute, if not held void as a whole, operates only against nonresidents. Since it seems that the rules of the common law are in force in Wyoming with respect to other nonresident aliens[15] an odd discrimination results between two classes of nonresident aliens. Nonresident aliens of races to which the privilege of naturalization is not extended are treated more severely by the statute than are other nonresident aliens by the common law.

The Arkansas legislature in 1943 enacted an anti-Japanese land law. It declares that "no Japanese or a descendant of a Japanese shall ever purchase or hold title to any lands in the State of Arkansas."[16] Nowhere does it use the word "alien" and on its face it applies to American citizens of Japanese ancestry as well as to alien Japanese. As applied to American citizens the statute manifestly violates the Fourteenth Amendment. As applied to *resident* Japanese aliens it violates the state constitution: "No distinction shall ever be made by law between resident aliens and citizens in regard to possession, enjoyment or descent of property."[17]

The statute is unique in that it expressly applies exclusively to Japanese. It makes no use of the concept "ineligible to naturaliza-

[7] By amending N. M. CONST. (1911) art. II, § 22.

[8] Idaho Laws 1923, p. 160; IDAHO CODE (1932) §§ 23.101-23.112.

[9] Mont. Laws 1923, p. 123; MONT. REV. CODE (1935) §§ 6802.1-6802.8.

[10] Ore. Laws 1923, p. 145; ORE. COMP. LAWS (1940) §§ 61.101-61.111.

[11] Kan. Laws 1925, p. 277; KAN. GEN. STAT. (Corrick, 1935) §§ 67.701-67.711.

[12] Utah Laws 1943, p. 127.

[13] Wyo. Laws 1943, p. 33.

[14] It was not until the Act of December 17, 1943, 57 STATS. (1943) 600, that Congress removed the racial bar to naturalization of Chinese aliens.

[15] See Bamforth v. Ihmsen (1922) 28 Wyo. 282, 308, 204 Pac. 345, 354.

[16] Ark. Acts 1943, p. 75.

[17] ARK. CONST. (1874) art. II, § 20.

tion" and consequently, if valid, it would apply to Japanese aliens even though Congress should make them eligible to naturalization. Accordingly, Arkansas is not counted as among the states that have "ineligible alien" land laws. Since those laws are in reality aimed at the Japanese, Arkansas raises to eleven the count of states that have anti-Japanese land laws. In 1925 the Arkansas legislature did enact an "ineligible alien" land law closely imitating the California law. The supreme court of the state held the statute void, apparently wholly void, as being in conflict with the provision of the constitution above quoted.[18] The Act of 1943 may also be held to be void as a whole. In any event it has no validity beyond its application to nonresident Japanese aliens.

The legislators of Wyoming and Arkansas will be greatly disappointed to discover that their statutes will not operate against resident Japanese aliens. While all of the "ineligible alien" land laws, except Wyoming's, operate against nonresident aliens, nonresidents were never mentioned in the propaganda advocating adoption of the laws. The avowed purpose of these laws has always been to discourage *residence* of "ineligible aliens" in the state. It seems that nonresident aliens were inadvertently embraced in the general term "ineligible aliens" used to define a class of residents who were to be discriminated against. From the standpoint of the constitutionality of these discriminatory laws, it is their operation in depriving a special class of residents of economic opportunities accorded to all other residents, whether aliens or citizens, that is important. The Fourteenth Amendment's command is that no state shall deny to any person *within its jurisdiction* the equal protection of the laws.

Before stating with more precision the scope of rights denied to "ineligible aliens" by these laws, let us look at their racial operation. Aliens of the brown or Malay race, except Filipinos[19] of the

---

[18] Applegate v. Lum Jung Luke (1927) 173 Ark. 93, 291 S.W. 978.

[19] The "ineligible alien" laws have never applied to Filipinos. Upon the cession of the Philippines to the United States all Spanish nationals residing there, except such of those born in European Spain as elected to retain Spanish nationality, became nationals of the United States. Thus they were not *aliens,* and the California law expressly applied to aliens only. Consequently it has been held that the California law did not apply to them. Alfafara v. Fross (1945) 26 Cal. (2d) 358, 159 P. (2d) 14. The *obiter dictum* of Justice Cardozo to the contrary was, therefore, an error. See Morrison v. California (1934) 291 U.S. 82, 95.

The privilege of naturalization, changing from the status of noncitizen national to the status of citizen, was granted to the white and negro natives of the Philippines, provided they came to reside in a state or "organized territory", by Act of June 29, 1906,

same race, and aliens of the yellow or Mongolian race, except Chinese of the same race, are denied rights which aliens of the white or Caucasian race, aliens of the black or Negro race, and aliens of the red or American Indian race are permitted to enjoy without limitation. Thus eligibility of aliens to possess these particular rights follows a very queer pattern, or rather, is patternless, like a crazy quilt. Note that brown and yellow patches may appear in the quilt if they are Filipino aliens or Chinese aliens.

There may also be some patches whose race or color is dubious. These are aliens of races indigenous to British India, called Hindus in the popular parlance of Americans. When naturalization was confined to white and Negro aliens, the Supreme Court held that Hindus are neither,[20] but surely they are not of the red, yellow, or brown races. Whatever their race, dark Hindu patches are included in the crazy quilt.

The patternless craziness does not end there. Even an alien whose blood is seven-sixteenths Japanese or Korean may acquire land in California if the other nine-sixteenths is wholly of the red, black, or white race, or Hindu, or Chinese, or Filipino, or a combination of any or all of these. So may any alien who is seven-sixteenths Malay if the rest of his blood is wholly of a qualifying kind or a combination of qualifying kinds. The fraction of seven-sixteenths is taken as an example. The actual rule is that if eligible blood preponderates, however slightly, the alien is eligible to acquire real property in California. Here we have the possibility of patches of intermediate color. On the other hand if Mongolian blood other than Chinese preponderates in the veins and arteries of an alien, or Malay blood other than Filipino predominates, that alien may not get into the quilt.

Yet I am talking law, and not indulging in a purely imaginative surrealistic painting.

To illustrate even more specifically the conception these states have of their yellow peril: if an alien is nine-sixteenths of Chinese blood and seven-sixteenths Japanese he may get into the quilt, but if

§ 30, 34 STAT. 606. Later the privilege was extended to those Filipinos regardless of race who enlisted in and served in the United States Navy, Marine Corps, or the Naval Auxiliary Services. Act of May 9, 1918, 40 STAT. 542, 547.

Now that the Philippines have become an independent foreign country, all Filipinos are aliens, except the few who became *citizens* of the United States under the statutes cited in the previous paragraph. But even so the "ineligible alien" laws do not now apply to them for with respect to all Philippine nationals the racial bar to their naturalization has now been abolished. Act of July 2, 1946; see *infra* note 21.

[20] United States v. Thind (1923) 261 U.S. 204.

the proportions are the reverse the line between safety and peril to the welfare of these states is regarded as having been crossed. This is not sarcastic humor. It is legal talk. It bears on the rationality of the discrimination made by these laws and therefore upon their constitutionality.

All of these diversities result from the fact that the laws of these states define the proscribed class as aliens who are ineligible to naturalization under the laws of the United States, and thereby adopt the vagaries of the naturalization law, set out in the footnote.[21]

HOW MANY "INELIGIBLE ALIENS" RESIDE IN THE UNITED STATES AND THE TEN STATES?

Prior to 1940, Census reports did not clearly divide our nonwhite population by citizenship and alienage. Formerly I estimated from figures in the Census of 1920 that there were 134,135 aliens residing in the continental United States that were racially ineligible to naturalization,[22] but that figure included 43,107 alien Chinese, 6,299 alien American Indians (foreign born) and some Hindus, classes which now are racially eligible to naturalization.

The number of aliens racially ineligible to naturalization under the present law who resided in the continental United States in 1940, and the number of American born citizens of the same races,[23] were:

	Aliens	American Citizens
Japanese	47,305	79,642
Korean	749	962
Polynesian	9	648
Other Asian	95	36
Total	48,158	81,288

[21] "The right to become a naturalized citizen . . . shall extend only to—

(1) white persons, persons of African nativity or descent, and persons who are descendants of races indigenous to the continents of North or South America or adjacent islands and Filipino persons or persons of Filipino descent;

(2) persons who possess, either singly or in combination, a preponderance of blood of one or more of the classes specified in clause (1);

(3) Chinese persons and persons of Chinese descent, and persons of races indigenous to India; and

(4) persons who possess, either singly or in combination, a preponderance of blood of one or more of the classes specified in clause (3) or, either singly or in combination, as much as one-half blood of those classes and some additional blood of one of the classes specified in clause (1)." 8 U. S. C. (1940) § 703, as last amended by PUB. L. No. 483, 79th Cong. 2d Sess. (July 2, 1946).

[22] McGovney, *Race Discrimination in Naturalization* (1923) 8 IOWA L. BULL. 211, 215.

[23] 16th Census of the United States: 1940, Characteristics of the Nonwhite Population, p. 2.

With the 47,305 Japanese aliens may be compared the 37,242 Chinese aliens and approximately 45,000 Filipinos in the United States in 1940, the two latter groups being not now racially ineligible to naturalization.

Since in 1940 there were 4,741,971 aliens residing in the continental United States,[24] the "ineligible aliens" were a trifle over one per cent of all our alien residents. Since entry into the United States by "ineligible aliens" for the purpose of permanent residence has been entirely cut off by our immigration law since 1924,[25] it is evident that death, deportation, and voluntary withdrawal have materially reduced the 1940 total of 48,158. I mention this number in the whole of the continental United States because it is the maximum number that can legally migrate into the ten states that have "ineligible alien" land laws, not that it is likely that all should do so.

It is more pertinent to inquire how many "ineligible aliens" reside in the ten states. How many of their residents are these states harassing? Let us look at California, the progenitor of this type of law, the one state that is now making extraordinary exertions to enforce it. California has a greater number of "ineligible alien" residents than any other state, although the number is small in comparison to her total population or to the total number of aliens residing in the state.

The Census of 1940 does not show how many Korean, Polynesian, Malay, or "other Asian" aliens resided in California. Inasmuch as there were only 853 of them, all told, in the continental United States, the number of them in California is too small to impeach the statement that her alien land law has no significance except as it operates against Japanese. Thus the law now operates solely against the race hostility toward which motivated its enactment. It is true that in the period of its origination, 1913-1920, there were other classes of aliens residing in California who, by the naturalization law as it then stood, were ineligible to naturalization. Of these the largest number were Chinese. By that time, however, the earlier hostility toward Chinese had almost wholly disappeared. In all the flood of hostile legislation against the Chinese in California which began in 1855 and ended in 1891 (see Appendix A) the legislature made no attempt to curtail the rights of Chinese aliens to hold realty, and in that respect they had equal rights with citizens. Although the

---

[24] REP. ATT'Y GEN. 1941, at 259.

[25] 43 STAT. (1924) 153, 162, 8 U. S. C. (1940) § 213(c).

propaganda in support of the anti-alien land law was aimed at "Oriental occupancy" of farm lands, it was conceded that Chinese holdings were slight.[26] The agitators never mentioned the six thousand foreign born and "ineligible alien" American Indians in California. While there was some reference to Hindus, the weight of decision in the lower federal courts[27] at that time was that Hindus were not racially ineligible to naturalization.[28] Furthermore the occupancy of farm lands by Hindus was insignificant.[29]

The Chinese aliens, the American Indian aliens, and the few resident Malay and Polynesian aliens were as a matter of indifference embraced within the law's generic term, "ineligible aliens". The law would have been manifestly unconstitutional if it had expressly applied exclusively to Japanese.

It is an indubitable historical fact that the "ineligible alien" land law would not have been enacted had it not been for the Japanese already in California, and the expectation of further immigration. In its initial decision in 1922 under this law, the supreme court of California alluded to "The object sought to be attained by these statutory provisions, that is, to discourage the coming of Japanese into this state . . . ."[30] "To discourage the coming" was an understatement, for the object was also to discourage the stay of those

---

[26] The statistics compiled by the State Board of Control in 1920 with regard to California city lots and farm lands occupied by Orientals, both American citizens and aliens, showed:

	City Lots	Farm Lands in Acres
Owned by Japanese or bought on contract	1,036	74,769
Owned by Chinese	546	12,076
Owned by Hindus	11	2,099
Totals	1,593	88,944
Under lease or crop contract:		
Japanese		383,287
Chinese		65,181
Hindus		86,340
Totals		534,808
Total acreages [of farm lands] occupied by Orientals		623,752

[The total acreage of farm lands in the state was reported as 27,931,444.] Rep. Cal. State Bd. Control, California and the Oriental (1920) at 47.

[27] McGovney, *op. cit. supra* note 22, at 145, n. 41.

[28] The decision of the Supreme Court holding Hindus racially ineligible to naturalization came in 1923. United States v. Thind, *supra* note 20.

[29] See *supra* note 26.

[30] Estate of Yano (1922) 188 Cal. 645, 658, 206 Pac. 995, 1001.

who had already come. The court readily took judicial notice of the current agitation and propaganda against the Japanese.[31]

The "Argument in Favor of Proposed Alien Land Law" in the pamphlet officially mailed to every voter before the election at which the Initiative Act of 1920 was to be voted on, said: "Its primary purpose is to prohibit Orientals who cannot become American citizens from controlling our rich agricultural lands . . . . Orientals, and more particularly Japanese, [have] commenced to secure control of agricultural lands in California . . . ." Further on is a reference to "Orientals, largely Japanese". These are the only references to Orientals in general, while repeatedly the argument is directed against the Japanese alone, without reference to other Orientals. Why should California "give to Japanese" rights which Japan denies to Americans in Japan, asks the Argument. There are statements about "long leases of these lands by Japanese"; "land is occupied by Japanese"; "control of the products of the soil by a unified interest such as the Japanese"; and "Japanese legitimately here may remain indefinitely . . . ."

This extrinsic evidence of the meaning of the law as understood by its enactors, in this case the state's electorate, is more persuasive than even committee reports on bills in legislatures, of which the courts take judicial notice to ascertain the intention of lawmakers.

The Census of 1940 reports that there were 33,569 Japanese aliens residing in California. This compares with 16,676 alien Chinese residents to whom the law no longer applies, and with 31,408 Filipinos to whom the law never applied,[32] to mention two groups which at times have also been objects of race prejudice in California.

The number of Japanese aliens in California is now materially less than in 1940. Death, deportation, voluntary return to Japan, and departures to other parts of the United States have greatly reduced the number. A careful estimate by highly informed students of the subject is that there are now only 25,000 alien Japanese in California.[33]

---

31 See McWilliams, Prejudice (1944) 14 *et seq.*

32 See *supra* note 19.

33 The following memorandum was made at my request by Professor Dorothy S. Thomas, Rural Sociologist on the Giannini Foundation of the Universitv of California, and Richard S. Nishimoto, Research Assistant, authors of The Spoilage, Japanese American Evacuation and Resettlement, University of California Press, 1946:

"All of the approximately 33,000 Japanese aliens resident in California at the outbreak of the war were ordered to evacuate the State. About 4,000 were interned by the Department of Justice (our estimate), about 700 were permitted to remain in the cus-

It is a notable fact that California has more aliens of all nationalities than any other state in the Union except New York.[34] In 1940 California's aliens numbered 526,937.[35] Assuming that only half a million of them are still aliens and reside in California today, only one in twenty is Japanese. It is this small fraction of her alien residents against which she discriminates.

It is pretended that California's welfare would be jeopardized if the 25,000 Japanese alien residents could legally acquire interests in agricultural land. The number of potential farm-owning family units is substantially less than the total figure because of marriages and other family relations in the group. Besides, the Census of 1940 shows that fifty-eight per cent of the alien Japanese in California resided in urban centers of 2,500 population and upward.[36] Furthermore, the occupational statistics showed large numbers of alien Japanese engaged in nonfarming occupations.[37] While it is true that the denial

---

tody of hospitals and institutions (our estimate), 1,315 voluntarily left the State (U. S. Army. Western Defense Command and Fourth Army. *Final Report. Japanese Evacuation from the West Coast, 1942*. Washington, Government Printing Office, 1943, p. 112.) The bulk of them were confined in relocation projects administered by the War Relocation Authority.

"How many of these 33,000 have since returned to California? The question cannot be answered directly and simply. The cohort of 33,000 had, according to our estimates, been reduced by death to 31,000; and by voluntary deportation to Japan to, probably, 29,000.

"When WRA camps closed during 1946, 20,788 Japanese aliens moved directly from camps to California communities, and 24 had earlier returned by individual Army permit. (U. S. Department of Interior, War Relocation Authority. *The Evacuated People*, p. 42.) There are numbers of Japanese aliens, formerly residents of California, who have resettled in other parts of the country and may or may not return to this area. There are, similarly, aliens, formerly residents of Washington and Oregon, some of whom are probably included in the 20,788, who came in the 1946 movement to California (since the statistics do *not* show whether or not the 20,788 were *formerly* residents of the State). If, on the most improbable assumption that *every* Japanese alien who left relocation projects for any destination whatsoever had decided, during the past year, to come to California, the total number could not exceed 38,000. (*The Evacuated People*, p. 42, shows the total number of aliens resettling anywhere in the U. S. from WRA camps as 38,351.) Our own considered judgment, which cannot yet be verified by statistics, is that there are not more than 25,000 alien Japanese now resident in the State."

[34] In 1940, 25.7 per cent of all aliens in the continental United States resided in New York, while 11.1 per cent resided in California. Pennsylvania had the next largest share, 7.6 per cent, and thirteen states had each only one-tenth of one per cent.

[35] REP. ATT'Y GEN. 1941, at 259.

[36] 16th Census of the United States: 1940, Characteristics of the Nonwhite Population, Table 33.

[37] The following table shows the occupations of the 23,208 alien Japanese, fourteen years of age and older, employed in California in 1940. For comparison it also shows

of land ownership has artificially affected their preferences, it is apparent that if the restriction were removed far less than 20,000 alien Japanese family units would become land owners.[38] There are further reasons why the number of alien Japanese farm owners would be small. The alien Japanese in the United States are aged people,[39] all having immigrated before 1924. In fact it is said by competent authority that almost half of them arrived before 1910.[40] In 1940 all but 2,760 of the alien Japanese in California were thirty-five years of age or older, which means that the minimum age of all but a few is now forty-two years. But many of them are older. In 1940, 20,869 were forty-five years of age or older; the minimum age of the survivors is now fifty-two. Seventeen per cent of them had passed their sixtieth birthday by 1942.[41] Many of these aged and aging Japanese

---

the occupation of the next largest nonwhite alien group, 22,961 Filipinos, fourteen years of age and over, a group to which the anti-alien land law does not apply.

CHARACTERISTICS OF NONWHITE POPULATION, 1940

	Japanese	Filipinos
Professional workers	589	109
Semi-professional workers	102	38
Farmers and farm managers	4,134	348
Proprietors, managers, and officials other than farm	3,169	251
Clerical, sales and kindred workers	1,454	241
Craftsmen, foremen and kindred workers	386	153
Operatives and kindred workers	1,340	732
Domestic service workers	1,407	1,187
Service workers, except domestic	1,619	5,420
Farm laborers (wage workers) and farm foremen	4,916	13,767
Farm laborers (unpaid family workers)	1,462	23
Laborers, except farm	2,493	626
Occupation not reported	137	66
	23,208	22,961

These statistics are taken from Tables 38 and 44 of the 16th Census of the United States: 1940, Characteristics of the Nonwhite Population.

38 The propensity of the alien Japanese to become farmers may be gauged somewhat by what the unrestricted citizen Japanese do. Out of 17,207 American citizen Japanese fourteen years of age, and older, employed in California in 1940, in other than emergency work, there were 1,663 farmers and farm managers, 2,791 farm wage workers and foremen, and 2,497 unpaid family farm workers, totaling 6,951, or 40.3 per cent. 16th Census of the United States: 1940, Characteristics of the Nonwhite Population, Table 38. The small number of farm owners among them may be partly due to the fact that their average age is much lower than that of the alien Japanese, resulting in lack of accumulated capital with which to buy land.

39 See 16th Census of the United States: 1940, Characteristics of the Nonwhite Population, Table 33.

40 Thomas and Nishimoto, The Spoilage (1946) 2.

41 *Ibid.* at 4.

aliens suffered heavy pecuniary losses incident to their evacuation during the war. Suddenly ordered to abandon their properties and their homes, many felt compelled to sell at sacrificial prices. Others lost through unfaithful custodianship of their properties during their absence. Confined to so-called relocation centers, they were cut off for nearly three years from any gainful employment. The result is that many of the well-to-do among them returned to California broken in fortune, with very few years of life left for financial recuperation.

Thus we have arrived at the size and character of what many Californians still regard as their yellow peril. It is this shrunken, and rapidly shrinking, small number of aged Japanese aliens, their fortunes, of those who had them, much depleted, to whom the California law denies the acquisition of any interest in agricultural land, and, probably, the ownership of any land for any purpose. Is it entirely irrelevant to add that many of these aged alien Japanese are the parents of American citizens who served in combat forces of the United States throughout the war and with marked distinction? Toward the end of the war a few alien Japanese were accepted as volunteers in the fighting forces, and all through the war many of them were employed by the War Department as language instructors, map readers, translators and in other capacities.

What is the size of the menace which threatens the welfare of the nine other states that have imitated California? The total number of Japanese aliens residing in all of those states in 1940 was 3,667. These states may, however, be retaining their "ineligible alien" land laws out of fear that some of the Japanese aliens now residing in other states may move into them. None can enter from abroad. The number residing at the present time in all the other states, including California, probably does not exceed 40,000. What probability is there that any considerable number of these aged persons will remove from the communities in which they have social and economic ties and settle in any single one of these nine states?

Judged by the number of Japanese aliens residing in any one of them, it takes a very prejudiced imagination to see a threat to a state's welfare. In no one of them can there be more than a handful of "ineligible aliens", other than Japanese, because there are now less than 853 residing in the continental United States. Arkansas, as we have seen, has a land law which discriminates exclusively against Japanese. In 1940 there were only two Japanese aliens among her total of 3,210 alien residents.

The following table shows the size of the Japanese menace in each of the nine states:

	Total Population	Total Resident Aliens	Resident Japanese Aliens
Arizona . . .	499,261	30,699	220
Louisiana . . .	2,363,880	16,601	13
New Mexico . .	531,818	12,123	72
Idaho	524,873	5,936	426
Montana . . .	559,456	13,639	227
Oregon	1,089,684	33,859	1,617
Kansas . . .	1,801,028	16,180	10
Utah	550,310	10,100	829
Wyoming . . .	250,742	5,745	253

The constitutional issue is whether California can pick out of her half-million alien residents, 25,000 Japanese aliens, together with an almost imperceptible number of Korean, Malay, and Polynesian aliens, and deny rights to them that she concedes to all others. Can Kansas deny to her ten Japanese alien residents rights which she grants to sixteen thousand other alien residents? Does such discrimination bear any rational relation to any purpose within the competency of the state?

To show the extraordinary narrowness of the discrimination made by the "ineligible alien" land laws, I shall review the origin in Anglo-American law of discrimination against aliens with respect to landholdings. I shall inquire whether the old common-law discrimination ever had any rational basis, although it was against all aliens without regard to race or national origin. I shall then review the law now in force in each of our states to determine what is the prevailing thought of our time with respect to the rationality of discrimination against any aliens with respect to land holdings.

THE ENGLISH COMMON LAW WITH RESPECT TO LANDHOLDING BY ALIENS

Under the common law as evolved by the end of the thirteenth century an alien could acquire goods and chattels in England, keep them, dispose of them, even by will, and if he died without a will his personalty went to his next of kin, even though they were aliens. Thus as to goods and chattels an alien stood on an equal footing with a subject of the King. But it was a different matter as to real property situated in England. An alien could not acquire such realty by inheritance. In the quaint language of the common law he lacked "inheritable blood". Nor could he acquire it by mere operation of law, but he could acquire it by act *inter partes*, as by gift to him, by sale to him, by devise, by lease, but he held it at the sufferance of the King, who might forfeit it to himself without compensation by the procedure called "inquest of office". And this at a time when all the King's property was his privately and not held in a governmental capacity in trust for the nation. The defeasible estate in realty which an alien might acquire he could convey to another. But the latter, alien or subject, in turn held it as a defeasible estate subject to forfeiture. If not transferred by the alien, at his death it escheated automatically to the King, for an alien was held to have no heirs.

The subtlety of the system! As Blackstone said, if an alien bought land from a subject the vendor could keep the price, for the conveyance was good to pass the vendor's title.[42] The King would have had no benefit had the rule been that the conveyance was void. As it was the alien lost both money and land if the King enforced the forfeiture.

Historians of the law of England say in explanation of the origin of these rules that "in the course of the thirteenth century our kings acquired a habit of seizing the lands of Normans and other Frenchmen" because, as they said, the Normans were traitors and the Frenchmen enemies. To these historians it seems that the King's later claim of right to seize the lands of aliens generally is an exaggerated generalization of his claim to seize the lands of his French enemies. "Such an exaggerated generalization of a royal right will not seem strange to those who have studied the growth of the king's prerogatives."[43]

After these rules had been established for two centuries Coke attempted to supply the reasons for them, both for seizures during war and during peace. During war, if aliens held land in England, "1. The secrets of the realm might thereby be discovered. 2. The revenues of the realm (the sinews of war, and ornament of peace) should be taken by strangers born. 3. It would tend to destruction of the realm." That destruction would consist in this, that "Strangers might fortify themselves in the heart of the realm" like "the Trojan horse in Vergil's Second Book of his Aeneid."[44]

In time of peace the condition of England would be equally desperate, for, said Coke, so much of the freehold of England would be held by aliens that there would not be enough English freeholders to man the juries and hence "there should follow a failure of justice."[45]

42 1 Bl. Comm. *372.

43 Pollock and Maitland, History of English Law (2d ed. 1898) 463.

44 Calvin's Case (1609) 77 Eng. Rep. 377.

45 *Ibid.*

It is to be noted that only the last reason is tied up with landholding, and that it is based on an absurd exaggeration. The other reasons all turn on the danger to the realm of having enemy aliens residing in England during war. They afford no adequate explanation why landholding alone should be denied to aliens, who were freely admitted to reside permanently in England, acquire and hold all other kinds of property, and engage in trade and all other pursuits on an equal footing with English subjects.

Wheaton, commenting upon similar early laws of other European countries, surmised that they originated during the regime of feudal tenures, with their incident of military service, when the notion was that the latter could be exacted only of subjects owing allegiance.[46] Blackstone offered the same explanation: "The design of introducing our feuds, the defense of the kingdom, would have been defeated" if lands had been suffered to be held by persons who owed no allegiance to the King.[47]

Writing in 1853, Chief Justice Redfield of Vermont said, "The escheat of estates to the sovereign, in consequence of a conveyance to an alien, is a result of purely feudal character. It was so held, because an alien, owing a foreign allegiance, was regarded as incapable of performing feudal military services to the king, as lord paramount of all the land in the realm."[48]

France abolished all discrimination against aliens with respect to holding real and personal property in 1819 and the British Parliament did so in 1870.

In the meantime the common law's discrimination against aliens had been received in the British colonies in America. Since the colonies were independent of each other, tied together only by their common subjection to the central government of the empire, each had its separate body of law. But the anti-alien law of one colony did not apply to a British subject residing in another colony, or elsewhere; a British subject was not an alien in the law of any British colony. After the colonies became states, in theory independent of each other as well as of Great Britain, a provision was adopted in the Articles of Confederation to forbid any state to impose the disabilities of alienage upon the citizens of any other state.[49] Our present

---

[46] WHEATON, INTERNATIONAL LAW (4th Eng. ed.) 134.

[47] 2 BL. COMM. *250.

[48] State v. Boston, Concord & Montreal R. R. Co. (1853) 25 Vt. 433, 438.

[49] Art. IV.

Constitution, as adopted in 1788, contains a like clause, for the same purpose: "The Citizens of each State shall be entitled to all Privileges and Immunities of Citizens in the several States."[50]

Inasmuch as there was no other equalitarian clause in the Constitution prior to the equal protection clause of the Fourteenth Amendment, ratified in 1868, the states were free to enforce the common law's discrimination against aliens. The dates at which its partial or complete abolition first occurred in the several states I have not traced. It is sufficient for our purposes to examine the extent to which it is abolished or partially retained at the present time.

STATE LAWS

An examination of the constitutional and statutory law[51] of the forty-eight states discloses that in sixteen states[52] all aliens, whether residents of the United States or not, and whether friendly or enemy aliens, are given equal rights with citizens to acquire, hold, and dispose of real property. In three other states the law is the same except that there is a restriction as to the *amount* of land an alien may hold: in Indiana,[53] not over three hundred and twenty acres; in Pennsylvania,[54] not over five thousand acres; and in South Carolina,[55] not over five hundred acres. As the permissible amounts are large there is slight distinction between these three states and the sixteen above

---

50 U. S. CONST., art. IV, § 2, cl. 1.

51 For digests of the laws of all states made by other writers, see 5 VERNIER, AMERICAN FAMILY LAWS (1938) §§ 289, 290, which follows a different scheme of analysis, and necessarily omits subsequent legislation; Miller, *Alien Land Laws* (1939) 8 GEO. WASH. L. REV. 1, apparently based on VERNIER, *loc. cit. supra.*

52 ALA. CONST. art. I, § 34; ALA. CODE (1940) tit. 47, § 1; COLO. CONST. art. II, § 27; COLO. STAT. (1935) c. 7, § 6; DEL. REV. CODE (1935) §§ 3655-3657; FLA. CONST., Declaration of Rights, § 18; FLA. STAT. (1941) § 731.28; ME. REV. STAT. (1944) c. 154, § 2; MASS. LAWS (1932) c. 184, § 1; MICH. CONST. art. XVI, § 9; MICH. COMP. LAWS (1929) § 13493; N. Y. REAL PROPERTY LAW (1945) § 10(2); N. C. GEN. STAT. (1943) § 64-1; N. D. REV. CODE 47-0111, 56-0116; OHIO CODE (Throckmorton, 1940) § 10503-13; R. I. GEN. LAWS (1938) c. 432; S. D. CONST. art. VI, § 14; S. D. CODE (1939) §§ 51.0205, 56.0120; TENN. CODE (Williams, 1934) §§ 7187-7190; VT. CONST. (1793) c. II, § 62; W. VA. CONST. art. II, § 5; W. VA. CODE (1943) § 3541. The Vermont constitution of 1793 gave resident aliens equal rights with citizens in landholding, and while no other constitutional or statutory provision abolished the common-law rules with respect to nonresident aliens, the supreme court of the state held in 1853 that no procedure for the forfeiture of the estates of aliens, resident or nonresident, was known to the law of the state. State v. Boston, Conrad & Montreal R. R. Co., *supra* note 48. The present attorney general of Vermont assures me that that is still true.

53 IND. STAT. (Burns, 1943) §§ 56-504, 56-505.

54 PA. STAT. (Purdon, 1936) tit. 68, §§ 22-32.

55 S. C. CONST. art. III, § 35; S. C. CODE (1942) §§ 8687, 8907, 8908, 7790; S. C. Laws 1945, p. 51.

mentioned. Four other states[56] grant equality with citizens to all aliens except enemy aliens. This transient disability of an alien during a war between the United States and his country is a slight qualification of the general rule. Thus there are twenty-three states which with substantial accuracy may be said to have completely wiped out the common law's discrimination against aliens with respect to acquiring and holding real property. That these states have acted affirmatively to abolish it shows that in the judgment of their lawmakers no rational basis for its retention exists. It is significant that New York is in this group although one-fourth of all the aliens in the forty-eight states reside in New York.[57]

In a twenty-fourth state, Wisconsin, the law is substantially the same.[58] All aliens have equal rights with citizens to acquire and hold realty, except that the amount of land an alien not residing in the United States may acquire is limited to three hundred and twenty acres, unless acquired by devise, inheritance, or in the collection of debts. In Iowa, a twenty-fifth state, the law is almost exactly the same as in Wisconsin.[59]

Nine other states join the above twenty-five in putting all aliens, resident or nonresident, on an equality with citizens with respect to acquiring and holding realty, *except aliens ineligible to naturalization* under the laws of the United States. These, as we have seen, are California and her imitators, Arizona, Idaho, Kansas, Louisiana, Montana, New Mexico, Oregon, and Utah. That is to say, the very states that discriminate against particular races or nationalities of aliens concede to aliens generally, whether resident or nonresident, equality with citizens in acquiring and holding realty, with only slight exceptions in Arizona[60] and Montana[61] with respect to acqui-

---

[56] GA. CODE (1933) § 79-303; MD. CODE (Flack, 1939) art. 3, § 1; N. J. REV. STAT. (Supp., 1941-1944) 46: 3-18 (not all enemy aliens are excepted, since the denial does not extend to enemy aliens who have permanent residence in the United States and are licensed or permitted by the federal government to engage in business transactions and are not under arrest or interned); VA. CODE (1936) § 66.

[57] REP. ATT'Y GEN. 1941, at 259.

[58] WIS. STATS. (1943) §§ 234.22, 234.23.

[59] A curious and slight difference is that in Iowa if a nonresident alien acquires land by devise from any alien or any *naturalized* citizen, he must dispose of it within twenty years, or become a citizen within that time. IOWA CODE (1946) § 567.1.

[60] An alien, other than an "ineligible alien", who acquires realty by devise or descent may hold it only five years, unless he becomes a citizen, saving, however, greater rights if the law of his country gives greater rights to American citizens. ARIZ. CODE (1939) § 39-111.

[61] An alien, other than an "ineligible alien", may take property in Montana by will

sitions by will or intestacy. Arkansas increases this group to ten for she also has the general rule of equal rights of aliens and citizens in landholding with the sole exception of nonresident Japanese aliens, and this exception will fall if the state supreme court holds the statute of 1943 void as a whole.

Thus there are thirty-five states that now see no virtue whatever in the common law's discrimination against aliens, except that ten of them retain something like the common-law system with respect to a small minority of aliens. Their narrow racial discrimination is an exception to a general policy of putting aliens, both resident and nonresident, upon an equal footing with citizens.

Five other states have abolished the common law with respect to all resident aliens, while retaining it more or less intact with respect to nonresident aliens. That is, all resident aliens are put on an equal footing with citizens with respect to acquiring and holding realty. These states are Connecticut, Mississippi, New Hampshire, Oklahoma, and Wyoming.[62] It should be noted that Connecticut gives such equal rights not only to aliens residing in the state but also to aliens who reside anywhere in the United States, barring only those who reside in foreign countries.

One other state, Minnesota, also accords substantial landholding rights to aliens, resident and nonresident, although the amount that may be held is restricted. Any alien, resident or nonresident, may hold land acquired by devise or by inheritance without limitation as to amount, but only 90,000 square feet, or about two acres, if the mode of acquisition is other than devise or inheritance. More pertinent to this article is the privilege Minnesota gives resident aliens to own farm lands. An alien may acquire a farm for his own occupancy by any mode known to the law and hold one hundred and sixty acres.[63] Thus resident aliens are encouraged to engage in agriculture in Minnesota. Moreover, there is no restriction whatever on an alien who has declared his intention to become a citizen.

In summary so far, it appears that while many states give all aliens, resident or nonresident, equal rights with citizens in landhold-

---

or by intestacy only to the extent that his country permits residents of the United States to so take property left by decedents in that country. Mont. Laws 1939, p. 220.

62 CONN. GEN. STAT. (1930) § 5055; MISS. CODE (1942) § 842; N. H. REV. LAWS (1942) c. 259, § 19; OKLA. CONST. art. XXII, § 1; OKLA. STAT. (1941) tit. 60, §§ 121-127; WYO. CONST. art. I, § 29; see *supra* p. 8 for a discussion of the Wyoming statute and constitution.

63 MINN. STATS. (1941) § 500.22.

ing, there are forty-one states that do so with respect to *resident* aliens, with the following exceptions: (1) four of them[64] limit the amount of land an alien may hold but nevertheless permit large holdings; (2) four of them[65] make a slight exception of enemy aliens; (3) nine of them[66] deny such equality to none but that small minority that consists of aliens racially ineligible to naturalization; and (4) one[67] denies such equality solely to nonresident Japanese aliens.

There remain only seven states in which the law approximates the common-law system with respect to both resident and nonresident aliens, but in none is that system preserved intact, although in a few the departures are slight. The remaining states are Illinois, Kentucky, Missouri, Nebraska, Nevada, Texas, and Washington. In Kentucky, Texas, and Washington the restrictions apply to both resident and nonresident aliens although an exception is made in favor of resident aliens who have declared their intentions to become citizens. In Texas there is the further remarkable exception that the law does not apply to aliens who are natural-born citizens of countries that have a common land boundary with the United States. It seems that Canadian and Mexican born aliens as landholders in Texas do not threaten the welfare of the state, but that aliens born elsewhere do. The law of the state of Washington will be stated more fully in the text when we come to consider the decision of the Supreme Court of the United States holding it not unconstitutional. The similarities to and departures from the common law in the other six states in this group are set forth in Appendix B.

ALIENS' PROPERTY RIGHTS IN CALIFORNIA PRIOR TO 1913

Under her first constitution (1849) California gave to resident aliens of every race and nationality a *constitutional guaranty* that they should enjoy complete equality of property rights with citizens.

Article I (Declaration of Rights) contained: "Section 17. Foreigners who are, or may hereafter become, *bona fide* residents of this State, shall enjoy the same rights in respect to the possession, enjoyment, and inheritance of property, as native born citizens."[68]

This *constitutional guaranty* was cut down in the constitution of

64 Indiana, Pennsylvania, South Carolina (*supra* notes 53-55), and Minnesota (*supra* note 63).

65 *Supra* note 56.

66 *Supra* notes 2, 3, 5-12.

67 *Supra* notes 16, 17.

68 Cal. Stats. 1849-1850, p. 25.

1879 to protect only white and Negro resident aliens: "Section 17. Foreigners of the white race or of African descent, eligible to become citizens of the United States under the naturalization laws thereof, while *bona fide* residents of this State, shall have the same rights in respect to the acquisition, possession, enjoyment, transmission, and inheritance of property as native-born citizens."[69]

By amendment, adopted November 6, 1894, this *constitutional guaranty* was further cut down to cover only property "other than real estate".[70]

I have emphasized that these were constitutional guaranties and thus affirmative grants of minimum rights which the legislature was forbidden to deny. They did not operate negatively to preclude the legislature from granting equal rights to other aliens or broader property rights to all aliens. In fact, these constitutional guaranties at no time defined the property rights of aliens in California. These rights were defined in section 671 of the Civil Code of 1872 which, after slight amendment in 1874,[71] read as follows: "Any person, whether citizen or alien, may take, hold, and dispose of property, real and personal, within this State."

This code section embodied the most liberal policy with respect to the property rights of aliens. It granted to all aliens irrespective of race or nationality, irrespective of residence or nonresidence,[72] equality with citizens in the acquisition and holding of property of every kind. The supreme court of California has many times held that this broad grant is in nowise in conflict with the minimum guaranties of the state constitution.[73] This code section continued in force after the constitution of 1879 was adopted, and indeed, has never been repealed. It is still the law of California with respect to all aliens except those ineligible to naturalization, first discriminated against by the statute of 1913. That discrimination is contained in the law now in force, the scope of which is next to be stated.

RIGHTS DENIED TO "INELIGIBLE ALIENS" BY PRESENT CALIFORNIA LAW

California's "ineligible alien" property law from its beginning in

[69] Cal. Stats. 1881, xxiv.

[70] *Ibid.* 1895, xxxii.

[71] Cal. Acts 1873-74, p. 218, which inserted the words, "and dispose of".

[72] Blythe v. Hinckley (1900) 127 Cal. 431, 59 Pac. 787; Estate of Pendergast (1904) 143 Cal. 135, 76 Pac. 962.

[73] Estate of Billings (1884) 65 Cal. 593, 4 Pac. 639; State v. Smith (1886) 70 Cal. 153, 12 Pac. 121; and cases cited *supra* note 72.

1913 has expressed itself in a "backhanded fashion".[74] Sections 1 and 2 of the Initiative Act of 1920, slightly amended in 1923, contain the more fundamental provisions now in force.[75] Section 1 affirmatively grants to aliens *eligible* to naturalization rights equal to those of citizens of the United States to "acquire, possess, enjoy, use, cultivate, occupy, transfer, transmit and inherit real property, or any interest therein, in this state, and have in whole or in part the beneficial use thereof." Section 2 proceeds, affirmatively also, to grant to "all aliens *other than* those mentioned in Section one" the same all inclusive rights with respect to real property "in the manner and to the extent, and for the purposes prescribed by any treaty *now existing* between the government of the United States and the nation or country of which such alien is a citizen or subject, *and not otherwise.*" (Emphasis added.) The last phrase is the negating bite of the statute. In effect the two sections declare that an alien ineligible to naturalization shall have no rights whatsoever with respect to "real property" in California other than those secured to him by a "now existing treaty" between the United States and his country, while all other aliens shall have the same rights as citizens.

The statute does not mention agricultural land specifically. Its denials are with respect to "real property" in general and of "any interest therein" and of "any beneficial use thereof", subject to then existing treaty rights. The expression "treaty now existing" was used in the statute of 1913, the Initiative Act of 1920, and in the statute of 1923, amending the latter, and is the wording of the law at the present time. The only treaty between Japan and the United States in those years was that of 1911,[76] and it was abrogated by the United States in 1940.[77] A California district court of appeal has held[78] that the abrogation of the treaty is of no significance, on the ground that its provisions were incorporated into the statute by the words "treaty now existing". The abrogation, however, has very substantial effect upon the law in several other of the "ineligible alien" land law states: those whose statutes made no reservation of "now existing treaty"

---

[74] Powell, *Alien Land Law Cases* (1924) 12 CALIF. L. REV. 259, 262.

[75] The law now in force is compiled in CAL. GEN. LAWS, Act 261.

[76] 37 STAT. (1911) 1504.

[77] On July 26, 1939, the United States served formal notice on the Government of Japan terminating the treaty six months from that date, *i.e.*, on January 26, 1940. Dept. of State Bull. (July 29, 1939) vol. I, p. 81.

[78] Palermo v. Stockton Theatres, Inc. (1946) 76 A. C. A. 26, 172 P. (2d) 103, hearing granted (Oct. 31, 1946).

rights.[79] In them Japanese nationals now unprotected by any treaty have no rights whatsoever with respect to realty—if the laws are valid.

If the above interpretation of the California law is correct, its negation of rights in real property to the Japanese is still qualified by the provisions of the abrogated treaty, just as it was qualified while the treaty was in force. By the treaty, Japanese nationals in the United States and American citizens in Japan were secured, so far as real property is concerned, rights "to own or lease and occupy houses, manufactories, warehouses and shops, . . . to lease land for residential and commercial purposes . . . ."

"It will be noted," said the recent Attorney General of California, "that the right to own land, for any purpose, is nowhere reserved."[80] He further said, "The escheat program now in progress [1944] is directed primarily at agricultural lands, at least for the present. This does not mean, however, that ownership of land for other uses and purposes will not be made the subject of scrutiny and action later on . . . ."[81]

According to this interpretation Japanese aliens can own or lease buildings for commercial and residential purposes, but can merely lease, not *own,* the land on which the buildings stand. Whether or not this is in accordance with the liberal construction which the Supreme Court of the United States holds should be given treaties, it may be a different question as to the interpretation of an abrogated treaty, the provisions of which merely survive as a part of a state statute into which they are incorporated by reference.

While the treaty with Japan reserved to Japanese aliens at least the right to own certain kinds of buildings and to lease land for commercial and residential purposes, even these rights are denied to "ineligible aliens" who are nationals of countries with whom the United States did not have at the crucial dates, and does not now have, any protective treaty.[82] No doubt the latter is an inadvertent effect of the law, its promoters being absorbed in curtailing the rights of Japanese aliens so far as the treaty with Japan permitted.

---

79 Louisiana, New Mexico, Montana, and Wyoming, *supra* notes 6, 7, 9, 13.

80 Robert W. Kenny, Attorney General of California, in a public address. Proceedings of the California Land Title Association, Thirty-eighth Annual Conference, June 7 and 8, 1944, Pasadena, California, pp. 91-101 [reprinted in Brief for Respondent, App. p. 6, People v. Oyama (1946) 29 A. C. 157, 173 P. (2d) 749.]

81 *Ibid.*

82 Limits of time have prevented investigation of the suggested question.

There has never been any question but that the treaty with Japan secured no rights to her nationals with respect to holding *agricultural* land, and while the statute of 1913 permitted "ineligible aliens" to "lease lands in this state for agricultural purposes for a term not exceeding three years", this privilege has been denied since the Initiative Act of 1920. Substantially all criminal prosecutions and escheat proceedings under the California law to date have presented issues with respect to the acquiring of some interest in agricultural lands by Japanese aliens. The advocates and defenders of the law have always emphasized that it kept the farm lands out of the hands of "ineligible aliens", particularly the Japanese. How far its terms do forbid farming by "ineligible aliens" is worth examination.

The strongest words of the law are those forbidding the proscribed class from acquiring "any interest" in real property or having "in whole or in part the beneficial use thereof." Since 1923 the law has also forbidden a member of the class from farming land under a crop-sharing contract, although technically such a contract confers no legal interest in the land. How this feature came into the law is interesting but is consigned to a footnote.[83]

The law, however, does not, and does not purport to, keep Japanese or other "ineligible aliens" off the farms of California. Any owner may hire an alien Japanese as farm-manager for wages other than a share in the crop. Any owner may employ Japanese aliens as farm laborers, including foremen. Indeed some proponents of the law de-

---

[83] The Initiative Act of 1920 (Cal. Stats. 1921, p. lxxxiii) did no more than prohibit the acquisition of "an interest" in real property. United States District Judge Dooling held in 1921 that "the cropper has no interest in the land, merely receiving his share of the crop as the price of his labor." O'Brien v. Webb (1921) 279 Fed. 117, 119. Nevertheless he assumed in a dictum "that the state has the power to inhibit an alien inadmissible to citizenship from making a contract to farm on shares . . . ." *Ibid.* at 124. On June 28, 1923, the supreme court of California also held that the Act of 1920 did not forbid crop-sharing contracts. *In re* Okahara (1923) 191 Cal. 353, 216 Pac. 614. Judge Dooling's decision was reversed by the Supreme Court of the United States (Nov. 19, 1923) on the ground that while such a contract gave no legal interest in the land it gave "use, control, and benefit of land . . . substantially similar to that granted to a lessee." Webb. v. O'Brien (1923) 263 U. S. 313, 324. The Court further held that the statute so construed was not unconstitutional. It had some difficulty in distinguishing the cropping contract before it from that in the California case above cited. The supreme court of California immediately revised its interpretation of the Act of 1920, accepting the United States Supreme Court's interpretation. Porterfield v. Webb (1924) 195 Cal. 71, 231 Pac. 554. In the meantime the California legislature, encouraged perhaps by the dictum of Judge Dooling, expressly declared that cropping contracts were within the prohibitions of the Act (Cal. Stats. 1923, p. 1023) and also amended section 2, to insert the words, "have in whole or in part the beneficial use" of real property. (*Ibid.*, p. 1021.)

sired Japanese farm workers and welcomed the reduction of the alien Japanese agriculturists to that status. Moreover, the law did not completely wipe out farm ownership by "ineligible aliens". It did not attempt to escheat farm lands owned by them before the statute of 1913 became effective, although further performance of executory contracts by which they were entitled to acquire land was held to be illegal.[84] Thus the Census of 1940, in reporting the occupations of persons fourteen years old and older, shows that over ten thousand alien Japanese were engaged in farming in California:[85]

Farmers and farm managers	4,134
Farm laborers (wage workers and farm foremen)	4,916
Farm laborers (unpaid family workers) . . .	1,462
	10,512

Japanese aliens in California may be farm managers, not only for hire, but as legally appointed guardians of estates including farm lands, despite the attempt in the Initiative Act of 1920 to forbid the appointment of any "ineligible alien" as "guardian of that portion of the estate of a minor" which consisted of real property that the "ineligible alien" could not himself legally acquire.[86] In *Estate of Yano*[87] a Japanese alien applied for appointment as guardian of the estate of his daughter, about three years of age, who was an American-born citizen, the estate consisting of fourteen acres of farm land. The superior court refused the appointment but was reversed by the supreme court of California. "It is settled law in this State," said the court, "that the father of a minor under the age of fourteen years is entitled as a matter of right . . . to the guardianship of such minor, unless shown to be incompetent."[88] The court then held that the attempt of the statute to make "ineligible aliens" incompetent was an irrational discrimination and therefore a denial of equal protection of the laws both to the alien parent and to his citizen child.

Later it was held that the law does not nullify a bona fide transaction by which an "ineligible alien" supplies the money to purchase land as a gift to a citizen or any other person who is not an "ineligi-

[84] See Mott v. Cline (1927) 200 Cal. 434, 253 Pac. 718; Delta Farms v. Chinese American Farms (1929) 207 Cal. 298, 278 Pac. 227.

[85] 16th Census of the United States: 1940, Characteristics of the Nonwhite Population, Table 38.

[86] Cal. Stats. 1921, p. lxxxiii.

[87] (1922) 188 Cal. 645, 206 Pac. 995.

[88] *Ibid.* at 648, 206 Pac. at 997.

ble alien", even though the grantee is the alien's minor child over whose estate the alien is entitled to be appointed guardian.[89] There is, however, a statutory "prima facie presumption" that where payment is by an "ineligible alien" and title is taken in another's name the transaction is not bona fide and is illegal.[90]

Amendments to the law in 1923 and 1943 have added several provisions[91] to prevent an "ineligible alien" appointed as guardian of his American-born minor child "or as guardian of any other person" from using his guardianship as a cloak for evasion of the law. Such guardian is required to administer the estate "solely for the use and benefit of the ward", and is not to receive directly or indirectly any of the proceeds of the estate for his own use. While he may be compensated, the court supervising the guardianship is given power to fix the amount, and also to fix the amount of the guardian's bond, without any statutory standard being prescribed to control the court's discretion. The guardian is required to make detailed annual reports of receipts and disbursements and such additional special reports from time to time as the court may require.

Complying with all the statutory requirements, an "ineligible alien" may lawfully be the manager of a farm which is owned by a ward of whom he is the guardian, and the recent Attorney General of California, after intensive investigation, said, "It is not inferred that *all* cases of Japanese ownership following the guardianship pattern are spurious . . . ."[92]

The procedures prescribed for enforcement of the law are: (1) escheat proceedings;[93] (2) criminal prosecutions;[94] and (3) injunction proceedings.[95] Prior to 1923, if an "ineligible alien" acquired a forbidden interest in real property and before escheat proceedings were begun sold it to any person legally competent to hold it, the latter acquired a good title.[96] In that year, however, the law was amended to make the escheat occur at the date of acquisition by the "ineligible alien", with the consequence that a transfer by him before

---

89 People v. Fujita (1932) 215 Cal. 166, 8 P. (2d) 1011.

90 This provision was held not to be a denial of due process of law in criminal trials [Cockrill v. California (1925) 268 U.S. 258] nor in civil trials [Haruko Takeuchi v. Schmuck (1929) 206 Cal. 782, 276 Pac. 345].

91 Cal. Gen. Laws, Act 261, § 4.

92 *Op. cit. supra* note 80, at 14.

93 Cal. Gen. Laws, Act 261, §§ 7, 7.5, 8, 9.

94 *Ibid.* § 10a.

95 *Ibid.* §§ 10b, 11a.

96 Mott v. Cline, *supra* note 84.

the state acts gives the transferee no title. Where the interest acquired by an "ineligible alien" is a fee, whether it is held by him or by a transferee, it may be seized by the state and sold at public auction for the benefit of the state. Where the alien acquires a leasehold, or where he has a crop-sharing contract, not only does his interest escheat, but also whatever interest the landlord has in the land escheats, whether it be a fee or a leasehold, and even though he is an "eligible alien" or a citizen, competent to hold land. The interests of both the "ineligible alien" and of the landlord are sold for the benefit of the state. No detail is overlooked.

When the 1923 amendment became operative, escheats in a sense became automatic, that is, by mere operation of law, although, to be sure, some proceeding by the state was necessary to establish the fact of violation and dispossess the holder of the escheated interest. But what of such escheats that may have occurred as long ago as 1924 and are not yet uncovered? The legislature in 1945 was greatly concerned lest proceedings to uncover them were barred by statutes of limitations, and in consequence amended the law to provide that "No statute of limitation shall apply or operate as a bar to any escheat action or proceeding now pending or hereafter commenced . . . ."[97] In what was perhaps a vain attempt to make this retroactive legislation appear not unconstitutional the amending statute declares that it "does not constitute a change in, but is declaratory of the pre-existing law."[98]

At the same session of the legislature a special appropriation of $200,000 was made to the attorney general for the investigation of possible evasions of the law. Moreover, to stimulate local interest in discovering facts justifying escheat, the statute was amended to give the county in which escheated land lies one-half of the proceeds of the sale.[99]

Such expenditures and painstaking legislation to root out an evil that threatens the welfare of California is highly commendable. It is of course probable that some of the small group of aged Japanese aliens in California are holding interests in real property forbidden by the law.

Prior to 1943 the only criminal offense under the law was a conspiracy of two or more persons to violate it.[100] Difficulty was encoun-

[97] Cal. Stats. 1945, p. 2177 (§ 1).

[98] *Ibid.* § 2.

[99] *Ibid.* p. 2165.

[100] Amendment of 1923, Cal. Stats. 1923, p. 1024.

tered in proving a conspiracy, particularly in cases where the alleged transfer to the alleged "ineligible alien" was by a white American citizen, one of the alleged conspirators. Statutory presumptions of the existence of some of the facts essential to establish guilt were enacted,[101] one of which was held unconstitutional by the Supreme Court of the United States.[102] In 1943 the criminal conspiracy provisions were repealed, and instead the act of any individual violating "any provision" of the act was made a crime, with a possible punishment of ten years in a penitentiary and a fine of $5,000.[103] Under the old common law the holding of real property by an alien was never a criminal offense.

We pass now to less well-known features of the law, those prohibiting certain corporations from acquiring interests in real property in California.[104]

The provision with respect to corporations is an affirmative grant to every corporation whatsoever, whether "organized under the laws of this state or any other state or nation", of equal rights with a citizen in acquiring and holding real property in California, without limit, with the single exception which denies such rights to a corporation "of which a majority of the members" are "ineligible aliens" "or in which a majority of the issued capital stock is owned by such aliens." Thus even a corporation formed under the laws of Japan may hold real property without limit in California if, for example, Chinese nationals are dominant as shareholders both in number and value of issued stock. It is apparent that California has no policy against corporate landholding, either with respect to domestic corporations or foreign corporations, using the latter term in its broadest sense.

No doubt this discriminatory provision against particular corporations because of the race of their shareholders is valid, if the Supreme Court of the United States continues to hold valid the other portions of the law directed at individual "ineligible aliens", inasmuch as the provision operates to prevent the latter from accomplish-

---

101 Cal. Stats. 1927, p. 881; CAL. GEN. LAWS, Act 261, §§ 9a, 9b.

102 Morrison v. California (1934) 291 U. S. 82. See Note (1934) 22 CALIF. L. REV. 420.

103 "Any person who violates any of the provisions of this act [the basic act of 1921, as amended] shall be punishable by imprisonment in the county jail not to exceed one year or in the State penitentiary not exceeding 10 years, or by a fine not to exceed five thousand dollars ($5,000), or both." Cal. Stats. 1943, p. 3002.

104 CAL. GEN. LAWS, Act 261, § 3.

ing forbidden objectives by incorporation. Realty held by a corporation that has the proscribed shareholdership escheats to the state.[105] By the terms of the law this may happen even with respect to a corporation which acquires land while all its shares are held by citizens or eligible aliens if "ineligible aliens" subsequently acquire the forbidden amount of shares, even though a remainder of the shares is still held by innocent shareholders who did not participate in the transfer to "ineligible aliens".

The restriction with respect to corporations is expressly subject to "now existing" treaty rights. Thus it has been held that the treaty right of individual Japanese nationals "to lease land . . . for commercial purposes, and generally do anything incident or necessary for trade upon the same terms as native citizens" gives alien Japanese the right to incorporate under California law for the purpose of *leasing* land upon which to operate a hospital as a business enterprise.[106]

In addition to the provision that a corporation's realty escheats if "ineligible aliens" are dominant in shareholding, there is a further provision that a single share acquired by an "ineligible alien" also escheats, if it is a share in any corporation authorized to acquire *real property,*[107] (and rare is the corporation that is not) unless the corporation is authorized to acquire no other interest in real property than such as an individual "ineligible alien" may acquire by a "now existing treaty". Thus it seems that a Japanese alien may not own a single share of stock in any corporation that is authorized to *own* land for any purpose, whether it is engaged in banking, insurance, retail trade, or any other business. But it seems that a Japanese alien may hold shares in a corporation authorized only to lease land, if its land is all held under a lease, and its corporate purposes are commercial, though not so if its leased land is held for agricultural purposes.

So thoroughgoing were the draftsmen of the California law that they regarded a share in a corporation as giving the shareholder a legal interest in the real property owned by the corporation, a peculiar instance of disregarding the separate corporate entity. They saw a menace to the welfare of California in a single "ineligible alien's" holding a single share in a corporation which owns land. What ra-

---

105 *Ibid.* § 7.

106 Tashiro v Jordan (1927) 201 Cal. 236, 256 Pac. 545, *aff'd* in Jordan v. Tashiro (1928) 278 U.S. 123.

107 CAL. GEN. LAWS, Act 261, § 8.

tional relation to what purpose has this discrimination which forbids an alien of particular racial blood or particular mixtures of racial blood to acquire a single share of stock in particular corporations, while aliens of other bloods or mixtures may acquire shares in the same corporations without restriction? Nevertheless the Supreme Court of the United States in 1923 held this feature of the law to be not unconstitutional.[108] It also held that a Japanese alien had no treaty right to acquire shares in a corporation that owned agricultural land.

Not only does a share of stock acquired in violation of the law escheat to the state but the alien violator is subject to the heavy criminal penalties prescribed by the law.[109]

In summary, the California law forbids Japanese aliens to hold any legal interest in land, except a leasehold for commercial and residential purposes, and the concept of a legal interest in land is stretched to include the holding of a share in a corporation that is authorized to own land, or that leases land for purposes not commercial within the meaning of the treaty, and is also stretched to include a sharecropper's contract of employment on farm land.

With respect to "ineligible aliens" who are nationals of countries that have no protective treaty with the United States, they may not acquire any kind of interest whatsoever in real property in California, nor hold a single share of stock in any corporation authorized to acquire real property in California for any purpose.

Thus while the California law is often defended as one that reserves the *agricultural* land for citizens, it does not do so because all the aliens in the world other than "ineligible aliens" may acquire agricultural land in California without limit, either as individuals or under corporate organization, and, moreover, the law's restrictions are not confined to interests in agricultural land.

THE CONSTITUTIONAL QUESTION

In 1923 the Supreme Court of the United States, in three cases, held that the California Initiative Act of 1920 was not unconstitutional, so far as it was not in conflict with any treaty, in denying to "ineligible alien" residents of the state, but to no other residents: (1) acquisition of any interest in real property in the state;[110] (2)

---

108 Frick v. Webb (1923) 263 U. S. 326.

109 *Supra* note 103.

110 Porterfield v. Webb (1923) 263 U. S. 225, *aff'g* (1921) 279 Fed. 114.

the farming of land under a crop-sharing contract;[111] and (3) the holding of a share of stock in any corporation authorized to hold real property.[112] All three of these cases reached the Supreme Court through the lower federal courts[113] and the supreme court of California had not passed upon the constitutionality of any of the above provisions.[114] In 1922 the latter court held that the guardianship provision of the act was unconstitutional as a denial of equal protection of the laws to "ineligible aliens".[115]

The Supreme Court of the United States is the authoritative decider of issues arising under the Constitution of the United States. Anyone who believes that it has committed error in decision should remain silent or give very cogent reasons for his disagreement. The burden of persuasion is a heavy one, and the attempt to discharge it here may exhaust the patience of the reader. The charge I make, however, is not the graver one that the Court misinterpreted the Constitution. The charge is that without announcing any novel doctrine of constitutional law, the Court misapplied a settled interpretation through failure to appreciate the peculiarities of the legislation it was considering. The reader will please keep that distinction in mind throughout the following discussion.

Every state law that discriminates against a particular class of residents must run the gauntlet of the Fourteenth Amendment's limitation: "No State shall . . . deny to any person within its jurisdiction the equal protection of the laws." Those words clearly embrace every resident of a state.

It is settled by Supreme Court decision that resident aliens as a class and as individuals are entitled to "equal protection"[116] as well

---

[111] Webb. v. O'Brien (1923) 263 U. S. 313, *rev'g* (1921) 279 Fed. 117.

[112] Frick v. Webb (1923) 263 U. S. 326, *aff'g* (1922) 281 Fed. 407.

[113] *Supra* notes 110-112.

[114] In 1922 the supreme court of California, after stating that no constitutional issue had been raised in the case [*In re* Akado (1922) 188 Cal. 739, 743, 207 Pac. 245, 246] said: "It is well settled that, in the absence of a treaty to the contrary, a state may forbid the taking or holding of property within their [sic] limits by aliens. (Blythe v. Hinckley, 127 Cal. 436)." Neither the dictum nor the case cited to support it touched at all the issue whether a state may set "ineligible alien" residents apart and deny to them rights which it concedes to all other residents. Indeed the cited case does not support the proposition that a state may deny to any alien the acquisition of realty. What it held was that a statute of California was valid insofar as it *conferred* upon a British national, not residing in California, the right to inherit California land and that such a statute did not invade the treaty power of the national government.

[115] Estate of Yano, *supra* note 87.

[116] Yick Wo v. Hopkins (1886) 118 U. S. 356; Truax v. Raich (1915) 239 U. S. 33.

as all other classes of residents. The expression "any person" in the clause was too clear to permit any other construction. Moreover, congressional legislation immediately after the ratification of the Fourteenth Amendment, enacted in furtherance of its provisions, discloses that the contemporary Congress understood that the equal protection clause extends to alien residents. Thus the Civil Rights Act of May 31, 1870, made it a criminal offense for any person "under color of any law" to deprive "any inhabitant of any State" of certain rights "on account of such person being an alien, or by reason of his color or race."[117] Moreover, it declared that no state should levy any tax on "any person immigrating thereto from a foreign country" that it did not impose equally upon immigrants from other countries.[118] Thus Congress assumed that the clause required states not to discriminate between aliens *inter se*—not to discriminate between the nationals of one foreign country and the nationals of another.

What is the "equal protection" that states are forbidden to deny to residents, aliens and all others? The Supreme Court's interpretation, which has been settled for at least fifty years,[119] is that no state shall make any discrimination against alien residents or any other class of residents that is not rational with respect to the purpose of

[117] 16 Stat. (1870) 140, 144.

[118] *Ibid.*

[119] The "rational basis" test was formulated at least as early as 1897 in Gulf, Colorado & Santa Fe Ry. Co. v. Ellis (1897) 165 U. S. 150. As there expressed, the equal protection clause does not "withhold from States the power of classification . . . yet it is equally true that such classification cannot be made arbitrarily." Classification "must always rest upon some difference which bears a reasonable and just relation to the act in respect to which the classification is proposed, and can never be made arbitrarily and without any such basis." *Ibid.* at 155. It seems that the Court's meaning would have been clearer if it had used the word "discrimination" where it used "classification". Usually classifications are not *made* by legislatures, but known and accepted classifications are made use of for statutory purposes. Thus the Court says, "The State may not say that all white men shall be subjected to the payment of the attorney's fees of parties successfully suing them and all black men not. It may not say that all men beyond a certain age shall be alone thus subjected, nor all men possessed of a certain wealth. These are distinctions which do not furnish any proper basis for the attempted classification" [discrimination]. *Ibid.* at 155. In Clarke v. Deckebach (1927) 274 U. S. 392, 396, Justice Stone said, "Although the Fourteenth Amendment has been held to prohibit plainly irrational discrimination against aliens . . . it does not follow that alien race and allegiance may not bear in some instances such a relation to a legitimate object of legislation as to be made the basis of a permitted classification" [discrimination]. It is true of course that an "invidious discrimination" made by a statute sometimes consists in arbitrary definition of the class given "special treatment", as in Skinner v. Oklahoma (1942) 316 U. S. 535, so that the two expressions, "arbitrary classification" and "arbitrary discrimination" are equally applicable.

the particular statute by which it is made. Not all state discriminatory laws are unconstitutional, for a class of persons may be singled out for different treatment provided the characteristics which distinguish the class rationally justify the difference in treatment.

Thus, a state statute which has for its purpose protection of the public health may prescribe qualifications of persons permitted to practice medicine, and exclude all others, provided the practice of medicine by persons lacking those qualifications may rationally be said to threaten the public health. If a state should prescribe citizenship as a qualification, the constitutional issue would be whether there is any rational ground for believing that alienage of a medical practitioner makes it likely that he will do acts prejudicial to public health, or in fact be less competent than citizen practitioners. Consequently, the purpose of a statute is a big factor in determining the constitutionality of any discrimination made by it against any particular class of persons. The irrationality or unreasonableness of a statutory discrimination is not tested in the abstract. Unreasonableness is always relative, and here it is a relation between the discrimination made by a statute and the purpose of the statute.

Had the Supreme Court held unconstitutional a state law which denies to all resident[120] aliens, regardless of race or national origin, the privilege of acquiring real property, on the ground that such a discrimination against resident aliens has no rational relation to the protection of the health, safety, morals, or general welfare of the inhabitants of the state, what fault could be found with that application of the equal protection clause? That question in effect is whether after the ratification of the Fourteenth Amendment in 1868, any state could constitutionally enforce the old common-law rules against resident aliens. It is true that the due process of law clauses have been construed "not to overthrow ancient practices even when hard to reconcile with justice", as Justice Holmes said,[121] but such leniency on the part of the Court in applying the vague requirement of "due" or proper procedure, a requirement which itself is rooted in history, seems inapplicable to the much more specific requirement of equality

[120] To the extent that the common-law rules operated against nonresident aliens, no question of the constitutionality of a state's adopting them would arise under the equal protection clause since it does not extend to persons not within the state's jurisdiction.

[121] Power Co. v. Saunders (1927) 274 U. S. 490, 498, doubtless referring to the decisions in Murray v. Hoboken Land Co. (1856) 59 U. S. (18 How.) 272, and Ownbey v. Morgan (1921) 256 U. S. 94.

with respect to all persons within a state's jurisdiction, which obviously was intended to be innovational.

No case questioning the power of a state to enforce the common-law rules against alien landholding after the adoption of the Fourteenth Amendment came to the Supreme Court before 1923. All that it had said on the point in the meantime had been dicta.[122] The question was raised in 1923 in *Terrace v. Thompson*,[123] in which the Court sustained the alien land law of the state of Washington. The Washington law denied the right to hold land in the state to all aliens whatsoever, resident and nonresident, except "an alien who has in good faith declared his intention to become a citizen of the United States."[124] The exception was the only substantial deviation from the common law, and was argued by counsel and discussed by the Court as the possible ground for holding that the statute made an unconstitutional discrimination between two classes of aliens, declarants and non-declarants. The validity of the law apart from this discrimination was given very slight consideration.

Justice Butler, delivering the opinion of the Court, seems to have assumed that it was settled by prior decisions. He said, " . . . each State, in the absence of any treaty provision to the contrary, has power to deny to aliens the right to own land within its borders. *Hauenstein v. Lynham*, 100 U. S. 483, 484, 488; *Blythe v. Hinckley*,

---

[122] The cases most often assumed to be in point are Hauenstein v. Lynham (1879) 100 U. S. 483, and Blythe v. Hinckley (1901) 180 U. S. 333. In the Hauenstein case the question was whether Swiss nationals, nonresidents of Virginia, could take lands in Virginia by inheritance. It was held that a treaty with Switzerland gave the Swiss heirs the right to inherit. It was assumed, though clearly not decided, that if there had been no treaty, Virginia law against nonresident aliens taking Virginia land by inheritance would have been valid. The sole remarks of the Court on this point were that by international law every government may give to foreigners only such rights with respect to immovable property as it sees fit, and "In our country, this authority is primarily in the States where the property is situated" (100 U. S. at 484), subject to being overriden by treaty.

In the Hinckley case the Court affirmed the decision of the California supreme court holding that a state statute *granting* to aliens the privilege of landowning does not infringe the treaty power of the national government (see *supra* note 114) and said, "This court has held from the earliest times in cases where there was no treaty that the laws of the State where the real property was situated governed the title and were conclusive in regard thereto." 180 U. S. at 341. For this were cited Clarke v. Clarke (1900) 178 U. S. 186, and De Vaughn v. Hutchinson (1897) 165 U. S. 566, which presented no issue whatever about aliens. Also Chirac v. Chirac (1817) 15 U. S. (2 Wheat.) 259 was cited, a case holding that a treaty supersedes a state statute in conflict therewith.

None of the cases passed on the question whether a state law which deprives resident aliens of the privilege of holding real estate is a denial of equal protection of the laws.

[123] (1923) 263 U. S. 197.

[124] WASH. REV. STAT. (Remington, 1933) §§ 10,581, 10,582.

180 U. S. 333, 340."[125] The cited cases contain nothing but meager dicta.[126]

After the above-quoted passage, Justice Butler gave a brief digest of the common-law rules, and added, "State legislation applying alike and equally to all aliens, withholding from them the right to hold land, cannot be said to . . . transgress the *due process* clause."[127] Turning to the equal protection clause he distinguished the decision in *Truax v. Raich*,[128] which he abstracted as holding that a state may not discriminate between citizens and resident aliens with respect to "the right to work for a living in the common occupations of the community." Then follows this sentence:

> "In the case before us, the thing forbidden is very different. It is not an opportunity to earn a living in common occupations of the community, but it is the privilege of owning or controlling agricultural land within the State."[129]

Since when did farming as a farm owner cease to be a "common occupation" as a means of earning a livelihood? At the time the Constitution was adopted it was estimated that nine-tenths of the gainfully employed people in America were engaged in agricultural pursuits,[130] and this was still substantially true in many states when the Fourteenth Amendment was adopted.

But passing that, we come to the next sentence:

> "The quality and *allegiance* of those who own, occupy and use farm lands within its borders are matters of highest importance and affect the safety and power of the State itself."[131]

In what respect does the ownership of some of the farm lands in a state by persons who owe no allegiance to the United States affect the safety of a state, either in time of peace or of war? Has this ancient idea by which early English law writers rationalized the exclusion of all but the King's subjects from certain feudal land tenures any validity in our time? Tenure by knight service, or military tenure, was then conceived of as something that none but persons under allegiance to the King might owe. But "by the end of the thirteenth

[125] 263 U. S. at 217.

[126] See *supra* note 122.

[127] 263 U. S. at 218. (Emphasis added.)

[128] (1915) 239 U. S. 33.

[129] 263 U. S. at 221.

[130] COXE, A VIEW OF THE UNITED STATES OF AMERICA (London ed. 1795) p. 6.

[131] 263 U. S. at 221. (Emphasis added.)

century, tenure by knight service had ceased to provide either soldiers or their pay."[132] Maitland says that if it had been abolished in 1300 the military strength of the realm would have been unaffected.[133] When the statute of 1660[134] completely abolished military tenure it was merely clearing away what had long been a dead letter so far as military service was concerned. A connection between tenure and military service had existed only in theory when Coke saw "destruction of the realm" in landholding by aliens. In our time liability to military service is not dependent upon allegiance. Resident aliens are now subjected to compulsory military service even in international warfare,[135] and nothing but legislative policy exempts enemy aliens. An alien is not exempt from draft because he owns farm land. So also Coke's Trojan-horse idea, that aliens owning land "might fortify themselves in the heart of the realm", never had any validity in the United States, certainly not since 1798. Congress then passed a statute,[136] ever since in force, authorizing the arrest, confinement, or removal of enemy aliens in wartime. It also authorized the President "to direct the conduct to be observed, on the part of the United States, toward" enemy aliens. During the war of 1812 with Great Britain, orders by the President and other officials acting under his authority directed all British nationals, fourteen years of age and over, residing within forty miles of tidewater to surrender to United States marshalls and be retired further into the interior of the country or to be kept in close confinement.[137] In terms of the greater rapidity of travel and transportation in our time, such removal was the equivalent of a removal of enemy aliens five hundred miles from the coast. The evacuation of Japanese enemy aliens from the Pacific Coast during the still legally existing war was not a novelty, although the evacuation of American citizens of Japanese ancestry was unprecedented.

The fact that an enemy alien owns farm lands in nowise affects his liability to evacuation. Indeed the ownership of any property by an enemy alien in the United States is an asset to us, rather than a liability or a handicap, in view of the authority given the Alien Prop-

---

[132] HOLDSWORTH, HISTORICAL INTRODUCTION TO THE LAND LAW (1927) 26.

[133] POLLOCK and MAITLAND, HISTORY OF ENGLISH LAW (2d ed. 1898) 276.

[134] 12 CAR. II (1660) c. 24.

[135] Formerly writers contended that international law was to the contrary. See MCGOVNEY, CASES ON CONSTITUTIONAL LAW (1935) 438.

[136] 1 STAT. (1798) 577; R. S. § 4067, 50 U. S. C. (1940) § 21.

[137] See Lockington v. Smith (1817) 15 Fed. Cas. 758.

erty Custodian to seize it, hold it, sell it or otherwise deal with it in the interest, and for the benefit, of the United States.[138]

Coke's Trojan horse now lives only in law books or in the minds of persons who unthinkingly accept antiquated "reasons" for the ancient discrimination that the common law made against aliens with respect to land holding.

Turning to peacetime, how does alien landholding then affect the safety of the state? I think the complete answer was given to that question by Chief Justice Redfield of Vermont in 1853. The question before the Vermont supreme court was whether the common law against landholding by aliens had been received, or had survived, in the state, and in particular whether Vermont law contained any procedure for the forfeiture of estates of aliens. The court held "no", the Chief Justice saying, "it must, I think, be regarded as questionable how far any such procedure could ever be enforced, for the mere purpose of escheating to the State the lands of a quiet resident or non-resident alien, in time of profound peace, where no danger was apparent, imminent, or even remotely threatened."[139]

If the allegiance of farm owners is of "highest importance" and the alienage of farm owners affects the safety of the state, the legislators of forty-one of our states[140] are lacking in statecraft, for by their laws the allegiance of those who own farm lands is regarded as of no significance whatever. Rightly included in the forty-one states are the nine "ineligible alien" land law states for they also regard the allegiance of landowners of no significance except in case of the small number of aliens racially ineligible to naturalization. So California lawmakers see no reason for denying to a half million alien residents the privilege of owning land without limit, though denying that privilege to less than thirty thousand other alien residents because of their race.

Consequently it seems that a strict application of the accepted interpretation of the equal protection clause would nullify any state law that confines landholding to citizens, because of its irrational discrimination against resident aliens. The Supreme Court, however, in *Terrace v. Thompson*[141] ,assumed the contrary upon slight consideration, and passed to what it conceived to be the only doubtful

---

138 U. S. Government Manual (2d ed. 1945) 70.

139 State v. Boston, Concord & Montreal R. R. Co. (1853) 25 Vt. 433, 440.

140 *Supra* pp. 21 *et seq.*

141 *Supra* note 123.

question in the case. This was whether the Washington law violated the equal protection clause because it discriminated between two classes of resident aliens, those who had and those who had not made declarations of intention to become citizens. On the premise assumed, that a state could restrict landholding exclusively to citizens, this was an easy question. The Washington law merely made a dispensation in favor of near-citizens, giving them the rights of citizens in landholding. It extended citizen rights to those aliens, regardless of race or national origin, who had "in good faith" made declarations of intention to become citizens. Since it is exceptional that such declarations are not followed through to final naturalization, declarants are rightly regarded as near-citizens, as persons in the process of becoming citizens. The dispensation in their favor is the same as that formally made in twenty-two states and territories[142] in granting declarant aliens the right to vote in anticipation of their acquiring citizenship within a few years. That the Washington lawmakers regarded declarants as near-citizens, with a high probability of soon becoming citizens, is shown by the requirement that the declaration of intention be made in good faith, coupled with the statutory presumption: "Unless an alien who has declared his intention to become a citizen of the United States be admitted to citizenship within seven years after his declaration was made, it shall be presumed that he declared his intention in bad faith."[143] It is curious that the only reported cases in which declarants have been found to have made their declarations in bad faith are those of two white aliens, nationals of Switzerland, and land acquired by them was forfeited.[144]

On the same day that the Supreme Court announced its decision on the Washington law, it announced its decision in *Porterfield v. Webb*,[145] upholding the basic features of the California law. The constitutional issue with respect to the latter was disposed of in less than a full page of the opinion, delivered by Justice Butler. The short passage opens with, "This case is similar to *Terrace v. Thompson*", and closes with, "Our decision in *Terrace v. Thompson* . . . controls the decision of all questions raised here."[146]

A patient examination of the two laws discloses that their dis-

---

[142] Aylsworth, *The Passing of Alien Suffrage* (1931) 25 Am. Pol. Sci. Rev. 114.

[143] Wash. Rev. Stat. (Remington, 1933) § 10,586.

[144] State v. Staeheli (1920) 112 Wash. 344, 192 Pac. 991; State v. Rychen (1920) 113 Wash. 90, 193 Pac. 220.

[145] (1923) 263 U. S. 225.

[146] *Ibid.* at 233.

criminations are very different both in the character of the aliens they affect and in the number of aliens affected. The language which the two laws use in defining their proscribed classes necessarily produces wide differences of application. The Washington law proscribes the alien who has not in good faith declared his intention to become a citizen. Its discrimination is not exclusively racial, whereas the California discrimination is that and nothing more. I doubt whether the Supreme Court fully appreciated the latter point. When we first read the California law which says, "All aliens eligible to citizenship under the laws of the United States" may acquire interests in realty, and other aliens may not, we assume that all aliens ineligible to naturalization are denied the privilege. Was the Supreme Court fully aware that California intended to make that mean only those aliens who are *racially* ineligible to naturalization? Taken at its face value the expression "aliens ineligible to naturalization" includes every alien who does not reside in the United States, regardless of race; and indeed every alien residing in the United States who has not resided here five years. But the California law is interpreted to permit every alien in the world to hold realty in California except aliens of the proscribed races.

Also, no alien is eligible to naturalization unless he speaks the English language, but the California law is interpreted not to make that requirement for landholding.

By interpretation California has read the law as saying "All aliens [racially] eligible to citizenship" may acquire interests in realty and others may not. Thus in its application to aliens residing in California it bars from acquiring any legal interest in realty about twenty-five thousand Japanese aliens and a very few Polynesian and Malayan aliens, and no other resident aliens.

The Washington law, on the other hand, while it also bars aliens racially ineligible to naturalization, because they are legally incompetent to make declarations of intention, bars them as a small portion of the millions of other aliens who are legally incompetent to make declarations of intention, for reasons apart from their race, as well as those who though competent, do not choose to make declarations. Thus no alien who does not reside in the United States may acquire realty in Washington, except by inheritance or in collection of a debt,[147] because a declarant is required to state a place of resi-

[147] But acquisitions by these excepted modes may be held for no more than twelve years. WASH. REV. STAT. (Remington, 1933) § 10,584.

dence in the United States and to declare that he intends to reside permanently in the United States.[148] The untold millions of aliens thus excluded from landholding in Washington regardless of their race are eligible to acquire realty in California except those who are members of particular races. Other requirements for a valid declaration of intention make some resident aliens ineligible to acquire land in Washington, regardless of their race. Thus a declarant must declare that he has reached the age of eighteen years. So also he must state facts establishing his lawful entry into the United States.[149] By contrast, aliens however young, and illegally entered aliens, are not forbidden to acquire realty in California unless they be of the proscribed races.

The reports of cases in the supreme court of Washington, to search no further, show that the Washington law has been applied to white aliens: a British national,[150] Swiss nationals,[151] and a German national.[152] Washington also, like California, bars certain corporations from acquiring realty. In California the proscribed corporations are those in which a majority of the stock is owned by aliens racially ineligible to become citizens. In Washington, the proscribed corporations are those in which a majority of the stock is held by nondeclarant aliens, and that rule has been enforced against corporations whose nondeclarant stockholders were obviously white although the reported cases do not specifically state that irrelevant fact.[153]

It is significant that the substantive rules of the Washington law were adopted before the agitation against the Japanese began in the Pacific coast states. They came in as article II, section 33 of the constitution of 1889,[154] which was self-operative and was judicially en-

---

148 8 U. S. C. (1940) § 731.

149 *Ibid.*

150 State v. O'Connell (1922) 121 Wash. 542, 209 Pac. 865.

151 State v. Staeheli; State v. Rychen, both *supra* note 144.

152 Abrams v. State (1907) 45 Wash. 327, 88 Pac. 327.

153 See Oregon Mortg. Co. v. Carstens (1896) 16 Wash. 165, 47 Pac. 421; State v. Hudson Land Co. (1898) 19 Wash. 85, 52 Pac. 574 (when the land was acquired a majority of the stock was owned by citizens, but later was bought by nondeclarant aliens, and the land was escheated); State v. Superior Court (1903) 33 Wash. 542, 74 Pac. 686. See also the threatened proceedings involved in Northport Power & Light Co. v. Hartley (1929) 35 F. (2d) 199.

154 "The ownership of lands by aliens, other than those who in good faith have declared their intention to become citizens of the United States, is prohibited in this State, except where acquired by inheritance, under mortgage or in good faith in the ordinary course of justice in the collection of debts . . . . Every corporation, the majority

forced, by forfeiture of realty acquired in violation of its provisions.[155] The statute of 1921 passed upon by the Supreme Court merely supplemented the constitutional provisions by adding procedural devices for enforcement.

The alien whose right to acquire land in Washington was under contest in *Terrace v. Thompson* was a Japanese. For that reason the effect of the Washington law to deny landholding to aliens legally incompetent to be declarants, as well as to the legally competent who abstained from making declarations, was discussed by Justice Butler. He pointed out that the criteria for classification in the Washington law was not racial eligibility to naturalization:

> "The inclusion of good faith declarants in the same class with citizens does not unjustly discriminate against aliens who are ineligible or against eligible aliens who have failed to declare their intention. The classification is based on eligibility *and purpose* to naturalize."[156]

He immediately proceeded to discuss the naturalization law's rules on *racial* eligibility to *naturalization.* He did not advert to the other requirements for making *a declaration of intention,* which as pointed out above, render legally incompetent millions of aliens regardless of race. He was fully aware, however, that aliens racially ineligible to naturalization are hit by the Washington law, because they fall within a wider category which includes them and countless others. Thus he says, "All persons of whatever color or race who have not declared their intention in good faith to become citizens are prohibited from so owning agricultural lands."[157] The size of the class in which the racially ineligible aliens are embraced is more fully

---

of the capital stock of which is owned by aliens, shall be considered an alien for the purposes of this prohibition."

By this provision Washington adopted a change of policy. By the Territorial Statute of January 27, 1864, all aliens had been given equal rights with citizens in acquiring and holding interests in realty. Wash. Stats. 1864, p. 12. This continued to be the law until 1886 when a statute excepted aliens "such as by the laws of the United States are incapable of becoming citizens." Act of January 29, 1886, Laws 1877-1888, p. 309. I have found no prior appearance of this idea in American law. It may have been the model for the California statute of 1913. Since there were few Japanese in the United States in 1886, the Washington statute may have been motivated by hostility to the Chinese. Compare article XV, section 8, of the Oregon constitution of 1859, declaring that "no Chinaman" should hold realty in Oregon, and see Chapman v. Toy Long (1876) 5 Fed. Cas. 497. There seem to be no reported cases arising under the Washington Statute of 1886, and it was supplanted by the very different provisions of the constitution of 1889.

[155] See cases cited *supra* notes 152, 153.

[156] 263 U. S. at 219. (Emphasis added.)

[157] *Ibid.* at 220.

seen when it is realized that it includes all nonresident aliens regardless of race. It was in this connection that Justice Butler wrote the oft-criticized statement:

> "Two classes of aliens inevitably result from the naturalization laws, —those who may and those who may not become citizens. The rule established by Congress on this subject, in and of itself, furnishes a reasonable basis for classification in a state law withholding from aliens the privilege of land ownership as defined in the act."[158]

Here the Justice may not have been thinking solely about the racial classification of the naturalization law, but of that together with all its other nonracial criteria of classification, such as continuous residence in the United States for five years, ability to speak English, ability to write one's name, attachment to the principles of the Constitution, and others.[159] More pertinent to the Washington case would have been the naturalization law's criteria for determining competency to make a declaration of intention.

On the other hand, unless the passage last quoted referred solely to the racial classification made by the naturalization law, how could Justice Butler justify his statement in *Porterfield v. Webb*, that "Our decision in *Terrace v. Thompson* controls the decision of all questions raised" by the California law?

The California law's discrimination between two classes of aliens is based solely and exclusively on the naturalization law's racial classification, disregarding all of its nonracial criteria for determining eligibility to naturalization.

In the Washington case, a state law is sustained which confines landholding to citizens and near-citizens, which denies the privilege to aliens racially ineligible to naturalization because they fall within a class not defined in terms of race, but one defined by very different criteria and which necessarily embraces a vast number of aliens irrespective of their race. In short, the Washington law closely approximates the common law's restriction of landholding to citizens, with a dispensation in favor of aliens in the process of becoming citizens.

How does sustaining that law necessarily determine the constitutionality of the California law? The latter law makes no attempt to confine landholding to citizens, or to citizens and near-citizens. Millions of nonresident aliens incompetent to make declarations of intention may acquire land in California; millions of nonresident

---

158 *Ibid.*

159 8 U. S. C. (1940) §§ 704, 707, 732.

aliens ineligible to naturalization may do so; even a half million resident aliens, regardless of whether they would or could become declarants and regardless of whether they could qualify for naturalization, may own and hold land in California. The sole exclusion by the California law is those aliens who are racially ineligible to naturalization.

How can it be said that a racial discrimination made by Congress in determining what aliens may become citizens "in and of itself, furnishes a reasonable basis for classification in a state law withholding from [some] aliens the privilege of land ownership"? A discrimination made for one purpose is necessarily rational for another purpose? A discrimination made for one purpose by a legislature that is subject to no equalitarian requirement justifies another legislature in making a like discrimination for another purpose although the latter is subject to an equalitarian requirement?

Justice Butler rightly said, "Congress is not trammeled, and it may grant or withhold the privilege of naturalization upon any grounds or without any reason, as it sees fit."[160]

He added, "But it is not to be supposed that its acts defining eligibility are arbitrary or unsupported by reasonable considerations of public policy."[161] Quite so, as an *a priori* supposition, but in reality it is difficult to find any reasonable considerations underlying the crazy quilt patternlessness of our naturalization law, which bars from naturalization because of their race Japanese Mongolians but not Chinese Mongolians, Malays if they are Siamese but not if they are Filipinos, and admits people indigenous to the Western hemisphere and to British India regardless of their ethnological classification. Moreover this patternless racial bar operates against individuals regardless of their culture, education, or personal fitness in other respects to exercise the privileges of citizenship. Moreover also, the public policies that are germane to determining what aliens should be permitted to become citizens lie in the field of political rights. The national government is concerned in determining what persons may become eligible to diplomatic protection of the United States and possibly also what persons shall become entitled to the protection which the Constitution gives citizens with respect to voting. The naturalization law expresses no judgment of Congress with respect to who should be permitted to own lands within the states, a matter

160 263 U. S. at 220.
161 *Ibid.*

not within the competency of Congress. To ascertain the judgment of Congress on that point we must look to its legislation for the Territories. There we find that "any alien who shall become a bona fide resident of the United States . . . shall have the right to acquire and hold lands in either of the Territories of the United States upon the same terms as citizens of the United States."[162]

Under the equal protection clause the validity of a state discriminatory law turns upon whether there is a rational relation between the discrimination and the purpose of *that* law.

Repeatedly the Court has said that a state law's discrimination to be constitutional must be "based on a real and substantial difference having a reasonable relation to the subject of the particular legislation."[163]

All that Justice Butler offered on the rationality of the "ineligible alien" land law was that it was enacted out of concern for the "safety of the state" in some unspecified respect. In *Webb v. O'Brien*,[164] sustaining the California law as one prohibiting ineligible aliens to farm under crop-sharing contracts, he said, "Conceivably, by the use of such contracts, the population living on and cultivating the farm lands might come to be made up largely of ineligible aliens. The allegiance of the farmers to the state directly affects its strength and safety."[165] Even if the allegiance of farmers had significance why is it of significance with respect to the less than thirty thousand "ineligible aliens" in California but of no significance with respect to a half million other aliens in California who may never seek or acquire citizenship? Moreover, the statement smacks of Coke's exaggeration when he said that if aliens could hold land in England, there would not be enough British freeholders to man the juries.[166] If all the "ineligible aliens" in California were to exhaust themselves in share cropping, there would be millions of acres of farm lands left for the citizens and other aliens. The same exaggeration is found in a statement with which Justice Butler said he agreed: "If one incapable of citizenship may lease or own real estate, it is within the realm of possibility that every foot of land within the state might pass to

---

162 8 U. S. C. (1940) § 72.

163 Power Co. v. Saunders (1927) 274 U. S. 490, 493; Quaker City Cab Co. v. Pennsylvania (1928) 277 U. S. 389, 400.

164 (1923) 263 U. S. 313.

165 *Ibid.* at 324.

166 *Supra* note 45.

the ownership or possession of noncitizens."[167] Even if that were a possibility the evil inherent therein is not specified.

Twice the supreme court of California has said that the purpose of her law is to reserve the lands of the state for citizens. Thus: "The ownership of the soil by persons morally bound by obligations of citizenship is vital to the political existence of a state."[168] "Unquestionably the farming of lands by ineligible aliens would give them a use, occupancy, and benefit of agricultural lands which in effect would amount to a deprivation of its use, enjoyment and occupancy by the citizen."[169]

In a recent case in the supreme court of California the state's Attorney General said: "We believe it may be said that, in a very real sense, ownership of the land by its citizens, or those qualified to become such, may be regarded as a *sine qua non* to the self-preservation of a free country."[170]

The denial of a common economic opportunity to a small portion of the residents of a state is essential to "the self-preservation of a free country"!

Are not all these remarkable assertions that the California law is intended to reserve the lands for its citizens belied by the fact that all the aliens in the world either as individuals or under corporate organization may legally acquire land in California without limit, unless the individuals be of particular races, or a majority of the corporate stock is held by aliens of particular races?

In vain we search for the purpose of the California law. Another former Attorney General of California, Ulysses S. Webb, asserted another purpose for it, and he had been active in drafting, and later in the enforcement of the law. In argument in *Frick v. Webb*[171] he said:

> "It was the purpose of those who understood the situation to prohibit the enjoyment or possession of, or dominion over, the agricultural lands of the State by aliens ineligible to citizenship,—in a practical way to prevent ruinous competition by the Oriental farmer against the American farmer."[172]

---

167 263 U. S. at 220.

168 Mott v. Cline, *supra* note 84, at 447, 253 Pac. at 724.

169 Porterfield v. Webb, *supra* note 83, at 82, 231 Pac. at 558.

170 Brief for Respondent, p. 11, State v. Oyama (1946) 29 A. C. 157, 173 P. (2d) 749.

171 *Supra* note 112.

172 *Ibid.* at 330.

No doubt this motive actuated some of the voters in approving the Initiative Act of 1920. The argument raises the issue whether prevention of competition is a constitutionally permitted purpose for which a common type of economic opportunity may be denied to a class of residents distinguished from all others solely by their race. The statutorily declared purpose "to protect the citizens of the United States in their employment against non-citizens of the United States" did not save Arizona's anti-alien law which was held invalid in *Truax v. Raich*[173] on the ground that it irrationally denied resident aliens a common type of economic opportunity.

Where a state discriminatory statute has a legitimate purpose the Supreme Court has paid great deference to the local legislature's judgment that the discrimination is rationally related to that purpose.[174] Such deference was shown in sustaining state legislation denying to all aliens, without distinction, licenses to operate pool and billiard rooms. Justice Stone, speaking for the Court, said:

> "The admitted allegations of the answer set up the harmful and vicious tendencies of public billiard and pool rooms, of which this Court took judicial notice in *Murphy v. California*, 225 U. S. 623. The regulation or even prohibition of the business is not forbidden. *Murphy v. California, supra.* The present regulation presupposes that aliens in Cincinnati are not as well qualified as citizens to engage in this business. It is not necessary that we be satisfied that this premise is well founded in experience. We cannot say that the city council gave unreasonable weight to the view admitted by the pleadings that the associations, experiences and interests of members of the class disqualified the class as a whole from conducting a business of dangerous tendencies.
>
> "It is enough for present purposes that the ordinance, in the light of facts admitted or generally assumed, does not preclude the possibility of a rational basis for the legislative judgment and that we have no such knowledge of local conditions as would enable us to say that it is clearly wrong. *Fort Smith Light & Traction Co. v. Board of Improvement, ante,* p. 387."[175]

If some evil condition in farming existed in any state, the state might set up a licensing system for farmers and prescribe qualifications deemed essential to overcome the evil, and the Supreme Court would doubtless pay deference to the local judgment on the ration-

---

173 (1915) 239 U. S. 33.

174 Missouri, Kansas & Texas Ry. Co. v. May (1904) 194 U. S. 267.

175 Clarke v. Deckebach (1927) 274 U. S. 392, 397.

ality of the discrimination made thereby. Thus if tillable land were scarce in California relative to the food needs of her population, the state might prescribe qualifications for farming that would exclude all not well qualified as productive operators. If such was the purpose of the California law it fits ill with the fact that the chief charge against "ineligible aliens", and the Japanese in particular, was that they were especially skillful and unduly industrious—particularly in intensive cultivation, involving hard personal labor. It would take a high degree of judicial deference to local judgment to believe that Japanese were the worst offenders in nonproductivity. There would be little room for applying the Court's doctrine: "If the law presumably hits the evil where it is most felt, it is not to be overthrown because there are other instances to which it might have been applied."[176]

The truth is that the real purpose of the California "ineligible alien" land law was to make the residence of Japanese in the state as little attractive as possible. Since the state lacked constitutional power to drive them across its borders by direct legislation, the attempt was made to approximate that objective by indirection. It had the same motive as the earlier agitation against the Chinese under the slogan "The Chinese must go".[177] In consequence the law denied to Japanese economic opportunity of a kind for which they had shown aptitude. Recent enactments of the legislature disclose that this motive persists, even against the small remnant of aged Japanese aliens now living in the state. One of these is a law with respect to who may obtain licenses for commercial fishing, enacted in 1943 and amended in 1945. A prior statute of 1933[178] granted this privilege to any "person", alien or citizen, "who has continuously resided within the United States for a period of one year immediately prior" to application. In 1943 this was amended to read, "A commercial fishing license may be issued to any person other than an alien Japanese."[179] In 1945 a committee of the legislature reported:

> "The committee, however, feels that there is danger of the present statute being declared unconstitutional, on the grounds of discrimination, since it is directed at alien Japanese. It is believed that this legal question can probably be eliminated by an amendment which has

---

[176] Radice v. New York (1924) 264 U. S. 292, 298.

[177] See Appendix A.

[178] Cal. Stats. 1933, p. 479 (§ 990).

[179] *Ibid.* 1943, p. 3040.

> been proposed to the bill which would make it apply to any alien who is ineligible to citizenship."

This recommendation resulted in enacting the provision now in force: "A commercial fishing license may be issued to any person other than a person ineligible to citizenship." Obviously that last phrase means racially ineligible and includes a trifling number of other alien residents of California along with the Japanese. Does this clever inclusion of a few other aliens, also determined by their race, save the law?

Will courts refuse to take judicial notice of the purpose of this law as shown by its legislative history? Even if they do refuse will it make any difference? The circumlocutionary phrase "ineligible to citizenship" has the same meaning as the phrase "aliens incapable of becoming electors of this State" in a California statute of 1880,[180] which prohibited fishing by such aliens. A circuit court of the United States held that the latter denied to Chinese the equal protection of the laws.[181] The court said, "It is obvious, . . . considered in connection with the public history of the times, that the act relating to fishing in question was not passed in pursuance of any public policy relating to the fisheries of the state as an end to be attained, but simply as a means of carrying out its policy of excluding the Chinese from the state, contrary to the provisions of the treaty."[182]

Likewise the statute of 1945 cannot be regarded as a fish-conservation measure since any person whatsoever may obtain a commercial fishing license except "ineligible aliens" of whom less than thirty thousand, men and women, reside in the state, and the persons eligible include a half-million other alien residents.

That to discourage the *residence* of alien Japanese in California is the legislative objective, and that the denial of particular economic opportunities is merely a means to that end, is further shown by the joint resolution of the legislature in 1944 petitioning Congress to provide for the deportation, at the end of the war, of all Japanese nationals residing in the United States.[183]

In the search for the purpose of California's discriminatory laws against "ineligible aliens" we end in finding that the purpose is to induce the withdrawal from the state of alien residents of a particular race or races, a purpose not within a state's competency. In con-

---

180 *Ibid.* 1880, p. 123.

181 *In re* Ah Chong (1880) 2 Fed. 733.

182 *Ibid.* at 737.

183 Cal. Stats. 1945, p. 101.

sequence, therefore, discussion whether the discrimination made in these laws has a rational relation to any legitimate state purpose seems uncalled for. How does this legislation differ from the San Francisco laundry ordinance under which none but Chinese were denied licenses? Of that ordinance the Supreme Court of the United States said:

> "The fact of this discrimination is admitted. No reason for it is shown, and the conclusion cannot be resisted, that no reason for it exists except hostility to the race and nationality to which the petitioners belong, and which in the eye of the law is not justified. The discrimination is, therefore, illegal, and the public administration which enforces it is a denial of the equal protection of the laws and a violation of the Fourteenth Amendment of the Constitution."[184]

A statute of the Philippines forbade "any person" to keep his business accounts "in any language other than English, Spanish, or any local dialect." The Supreme Court took judicial notice of the legislative history of the act, and said:

> "Nor is there any doubt that the Act, as a fiscal measure, was chiefly directed against the Chinese merchants. The discussion over its repeal in the Philippine Legislature leaves no doubt on this point. So far as the other merchants in the Islands are concerned, its results would be negligible and would operate without especial burden on other classes of foreign residents."[185]

The Court quoted[186] from a former opinion: "The question in each case is whether the legislature has adopted the statute in exercise of a reasonable discretion, or whether its action be a mere excuse for an unjust discrimination, or the oppression, or spoliation of a particular class."[187]

The Court concluded that the Philippine statute was "obviously intended chiefly to affect" the Chinese and was a denial to them of equal protection of the laws.[188] The opinion by Chief Justice Taft makes it clear that if the Philippine statute had confined its requirement to the keeping of particular accounts in a language known to public officials for the *purpose* of aiding detection of sales-tax evasions and had allowed Chinese to keep duplicates in their own lan-

---

184 Yick Wo v. Hopkins (1886) 118 U. S. 356, 374.

185 Yu Cong Eng v. Trinidad (1926) 271 U. S. 500, 514.

186 *Ibid.* at 526.

187 Holden v. Hardy (1898) 169 U. S. 366, 398.

188 271 U. S. at 528.

guage, the statute might have been sustained. The Court, however, found no purpose for the sweeping provision of the statute to which its discrimination was rationally related.

In 1925 Justice Butler, in summarizing his three opinions of 1923, in which the California law had been sustained, said that they rested on the proposition that "The State has a wide discretion and may classify persons on bases that are reasonable and germane having regard to the purpose of the legislation."[189]

In thus supposing that the long-settled interpretation of the equal protection clause had been applied in those decisions there seems to be error, through failure of the Court to penetrate to the purpose of the California law and through failure to fully consider whether it had any legitimate purpose to which its narrow and purely racial discrimination is germane.

APPENDIX A

THE ANTI-CHINESE LEGISLATION OF CALIFORNIA

California legislation against Orientals prior to 1913 was directed against the Chinese. In all the flood of discriminatory measures, however, the legislature made no attempt to curtail the rights of Chinese to hold land, and in that respect Chinese aliens in California had equal rights with citizens.

The period of anti-Chinese legislation ran from 1855 to 1891. At the end of that period there were about 107,000 Chinese in the continental United States, or 126,778 in the United States including Alaska and Hawaii.[190] Of these, 72,472, mostly aliens,[191] resided in California. This was a decrease since 1880, and so rapidly did the number continue to decrease that in 1910 there were only 27,778 alien Chinese and 8,470 American-citizen Chinese in the state. In 1890 it was believed by local observers that there were "twenty-odd thousand" Chinese in San Francisco, the chief center of anti-Chinese agitation.[192]

During the period of anti-Chinese legislation there were few Japanese in California. In 1860 there were none, in 1870, 33; in 1880, 86; in 1890, 1147, almost all foreign-born. The census shows no American-born Japanese in California until 1900, the number then being 143. In that year 10,008 alien Japanese were reported as residing in California. In 1910 the number was 38,184. By that time California's hostility had shifted from the Chinese to the Japanese. It may be added that by 1920 the number of alien Japanese in California had increased to 51,138, which was the peak,

---

189 Cockrill v. California (1925) 268 U. S. 258, 262.

190 12th Census of the United States: 1900, Population, Vol. I, p. cxxiii.

191 The Census of 1890 did not distinguish between the foreign born and the American born, except with respect to males, giving 64,065 as the number of China-born males residing in California.

192 See *In re* Lee Sing (1890) 43 Fed. 359, 361, and Wong Wai v. Williamson (1900) 103 Fed. 1, 6.

for the number has progressively declined ever since. At no time were the alien Japanese as numerous in California as were the Chinese in 1880, then numbering about 75,000.

The anti-Chinese laws and ordinances in some instances *expressly* named the Chinese as the only persons affected, while in other instances phrases of "indirection and circumlocution", as United States Circuit Judge Sawyer called them,[193] were used for the same purpose. Both the state and federal courts were astute to take judicial notice that it was the intention of the lawmakers to hit the Chinese only, and dealt with these laws and ordinances accordingly. The intentions of the American people in adopting the equal protection clause of the Fourteenth Amendment were fresh in the minds of these judges and they applied it in accordance with those intentions, although some of the anti-Chinese legislation was held to violate other provisions of the Constitution, particularly the commerce clause, and some of it to be in violation of treaty rights of the Chinese. The motives of the legislation against the Chinese were the same as those of the later legislation against the Japanese: to prevent or discourage their coming, and to induce those who had come to depart. At bottom the tactics were the same: to hit them where it hurt most, to deny them economic opportunities of the kinds they preferred. The Chinese, however, were not denied the right to own farm land because few of them engaged in farming.

A brief summary of California's anti-Chinese legislation follows.[194]

A statute of 1855[195] required any shipmaster who brought into California "any persons who are incompetent by the laws of the United States . . . to become citizens" to pay a fifty dollar tax for each person. The California supreme court held that this statute was an invasion by the state of the exclusive power of Congress under the commerce clause, and said, "We, therefore, decide that the act of this State, laying a tax of fifty dollars each on Chinese passengers, is invalid and void."[196]

In 1853 a uniform license fee was imposed upon all alien gold miners,[197] without distinction, but a statute of 1855 made a discrimination by imposing upon "each foreigner ineligible to become a citizen of the United States" a much heavier tax than on other alien gold miners.[198] Obviously it was the Chinese gold miner who was hit. The discrimination, however, was repealed the following year.[199] A statute of 1858[200] made it unlawful for "any person, or persons, of the Chinese or Mongolian races" to enter or be brought into the state. This statute it seems was held unconstitutional by the state supreme court in an unreported case.[201] In 1860 the legislature enacted that

[193] *In re* Ah Chong (1880) 2 Fed. 733, 740.

[194] See also, Weinstock and Landis, *Right of Chinese Aliens to Take Title to Land* (1944) 19 CAL. ST. BAR J. 19.

[195] Cal. Stats. 1855, p. 194.

[196] People v. Downer (1857) 7 Cal. 169, 171.

[197] Cal. Stats. 1853, p. 62.

[198] *Ibid.* 1855, p. 216.

[199] *Ibid.* 1856, p. 141.

[200] *Ibid.* 1858, p. 295.

[201] See Lin Sing v. Washburn (1862) 20 Cal. 534, 539.

"no Chinese or Mongolian" should take fish from the waters of the state without paying a monthly license fee.[202] This law was entitled "An Act for the Protection of Fisheries".

An act entitled "An Act to protect Free White Labor against competition with Chinese Coolie Labor, and to discourage the Immigration of the Chinese into the State of California" was passed in 1862.[203] It levied on "each person, male and female, of the Mongolian race of the age of eighteen years and upward", except those engaged in a few specified occupations, a monthly tax of $2.50, to be known as the "Chinese Police Tax". It is obvious that the legislature used the words "Mongolian" and "Chinese" as synonymous. The state supreme court bore down upon the declared purpose of this act "to discourage the immigration of Chinese" and held it a violation of the commerce clause,[204] notwithstanding that the statute did nothing to accomplish that purpose other than to lay a discriminatory tax on Chinese residents. The Fourteenth Amendment with its equal protection clause had not yet been adopted.

In 1850 the legislature had enacted a statute familiar in America from colonial times: "No black or mulatto person, or Indian, shall be permitted to give evidence in favor of, or against, any white person."[205] In 1863 the legislature, shifting its race prejudice, struck out the words "black or mulatto" and substituted "Mongolian, or Chinese". In 1870 the supreme court of California held that this statute did not deny to Chinese the equal protection of the laws,[206] this being the first decision in which that court failed to protect the Chinese from discriminatory legislation.

The constitution of 1879 was adopted at the height of the agitation against the Chinese. In confining to whites and Negroes its guaranty (article I, section 17) that resident aliens should have the same property rights as citizens, it obviously was intended to permit the legislature to restrict the property rights of resident aliens of other races, including Chinese, but prior to 1913 no such legislation was enacted.[207]

Article XIX of the constitution, headed "Chinese", directed the legislature to pass all necessary laws: (1) to forbid any corporation formed under the laws of the state to "employ, directly or indirectly, in any capacity, any Chinese or Mongolian"; (2) to forbid employment of "Chinese" on any state, county, municipal, or other public work; (3) to empower cities and towns to require "Chinese" either to remove from them or live in segregated areas therein; and (4) in general to do all in its power to discourage the immigration of "foreigners ineligible to become citizens" and in particular "to prohibit the introduction into this State of Chinese."

The legislature of 1880 hastened to act upon these mandates. Its statute[208] against employment of Chinese by domestic private corporations was

[202] Cal. Stats. 1860, p. 307.

[203] *Ibid.* 1862, p. 462.

[204] Lin Sing v. Washburn, *supra* note 201.

[205] Cal. Stats. 1849-1850, p. 230.

[206] People v. Brady (1870) 40 Cal. 198.

[207] See *supra* pp. 24-25.

[208] Acts Amendatory of the Penal Code, 1880, p. 1.

held invalid by a United States circuit court as being in conflict with a treaty with China, and also as a denial of equal protection of the laws.[209]

Another statute[210] authorized cities to enact ordinances to drive out the Chinese or segregate them, though it is now obvious that such ordinances would be unconstitutional.[211] By a third statute[212] the catching of fish for sale was forbidden to "all aliens incapable of becoming electors of this State." The use of this formula to define the proscribed class was doubtless suggested by article II of the constitution of 1879 which declared that "no native of China . . . shall ever exercise the privilege of an elector in this State."

United States Circuit Judge Sawyer, in holding this statute both in conflict with a treaty and a denial of equal protection, said that it was passed not "in pursuance of any policy relating to the fisheries of the state as an end to be attained, but simply as a means of carrying out its policy of excluding the Chinese from the state . . . ."[213] He took judicial notice of the history of the times to conclude that the statute's words, "all aliens incapable of becoming electors", meant Chinese, and said that the state could not accomplish an unconstitutional purpose "by indirection and circumlocution".[214]

Judge Sawyer also intimated that a fourth statute[215] of 1880 was unconstitutional for the same reason. It forbade state or local officials to issue a license "to transact any business or occupation . . . to any alien not eligible to become an elector of this State."

In 1891 the legislature prohibited "the coming of Chinese persons into the State, whether subjects of the Chinese Empire or otherwise."[216] The supreme court of the state held that this statute was "plainly in excess of the power of the State."[217]

This was the last act of the legislature directed at the Chinese. Several city ordinances against them were also frustrated by the federal courts. Three of them were intended to drive Chinese out of the humble occupation of laundryman [*In re Quong Woo*,[218] *In re Tie Loy* (The Stockton Laundry case)[219] and *Yick Wo v. Hopkins*[220]]. In the last case the ordinance was expressed in nondiscriminatory words but arbitrarily administered to deny laundry licenses to none but Chinese and for that reason was held a denial to them of equal protection of the laws. The Supreme Court of the United

[209] *In re* Parrott (1880) 1 Fed. 481.
[210] Cal. Stats. 1880, p. 22.
[211] Buchanan v. Warley (1917) 245 U. S. 60.
[212] Cal. Stats. 1880, p. 123.
[213] *In re* Ah Chong (1880) 2 Fed. 733, 737.
[214] *Ibid*. 737, 740.
[215] Cal. Stats. 1880, p. 39.
[216] *Ibid*. 1891, 185.
[217] *Ex parte* Ah Cue (1894) 101 Cal. 197, 198, 35 Pac. 556, 557.
[218] (1882) 13 Fed. 229.
[219] (1886) 26 Fed. 611.
[220] (1886) 118 U. S. 356.

States said, "No reason for it [the discrimination] is shown, and the conclusion cannot be resisted, that no reason for it exists except hostility to the race and nationality to which the petitioners belong, and which in the eye of the law is not justified."[221]

Another ordinance of San Francisco ordered "all Chinese", both aliens and American citizens, either to move out of the city or to segregate themselves, both for residence and the carrying on of business, within a prescribed area of the city, and was held invalid by a federal court.[222] Two other San Francisco ordinances met the same fate because of their discrimination against the Chinese.[223]

Of all the San Francisco anti-Chinese ordinances the "queue ordinance" of 1876 is the most notorious. On its face it applied to "every male person" imprisoned in the county jail, and provided that upon arrival the hair of his head should be "cut or clipped to an uniform length of one inch from the scalp." In holding that the ordinance denied to Chinese the equal protection of the laws Justice Field took judicial notice of the fact that at that time Chinese men regarded deprivation of their queues a mark of disgrace and that in spite of the generality of its wording "the ordinance was intended only for the Chinese." This was, he said, the intention avowed by the supervisors on its passage, and was so well understood by everyone, that it was known in the community as the "queue ordinance". He said:

> "When we take our seats on the bench we are not struck with blindness, and forbidden to know as judges what we see as men; and where an ordinance, though general in its terms, only operates upon a special race, sect or class, it being universally understood that it is to be enforced only against that race, sect or class, we may justly conclude that it was the intention of the body adopting it that it should only have such operation, and treat it accordingly."[224]

It will be noted that some of the statutes and ordinances against the Chinese were enacted after Congress had passed the Chinese Exclusion Act of 1882[225] which was unsatisfactory to anti-Chinese agitators in California because it merely suspended the immigration of Chinese *laborers,* and for ten years only. The suspension was extended for another ten years in 1892.[226] In 1902 Chinese laborers, skilled as well as unskilled, were excluded for the indefinite future.[227] By the Act of May 26, 1924,[228] all other classes of Chinese were denied entry as "immigrants", that is, for permanent residence. Before the last enactment, however, race prejudice in California had ceased to be directed toward the Chinese. The last remnant of San Francisco's discrimination against them, the segregation of Chinese chil-

[221] *Ibid.* at 374.

[222] *In re* Lee Sing, *supra* note 192.

[223] Wong Wai v. Williamson, *supra* note 192; Jew Ho v. Williamson (1900) 103 Fed. 10.

[224] Ho Ah Kow v. Nunan (1879) 12 Fed. Cas. 252, 255.

[225] Act of May 6, 1882, c. 126, § 1, 22 STAT. (1882) 58.

[226] 27 STAT. (1892) 25.

[227] 32 STAT. (1902) 176.

[228] § 13(e), 43 STAT. (1924) 162.

dren, citizens as well as aliens, in the public schools of the city, has fallen quietly into desuetude. The era of the opprobrious epithet, "the heathen Chinee", has become a shameful memory. In 1943 Congress removed the bar of racial ineligibility for naturalization of Chinese, repealed the Chinese Exclusion Acts, and assigned to the Chinese a quota of annual immigrants.[229] This abolition of discrimination against the Chinese met with hearty approval in California. The fact that making them racially eligible to naturalization causes the "ineligible alien" land acts of 1913 and 1920 no longer to apply to them arouses no resentment. It is a curious commentary upon the earlier dogma that Chinese are unassimilable in America, and upon the former intolerance of Chinese culture and customs, that the Chinese are now encouraged to display the latter, as in their celebration of the Chinese New Year, adding color and picturesqueness to the life of the community.

APPENDIX B

Illinois adheres to the common-law rules with respect to *all* aliens more closely than any other state. Her deviations from the common law are slight: an alien may acquire realty by descent, and realty held by an alien at his death will pass by his devise or, if he dies intestate, to his heirs. But however acquired, realty held by an alien is subject to forfeiture to the state, as at common law, with this further deviation that the alien is assured a six-year period of holding before forfeiture proceedings may be begun, to enable him to sell in good faith, giving an indefeasible title, or to preserve his holding by becoming a citizen.[230]

In Kentucky alien declarants have equal rights with citizens in acquiring, holding and transmitting realty, unless they are enemy aliens.[231] Other aliens, if residents, may "take and hold" land for a period of twenty-one years for any purpose, it seems, other than agricultural.[232] In no case is real estate "purchased" by an alien subject to forfeiture until after he has held it eight years and during that time and until actual forfeiture he may alienate an indefeasible title to a purchaser, lessee, heir or devisee, provided the transferee is a citizen. Moreover, the alien may keep the realty if he becomes a citizen within the eight-year period.[233] The common law is also modified with respect to nonresident aliens by allowing them to take Kentucky realty by descent, but they must alienate it within eight years to escape forfeiture.[234]

Missouri's departures from the common law against realty-holding by aliens are slight. Any alien may acquire realty in Missouri by inheritance, by devise, and by proceedings for the collection of debts, and hold realty so acquired without liability to forfeiture. The statute makes an unclear

[229] Act of December 17, 1943, 57 STAT. (1943) 600.

[230] ILL. REV. STAT. (1943) c. 6, §§ 1, 2.

[231] KY. STAT. (1942) § 381.290.

[232] *Ibid.* § 381.320.

[233] *Ibid.* § 381.300.

[234] *Ibid.* § 381.330.

reference to alien declarants as if they might have greater rights than other aliens.[235]

So also Nebraska retains much of the common law against the holding of realty by aliens. Any alien, however, may acquire and hold a leasehold in any realty for a term not exceeding five years. A resident alien may acquire title to any realty by devise or descent and hold for five years, or he may acquire title in the course of proceedings to collect a debt due him, and hold for ten years.[236] Any alien may "purchase" and hold as much real estate as is necessary for manufacturing establishments or for the storage and sale of petroleum products.[237]

Nevada formerly gave both resident[238] and nonresident aliens[239] equal rights with citizens to acquire and hold realty, but since 1924 has made the surprising discrimination of reverting to the common law with respect to resident aliens while still giving nonresident aliens "except subjects of the Chinese empire" equal rights with citizens, with the exception that the acquisition of property by will or by intestacy by a nonresident alien is made dependent upon reciprocal treatment of American citizens by an alien's country.[240]

In Texas the common law against landholding by aliens is in force with some exceptions: (1) it does not apply to land in an incorporated town or city; (2) it does not apply to certain classes of aliens so long as they are residents of the state, *viz.*, (a) alien declarants; (b) aliens who are natural-born citizens of countries that have a common land boundary with the United States; and (3) any alien prohibited from holding is in reality allowed to hold a minimum of five years if he acquires the realty by descent, devise, or in collection of a debt. In other cases forfeiture proceedings may be begun at any time. In any case an alien who acquires a defeasible title may prior to institution of forfeiture proceedings convey an indefeasible title if the conveyance is to a citizen.[241]

---

235 Mo. Rev. Stat. (1939) §§ 15228, 15230.

236 Neb. Rev. Stat. (1943) §§ 76-402, 76-405, 76-411.

237 Neb. Laws 1945, p. 573.

238 Nev. Const. (1864) art. I, sec. 16, repealed Nov. 4, 1924.

239 Act of February 27, 1879, still in force. Nev. Comp. Laws (Hillyer, 1929) § 6365.

240 Act of March 28, 1941. Nev. Comp. Laws (Hillyer, Supp. 1931-1941) § 9894.

241 Tex. Stat. (Vernon, Centennial ed. 1936) arts. 166 *et seq.*

European Immigrant and Oriental Alien: Acceptance and Rejection by the California Legislature of 1913

SPENCER C. OLIN, JR.

The author is assistant professor of history in the University of California, Irvine.

AFTER THE POLITICAL CATHARSIS of the Bull Moose campaign of 1912, many California progressives had had enough of reform. Their original reform goals had been three: "turn out the railroad villains," "purify" the administration of governmental affairs, and "democratize" the political system. Such a general program had offended few people and had received enthusiastic endorsement by a large majority of the state's citizens. In fact, the great strength of the California reform movement of 1910–1911 was due to the relatively uncontroversial nature of its "ideology" and to its consequent broad appeal. But by 1913 the pledges of the 1910 campaign had been fulfilled. The Southern Pacific Railroad Company had been kicked out of politics, state agencies had been fumigated by a newly created Board of Control, and the people had been given additional political power through direct legislation measures. Was there more to be done? Could more be asked of them?

Before the legislature of 1913 convened, it had become quite apparent that the basic unity which characterized the California progressive movement in the earlier years no longer existed. Conflict was inevitable between those legislators who felt that reform had gone far enough and those who recognized the necessity for additional legislation. Governor Hiram Johnson's opening address to the session seemed designed to pacify the former element, as he asked only for two specific measures: higher corporate taxes and the creation of a state administrative board to manage all state institutions and to have powers commensurate with the financial jurisdiction of the Board of Control. But if Johnson did not publicly urge the 1913 legislature to enact sweeping reforms, and if he had no well-formulated legislative program of his own, it is to his credit that he supported and helped push through the legislature several progressive measures advocated by various pressure groups and influential citizens.

The session of 1913, though less memorable than that of 1911, considered and passed a significant body of legislation. Among the most important was the establishment of three new state agencies—an Industrial Welfare Commission, an Industrial Accident Commission, and a Commission of Immigration and Housing—and the passage of an Alien Land Law. Neither the Industrial Welfare Commission nor the Industrial Accident Commission will be discussed here. Rather, discussion centers on the concern for the plight of the European immigrant, expressed in the creation of a Commission of Immigration and Housing, and on the simultaneous disregard for the rights of the Oriental alien, expressed in the passage of an Alien Land Law.

It is true that the living conditions of Japanese workers engaged in agricultural labor were also improved by accomplishments of the Commission of Immigration and Housing. Yet when these same Orientals began to buy their own land, and to monopolize cheap farm labor, they presented an economic threat to American farm owners which could not be ignored.

California agriculture has always been dependent upon a large, mobile supply of cheap labor. As Henry George pointed out in *Progress and Poverty*, published in 1879, the early agricultural development of the state resulted in large-scale farming units worked by wage laborers, and not in extensive farm tenancy.[1] Such an agricultural system attracted thousands of unskilled aliens to California and dictated the substandard living conditions of a large portion of this population. Chinese, Japanese, Mexicans, Filipinos, and native migrants followed the harvests, living in camps or "jungles." Inadequate housing conditions and poor sanitary facilities resulted in

[1] Charles A. Barker, "Henry George and the California Background of *Progress and Poverty*," *California Historical Society Quarterly*, XXIV (1945), 109.

sporadic uprisings in California's "factories in the fields," such as the famous Wheatland hop fields riot of 1913.[2]

In addition, thousands of immigrants from southern and eastern Europe flocked to California, lured by the advertised promise of wealth, health, and happiness. Once here, however, they often found that the Golden State for the immigrant was a kind of Hell. For them life was dismal; they were underfed, underpaid, exploited, and ignorant of the language and of their rights under American law. Many returned to their native lands, but many stayed, hoping for a better future.

These aliens, whether living with their families in rural labor camps or in urban slums, constituted a serious challenge to an administration concerned with social amelioration. The Johnson administration accepted the challenge, and a liberal reformer named Simon Lubin provided the main thrust. The result was the creation of perhaps the most important of the three social welfare agencies established in 1913—the Commission of Immigration and Housing. Launching a program of immigrant assimilation unparalleled in the United States at that time, this agency was a pioneer not only in immigrant housing, but in education and labor camp inspection.

"To Simon Lubin more than any man," writes Samuel E. Wood, a specialist on problems created by immigration, "must be credited the creation of the Commission of Immigration and Housing. He insisted upon an independent agency, invested with powers adequate to cope with the complexity of the immigration problem in this state." [3] Lubin selected the personnel of the commission and as its president was instrumental in determining the policy and charting the activities of the agency for ten years.

Simon Lubin, born in Sacramento in 1876, was the son of David Lubin and the nephew of Harris Weinstock, both prosperous Sacramento merchants and crusaders for industrial and agrarian reform.[4]

---

[2] Charleton H. Parker's report to Governor Hiram Johnson on the causes of the Wheatland riot, reprinted in his *The Casual Laborer and Other Essays* (New York, 1920), 171–199. His account of the Wheatland episode in Chapter II is most informative. Parker was executive secretary of the Commission of Immigration and Housing.

[3] See the excellent and neglected work by Samuel E. Wood, "The California State Commission of Immigration and Housing: A Study of Administrative Organization and the Growth of Function" (unpublished Ph.D. dissertation, University of California, Berkeley, 1942), p. 82.

[4] For a biography of David Lubin see Olivia Rossetti Agresti, *David Lubin: A Study in Practical Idealism* (Berkeley, 1941). Lubin and his stepbrother, Harris Weinstock, opened a dry goods store in Sacramento in 1874. Within ten years it was the largest department store and mail order house on the Pacific coast. Lubin was also a founder of

Educated at Harvard, Simon Lubin spent his college vacations working in the lower East Side of New York. From 1903 to 1904 he was a resident of South End House, a Boston social settlement. During his last two years at Harvard he made special investigations of immigrant problems in New York and Boston. In 1906 he returned to California. From then until his death in 1936 he was secretary and manager of Weinstock, Lubin, and Company of Sacramento. The employee-employer relationships of this company were characterized by advanced schemes of management—employee representation, credit unions, and retirement systems. Much of California's social legislation during this period was drafted by Lubin at his desk in the company offices.[5]

Lubin's first conversation with Governor Johnson regarding a state program directed at the immigrant problem was just prior to the Bull Moose convention in 1912. Johnson discussed Lubin's suggestions with "some of those in whom I have confidence" during the convention and after his return to California.[6] The social worker-businessman continued to urge immediate action and finally prevailed upon Johnson to appoint a special committee which would submit a report to the next session of the legislature. On August 21, 1912, Lubin received his appointment to this committee. At the same time, Johnson wrote Lubin his own personal thoughts on planning for the future. "My hope," explained the governor, "is that by timely action on our part, even if the immigration diverted to us by the opening of the Panama Canal shall be as great as that which in recent years has come to the Atlantic Coast, we may prevent the dreadful conditions of poverty that prevail in the great cities there." [7]

The temporary agency recommended legislation to create a permanent commission rather than attempting to strengthen existing state agencies. Lubin prepared a rough draft of an act creating an unpaid Commission of Industries and Labor, consisting of five members appointed by the governor. This commission was to direct and

---

the International Institute of Agriculture in Rome and devoted much of his life after 1885 to agricultural matters.

[5] Wood, "The California State Commission of Immigration and Housing," 83–85. All Lubin letters mentioned hereafter are cited in this dissertation. The Lubin Papers are housed in the Bancroft Library, but certain sections are restricted.

[6] Johnson to Simon Lubin, Aug. 15, 1912, Lubin Papers.

[7] Johnson to Simon Lubin, Aug. 20, 1912, Lubin Papers. Other appointees included Robert Watchorn and Reverend Dana W. Bartlett of Los Angeles and Katherine Felton and Robert N. Lynch of San Francisco. Also see Franklin Hichborn's article in the Sacramento *Bee*, March 8, 1913.

supervise a Bureau of Industry and Immigration and appoint all its employees.[8]

Lubin met with Johnson in late November, 1912, after which he reported to a fellow committeeman that he was sure the governor had "caught the spirit of the act." Johnson liked the idea of an unpaid commission which would determine policy and hire paid experts to administer the program. He advised Lubin to prepare a memorandum for the Board of Control, explaining the organization and proposed expenditures of the commission. In this memorandum Lubin recommended an appropriation of $50,000.00 a year to support the commission.[9]

While Johnson officially sponsored the measure and chose specific legislators to lead the fight in the Senate and assembly, he left the mobilization of pressure and the handling of the opposition to Lubin and his fellow committeemen. During the spring of 1913 Lubin remained in Sacramento to press for the passage of his bill. He arranged for witnesses to appear at committee hearings. He convinced C. K. McClatchy to wage an editorial battle for the bill in the Sacramento *Bee*. He prepared articles for newspapers and saw to it that letters were written to key legislators.[10] The legislature, responding favorably, passed the measure (which included a $50,000.00 appropriation for the gathering of information and data), and sent it to the governor in June.[11]

Members of the new commission were well aware of the general conditions under which aliens lived in California. But they lacked factual data upon which to base a specific remedial program. The first order of business, therefore, was to employ housing experts and special investigators to make field surveys. Between April 1 and August 11, 1914, 641 labor camps in every county of the state, housing over 41,000 laborers, were inspected. Of the total number, 188 were found to be in dangerous sanitary condition, and only 195 met the modest minimum sanitation standards established by the commission. In addition to labor camps, the commission's experts investigated lodging houses and tenements in the larger cities, into which newly arrived Spanish, Mexican, Portuguese, and Italian families were

[8] Lubin to commissioners, Nov. 2, 1912, Lubin Papers.

[9] Lubin to Robert Lynch, Nov. 23, 1912, Lubin Papers. Also see Wood, "The California State Commission of Immigration and Housing," 95.

[10] Wood, *op. cit.*, 102.

[11] By September, Johnson had announced his appointments to the new commission: Simon Lubin as Chairman, Reverend Edward J. Hanna, Paul Scharrenberg, Mrs. Frank A. Gibson, and Authur J. Fleming.

packed like sardines.[12] These various surveys resulted in thirty-five special reports, three of which were eventually published.[13]

The commission's *Report on Unemployment*, published in December, 1914, called for the creation of a state bureau of labor exchanges with branch offices in major cities. It urged the passage of adequate camp sanitation laws and a complete revision of the state's housing laws. It also recommended legislation to prevent and punish fraud and misrepresentation in the sale of agricultural land. Governor Johnson was very enthusiastic about this report, and Lubin described his reaction in a letter to Mrs. Frank Gibson, a fellow commissioner:

> In all my contact with the Governor I never saw him so enthusiastic. He asked a great many questions, and then began to give again his opinion of the value of our work in the state, saying that he thought the real fruits of our efforts would not be seen until most of us had passed away. . . . He said that we could expect his cooperation at every stage of the game, and that he wants us to know that he is in entire sympathy with all we are trying to do.[14]

It was not until 1915 that the legislature authorized the Bureau of Labor Statistics to establish free employment bureaus in specific cities, passed a Labor Camp Act which required proper bedding, bathing, and eating facilities in all labor camps, and created a State Colonization and Rural Credits Committee.[15] But a substantial beginning was made during 1913 and 1914 to ameliorate the conditions under which immigrants in California were forced to live. Californians had invited the world to share the blessings of their state. The least the legislature could do was to insure that those blessings could be enjoyed by all who accepted that invitation.

---

[12] Charleton H. Parker, "State Commission of Immigration and Housing," *Labor Clarion*, XIII (Sept. 4, 1914), 56–57. For a thorough discussion of the commission's remarkable activities with respect to labor camp inspection, immigrant education, and housing see the *Second Annual Report of the Commission of Immigration and Housing, January 2, 1916* (Sacramento, 1916), *passim*.

[13] Wood cites the *Report on Unemployment to His Excellency. Governor Hiram Johnson* (Sacramento, 1914), which includes two studies: "Life-History Statistics" and "Employment Agency Situation in California." The third published report was "The Wheatland Hop Field Riot," which may be found in U. S., Senate, Subcommittee of the Commission on Education and Labor, *Hearings, Agricultural Labor in California*, 76th Cong. 3rd sess., Part 54, 20069–20072. Summaries of all the surveys are found in the Annual Reports of the Commission of Immigration and Housing for 1915 and 1916.

[14] Lubin to Mrs. Frank Gibson, (undated), 1915, Commission File, cited in Wood, "The California State Commission of Immigration and Housing," 258n.

[15] See Earl C. Crockett, "The History of California Labor Legislation, 1910–1930" (unpublished Ph.D. dissertation, 1931), 240 and Wood, *op. cit.*, 188–189. For the early activities of the free employment bureaus see the *Labor Clarion*, Sept. 1, 1916, 8–10.

It may seem strange that an administration so concerned about the plight of the immigrant would at the same time support legislation designed to restrict the activities of a large portion of the state's alien population, the Orientals. Yet twice within a period of seven years, Californians, by their actions against the Japanese, embarrassed the national government and involved it in international difficulties.

There had been no significant anti-Japanese legislation passed in California prior to 1913, but there had been a long struggle for Japanese exclusion.[16] This struggle was highlighted, in 1905, by the formation of the Asiatic Exclusion League in San Francisco, and, in 1906, by the San Francisco school board's segregation of Japanese and Korean students from American. The Gentlemen's Agreement of 1907 temporarily decreased Japanese immigration, but California exclusionists were not completely satisfied.

So long as the Japanese remained wage laborers, agitation against them came largely from nonfarm groups which feared competition from "cheap labor." Farmer-employers, on the other hand, welcomed this source of mobile, cheap labor. As one Fresno fruit grower explained in January, 1907: ". . . we are wholly dependent upon [Japanese] labor. If they are excluded, we shall have to give up our farms and go out of business." [17]

However, a shift of Japanese population from urban to rural areas after 1908 increased anti-Japanese feeling in those districts, especially in the Central Valley. The Japanese began to acquire land and to employ as workers members of their own race exclusively, thereby reducing the farm labor pool. As Japanese land owners began to monopolize such cheap farm labor, they incurred the animus of both large and small growers. The Japanese were no longer merely a convenient source of manpower, but had gradually become active competitors for farm labor, farm land, and agricultural markets. "The real prejudice against the Japanese," writes Carey McWilliams, "dates from the time when they began to be small owners, rather than farm laborers." [18]

Yet in 1909 there were still approximately 30,000 Japanese occu-

---

[16] For a good account of anti-Orientalism during the Johnson administration see Roger B. Daniels' *The Politics of Prejudice: The Anti-Japanese Movement in California and the Struggle for Japanese Exclusion* (Berkeley, 1962), particularly pp. 16–64.

[17] See Herbert B. Johnson, *Discrimination against Japanese in California* (Berkeley, 1907), 42, quoting from the San Francisco *Chronicle*, Jan. 2, 1907.

[18] Carey McWilliams, *Factories in the Field* (Boston, 1939), 111. Also see Fred H. Matthews, "White Community and 'Yellow Peril,' " *Mississippi Valley Historical Review*, (1964), 618.

pied in agricultural labor in California. They were employed chiefly during cultivation and harvest, but were far more difficult to manage than the Chinese had been. Their characteristic independence was bemoaned by large growers, one of whom expressed his dismay in this manner:

> The Chinese when they were here were ideal. They were patient, plodding, and uncomplaining in the performance of the most menial service. They submitted to anything, never violating a contract. The exclusion acts drove them out. The Japanese now coming are a tricky and cunning lot, who break contracts and become quite independent.[19]

These feelings of irritation at the continued threat to the existence of large units of production and dismay at the decrease in the supply of cheap, manageable labor were manifested in increased anti-Japanese activity in the California legislature. When such economic pressures were merged with latent social and racial hostility, the issue was sure to become of prime political importance.

During the 1910 campaign, Democrats monopolized the anti-Oriental issue. Hiram Johnson decided not to take a public stand on the question and turned down invitations to address the Asiatic Exclusion League. But he did assure A. E. Yoell, the League's secretary, that he favored exclusion.[20] Once elected, however, Johnson informed Philander Knox, President Taft's secretary of state, that he would do everything he could to prevent the passage of anti-Oriental legislation in 1911. Johnson successfully bottled up such legislation in committee and no measures passed.[21]

In 1913, California business leaders in charge of organizing the Panama-Pacific International Exposition worked to quash further discriminatory legislation for fear it might impair trade relations with Japan and China. Chester Rowell, a member of the exposition's Advisory Council and a close friend of Johnson, explained to him in January, 1913, that the Japanese Diet was about to convene and would be debating its proposed budget. Included in that budget was an appropriation of some $1,500,000.00 for the exposition. Rowell

---

[19] California Fruit Growers' Convention *Proceedings,* 1907, p. 69, as quoted in the California State Relief Administration's study, *Migratory Labor in California* (Sacramento, 1936), 22. Chester Rowell repeated this charge in 1909: "The one overshadowing contrast is this: The Chinese will keep a contract; the Japanese will not." See "Chinese and Japanese in America," *The Annals of the American Academy of Political and Social Science,* XXXIV (1909), 5.

[20] Johnson to A. E. Yoell, May 18 and July 29, 1910, Johnson Papers.

[21] Johnson to Knox, Jan. 6, 1911, Johnson Papers.

and his fellow commissioners feared that if that item were defeated or slashed, it might seriously harm the exposition. Johnson was urged to press for postponement of anti-Oriental legislation. "There is no immediate urgency in passing the bill at all," Rowell declared. "The law must be passed ultimately, if California is not to be Hawaiianized, but there is no emergency so long as Japan continues in good faith to carry out the present arrangement." [22]

Johnson, in turn, suggested that a committee from the exposition come to Sacramento and address a conference of legislators. The commissioners were reluctant initially, fearing that such action might over-dramatize the issue and provoke adverse reaction.[23] Eventually they agreed to accept the governor's suggestion and met with him prior to the opening of the legislative session. Johnson assured the nine-man delegation that he would support their efforts to head off an alien land act. The delegation then met individually with nearly every senator and assemblyman in an effort to quash any legislation dealing with aliens.

Their efforts were in vain, for when the session opened anti-Japanese measures were submitted by Democrats and Republicans in both houses. Johnson later explained to Theodore Roosevelt that the exposition officials might have succeeded in their task had not many legislators, up to that time uncommitted, been persuaded by the impressive testimony of farmers from various communities in the state. "These farmers insisted that an alien land bill was absolutely essential for their protection, and necessary for the future welfare of California," Johnson reported.[24]

Perhaps equally important was the challenge presented to Johnson and California politicians by the federal government's intervention in April, 1913. For Johnson, this intervention was a major event, marking "the breaking down of the barrier that has heretofore existed between the national government and legislation in the states." [25]

After Woodrow Wilson had taken office, Johnson had informed Rowell of his suspicions that such pressures would be exerted to

---

[22] Rowell to Johnson, Jan. 6, 1913, Rowell Papers.

[23] Rowell to Johnson, March 16, 1913, Rowell Papers.

[24] Johnson to Roosevelt, June 21, 1913, Johnson Papers. As Robert Kelley points out in a recent article, V. S. McClatchy, president of the Sacramento *Bee* and owner of 1,200 acres of land in the Sutter Basin, was an avid opponent of Japanese immigration: ". . . If he was creating a farm empire for the purpose of preserving what agrarians always regarded as the bedrock of American society, the family farm, the families on them had also to be traditionally American, not Japanese." *Pacific Historical Review*, XXXIV (1965), 46–47.

[25] Johnson to Roosevelt, June 21, 1913, Johnson Papers.

block discriminatory legislation.[26] Much to Johnson's surprise, however, Wilson did not immediately intervene to thwart anti-Oriental measures. In fact, the President even encouraged Democratic politicians in California to continue their course: "I have never been inclined to criticize," Wilson wrote James D. Phelan. "I have only hoped that the doing of the thing might be so modulated and managed as to offend the susceptibilities of a friendly nation as little as possible." [27]

Rather than intervene directly in California's affairs, Wilson chose to express his point of view to Representative William Kent, a progressive from northern California. During an interview held the first week of April, 1913, Wilson suggested to Kent that California legislators might frame their bill in less offensive form by excluding from land ownership those persons who had not applied for American citizenship, without singling out the Japanese. Kent relayed this suggestion to Hiram Johnson, and the doughty governor replied that Wilson should communicate with him directly if he had anything to propose.[28]

The President's dilemma was temporarily resolved when Johnson agreed to his request that Secretary of State William Jennings Bryan consult with the California governor. But Bryan's mission was hopeless from the beginning, for the legislature was more than ever determined to pass an anti-alien measure. By the time Bryan arrived in Sacramento, substantial progress had been made preparing a bill for passage.

During a period of one week Bryan summoned various senators and assemblymen for personal interviews, discussing with them the diplomatic consequences of anti-Oriental legislation and urging them to reconsider their views. His overtures were completely disregarded. In early May the Alien Land Bill passed the Senate by a vote of 35 to 2 and the Assembly 72 to 5.[29] Limiting leases of agricultural land to Japanese to maximum terms of three years, the law barred further land purchases by Japanese aliens. Aliens eligible for citizenship, on the other hand, could own property without limitation.

---

[26] Johnson to Rowell, March 17, 1913, Rowell Papers.

[27] Wilson to Phelan, April 9, 1913, Wilson Papers, as quoted in Arthur S. Link, *Wilson: The New Freedom* (Princeton, 1956), 290.

[28] See William Kent, "Some Reminiscences of Hiram Johnson," manuscript in the Kent Papers, Yale University; Kent to Johnson, April 7, 1913, Wilson Papers, Library of Congress; and Johnson to Kent, April 8, 1913, Kent Papers—all cited in Link, *op. cit.*, 290–291.

[29] *Journal of the Senate, 1913*, p. 2324; *Journal of the Assembly, 1913*, p. 2495.

Johnson promised Bryan that he would not sign the bill until the secretary had conferred with President Wilson. On May 11, 1913, Bryan sent Johnson a telegram suggesting that the bill be vetoed. In his lengthy reply, Johnson clearly stated California's position, stressing the fact that, in his opinion, the federal government had established the precedent for Oriental discrimination. It was California, not the Oriental, which was being discriminated against. Accordingly, on May 19, 1913, Johnson signed the bill.[30]

The Asiatic Exclusion League immediately announced that it intended to invoke direct legislation against the Alien Land Act and to substitute a law prohibiting Japanese from either owning or leasing any land in California. Despite some dissatisfaction with the bill, however, most Californians seemed to feel that the problem of Orientals had been laid to rest. As a result, there was very little anti-Japanese agitation for the remainder of Johnson's tenure in office.

What role did Johnson play in the passage of the Alien Land Act of 1913? What beliefs and political calculations motivated him? In late March of 1913 he had assured the Panama-Pacific Exposition delegation that he would support their efforts to head off the alien land bill. Yet Roger Daniels, author of a detailed study of the movement for Japanese exclusion in California, reports: "it is now quite clear that from the middle of March Johnson was the behind-the-scenes manager of the alien land bill.[31] In support of this statement Daniels cites a telegram of March 23 from Johnson to Rowell: "HAVE INFORMED [Assemblyman E. S.] BIRDSALL [sponsor of a general anti-alien bill] THAT HE MAY ACT IF HE DESIRES." [32] What caused Johnson to so instruct Birdsall? What prompted him to renege on his promise to the Panama-Pacific Exposition delegation? Daniels does not discuss the reasons for Johnson's switch from opposition to support of the bill, but several may be advanced.

Johnson obviously enjoyed his skirmish with the federal govern-

---

[30] See Johnson's reply to Bryan of May 14, 1913, Johnson Papers. Also see Thomas A. Bailey, "California, Japan, and the Alien Land Legislation of 1913." *Pacific Historical Review*, (1932), 40.

The Naturalization Act of 1906 restricted naturalization to white persons and persons of African descent, and by a special Act of Congress Chinese were specifically barred. There was no direct provision relating to Japanese, but, West Coast exclusionists assumed that the Japanese, being neither white nor of African descent, were not entitled to naturalization.

[31] Daniels, *The Politics of Prejudice*, 59.

[32] *Ibid.*, 135, note 66.

ment, although he admitted afterwards that he had never "skated on thinner ice than . . . in the contest with Mr. Bryan."[33] Writing to Theodore Roosevelt, Johnson exulted: "We have shown the Democratic doctrine of 'State's rights' to be sham and pretense, insisted upon when it is their state that is affected but denied when they represent the federal government and our State is affected."[34] In waging a victorious battle against the federal government on behalf of "states rights," Johnson not only succeeded in embarrassing the Wilson administration but also in attracting national publicity.

It is also probable that Johnson saw the handwriting on the wall: if the legislature were bound and determined to pass the Alien Land Law, why should he risk his political neck to fight for its defeat? What must be stressed is Johnson's belief that the passage of the bill was essential for his own political survival. In a particularly revealing letter to Meyer Lissner, Johnson commented on recent progressive defections:

> You can not make people be good faster than they want to be good. . . . Communities will stand just so much reform legislation at one time, and wise is the man who intuitively has some conception of just how far he can go. . . . Indeed, our legislation had brought us to the very verge of disaster. . . . The alien land bill rehabilitated us north of Tehachapi; but aside from the right of the alien land bill, its necessity etc., it was the most fortunate thing that ever occurred from a political standpoint.[35]

Anti-Oriental legislation thus became the means by which Johnson could regain the esteem which he felt had been lost by his support of "excessively radical" legislation. Such demagoguery was not uncharacteristic of Johnson, but the fact that he was willing to involve the United States government in international difficulties mainly to enhance his own political position makes his actions seem quite irresponsible.

Daniels has pointed out that Johnson's support of the alien land bill was particularly wanton because he "knew well that Japanese land tenure in California would not be seriously affected by it."[36] As Californians quickly discovered, the Alien Land Law was rendered ineffective when the Japanese continued to buy and lease land in the names of their children who were American citizens. Orientals

[33] Johnson to Lissner, May 7, 1913, Johnson Papers.
[34] Johnson to Roosevelt, June 21, 1913, Johnson Papers.
[35] Johnson to Lissner, June 9, 1913, Johnson Papers.
[36] Daniels, *The Politics of Prejudice*, 63.

also formed corporations and bought or leased land in the corporate name, after issuing a majority of the capital stock to American citizens, who served as trustees. In 1920 a new land law remedied these "defects": Japanese were thereafter prohibited from buying or selling land in the names of their children or through the medium of corporations.[37]

While it was possible to evade the law, it must not be assumed that Japanese farmers were not seriously affected by the Alien Land Law. Often the Japanese would win their court cases and be impoverished in the process. The anti-alien laws made land ownership uncertain and subject to the whims of politicians and district attorneys.[38] Progressives of both parties were responsible for this unfortunate affront to the dignity of the Japanese people. Ostensibly dedicated to the principles of democracy, yet blinded by racial prejudice, these "reformers" were so influenced by unfounded fears of Oriental inundation that they participated in an essentially undemocratic act.

Despite the reluctance of many progressive legislators to proceed farther along the reform path, the 1913 legislature established an impressive record, marred only by the Alien Land Law. Social welfare legislation set the pattern for the session, and individuals such as Simon Lubin provided the main impetus for the passage of these measures. Characteristic of the California progressives' "scientific" approach to social and economic problems was the creation of numerous commissions—the Industrial Welfare Commission, the Industrial Accident Commission, and the Commission of Immigration and Housing. Yet it was the Johnson Administration's commitment to the immigrant, in the form of a special commission, which was most unique and significant. The activities and accomplishments of Simon Lubin's Commission of Immigration and Housing expressed a deep concern for the plight of the immigrant, especially the immigrant of European stock. It is unfortunate, though typically in character, that the progressives' concern was not coupled with an understanding of the aspirations of nonwhite aliens.

---

[37] *Ibid.* Also see the State Board of Control report, *California and the Oriental* (Sacramento, 1920), 135; U.S., H.R., Committee on Immigration and Naturalization, *Hearings on Japanese Immigration 1920,* 66th Cong. 2d sess., pp. 98–99; and T. Iyenaga and Kenoske Sato, *Japan and the California Problem* (New York, 1921), 139–140. The 1913 Alien Land Law is reprinted in its entirety on pp. 204–206 of the latter work; the 1920 law on pp. 207–215.

[38] See T. Scott Miyakawa's review of *The Politics of Prejudice* in the *Southern California Quarterly,* XLVI (1964), 107–108.

California Law Review

Volumn XII. MAY, 1924 Number 4

Alien Land Cases in United States Supreme Court

In four cases involving statutes of Washington and of California the Supreme Court of the United States has sustained the power of the states, under existing treaties with Japan, to prevent Japanese subjects from becoming lessees of agricultural land,[1] from becoming stockholders in a corporation authorized to own agricultural land,[2] and from making so-called "cropping contracts" for cultivating such land.[3] The major issues involved in these decisions have already been treated in the pages of this Review[4] and the discussion here will content itself with an exposition and analysis of the Supreme Court opinions in the recent cases. The most serious problem was presented by the "cropping-contract" case from California. In this case the Supreme Court quite patently misinterpreted the California statute of 1920[5] and inadequately distinguished the decision of the Supreme Court of California in the Okahara Case[6] which put upon that statute a binding interpretation. Whether these intellectual mishaps rendered the Supreme Court decision erroneous is another and more difficult question. This, however, is of speculative rather than of practical significance, for the California statute of 1923[7] explicitly interdicts such cropping contracts.

I.—The Question of Injunctive Relief.

The issue in each of these cases arose through a bill brought by a citizen and alien jointly to restrain state officers from threatening interference with the carrying out of proposed contracts. Justices McReynolds and Brandeis dissented in each case on the ground that

[1] Terrace v. Thompson (1923) 263 U. S. 197, 68 L. Ed.—,44 Sup. Ct. Rep. 15; Porterfield v. Webb (1923) 263 U. S. 225, 68 L. Ed. —, 44 Sup. Ct. Rep. 21.

[2] Frick v. Webb (1923) 263 U. S. 326, 68 L. Ed. —, 44 Sup. Ct. Rep. 115.

[3] Webb v. O'Brien (1923) 263 U. S. 313, 68 L. Ed. —, 44 Sup. Ct. Rep. 112.

[4] See 10 California Law Review, 56, 94, 494.

[5] Cal. Stats. 1921, p. lxxxvii.

[6] In the Matter of Okahara (1923) 66 Cal. Dec. 15, 216 Pac. 614.

[7] Cal. Stats. 1923, p. 1020.

there was no justiciable question and that the case should therefore have been dismissed. They have dissented in earlier cases on the same ground, but the majority of the court seems to be convinced that this is an appropriate method of raising constitutional issues. The practice was employed in a number of cases without being questioned in the Supreme Court. The Arizona anti-alien statute,[8] the Adamson Law[9] and the first federal Child Labor Law[10] came before the court in similar proceedings. The War Prohibition Act was sustained in a proceeding against a federal district attorney and Mr. Justice Brandeis wrote the opinion in Ruppert v. Caffey[11] without objecting to the way in which the issue came before him. On the strength of these and other cases[12] the Supreme Court in Kennington v. Palmer[13] enjoined the attorney general from seeking to enforce the Lever Act. This seems to be the first decision outside of rate cases in which the point of procedure was explicitly adjudicated by the Supreme Court. Mr. Justice McReynolds filed no indication of dissent. Chief Justice White did not discuss the matter but contented himself with referring in the margin to the cases in which the practice had developed Topsy-like without evoking comment. Now that the practice is approved by so large a majority of the court, it should cease to provoke further dissent which may deprive the quondam objectors of full freedom in expressing themselves on the substantive issues raised thereby.

Obviously the practice has great advantages. It would have been most unfortunate if no proceeding to test the constitutionality of the Adamson Law could have been started until after the law had become in force and been violated. Even with this method of raising the objections to the War Prohibition Act, the decision rejecting part of the Government's interpretation of the statute was not rendered until after the Act had been succeeded by superseding legislation. It is far from business-like to have a statute that may ultimately be declared unconstitutional standing meanwhile on the books as a continuing menace to all inhibited transactions. This sort of

[8] Truax v. Raich (1915) 239 U. S. 33, 60 L. Ed. 131, 36 Sup. Ct. Rep. 7.

[9] Wilson v. New (1917) 243 U. S. 332, 61 L. Ed. 755, 37 Sup. Ct. Rep. 298.

[10] Hammer v. Dagenhart (1918) 247 U. S. 251, 62 L. Ed. 1101, 38 Sup. Ct. Rep. 529.

[11] (1920) 251 U. S. 264, 64 L. Ed. 260, 40 Sup. Ct. Rep. 141.

[12] Adams v. Tanner (1917) 244 U. S. 590, 61 L. Ed. 1336, 37 Sup. Ct. Rep. 662; Hamilton v. Kentucky Distilleries Co. (1919) 251 U. S. 146, 64 L. Ed. 194, 40 Sup. Ct. Rep. 106; Ft. Smith & Western R. R. Co. v. Mills (1920) 253 U. S. 206, 64 L. Ed. 862, 40 Sup. Ct. Rep. 526.

[13] (1921) 255 U. S. 100, 65 L. Ed. 528, 41 Sup. Ct. Rep. 303.

suspended inanimation will actually prevent many enterprises that may not constitutionally be forbidden. It leaves business men uncertain what to do and promotes insecurity where security is important. Injunctions against prosecuting officers seem much more desirable modes of raising constitutional issues than injunctions by stockholders against corporations[14] or defenses to actions for specific performance by those who have agreed to buy for certain uses forbidden by the legislation in issue.[15] Under both procedures, contracts are devised for the express purpose of testing the constitutionality of the statute by which they are inhibited. Conceivably such a contract might be made and a judicial proceeding started by parties who desired the legislation to be sustained and who hired able lawyers to write feeble briefs on their behalf. This is equally possible in test cases started in other ways. Others genuinely opposed may initiate other proceedings and introduce their advocates as *amici*. Any complaint that the suit is one against the state has long since been answered by the decisions holding that, if the action of the state officer is unwarranted by the statute because the statute is unconstitutional, the action is not against the state but against the unjustified officer.[16] There may have been some difficult metaphysics about this in the beginning, but, unlike most metaphysics, its difficulties have been resolved by adjudication. This leaves the only objection one of equity practice, and equity practice ought of all things to be sensible.

To this unsolicited wisdom of the writer there remains only to add the wisdom of Mr. Justice Butler in justifying the injunctive proceedings in the cases under review. He recognizes that the unconstitutionality of the statute is not alone ground for equitable relief, but that it must be clear that the remedy at law is inadequate. He adds, however, that "the legal remedy must be as complete, practical and efficient as that which equity could afford."[17] Manifestly the chance of a later gamble on getting the statute annulled or suffering imprisonment and forfeiture is not as adequate a remedy as advance advice as to what can be done. As Mr. Justice Butler puts it:

> "No action at law can be initiated against them until after the consummation of the proposed lease. The threatened enforce-

---

[14] Pollock v. Farmers' Loan & Trust Co. (1895) 158 U. S. 601, 39 L. Ed. 1108, 15 Sup. Ct. Rep. 912.

[15] Buchanan v. Warley (1917) 245 U. S. 60, 62 L. Ed. 149, 38 Sup. Ct. Rep. 16.

[16] Ex parte Young (1908) 209 U. S. 123, 155, 162, 52 L. Ed. 714, 28 Sup. Ct. Rep. 441.

[17] Terrace v. Thompson (1923) 263 U. S. 197, 214.

ment of the law deters them. In order to obtain a remedy at law, the owners, even if they would take the risk of fine, imprisonment and loss of property must continue to suffer deprivation of their right to dispose of or lease their land to any such alien until one is found who will join them in violating the terms of the enactment and take the risk of forfeiture. Similarly Nakatsuka must continue to be deprived of his right to follow his occupation as farmer until a land owner is found who is willing to make a forbidden transfer of land and take the risk of punishment. The owners have an interest in the freedom of the alien, and he has an interest in their freedom, to make the lease. The state act purports to operate directly upon the consummation of the proposed transaction between them, and the threat and purpose of the Attorney General to enforce the punishments and forfeiture prescribed prevents each from dealing with the other. .... They are not obliged to take the risk of prosecution, fines and imprisonment and loss of property in order to secure an adjudication of their rights. The complaint presents a case in which equitable relief may be had, if the law complained of is shown to be in contravention of the Federal Constitution."[18]

II.—The California Statute of 1920 and the Cropping Contract

The California statute of 1920 puts its prohibition in backhanded fashion. The only prohibition contained in the pertinent second section is found in the words "and not otherwise." We have to discover what ineligible aliens may not do by discovering what others may do. This second section reads as follows:

> "All aliens other than those mentioned in section 1 of this act [aliens eligible to citizenship] may acquire, possess, enjoy and transfer real property, or any interest therein, in this state, in the manner, and to the extent, and for the purpose prescribed by any treaty now existing between the government of the United States and the nation or country of which such alien is a citizen or subject, and not otherwise."[19]

To get the straight sense, this may be transformed to read: "No alien who is ineligible to citizenship may, except as allowed by treaty between the United States and the country of which he is a citizen, acquire, possess, enjoy and transfer real property, or any interest therein." Another version might be: "All aliens ineligible to citizenship are forbidden, except as allowed by treaty etc., to acquire, possess, enjoy and transfer real property, or any interest therein."

---

[18] Ibid., 215-216.
[19] Cal. Stats. 1921, p. lxxxvii.

This may be thought of as a prohibition with an exception in favor of treaty rights or as a prohibition with two elements in its definition. In either case the legal results are identical. If we take one of the elements of the prohibition to be the acts not sanctioned by appropriate treaty, we still have the other element of the acts enumerated in the statute. Clearly the statute does not forbid everything not sanctioned by treaty. To bring the ineligible alien within its prohibition, it must be shown also that in doing the thing not sanctioned by treaty he may be said to acquire, possess, enjoy or transfer real property or some interest therein.

As a purely verbal matter an alien might be said to possess or enjoy real property without acquiring any technical interest therein. Certainly the additional reference to an "interest" would seem designed to add something to what went before rather than to qualify it. Therefore, even if the word "interest" were to be interpreted in some technical fashion, one who had acquired no technical interest in the land might still have contract rights which enabled him to "possess" or "enjoy" it. On the other hand a technical restriction might be given to the words "possess" and "enjoy" as well as to the word "interest." This in substance is what the California Supreme Court did in In the Matter of Okahara[20] decided on June 28, 1923. After holding that the cropping contract there involved did not amount to an interest in the land, Judge Seawell said as to the two other words under consideration:

> "'Possess' used in reference to land titles and estates means to own; have as a belonging; property. . . . The word 'enjoy' is one frequently found in instruments of transfer and means to make such use of the thing transferred as is consistent with the tenure by which it is held."[21]

This says that to enjoy requires something more than to have fun with or to have some advantage from; it demands some use incident to some holding of the land. Unless there is some technical holding of the land or technical interest therein, there is no enjoyment within the meaning of the statute; for the phrase "to enjoy" is also a technical word of art. A similar attitude must have been held by the three federal judges who sat in the district court when O'Brien v. Webb[22] came before it, for they

---

[20] Supra, n. 6.
[21] In the Matter of Okahara (1923) 66 Cal. Dec. 15, 20.
[22] (1921) 279 Fed. 117.

decided that the cropping contract there involved did not violate the California statute. Thereby they were relieved from passing on the question whether the statute infringed upon treaty rights or upon the Fourteenth Amendment.

This case came to the Supreme Court of the United States on appeal from the District Court, and in Webb v. O'Brien[23] Mr. Justice Butler ordered the reversal of the decision below. It is difficult to tell what was the basis of his action. He considers the California decision in the Okahara Case and undertakes to distinguish it on two grounds. Both grounds seem wholly untenable. Without analysis he says that "the contract in that case differs in important particulars from the one before us."[24] The California Supreme Court, however, in the Okahara Case had declared:

> "In form and in substance this contract follows closely a contract considered and upheld by the United States District Court, Northern District of California, in the case of *O'Brien v. Webb, supra,* and we entertain no doubt but that it was patterned after that contract and its drafters were aided by the discussion of the question therein made."[25]

Clearly therefore the California Supreme Court thought that the O'Brien contract and the Okahara contract were alike immune from the California statute. No one contests that a state court's interpretation of a state statute is to be accepted and followed by the Supreme Court of the United States.

To comprehend the other reason which Mr. Justice Butler gives for not following the Okahara Case we should have his words in full. After quoting from the Okahara opinion to the effect that the cropping contract confers no interest in real property, he continues:

> "The court held that the contract did not violate § 10 and discharged Okahara. The contract in that case differs in important particulars from the one before us; but in the view we take of this case, we need not determine whether, within the meaning of the act, the contract between O'Brien and Inouye, if executed, would effect a transfer of an interest in real property. The question in this case is not whether the proposed contract is prohibited by § 10, but it is whether appellees have shown they have a right under the Constitution or treaty to make and carry out the contract, and are entitled to an interlocutory injunction against the officers of the state.

---

[23] Supra, n. 3.
[24] Webb v. O'Brien (1923) 263 U. S. 313, 325.
[25] In the Matter of Okahara (1923) 66 Cal. Dec. 15, 18.

> The privilege to make and carry out the proposed cropping contract, or to have the right to the possession, enjoyment and benefit of land for agricultural purposes as contemplated and provided for therein, is not given to Japanese subjects by the treaty. The act denies the privilege because not given by the treaty. No constitutional right of the alien is infringed. It therefore follows that the injunction should have been denied."[26]

Here is confusion. From parts of the paragraphs quoted it might be thought that the Supreme Court did not care whether the proposed contract was forbidden by the statute so long as there was no federal right to make such contracts. Then, however, Mr. Justice Butler insists that "the act," meaning plainly the California statute, "denies the privilege because not given by the treaty."[27] The California court, however, holds that the statute does not deny the privilege, even if not given by the treaty, unless it amounts to the enjoyment of an interest in land. On this question the California court is the authorized mentor of the Supreme Court. If, therefore, Mr. Justice Butler in denying the injunction thought that the statute actually forbade the proposed contract, and not merely that the legislature might by some other statute constitutionally forbid it, he is guilty of an obvious blunder.

When Mr. Justice Butler says that "the question in this case is not whether the proposed contract is prohibited by § 10",[28] he seems about to distinguish the Okahara Case on the ground that it involved only the conspiracy section which is confined to a conspiracy "to effect a transfer of real property, or of an interest therein, in violation of the provisions hereof."[29] This would have been unwarranted, for the Okahara Case held very clearly that the conspiracy there involved would not, if fully consummated, have created any possession or enjoyment in violation of the prohibitory clause of section two. This blunder Mr. Justice Butler avoids in favor of the blunder that that statute forbids all contracts not secured to the alien by treaty. If it were not for this one unfortunate sentence introduced in the succeeding paragraph, we should have understood him to go on the ground that the only question was whether the immunity claimed by the alien was secured to him by the Constitution or by treaty. Possibly he meant to base his decision on this ground and intended his final paragraph merely as corroboratory. Let us, then,

[26] Webb v. O'Brien (1923) 263 U. S. 313, 325-326.
[27] Passage cited in note 26, supra.
[28] Ibid.
[29] Cal. Stats. 1921, p. lxxxix.

cast the mantle of charity over his slip and inquire whether, in spite of it, his judgment denying the injunction is warranted.

It is established that a lower federal court having a case before it on federal grounds may decide the case on a state ground, as the district court did when in O'Brien v. Webb[30] it held that the California statute did not forbid the proposed contract. On appeal the Supreme Court also may take its stand on state ground whenever this leads to a desirable disposition of the case. When there is involved a money judgment, the Supreme Court should not sustain a judgment unauthorized by either federal or state law. The O'Brien case, however, involved no money judgment. It was a bill to enjoin a state officer from making threats. It was started in the federal court on the ground that the threats were in contravention of the federal Constitution and a national treaty. The Supreme Court found no such contravention. It held, as it was within its power to hold, that the state might frown upon such contracts if it wished. There was therefore no secure right to federal relief against the threats in issue. It seems, then, that the Supreme Court might properly have confined itself to the decision of the federal question and denied the injunction against the state attorney-general, leaving the complainants to fight out in the state courts any remaining state issues. This would have been a sensible enough disposition of the O'Brien Case even if at the time of the decision in the Supreme Court the California statute of 1920 was all that applied to the situation. It would have been much more sensible than it was to say erroneously that the statute of 1920 denies the privilege because not given by the treaty.

There is another element in the situation which satisfies us that the Supreme Court perhaps unwittingly blundered into a sensible disposition of the procedural problem in the case. The Act of 1920 was amended by the Act of 1923, approved on June 20, 1923. This explicitly forbids cropping contracts.[31] The O'Brien case was argued in the Supreme Court on April 23, 24, 1923. Hence the Supreme Court may not have been aware of the later

---

[30] Supra, n. 22.

[31] The amendment to section 2 adds the words "cultivate" and "occupy" to those in the Act of 1920, and refers also to having "in whole or in part the beneficial use thereof." Section 8 of the Act of 1923 provides for the forfeiture of "any leasehold or other interest in real property less than a fee, including cropping contracts which are hereby declared to constitute an interest in real property less than the fee." Cal. Stats. 1923, ch. 441, pp. 1020, 1021, 1023.

California statute of June 20, 1923, when it decided the case on November 19, 1923. The statute, however, if duly called to the attention of the Supreme Court, would justify the denial of the injunction. An injunction speaks *in futuro,* and it would do O'Brien and Inouye no good to enjoin General Webb from threatening to enforce the superseded statute of 1920 when he would remain free to enforce the superseding statute of 1923. All that the two complaining gentlemen suffered by any Supreme Court misapprehension was their right to costs.

III.—The Alien Land Laws and the Treaty with Japan

It is elementary that the treaty-making power of the national government may prescribe the privileges of aliens with respect to lands in the United States[32] and that any state statute in conflict with a national treaty is inapplicable.[33] In Terrace v. Thompson[34] the Supreme Court interpreted the existing treaty with Japan[35] and found that it conferred no privilege of leasing agricultural land. It does confer the "liberty . . . to lease land for residential and commercial purposes."[36] This by the aid of the maxim *expressio unius exclusio alterius* may readily be taken to negative a liberty to lease land for any other purposes. Of course this maxim is without absolute or universal validity and it has to lock horns with the competing maxim *ex abundantia cautelae.* The Supreme Court uses now one maxim and now the other as best befits its judgment in the particular controversy. Such is one of the delights of that universal right reason which is the law. The issue is one of judgment rather than of the dictionary or the grammar. In the present cases the judgment of the Supreme Court seems to be a reasonable one and it is enough to quote what it says.[37] It is but a step farther

[32] Hauenstein v. Lynham (1880) 100 U. S. 483, 25 L. Ed. 628.
[33] Ibid.
[34] Supra, n. 1.
[35] 37 U. S. Stats. at L. 1504-1509.
[36] Quoted in Terrace v. Thompson (1923) 263 U. S. 197, 222.
[37] "The only provision that relates to owning or leasing land is in the first paragraph of Article I, which is as follows:

'The citizens or subjects of each of the High Contracting Parties shall have liberty to enter, travel and reside in the territories of the other to carry on trade, wholesale and retail, to own or lease and occupy houses, manufactories, warehouses and shops, to employ agents of their choice, to lease land for residential and commercial purposes, and generally to do anything incident to or necessary for trade upon the same terms as native citizens or subjects, submitting themselves to the laws and regulations there established.'

to affirm in the cropping contract case of Webb v. O'Brien[38] that "the treaty gives no permission to enjoy, use or have the benefit of land for agricultural purposes."[39]

IV.—The Inhibitions of the Fourteenth Amendment

The other constitutional issue which these alien land laws raise is whether they deprive any person of rights or privileges secured by the Fourteenth Amendment. It is settled that aliens may invoke

---

For the purpose of bringing Nakatsuka within the protection of the treaty, the amended complaint alleges that, in addition to being a capable farmer, he is engaged in the business of trading, wholesale and retail, in farm products and shipping the same in intrastate, interstate and foreign commerce, and, instead of purchasing such farm products, he has produced, and desires to continue to produce, his own farm products for the purpose of selling them in such wholesale and retail trade, and if he is prevented from leasing land for the purpose of producing farm products for such trade he will be prevented from engaging in trade and the incidents to trade, as he is authorized to do under the treaty.

To prevail on this point, appellants must show conflict between the state act and the treaty. Each State, in the absence of any treaty provision conferring the right, may enact laws prohibiting aliens from owning land within its borders. Unless the right to own or lease land is given by the treaty, no question of conflict can arise. We think that the treaty not only contains no provision giving Japanese the right to own or lease land for agricultural purposes, but, when viewed in the light of the negotiations leading up to its consummation, the language shows that the high contracting parties respectively intended to withhold a treaty grant of that right to the citizens or subjects of either in the territories of the other. The right to 'carry on trade' or 'to own or lease and occupy houses, manufactories, warehouses and shops,' or 'to lease land for residential and commercial purposes,' or 'to do anything incident to or necessary for trade' cannot be said to include the right to own or lease or to have any title to or interest in land for agricultural purposes. The enumeration of rights to own or lease for other specified purposes impliedly negatives the right to own or lease land for these purposes. A careful reading of the treaty suffices in our opinion to negative the claim asserted by appellants that it conflicts with the state act.

But if the language left the meaning of its provisions doubtful or obscure, the circumstances of the making of the treaty, as set forth in the opinion of the District Court (*supra*, 844, 845), [274 Fed. 841, 844, 845] would resolve all doubts against the appellants' contention. The letter of Secretary of State Bryan to Viscount Chinda, July 16, 1913, shows that, in accordance with the desire of Japan, the right to own land was not conferred. And it appears that the right to lease land for other than residential and commercial purposes was deliberately withheld by substituting the words of the treaty, 'to lease land for residential and commercial purposes' for the more comprehensive clause contained in the earlier draft of the instrument, namely, 'to lease land for residential, commercial, industrial, manufacturing and other lawful purposes." (263 U. S. 197, 222-224.)

[38] Supra, n. 3.

[39] 263 U. S. 313, 323. In applying the same conclusion to the right to own stock in an agricultural corporation, Mr. Justice Butler in Frick v. Webb, supra, n. 2, at page 334 declared: "The right to 'carry on trade' given by the treaty does not give the privilege to acquire the stock above described. To read the treaty to permit ineligible aliens to acquire such stock would be inconsistent with the intention and purpose of the parties."

the protection of the Amendment[40] although the protection need not necessarily be the same for aliens as for citizens.[41] The laws in question of course deny the legal capacity of citizens to grant as well as that of aliens to receive, and in each of the four cases under review one of the complainants was a citizen. Conceivably it might be held that the restraint upon citizens is unconstitutional even though the aliens may not successfully complain of any frustration of their hopes. To defeat the alien it might be sufficient to show that his alienage disentitles him to the protection claimed. To defeat the citizen it might be necessary to show that there is an adequate public advantage in suppressing alien holdings. Mr. Justice Butler hardly gives adequate consideration to the problem when he confines himself to saying that "the Terraces, who are citizens, have no right safeguarded by the Fourteenth Amendment to lease their land to aliens lawfully forbidden to take or have such lease."[42] His circular statement is safe enough, as are all circular statements, but the denial of the complaint of the alien does not necessarily settle that of the citizen.

Though this may smack of somewhat arid logic, no one is likely to contest it in so far as it is confined to the complaint of the alien that he is selected for a discriminatory exclusion in violation of the equal-protection clause. There may be no vice in excluding some aliens rather than all aliens and yet be abundant vice in restraining citizens from making contracts which they deem advantageous. It is clear, therefore, that the rejection of the alien's complaint of unconstitutional discrimination does not get us far. The question still remains why alien ownership of agricultural land or alien cultivation of such land under a cropping contract present so serious a public menace that citizens may be deprived of the advantages that free bargaining may give them. On this question we shall seek the judicial light after disposing of the subsidiary issue of discrimination.

A.—THE EQUAL-PROTECTION COMPLAINT

The Washington statute sustained in Terrace v. Thompson[43] confined its inhibition to aliens who have not in good faith declared

---

[40] Yick Wo v. Hopkins (1885) 118 U. S. 356, 30 L. Ed. 220, 6 Sup. Ct. Rep. 1064; Truax v. Raich (1915) 239 U. S. 33, 60 L. Ed. 131, 36 Sup. Ct. Rep. 7.
[41] Patsone v. Pennsylvania (1914) 232 U. S. 138, 58 L. Ed. 539, 34 Sup. Ct. Rep. 281.
[42] 263 U. S. 197, 221.
[43] Supra, n. 1.

their intention to become citizens.[44] The California statute sustained in Porterfield v. Webb,[45] Webb v. O'Brien[46] and Frick v. Webb[47] was still milder and affected only aliens ineligible to citizenship.[48] Both statutes permit some aliens to own and lease land; both, therefore, discriminate against some aliens in favor of other aliens and in favor of all citizens. Neither state regards mere alienage as a sufficient sign of sepsis. Washington diagnoses all alienage as a suspicious symptom and imposes a quarantine until the prophylaxis of first papers. California confines her fears to chronic incurable alienage externally imposed; she sees no menace in a voluntary acute alienage readily remedied by the application of New Thought. Since in neither state is there drawn a sharp line between citizenship and alienage, the discrimination cannot find complete justification in any common-law attitude toward all aliens or in any state power over all aliens. No such power has been exercised. Whatever power the state has over all aliens has been exercised over less than all. If those who have been selected for suffering can complain of the discrimination on the ground that others equally noxious have been more favorably treated, they may rightfully require some other justification than the fact that they are aliens.

Evidently the Supreme Court deems it necessary to justify the favors accorded to other aliens, for Mr. Justice Butler declares that "the inclusion of good faith declarants in the same class with citizens does not unjustly discriminate against aliens who are ineligible or against eligible aliens who have failed to declare their intention."[49] He notes earlier that a number of statutes have conferred privileges and imposed duties on declarant eligibles that are not extended to nondeclarant eligibles, and he observes that "the alien's formally declared bona fide intention to renounce forever

---

[44] The pertinent sections of the Washington constitution and the Washington statute are quoted in 263 U. S. 197, 212-213.

[45] Supra, n. 1.

[46] Supra, n. 3.

[47] Supra, n. 2.

[48] Section 1 of the statute gives to aliens eligible to citizenship the same powers over real property as those possessed by citizens, "except as otherwise provided by the laws of the state." Section 2 reads as follows:

> "All aliens other than those mentioned in section one of this act may acquire, possess, enjoy and transfer real property, or any interest therein, in this state, in the manner and to the extent and for the purpose prescribed by any treaty now existing between the government of the United States and the nation or country of which such alien is a citizen or subject, and not otherwise." (263 U. S. 225, 232.)

[49] 263 U. S. 197, 219-220.

all allegiance and fidelity to the sovereignty to which he lately has been a subject, and to become a citizen of the United States and permanently to reside therein markedly distinguishes him from an ineligible alien or an eligible alien who has not so declared."[50] If the ineligible cannot complain because citizens are favored, he cannot complain because the favor is extended to the pollywog who will soon become a frog. Obviously he is not discriminated against because the nondeclarant eligible is not favored. Nevertheless, perhaps in anticipation of a future action brought by a nondeclarant eligible, Mr. Justice Butler observes that "it is clearly within the power of the State to include nondeclarant eligible aliens and ineligible aliens in the same prohibited class,"[51] and that "reasons supporting discrimination against aliens who may but who will not naturalize are obvious."[52] These affirmations are preceded by an approving incorporation of a selection from the opinion of the district court. To mere affirmation this adds something of specification when it says:

> "It is obvious that one who is not a citizen and cannot become one lacks an interest in, and the power to effectually work for the welfare of, the state, and, so lacking, the state may rightfully deny him the right to own and lease real estate within its boundaries. If one incapable of citizenship may lease or own real estate, it is within the realm of possibility that every foot of land within the state might pass to the ownership or possession of non-citizens."[53]

This apprehension does not unduly exalt the resourcefulness of those who are prone to call themselves 100% Americans. It overlooks the power of Congress to halt immigration in season to save several sections of soil for those who need legislation to help them. One wonders, too, just what is meant by interest in the state and power to work effectually for its welfare. Ineligible aliens could not of course hope to become effective political supporters of the Farm Bloc, and from the standpoint of this group it may be desirable to have the farms in the possession of voters. If the voters are crowded off the farms and become law professors or laborers, their allegiance to the state may take a form different from that of the agricultural group. Yet an increase in the number of

[50] Ibid., 219.
[51] Ibid., 221.
[52] Ibid.
[53] Ibid., 220-221.

Japanese farmers does not disfranchise the citizens whom they displace and the ineligible alien can hardly acquire added interest in the state or greater power to work for its welfare by being legislated into landlessness. These judicial affirmations of the "obvious" need to be supplemented by some demonstration or assertion that ineligible aliens and nondeclarant eligibles are more of a menace on the land than in the factory, shop and kitchen. Such assertion appears a little later when Mr. Justice Butler observes that "the quality and allegiance of those who own, occupy and use the farm lands within its border are matters of highest importance and affect the safety and power of the state itself."[54] Again we are not told why. One sees readily that allegiance has a close relation to matters within the scope of national authority, but its peculiar relation to fruit raising is less evident.

If we grant that political reasons justify favoring citizens it is easy to find justification for favoring also those soon to acquire this status. Thus the favorable discrimination in the Washington statute stands or falls with the wisdom of drawing the line between citizens on the one hand and confirmed aliens on the other. Yet if Mr. Justice Butler is justified in saying that "reasons supporting discrimination against aliens who may but who will not naturalize are obvious,"[55] he sets something of a task for himself when he comes to the discrimination against those who cannot become citizens in favor of those who can but do not choose to do so. His monition on the menace of those who have not renounced allegiance to a foreign power makes it hard to justify the favor extended by California to those whose recusance is voluntary. It would be an exaggeration to accord him unstinted praise for his method of meeting the difficulty when, in comparing the Washington and the California favors, he confines himself to saying:

> "There the prohibited class was made up of aliens who had not in good faith declared intention to become citizens. The class necessarily includes all ineligible aliens and in addition thereto all eligible aliens who have failed so to declare. In the case before us the prohibited class includes ineligible aliens only. In the matter of classification, the states have wide discretion. Each has its own problems, depending on circumstances existing there. It is not always practical or desirable that legislation shall be the same in different states. We cannot say that the

---

[54] Ibid., 221.
[55] Ibid.

> failure of the California Legislature to extend the prohibited class so as to include eligible aliens who have failed to declare their intention to become citizens of the United States was arbitrary or unreasonable."[56]

"There's a Reason", says the learned Justice, but he seems not to have it so clear in his mind at the moment as to be able to tell us what it is. In Terrace v. Thompson,[57] however, in discussing the different discrimination of the Washington statute, he points somewhat more clearly to considerations which might justify California in favoring those who do not choose to naturalize. After observing that the classification in the Washington statute "is based on eligibility and purpose to naturalize", he continues:

> "Eligible aliens are free white persons and persons of African nativity or descent. Congress is not trammelled, and it may grant or withhold the privilege of naturalization upon any grounds or without any reason, as it sees fit. But it is not to be supposed that its acts defining eligibility are arbitrary or unsupported by reasonable considerations of public policy. The state properly may assume that the considerations upon which Congress made such classification are substantial and reasonable. Generally speaking, the natives of European countries are eligible. Japanese, Chinese and Malays are not. Appellants' contention that the state act discriminates arbitrarily against Nakatsuka and other ineligible aliens because of their race and color is without foundation. All persons of whatever color or race who have not declared their intention in good faith to become citizens are prohibited from so owning agricultural lands. Two classes of aliens inevitably result from the naturalization laws,—those who may and those who may not become citizens. The rule established by Congress on this subject, in and of itself, furnishes a reasonable basis for classification in a state law withholding from aliens the privilege of land ownership as defined in the act."[58]

This adds to "There's a Reason" the further admonition: "Ask Congress; it knows." Doubtless most of the readers of this article who can surmise what Congress might give for reasons will find it in their hearts to respond: "They satisfy." It is perhaps sufficient here to say that Mr. Justice Butler's two opinions disclose no satisfactory reasons, since when taken together they destroy the only reason suggested. They proceed along the path of political allegiance. They tell us that it is obvious that one who chooses not to

---

[56] In Porterfield v. Webb, 263 U. S. 225, 233.
[57] Supra, n. 1.
[58] 263 U. S. 197, 220.

be naturalized may be put in the same class as one who cannot be naturalized, and thus imply that the former as a farmer is as much of a menace as the latter. Then they bid us to trust Congress for the conclusion that one who is a voluntary alien may be accorded more favorable treatment than one who is an alien by compulsion. They say that the Japanese in Washington are not discriminated against on account of their race or color because those of other races and other colors who choose not to become naturalized are treated in like fashion. In California they are not treated in like fashion. Here, then, the reason fails. In the opinion in the California case, race and color are not mentioned. They might, however, be mentioned with safety, for they are not mentioned in the Fourteenth Amendment. It is in the Fifteenth Amendment that the words "race" and "color" occur, and there they relate only to the rights of citizens of the United States to vote.

Enough has been said to show the artificiality of seeking to justify the discrimination against ineligible aliens on purely political grounds. If under the equal-protection clause we must, as Mr. Justice Butler seems to assume, justify discriminations that are favorable as well as those that are unfavorable, the political justifications fail when we come to discrimination in favor of aliens who with the opportunity to take steps toward citizenship prefer not to do so. It must seriously be questioned also whether political considerations underlie any of the discriminations in the alien land laws. Incapacity for suffrage can hardly be regarded as a menacing sign of lack of interest in the state or lack of power to work for its welfare when women were so long left unfranchised and yet not thought of as a menace on the land. The state is a community as well as a political entity, and interest in and work for the welfare of the community are not precluded by exclusion from political power as they are not ensured by possession of political power. Foreign allegiance is a bird of different feather, but foreign allegiance is not California's line of demarcation. Moreover it is hard to see how from any distinctly state point of view foreign allegiance is of more significance on the farm than in the mine or factory. There is an incomplete *sequitur* in the assumption that proper canons for the exercise of national power are necessarily proper canons for the exercise of state power.

This is not to say that the canons for the exercise of state power are necessarily different from those for the exercise of national power. It is quite possible that there is something in common in the test of a desirable citizen and the test of a desirable farmer. It would of course be monstrous for a state to withhold all means of livelihood from aliens whom Congress chooses to admit, as the Supreme Court has fully recognized.[59] Yet it is still open to proof that reasons motivating denial of citizenship may be sufficient reasons for exclusion from certain occupations. A Maryland court was of the opinion that even in 1890 there was a sufficient relation between the Constitution and the liquor traffic so that the legislature might wisely confine saloon-keepers to "those who, being natives of the country, might reasonably be supposed to have a regard for its welfare; or who, not being natives, had, as required by the naturalization law, proven by credible testimony before a Court of Justice, that they were attached to the principles of the Constitution of the United States, and were well disposed to their good order and happiness."[60] So it may be with farming. That the President and the Senate have some such idea may be inferred from their failure to include farming in the occupations listed in the Treaty with Japan. Again, however, such reasons can not be deemed purely political. Thus we are still left with our conclusion that Mr. Justice Butler's references to political distinctions afford no adequate justification for California's choice of farming as the one occupation in which noneligible aliens are restricted or for California's favor to the nondeclarant eligible as contrasted with the ineligible.

There is, however, a more fundamental question which remains for answer. Do we need any justification for favorable discrimination? If there are adequate reasons for excluding the noneligible alien, what concern is it of his whether others who might also have been excluded have been left to their own devices? Does the discrimination in favor of others render more onerous the discrimination against him? Some favorable discriminations undoubtedly have this effect. Sometimes a restraint is less irksome if it is more general. Barbers forbidden to work on Sunday can hardly care that legal writers may still ply their trade on that special day, but they may seriously object to an an exception in favor of barbers who work in hotels. They may very wisely wish that all possible Sunday shaves be saved for Monday. When the complaint is made on the ground of discrimination, should it not appear that the person restrained is really prejudiced because the restraint is not

---

[59] Cases cited in note 40, supra.
[60] Trageser v. Gray (1890) 73 Md. 250, 254, 20 Atl. 905.

wider? Should one be entitled to relief under the equal-protection clause on the ground of unfavorable discrimination when one would not be a bit happier if the discrimination were removed by making the restraint universal?

From the cases it is clear enough that discriminatory restraint can run afoul of the equal-protection clause even though all that the complainant really objects to is the restraint. Quite often it seems that courts place their decisions on the ground of unconstitutional discrimination where their aversion is really to the restraint on individual liberty and yet the restraint is not such as to make it wanting in due process of law under established precedents. An effort to systematize the decisions under the equal-protection clause is not likely to meet with much success. The cases represent a congeries of particular judgments rather than any uniform line of doctrine. Yet it seems clear that a discriminatory restraint such that the restraint would not be mitigated by extension of it to others requires much less justification than one which imposes additional hurt because of the discrimination. What the ineligible alien really objects to is that he loses desired access to the land rather than that some other aliens do not. When, Sampson-like, he seeks to share his fate with others, he deserves but slight consideration. Mr. Justice Butler's justifications for the favorable treatment accorded to other aliens may not be very good and still be good enough for practical purposes. In the absence of hampering treaties, the alien land laws might be extended to all aliens. It would be going rather far to say that California, because it had done less than it might, had done more than it could.

One discrimination which the ineligible alien did not see fit to complain of is that between agricultural land and other land. Some ingenious advocate might have urged that an ineligible alien suffered an unconstitutional injury under the equal-protection clause because he was restrained only in respect to agricultural land and not in respect to all land. Such an absurdity would hardly be worth mentioning but for the fact that a similar one has had the august sanction of the Supreme Court. In Truax v. Corrigan[61] Chief Justice Taft lays down that employers are denied the equal protection of the laws by being foreclosed from enjoining picketing employes when they still may pursue that remedy against others.

---

[61] (1921) 257 U. S. 312, 66 L. Ed. 254, 42 Sup. Ct. Rep. 124.

Certainly the employer is not prejudiced because his loss of injunctive relief is partial rather than complete; and the minority of the court were justified by all the precedents in declaring that the plaintiff can not complain of a discrimination from which he does not suffer. The employer is himself treated differently in different situations and the essence of his equal-protection objection is that he is not treated as harshly in all cases as he is in some. Yet Chief Justice Taft asserts that equal protection means equal protection against all similarly situated as well as for all similarly situated. This is one of the clearest cases in which an inhibition disliked for intrinsic reasons not sufficient to declare it unconstitutional under the due-process clause is found wanting under the equal-protection clause on fantastic reasoning. In logic this was no more absurd than it would have been to grant the ineligible alien relief under the equal-protection clause because he suffers only in respect to agricultural land rather than in respect to all land. It certainly would have been unwarranted for the court to have pursued such logic for the benefit of those who lack "interest in, and the power to effectually work for the welfare of, the state."

It may be questioned whether the equal-protection issue was worth the preponderant attention which it receives in Mr. Justice Butler's opinions. His discussion follows a terse rejection of the due-process complaint. This is by far the more fundamental one from the standpoint of the suffering alien. His interest in what happens to him is far more vital than his interest in what does not happen to somebody else. It is clear enough that citizens could not be kept from acquiring an interest in agricultural land. Once it is established that an alien has no due-process objection to such exclusion, the discrimination against him in favor of citizens is readily justified. It needs but little additional justification to sustain the discrimination in favor of embryo citizens. Yet Mr. Justice Butler adduces reasons of a political character which fail completely when he comes to the discrimination in favor of aliens who might renounce their foreign allegiance but do not choose to do so. In so doing he calls in question the character of the political justification on which the due-process issue was decided. He invites inquiry whether the reason relied on to justify the discrimination and the restraint was the real reason motivating the legislation or merely a fortunate excuse.

B.—THE DUE-PROCESS OBJECTION

If the canons of equal-protection are amorphous, those of due-process are almost equally so. The problem in each case is one of comparing the detriment to the individual with the benefit to the public. If the injury is slight the compensating benefit need not be so great as where the injury is more serious. So, too, if the legal quality of the individual interest is precarious, it requires less justification to curb it or qualify it than it does to deal adversely with an interest of higher legal order. Thus corporations which depend for their continued existence on the grace of the state have less protection against burdensome regulation than does an individual. Inheritances which might be prohibited may be taxed more whimsically than property generally. Drastic regulations of foreign commerce are sustained where equally drastic regulations of interstate commerce would be seriously suspected, since Congress might put an embargo on all foreign commerce but not on all interstate commerce. In pre-arid times it was fully recognized that the power to forbid the liquor traffic carried with it a power to impose all sorts of drastic and vexatious restrictions on any traffic that was permitted. Where the enterprise or the enterpriser is in a general state of constitutional insecurity, courts are not very fussy in finding justification for restraints less onerous than others that might constitutionally be imposed. Thus constitutional complaints are sometimes dismissed because the complainant is not entitled to much consideration, without any careful inquiry into the question whether what has been done to him has sufficient inherent justifications of its own.

In this class of cases fall those with which we are now dealing. The alien was something of a pariah at common law and it has always been assumed in this country that "each state, in the absence of any treaty provision to the contrary, has power to deny to aliens the right to own land within its borders."[62] This recital leads Mr. Justice Butler easily to the affirmation that "state legislation applying alike and equally to all aliens, withholding from them the right to own land, cannot be said to be capricious or to amount to an arbitrary deprivation of liberty or property, or to transgress the due-process clause."[63] This rests the due-process part of the decision solely on the inherent weakness in the position of the alien. It is only when

---

[62] Terrace v. Thompson (1923) 263 U. S. 197, 217.
[63] Ibid., 218.

Mr. Justice Butler comes to the consideration of the equal-protection question and to the dismissal of Truax v. Raich[64] that he adduces the consideration that "the quality and allegiance of those who own, occupy and use the farm lands within its borders are matters of highest importance and affect the safety and power of the state itself."[65] We have already dealt with the inadequacy of this as a justification for the California discrimination in favor of nondeclarant eligible aliens. Its weakness in that connection has slight, if any, bearing upon the due-process complaint of the noneligible alien. If the alien is really a menace on the farm, it does not matter from a due-process standpoint that California has refrained for the moment from dealing with all the menace that it might. Legislation is not wanting in due process of law merely because it is less general or less complete than it might be.

A tight technician might see added difficulties in the restraint on alien ownership of stock in corporations authorized to own agricultural land, which was sustained in Frick v. Webb.[66] Are we not assured that the property of the corporation is wholly distinct from the property of the stockholder? Are we not frequently warned of the danger and the confusion which will result if we intrusively pierce the veil of the corporate entity? We are. Still the courts do it whenever they think it is a good thing to do. Jural prestidigitation finds this one of the easiest exemplifications of "Now you see it, now you don't." No logical difficulties disturb the performer of the feat. The manipulation is a simple exercise of judgment and of will. Nothing more was needed in the present case than Mr. Justice Butler's two assertions that "as the state has the power to . . . prohibit, it may adopt such measures as are reasonably appropriate and needful to render exercise of that power effective"[67] and that "it may forbid indirect as well as direct ownership and control of agricultural land by ineligible aliens."[68] With this there can be no legitimate quarrel. It would certainly be absurd to characterize alien landholding as a menace and then to find in the sheerest of technicalities an insuperable due-process objection to a statute which is essential if the menace is to be suppressed.

---

[64] Supra, n. 8.

[65] Terrace v. Thompson (1923) 263 U. S. 197, 221.

[66] Supra, n. 2.

[67] Frick v. Webb (1923) 263 U. S. 326, 333, quoted from Crane v. Campbell (1917) 245 U. S. 304, 307, 62 L. Ed. 304, 38 Sup. Ct. Rep. 98.

[68] Frick v. Webb (1923) 263 U. S. 326, 334.

The more difficult due-process question was presented by the cropping-contract case of Webb v. O'Brien.[69] Mr. Justice Butler treats it as follows:

> "The term of the proposed contract, the measure of control and dominion over the land which is necessarily involved in the performance of such a contract, the cropper's right to have housing for himself and to have his employees live on the land, and his obligation to accept one-half the crops as his only return for tilling the land clearly distinguish the arrangement from one of mere employment. The case differs from *Truax v. Raich,* 239 U. S. 33. In that case, a statute of Arizona making it a criminal offense for an employer of more than five workers, regardless of kind or class of work or sex of workers, to employ less than eighty per cent. native born citizens of the United States was held to infringe the right, secured by the Fourteenth Amendment, of a resident alien to work in a common occupation—cooking in a restaurant. The right to make and carry out cropper contracts such as that before us is not safeguarded to ineligible aliens by the Constitution. A denial of it does not deny the ordinary means of earning a livelihood or the right to work for a living. The practical result of such contract is that the cropper has use, control and benefit of land for agricultural purposes substantially similar to that granted to a lessee. Conceivably, by the use of such contracts, the population living on and cultivating the farmlands might come to be made up largely of ineligible aliens. The allegiance of the farmers to the State directly affects its strength and safety. *Terrace v. Thompson, supra.* We think it within the power of the state to deny to ineligible aliens the privilege so to use agricultural lands within its borders."[70]

With the difference to the alien between being excluded from one occupation and being excluded from all, we may be satisfied without further comment. The difference between the cropping contract and contracts of employment generally is equally manifest. The difference, like most differences, is one of degree; but it is one of considerable degree. The alien's constitutional position may be strong enough to save him from state-imposed starvation and still be weak enough to afford him no refuge from interdiction of certain forms of agricultural enterprise.

Distinctions, however, should be more than stated. They should be analyzed and justified. Mr. Justice Butler's declaratory diction

---

[69] Supra, n. 3.
[70] Webb v. O'Brien (1923) 263 U. S. 313, 324.

does not venture into these further enterprises. This "take-it-from-me" temper has more justification in opinions sustaining legislation than in opinions declaring statutes unconstitutional, but it still has something of an unsatisfactory flavor. We must wonder why the question of allegiance has anything to do with the case when those whose un-allegiance or perhaps dis-allegiance is voluntary are left without restraint and when those restrained from farming are left free for other pursuits. We must wonder what is the ineligible alien's peculiarly defective qualification for farming as compared with other occupations. Mr. Justice Butler gives no hint that ineligible aliens are such mal-adroit cultivators of the soil that they are likely to turn it into waste places and in consequence to become charges on public charity. In short, he tells us substantially nothing that can be dignified by the name of a reason. We get our only helpful pointers from the reference to the canons chosen by Congress in designating ineligible aliens and from the fact that the treaty-making power has put agriculural enterprise in a class by itself.

If the Supreme Court chooses to refuse to satisfy the curiosity of Californians, I may be pardoned for following its example. It would be ungracious for a visitor to suggest that a substantial justification for the particular picking on farming might be that the ineligible alien is competent rather than incompetent. No one unfamiliar with local conditions would be fitted to pass judgment on such a matter. Yet one who is curious about constitutional issues might well wish to speculate on the hypothetical question whether the police power of the state extends to excluding a class from some pursuit for the reason that in that particular calling they have shown themselves unusually efficient. Our anti-trust legislation has behind it the idea that there may be a menace in extreme effectiveness in individually successful methods of competitive enterprise. Much of our labor legislation proceeds upon a recognition that the economically strong must be curbed for the protection of the economically weak. Legislation against fraud restrains those with a type of superior endowment for the benefit of others who lack the acumen to perceive the wiles of the smart. A protective tariff seeks to bolster up the weak by putting barriers against the strong. Even in horse racing we put weights upon the fleet. An aversion to letting the devil take the hindmost is common in legislation as in life. This is often sought to be justified or rationalized by a profession that it springs from no mawkish sentimentality for the hindmost but from a conviction that the welfare of the hindmost is vital to the welfare of us all. Hence our hypothetical constitutional question will find legislative and judicial precedents in favor of an affirmative answer. If such an answer be given, it is in turn a precedent for other legislation such as a minimum-wage law which has behind it a widely felt need that the general public welfare is served by protecting those with inferior bargaining power from the bargains which those with superior power might induce.

In so far as the restraint upon the alien is justifiable merely because of his alienage, these other considerations need not enter. Yet it seems that some genuine realistic menace should be found in the inhibited form of alien cultivation in order to justify the restraint upon citizens who lose the opportunity to contract as they desire. Freedom of contract has been so exalted in some recent Supreme Court opinions and is so often extolled as one of the inalienable and fundamental constitutional rights of American citizens that Messrs. Terrace, Porterfield, O'Brien and Frick may well be wondering why Mr. Justice Butler has given them no better reasons for the frustration of their hopes. Perhaps in their hearts they know, without being told. If perchance their self interest blinds them to a full realization, there may still be others who appreciate the significance and the weight of possible considerations underlying the recent Supreme Court judgments which failed to find expression in the opinions. These considerations are not a fine flowering of a secure constitutional concept of liberty of contract. The cases recognize that important social ends may sometimes be better served by restraint of contract than by liberty of contract. The land legislation before us is of the type often denounced as socialistic. It is restraint upon individuals for an assumed general good. So is practically all legislation. Perhaps a fuller realization of this in connection with legislation widely welcome may serve to shut off some of the loose talk about similar legislation less pleasing. It may thereby turn us from denunciatory shibboleths to a more careful and more practical analysis of the competing benefits and burdens and the contending merits and defects to be found in other legislation which comes before us for judgment.

Thomas Reed Powell.

School of Jurisprudence,
University of California.

Civil Rights and Anti-Japanese Discrimination

In *Terrace* v. *Thompson*,[1] the Supreme Court of the United States considered a Washington statute which forbade any kind

[1]263 U. S. 197, 44 Sup. Ct. 15, 68 L. Ed. 255 (1923).

of legal or equitable ownership of land in that state by aliens other than those who in good faith had declared their intention to become citizens of the United States, including corporations and groups of persons a majority of whose members were aliens. Since certain groups of aliens were ineligible to become United States citizens, particularly the Japanese,[2] the classification of those who were ineligible to hold land in Washington fell into two main groups; namely, the Japanese (and a few other minority groups[3]) and those aliens who were eligible for citizenship but who had not declared their intention of becoming citizens.

A suit for an injunction against the enforcement of this act by state officials was brought in the United States District Court for the Western District of Washington by Terrace, a United States citizen, who owned land in Washington; and Nakatsuka, an alien Japanese who desired to lease such land for agricultural purposes.[4] The suit was dismissed and an appeal was taken from its dismissal.

The plaintiffs first contended that the act contravened the due process clause of the Fourteenth Amendment,[5] in that it prohibited owners of land from making a lawful disposition or use of their land by making it a criminal offense for such owners to lease their land to an alien,[6] with the result that it prohibited the alien from following the occupation of farmer.[7]

In answer to that contention the Supreme Court said that the Fourteenth Amendment does protect owners of property, in their right to lease or otherwise dispose of it for lawful purposes, from arbitrary action of the state; and it does, likewise, prohibit the state from arbitrary action in interfering with the alien resident in his right to earn a living by following the ordinary occupations of the community;[8] but it does not restrict the state in the exercise of its police powers which are not in conflict with the supreme

---

[2] 8 U. S. C. A. § 703 (1922), prior to amendment.

[3] *Ibid.*

[4] 274 Fed. 841 (D. C. Wash. 1921).

[5] U. S. CONSTITUTION, Art. XIV, Sec. 1.

[6] California Laws 50 (1921).

[7] Truax v. Raich, 239 U. S. 33, 36 Sup. Ct. 7, 60 L. Ed. 131 (1915).

[8] *Ibid.*

law of the land.[9] In the exercise of this police power the state has wide discretion in determining what measures are necessary for its own protection and for the general welfare of its citizens. Hence, such legislation which applies equally and alike to all aliens who have not declared their intention to become citizens, and, *a fortiori*, to aliens who cannot become citizens, is a proper exercise of a state's police power, and cannot be said to be arbitrary or capricious so as to amount to deprivation of property without due process of law.

The plaintiffs also contended that the act contravened the equal protection clause of the Fourteenth Amendment in that the clause secures equal protection to all in the enjoyment of their rights, whether United States citizens or not. In disposing of this contention the Supreme Court said that the equal protection clause does not prohibit every distinction between citizens and alien residents by states' laws,[10] but only those distinctions which are arbitrary and bear no proper relation to a proper governmental purpose. The issue, therefore, was reduced to the question of whether the classification in the Washington law was proper. The Supreme Court concluded that it was a proper classification in that the United States Congress had established similar broad classifications as a basis for determining who might or might not become citizens. Thus such a classification adopted by a state in determining who might or might not own agricultural land in that state cannot be said to be unreasonable. Particularily, the Court said, such an ineligible person lacks an interest in and the power to work effectively for the welfare of the state and may therefore be properly excluded from the right to own or lease real estate within that state. Further, it is theoretically possible that all the land in the state might pass to such an ineligible group (ineligible for citizenship), and it cannot be said to be an unreasonable classification when the result of such classification would be to prevent such a possibility and work for the welfare of its citizens.

---

[9]Corfield v. Coryell, 4 Wash. C. C. 371, Fed. Cas. No. 3230 (1825); Geer v. State of Connecticut, 161 U. S. 519, 16 Sup. Ct. 600, 40 L. Ed. 793 (1896).

[10]263 U. S. 197, 218, 219 (1923).

The Court then concluded that the statute in question here is not analogous to the statute declared invalid in *Truax* v. *Raich.*[11] In that case the Arizona legislature passed a statute making it a criminal offense for an employer of more than five workers to employ less than eighty per cent qualified electors or native-born citizens of the United States. That statute was held to be unconstitutional as being opposed to the Fourteenth Amendment. While the factual background did not relate to the devolution of real property, the Court did say that the right to work at the common occupations of the community was secured by the Fourteenth Amendment. The Court here did recognize that fact but pointed out that the problem was not the right of an alien to work at farming, a common occupation of the community wherein the plaintiffs resided, but rather of ownership of agricultural land. The significance seems to be real because the problem of ownership of a state's agricultural lands is wholly within the province of the state to determine for its own welfare and safety so that the arbitrary exclusion of aliens in that respect does not contravene the equal protection clause. Indeed the distinction does seem to be real, because such an approach by the Supreme Court resulted in the ineligible alien being able to pursue only the most menial jobs in farming. This does not sound like the equal protection that *Truax* v. *Raich* announces that the Fourteenth Amendment secures.[12] There is a distinction, however, in the cases on their facts and the type of statute involved.

A similar statute was enacted in California in 1913, which forbade aliens ineligible for naturalization to own agricultural lands in that state.[13] This act was amended in 1920 to plug existing loopholes and to place the further restriction on such aliens of being unable to lease agricultural lands. It also provided that any property acquired in violation of the statute should escheat as of the date of acquisition, and that any transfer made with intent to circumvent the statute would likewise escheat. In addition, such a fraudulent intent was prima facie presumed whenever an ineligible alien paid the consideration for a transfer to a

[11]Truax v. Raich, 239 U. S. 33, 36 Sup. Ct. 7, 60 L. Ed. 131 (1915).

[12]*Ibid.*

[13]1 California General Laws, Act 261.

citizen or eligible alien.[14] Shortly after *Terrace* v. *Thompson*, and strictly in accordance with it, the Supreme Court upheld the constitutionality of the provision of the California statute prohibiting aliens from leasing agricultural lands.[15] In a similar vein and in short succession thereafter, the Supreme Court upheld the provision of the California statute relating to share-cropping by ineligible aliens,[16] and the inability of an ineligible alien to acquire stock in a corporation holding agricultural land.[17]

Two recent Supreme Court cases on the subject were decided during the last term, *Oyama* v. *California*[18] and *Torao Takahashi* v. *Fish and Game Commission*.[19] These cases present the perplexing question of whether *Terrace* v. *Thompson* and the companion decisions on the California statute are still the law, or whether they are again distinguishable on their facts, as the Supreme Court said *Terrace* v. *Thompson* was distinguishable from *Truax* v. *Raich*.

Oyama v. *California* involves an interpretation of the California statute which had not been litigated in the prior decisions. The facts in brief were as follows. One of the petitioners, Kajiro Oyama, father and guardian of the other petitioner, Fred Oyama, was a Japanese citizen ineligible for naturalization. The son, Fred, was an American citizen, having been born in the United States. The father paid the consideration involved for the purchase of two tracts of agricultural lands, which lands were conveyed to the son in the son's name. This occurred in 1934, when the son was six years old. The father petitioned the California court to be appointed guardian of his son, which appointment was made. In 1942 Fred and his family were evacuated from the Pacific coast in accordance with war precautionary measures. In 1944, when Fred was sixteen and still forbidden to return home, the state of California started escheat proceedings of the two parcels on the ground that the conveyances in 1934 and 1937 were made with intent to violate and evade the Alien Land Law. From

---

[14]California Alien Land Law, Sec. 9 (a).

[15]Porterfield v. Webb, 263 U. S. 225, 44 Sup. Ct. 21, 68 L. Ed. 288 (1923).

[16]Webb v. O'Brien, 263 U. S. 313, 44 Sup. Ct. 112, 68 L. Ed. 318 (1923).

[17]Frick v. Webb, 263 U. S. 326, 44 Sup. Ct. 115, 68 L. Ed. 323 (1923).

[18]92 L. Ed. 257, 68 Sup. Ct. 269 (1948).

[19]68 Sup. Ct. 1138, 92 L. Ed. 1096 (1948).

the time of the two conveyances until the date of trial, Kajir had not filed the annual reports which the Alien Land Law required of all guardians of minor children of ineligible aliens when such minor children owned agricultural land. The only evidence offered on trial was that of the person who had been left in charge of the land when Fred was forced to abandon the land. He testified that he had made all rental checks payable to the son, Fred, and understood that all moneys he did pay went to Fred. The petitioners contended that the statute deprived Fred of the equal protection of the laws as an American citizen; that it denied Kajiro equal protection of the laws as secured by the Fourteenth Amendment; and that it contravened the due process clause by sanctioning a taking of property after expiration of the applicable limitations period.

The opinion of the Court was rendered by Mr. Chief Justice Vinson, with whom Mr. Justice Frankfurter appeared to concur *sub silentio*. Mr. Justice Black, with whose opinion Mr. Justice Douglas agreed, concurred with the opinion of the Court, but preferred to state broader reasons for his position. Mr. Justice Murphy, with whom Mr. Justice Rutledge joined, likewise expressed his concurrence but for different reasons. Mr. Justice Reed, together with Mr. Justice Burton, dissented. Mr. Justice Jackson likewise dissented but for different reasons.

Mr. Chief Justice Vinson stated that the statute unconstitutionally discriminated against Fred because of his father's nationality in that it placed on him a burden of proof not generally borne by other minors in California when their parents purchased property for them. Thus Fred was denied the equal protection of the laws that the Fourteenth Amendment secures. This was so because, in the ordinary situation where the parent pays the consideration for a transfer of land to his minor child, a gift is presumed. There is no presumption of a resulting trust for the benefit of the parent. The burden, therefore, falls on the party who would attack the validity of the gift. But in Fred's situation the statute prima facie presumed that no gift was intended; and even more, that there was an intent to evade or avoid the statute because the consideration was paid by an ineligible alien for the transfer to a United States citizen or an eligible alien. Thus the burden fell on Fred to overcome this prima facie presumption, a burden, as just pointed out, not borne by other California children.

The most significant portion of this decision lies in the opinions of the four other justices, who concurred in the judgment of the Court, but who preferred to declare the statute unconstitutional on broader grounds. Mr. Justice Black, with whose opinion Mr. Justice Douglas agreed, felt that the basic provisions of the statute (forbidding ownership or leasing of agricultural lands by ineligible aliens) violated the equal protection clause of the Fourteenth Amendment. He felt that while the statute did not single out the Japanese by name to discriminate against, the purpose and effect of the statute was to discriminate against this racial group. It prohibited a Japanese from even owning a home in California if the land was at all suitable for cultivation, he continued, stating that the statute left open only the possibilities of working on agricultural lands as a servant or a hired hand. In effect then, he said, it suppressed him to the lowest possible economic levels. In his opinion this was not affording the Japanese the equal protection of the laws and the right to work at the common occupations of the community that the Fourteenth Amendment secures. "I would now overrule the previous decisions of this Court that sustained state land laws which discriminate against people of Japanese origin residing in this country," he emphatically concluded.[20]

Mr. Justice Murphy, in whose opinion Mr. Justice Rutledge joined, traced the historical growth of these laws, and then set about to dispell the arguments advanced in *Terrace* v. *Thompson*. He dispells the first argument that such laws were necessary to protect the safety of the state and the welfare of its citizens from the possibility of Japanese owning or occupying all the agricultural lands in the state by saying that such a possibility lies in the realm of theory only and not of reality. Another argument, heeded in *Terrace* v. *Thompson*, that such classification was proper because it was patterned after a similar classification adopted by the United States Congress in determining who might or might not become citizens, is likewise dispelled by Mr. Justice Murphy when he states that such a classification is not proper for a state to determine who might or might not own its agricultural lands when in fact such classification works to deprive the residents of that state of the equal protection of the laws.

---

[20] 92 L. Ed. 257, 265, 266, 68 Sup. Ct. 269, 276, 277 (1948).

The other case on the subject, *Tarao Takahaski* v. *Fish and Game Commission*,[21] decided by the Supreme Court during the last term, involved the question of the validity of a recent amendment to the California Fish and Game Code prohibiting the issuance of any license to any person ineligible for United States citizenship. The amendment, as originally adopted in 1943 when feeling was high against the Japanese as a result of the recent hostilities, was specifically directed against the Japanese. But in 1945, the legislature, feeling that such a classification might be declared discriminatory and hence uncononstititional, adopted the present classification prohibiting any person not eligible for citizenship from obtaining a license.[22] Takahashi brought this action in mandamus to compel the commission to issue a license to him. The California Supreme Court, when the case finally reached it on appeal, held the statute to be constitutional, with three dissenting opinions therefrom,[23] on the grounds that the state of California had a special proprietary interest in the fish off its shores which justified the state in protecting this property interest for the benefit of its own citizens, and as a conservatory measure therefor. The Supreme Court granted certiorari, as the state decision was based on the interpretation of a federal question.

The Supreme Court likened this case to the factual situation presented in *Truax* v. *Raich*, and said that the amendment would clearly be unconstitutional on the basis thereof had not *Truax* v. *Raich* gone further and announced that distinctions between aliens and citizens were valid when necessary to protect special interests of the state or its citizens. The Court here gave several examples of what had been held to be such special interests, but blandly concluded that there was no such special property interest;[24] that the argument that it was enacted wholly as a fish conservatory measure is wholly without merit in view of the original statement of the statute (prior to the 1945 amendment) when it was specifically directed against the Japanese; and that, therefore, it is a discriminatory classification which denies the

---

[21]68 Sup. Ct. 1138, 92 L. Ed. 1096 (1948).

[22]CAL. STATS., 1943, Ch. 1100, as amended in CAL. STATS., 1945, ch. 181.

[23]30 Cal. 2d 719, 185 P. 2d 805 (1947).

[24]McCready v. Virginia, 94 U. S. 391, 24 L. Ed. 248 (1876); Patsone v. Pennsylvania, 232 U. S. 138, 34 Sup. Ct. 281, 58 L. Ed. 539 (1914).

equal protection of the laws that the Fourteenth Amendment secures, and hence is unconstitutional.

The Court then passed to the argument that *Terrace* v. *Thompson* is controlling, and said, ". . . assuming the continued validity of these cases, we think they could not in any event be controlling here."[25] The Court distinguished *Terrace* v. *Thompson* as resting upon the power of states to control the devolution of real property within its borders.

Is this distinction real? Can it safely be concluded that the prior law on the subject, as announced in *Terrace* v. *Thompson* and the earlier California decisions, is still the law, or that *Oyama* v. *California* and *Tarao Takahashi* v. *Fish and Game Commission* supersede these cases, or that all these are cases distinguishable on their facts and hence in harmony? The conclusion seems inescapable that *Terrace* v. *Thompson* is no longer the law. It will be interesting to note what the Supreme Court will do when it is squarely confronted with the problem.

RICHARD A. GOATER.

---

[25]68 Sup. Ct. 1138, 1144 (1948).

AMERASIA 5:1 (1978), 39-56

Politics, Education, and Language Policy: The Case of Japanese Language Schools in Hawaii

JOHN N. HAWKINS

In culturally diverse societies, national language policy, especially as it relates to the function of schooling, is one of the most complex and at times emotionally-charged educational issues. Traditionally, the bulk of research on this controversial issue has focused on the psychological or linguistic dimensions of multilingual education.[1] In recent years, new studies are appearing that attempt to account for the larger social context in which language policy is formulated. Other studies are directing their attention to the thousands of recent bilingual and multilingual programs that have emerged outside of North America, often in the wake of intense social unrest.[2] Indeed, debates on the positive and negative aspects of bilingual or multilingual educational policy are worldwide. Viewed on an international scale, the complexity of issues concerning intergroup ethnic relations, and language policy specifically, are sharply apparent.[3] Hence, reinterpretations of existing data as well as case studies analyzing the influence of political, economic, and social forces on the formation of education and language policy are sorely needed. This case study of the early Japanese language schools in Hawaii is one attempt to meet such a need.

The study will focus on the political struggle of the Japanese immigrant community in the early twentieth century to maintain

JOHN N. HAWKINS is assistant professor of comparative and international education at the University of California, Los Angeles.
© 1978 by John N. Hawkins

their autonomous Japanese language schools in the face of strong opposition from the Hawaiian Territorial Government, controlled by the *haole* (white) elite.

After a long, drawn-out judicial process, the Japanese immigrant community won their case. This study will not examine, however, the legal aspects of the conflict, but will trace instead the intense period of political mobilization preceding the legal victory. Both proponents and opponents of the Japanese language schools mobilized their respective forces to maximize their access to educational policy making. Because the conflict was eventually decided in favor of the Japanese language schools, examining the political reasons for this policy outcome may shed light on language policy formation in general.

At the outset it is necessary to clarify some terms and concepts that are already referred to above and often used in analyzing language policy formation and the politics of education. Central to such study is the significant question of who has access to the formal and informal political institutions to change, modify, and adapt other institutions and resources. According to Lutz, there are three basic characteristics of educational decision making involving subordinate and dominant groups: 1) politics and power are integral to understanding any given educational decision; 2) power holders tend to maximize their own values and interests; and 3) subordinate groups, despite democratic and ideological exhortations to the contrary, are seldom represented politically in an equitable manner.[4] While these observations are not surprising, they represent the social and political conditions which existed in Hawaii at the turn of the century. During this period, in general, the *haole* elite utilized their monopoly on formal political and economic institutions to promote their own values and interests at the expense of the numerous subordinate populations (Hawaiians, Portuguese, Pilipino, Japanese, Korean, Chinese). These conditions and their concrete manifestations led supporters of the Japanese language schools to begin a process of political mobilization and participation in an effort to gain access to and ultimately influence the educational decision making.

What do we mean by mobilization and participation? Mobilization suggests participation, and several authors have insisted that regardless of how the politics of education is conceptualized (ranging from systems theory to psychological models), the interlinking thread inherent in all models is the degree of participation present and visible in the people involved.[5] Yet participation is a deceptive and elusive phenomenon. To "participate" politically conjures up images of actors playing roles in the numerous voluntary associations normally associated with politics and decision making, yet this range of possibilities is vague. In order to equate participation with a "share in the power" of decision making in education, we must distinguish between conventional concepts of participation (which Schermerhorn terms activation)[6] and the use of critical resources in the direct interests of the group attempting to influence policy making. In this case, supporters of Japanese language schools succeeded in mobilizing a critical number and variety of resources directly related to the preconditions mentioned above. This form of participation (not simply numbers of actors, since many Japanese did not support the struggle) was crucial to mounting an effective campaign around the issue of control of the language schools. Additional minimum conditions from the perspective of the subordinate group included a shared target of hostility (the Territorial Government and the *haole* elite), feelings of grievance and hardship, and a sense of collective oppression. In addition, an organizational base was available along two horizontal lines: traditional lines of ethnicity and secondary group lines of occupation and religion.

The terms "subordinate group" and "dominant group" are, of course, generalizations useful only to describe general patterns of relations. The Japanese community was never wholly united in support of the language schools, and the *haole* sector of the population experienced internal dissension as well. On the Japanese side, one major Japanese newspaper, and especially its editor (Kinzaburo Makino of the *Hawaii Hochi*), provided much of the leadership toward preserving the language schools and was backed by much of the Buddhist clergy. The Japanese Consul General's office and the other major Japanese newspaper, *Nippo Jiji,* wavered and at times opposed the struggle. On the American side, both newspapers and their editors, specifically Allen of the *Star Bulletin* and Irwin of the *Advertiser,* were vocal in their opposition to the schools. They were backed by Territorial Government officials associated with the Department of Public Instruction as well as elected officials in the legislature and the Governor's office. However, labor and plantation interests were at times opposed to the government's efforts to regulate the schools. Despite these apparent divisions in both communities (and we shall discuss them in more detail), they were in fact two different communities, overlapping very little institutionally, with separate communications channels and separate social organizations.

These characteristics of Hawaiian society during the early 1900s and the concepts of mobilization and participation as discussed above provide a loose framework for analyzing some salient aspects of the politics of educational decision making, especially as this process relates to cultural diversity and language policy.

Japanese Language Schools in Hawaii: A Brief Survey

In the following sections we will first examine the social and political context in which the language schools developed, and second, look at the mobilization efforts of the parties involved to acquire or maintain control over the schools. The history and characteristics surrounding the rise of the language schools were important factors in convincing the Territorial Government that they must be regulated and ultimately abolished.

Following a major period of Japanese immigration to Hawaii in the late 19th century and the subsequent rise of a new second generation, the Japanese community developed independent, private language schools which were designed to promote a sense of community through the study of Japanese culture and language, as well as to perpetuate Japanese culture and values.[9] The first schools were founded in the late 1800s on Maui and in Honolulu by both Buddhist and Christian representatives.[10] Although initially the schools were strongly tied to formal religious organizations, independent schools eventually dominated. Of the 181 Japanese language schools established in Hawaii by 1934, 76 percent were independent, 22 percent Buddhist, and 2 percent Christian.[11] Reverend Okumura's school in Nuuanu, considered by some as the model, included the following items in the school regulations: "The purpose of this school is to give children Japanese education...the subjects taught are reading, calligraphy, and composition. In addition, moral education and physical education will be given. Textbooks used for reading will be those approved by the Japanese Ministry of Education."[12] Children in these early schools observed major Japanese holidays and were at those times absent from the American public schools, which according to law they were required to attend. They bowed to the Emperor's picture, sang the Japanese national anthem, and studied the Imperial Rescript on Education.[13] This type of instructional activity continued down to 1915. As a result of increasing criticism by American educational authorities, from 1916 onward most schools made efforts to discard the image of being a separate educational track. They changed their names from Japanese Elementary Schools to Japanese Language Schools and discontinued use of Japanese Ministry of Education instructional materials; a period of curricular reform began.[14]

An umbrella organization, the Japanese Education Association, was founded in 1914 and included both Christian and Buddhist representatives (led by Okumura and Imamura respectively). Both groups within the Japanese community recognized the need for curriculum reform, and in 1915 a distinguished group of Japanese educators met to formulate a revision plan (Rev. Okumura, Bishop Imamura, Professor Haga of Tokyo University, R. Tsunoda of Honpa Hongwanji). Later, in 1916, Japanese Consul General Rukuro Moroi spearheaded a Central Educational Association which worked in cooperation with the Territorial Government to standardize the curriculum. At this early date a slight rift occurred within the Japanese community when Okumura introduced a new issue apart from the question of curriculum revision. Essentially, he suggested that all Japanese Language Schools be converted into independent schools under the joint supervision of American and Japanese educators. The Central Commission eventually disbanded. In any case, the revised texts that appeared after 1916 were "Hawaiianized versions" of the previous materials. These revisions made by the Japanese schools can be seen as a political strategy to relieve the pressure from American authorities.[15] Concomitantly, the revised curriculum may also be viewed as a reflection of the changing world view of the Japanese immigrants toward themselves, from sojourners to settlers with a political and economic status in Hawaii.

Apart from the criticism directed against the curriculum, the schools drew little attention from authorities in the Territorial Government and expanded steadily. By 1917, the majority of Japanese school-age children attended the public schools during the day and the Japanese language schools in the late afternoon and on weekends. The end of World War I brought a high degree of national chauvinism to Hawaii which, coupled with rising suspicion of the Japanese community in the 1920s (related in some measure to Japan's actions in China), created conditions for the conflict around the issue of control and regulation of the language schools. An additional factor raised repeatedly by the *haole* elite was the role played by Japanese strike leaders in the 1909 and especially the

1920 sugar plantation strikes. Even though the latter strike was broken and the leaders publicly humiliated the specter of a unified and mobilized Japanese labor force alarmed Hawaii's dominant groups, who viewed the language schools as an institutional organizational base of un-Americanism. An editorial in the *Star Bulletin* somewhat hysterically warned against "the priests of Asiatic paganism who were in an unholy alliance with foreign language schoolteachers and Japanese editors to control the industrialism of Hawaii."[16] On underlying cause for the tension that developed between the dominant leadership in Hawaii and the Japanese was fear on the part of the *haole* elite that the Japanese were getting out of hand economically and politically. The Buddhist temples and the language schools were considered the most dangerous manifestation of this trend.[17]

Throughout the struggle over regulation of the schools, Japanese supporters of the schools, particularly the *Hawaii Hochi,* maintained that the basic problem was the religious differences between Buddhist and Christian communities. Supporters of regulatory legislation, however, argued that religion had nothing to do with the struggle and instead stressed institutional and pedagogical problems related to the language schools. Despite some outward displays of religious tolerance, the record of *haole* antagonism toward non-Christian religions coupled with anti-foreign sentiment during this period made it easier for government officials and American educators to attack the language schools. The Territorial Government could and did interfere often on educational matters, and educational agencies in Hawaii increasingly saw the Japanese language schools as obstacles to their attempts to inculcate American values and attitudes in Japanese as well as other ethnic groups (especially Chinese and Koreans, who also maintained separate language schools).[18]

By 1919, legislation and proposals began to appear, calling for the certification of teachers on the basis of "ideals of democracy and knowledge of English."[19] This represented the first of several moves to monitor and limit the number of Japanese teachers (the majority of whom spoke only Japanese) and thereby further regulate the schools. The following excerpt from the Judd proposal appeared in the 4 January 1919 edition of the *Pacific Commercial Advertiser* and elaborated on additional preconditions for teacher certification in any school, public or private:

> To prescribe certain qualifications for school teachers and for the purpose of safeguarding American citizenship in the Territory of Hawaii.

> Be it enacted by the legislature of the Territory of Hawaii. *Section 1.* No person shall serve as a teacher in any school, without first having obtained a certificate from the Department of Public Instruction... Before issuing a certificate to any teacher, the department shall satisfy itself that such teacher possesses ideals of democracy and has a knowledge of the English language, American history, and methods of government...*Section 3.* The department may revoke a certificate, when satisfied that the holder thereof is unable to qualify under Section 1 of this Act... *Section 4.* Whoever shall serve as a teacher, without first having obtained such certificates, shall be punished by a fine.

Other legislation was introduced to abolish the schools entirely, but such efforts were haphazard and immediately opposed by leaders in the Japanese community. The Japanese response to the Judd proposal (January 1919), and later the Andrews bill (March 1919), was attacked by the *Advertiser* and American officials as "intemperate." The Japanese community was warned that such an attitude might result in further regulatory legislation. In fact, the Japanese response was quite temperate and consisted of petitions, mass meetings (Asahi Theatre, 10 March 1919), and a formal request from the Japanese Education Association (Ryuhei Mashimo) to officials requesting that the bills be withdrawn. The Hongwanji Educational Home Committee also submitted a formal resolution. Consequently, till 1920 all such acts, including the Lyman proposal which was more strongly phrased, were either tabled or defeated.[20] These measures were the first overt efforts to wrest control of the schools from the Japanese and met with the first instance of mobilized opposition. A "veritable flood of petitions" was sent to the legislature, Japanese workers on the plantations threatened to leave their jobs, and even the Chinese and Korean communities supported efforts to defeat the measures.[21]

Both sides had, however, made their positions clear. The Territorial Government realized that a planned, concerted effort was required to obtain control of the language schools. The Japanese community had, on the other hand, realized that only through effective mobilization could they influence educational decision making. The lines were thus drawn between those (including some Japanese) who increasingly favored control or abolition of language schools—accompanied as rapidly as possible with total assimilation of the Japanese into American society—and those, primarily in the Japanese community, who argued for cultural preservation and saw the language schools as the principal vehicle to achieve this goal.

The crisis accelerated during the period from 1919 to 1921. The defeat of the Judd and Andrews bills encouraged the Governor to invite the United States Commissioner of Education to investigate all public and private schools in the Territory in order to build a base for elimination of the private language schools. The 1920 labor strike also had the effect of inflaming opinion against the Japanese. Irwin of the *Advertiser* (he was also Territorial Attorney General) charged that teachers in the Japanese Language Schools had taken an active role in the strike, and McNally of the *Star Bulletin* argued that the previous bills had been defeated because of fear of further labor unrest. Both newspapers implied that a lobby group composed of labor and plantation interests had convinced the legislature of the danger of abolishing the separate schooling system for the Japanese, and of the need to maintain them. Legislation to eliminate the schools would adversely affect labor conditions, they argued, since the Japanese would become Americanized to the point where they would acquire the skills and abilities which would allow them to leave the fields for more lucrative and professional occupations. Members of this sector of the business community clearly were firm believers in the transformational power of education and sought to isolate the Japanese (and other Asian laborers) from the mainstream educational system, and by extension, from access to political and economic power. Here we see one example of the split in the *haole* community over regulation of the Japanese Language Schools.[22]

Reportedly at the request of the Chamber of Commerce, the Territorial Attorney General, Harry Irwin, drafted a proposal which was presented at a special session of the Territorial legislature on 20 November 1920. This proposal urged the total abolition of all foreign language schools and was the harshest legislation yet presented.[23] The response by moderate members of both the Territorial Government and the Japanese community was a compromise proposal known as Act 30. This measure, and what the Japanese later considered to be a betrayal of its contents, led to an open struggle and eventually a complicated legal battle over the issue of control of the Japanese language schools.

The Struggle for Control of the Japanese Language Schools

Educational officials, government authorities, and other leading members of the Territory of Hawaii set the stage for the legislative struggle that was to follow by a variety of both direct and indirect means. Direct efforts were made to remove the financial base of the language schools by such organizations as the Committee of the

Japanese Section of the Hawaiian Evangelical Association. This committee passed a resolution to discontinue plantation owners' subsidies to Japanese Language Schools operated by non-Christian organizations (i.e., the majority Buddhist schools).[24] Meanwhile, a series of media reports and statements ultimately removed any doubt regarding the overall goals of American society and the specific function of schooling as viewed by the Territorial Government and other opinion leaders in the *haole* elite. An annual government report issued in 1919 stated: "There can neither be national unity in ideals nor in purpose unless there is some common method of communication through which may be conveyed the thought of the nation. All Americans must be taught to read and write and think in one language; this is a primary condition to that growth which all nations expect of us and which we demand of ourselves."[25] The report goes on to lament a democracy which allows multi-language instruction in the schools and added that the machinery for effective Americanization is to be found in public education. The Territorial Superintendent was no less direct. Henry Kinney urged voters to support legislation aimed at controlling the Japanese language schools and declared that those Japanese who supported the schools were "troublemakers and agitators."[26] He predicted that the language schools would eventually die, killed off by second and third generation Japanese who would not attend: "The task of the Department of Public Instruction is to weld the large Japanese factor... into an integral part of our American body politic."[27] Eliminating the language schools was the first step. Other non-governmental institutions followed this lead and some, such as the YMCA, took active steps to promote the Americanization of the Japanese as quickly as possible.[28]

Supporters of the language schools at this time were represented primarily by the Hawaii Kyoiku Kai (Hawaii Education Association, also known as Japanese Education Association) founded in 1914.[29] The Association had been forewarned of the potential dangers of stressing cultural preservation and language integrity by Japanese Consul General Arita. In 1916, the Association began to revise the curriculum to remove clauses overtly stressing Japanese citizenship. A parallel move to separate the language schools from religious affiliation also took place.[30] However, these compromise actions had little effect as several bills introduced in 1919–1920 proposed either the abolishment or regulation of the language schools. The Japanese community responded with a series of volatile mass meetings during which race discrimination was denounced, petitions were drawn up and presented to a wide range of government authorities (including President Wilson), and appeals were made through the Japanese language newspapers (*Hawaii Hochi* and *Nippo Jiji*) to the community to fight the legislation.[31] The first signs of a split in the Japanese community emerged at this time. Increasingly, the language of protest shifted to suggestions that perhaps the existence of the language schools would actually promote Americanization and that for this reason the Territorial Government should retreat from its position on elimination of the schools. By 1920, however, the Japanese community was effectively mobilized and able to call mass meetings that were well attended, as well as reach organized labor groups and utilize the Japanese language media as an information channel.[32]

In the face of such widespread mobilization by the Japanese, Territorial Government officials, especially the Office of the Superintendent of Public Instruction, did not expect to successfully promote legislation that would entirely abolish the language schools. They were successful, however, in introducing and eventually signing into law the compromise measure, Act 30. The committee which drafted the measure included both moderate government officials and moderate members of the Japanese community. The Act stated that the government and the Office of the Superintendent of Public Instruction would be allowed to: "Regulate and not to prohibit the conducting of foreign language schools and the teaching of foreign languages; but to regulate the same so that the Americanism of the pupils be promoted."[33] The measure thus satisfied a broad segment of both communities, the *haole* elite who were concerned about the Americanism of Japanese youngsters, and the Japanese community who were now assured that the schools would not be eliminated but only "regulated." However, in a move the retriggered the conflict, American members of the committee proposed and added a clause to Act 30 that restricted the student enrollment in language schools to students who had reached the third grade of the public schools.[34] The Japanese members of the committee first opposed this action and then reluctantly agreed to support the entire document. Thus, it became obvious that the original intention of eliminating the schools was still in the minds of the American members of the committee, who justified their actions in the following manner:

> Practically all of the pupils are American citizens [second generation], and almost none of them will return to Japan to become Japanese residents or subjects. We shall hold these children more and more to

> American standards of manners, conduct, speech and habits of thought. We should be unjust to them if we allowed them to be surrounded by preventable alien influence, and forced them to enter the competitive American life under the resulting handicap...Assume if you choose, that the Japanese educational, social and political system is superior. The fact remains that there is a place for both civilizations, and the place for Japanese civilization is in Japan, not in the United States. In the interests of social harmony and good will, it is inexpedient that we should have, as a permanent institution, a system of schools managed and taught by aliens, even with the best of intentions on their part. We believe that the proper answer to the desire of Americans of oriental ancestry to learn the language of the orient is by offering instruction therein in the public schools, and charging tuition if necessary.[35]

Apart from the patronizing tone of the statement, it was clearly out of spirit with the original intent of Act 30, at least from the Japanese point of view. After all, they had complied with the certification and licensing requirements, had formed a joint committee to revise the curriculum, and had compromised on a variety of other issues. Despite disapointment, frustration, and outrage at what some members of the Japanese community believed to be a betrayal of their trust, in a compromise solution the Act was signed into law and became effective 1 January 1923.

Dissension in the Japanese community took place over the course of what future action, if any, ought to be taken. The possibilities ranged from complete acquiescence to mass protest and violence. One group, supported and encouraged by the Japanese Consul General and several prominent members of the Japanese community, urged the community not to fight the issue at this time but to assure government officials that they would Americanize as quickly as possible and reorganize the language schools accordingly. They argued that only through this method could the language schools be saved from complete elimination. Japanese Premier Hara and a number of other high officials in Japan also supported Americanization. Japanese in Hawaii were encouraged by this group to eliminate their "pagan" ways, give up persistent customs and manners (e.g., "noisy festivals and wrestling tournaments that disrupt the quiet Sundays") and generally "forget the idea of Japanese and always think and act from the point of view of the American people."[36] One prominent leader in the Japanese community challenged Japanese in Hawaii to become American in all ways except physical features and suggested that those parents who wanted their children to preserve Japanese manners and customs (including language) send them to Japan permanently.[37] It is difficult to determine from existing sources how widespread these sentiments were. Support for Act 30 and rapid Americanization clearly existed. Among officials of the Japanese government (the consulate in Hawaii and officials in Japan), fifty *nisei* (second generation) students at the University of Hawaii signed a petition in support of the Act, and seven of sixteen members of the committee appointed by the Superintendent's office to revise the curriculum of the language schools supported the legislation.[38] In addition, one of three Japanese language newspapers supported the Act.

The forces in the community opposed to the Act realized that the dissension over the issue of litigation seriously retarded the momentum that had built up since the Territorial Government began introducing regulatory legislation. The range of opinion was wide. One prominent Buddhist priest (Ninryo Nago) commented that the cultural differences between Japanese and Americans were simply too great and probably irreconcilable. For this reason he opposed control or elimination of the language schools on the grounds that it would be disastrous to the cultural integrity of Japanese in Hawaii. In fact, he stated, Japanese should look to Japan for identity and security, and if a choice should ever have to be made in terms of loyalty, it should be made in favor of Japan.[39] Others were more hopeful that a less extreme position could be found. The Japanese Society of Hawaii, a large umbrella organization of Japanese public opinion, met several times and reached the conclusion that further protest was necessary; that the language schools should be supported. At the same time, their argument shifted to emphasize the positive role the schools could play in creating good American citizens (not necessarily "Americanized," however). Moreover, they took the position that if the schools were eliminated, social disorder could result, especially among Japanese youth. Here we see one of the first important expressions of a threatened sanction to both the non-Japanese and Japanese communities in Hawaii: youth violence. Their opinion was formulated in a petition and sent to the Superintendent of Public Instruction, along with the veiled threat that enforcement of the Act could lead to social chaos.[40] The Japanese media (primarily the *Hawaii Hochi* and *Hawaii Shinpo*) directed their attention to the Japanese community itself.[41] In a series of articles from February to May 1923, the *Hawaii Hochi* encouraged the community to fight the legislation and stand up for their rights. Writers played on the theme of "manhood" and derided those who succumbed to the Territorial Government's actions as "weak Japanese." Other writers were more vehement, suggesting that those Japanese who submitted to the legislation should be despised as *chorinbo,* or outcasts.[42] Editorials encouraged Japanese labor to apply pressure on the Sugar Planter's Association and reminded the Association of the 1920 strike and the potential danger of a similar strike over the school issue. The paper urged a frontal assault against the Territorial Government, extending from formal litigation to pressure on the labor community and the educational establishment.[43] All of these plans sufficiently alarmed the Government, the *haole* elite, and the sugar plantation owners for whom the labor strike of 1920 was still a fresh memory. The situation was described by Governor Farrington as "delicate." Other influential *haoles* urged the Governor to proceed with caution, and the entire situation was "touchy."[44] So while the Japanese community was clearly divided over the issue of further protest, the opponents of the schools, primarily government officials and educators, were also beginning to waver. The combined threats of labor unrest (in actuality more in the minds of the *haole* elite than most Japanese), youth violence, and social instability within the Japanese community had the effect of weakening support for Act 30 and regulation of the language schools in general.

Although the initial response of the Japanese community toward the idea of formal legal action was not widespread, (only eleven out of one hundred and thirty language schools voted to join a lawsuit), a test case was entered. As litigation proceeded and community pressure grew in favor of fighting the Act, more schools joined, so that by August 1923 eighty-seven supported the test case.

Prior to the signing of Act 30, the legal firm of Lightfoot and Lightfoot, representing the Japanese Society of Hawaii, filed a brief with the Governor's office challenging the constitutionality of the new regulations. The Hawaii Circuit Court tried the case, and the constitutionality of Act 30 was upheld by Judge James Banks. In the meantime, a landmark case, *Meyers* v. *Nebraska,* was decided in favor of an elementary school teacher who taught the subject of reading in German. The Nebraska State Supreme Court had originally upheld a state ruling prohibiting "teaching any subject to any person in any language other than the English language." In this case there was clearly no religious argument; the State of Nebraska instead focused on the foreign language threat to order and stability. The Supreme Court of the United States finally reversed the ruling in 1923, on the grounds that it violated the 14th Amendment.

In Hawaii by 1925, eighty-four of a hundred and forty Japanese language schools joined the litigants. The Japanese community was able to raise over $25,000 to fight the case. On 21 February 1927 the United States Supreme Court finally decided in favor of the Japanese language schools. The judgment of the Court was particularly harsh toward Territorial officials. After detailing the various attempts to control the language schools, the court ruled: "...all are parts of a deliberate plan to bring foreign language schools under a strict governmental control for which the record discloses no adequate reason." Both parties avoided the religious issue and focused instead on loyalty, stability, and threats to the state.[45] The seven year effort to preserve the schools and to maintain autonomous control over the curriculum and administration was successful. This was an impressive example of a clearly subordinate group effectively mobilizing available resources, coping with a damaging split in the mobilization effort, and finally emerging victorious.

Twenty years later, in 1947 an attitudinal survey revealed that although first and second generation Japanese generally agreed that the preservation of the language schools was a positive development, considerable disagreement existed regarding other aspects of the language school issue. The disagreement as revealed in the questionnaire was directly correlated with generation and had little to do with other measures (e.g., occupation, sex, religion, education, etc.). First generation Japanese favored the schools for most of the reasons stated earlier (knowledge of Japanese was essential to maintain linkages between generations, the schools promoted good will and assisted in the Americanization process, moral training in the schools was important for community solidarity, and so on). However, the statements of second generation Japanese were more critical. The schools, they charged, caused far too much stress in children (one of the earlier *haole* arguments), and in fact hindered Americanization; the schools were too small and run inefficiently; curricular objectives were not coordinated with the public schools, creating confusion in the child; and the language schools generally did a poor job of teaching the language.[46]

On the surface it might appear that the preservation of Japanese language schools was the result of well-argued litigation and an equitable judicial system. And in fact it was through the courts that supporters of the language schools were finally able to gain access to the educational decision-making structure. Yet the road to the first test case, as we have seen, was long and arduous. An earlier point stressed the importance of mobilization as the key to access, and the court action, while critical, could not have occurred had not other conditions been present. What were these conditions and what judgments can be made in relation to language policy formation in general? We cannot generalize on the basis of one case study;

nonetheless, in the case of the language schools, at least two sets of conditions seemed to be present.

First, the attempt by the Territorial Government to regulate and eliminate the foreign language schools was only one of many such efforts to maintain dominance over the many subordinate ethnic groups in Hawaii. This attempt came, however, at a time when the Japanese realized the political resources available to them and were also aware of their ability to mobilize these resources. Control of language schools was an issue that prompted the Japanese community to increasingly participate and mobilize in opposition to the dominant elite. A mobilization effort of this kind is not necessarily the result of conscious leadership, at least at the beginning.[47] In the Hawaii case it is difficult to isolate individual leaders, aside from Makino of *Hawaii Hochi,* who from the start agitated for struggle on the language issue. Rather, we see larger organizations and institutions (the Buddhist church, the Japanese media, the Hawaii Education Association, labor groups, etc.) responding to a perceived threat, and later duplicity on the part of the *haole* elite. As the struggle progressed, the Japanese were able to mobilize power resources and threaten sanctions, satisfying the preconditions of mobilization as we have discussed.[48] This combination of activities (inter- and intra-group struggle, intensive participation, mobilization of available resources, and the threat of sanctions) laid the basis for the successful court action that was to come.

Second, the dominant group in Hawaii (the *haole* elite) had increasingly experienced a lessening of social control over the Japanese as well as other subordinate ethnic groups. The success of Japanese labor organizers in the early 1900s (culminating in the 1909 strike which was 100 percent Japanese), and the joint Japanese-Pilipino strike in 1920 contributed to the alarm the *haole* elite were beginning to feel about their own ability to maintain control over the industrial and political institutions of the Territory. On another level, the Territorial Government was having increasing difficulty dealing with higher level officials in Washington, upon whose legitimacy they depended. Attempts to convince Washington officials to lift immigration laws at this time (1920s) in order to allow more Chinese labor into the islands (an action designed to weaken Japanese labor solidarity and control) ran into severe difficulties.[49] In short, the Japanese endeavor was aided by the weakening social control of the *haole* elite.

This dual set of circumstances—political mobilization of the oppressed group and weakening of social control on the part of the dominant elite—appears to be the essential element in the Japanese community's maintaining control of the language schools. The implications of this study for language policy formation in general is probably limited to experiences that are at least somewhat similar in context. Yet clearly the institutional survival of the language schools and the opening of access to educational decision making were directly related to the politics of mobilization and participation by a subordinate group. This experience, along with subsequent struggles, contributed to the eventual emergence of a more equitable political and economic relationship between the Japanese and *haoles* in Hawaii.

NOTES

1. Joshua A. Fishman, *Bilingual Education: An International Sociological Perspective* (Rowley, Mass., 1976), 108.

2. Kellman's study suggests that depending upon the kind of attachment that groups and subgroups may have to the national system, language can either serve an integrative or disintegrative function. Herbert C. Kellman, "Language as Aid and Barrier to Involvement in the National System," *Conference on Language Planning and Processes, East West Center,* Honolulu (1969). Additional recent cross-national studies include: Alfa Ibrahim Sow, *Languages and Linguistic Policies in Black Africa: The Experience of UNESCO* (Paris, 1977); M. L. Marasinghe, "Some Problems Associated with a Language Switchover in the Third World," *Law and Modernization,* No. 4 (1978); Istvan Fodor and Claude Hagege, *Language Reforms of the Past and in the Developing Countries* (Hamburg, Germany, 1978).

3. Fishman, 1976; Bernard A. Spolsky and Robert L. Cooper, eds., *Case Studies in Bilingual Education* (New York, 1977).

4. Frank Lutz, "Methods and Conceptualizations of Political Power in Education" in J. Scribner, ed., *The Politics of Education* (Chicago, 1977), 33.

5. Kjell Eide, "Participation and Participatory Planning in Educational Systems," in *Participatory Planning in Education* (Paris, 1974); Lutz, "Methods and Conceptualizations of Political Power in Education;" R. A. Schermerhorn, *Comparative Ethnic Relations: A Framework for Theory and Research* (New York, 1970).

6. Schermerhorn, *Comparative Ethnic Relations,* 130.

7. Hubert M. Blalock, *Toward a Theory of Minority-Group Relations* (New York, 1967), 110-112.

8. Anthony Oberschall, *Social Conflict and Social Movements* (New Jersey, 1973), 120. The term "*haole* elite" refers to those Caucasians who constituted an elite group, around 5 percent of the population in 1900, of American or British background. Of primarily missionary or business background, they sought and acquired political and economic control of the islands by the 1920s. A small core of families dominated the inner group of all *haoles* (in 1935 about 20 percent of the population). For a detailed analysis of the role of the *haole* elite in Hawaii see: Lawrence H. Fuchs, *Hawaii Pono: A Social History* (New York, 1961).

9. Koichi Glenn Harada, "A Survey of Japanese Language Schools in Hawaii," (M.A. thesis, University of Hawaii, 1934), 33; John E. Reinecke, "Feigned Necessity: Hawaii's Attempt to Obtain Chinese Contract Labor, 1921-1923," (M.A. thesis, University of Hawaii, 1967), 32.

10. Reverend Yonichi established the Buddhist Hongwanji mission in 1887, and Reverend Okumura founded the Nuuanu Japanese Church in 1890; both were bases for the eventual proliferation of Japanese language schools: Harada, "A Survey of Japanese Language Schools in Hawaii," 42; Katsumi Onishi, "A Study of the Attitudes of the Japanese in Hawaii Toward the Japanese Language Schools," (M.A. thesis, University of Hawaii, 1948), 7.

11. Harada, "A Survey of Japanese Language Schools in Hawaii," 42.

12. Hawaii Nihonjin Iminshi Kauko Iinkai, ed., *Hawaii Nihonjin Iminshi* (Honolulu, 1964), 232.

13. Hawaii Nihonjin Iminshi Kauko Iinkai, ed., *Hawaii Nihonjin Iminshi,* 232. The Imperial Rescript was promulgated on 30 October 1890 and became the basic statement of official educational aims in Japan. Stressing filial piety, harmony, and morality, it was essentially a neo-Confucian pedagogical statement: Herbert Passin, *Society and Education in Japan* (New York, 1965), 151.

14. *Ibid.*, 232-233.

15. Louise H. Hunter, *Buddhism in Hawaii* (Honolulu, 1977), 99.

16. Fuchs, *Hawaii Pono,* 219.

17. Reinecke, "Feigned Necessity," 34.

18. *Ibid.*

19. *Ibid.*, 37.

20. Harada, "A Survey of Japanese Language Schools in Hawaii," 63; Hunter, *Buddhism in Hawaii,* 109.

21. Reinecke, "Feigned Necessity," 39.

22. Hunter, *Buddhism in Hawaii,* 110.

23. Hawaii Nihonjin Iminshi Kauko Iinkai, ed., *Hawaii Nihonjin Iminshi,* 235-238.

24. *Ibid.*, 228-229.

25. *Advertiser,* 4 January 1919.

26. *Advertiser,* 13 March 1919.

27. *Ibid.*

28. For example, the YMCA published English language books for plantation workers and established special classes with the expressed desire to further the Americanization process: *Advertiser,* 6 January 1919.

29. Onishi, "A Study of the Attitudes of the Japanese," 15.

30. *Ibid.*, 16.

31. *Advertiser,* 11 March 1919; *Advertiser,* 12 March 1919.

32. *Ibid.*

33. Reinecke, "Feigned Necessity," 398.

34. *Ibid.*, 400.

35. *Ibid.*, 399.

36. Takie Okumura and Umetaro Okumura, *Hawaii's American-Japanese Problem* (Honolulu, 1927), 9.

37. *Ibid., 17.*

38. Reinecke, *Feigned Necessity,* 390.

39. *Hawaii's Buddhism* (Honolulu, February 1923).

40. *A Brief Survey of the Foreign Language School Question.* (Honolulu, 1923), 14.

41. The Superintendent's office regularly had selections of the Japanese newspapers translated in order to keep abreast of sentiment in the Japanese community.

42. Reinecke, "Feigned Necessity," 402.

43. *Hawaii Hochi,* 23 February, 20 March, 21, 23, 25, 28 April, 3 May, 1923.

44. Reinecke, "Feigned Necessity," 401-402.

45. Harada, "A Survey of Japanese Language Schools in Hawaii"; Onishi, "A Study of the Attitudes of the Japanese." *Meyers* v. *Nebraska.* Supreme Court of the United States, 1923. 262 U.S. 390, 43 S.Ct. 625; 67 L.Ed. 1024, 281-286. *Farrington* v. *Tokushige.* Supreme Court of the United States, 1927. 465 U.S. 273, 284-299.

46. Onishi, "A Study of the Attitudes of the Japanese."

47. This point is made by Oberschall, *Social Conflict and Social Movements,* 146-148.

48. Schermerhorn, *Comparative Ethnic Relations,* 130.

49. Fuchs, *Hawaii Pono,* 228-229.

AMERASIA 4:2 (1977), 1–22

The Early Japanese Immigrant Quest for Citizenship: The Background of the 1922 Ozawa Case

YUJI ICHIOKA

Denied the right of naturalization, Japanese immigrants were so-called "aliens ineligible to citizenship" for decades. In the noted case of Ozawa Takao, the United States Supreme Court upheld the ineligibility of the Japanese in a 1922 landmark decision that stood unchallenged until the McCarran Act of 1952 altered their legal status and finally admitted them into citizenship. The literature in English on the early history of the immigrants is one-sided.[1] Principally devoted to the movement to exclude the Japanese from the United States in the first quarter of the twentieth century, it covers the origins, causes, and development of the exclusion movement and the adverse repercussions it had on United States-Japan relations. Highlighting the *excluders* rather than the *excluded,* the literature rarely touches on how the immigrants felt, thought, and reacted to being excluded. Slighting them, past studies give at best the false impression of their having been merely a victimized mass. Japanese immigrants were anything but passive victims; on the contrary, they actively fought the exclusion movement. As a part of their long and bitter struggle, they supported the Ozawa case in the

YUJI ICHIOKA, editor of *A Buried Past: An Annotated Bibliography of the Japanese American Research Project Collection* (Berkeley, 1974), is currently doing primary research on the history of Japanese immigrant society in America before World War II using Japanese-language sources.

A Ford Foundation grant, administered by the Institute of American Cultures, University of California at Los Angeles, made possible the research for this essay.
© 1977 by Yuji Ichioka

hope of gaining the right of naturalization. Presenting the immigrant background of the case, this essay will examine the initial abortive Japanese quest for naturalization rights.[2]

Barring Asians from acquiring American citizenship, early naturalization statutes formed the legal framework of the Ozawa case.[3] In 1790 Congress restricted the right of naturalization to an alien who was a "free white person" in the very first naturalization act. Subsequent enactments, legislated during the nineteenth century, all contained this racial condition which defined an alien's general eligibility for admission into citizenship. Extending the right of naturalization to former slaves, in 1870 Congress made "aliens of African nativity and persons of African descent" also eligible. In force at the time of the Ozawa decision, both the white and African categories of eligibility were embedded in section 2169 of Title XXX of the Revised Federal Statutes of 1875. The Act of 29 June 1906 standardized naturalization requirements and procedures. Directly bearing on the Ozawa case, this legislation regulated nonracial requirements, but did not rescind the preceding racial limitations of section 2169. Thus only two types of aliens were eligible to become American citizens when Ozawa Takao filed for naturalization in 1914, namely, persons of white and African descent.

Despite the racial restriction, the eligibility of the Japanese was subject to debate before the Ozawa decision. Though the Japanese definitely were not of African descent, the question of whether they might be classified as so-called free white persons remained. This racial category was not defined precisely. What was meant by *free*? And, more significantly, what was meant by *white*? Was the category inclusive or exclusive? Could the Japanese be classified, not as mongolian, but as caucasian? Neither Congressional legislation nor any United States Supreme Court decision provided unequivocable answers to such key questions. The fate of the Chinese offered a clue but less than definitive answers. In the Chinese Exclusion Act of 1882, Congress declared the Chinese inadmissible into citizenship, but the act made no mention of the Japanese. Due to the ambiguous meaning of a free white person, some lower federal courts issued naturalization papers to a number of Japanese. According to the census of 1910, four hundred twenty were naturalized.[4] One of the first was Kaneko Shinsei, a resident of Riverside, California, who received his preliminary papers in 1892. Obtaining his final papers in 1896, Kaneko exercised his American citizenship by voting and serving as a juror. He even had an American passport issued to him with which he travelled abroad.[5] In 1906, in conjunction with the passage of the Act of 1906, the United States Attorney General ordered federal courts to cease issuing naturalization papers to Japanese applicants, which ended the practice that permitted the handful to become naturalized. Yet this administrative measure did not have the weight of a final judicial ruling, leaving doubts as to the eligibility of the Japanese under existing statutes.

The anti-Japanese exclusion movement first brought the question of naturalization rights for the Japanese into prominence. In late February 1905 the San Francisco *Chronicle* launched a front-page editorial crusade against the influx of Japanese laborers. Organized labor followed suit in May by establishing the Japanese and Korean Exclusion League (later known as the Asiatic Exclusion League), and intensified the agitation calling for the exclusion of Japanese laborers. After the disastrous earthquake of April 1906, many anti-Japanese outbursts occurred. Precipitating an international crisis, the major event took place in October when the San Francisco School Board resolved to segregate Japanese pupils in the public schools. The Japanese government lodged a vigorous protest. In response to the ensuing crisis, President Theodore Roosevelt on December 3 denounced the Board's action as "a wicked absurdity" in his annual message to Congress.[6] While lauding the Japanese people to placate the Japanese government and public opinion in Japan, he recommended legislation to grant the Japanese in the United States the right of naturalization. Whatever his motives were, Roosevelt's recommendation riveted sudden attention to this matter.[7]

Japanese diplomats were aware of the questionable status of the Japanese immigrants with respect to naturalization. Even before Roosevelt's message, Consul Uchida Sadatsuchi of New York City in the spring of 1906 noted that the Supreme Court had yet to rule on the eligibility of the Japanese under existing statutes. Only lower court decisions and administrative interpretations excluded them. Uchida favored naturalization rights for Japanese immigrants, but felt that "it was advisable to defer the solution to this question for a while until an opportune time arrives."[8] Aoki Shūzō, Japanese Ambassador to the United States, believed that such a moment had come with the school crisis. Accordingly, independent of instructions from the Foreign Ministry, he broached the subject of naturalization with Secretary of State Elihu Root in late October. Shown a draft of Roosevelt's message to Congress, Aoki reported optimistically to the Foreign Ministry that the Roosevelt administration was disposed to granting the Japanese the right.[9] Acknowledging that its acquisition would be "the basic solution to the immigration issue," Foreign Minister Hayashi Tadasu on November 18 thereupon ordered Aoki to explore the matter further with the Secretary of State.[10]

Diplomatic efforts to negotiate the right were short-lived. In early January 1907 Foreign Minister Hayashi instructed Ambassador Aoki to ascertain how the American government intended to solve the school and naturalization issues. Queried by Aoki about naturalization, Secretary of State Root refused flatly to consider it, contending that a bill of the kind recommended by the President could not be introduced in time for Congressional action.[11] Undeterred by this rebuff, towards the beginning of February, the Foreign Ministry laid down the condition that, upon satisfactory solution of the school issue, it would be willing to negotiate the curtailment of Japanese immigration in exchange for the right of naturalization. The American side never accepted the condition; both Secretary of State Root and American Ambassador Luke E. Wright in Tokyo persisted in refusing adamantly to discuss naturalization. Confronted by the unyielding stance, Foreign Minister Hayashi conveyed to Ambassador Aoki on February 23 that "I consider naturalization is impossible at this juncture."[12] Aoki reached an identical conclusion. On the following day he reported that "the present juncture is most unsuitable for effecting any favorable arrangement."[13] Judging any further pursuit of the matter as futile, however the immigration issue might be finally settled, the Foreign Ministry henceforth dropped the naturalization issue altogether.

Simultaneously, immigrant leaders considered the naturalization question. Kawasaki Minotarō, editor of the *Nichibei Shimbun* of San Francisco, the most influential immigrant newspaper, recognized the Japanese immigrants' uncertain legal status. To make them clearly admissible into citizenship, he proposed in July 1905 that the Japanese government negotiate naturalization rights with the American government.[14] When President Roosevelt's message to Congress was publicized, the *Shin Sekai,* another San Francisco immigrant newspaper, editorially heralded his recommendation with great elation.[15] Later in January 1907, with a growing interest in naturalization, the newspaper published an extensive article on the legal aspect of the question by Miyakawa Masuji.[16] A practicing attorney in San Francisco, Miyakawa, who had acquired citizenship in 1905, was among the handful of naturalized Japanese. Congress amended immigration statutes in mid-February 1907 and authorized the President to halt the migration of Japanese laborers from the

Hawaiian Islands. The day after the Congressional action, and as the Foreign Ministry was trying to negotiate the naturalization issue, the Japanese Association of Washington wired Foreign Minister Hayashi, appealing to him to seek the right of naturalization in exchange for any immigration restrictions.[17] In April Takahashi Tetsuo, president of the Washington association, submitted a formal petition to Ambassador Aoki in which he stated that "the acquisition of naturalization rights would undercut the arguments for exclusion."[18] Immigrant leaders in San Francisco acted similarly. They dispatched Noda Otosaburō to Washington, D.C., also in April, to impress upon Aoki "the urgency of acquiring naturalization rights."[19] And in June Karl K. Kawakami published an article entitled "The Naturalization of Japanese" in the *North American Review*. The foremost immigrant publicist in English, he argued for naturalization rights for professionals, merchants, and farmers.[20]

This initial interest subsided as suddenly as it emerged. In accordance with the Congressional authorization, President Roosevelt issued an executive order on 14 March 1907 prohibiting Japanese (and Korean) laborers, whose passports had been issued for destinations other than the United States, to enter the country via insular possessions, the Canal Zone, or other nations. Separate from the naturalization issue, the Japanese government consented to terminate all labor immigration to buttress the executive order. Based upon the Gentlemen's Agreement, the Foreign Ministry stopped issuing passports to laborers for the continental United States. During negotiation of the agreement in the winter of 1907–1908, Japanese diplomats never raised the naturalization issue.[21] Nor did they bring it up in later talks to conclude the United States-Japan Treaty of Commerce and Navigation of 1911. Immigrant leaders did not push for naturalization rights once the international crisis passed. Destined to be the main political organization of the Japanese immigrants in California, the Japanese Association of America was organized in February 1908.[22] The naturalization question appeared on the agenda of its first official conference with affiliated local Japanese associations held in January 1909. No specific course of action was adopted. Japanese association leaders simply referred it to a study committee where it languished from want of action.[23]

The California Alien Land Law of 1913 revived the interest of the immigrants in naturalization rights. Employing the phrase "aliens ineligible to citizenship," the law avoided direct reference to the Japanese, but the language was devised clearly with them in mind. Stripped of legal jargon, the law prohibited individual Japanese and corporate bodies, the majority of whose members or stockholders were Japanese, to purchase agricultural land, and limited the leasing of such land to no more than three years. Moreover, it forbade the Japanese to bequeath or sell agricultural land they already owned to fellow immigrants. Enacted by the state legislature at the beginning of May 1913, it was signed officially into law on the nineteenth. The *Nichibei Shimbun* voiced the anger felt by the immigrants. It editorially opined that the law manifested the "height of discriminatory treatment" to which the immigrants were subjected. Ostensibly a people of a first-rate power, the Japanese were "accorded worse treatment than people of third-rate southern and eastern European nations living in the United States."[24]

Since the new law singled out ineligible aliens, the immigrants turned naturally to the old question of naturalization. If somehow they were able to acquire citizenship, so they reasoned, the law would not apply to them. Reflecting the turn of events, an intense, widespread discussion of the question arose. The immigrant press analyzed it in great depth in the spring and early summer months of 1913. All immigrant newspapers have not been preserved, but the available ones championed the idea of seeking naturalization rights. The *Nichibei Shimbun* was at the forefront. "Japanese diplomats and other notables say that we should wait until the opportune time comes," the newspaper granted, but avowed that "we cannot agree with the position of waiting for that moment."[25] Admittedly, seeking the right would require time and careful study; but concluding that its acquisition would be "the basic solution" to the alien land law, the *Nichibei Shimbun* dismissed a policy of stoic inaction and called upon immigrant leaders to initiate a long-term drive to secure the right. Using the same language, the *Shin Sekai* interpreted "the acquisition of naturalization rights" as "the basic solution" to the legislation.[26] The *Kororado Shimbun* of Denver echoed the editorials of the San Francisco immigrant dailies.[27] The *Taihoku Nippō* of Seattle dissented conspicuously. Against any drive to seek the right, it believed that such a quest was foreordained to fail and, contrary to being a solution, would arouse more hostility towards the Japanese.[28]

Other groups and individuals joined in supporting the idea of seeking naturalization rights. Headquartered in San Francisco with immigrant Christian churches under its jurisdiction, the Japanese Interdenominational Board of Mission endorsed the idea through its official organ, the *Shin Tenchi.*[29] Expressing the position of the

Buddhist Mission of America, the *Beikoku Bukkyō* came out in favor of naturalization too.[30] More explicitly, Chiba Toyoji proposed a naturalization test case as the best way of gaining the right.[31] As editor of the *Hokubei Nōhō,* a monthly journal devoted to the promotion of immigrant agriculture, Chiba was a prominent figure in the Japanese Agricultural Association. Immediately after the passage of the land bill, individuals in San Francisco favoring naturalization founded the Shiminken Kakutoku Kisei Dōshikai (Society for Promoting Acquisition of Citizenship), the very name of the organization denoting the purpose to which it was dedicated.[32] Addressing the general American public in May, Karl K. Kawakami wrote: "The only salvation for the Japanese lies in their admission into citizenship"; and in his book of 1914, *Asia At The Door,* he restated his belief that the Japanese should be allowed to naturalize.[33]

The Japanese Association of America and its affiliated locals also affirmed support. Just as the state legislature was about to enact the land bill, Japanese association leaders met at the end of April to discuss ways of coping with it at an emergency conference.[34] The naturalization question was a major agenda item, and the deliberation on this subject mirrored the on-going discussion within immigrant society. No delegate disputed that naturalization presented a fundamental solution; nor did anyone object to seeking the right. Accepting the desirability of the goal, the delegates debated the means of achieving it. As a result of the proceedings, a fifteen-man committee was appointed and empowered to explore all possible countermeasures to the pending bill, including the acquisition of naturalization rights. The 1906 school imbroglio generated a sudden, brief interest in naturalization. The California Alien Land Law of 1913 resuscitated the interest permanently, producing a wide consensus among immigrant leaders that they should embark on actually seeking the right.

Three ways of obtaining naturalization rights were aired.[35] The first was through diplomatic channels. The immigrants would depend on the Japanese government to conclude a special convention granting the right with the American government. During the school crisis, the Japanese government had offered to curtail labor immigration in exchange for naturalization rights, only to have abandoned this condition in the face of stiff American opposition. For the immigrants this alternative meant they had to wait for Japanese diplomats to take the initiative. The second way was to lobby for Congressional legislation. The immigrants would campaign for a law specifically admitting them into citizenship. A leading proponent of this idea was Masukawa Takeji of New York City who addressed immigrant audiences up and down the Pacific Coast in the summer of 1913 to marshall support for it. Realistically, the prospect for such legislation was dim, if not nil, in the light of American public opinion. That left a third choice. The immigrants would seek the right through litigation. To get a final judicial ruling regarding their eligibility under existing statutes, they could take a naturalization test case to the Supreme Court. Aside from the question of securing a favorable decision, this last option had an attractiveness. It did not hinge directly on either the initiative of Japanese diplomats or the state of American public opinion. The immigrants themselves were in a position to pursue it.

Leading up eventually to the Ozawa case, two important events transpired following the emergency parley of the Japanese Association of America and its affiliated locals. First, the newly appointed fifteen-man committee sent two representatives to Washington, D.C. to confer with the Japanese Ambassador who then was Chinda Sutemi. The two emissaries were Abiko Kyūtarō, publisher of the *Nichibei Shimbun,* and Ushijima Kinji, commonly known outside of immigrant society as George Shima, the Potato King. To overcome the adverse effects of the exclusion movement, Japanese association leaders decided to undertake, what they labelled, "a campaign of education" to enlighten the American public about Japan and the Japanese immigrants as well as to educate the immigrants themselves about the United States. Beyond seeking the right of naturalization, they deemed such a broad educational program necessary in order to foster a favorable climate of opinion. The two men were entrusted with a three-fold mission: to outline the campaign to Ambassador Chinda, to inform him of the condition of the immigrants in California, and to elicit from him the Japanese government's stand on naturalization.

Abiko and Ushijima met with Ambassador Chinda in mid-June 1913 as he was protesting the enactment of the alien land law. Chinda submitted his first protest note to Secretary of State William Jennings Bryan on May 9 in which he said nothing about naturalization. Eight days later Foreign Minister Makino Shinken instructed him to feel Bryan out on the subject.[36] Chinda did so immediately, and Bryan declined emphatically to consider it, as Secretary of State Elihu Root had in 1907.[37] In his second protest note of June 4, Chinda described the ineligibility of the Japanese as "mortifying to the Government and people of Japan" because it had been manipulated to restrict the Japanese immigrants' "civil" right in regards to land tenure. As long as the "distinction" had been "employed in relation to rights of [a] purely political nature," he stated, his government had "had no occasion to approach the Government of the United States on the subject."[38] Conceding naturalization was a domestic matter, Chinda couched his reference to it in these oblique terms. Having been rebuffed by Bryan, he never insisted on negotiating naturalization rights.

Chinda was awaiting a reply to his second protest note from Bryan when he received Abiko and Ushijima. Informed by them of the Japanese associations' plan for an educational campaign, Chinda heartily endorsed it. As to naturalization rights, according to the two emissaries, he averred that, in principle, his government favored it, but the American public was not ready to accept it. Rather than precipitately seeking the right, the groundwork of changing public opinion had to be done beforehand.[39] Chinda indicated the reluctance of his government to force the issue, a stance to be reiterated later by other Japanese diplomats. On July 16 Secretary of State Bryan answered Chinda's second note. Surmising that Chinda did not have instructions "to press the matter," Bryan ignored the subject.[40] A week later Foreign Minister Makino advised Chinda to shelve the naturalization issue.[41] In the estimate of Japanese diplomats, the diplomatic possibility of negotiating naturalization rights was not present. As it had been in 1907, for them the time still was inopportune, making it evident to immigrant leaders that they could not count on the Japanese government to take the initiative.

The founding of the Pacific Coast Japanese Association Deliberative Council was the other event of importance. At the emergency April 1913 conference, Japanese association leaders also adopted a proposal to establish a broader, national organization, embracing at least all immigrants on the Pacific Coast and in the western states. To implement this proposal, a preliminary meeting in San Francisco was held in November 1913. Then, in July 1914, representatives from Seattle, Portland, San Francisco, and Vancouver, Canada convened in Portland to form the Council. As it was organized, the Council was not a new organization but a higher coordinating organ of the existing so-called central bodies to which all local Japanese associations were affiliated. The United North American Japanese Association was the central body in Seattle to which locals in Washington and Montana were affiliated.[42] The Japanese Association of

America, the largest central body, had all locals in California, Nevada, Utah, Colorado, and Arizona affiliated to it. Based in Portland, the Japanese Association of Oregon had locals in Oregon, Idaho, and Wyoming under its jurisdiction. These three central bodies combined with the Japanese Association of Canada to constitute the Pacific Coast Japanese Association Deliberative Council whose purpose was to solve problems held in common by all associations. Founded in 1915, the Central Japanese Association of Southern California, with affiliated locals in southern California and Arizona, joined the Council in 1916.[43] From 1914 the Council convened at least once a year. Inasmuch as the naturalization problem was shared by all immigrants in the United States, it was this body which assumed responsibility for solving it. At its inception, indeed, the Council adopted a resolution that read:

> Whereas, recognizing the present urgency of solving the naturalization question, be it hereby resolved that a test case be instituted at an appropriate time in pursuit of the just legal goal of acquiring the right of naturalization for the Japanese.[44]

In order to go to court, the first task was to find an ideal test case both in a political and legal sense. That case proved to be that of Ozawa Takao which originated in Hawaii.[45] His was unquestionably ideal in a political sense. Born 15 June 1875, Ozawa was a native of Kanagawa Prefecture who landed in San Francisco as a young man in 1894. Working as a school boy, he attended various schools and graduated from Berkeley High School in Berkeley, California. He also studied at the University of California for three years until 1906, after which he discontinued his studies and moved to Honolulu where he resided. He worked for an American company and had outstanding references to his moral character from his associates. He was married with two children. To argue his own case, Ozawa authored two legal briefs. Vouching for his own personal character, he unabashedly wrote in one of them:

> I neither drink liquor of any kind, nor smoke, nor play cards, nor gamble, nor associate with any improper persons. My honesty and my industriousness are well known among my Japanese and American acquaintances and friends; and I am always trying my best to conduct myself according to the Golden Rule. So I have all [the] confidence in myself that as far as my character is concerned, I am second to none.

Attesting to his single-minded attachment to the United States, he continued:

> In name, General Benedict Arnold was an American, but at heart he was a traitor. In name, I am not an American, but at heart I am a true American. I set forth the following facts that will sufficiently prove this. (1) I did not report my name, my marriage, or the names of my children to the Japanese Consulate in Honolulu; notwithstanding all Japanese subjects are requested to do so. These matters were reported to the American government. (2) I do not have any connection with any Japanese churches or schools, or any Japanese organizations here or elsewhere. (3) I am sending my children to an American church and American school in place of a Japanese one. (4) Most of the time I use the American (English) language at home, so that my children cannot speak the Japanese language. (5) I educated myself in American schools for nearly eleven years by supporting myself. (6) I have lived continuously within the United States for over twenty-eight years. (7) I chose as my wife one educated in American schools . . . instead of one educated in Japan. (8) I have steadily prepared to return the kindness which our Uncle Sam has extended me . . . so it is my honest hope to do something good to the United States before I bid a farewell to this world.[46]

Ozawa was a paragon of an assimilated Japanese immigrant, a living refutation of the allegation of Japanese unassimilability. He could speak, read, and write English; he sent his children to American institutions and spoke English with them; he had no ties to the Japanese community and Japanese government; he married an American-educated woman; and his character was beyond reproach. Immigrant leaders were able to support him without fear his case would fail by virtue of the elementary political fact that he was not assimilated. From this perspective Ozawa was an excellent candidate to be the central figure in a naturalization test case.

Legally, his case was also considered ideal. Ozawa fulfilled all the nonracial requirements for naturalization set by the Act of 1906. According to this statute, an applicant had to file a petition of intent to naturalize at least two years prior to formal application. Ozawa filed for naturalization on 16 October 1914, and he had filed his petition of intent on 1 August 1902 in Alameda County, California. He satisfied the five-year continuous residency requirement having lived in the United States or its territory for over twenty years. His personal character and English fluency needless to say met the requirements related to moral fitness and knowledge of the English language. Fully qualified in terms of the Act of 1906, his case was impeccable from a legal point of view.

Nevertheless Ozawa was unsuccessful at the lower court level. His petition to naturalize having been denied, he took his case to the United States District Court for the Territory of Hawaii. On 25

March 1916 Judge Charles F. Clemons rendered his decision in these words:

> The court finds that the petitioner is not qualified under Revised Statutes, section 2169, and must therefore deny his petition; and it is so ordered, in spite of the finding hereby made that he has fully established the allegation of his petition, and, except as to the requirements of section 2169, is in every way eminently qualified under the statutes to become an American citizen.[47]

Translated into ordinary language, classified as a member of the mongolian race, Ozawa was excluded by the racial restrictions of section 2169, and therefore ineligible to citizenship. Notwithstanding his obvious qualifications, he was not considered a free white person, which alone disqualified him. Ozawa filed an appeal that was granted on 25 September 1916, and his case then passed on to the Ninth Circuit Court of Appeals in San Francisco. Without handing down a decision, the appellate court referred it to the Supreme Court on 31 May 1917.[48] Up to the point of his appeal, Ozawa on his own contested the denial of his petition to naturalize. Save for a few close friends and associates, he did not have the backing of any organized immigrant group. When he appealed to the Ninth Circuit Court, his case drew the notice of immigrant leaders on the Pacific Coast. While looking for an ideal test case, it suddenly loomed before them.

The Pacific Coast Japanese Association Deliberative Council first discussed the Ozawa case in August 1916.[49] Kanzaki Kiichi, General Secretary of the Japanese Association of America, presented a report on it. With a possible test case in mind, the Council voted to obtain the court transcript from Honolulu. Kanzaki agreed to solicit the legal opinions of the counsels to the Japanese Association of America and to circulate all information, including copies of the transcript, to the other central bodies. In the meantime the Council resolved not to publicize the case before it had a chance to study it fully. In April 1915 Consul Numano Yasutarō of San Francisco had requested instructions from the Foreign Ministry on any test case. Foreign Minister Katō Takaaki ordered him "to take steps to prevent the Japanese within your jurisdiction from undertaking a test case campaign."[50] This order was in keeping with the Foreign Ministry's view, stated by Ambassador Chinda Sutemi in 1913, that the time was inappropriate to pursue any course in the matter of naturalization. Consul Moroi Rokurō of Honolulu even tried to persuade Ozawa to withdraw his appeal.[51] Aware of the Japanese government's attitude, the Council understandably held back publicity until it reached a final decision on the case.

The immigrant press covered the Ozawa case widely in the summer of 1917. Before the Ninth Circuit Court referred it to the Supreme Court on May 31, the *Nichibei Shimbun* maintained pointedly that "the Japanese are considered aliens ineligible to citizenship . . . because we are presumed to be an inferior race" which was "an insulting treatment." Since ineligibility was at the root of "discriminatory legislation," the case "warranted as much support as possible."[52] Expecting the Ninth Circuit Court to rule on it, the newspaper was startled by the court's action. But realizing the case was heading for the highest tribunal, regardless of its own reservations and possible outcome, in June it exhorted everyone to cooperate and pull behind it.[53] Like it or not, Ozawa had become the representative of all Japanese immigrants. The *Shin Sekai* and the *Rafu Shimpō* of Los Angeles concurred with the *Nichibei Shimbun.*[54] The Ozawa case was no longer a private legal battle. Passed on to the Supreme Court, the decision at this level would affect every Japanese in the United States. All three newspapers urged the Pacific Coast Japanese Association Deliberative Council, scheduled to convene in July, to assume the leadership on behalf of the immigrants and support the case.

The Council met for two days on July 26–27 in Los Angeles. Upon weighing carefully the implications, it voted unanimously to support Ozawa Takao. To carry out the decision, a four-man naturalization committee was appointed, composed of one representative from each central body (except Canada) and headed by Yamaoka Ototaka of Seattle.[55] This new committee went quickly to work. Along with other immigrant leaders, in mid-August Yamaoka conferred with Viscount Ishii Kikujirō in San Francisco. Ishii had just arrived as Ambassador Extraordinary and Plenipotentiary, leading a special diplomatic mission to Washington, D.C. to negotiate affairs relating to China. Taking advantage of his timely presence, a petition was submitted to him which asked for, among other things, assistance from the Japanese government in the forthcoming litigation. On Ishii's way back to Japan in November, Yamaoka conferred with him again. At the time of this second meeting, Ishii requested the naturalization committee to suspend support of the Ozawa case. Yamaoka reported his saying:

> All eminent persons in the executive branch of the American government and in every political party and faction believe that the Japanese

> should be allowed to naturalize as a matter of justice and humaneness. But public opinion at large is not ready so no one will come out and take a public stand on the question. Thus it is better to postpone the case until the right time comes.[56]

Ishii's remarks left no room for doubt—Japanese diplomats were opposed unalterably to the Ozawa case. The committee could not bank on any help from the Japanese government.

Specific preparations were made in the next year. In April Yamaoka placed Ishii Kikujirō's request before the committee as a formal resolution which it rejected summarily.[57] Electing to proceed with the case, the committee retained David L. Withington, Ozawa's attorney, but as principal counsel selected George W. Wickersham, onetime United States Attorney General. After this decisive meeting, Yamaoka travelled to Honolulu where he spoke directly with Ozawa and his attorney. In late 1917 Ozawa had been asked by Horikoshi Zenjūrō, a New York City businessman, and Ishii himself to defer his appeal.[58] A foe of litigation, Horikoshi returned to Japan towards the end of that year. Stopping off in Honolulu en route, he tried to convince Ozawa to discontinue his appeal. With the same objective in mind, Ishii talked with him on his own return voyage to Japan. Ozawa turned a deaf ear to their suggestion. When Yamaoka consulted with him, he categorically said that he would neither postpone nor withdraw his case under any circumstance, even in "the face of death."[59] In June the committee settled on final terms with George W. Wickersham for his legal service. All necessary preparations seemingly had been completed.

Concurrent events proved otherwise. The preparations were made in the midst of a new debate over the merits of the Ozawa case. The *Nichibei Shimbun* set off the debate by doing an abrupt turnabout. Beginning with an editorial in January 1918, it predicted inevitable defeat in the case since "public opinion greatly influences the judiciary." The wisest policy was "to promote first a favorable public opinion" and then to seek naturalization rights through "legislation" instead of litigation.[60] In March the newspaper put forth a concrete, legal objection to the case, citing the Supreme Court decision in the Antonio Morena case.[61] Handed down on 7 January 1918, this decision involved the time lapse between the filing of a petition of intent and of a petition to naturalize. The Act of 1906 stipulated that an applicant had to file the latter at least two years but no more than seven years upon filing the former. The court upheld the constitutionality of this procedural requirement in the Morena case.[62] Ozawa filed his petition of intent on 1 August 1902 and his petition to naturalize on 16 October 1914. Twelve years separated the two filings, five more than the allotted maximum of seven years. The *Nichibei Shimbun* pointed to this unforeseen snag as a compelling legal reason to forego the Ozawa case.

A polemical debate over the case then ensued. The *Nichibei Shimbun* forcefully recommended postponement or withdrawal of the case prior to the April meeting of the naturalization committee. Once the committee decided to proceed with the case, it assailed the decision as "utterly regrettable," going so far as to condemn it as "arbitrary" and "undemocratic" and accusing the committee of exercising unauthorized power.[63] In May the newspaper opened its columns to opponents of the case and printed many anti-Ozawa articles in order to rally the opposition. The *Shin Sekai* took up the cause of the opposite side. Contrary to the accusation of improper conduct, according to its opinion, the naturalization committee was duly appointed and acted within prescribed authority, and the Morena decision was not an insurmountable obstacle. Charging the *Nichibei Shimbun* with "inconsistency" and "undue pessimism," the *Shin Sekai* likewise gave space to the immigrant public and published innumerable pro-Ozawa articles.[64] It even sponsored a public forum on naturalization in early May. And to prove the immigrant press supported the Ozawa case, it reprinted editorials from many other newspapers.[65] In the Sacramento area the *Ōfu Nippō* claimed that the majority of the Japanese there were inclined towards postponing the case, while the *Kakushū Jiji* of Denver advocated going ahead with it.[66] The *Rafu Shimpō* took the *Nichibei Shimbun* to task severely for reversing its position and lined up solidly behind the *Shin Sekai.*[67]

After the controversy died down, the naturalization committee temporarily deferred the Ozawa case on the advise of George W. Wickersham. The Morena decision did affect the legal status of the case. As pointed out by the *Nichibei Shimbun,* Ozawa had not satisfied the procedural requirement regulating the time interval between the filing of a petition of intent and of a petition to naturalize. Wickersham feared the case might be declared moot by the Supreme Court on this technicality. Reasoning he needed another case upon which to fall back to be prepared for the possibility, he advised Yamaoka in December 1919 to begin a formal search for a second case.[68] With Yamaoka carrying the main burden in the Pacific Northwest, the naturalization committee examined possible cases throughout 1920. Meanwhile in November 1920, Californians passed an initiative amending the Alien Land Law of 1913. The 1920 enactment prohibited aliens ineligible to citizenship to purchase or lease agricultural land, to hold stocks in agricultural land companies, to transfer or sell agricultural landholdings to each other, and disqualified them from being appointed as guardians of minors who had title to such land. Written to plug up the loopholes of the earlier legislation, it had the undisguised aim of driving Japanese immigrants out of California agriculture. Together with a similar Washington State law enacted in March 1921, this ominous new development made the search for a second case at once more pressing.

The naturalization committee thus instituted another case in May 1921. On behalf of the committee, Corwin S. Shank, a Seattle attorney, in cooperation with George W. Wickersham, brought the case of Yamashita Takuji and Kono Hyōsaburō before the Washington State Supreme Court.[69] The essence of this case was simple. In 1902 both Yamashita and Kono had been naturalized in Pierce County, Washington. Forming a real estate company, they filed articles of incorporation on 14 May 1921 with the Secretary of State. His office refused to accept the articles on the grounds that the two men had not been naturalized legally and were unable consequently to form such a company under the laws of the state. Yamashita and Kono applied promptly for a writ of mandate with the State Supreme Court in order to compel the Secretary of State to accept the articles of incorporation. The court declined to issue the writ on June 28 at which point the two men appealed to the United States Supreme Court. The naturalization committee initiated this case as the companion to the Ozawa case because it was the shortest, and hence fastest, way of reaching the high tribunal.[70] Though the legal details differed, it nonetheless required the Supreme Court to rule on the question of Japanese eligibility under existing naturalization statutes. All preparations were complete at last. The years of controversy and of legal uncertainty were to become history with the long-awaited decision.

The Supreme Court pronounced the fateful decision in November 1922. Despite Wickersham's apprehension, the court heard the Ozawa case and ruled upon it first. The court held that Ozawa Takao was ineligible to citizenship. Judged to be neither a free white person nor an African by birth or descent, he did not have the right of naturalization as a mongolian.[71] The Yamashita and Kono case was decided in accordance with the Ozawa ruling. In general, the immigrant press expressed controlled anger but little surprise at the decision. The leading champion of the Ozawa case, the *Shin Sekai* commented indignantly: "The slim hope that we had entertained . . . has been shattered completely." "We are not too surprised," it continued, "for we have been treated for a long time as if we did not have the right in fact."[72] The *Ōfu Nippō* deplored the decision as an expression of "racial prejudice" at odds with the "original founding spirit of the nation," but saw no purpose in becoming "irate."[73] The *Rafu Shimpō* interpreted it with a touch of irony. Since this newspaper did "not believe whites are the superior race," in one sense, it was "delighted" the high tribunal "did not find the Japanese to be free white persons."[74] The *Taihoku Nippō* voiced a lack of astonishment, asserting that it had not expected any other decision.[75] The *Nichibei Shimbun* stated that "the expected decision has been handed down as expected," but felt no need for "pessimism" or "indignation."[76] In his capacity as head of the naturalization committee, Yamaoka Ototaka decried the decision as a "national humiliation" that cast the Japanese people in a humiliating light, but concluded that the Ozawa case had had the merit at least of clarifying, once and for all, the ineligibility of the Japanese.[77] The Supreme Court decision left not a shadow of doubt. On this anticlimactic note, the early Japanese immigrant quest for naturalization rights came to a close.

To grasp the full meaning of the Ozawa case, the larger historical context must be taken into account. The term *kimin* often appears in the writings of Japanese immigrants. Meaning "an abandoned people," this special term stems from the immigrants' profound sense of rejection. It refers, on the one hand, to the failure of the Japanese government to come to their aid in times of need. Japanese diplomats usually sacrificed the immigrants' welfare for the sake of what they perceived as diplomatic necessity. An instance was their reluctance to negotiate naturalization rights for the immigrants. Prejudiced by class and bureaucratic biases, many Japanese officials and prominent persons in Japan indeed looked down with arrogant contempt upon their uprooted countrymen as an uneducated, ignorant lot and blamed them for the animosity of white Americans. Such individuals felt that the immigrants, by their own conduct in the United States, were responsible for causing the exclusion movement.

On the other hand, *kimin* refers to the American repudiation of the immigrants, especially after 1922. Parallel to the Ozawa case, the immigrants instituted land litigation to contest the 1920 California and 1921 Washington alien land laws. Three types of cases pended before the Supreme Court in 1922 which tempered the immigrant response to the Ozawa decision. For the prevailing opinion among immigrant leaders was that they would win the separate land cases, even if they lost the naturalization test cases. To their utter dismay, the immigrants suffered total defeat in the land cases in 1923 which undermined the livelihood of many tenant farmers. Terminating all Japanese immigration to the United States, the Immigration Act of 1924 was the culminating event. Prohibiting the entry of all aliens ineligible to citizenship, the immigrants interpreted this enactment as America's final rejection of them. The Ozawa decision was rendered within this broad historical context. Viewed from the vantage of the immigrants themselves, it was one of many events that contributed to their sense of having been reduced to "an abandoned people" forsaken by both the mother country and the immigrant land.

NOTES

1. Yuji Ichioka *et al.*, *A Buried Past: An Annotated Bibliography of the Japanese American Research Project Collection* (Berkeley and Los Angeles, 1974), 3-11; and Roger Daniels, "American Historians and East Asian Immigrants," *Pacific Historical Review*, 43 (November 1974), 449-472.

2. For the exclusion movement and the naturalization issue, see Sidney L. Gulick, *The American Japanese Problem* (New York, 1914), 281-307; H.A. Millis, *The Japanese Problem in the United States* (New York, 1915), 276-312; Sidney L. Gulick, *American Democracy and Asiatic Citizenship* (New York, 1918); Roy Malcolm, "American Citizenship and the Japanese," *Annals of the American Academy of Political and Social Science*, 93 (January 1921), 77-81; Raymond L. Buell, "Some Legal Aspects of the Japanese Question," *American Journal of International Law*, 17 (January 1923), 29-49; Valentine S. McClatchy and Raymond L. Buell, "May Japanese Become Citizens?," *The Forum*, 72 (September 1924), 289-305; R.D. McKenzie, *Oriental Exclusion: The Effects of American Immigration Laws, Regulations, and Judicial Decisions Upon the Chinese and Japanese on the American Pacific Coast* (Chicago, 1928), 66-78; and Eliot G. Mears, *Resident Orientals on the American Pacific Coast* (Chicago, 1928), 96-118. Summaries of the Ozawa case in immigrant language sources can be found in Takeuchi Kōjirō, *Beikoku Seihokubu Nihon Iminshi* (Seattle, 1929), 255-274; and Zaibei Nihonjinkai, *Zaibei Nihonjinshi* (San Francisco, 1940), 1091-1096. This essay will not cover the naturalization of Japanese World War I veterans. For this topic, see Harry M. Naka, "The Naturalization of Japanese War Veterans of the American World War Forces," unpublished M.A. thesis (Berkeley, 1938).

3. For details of the legal background, see Mears, *Resident Orientals on the American Pacific Coast*, 96-118; Buell, "Some Legal Aspects of the Japanese Question," 29-49; and Milton R. Konvitz, *The Alien and the Asiatic in American Law* (Ithaca, 1946), 79-116. For the briefs of the Ozawa case, see San Francisco Consulate General of Japan, *Documental History of Law Cases Affecting Japanese in the United States, 1916-1924* (San Francisco, 1925), I, 1-120; and Japanese American Research Project Collection, Japanese Foreign Ministry Archival Documents, U.C.L.A., reel 39 (hereafter cited as JARP, JFMAD).

4. U.S. Bureau of the Census, *Chinese and Japanese in the United States, 1910*, bul. 127 (Washington, D.C., 1914), 10-11.

5. Fujioka Shirō, *Minzoku Hatten no Senkūsha* (Tokyo, 1927), 107-109.

6. U.S. Department of State, *Papers Relating to the Foreign Relations of the United States, 1905/1906* (Washington, D.C., 1909), xlii.

7. Roger Daniels, *The Politics of Prejudice* (New York, 1968), 39, interprets Roosevelt's message as "chiefly for Japanese consumption" which he made "in order to have an advanced position from which to retreat in his dealings with California."

8. Uchida Sadatsuchi to Hayashi Tadasu, 31 May 1906, Nihon Gaimushō, *Nihon Gaikō Bunsho, 1906* (Tokyo, 1959), II, 400 (hereafter cited as *NGB*).

9. Aoki Shūzō to Hayashi, 1, 10 November 1906, *ibid.*, 454-455, 477.

10. Hayashi to Aoki, 18 November 1906, *ibid.*, 499.

11. Aoki to Hayashi, 10 January 1907, *NGB, 1907* (Tokyo, 1961), III, 269.

12. Hayashi to Aoki, 23 February 1907, *ibid.*, 345.

13. Aoki to Hayashi, 24 February 1907, *ibid.*, 346. This brief diplomatic effort to negotiate naturalization rights is also covered within the broader context of the school and immigration issues by Raymond A. Esthus, *Theodore Roosevelt and Japan* (Seattle, 1966), 128-195; and Charles E. Neu, *An Uncertain Friendship: Theodore Roosevelt and Japan, 1906-1909* (Cambridge, Mass., 1967), 52-88.

14. Kawasaki Minotarō presented his opinion in a leading journal published in Japan. See Kawasaki Minotarō, "Zai-Bei Nihonjin no Kikaken," *Taiyō*, 11:10 (July 1905), 74-80. Unfortunately, early issues of the *Nichibei Shimbun* have not been preserved. As early as 1903 Negishi Motoyuki, a student at the University of California, analyzed the questionable legal status of the Japanese in another journal published in Japan. See Negishi Motoyuki, "Beikoku ni Okeru Nihonjin no Shiminken," *Nihonjin*, no. 196 (October 1903), 28-31.

15. *Shin Sekai*, 6 December 1906.

16. *Ibid.*, 12 January 1907.

17. Shatoru Nihonjinkai to Hayashi, 19 February 1907, *NGB, 1907*, III, 333.

18. Hisamizu Saburō to Hayashi, 29 April 1907, enclosure "Kashū Nihonjinkai Chinjōsho," April 1907, JARP, JFMAD, reel 7. This petition also is appended to Takahashi Sakue, *Nichi-Bei no Shin Kankei* (Tokyo, 1910), 350-374.

19. Matsubara Kazuo to Hayashi, 21 April 1907, *NGB, 1907*, III, 401-402.

20. K.K. Kawakami, "The Naturalization of Japanese," *North American Review*, 185 (21 June 1907), 394-402. Not all Japanese immigrants favored naturalization. Ōtsuka Zenjirō, for example, was critical of immigrant leaders who advocated naturalization. A conservative and reporter for the *Sōkō Shimbun* of San Francisco, he felt that "naturalization was an act which reflected a lack of Japanese patriotism." See Ōtsuka Sokumei, "Kashū Iminron," *Nihon Oyobi Nihonjin*, no. 463 (July 1907), 17-21.

21. For details of the negotiation, see Esthus, *Theodore Roosevelt and Japan*, 146-166, 196-228; and Neu, *An Uncertain Friendship*, 163-180.

22. For the formation of the Japanese Association of America, see Yuji Ichioka, "Japanese Associations and the Japanese Government: A Special Relationship, 1909-1926," *Pacific Historical Review*, 46 (August 1977), 409-437.

23. *Shin Sekai*, 26 January-1 February 1909. This immigrant newspaper published the proceedings in great detail. Accounts of later conferences are also taken from this source.

24. *Nichibei Shimbun*, 26 April 1913.

25. *Ibid.*, 30 March 1913. See also 28 March, 15, 16 April 1913.

26. *Shin Sekai*, 8 March, 7 April, 14, 31 May, and 2 June, 1913.

27. *Kororado Shimbun*, 9 May 1913.

28. *Taihoku Nippō*, 16-18, 20, 21, 23-28 June 1913.

29. *Shin Tenchi*, 4:5 (1 May 1913), 1.

30. *Beikoku Bukkyō*, 14:5 (1 May 1913), 1. Bishop Uchida Kōyū, head of the Buddhist Mission of America, also published his opinions in the immigrant press. See, for example, *Nichibei Shimbun*, 27, 29 April 1913.

31. Chiba Toyoji, *Hai-Nichi Mondai Kōgai* (San Francisco, 1913), 110-126.

32. Shiminken Kakutoku Kisei Dōshikai, *Nichi-Bei Mondai ni Taisuru Wagato no Shuchō* (San Francisco, 1913).

33. Kiyoshi K. Kawakami, "How California Treats the Japanese," *The Independent*, 74 (8 May 1913), 1022; and Kiyoshi K. Kawakami, *Asia at the Door* (New York, 1914), 87-89.

34. *Shin Sekai*, 30 April-1 May 1913.

35. For example, see *Nichibei Shimbun*, 16 April 1913; *Shin Sekai*, 24 May 1913; Chiba, *Hai-Nichi Mondai Kōgai*, 119-125; and the proceedings of the Japanese Association of America and its affiliated local Japanese Associations published in the *Shin Sekai*, 30 April-1 May 1913.

36. Makino Shinken to Chinda Sutemi, 17 May 1913, *NGB, 1913* (Tokyo, 1965), III, 211-212.

37. Chinda to Makino, 18 May 1913, *ibid.*, 214-215. See also Paolo E. Coletta, " 'The Most Thankless Task': Bryan and the California Alien Land Legislation," *Pacific Historical Review*, 36 (May 1967), 163-187.

38. Chinda to William Jennings Bryan, 4 June 1913, *NGB, 1913*, III, 262-263. This protest note and others can also be found in U.S. Department of State, *Papers Relating to the Foreign Relations of the United States, 1912/1913* (Washington, D.C., 1920), 629-653.

39. *Shin Sekai*, 30 June, 18 August 1913.

40. Bryan to Chinda, 16 July 1913, *NGB, 1913*, III, 295.

41. Makino to Chinda, 23 July 1913, *ibid.*, 323-324.

42. The name of this central body was changed to the Northwest American Japanese Association in 1920.

43. The affiliated locals of the Central Japanese Association of Southern California were linked formerly to the Japanese Association of America.

44. Taiheiyō Engan Nihonjinkai Kyōgikai, "Gijiroku," 15-16 July 1914, JARP.

45. In 1914 Japanese association leaders considered the case of Kaneko Shinsei. In late January the Deputy United States District Attorney of southern California filed a complaint in the United States District Court compelling Kaneko to show cause why he should not give up his naturalization papers. For unexplained

reasons, the complaint was withdrawn in February. See Fujioka, *Minzoku Hatten no Senkūsha,* 108. See also *Nichibei Shimbun,* 30 January, 8, 19 February 1914; *Shin Sekai,* 31 January 1914; and Los Angeles *Times,* 22 January 1914.

46. Takao Ozawa, "Naturalization of a Japanese Subject," undated brief, JARP, JFMAD, reel 39.

47. San Francisco Consulate General, *Documental History of Law Cases Affecting Japanese in the United States, 1916–1924,* 8-9.

48. The Ninth Circuit Court asked the Supreme Court to rule basically on two legal questions. First, was the Act of 1906 complete in itself or limited by section 2169 of the Revised Federal Statutes which restricted eligibility to free white persons and persons of African descent? Secondly, if the Act of 1906 was so limited, then were the Japanese eligible under this restriction?

49. Taiheiyō Engan Nihonjinkai Kyōgikai, "Gijiroku," 12-14 August 1916.

50. Nihon Gaimushō, "Ozawa Takao Kika Soshō Jiken . . . ni Kansuru Ken," December 1919, JARP, JFMAD, reel 39. This document summarizes the Foreign Ministry's position on the Ozawa case.

51. *Ibid.*

52. *Nichibei Shimbun,* 30 May 1917.

53. *Ibid.*, 1, 4, 26 June and 11 July 1917.

54. *Shin Sekai,* 2, 3, June 1917; and *Rafu Shimpō,* 3 June, 3 July 1917.

55. Taiheiyō Engan Nihonjinkai Kyōgikai, "Gijiroku," 26-27 July 1917.

56. Taiheiyō Engan Nihonjinkai Kyōgikai, "Gijiroku," 1-3 July 1918.

57. *Ibid.*

58. *Nichibei Shimbun,* 31 January 1918; and Nihon Gaimushō, "Ozawa Takao Kika Soshō Jiken . . . ni Kansuru Ken," December 1919.

59. *Shin Sekai,* 7 May 1918.

60. *Nichibei Shimbun,* 1, 8 January 1918.

61. *Ibid.*, 7 March 1918.

62. United States v. Morena, 38 Sup. Ct. 151 (1918).

63. *Nichibei Shimbun,* 15, 18, 20 April 1918.

64. *Shin Sekai,* 11, 12, 14 April, May, 1918. Hardly a day passed without a pro-Ozawa article in the month of May.

65. *Ibid.*, 12-14 May 1918. The editorials were from the Ōshū Nippō of Portland, the *Hokubei Hōchi* and Rafu Asahi of Los Angeles, the *Taimusu* of Stockton, the *Nippu Jiji* of Honolulu, and the *Hokubei Jiji* of Seattle.

66. *Ōfu Nippō,* 9 May 1918; and *Kakushū Jiji,* 15, 16 May 1918.

67. *Rafu Shimpō,* 12 May 1918.

68. Taiheiyō Engan Nihonjinkai Kyōgikai, "Gijiroku," 24-26 June 1920. See also Beikoku Seihokubu Renraku Nihonjinkai, *Kaimu Oyobi Kaikei Hōkoku, 20 August 1920–28 February 1921* (Seattle, 1921), 22-23.

69. For the briefs of the Yamashita and Kono case, see San Francisco Consulate General, *Documental History of Law Cases Affecting Japanese in the United States, 1916–1924,* 121-175.

70. Taiheiyō Engan Nihonjinkai Kyōgikai, "Gijiroku," 18-21 July 1921. See also Beikoku Seihokubu Renraku Nihonjinkai, *Kaimu Hōkoku, 1 March–31 August 1921* (Seattle, 1921), 78-82.

71. In terms of the legal questions raised by the Ninth Circuit Court, the Supreme Court ruled that section 2169 of the Revised Federal Statutes limited the Act of 1906 and that Ozawa was excluded by the racial restrictions of that section.

72. *Shin Sekai,* 14 November 1922.
73. *Ōfu Nippō,* 18 November 1922.
74. *Rafu Shimpō,* 15-17 November 1922.
75. *Taihoku Nippō,* 14 November 1922.
76. *Nichibei Shimbun,* 14, 15 November 1922.
77. Taiheiyō Engan Nihonjinkai Kyōgikai, "Gijiroku," 10-12 July 1923.

1947-48 TERM OF THE SUPREME COURT: THE ALIEN'S RIGHT TO WORK

In virtually every state and the District of Columbia, legislation exists which prohibits either all aliens, or aliens who have not legally declared their intention of becoming citizens, from engaging in numerous occupations.[1]

---

1. See KONVITZ, THE ALIEN AND THE ASIATIC IN AMERICAN LAW 190-207 (1946);

Though the constitutionality of these statutes has been questioned by writers,[2] most of this legislation has gone unchallenged in the courts. However, re-examination of the subject is warranted as a result of two important decisions handed down by the Supreme Court during its past term. By striking down discriminatory legislation against Japanese resident aliens in California in *Takahashi v. Fish and Game Commission*[3] and *Oyama v. California*,[4] the Court overturned traditional concepts of the proprietary power of the states in favor of the aliens' right to the equal protection of the laws.[5] Of the two cases, the *Takahashi* decision is the more significant because of its strong reaffirmation of the alien's right to work.[6] The purpose of this Note will be to analyze these cases and to determine the present scope of legislative power to place limitations upon the right of an alien to participate in the common callings of the community.

The statute under consideration in the *Takahashi* case denied commercial fishing licenses to all aliens ineligible to become citizens. The State of Califor-

---

Brause, *State Laws Barring Aliens from Professions and Occupations,* 3 IMMIG. AND NAT. SERV. MO. REV. 281, 283-84 (1946) ; 5 VERNIER, AMERICAN FAMILY LAW 383-87 (1938). For statutes limiting the employment of aliens on public works, see 5 VERNIER, *supra,* at 378-81. For statutes limiting the right of aliens to hunt and fish, see *id.* at 395-97.

For an idea as to the scope of this discrimination, the restrictions found in the New York statutes are set out below. This does not include the multitude of city ordinances which may also be discriminatory.

Occupations limited to citizens and declarants (Here it must be remembered that the prohibition is absolute as to Japanese since they cannot become declarants.) : Architect [N.Y. EDUCATION LAW § 7304(1)]; billiard room operator (N.Y. PENAL LAW § 345); certified public accountant (N.Y. EDUCATION LAW § 7404); certified shorthand reporter (N.Y. EDUCATION LAW § 7502); dentist (N.Y. EDUCATION LAW § 6608); engineer [N.Y. EDUCATION LAW § 7205(1)(b)]; land surveyor [N.Y. EDUCATION LAW § 7205(2)(b)]; nurse [N.Y. EDUCATION LAW §§ 6905(1)(c), 6906(1)(c)]; osteopath (N.Y. EDUCATION LAW § 6506); pharmacist [N.Y. EDUCATION LAW § 6803(1)(h)]; physiotherapist (N.Y. EDUCATION LAW § 6506); physician (N.Y. EDUCATION LAW § 6506); realtor (N.Y. REAL PROPERTY LAW § 440-a); teacher [N.Y. EDUCATION LAW § 3001(3)].

Occupations restricted only to citizens: Attorney (N.Y. JUDICIARY LAW §§ 460, 467); bank director [N.Y. BANKING LAW §§ 116(4), 246(3)(a), 325, 397(1), 441(1)]; embalmer (N.Y. PUBLIC HEALTH LAW § 293); guide (fish and game) (N.Y. CONSERVATION LAW § 183); investigator (N.Y. GENERAL BUSINESS LAW §§ 70, 72); liquor dealer [N.Y. ALCOHOLIC BEVERAGE CONTROL LAW § 1126(3)(4)]; pawnbroker (cities) (N.Y. GENERAL BUSINESS LAW §§ 40, 41); pilot (vessel) (N.Y. NAVIGATION LAW § 64); private detective (N.Y. GENERAL BUSINESS LAW §§ 70, 72); race track employee (N.Y. UNCONSOLIDATED LAWS §§ 7582, 7610); watchman (N.Y. GENERAL BUSINESS LAW §§ 70, 72).

Public Works. Preference is given to citizens in employment (N.Y. LABOR LAW § 222).

Fish and Game. Aliens are charged higher license fees [N.Y. CONSERVATION LAW §§ 180(7), 182, 185(1)].

Land. No discrimination (N.Y. REAL PROPERTY LAW § 10).

2. See, *e.g.*, KONVITZ, *op. cit. supra* note 1, at 188-89; Fellman, *The Alien's Right to Work,* 22 MINN. L. REV. 137, 175-76 (1938) ; Note, *Constitutionality of Legislative Discrimination Against the Alien in his Right to Work,* 83 U. OF PA. L. REV. 74, 82 (1934).

3. 334 U.S. 410 (1948).

4. 332 U.S. 633 (1948).

5. U.S. CONST. AMEND. XIV, § 1; Yick Wo v. Hopkins, 118 U.S. 356, 369 (1886).

6. For a strong affirmation of the alien's right, generally, not to be discriminated against, see Truax v. Raich, 239 U.S. 33 (1915). See also Yu Cong Eng v. Trinidad, 271 U.S. 500 (1926) ; Fraser v. McConway & Torley Co., 82 Fed. 257 (C.C.D. Pa. 1897) ; *In re* Case, 20 Idaho 128, 116 Pac. 1037 (1911) ; Juniata Limestone Co. v. Fagley, 187 Pa. 193, 40 Atl. 977 (1898) ; Ade v. County Commissioners, 7 Pa. Dist. 199 (1898).

nia argued that the denial was justified by the long established principle of *McCready v. Virginia,*[7] that a state holds the fish in its tidal waters in trust for its citizens and can limit fishing rights solely to these citizens. Rejecting this contention, the Court said: "[W]e think that 'ownership' is inadequate to justify California in excluding *any or all aliens*[8] who are lawful residents of the State from making a living by fishing in the ocean off its shores while permitting all others to do so."[9] Since prohibitions directed at a particular race or nationality generally are in clear conflict with the equal protection clause,[10] it is significant that the Court did expressly recognize that the statute, by excluding ineligible aliens, in effect only impinged upon the rights of Japanese.[11] Moreover, it cited, but did not rely upon, a case involving practically the identical situation in which it was said: "To subject the Chinese to imprisonment for fishing in the waters of the state, while aliens of all European nations under the same circumstances are exempt from any punishment whatever, is to subject the Chinese to other and entirely different punishments, pains, and penalties than those to which others are subjected, and it is to deny to them the equal protection of the laws contrary to those provisions of the Constitution."[12] Under this reasoning, a prohibition against particular aliens would be invalid and yet the same prohibition applying to all aliens might not be. Despite the Court's obvious awareness of the availability of this narrow ground for its decision, a majority of the justices declined to so confine their holding, and, by referring to "any or all aliens," gave this decision a much broader scope than the facts actually required. The breadth of this holding is further emphasized by a comparison with the concurring opinion,[13] which would have achieved the same result on the more narrow ground that the statute was the product of racial antagonism.

The foregoing analysis would lose much persuasiveness if the Court intended to indicate not so much the vigor of the right of the alien to work but rather the weakness of the proprietary theory expounded in *McCready v. Virginia.* State courts have consistently followed the *McCready* rule[14] which

7. 94 U.S. 391 (1877); *cf.* Geer v. Connecticut, 161 U.S. 519 (1896).

8. Italics added.

9. 334 U.S. 410, 421 (1948).

10. Yick Wo v. Hopkins, 118 U.S. 356 (1886); *In re* Tie Loy, 26 Fed. 611 (C.C.D. Cal. 1886); Ho Ah Kow v. Nunan, 12 Fed. Cas. 252, No. 6546 (C.C.D. Cal. 1879); Begay v. Sawtelle, 53 Ariz. 304, 88 P.2d 999 (1939); *In re* Opinion of the Justices, 207 Mass. 601, 94 N.E. 558 (1911); *see* Rok v. Legg, 27 F.Supp. 243, 246 (S.D. Cal. 1939).

11. "Free white persons", "persons of African descent", "descendants of races indigenous to the Western Hemisphere", "persons of Chinese descent", Filipinos, and Indians are eligible for citizenship. Japanese are among the few groups not eligible, and in 1940 constituted the great majority of resident aliens ineligible for citizenship. 334 U.S. 410, 412 n. 1 (1948).

12. *In re* Ah Chong, 2 Fed. 733, 737 (C.C.D. Cal. 1880).

13. 334 U.S. 410, 422 (1948) (Justices Murphy and Rutledge).

14. Commonwealth v. Hilton, 174 Mass. 29, 54 N.E. 362 (1899); People v. Loundes, 130 N.Y. 455, 29 N.E. 751 (1892); State v. Catholic, 75 Ore. 367, 147 Pac. 372 (1915); State v. Medbury, 3 R.I. 138 (1855); Chambers Bros. v. Church & Co., 14 R.I. 398

permits a state to discriminate in favor of its citizens in regard to fish and game privileges against citizens of other states without contravening the privileges and immunities clause.[15] Prior to the *Takahashi* case, this rule had been regarded as authorizing similar discrimination against resident aliens,[16] even against right to work objections grounded on the equal protection clause.[17] However, *Toomer v. Witsell*,[18] decided the same day as *Takahashi*, seriously impaired the vitality of the proprietary principle. In that case, the Court refused to "extend" the application of the *McCready* rule from non-migratory fish in inland waters to free-swimming shrimp off the South Carolina coast, even though other courts had considered this situation within the rule.[19] Nevertheless, the Court in the *Takahashi* case did not rely on the diminished force of *McCready v. Virginia*. On the contrary, by indicating that the proprietary rule was still operative,[20] though limited by *Toomer v. Witsell*, the Court made it clear that the controlling rationale of its decision was the overriding importance of vindicating the alien's right to work.

The *Takahashi* case may have a substantial influence on the validity of exclusionary state laws or practices in certain analogous situations. State exclusion of aliens from employment on public works[21] had previously been upheld by the Supreme Court.[22] In reaching this result the Court considered the state to have the same rights as an individual employer. This position has been criticized as completely nullifying the effect of the equal protection clause,

---

(1884); *cf.* Haavik v. Alaska Packers Assn., 263 U.S. 510 (1924) (Alaska). However, control of wild game by the state does not go so far as to deprive a non-resident landowner of his property interests. Pavel v. Richard, 28 F.Supp. 992 (W.D. La. 1938); Pavel v. Pattison, 24 F.Supp. 915 (W.D. La. 1938).

15. U.S. Const. Art. IV, § 2. Objections based upon the commerce clause [U.S. Const. Art. I, § 8] were also rejected. McCready v. Virginia, 94 U.S. 391 (1877).

16. State v. Kofines, 33 R.I. 211, 80 Atl. 432 (1911); Bondi v. MacKay, 87 Vt. 271, 89 Atl. 228 (1913).

17. Lubetich v. Pollock, 6 F.2d 237 (W.D. Wash. 1925); *Ex parte* Gilletti, 70 Fla. 442, 70 So. 446 (1915); Alsos v. Kendall, 111 Ore. 359, 227 Pac. 286 (1924).

Once the wild life has been lawfully reduced to private possession, the proprietary interest of the state ceases. Accordingly, the *McCready* rule affords no basis for excluding aliens from becoming wholesale fish dealers. Poon v. Miller, 234 S.W. 573 (Tex. Civ. App. 1921).

18. 334 U.S. 385 (1948).

19. Toomer v. Witsell, 73 F.Supp. 371 (E.D.S.C. 1947), *rev'd*, 334 U.S. 385 (1948); Dodgen v. Depuglio, 209 S.W.2d 588 (Tex. 1948); Brownsville Shrimp Co. v. Miller, 207 S.W.2d 911 (Tex. Civ. App. 1947).

20. 334 U.S. 410, 420-21 (1948).

21. "The Constitution that permits the bar of aliens from public works surely must permit their bar from state fishing rights." Takahashi v. Fish and Game Commission, 334 U.S. 410, 431 (1948) (dissenting opinion). Will the Constitution which forbids barring aliens from fishing rights equally forbid barring them from public works?

22. Heim v. McCall, 239 U.S. 175 (1915). See also Crane v. New York, 239 U.S. 195 (1915); Lee v. Lynn, 223 Mass. 109, 111 N.E. 700 (1916); People v. I.M. Ludington's Sons, 74 Misc. 363, 131 N.Y. Supp. 550 (Orleans Co. Ct. 1911); Cornelius v. Seattle, 123 Wash. 550, 213 Pac. 17 (1923); *cf.* Rok v. Legg, 27 F.Supp. 243 (S.D. Cal. 1939) (upholding denial of W.P.A. employment to aliens). *Contra:* People v. Warren, 13 Misc. 615, 34 N.Y.Supp. 942 (Super. Ct. of Buffalo 1895).

which is a prohibition against states and not individuals.[23] Moreover, the Supreme Court itself recently recognized restrictions on Congressional racial or religious discrimination in federal employment,[24] and no reason exists why these same limitations should not be applicable to states. Assuming that the Court's original rationale of state exclusion of aliens from public works employment is at present extremely dubious, an attempt may still be made to justify the result by invoking the proprietary doctrine employed by Justice Cardozo while a member of the New York Court of Appeals.[25] Relying on cases dealing with natural resources to support this doctrine, Cardozo concluded that employment on public works was a privilege which could be limited to citizens. But discrimination affecting the distribution of resources can be more readily justified than discrimination affecting the distribution of employment. In the latter instance the state receives a quid pro quo in the form of services rendered, and the alien makes a pro rata contribution to the taxes which help finance the public work. On the other hand, sharing in the natural resources of a state is a benefit usually inuring primarily to the individual. Under this view, therefore, the reasoning of the *Takahashi* case should apply *a fortiori* to the exclusion of aliens from employment on public works.

Another situation which may be influenced by the *Takahashi* case involves a state's exclusion of aliens from ownership of land. Such discrimination directly limits an alien's right to work where it prevents his acquisition of interests in agricultural land so as to preclude him from ever rising above the status of a hired farm hand. Nevertheless, statutes barring either nondeclarant aliens[26] or aliens ineligible for citizenship[27] from taking or holding interests in land have been sustained by the Supreme Court on the ground that the state's interest in the preservation of its "safety and power"[28] permitted it to determine who should own its land. Moreover, the classification formulated by Congress for determining those who were eligible to become citizens was declared to be a reasonable one for the state to adopt for purposes of land ownership.[29] However, the recent decision in *Oyama v. California* together with the *Takahashi* case placed the continued validity of the alien land laws in extreme doubt.[30] The opinion of the Court in the *Oyama* case went only so far as to

---

23. See, *e.g.*, Powell, *The Right to Work for the State,* 16 COLUMBIA L. REV. 99 (1916) ; KONVITZ, *op. cit. supra* note 1, at 182-86.
24. *See* United Public Workers v. Mitchell, 330 U.S. 75, 100 (1947).
25. People v. Crane, 214 N.Y. 154, 108 N.E. 427 (1915), *aff'd,* 239 U.S. 195 (1915).
26. Terrace v. Thompson, 263 U.S. 197 (1923).
27. Porterfield v. Webb, 263 U.S. 225 (1923) ; Frick v. Webb, 263 U.S. 326 (1923) ; Webb v. O'Brien, 263 U.S. 313 (1923).
28. *See* Terrace v. Thompson, 263 U.S. 197, 221 (1923).
29. *Id.* at 220.
30. As a result of the decision, the California Attorney General cancelled all escheat actions pursuant to the land law. Frank, *The United States Supreme Court: 1947-48,* 16 U. OF CHI. L. REV. 28 (1948). Prior to the *Oyama* decision the announced intention of California to vigorously enforce the land laws against returning Japanese war-evacuees

hold that the application of the statutory presumption of intent to evade the land law arising when an alien ineligible to hold land pays the consideration to an owner of realty for a transfer of land to another, denied the equal protection of the law to the minor son of the alien, an American citizen, who was the transferee and recipient of the gift.[31] However, Justices Black and Douglas, and Murphy and Rutledge, in two concurring opinions,[32] stated that they thought the entire alien land law was racial discrimination and an unreasonable classification violative of the equal protection clause. Three dissenting justices[33] did not consider the validity of the land law, but stated that unless it were to be declared unconstitutional, the presumption, being only a legitimate means of effectuating the Act, should not be invalid. Thus, should the dissenters be willing to accept the *Oyama* decision as a controlling precedent, logically their position would be that the alien land law has been impliedly declared unconstitutional. Furthermore, the *Takahashi* case makes it clear that a classification made by Congress in enacting naturalization laws may not be a reasonable one for a state to adopt in other situations.[34] It is, therefore, not unreasonable to expect that a direct challenge to the alien land laws, brought before the Supreme Court, may bring about the overruling of prior precedents.

Discrimination against aliens engaging in private occupations, where such occupations were totally unrelated to any proprietary interest the state might have had in its natural resources or the public payroll, has been sustained only where a rational connection existed between the discriminatory classification and the preservation of the health, safety and morals of the people of the state.[35] By undermining the proprietary doctrine, which, if applicable, would

---

brought forth strong comment insisting on the unconstitutionality of these acts. See, *e.g.*, McGovney, *The Anti-Japanese Land Laws of California and Ten Other States*, 35 CALIF. L. REV. 7 (1947); Ferguson, *The California Alien Land Law and the Fourteenth Amendment*, 35 CALIF. L. REV. 61 (1947); Note, *The Alien Land Laws: A Reappraisal*, 56 YALE L. J. 1017 (1947).

31. Where the transfer had been to a stranger, an American citizen, to hold for the alien's minor child, who was also a citizen, the presumption had previously been held constitutional. Cockrill v. California, 268 U.S. 258 (1925). This case was distinguished by the Court in the *Oyama* case on the grounds that in the case at bar there was discrimination as between citizen children of a Japanese father and citizen children of fathers of other nationalities when a gift of land was received from their father, while in the previous case there was no discrimination as between strangers taking from the same transferor. However, a deeper analysis shows that the child in the *Cockrill* case, the ultimate beneficiary of the gift, was under the same disabilities in enjoying the advantages of his gift as the child in the *Oyama* case, and therefore was denied equal protection to the same extent. That in one case the child was the direct transferee while in the other only a beneficiary seems to be an illusory distinction, because the denial of the benefits of the gift are precisely the same in both.

32. 332 U.S. 633, 647, 650 (1948).

33. *Id.* at 674, 684 (Justices Reed, Burton, and Jackson).

34. *See* 334 U.S. 410, 420 (1948); note 37 *infra*; Oyama v. California, 332 U.S. 633, 664-65 (1948) (concurring opinion).

35. *E.g.*, Anton v. Van Winkle, 297 Fed. 340 (D. Ore. 1924); Bloomfield v. State, 86 Ohio St. 253, 99 N.E. 309 (1912); *cf.* Truax v. Raich, 239 U.S. 33 (1915).

in itself justify discrimination,[36] the *Takahashi* case leaves the rational basis test as the sole criterion for determining permissible discrimination in any future case.[37]

Only once prior to *Takahashi,* in a case[38] involving the validity of an ordinance which prevented aliens from operating pool rooms, was the Supreme Court called upon to apply this test directly to a particular occupation. In that case the Court upheld the ordinance, since it had not been shown that no rational basis existed for the classification.[39]

A number of state cases in which the test has been applied have differed widely in their results. While all courts that have passed on the point have upheld the denial of liquor licenses to aliens,[40] the courts have split concerning the validity of legislation discriminating against aliens in the sale of soft drinks,[41] and also in the licensing of peddlers.[42] Moreover, it has been held constitutional to deny an alien a bus driver's license,[43] but unconstitutional to preclude him from obtaining a chauffeur's license.[44] Two cases have ruled that the occupation of barber could not be limited to citizens,[45] and one indicated that the same would hold true for the profession of doctor,[46] but an-

---

36. Terrace v. Thompson, 263 U.S. 197 (1923) ; *cf.* McCready v. Virginia, 94 U.S. 391 (1877).

37. California contended that its denial of licenses to aliens who were "ineligible to citizenship" was a reasonable classification by virtue of the fact that the federal government had utilized the very same classification in its naturalization laws. This contention was rejected by the Supreme Court on the ground that Congress had broad constitutional powers to enact such laws whereas the states did not.

38. Ohio *ex rel.* Clarke v. Deckebach, 274 U.S. 392 (1927).

39. Previously, when dealing with a statute prohibiting aliens from killing wild life where no infringement of the right to work was claimed, the Court had used the same approach, indicating that it did not have sufficient knowledge of local conditions to justify it in declaring that aliens were not the peculiar source of the evil which the conservation measure was designed to prevent. Patsone v. Pennsylvania, 232 U.S. 138 (1914). In both these cases it would seem that the Supreme Court might have examined more zealously the rational basis for the classification employed in the legislation therein considered.

40. Kaname Tokaji v. State, 20 Cal. App.2d 612, 67 P.2d 1082 (2d Dist. 1937) ; Bloomfield v. State, 86 Ohio St. 253, 99 N.E. 309 (1912) ; Trageser v. Gray, 73 Md. 250, 20 Atl. 905 (1890). The rationale of the last case, that where a state can prohibit a business entirely it can restrict it in any way it chooses, seems wholly unjustified. *See* Tittsworth v. Akin, 118 Fla. 454, 459-61, 159 So. 779, 780-81 (1935) ; C. Tisdall Co. v. Board of Aldermen of City of Newport, 57 R.I. 96, 103, 188 Atl. 648, 652 (1936).

41. *Compare* George v. Portland, 114 Ore. 418, 235 Pac. 681 (1925), *with* Miller v. City of Niagara Falls, 207 App. Div. 798, 202 N.Y. Supp. 549 (4th Dep't 1924).

42. *Compare* Commonwealth v. Hana, 195 Mass. 262, 81 N.E. 149 (1907), *with* State v. Montgomery, 94 Me. 192, 47 Atl. 165 (1900).

43. Gizzarelli v. Presbrey, 44 R.I. 333, 117 Atl. 359 (1922) ; *cf.* Morin v. Nunan, 91 N.J.L. 506, 103 Atl. 378 (Sup. Ct. 1918).

44. Magnani v. Harnett, 282 N.Y. 619, 25 N.E.2d 395 (1940), *cert. denied,* 310 U.S. 642 (1940).

45. Templar v. State Board of Examiners of Barbers, 131 Mich. 254, 90 N.W. 1058 (1902) ; State *ex rel.* Quisor v. Ellis, 184 P.2d 860 (Ore. 1947) ; *see* Matter of Wormsen v. Moss, 177 Misc. 19, 23-24, 29 N.Y.S.2d 798, 803-04 (Sup. Ct. 1941) (massage operator).

46. *See* Templar v. State Board of Examiners of Barbers, 131 Mich. 254, 257, 90 N.W. 1058, 1060 (1902).

other court has held that aliens could be excluded from practicing pharmacy.[47] On the other hand, the states are uniform in denying admission to the bar to aliens,[48] because an attorney is considered an "officer of the court," and on similar reasoning an alien has been denied the right to be an auctioneer.[49] The cases upholding the discrimination find a reasonable basis for the classification in the alien's purported lack of devotion to, or lack of knowledge of, the principles of the American tradition.[50] Those which condemn the discrimination find no rational connection between the classification and the occupation in question. By rejecting the classification contained in the naturalization laws as, ipso facto, a reasonable one for a state to invoke in order to justify interference with an alien's right to work, the *Takahashi* case seems to imply that it is virtually impossible to characterize aliens as a class. Aliens will, in fact, differ in allegiance, intelligence, education, and honesty just as any other group of individuals will differ. It would seem that no rational basis can exist for the exclusion of aliens from any occupation other than one involving a position of trust in government or military establishments. Educational standards, examinations, bonding, and affidavits of good character, applying to aliens and citizens alike, should adequately protect the public in those vocations requiring regulation.

Moreover, the alien, lacking suffrage, is unprotected in the legislatures against pressure groups attempting to better their economic position at his expense. To afford him adequate protection it would seem necessary to remove the presumption of validity of statutes which discriminate against aliens in their right to work.[51] The *Takahashi* and *Oyama* cases have pointed the way, and it should not be long before the alien enjoys the equality of opportunity which has long been the promise of the American tradition.

---

47. Sashihara v. State Board of Pharmacy, 7 Cal. App.2d 563, 46 P.2d 804 (2d Dist. 1935).

48. *In re* O'Sullivan, 267 Fed. 230 (D. Mont. 1920); Large v. The State Bar, 218 Cal. 334, 23 P.2d 288 (1933); *In re* Hong Yen Chang, 84 Cal. 163, 24 Pac. 156 (1890); *In re* Admission to Bar, 61 Neb. 58, 84 N.W. 611 (1900); In the Matter of O'Neill, 90 N.Y. 584 (1882); *Ex parte* Thompson, 10 N.C. 355 (1824); *In re* Takuji Yamashita, 30 Wash. 234, 70 Pac. 482 (1902).

49. Wright v. May, 127 Minn. 150, 149 N.W. 9 (1914).

50. It must be remembered that the existence of a treaty made by the United States with a foreign country may preclude the states from denying equal work opportunities to aliens of that country residing here. Asakura v. Seattle, 265 U.S. 332 (1924) (pawnbroking); *In re* Naka's License, 9 Alaska 1 (1934) (liquor license); *In re* Tiburcio Parrott, 1 Fed. 481 (C.C.D. Cal. 1880) (excluding Chinese from employment by corporations); Baker v. Portland, 2 Fed. Cas. 472, No. 777 (C.C.D. Ore. 1879) (excluding only Chinese from public works).

The federal treaty power overrides both the state's police and proprietary powers. Asakura v. Seattle, *supra*; Missouri v. Holland, 252 U.S. 416 (1920). See Note, 48 Columbia L. Rev. 890 (1948).

51. See Konvitz, *op. cit. supra* note 1, at 180-81. An additional reason for removing the presumption is the practical impossibility, in many cases, of producing sufficient proof to overcome the presumption that the classification discriminating against aliens has a rational basis.

Acknowledgments

Buell, Raymond Leslie. "Some Legal Aspects of the Japanese Question." *American Journal of International Law* 17 (1923): 29–49. Reprinted with the permission of the *Amerasia Journal*. Courtesy of Yale University Seeley G. Mudd Library.

Buell, Raymond Leslie. "The Development of the Anti-Japanese Agitation in the United States." *Political Science Quarterly* 37 (1922): 605–83. Courtesy of Yale University Law Library.

Buell, Raymond Leslie. "The Development of Anti-Japanese Agitation in the United States II." *Political Science Quarterly* 38 (1923): 57–81. Courtesy of Yale University Law Library.

Woolsey, Theodore S. "The California-Japanese Question." *American Journal of International Law* 15 (1921): 55–9. Courtesy of Yale University Seeley G. Mudd Library.

Pritchard, Earl H. "The Japanese Exclusion Bill of 1924." *Research Studies of the State College of Washington* 2 (1930): 65–77. Courtesy of Yale University Sterling Memorial Library.

Bailey, Thomas A. "California, Japan, and the Alien Land Legislation of 1913." *Pacific Historical Review* 1 (1932): 36–59. Courtesy of Yale University Sterling Memorial Library.

Carrott, M. Browning. "Prejudice Goes to Court: The Japanese and the Supreme Court in the 1920s." *California History* 62 (1983): 122–38. Reprinted with the permission of the California Historical Society. Courtesy of Yale University Sterling Memorial Library.

Coletta, Paolo E. "'The Most Thankless Task': Bryan and the California Alien Land Legislation." *Pacific Historical Review* 36 (1967): 163–87. Reprinted with the permission of the University of California Press. Courtesy of Yale University Sterling Memorial Library.

Anon. "Constitutional Law: Equal Protection of the Laws: Presumption of Intent to Evade Escheat in California Alien Land

Law." *California Law Review* 36 (1948): 320–25. Courtesy of Yale University Law Library.

Ferguson, Edwin E. "The California Alien Land Law and the Fourteenth Amendment." *California Law Review* 35 (1947): 61–90. Courtesy of Yale University Law Library.

Higgs, Robert. "Landless by Law: Japanese Immigrants in California Agriculture to 1941." *Journal of Economic History* 38 (1978): 205–25. Reprinted with the permission of Cambridge University Press. Courtesy of Yale University Sterling Memorial Library.

Ichioka, Yuji. "Japanese Immigrant Response to the 1920 California Alien Land Law." *Agricultural History* 58 (1984): 157–78. 1984, by the Agricultural History Society. Reprinted from *Agricultural History*, Vol.58 No.1 1984, pp.157–78 by permission. Courtesy of Yale University Seeley G. Mudd Library.

Note. "The Japanese Problem in Oregon." *Oregon Law Review* 24 (1945): 208–19. Courtesy of Yale University Law Library.

LePore, Herbert P. "Prelude to Prejudice: Hiram Johnson, Woodrow Wilson, and the California Alien Land Law Controversy of 1913." *Southern California Quarterly* 61 (1979): 99–110. Reprinted with the permission of the Historical Society of Southern California. Courtesy of Yale University Sterling Memorial Library.

McGovney, Dudley O. "The Anti-Japanese Land Laws of California and Ten Other States." *California Law Review* 35 (1947): 7–60. Courtesy of Yale University Law Library.

Olin, Spencer C., Jr. "European Immigrant and Oriental Alien: Acceptance and Rejection by the California Legislature of 1913." *Pacific Historical Review* 35 (1966): 303–15. Reprinted with the permission of the University of California Press. Courtesy of Yale University Sterling Memorial Library.

Powell, Thomas Reed. "Alien Land Cases in United States Supreme Court." *California Law Review* 12 (1924): 259–82. Courtesy of Yale University Law Library.

Goater, Richard A. "Civil Rights and Anti-Japanese Discrimination." *University of Cincinnati Law Review* 18 (1949): 81–9. Reprinted with the permission of the University of Cincinnati Law School. Courtesy of *University of Cincinnati Law Review*.

Hawkins, John N. "Politics, Education, and Language Policy: The Case of Japanese Language Schools in Hawaii." *Amerasia*

Journal 5 (1978): 39–56. Reprinted with the permission of the *Amerasia Journal*. Courtesy of Yale University Sterling Memorial Library.

Ichioka, Yuji. "The Early Japanese Immigrant Quest for Citizenship: The Background of the 1922 Ozawa Case." *Amerasia Journal* 4 (1977): 1–23. Reprinted with the permission of the *Amerasia Journal*.

Anon. "1947–48 Term of the Supreme Court: The Alien's Right to Work." *Columbia Law Review* 49 (1949): 257–64. Courtesy of Yale University Law Library.